The Unfinished Peace after World War I

This is a highly original and revisionist analysis of British and American efforts to forge a stable Euro-Atlantic peace order between 1919 and the rise of Hitler. Patrick O. Cohrs argues that this order was not founded at Versailles but rather through the first 'real' peace settlements after World War I – the London reparations settlement of 1924 and the Locarno security pact of 1925. Crucially, both fostered Germany's integration into a fledgling transatlantic peace system, thus laying the only realistic foundations for European stability. What proved decisive was the leading actors' capacity to draw lessons from the 'Great War' and Versailles' shortcomings. Yet Cohrs also re-appraises why they could not sustain the new order, master its gravest crisis – the Great Depression – and prevent the onslaught of Nazism. Despite this ultimate failure, he concludes that the 'unfinished peace' of the 1920s prefigured the terms on which a more durable peace could be built after 1945.

PATRICK O. COHRS is a fellow at the John F. Kennedy School's Belfer Center for Science and International Affairs at Harvard University and a research fellow at the History Department of Humboldt University Berlin. He has been a post-doctoral scholar at the Center for European Studies, Harvard University, in 2002 and 2003.

The Unfinished Peace after World War I

America, Britain and the Stabilisation of Europe, 1919-1932

Patrick O. Cohrs

CAMBRIDGE
UNIVERSITY PRESS

CAMBRIDGE UNIVERSITY PRESS
Cambridge, New York, Melbourne, Madrid, Cape Town, Singapore, São Paulo

Cambridge University Press
The Edinburgh Building, Cambridge CB2 2RU, UK

Published in the United States of America by Cambridge University Press,
New York

www.cambridge.org
Information on this title: www.cambridge.org/9780521853538

First published 2006

Printed in the United Kingdom at the University Press, Cambridge

A catalogue record for this book is available from the British Library

ISBN-13 978-0-521-85353-8 hardback
ISBN-10 0-521-85353-2 hardback

For My Mother
&
Erica

Contents

Acknowledgements

This study was begun at St Antony's College, Oxford, and completed at the Center for European Studies, Harvard University, which provided a very stimulating environment throughout. When I embarked on my research my subject seemed to many, including myself, far too wide in scope to be treated sensibly, perhaps even a recipe for an unfinished analysis of the unfinished peace of the 1920s. For whatever sense I have been able to make of it since then I owe immense gratitude to Tony Nicholls and Jonathan Wright, who unfailingly encouraged my project in its early stages, and to Charles Maier for his advice and support in the latter stages. I owe special thanks to Jonathan Wright for his thorough and always helpful comments.

For their constructive criticism and comments I would like to thank Paul W. Schroeder, Samuel Wells, Ernest May, Akira Iriye, Niall Ferguson, Kathleen Burk, John Darwin, Avi Shlaim, Timothy Garton Ash, Kenneth Weisbrode and Peter Hall. I am particularly indebted to Samuel Wells for his kindness and support during my research in the United States both in 1999 and 2000, where I could not have found a better base than the Woodrow Wilson Center in Washington. St Antony's College and Lincoln College furnished a pleasant setting for my research at Oxford. Finally, I would like to thank Professor Dr Klaus Hildebrand for supervising my MA thesis at the University of Bonn, which led me to think harder about the prospects and limits of European stabilisation after 1918. I am also glad to acknowledge the unswerving support of Christoph Studt.

I am grateful to the Trustees of the Michael Wills Scholarship (Dulverton Trust), the German Academic Exchange Service (DAAD), the Friedrich Naumann Foundation, the Fritz Thyssen Foundation, the Cyril Foster and Related Funds, the Lord Crewe Trustees, Lincoln College, the German Historical Institute, Paris and the Woodrow Wilson Center for generous financial assistance. I am particularly grateful to the Fritz Thyssen Foundation for its contribution to the publication of this book. Last but not least, I would like to thank Linda Randall and Jackie Warren for their much appreciated help with the final editing of this book and Fran Robinson for her thorough work on the index. No less, I would like to thank Michael Watson and the Syndics of

Cambridge University Press for agreeing to publish such an inordinately long book; and I gratefully acknowledge the support of the Fritz Thyssen Foundation, which generously contributed to its publication.

Grateful acknowledgement is also made to the following archives for permission to quote material: Houghton Research Library and Baker Library, Harvard University, Cambridge, Massachusetts; Hoover Institution, Stanford, California, and Hoover Presidential Library, West Branch, Iowa; Minnesota Historical Society, St Paul, Minnesota; Sterling Library, Yale University, New Haven, Connecticut; Pierpont Morgan Library, New York; Federal Reserve Bank Archives, New York: University of Birmingham Library.

I warmly thank all my friends for their kindness and patience during the many years and travels it took me to finish this book – especially Peter, Florian, Gerd and, also for his generous hospitality in Paris, Jean. I am also glad to take this opportunity to thank Gesche, Fritz and Malte Lübbe for their friendship and support over many years when the thought of writing this book was still but a faint idea. My sister Dörthe I thank, with love, for putting up with her s.o. brother.

In particular, I wish to express my heartfelt gratitude to my uncle Dieter Grober for his generous support, which contributed decisively to enabling the publication of this book in its final form. And finally I also, and most warmly, thank my uncle Heini Witte-Löffier for supporting my work when it mattered most, at the outset of my studies. I am also grateful to my father, if for different reasons.

To my wife Erica I owe more than I could possibly acknowledge here. She has probably shown me more than anyone else what learning processes really mean – far beyond the scope of this book. I especially thank her for reminding me time and again that there are (even) more important things in life than international history. Finally, I thank my mother for all she has done for me. To her and Erica I dedicate this book. Its shortcomings are mine alone.

Abbreviations

AA	Auswärtiges Amt (German Foreign Office), Berlin
ADAP	*Akten zur deutschen auswärtigen Politik*
AHR	*American Historical Review*
AR	*Akten der Reichskanzlei*, Berlin
BHR	*Business History Review*
CAB	Cabinet Office Papers, National Archive, London
CEH	*Contemporary European History*
CID	Committee of Imperial Defence
DBFP	*Documents on British Foreign Policy*
DH	*Diplomatic History*
EHQ	*European History Quarterly*
EHR	*English Historical Review*
FA	*Foreign Affairs*
FO	Foreign Office
FO 371	Foreign Office Political Files, National Archive, London
FRBNY	Federal Reserve Bank of New York
FRUS	*Papers relating to the Foreign Relations of the United States*
GG	*Geschichte und Gesellschaft*
GWU	*Geschichte in Wissenschaft und Unterricht*
Hansard	*Hansard*, Parliamentary Debates: House of Commons
HC	House of Commons
HJ	*Historical Journal*
HZ	*Historische Zeitschrift*
IHR	*International History Review*
IMCC	Inter-Allied Military Commission of Control
IO	*International Organization*
JAH	*Journal of American History*

JAS	*Journal of American Studies*
JBIIA	*Journal of the British Institute of International Affairs*
JCEA	*Journal of Central European Affairs*
JCH	*Journal of Contemporary History*
JEH	*Journal of Economic History*
JMH	*Journal of Modern History*
JOC	*Journal Officiel, Chambre des Deputés*
JOS	*Journal Officiel, Sénat*
Locarno-Konferenz	*Locarno-Konferenz, 1925. Eine Dokumentensammlung* (Berlin, 1962)
MAE	Archives du Ministère des Affaires Etrangères (French Foreign Ministry), Paris
MF	Archives du Ministère des Finances, Archives Nationales, Paris
NA RG 59	National Archives, Maryland, Record Group 59 (Department of State, General Files)
NAL	National Archive, London
NN	*Nations and Nationalism*
NPL	*Neue Politische Literatur*
PA	Politisches Archiv des Auswärtigen Amts, Berlin
PHR	*Pacific Historical Review*
PWW	A.S. Link (ed.), *The Papers of Woodrow Wilson*, 69 vols. (Princeton, 1977)
RHD	*Revue d'Histoire Diplomatique*
RI	*Relations Internationales*
RIS	*Review of International Studies*
RP	*Review of Politics*
SB	*Stenographische Berichte über die Verhandlungen des Reichstags* (minutes of the German parliament)
SB, Nationalversammlung	*Stenographische Berichte über die Verhandlungen der verfassunggebenden Deutschen Nationalversammlung* (minutes of the German constitutional national assembly, 1919)
UF	*Ursachen und Folgen* (Berlin, 1959ff)
VfZg	*Vierteljahrshefte für Zeitgeschichte*
WP	*World Politics*

A note on the footnotes and bibliography

To save space, all works in the footnotes are cited only by the last name of the author, or editor, and the year of publication. These abbreviated citations correspond to works listed, and cited in full, in the bibliography.

Introduction

> What will now happen – once the phase of exhaustion has passed – is that *peace, not war, will have been discredited* . . .
> Politics means slow, strong drilling through hard boards, with a combination of passion and a sense of judgement . . . It is of course entirely correct, and a fact confirmed by all historical experience, that what is possible would never have been achieved if, in this world, people had not repeatedly reached for the impossible. But the person who can do this must be a leader; not only that, he must, in a very simple sense of the word, be a hero.
>
> (Max Weber, 'The Profession and Vocation of Politics', January 1919)[1]

This study is based on a simple premise: what needs to be re-appraised when examining the history of international politics in the aftermath of World War I, the twentieth century's original cataclysm, is *not* crisis or the demise of international order. It is, rather, the contrary: the achievement of any international stabilisation in Europe – even if it was to prove relative and ultimately unsustainable.[2] Grave crises can engender a fundamental transformation of the mentality and practices of international politics. This in turn can alter, and improve, the very foundations of international stability.[3] As has been shown, such a transformation gave rise to the durable Vienna system of 1814/15, forged after decades of revolutionary, then Napoleonic, wars.[4]

To underscore the deficiencies of peacemaking in the twentieth century, particularly those of British and American quests to re-establish international order after the Great War, scholars of the 'twenty years' crisis' have mainly pointed to negative lessons – routes to disaster then largely avoided in achieving greater stability after 1945. They have not only expounded the 'lessons of Versailles' and 'appeasement' in the 1930s but also, and notably, those of Europe's 'illusory peace' in the 1920s.[5] Is it really tenable to conclude that a crisis of the magnitude of World War I did not lead to any forward-looking

---

[1] Weber (1994), pp. 359, 369.
[2] Cf. the underlying premise of Maier (1988), p. 3.
[3] For the wider context see Ikenberry (2001); Kennedy and Hitchcock (2000).
[4] See Schroeder (1994).
[5] See Marks (1976), pp. 143–6; Carr (1939), pp. 208–39; Ikenberry (2001), pp. 117ff.

1

reorientations in international politics? Did those who sought to stabilise Europe in the 1920s, the first and crucial decade after the war – and before the Great Depression – fail to make any substantial advances, comparable to those of 1814/15?

To be explored here is what was the closest approximation of a viable Euro-Atlantic peace order after the Great War. Was it, for all its shortcomings, the treaty system of Versailles?[6] Or was it rather – as this analysis seeks to show – the result of a fundamental recasting of transatlantic relations following a drawn-out postwar crisis, which led to the emergence of a qualitatively differ-ent international system? If the latter, then it was a system built half a decade after Versailles – and on two main pillars: the London reparations settlement of 1924 and the Locarno security pact of 1925. Essentially, this study seeks to shed new light on these agreements and what they founded: the 'real' post-World War I peace order. What it envisages has not been attempted within one analytical framework before. It will first re-appraise what made the advances of the mid-1920s possible and set them apart from all previous attempts to pacify Europe. Then, it will re-assess how far they could be sustained in the ultim-ately brief period of 'relative' European stability between 1924 and the World Economic Crisis of 1929–32.

The progress policymakers made along this stony path in the 'era of London and Locarno' was indeed striking. But a comprehensive analysis also has to re-examine two even more important questions, namely: why they ultimately failed to transform the settlements of the mid-1920s into a more robust international order, one that could have prevented Hitler; and why the system of London and Locarno dissolved so rapidly under the impact of the Great Depression – because of inherent limits, overwhelming pressures or indeed a combination of both.

As I seek to substantiate, the remarkable degree of international stability achieved in the decade after 1918 resulted from a formative transformation process in the history of international politics: the most far-reaching attempts *after* Versailles to create a peace system *that included Germany*. Yet I also seek to illuminate why this hitherto misunderstood or disregarded process could not be sufficiently advanced, and legitimated, further in the latter 1920s – why it remained unfinished. I hope to show, first, that the sharpest – and neglected – focus for analysing this process can be found in a comparative examination. It centres on the two bids for European consolidation that, for all their inherent shortcomings, can be called the most far-reaching approaches to this end in the interwar period. It is an analysis of two compatible and interdependent

---

[6] For recent, overall benign evaluations see Boemeke, Feldman and Glaser (1998); Macmillan (2001).

yet also markedly distinct stabilisation policies, the ideas underlying them, and their impact on Europe between 1919 and 1932. These were, on the one hand, Britain's quest for appeasement and a new European equilibrium and, on the other, America's pursuit of a 'Progressive', economically orientated transformation of an Old World destroyed by the Great War. What I thus pursue is, in essence, a study of two policies of peaceful change that have not been systematically compared before.[7]

I hope to show, second, that the most illuminating way of assessing the prospects *and limits* of these approaches is to evaluate how far Anglo–American policymakers, and their continental European counterparts, coped with the problem arguably lying at the heart of Europe's inherent instability after 1918: the unsettled 'Franco–German question' of the 1920s. What I term as such is the core problem, unresolved in Versailles, of finding a balance between the removal of France's preponderant security concerns – its anxieties on account of *les incertitudes allemandes* – and the international integration of a vanquished, originally revisionist and only newly republican Germany. This problem was inseparably linked with a second key question of postwar international politics, namely the 'Polish–German question'. What I term as such was the core problem, also created at Versailles, how, if at all, a peaceful settlement of the Polish–German dispute over the contested border of 1919 and the status of German minorities in Poland could be achieved. Both central postwar questions thus had one common root: the challenge of reconciling Weimar Germany's accommodation with the security of its neighbours.

Throughout the 1920s, the Franco–German question remained crucial, and ⸻ll be at the centre of this study. But the *status quo* between Germany and ⸻ even more unsettled. And the situation in the east was in turn ⸻d by the question of whether pacific change in the west could ⸻ constructive relations between the western powers, Germany ⸻ssia, superseding early tendencies of Soviet–German alliance-⸻ Versailles. The ramifications of such eastern questions will ⸻ered. They became particularly important from the time of ⸻ that was also the first time when genuine, if still precarious, ⸻r pacifying eastern Europe were opened up. In sum, then, my ⸻ to shed new light on Anglo–American efforts to recast the unstable Versailles system and foster stability not only in western but also in eastern Europe. Thus, I hope to elucidate interdependencies between two areas previously often regarded as two sides of a dichotomy.

---

[7] There have been valuable studies of British *or* American policies towards Europe and Anglo-American relations in the 1920s. See Leffler (1979); Costigliola (1984); Grayson (1997); McKercher (1984) and (1999).

The interpretative context: previous interpretations and the need for a new approach

The reality and extent of such international stabilisation as was achieved after 1918 have remained contested ever since, particularly since 1945. This study intends to complement but also, and principally, challenge prevalent interpretations shaping today's understanding of Europe's 'relative' pacification in the 1920s. Broadly speaking, most previous attempts to explain its prospects, and notably its limits, have taken the form of either nationally focused or Eurocentric analyses. Some have claimed that Versailles and the agreements following it led to a 'European restoration', which was then undermined by the Great Depression. Most, however, have emphasised the 'illusion of peace' in the interwar period, making it part of a new 'Thirty Years' War' that only ended in 1945. And they have particularly criticised the Anglo-American failure to reinforce Versailles and ultimately forestall Hitler.[8]

Comparatively subdued more recently has been the 'idealist' critique of British and American policies after 1918. It hinges on the assertion that a 'western' diplomacy relying on a great-power accommodation with Germany undercut what the League of Nations could have become: Europe's central agency of collective security safeguarding in particular the integrity of its smaller nation-states.[9]

What has been more influential – and what this analysis mainly seeks to challenge – can be subsumed under the 'realist' critique of 1920s international politics.[10] Through the prism of the 1930s, 'realist' studies have branded the accords of London and Locarno as centrepieces of misguided Anglo-American policies that paved the way for Nazi German expansionism. For they allegedly undermined the Versailles system and with it any chances of re-establishing a balance of power to check Germany's 'inherent' revisionism.[11] Although never systematically compared, both settlements have thus been implicitly linked. Probably most far-reaching remains Stephen Schuker's claim that, in forcing the Dawes plan on France, Anglo-American politicians and financiers inflicted the decisive 'defeat' on French postwar policy – which was then merely confirmed at Locarno. They would thus shatter Europe's best hope for stability:

---

[8] See Bell (1986), pp. 14–47. A still useful synopsis is provided by Jacobson (1983a).

[9] See the overview in Steiner (1993); Dunbabin (1993); Fleury (1998), pp. 507–22.

[10] It is characterised by a reliance on the balance-of-power paradigm to determine the stability of international order. See Kissinger (1994), pp. 17ff; Mearsheimer (2001), pp. 42–51.

[11] 'Realists' thus distribute responsibility for the 'illusory peace' among national foreign-policy approaches. See Marks (1976), pp. 143ff; Kissinger (1994), pp. 266–87; Schuker (1976), pp. 385ff. This has mainly been challenged by studies of German policy. See Krüger (1985); Wright (2002). Studies of French policy still largely follow 'old' realist premises. See Keeton (1987); Pitts (1987).

France's bid to achieve it by containing or ultimately even fragmenting Germany.[12]

In a similar vein, it has been asserted that Anglo-American policies had a clearly detrimental effect on central and eastern Europe, particularly the security of Poland and Czechoslovakia. For their net effect, or so it has been claimed, was to dismantle France's eastern alliance system, diminishing the eastern powers' status as allies of the west in restraining Germany. They thus allegedly eroded the 'eastern barrier' against a revisionist *entente* between Germany and Bolshevik Russia.[13]

From a different angle, recent perspectives of research have focused on the structural conditions and *forces profondes* affecting post-World War I stability. One has essentially explained its impermanence by highlighting fundamental contradictions within the transatlantic states-system, especially the tensions between 'revisionist' and '*status quo*' powers.[14] Invoking either the 'primacy of internal politics' or that of economics, the other has pointed to postwar nationalism, domestic crises or staggering financial impediments, particularly in France and Germany.[15]

Concentrating on European diplomacy, some have claimed that the 'edifice' of Locarno essentially rested on sound foundations and only incisive 'extraneous events', namely the Great Depression, made it collapse.[16] Overall, however, most previous analyses have sought to show why ultimately all bids to pacify Europe only produced a 'semblance' of peace. In the 'realist' interpretation, the Locarno system's demise was inevitable because its principal powers, and particularly Britain, never corrected its basic flaw – the disregard for the European balance of power; at the same time, the structural antagonism between France's search for a secure *status quo* and German revisionism remained indelible.[17]

Focusing on America's approach to European reconstruction, some scholars have tried to establish causal links between Republican pursuits after 1919 and the catastrophe of 1929.[18] Did US decisionmakers indeed adopt reckless loan

---

[12] See Schuker (1976), pp. 3ff, 385–93, which remains the most thorough study of the Dawes settlement.

[13] It is also still a predominant view that in reaction to the western powers' 'appeasement' of Germany and Warsaw's 'subjective defeat' at Locarno, Polish policymakers were driven to ever more nationalistic policies, especially under Marshal Piłsudski. See Wandycz (1961) and (1988); Cienciala and Kormanicki (1984); Schattkowsky (1994c).

[14] See Clark (1997), pp. 75–98; Nye (1993), pp. 77–88; Girault and Frank (1988), pp. 121–62; Maier (1981), pp. 327–52.

[15] See Ferguson (1997); Feldman (1993); Knipping (1987); Becker and Berstein (1990), pp. 155–343.

[16] See Grayson (1997), pp. 138–9; Jacobson (1983a).

[17] See Jacobson (1972b), pp. 367–73, yet also the more recent and affirmative interpretation in Jacobson (2004); Marks (1976), pp. 143–6; Kissinger (1994), pp. 266ff.

[18] See Kindleberger (1973), pp. 1–13; Kent (1989), pp. 373–90; Friedmann and Schwartz (1963).

policies? Did they simply fail as leaders of the world economy's new pre-eminent power? Melvyn Leffler has concluded that Washington ultimately pursued incompatible objectives: political aloofness *and* a US-dominated economic order, German revitalisation *and* French security. Is this what produced catastrophic unintended consequences in the 1930s?[19]

Finally, it should be noted that notwithstanding valuable contributions to 1920s international history from both economic and 'classic' diplomatic historians a certain dichotomy has emerged. The former have mainly focused on US efforts at financial stabilisation, especially in Germany, and informal cooperation among Anglo-American elites. In their view, the causes for Europe's 'relative' stabilisation *and* its failure have to be sought in the 'crucial' area of financial and economic reconstruction, *not* in the political realm.[20] By contrast, diplomatic historians have emphasised America's political 'isolationism' after 1919, concentrating instead on security relations between the 'Locarno powers'.[21] Arisen from this has, arguably, a certain tendency to separate two processes that ought to be seen as interconnected and indeed interdependent. On the one hand, there was a process of financial-cum-political stabilisation chiefly but not exclusively propelled by America. On the other, there was a process of political and strategic accommodation decisively advanced by Britain – yet inconceivable without US support. This study seeks to examine both processes in one analytical framework and to re-appraise how far on their own terms, and in their combined effect, they contributed to more than a 'semblance' of peace in Europe.

The main theme and theses of my study

Departing from both idealist and realist analyses previously undertaken, this study seeks to open up a different, third perspective. It will pursue one underlying theme: what progress there was towards Europe's pacification in the 1920s stemmed by no means from a – *de facto* elusive – return to pre-1914 balance-of-power politics. Nor were they, however, the result of imposing a radically altered 'Wilsonian world order' underpinned by the League and universal, supranational norms of collective security. Rather, the modicum of European stabilisation achieved by late 1925 was the outcome of significant, but ultimately unsustainable, advances in the pacific settlement of international conflicts and integrative co-operation between states: the making of the unfinished transatlantic peace order after World War I. These advances were made

[19] Leffler (1979), pp. 362–8. See also Link (1970), pp. 620ff.
[20] See Eichengreen (1992); Kindleberger (1973), pp. 14–69; Silverman (1982); Orde (1990); Burk (1981); Hogan (1991); James (2001).
[21] See Jacobson (1972b); Bariéty (1977); Krüger (1985).

by those who, in collaboration with Anglo-American financiers and in negotiation with French and German policymakers, altered not only British and American policies but also the course of international politics after 1923. Their efforts were premised on distinct British and American principles of peaceful change and political-cum-financial consolidation. Crucially, they began to foster new ground-rules for reforming the ill-founded peace of Versailles and integrating Weimar Germany into a recast western-orientated peace order – on terms acceptable to France, improving Polish security and prevailing over both communist and autocratic challenges in the 1920s. These terms indeed prefigured those on which more durable Euro-Atlantic stability would be founded after 1945.[22]

Yet by the end of 1925 the edifice of London and Locarno was by no means already firmly entrenched. It was not yet a robust international system of security and economic stabilisation. The main threat to its consolidation was not that it merely concealed underlying – and essentially irreconcilable – Franco-German differences or that it rested on such contradictory premises that it sooner or later had to collapse. Nor did this threat emanate from Bolshevik Russia. By 1923, it had become obvious that Lenin's postwar bid to spread the Bolshevik revolution and draw the states of central and western Europe into a European federal 'Union' of Soviet-style republics had failed. And in the latter 1920s Stalin prevailed with his maxims to concentrate on building 'socialism in a single country' and to insulate Soviet Russia from involvement in disputes between the capitalist powers, because he feared they would only conspire to undermine Europe's pariah regime in Moscow.[23] The main risk was instead that policymakers on both sides of the Atlantic failed to develop, and thus legitimate, further what they had begun to build in the mid-1920s: the system of London and Locarno. What was thus all the more, not less, indispensable after Locarno was a sustained forward engagement of this system's pivotal powers: Britain as the 'honest broker' of the fledgling European concert, America as the arbiter of financial-cum-political stabilisation under the Dawes regime and chief creditor of France. The Franco-German peace process could not be advanced decisively without a powerful third party – an arbiter willing and able to mediate, using what political and economic leverage it commanded. The same held true for Polish–German accommodation and, essentially, for the Euro-Atlantic peace order as a whole.

This study seeks to consider all actors who decisively influenced the formulation and implementation of international stabilisation strategies after 1918. But it deliberately concentrates on individual decision-makers rather than entire elites. And it focuses on policymakers rather than financial leaders.

[22] See Cohrs (2003).   [23] Cf. Service (2000), pp. 412–13, and (2005), pp. 380–1.

For there were indeed certain actors who can be called the political protagonists of peaceful change in Europe. To be sure, they faced political and strategic
challenges of European instability that to an unprecedented degree were
intertwined with financial problems – not only in the central areas of reparations and inter-allied war-debts. But, as will be argued here, all of these
questions ultimately demanded not only financial expertise but also, and
essentially, *political* answers.

In the final analysis, policymakers, not financiers, were called upon – not
least by bankers like the Dawes loan's main underwriter, J.P. Morgan – to
create the indispensable framework in which financial and political stabilisation
could be advanced. And they were the only actors in a position to tackle the
critical European security question, which underlay everything else. Finally,
they were the only ones who – if anyone – could perform one newly central task
of diplomacy in the first era of Euro-Atlantic history that really was an era of
democratic mass politics, namely to legitimate painstakingly forged international compromises domestically. In fact, they had to do so in highly
disparate domestic theatres on both sides of the Atlantic. It is from their
perspective, then, that the making of the 'system of London and Locarno' will
be traced. There were no heroes, and hardly any charismatic leaders, among
those seeking to reshape the western powers' relations with Germany in the
decade after World War I. But they certainly had to drill through hard boards
to achieve any stabilisation.

On these premises, the prologue ought to show that, though Woodrow
Wilson and David Lloyd George strove hard at Versailles to forge a peace 'to
end all wars', neither became a principal peacemaker after the Great War.
A stronger claimant to this epithet was American secretary of state Charles
E. Hughes who sought to foster a transatlantic 'community of ideals, interests
and purposes' in 1923/4.[24] And the same could be said for the British prime
minister Ramsay MacDonald and his evolutionary approach to rebuilding a
comity of states 'beyond Versailles' that included both Germany and the
United States.[25] A re-appraisal of their efforts will be at the heart of this
study's first part.

Then will follow what I believe is a new interpretation of Anglo-American
attempts to foster European stability between 1925 and 1929. It will focus on
the British foreign secretary Austen Chamberlain, who prepared the ground
for Britain's 'noble work of appeasement' between France and Germany.[26] And
it will focus on his US counterpart Frank B. Kellogg, who defined America's

---

[24] Thus Hughes in a 1922 address, in Hughes (1925).

[25] The policies of the Conservative foreign secretary Lord Curzon will also be considered. Yet he
was only cursorily involved in the main developments analysed here. See chapter 7.

[26] Chamberlain speech in the Commons, 18 November 1925, *Hansard*, 5th series, vol. 188, col. 420.

role in Europe as that of a benign, but also distinctly aloof, arbiter in the European dispute, which guarded its 'freedom of action'.[27] Yet it will also analyse a newly powerful approach to international relations already shaping US policy after Wilson's fall and finally ascendant in the latter 1920s. It was the bid of Herbert Hoover, first as US secretary of commerce, then as president, to recast Europe after the Progressive model of America's 'New Era' and to replace old-style European diplomacy by a rational, 'economic' *modus operandi*.[28]

The first main thesis to be substantiated is that the reorientation of American policy under Hughes and a new mode of Anglo-American co-operation fostered by MacDonald paved the way for what was indeed the first 'real' peace settlement after 1918: the London reparations settlement of 1924. Negotiated between the western powers and Germany, it laid the foundations for the Dawes regime and Europe's 'economic peace' of the mid-1920s. Yet, thus the second main thesis, this *Pax Anglo-Americana* would not have endured without the second formative postwar settlement, the Locarno pact of 1925. Locarno, in turn only made possible through the breakthrough of London, essentially became its political security framework. At its core emerged a western-orientated concert of Europe – a concert incorporating Germany. With significant American support, it was forged under the aegis of British diplomacy, reshaped under Chamberlain.

Based on this re-appraisal the study's final part seeks to show that British and American attempts to consolidate the system of London and Locarno between 1926 and 1929 were by no means inherently flawed. They were not doomed to be as limited in effect as the 1928 Kellogg–Briand Pact for the Outlawry of War or as short-lived as the Young plan. Nor did they initiate a pacification process by nature limited to western Europe, accentuating a new dividing-line between a more or less functioning peace system in the west and a destabilised *Zwischeneuropa* in the east. Rather, Euro-Atlantic co-operation after 1925 opened up the best prospects for stabilising Weimar Germany, and thus post-World War I Europe, by fostering its progressive integration into the new international system – both politically and economically. Further notable advances in this direction were made through the Young settlement and the Hague accords of 1929.

Crucially, Anglo-American policies began to draw Germany away from the pursuit of revisionism by force, reinforcing instead Berlin's commitment to moderate and economically underpinned policies of peaceful change in western *and* eastern Europe. They also began to stimulate what remained difficult reorientation processes in France and Poland, steering policymakers there away

[27] Kellogg to Coolidge, 7 October 1924, Kellogg Papers.
[28] Hoover address, 14 December 1924, Hoover Papers, box 75.

from enforcing Versailles and towards accommodation with Germany. They thus indeed initiated what became a genuine, if arduous, Franco-German peace process in the latter 1920s. And they created the most favourable – if still far from auspicious – preconditions for an 'eastern Locarno', especially a pacific settlement of the Polish–German question, in the interwar period. Yet, while having most, but not all, essential means, British and American policymakers could not *sustain* these transformation processes after 1925. Once Europe's postwar crisis seemed contained, and its overall stabilisation assured, they lacked the strategic interest, concrete incentives and political will to pursue further forward engagement. They did not make the necessary commitments to extend the limited Euro-Atlantic concert of 1925 into a wider, and more robust, system of security and economic consolidation. There were no concrete initiatives to settle what was at the core of the Polish–German antagonism, the precarious border and minority questions. A Locarno-style agreement for eastern Europe remained elusive.

Against the background of the cardinal European security question, finally addressed yet not resolved by the mid-1920s, the main impulses for the still arduous Franco-German accommodation process could not come from Paris or Berlin. Nor could they come 'only' from Locarno politics or US-led reconstruction efforts. Essentially, while also requiring time and domestic legitimacy, European stabilisation in west and east could only be genuinely advanced through further strategic bargains. In other words, it required settlements comprising both political and financial elements akin to those of 1924 and 1925. Yet those powers alone capable of doing so, America and Britain, no longer took the lead in forging such bargains, at least not until 1929 when – in hindsight – it proved too late and when, crucially, Hoover and his secretary of state Henry Stimson placed financial interests and progressive aloofness over political engagement in Europe. Though MacDonald and his foreign secretary Arthur Henderson strove hard to turn the Hague accords into a further and more far-reaching London-style settlement, it was beyond their means to fill the gap that US disengagement left. All in all, the Anglo-American powers thus only partially fulfilled their critical roles within the changing post-World War I international order. In one respect, this was precisely due to the fact that the peace settlements of London and Locarno had been so successful. There were no further immediate crises spurring Anglo-American policymakers into sustaining or even intensifying their stabilisation efforts.

They were thus even less in a position to master the gravest crisis facing the international system of the 1920s, the Great Depression. It was not a crisis *of* this system as such; yet nor was it a calamity whose origins lay entirely beyond what political actors, namely the leading Republican policymakers of the 'New Era', could have influenced decisively. Crucially, their decision not to underpin the Dawes and Young regimes through political guarantees had a significant part in turning the US stock-market crash into a world crisis. Even more detrimental proved Washington's unwillingness to establish international mechanisms for concerted crisis management in the world economic system. While after 1929 Britain also shifted towards policies devised to safeguard more narrow national interests rather than the Locarno concert, the second MacDonald government's room to manoeuvre was as limited as that of the national governments following it. US policies contributed more to eroding the peace order of the 1920s, which also precipitated the demise of Weimar Germany. Ultimately, however, the system of London and Locarno could only have been sustained if *all* of its principal powers had made a stronger commitment to fortifying it – and if they had developed it further.

Analysing the evolution of international politics between 1919 and 1932 we can thus discern all the more distinctly the constraints imposed on European consolidation after World War I. They were not only imposed by adverse domestic conditions but also by distinct national traditions and foreign-policy cultures in Britain, America and continental Europe. Ultimately, the Anglo-American powers could not achieve a more fundamental reform of the Versailles system – a reform that buttressed Germany's international rehabilitation and made its revitalisation as a great power compatible with European stability. Neither Anglo-American nor French, German or Polish reorientations gained sufficient impetus to overcome various forms of postwar nationalism and reticence towards more forceful international engagements. As a result, peaceful change could not gain decisive momentum in the brief period of respite the unfinished transatlantic peace order warranted prior to its disintegration in the 1930s.

Methodological premises: reorientations and learning processes

In sum, as indicated, I posit that the underlying significance of London and Locarno can only be gauged if they are understood as part of a wider, essentially transatlantic recasting of international politics. This study proposes a methodological approach to this end whose premises differ considerably from those informing previous interpretations. The underlying premise is that in order to assess the degree of stabilisation British and American policymakers did and could achieve after 1918 one not only has to interpret their policies in a new light, one also has to re-assess the postwar international system, the roles Britain and the United States had within it – and the principal challenges they faced.

Overall, my study is intended as a contribution to the historical and hence essentially empirical examination of international conflicts and peace systems in a critical era of transatlantic relations in the twentieth century. It is written in 'an analytical mode'. In other words, its main aim is not to provide a unified 'grand narrative' of international politics in the first decade after World War I. Rather, based on empirical research I have sought to formulate core analytical questions, develop a methodological approach and pursue appropriate levels of analysis so as to find, ultimately, answers that can be substantiated empirically as well. My analysis proceeds on two main levels that it seeks to interrelate, combining two methodological approaches. On the one hand, it pursues a systematic, comparative approach in order to draw parallels, and mark distinctions, between British and American approaches to European pacification after 1919. On the other, it uses methods of *systemic* diplomatic history in order to embed this comparison in an appraisal of the wider Euro–Atlantic international system in the 1920s and 1930s.[29]

Building on Paul W. Schroeder's conceptual innovation, my study is based on the premise that only one level of the international system can be described, classically, as the interaction of state actors within a given geo–political setting and the distribution of power among them.[30] On a more formative level, the *system of international politics* can indeed be characterised as the constituent principles and rules of a 'shared practice' or common pursuit, which in turn are shaped by certain constituent ideas and assumptions.[31] In my interpretation, this system is thus constituted by the ideas and – often unspoken – assumptions actors develop, the principles they formulate and the rules they cultivate in pursuing their individual aims in the framework of a common practice – here: the conduct of international politics, pursued within the specific geo–political constellation of the post–World War I era. Alternatively, such rules could also be called the rules of a game, which is fundamentally the same for all the players involved. They are often determined by the most powerful players more than by others. But the game itself is mainly shaped through the goals not only they but also the smaller players pursue, the means they employ and the possibilities they create within it.

What has to be considered when examining twentieth-century international politics, however, is that in contrast to 1814/15 there was a further and ever more important dimension to this 'game': a new dimension of legitimacy, particularly domestic legitimacy. In an era of international relations between

---

[29] My study especially takes into account categories for the analysis of twentieth-century Europe developed by Charles Maier and above all those advanced for nineteenth-century international history in Schroeder (1994) and Krüger and Schroeder (2001). But in contrast to Maier (1988) I naturally focus on international rather than domestic politics. See Schroeder (1994), pp. vii–xiii, and (1993). See also Kennedy (1980), pp. xi–xii. I also consider relevant international relations theory, such as hegemony and interdependence theory, yet only to illuminate historical developments, not vice versa.

[30] See. Mearsheimer (2001), pp. 42–51; Waltz (1979); Snyder and Diesing (1977), p. 28.

[31] See Schroeder (1994), p. xii. Cf. also Ikenberry (2001), pp. 21–9.

democracies on both sides of the Atlantic, including the originally very un-stable Weimar Republic, pacification efforts were only sustainable if they produced outcomes that were not only viable in the international sphere but could also be legitimised in very disparate domestic settings.

Seeking to emphasise the centrality of ideas in the shaping of historical processes, this analysis rests on one central premise. It is the premise that one, if not *the*, central area in which to look for the origins of relative stagnation or transformation in any system of international politics is the field of individual outlooks and collective mentalities.[32] I argue that the decisive changes which initiated Europe's 'relative stabilisation' in the mid-1920s, and later con-strained it, originated at this level: at the level of ideas and assumptions informing not only Anglo-American approaches to the two-dimensional pro-cess of effecting and legitimating peaceful change in the western powers' relations with Germany. As I hope to substantiate, of crucial importance in this respect was the leading actors' capacity to embark on individual and collective learning processes: to conceive of new rules and pursue new and different practices, if what had been thought and practised before had failed or proved insufficient.[33] And by 1923, in the minds of decisionmakers both in London and Washington, postwar peacemaking clearly had. How relevant were the lessons they drew from the war and the crises following it? And how conducive were the conclusions they (and financiers) drew from the advances of the mid-1920s to achieving more than two significant settlements? How far could they build on the premises of London and Locarno to turn these settlements into a durable international system?

An exploration of my subject thus requires a systematic comparison of the rationales and aims of those who shaped Anglo-American policies – key policy-makers as well as their principal advisers in the Foreign Office, the State Department and other government branches. As I seek to show, what informed these policies were not only traditional ideas about external relations. There were also novel concepts in the field of international politics, such as new modes of economic diplomacy, advanced in reaction to the specific challenges of the 1920s. Of particular interest will be tracing the crucial 'unspoken assumptions' informing British, American and continental European policies as well as each side's perceptions of the Franco-German question, the Polish–German problem and Europe's general instability. This also involves examining

---

[32] It may be noteworthy here that recent cold war historiography has also emphasised the relevance of ideas, both for Soviet and US conduct. See Gaddis (1997), pp. 288–92; Leffler (1999), pp. 501–4.

[33] For an approach to historical analysis highlighting the 'use and misuse' of historical 'lessons', in this case by American policymakers in the era of World War II, see May (1973), pp. ix–xii, 3–18, 19–51. For a theoretical rather than historical approach to learning processes in international politics, see Jervis (1976), pp. 271–87.

the British 'official mind' and its post-1918 attitude towards the United States and perceptions of Britain prevalent among US policymakers and financial elites. In particular, it will be re-assessed how far Anglo-American co-operation was determined by a natural concord in stabilising the postwar order – a concord premised upon the notion of a common history and strong political as well as cultural links. And it will be evaluated how far this co-operation was ultimately limited by bilateral rivalry and each side's pursuit of narrower national interests.

Finally, I focus on an even more critical – yet often neglected – aspect: the comparison of contemporary perceptions of *the international system as a whole*, especially the outlooks of Anglo-American decisionmakers on what kind of system they desired to create. No less, however, I seek to bring out time and again how this system's configuration influenced their decisions as well as particular outcomes. And I seek to show how internal constraints that all policymakers faced one way or another – notably security concerns, financial constraints and the (perceived) force of 'public opinion' – affected international accommodation.

Yet what, if any, could be the guiding principle for a stable and legitimate postwar system after 1919? As noted, most persistently advocated by 'realist' historiography has been the all-embracing phrase 'balance of power'.[34] What I propose as a concept to replace it and to reveal the limits of this paradigm in the field of twentieth-century international history is the concept 'legitimate equilibrium'. While this term may appear equally abstract, it seems more appropriate to capture what *some* Anglo-American policymakers in the 1920s sought to achieve. Paul W. Schroeder's works have firmly established the concept 'political equilibrium' in the analysis of nineteenth-century European politics. For the era after World War I, I shall define 'legitimate equilibrium' as a maxim of reciprocity: a balance of rights, security, reciprocal satisfactions and responsibilities within the international system – a balance deemed legitimate and fundamentally fair not only by international policymakers but also by those on whose domestic support their policies depended.[35]

With this yardstick, it is to be assessed how far British and American policies could actually provide something approaching hegemonic stability after 1918, within a Euro-Atlantic system comprising states of vastly unequal power capabilities and postwar positions. Conversely, it is to be examined how far the systemic conditions then prevailing allowed for the construction of an order not resting on a crude balance of power, impossible to attain, but a new postwar equilibrium. Crucially, to be sustainable the new international system had to gain legitimacy in the eyes of all the principal actors: the victors *and*

---

[34] See Waltz (1979), pp. 84ff.   [35] Schroeder (1994), p. 582.

the vanquished; political decisionmakers, key interest-groups *and* electoral majorities.

Analytical premises: Britain and America in the post-World War I international system

This study thus argues that Europe's consolidation in the 1920s ultimately depended, not on an 'effective' balance of power, elusive after 1918, but on how adequately the international system's *de facto* pivotal powers fulfilled their roles of fostering stability and peaceful change. More precisely, it hinged on how far their principal policymakers learned to fulfil these roles – and to what extent they were not only willing but also in a position to make the political, financial and strategic commitments this entailed. In turn, this depended to a considerable degree on how far they could, or felt they could, legitimate such commitments internationally and domestically.

Yet what made the policies implemented by Britain and the United States from 1923 'policies of peaceful change' under the specific conditions of the 1920s? For purposes of orientation, I propose the following 'working definition': each approach was essentially characterised by one underlying rationale. It was the rationale to establish, first, new rules of pacific settlement and conflict-resolution within a *given* international order, underpinned by existing treaties and provisions of international law – here: the peace order, or disorder, of 1919. Their second and final purpose, however, was to apply and reinforce these rules so as to alter, in a peaceful manner, the existing order and to replace it, ultimately, by a qualitatively new international system. Here, as described, it was to be a system no longer based on containing and excluding Germany but constructed to ensure its stabilising integration.[36]

If borne out, the approach informing this analysis may elucidate what constituted, and what constrained, the effective exercise of stabilising preponderance in post-World War I Europe. And it may permit us to gauge how far some of the calamities facing Europe – though by no means all of them – can be explained by the fact that the 1920s were a fulcrum stage in a protracted transition process. It was the transition from the 'constructive' British hegemony of the early nineteenth century to the American hegemony of the latter twentieth century, from the pre-1914 *Pax Britannica* to the post-1945 *Pax Americana*.[37] As will be

---

[36] Cf. Carr (1939), pp. 208–39; Claude (1964), p. 232; Link (1970), p. 618; Kennedy (1983), pp. 21ff.

[37] Cf. the different periodisation in McKercher (1999), pp. 1–5. For the wider debate about the transition, and comparison, between two distinct hegemonies, the *Pax Britannica* and the *Pax Americana*, see Kennedy (1988), pp. 193–203, 665–92; May (1961); Schroeder (2004c); Maier (1987), pp. 148–52, and (2002); Ferguson (2003); Ikenberry (2001), pp. 80–116, 163–214; Kupchan (2003), pp. 247–62.

shown, there was no clear, let alone a benign, hegemon in the post–World War I system. Yet for all the difficulties this and the general transition process caused Britain and America were the only powers capable of shaping *and transforming* the ground-rules of international politics in Europe. Further, and crucially, they were the only powers that could induce France and Germany to accept these rules and endorse peaceful change. Even though each was in its own way constrained – Britain, financially; America, politically – they could do so not only due to their power capabilities but also by virtue of their foreign-policy approaches and systemic leverage.

The Great War had thrust the United States into the role of the newly pre-eminent financial power and 'world creditor', not least of substantial war-debts owed by the former allies Britain and France.[38] At the same time, through the war the centre of gravity in the international monetary system had shifted from London to New York. The old pre-eminence of the City of London and pound sterling as the determinant of the international gold standard was more and more replaced by the US gold-dollar system – a process which culminated in Germany's inclusion within this system in 1924.[39] America was hence also in a predominant position to set the rules for a liberal-capitalist world economy. At the same time, however, it faced the challenge of providing political leadership in accordance with the power it wielded.

Contrary to the rising American power, the real potential hegemon of the post–World War I era, the British Empire had emerged from the war victorious but by no means strengthened. Even if after the Treaty of San Remo the Empire's extension had reached its all-time zenith in 1920, Britain's altered role in the post-1918 constellation was marked by the accentuated 'Janus-faced' nature of her position. What appeared on the imperial horizon was the danger of strategic 'over-extension', a widening gap between her expanding commitments and the relative diminution of her resources, not least due to the postwar contraction of the 'Victorian economy', which was underscored by Britain's war-debts.[40] Yet Britain remained, not only in Chamberlain's view, Europe's pivotal balancing power, positioned to play a decisive role in overcoming the Franco-German antagonism. It could fulfil this role, and was called upon to do so, not so much through military deterrence as by bringing its to bear its diplomatic weight to further peaceful change.[41]

---

[38] Cf. Burk (1985), pp. 10ff; Reynolds (1991), pp. 105ff; Artaud (1979).
[39] Cf. Rowland (1975); Orde (1990), p. 11. See chapter 11.
[40] Cf. Ferguson (1998b), pp. 395–6; Kennedy (1988), pp. 407–13; Hobsbawm (1969), p. 204. The San Remo Treaty added large-scale mandates in the Middle East. Cf. Monroe (1981), p. 74.
[41] Chamberlain to Howard, 18 March 1925, *DBFP*, I, XXVII, no. 256.

Introduction

The 'architecture' of this study

On these methodological and analytical premises, this study is st
systematically yet also follows an overall chronological pattern. Follo ...ᵦ ᴜᴇ
introductory prologue, it falls into three main parts and an epilogue, which
each pursue one principal theme. Each part comprises systematic 'blocs' of
comparative examinations and, subsequently, chapters centring on the systemic analysis of core developments in international politics between 1919 and
1932. I thus hope to capture not only the dynamism of change but also the *per
se* more static systemic and structural features marking international relations
after 1918.

Prologue

The prologue sets out by analysing the challenges of peacemaking in the
aftermath of the Great War and the long period of widening imperialist
competition and nationalist antagonism preceding it. And it compares the
two first British and American attempts to build a new peace order on the
carnage of 1918: Lloyd George's bid for a moderate settlement with Germany
and a new directorate of great powers; and Wilson's quest for an entirely novel
peace system, anchored in the League of Nations and based on national self-
determination and collective security. It then re-appraises the 'truncated peace'
of Versailles and its consequences, showing why neither British nor American
peace efforts in 1919 could found anything even coming close to a sustainable
postwar order for Europe.

First part

On these premises, the first part of my study explores what those policymakers
who followed Wilson and Lloyd George perceived as the core problems
causing European instability after 1919 – those left behind by the war but also
those created or exacerbated at Versailles. It then analyses what concepts each
side developed to settle the cardinal problem of the 1920s: the unresolved
Franco-German question. And it shows how each side sought to come to terms
with the climactic Franco-German conflict over the Ruhr – as well as the larger
problems of reparations and European insecurity underlying it. Then follows a
re-appraisal of what impact British and American stabilisation strategies had on
the recasting of postwar relations between the western powers and Germany
after the *caesura* of 1923. Finally, my analysis seeks to shed new light on the
making of the Dawes plan and the 1924 London settlement, re-evaluating it as
the first 'real' peace settlement in Europe after the Great War.

Second part

In the second part, the main aim is to build on these findings to re-assess the path to, and making of, the second substantial peace settlement in post-World War I Europe, the Locarno accords. By placing this process in a wider transatlantic context, the pact of October 1925 is re-interpreted as part of a more far-reaching consolidation process – and as the second pillar of an essentially Euro-Atlantic peace system emerging in the mid-1920s. As outlined above, my overriding interest in all three parts will be to elucidate, first, what – if any – lessons British and American policymakers drew not only from the war and Versailles but also from the European crises following it.

Then, it will be re-assessed how far the strategies decisionmakers in Washington and Whitehall pursued *de facto* furthered a more general reorientation towards shared – broadly speaking, Anglo-American – principles and rules of pacific settlement and peaceful change in international politics. What is to be examined, then, is – first – their effect on, and compatibility with, the western-orientated policy of peaceful revision pursued by Weimar Germany's pre-eminent foreign minister Stresemann. And it is to be examined – second – how far they were reconcilable with France's more *status quo*-orientated but also changing security policy. Already readjusted under the Third Republic's pre-eminent postwar premier, Raymond Poincaré, it was mainly altered by his successor, Edouard Herriot, and above all the subsequent foreign minister, Aristide Briand.

Thus, a particular emphasis will be on evaluating – both from the French and the German perspectives – what influence Anglo-American policies, and leverage, had on policymaking in Paris and Berlin. In particular, I consider how far they could spur concomitant reorientations on the part of those who sought Franco-German reconciliation in the 1920s. A similar approach will be pursued to re-assess the Polish–German problem and its repercussions for Locarno politics. Not least, it will be examined what impact Anglo-American policies had on Poland's postwar quest for security between Germany and Bolshevik Russia. And it will be analysed how those who led it, chiefly Marshal Jozef Piłsudski and the foreign ministers Aleksander Skrzińsky and August Zaleski, responded to the changes initiated at London and Locarno.

Third part

The study's final part and its epilogue seek to provide new answers to two cardinal questions. How far could the emerging transatlantic peace order of the mid-1920s be sustained? And why was it undermined so quickly and thoroughly by the colossal shock-waves of the Great Depression? To this end, it will first re-examine the limited yet remarkable consolidation of Europe's nascent *Pax Anglo-Americana* in Europe's period of 'relative stability' (1926–9). Often called the 'Locarno era', it was more precisely the era of London and Locarno, the Dawes regime and the security pact.

At the outset, the remaining challenges of Euro-Atlantic stabilisation will be assessed. Also to be analysed, however, is a further stage in the reorientation of Anglo-American stabilisation policies: essentially the retreat from further forward engagement on behalf of peaceful change after Locarno, which was not reversed until late 1928. Then, it will be assessed what this meant for the consolidation not only of western but also of eastern Europe. The main focus will again be on Franco-German relations, particularly on both powers' attempt to forge a 'final postwar settlement' at Thoiry in 1926. Further, concentrating on the negotiations over the Kellogg–Briand Pact of 1928, the prospects of widening the Locarno concert into a broader Euro-Atlantic security system will be assessed. What effect all of these developments had for Polish–German relations – and vice versa – will also be considered. Finally, I shall re-appraise what can essentially be seen as attempts to build on the precedent of the 1924 Dawes accords in order to achieve a 'final settlement' of reparations and the pivotal Rhineland question. These led to the final transatlantic 'grand bargains' of the interwar period: the Young plan and the Hague settlement of 1929.

Epilogue

The epilogue will focus on the eventual dissolution of the 'unfinished transatlantic peace order' after the onset of the World Economic Crisis in 1929. It will re-evaluate how far Anglo-American policymakers and their continental European counterparts could find ways to manage a crisis of such unprecedented proportions and how far they had room for manoeuvre to salvage the international system of the 1920s. Re-evaluating the *caesura* of the 1931 Hoover Debt Moratorium, my analysis will end with the demise of the Weimar Republic, and world order, in 1932/3. My main interest lies in re-appraising how far this outcome was inescapable, not least due to the 'inherent contradictions' of Anglo-American attempts to recast the system of 1919 *and* constrain German power – or whether this hitherto predominant interpretation has to be revised.

Prologue: the truncated peace of Versailles and its consequences, 1919–1923

If there was a peace settlement after World War I, it was not forged in 1919. The Paris Peace Conference did not, and could not, lay the foundations for a stable and peaceful international order, certainly not in Europe. It could not even achieve what alone was in the realm of the possible so shortly after the unprecedented catastrophe of 1914–18: to establish a basic framework for postwar security, political stabilisation and economic reconstruction in a shattered Old World. It appears more illuminating to interpret the Versailles settlement as the first yet by no means the most balanced or far-reaching attempt to cope with the legacy of the Great War – and to establish a stable and legitimate peace system for the emerging Euro-Atlantic world of the 'short twentieth century'.

The peacemakers of Versailles were not only unable to come to terms with the most critical problems and core structural challenges of the postwar era – notably the lack of international security – but effectively exacerbated them. This crystallised in the unresolved German question – the question of what shape and what place the vanquished power was to have in the postwar international system. It could only be addressed after an extended period of post-Versailles crisis, and on different premises, when – from 1923 – concrete lessons were drawn from the deficiencies of what had been decided in 1919.

Appraisals of Versailles have come a long way from early, heavily politicised indictments of the treaty that portrayed it essentially as either too draconian or far too lenient. Most recent studies, by contrast, have given rise to a basic, albeit still far from complete, consensus: namely that the settlement represented 'the best compromise' that could have been forged under the conditions of 1919.[1] Then, one of the harshest and most influential critics of the peace, the economist John Maynard Keynes, concluded in his famous *Economic Consequences of the Peace* that what the victors had imposed on Germany amounted to a 'Carthaginian peace'. As Keynes, a representative of the British Treasury at Versailles, saw it, the Big Three had utterly failed to lay proper foundations

---

[1] Boemeke, Feldman and Glaser (1998), p. 3. Cf. Sharp (1991); Macmillan (2001); and the special *JMH* issue on Versailles, 51 (1979).

for peace, which should have been rational economic foundations. Instead, Wilson had given in to the statesmen of the old Europe and what they produced was predicated on flawed political precepts – 'preoccupations' that related to 'frontiers and nationalities', the 'balance of power' and 'the future enfeeblement of a dangerous enemy'. He admonished that the treaty, and particularly its call for reparations, was not only 'reducing Germany to servitude for a generation' but thereby also eliminating 'central support of the rest of Europe' and thus 'sowing the decay of [its] whole civilized life'. Unless corrected, it would thus plunge Europe into economic chaos and a 'war of vengeance'.[2] Keynes' critique sparked a flurry of 'revisionist' interpretations of the treaty from the 1920s onwards.[3]

Yet there has also been a fundamental and even more enduring 'realist' critique of Versailles in general and of Wilson's role and policy in particular. First voiced in post-World War I France, it was later, in the 1940s, formulated most powerfully by Hans Morgenthau and Walter Lippmann and subsequently refined by those who followed in their wake. It has centred on the claim that, chiefly under Wilson's influence, the peacemakers of 1919 failed to establish a powerful balance of power against German revisionism – an order that essentially reined in the defeated power by force, on the basis of a firm alliance of the victors. In the judgement of Morgenthau and Lippmann, the very premises of Wilsonianism and its emphasis on collective security and the power of public opinion were flawed. Wilson's main failure was that he did not comprehend that there was no tenable alternative to the pursuit of power politics to re-establish international order after World War I. And foremost among these was, of course, particularly when seen against the horizon of the 1930s, the problem of German power. Morgenthau thus concluded, historically hardly accurately, that at Versailles Wilson betrayed the 'traditional' US interest in re-erecting a 'viable' balance of power in Europe.[4]

Recent attempts at reconsidering the negotiations and settlement of 1919 have cast them in a far more benign light. They have emphasised the – indisputably severe – domestic and international constraints under which the principal peacemakers had to operate. And they have underlined that all sides had to make certain compromises if they wanted to salvage some essentials of their peace programmes. Thus, notably Wilson had no choice but to accept some of Georges Clemenceau's harsher demands vis-à-vis Germany for the sake of salvaging the League. Indeed, with a view to the German problem, it has been asserted that the victors of 1918 did not at all aim to impose an

[2] Keynes (1919), pp. 9–10, 35ff. Cf. Skidelsky (1983), pp. 384–8.
[3] Cf. Fry (1998), pp. 587ff; Boemeke, Feldman and Glaser (1998), pp. 6–10.
[4] Morgenthau (1952), pp. 4–27. Cf. Lippmann (1944), pp. 180–1, and (1943), pp. 6–8; Smith (1994), pp. 103–4.

outright punitive treaty on Germany, let alone to dismantle it. Rather, they sought to constrain German power while preserving its integrity as far as possible – and genuinely struggled to found a stable international order.[5]

In many respects, the peacemaking efforts of Versailles were indeed remarkable attempts to overcome the imperialism, power politics and rivalries that had plunged Europe and the world into the Great War. And notably Wilson's was a remarkable and sincere quest to construct a radically new and better world order, one based on tenets of national self-determination, collective security and enlightened public opinion. Yet the agreement he, Lloyd George and Clemenceau managed to hammer out remained beset by fundamental difficulties. It not only failed to cope with cardinal issues, above all the future of Germany. It also created some of the most virulent problems and fault-lines of the postwar period: above all the reparations conundrum and the precarious situation on Germany's western and eastern borders.

The main reason why Versailles fell short of a 'good peace' was not that it failed to satisfy the essentially economic requirements of postwar stability. Nor was its cardinal flaw that it failed to establish a functioning balance-of-power system that kept German revisionism in check – nor that it failed to follow early French proposals and eliminate the German threat once and for all by dismembering the defeated power. Rather, the settlement of 1919 could not found postwar stability, certainly not in Europe, because it remained, in essence, a truncated peace. More precisely, it even remained a 'doubly truncated' peace. For the system it established, the system of Versailles, was marred by two fundamental shortcomings. What mattered most was that the leaders of Britain, France and the United States, who became the decisive peacemakers in 1919, could not even begin to settle the central question they faced – the question how the vanquished Germany was to be treated and how its treatment could be reconciled with the creation of a sustainable European peace order. Yet what in many ways proved no less decisive was that the victors, and especially the American president Woodrow Wilson, could neither establish a 'new world order' underpinned by the newly pivotal power in European and world politics, the United States.

That no solution emerged from Versailles as to how to deal with Bolshevik Russia or, in Keynes' verdict, how to 'regain' the then still civil-war torn country for the western world, compounded the difficulties. But it was not one of the major shortcomings of 1919 because there was as yet no way of 'regaining' Russia. The western victors of the war were at that point still bent on overthrowing the Bolshevik regime, which they regarded as a temporary yet potentially contagious menace. But all their efforts to contain the Russian

---

[5] Thus the summary of recent scholarship in Boemeke, Feldman and Glaser (1998), p. 2.

revolution by drying up its source, both through direct intervention in the Russian civil war and the support of counterrevolutionary forces, were to fail. Nor, however, were there even rudiments of a common platform on which to build a peace order *with* Bolshevik Russia. Obviously, not only Wilson's blueprint for peace clashed violently with Lenin's aspirations for a federal Soviet Union of Europe. Denied diplomatic recognition, the Bolshevik regime remained excluded from the peace negotiations; and, for the foreseeable future, Bolshevik Russia remained an ostracised power and cardinal factor of uncertainty in postwar international politics.[6]

Under the circumstances, it was impossible for the principal plenipotentiaries assembled at Versailles to forge a settlement that created a stable *status quo* in Europe. And it was likewise all but inconceivable to forge a legitimate peace – to agree on peace terms that, however harsh or lenient, not only suited the differing aims of the victors but were also even remotely acceptable to the vanquished. In the final analysis, an insurmountable dilemma emerged: Wilson, the British prime minister Lloyd George and the French premier Clemenceau, who came to be known as the 'Big Three' of Versailles, could not (yet) approach a solution to the German problem *with* the leaders of the defeated, only newly republican Germany. Yet nor did they manage do so *without* them, once it became clear that Germany would not be represented at the negotiating table.

In a wider perspective, the victors could not even agree on something more fundamental amongst themselves: the basic mechanisms and ground-rules of a postwar system of international politics. They failed even to lay the groundwork for a system through which, over time, they and the vanquished could seek to forge what was indispensable: mutually tenable compromises. For such compromises were indispensable for the consolidation of post-World War I Europe. Above all, it had to be a system that eventually permitted the integration of Germany. For, as both Wilson and Lloyd George came to realise ever more acutely in 1918/19, no European peace could be sustained, without Germany's co-operation.[7] This was especially critical for addressing the lack of international security that lay at the root of the European crisis after 1918.[8] In short, then, Versailles opened up no prospects for what Europe's stabilisation required more than anything else: strategic bargains with Germany over

---

[6] Keynes (1919), p. 211. Cf. Mayer (1967), pp. 21–30, 284ff; Service (2000), pp. 412–13; Jacobson (1994), pp. 11–36; Jacobson (1998).

[7] Wilson, 'Fourteen Points', *PWW*, XLV, pp. 534–9; Imperial War Cabinet minutes, 30 December 1918, *PWW*, LIII, p. 568; Wilson's and Lloyd George's statements in the Council of Four, 27 March 1919, Mantoux (1992), I, pp. 31–2, 39–40.

[8] This was clearly perceived not only by Wilson and Lloyd George. See Crowe memorandum, 7 December 1918, cited in Rothwell (1972), p. 254; Colonel House diary, 19 December 1918, *PWW*, LIII, pp. 448–9; Bowman memorandum, 10 December 1918, in Seymour (1926–8), IV, pp. 280–1.

the shape of the postwar order, the basis of European security – and over how to distribute the costs of a war of unprecedented destructiveness.

As a result, international instability was aggravated rather than overcome in 1919. It was aggravated in particular because the Versailles system rested on what remained a precarious compromise between three disparate and to a large extent conflicting approaches to peace. Wilson's aspiration to 'make the world safe for democracy' was doubtless the most radical and progressive. He sought to effect no less than a transformation of what he regarded as a bankrupt prewar order. His vision was to replace it by a new order based on the principle of national self-determination and a supranational system of collective security under the Covenant of the newly established League of Nations, which also was to include – as soon as possible – a democratic Germany.[9] This reached much further than, yet was not wholly incompatible with, Lloyd George's quest for building peace through a new directorate of great powers and moderation vis-à-vis Germany. It was harder to reconcile with Britain's claims for 'full reparation'. Most importantly, however, both American and British peace aims were in cardinal aspects irreconcilable with Clemenceau's peace agenda – his quest for *sécurité*, to be achieved by establishing a new balance of power against German revisionism and preferably also by substantially dismembering the *voisin d'outre-Rhin*.

It is not surprising in view of these differences that what 'Big Three' hammered out at Versailles ultimately became an ill-founded settlement. Not only did the peace of 1919 leave Bolshevik Russia outside what was to become the postwar international order. Crucially, it was indeed imposed on *and excluded* the vanquished power Germany. The latter, in a process of transition to an as-yet highly unsettled Weimar Republic, would hence be isolated and beset by a 'revision syndrome' regarding the peace treaty.[10] At the same time, an inescapably less than even-handed application of the self-determination principle left central and eastern Europe structurally unstable, with the newly recognised nation-states Poland and Czechoslovakia encompassing German minorities and sharing contested borders with their western neighbour. As Wilson's key adviser and America's most seasoned foreign-policymaker at the time, Colonel House, laconically remarked after Versailles, 'empires cannot be shattered and new states raised upon their ruins without disturbance'.[11] Finally, whatever designs there were to remedy these problems through the Versailles system collapsed, or were at least severely impaired, when it 'lost' what was to have been its principal power. Wilson's failure to gain the US Senate's approval for the Treaty of Versailles – and the Anglo-American security pact with France – all but undermined the edifice of Versailles before it could even begin to consolidate.

[9] Wilson Senate address, 22 January 1917, *PWW*, XL, pp. 539ff.
[10] Cf. Salewski (1980); Krüger (1993).
[11] House diary, 29 June 1919, Seymour (1926–8), IV, pp. 488–9.

1 The wider challenges

The legacy of the Great War and the era of

Yet the cardinal reasons for why the efforts of 1919 could found no durable peace lie far deeper. This was due neither to Clemenceau's pursuit of harmful designs on Germany nor, primarily, to the fact that Wilson's principles were too rigid to make for workable solutions to Europe's underlying postwar problems, chiefly that of security. Rather than focus on explaining what the peacemakers at Versailles did or did not achieve, a re-appraisal of their efforts should elucidate what they *could* – and more importantly what they *could not* – achieve under the conditions of 1919. Answering this latter question requires not only a fresh look at the protagonists' aims and strategies as well as the constraints they faced, both international and domestic. It also requires placing the Paris negotiations in their proper historical context – against the back-ground of how the international system had evolved in the 'long' nineteenth century. Crucially, Versailles followed a long period of escalating imperialist rivalry preceding the July crisis of 1914. This historical canvass can only be sketched in broad brushstrokes here; but it is indispensable.

What, then, were the most critical issues facing Anglo-American policy-makers? And what were the main structural challenges that, to a greater or lesser extent, figured on their 'mental maps'? In short, they not only had to cope with the immense human and material costs of the war on both sides of the trenches – unprecedented death tolls, devastation on the battle-fields and the immense political, economic and social consequences of a conflict that nearly ruined all major European belligerents. Nor did they 'merely' have to cope with the nationalist fervour whipped up in all warring countries to mobilise entire populations for four gruelling years of trench-warfare – and with these popula-tions' heightened expectations as to the dividends of the peace. Policymakers also had to come to terms with a yet more daunting legacy. For beyond its immediate causes and key factors like Germany's aggressive militarism, the war was the outcome of decades of growing power-political rivalries under the banner of imperialism.[1] And behind these lay, in modern European history,

---

[1] For the interminable debate on German war-guilt see Fischer (1967); Berghahn (1993). For the wider debate over the origins of the Great War see Strachhan (2001); Joll (1992); Schroeder (2004b).

three centuries of intermittent yet continually widened international conflicts within a for the most part competitive, war-prone state-system.

This system had been fundamentally recast in 1814/15. Some scholars have argued that the Congress of Vienna established a balance of power on which the order of nineteenth-century Europe rested. And they claim that it was the 'abdication' of its principles that caused World War I. In this interpretation, European leaders failed to keep the continental balance sufficiently flexible to prevent great-power conflicts from spinning out of control.[2] But, as has been shown more recently, the Vienna system was sustained, not by a balance of power but by a new political equilibrium of rights and satisfactions, guarded by its key mechanism, the Concert of Europe. Underpinned by a moderate and overall stabilising British hegemony, and a comparatively restrained Russian hegemony in the east, this provided the framework for a remarkably long period of European peace.[3]

In the light of this, it seems more accurate to conclude that the wider origins of the catastrophe of 1914 have to be sought in a momentous shift occurring in the latter half of the nineteenth century: the shift from the European concert to a war-prone balance-of-power system after the Crimean War (1853–6). While still – albeit precariously – moderated through Bismarckian *realpolitik*, competition between Europe's great powers intensified after the Franco-Prussian war and the German unification of 1871.[4] Yet it was the globalisation of this competition in the core period of imperialism (1880–1914) that ultimately led to the erosion of the Vienna system. It was replaced by an inherently unstable (im)balance between two increasingly rigid alliance blocs. In the imperialist order, Britain could no longer fulfil the vital hegemonic role that it had played earlier in the nineteenth century in equilibrating the European international system. At the same time it proved ever harder, and in the end impossible, to develop effective mechanisms for settling great-power conflicts – mechanisms that could have prevented the cataclysm of 1914.[5]

Undoubtedly, the imperialist era saw striking instances of the great powers managing to prevent the escalation of local crises to all-out war, notably in the Balkans.[6] Yet it also saw the culmination of one ultimately far more detrimental trend: all European powers increasingly prepared themselves not for crisis management but for war. To defend their security, status and interests vis-à-vis their international competitors, they came to rely chiefly on secret diplomacy, armed strength and alliances serving ever less to manage conflicts and

---

[2] See Kissinger (1994), pp. 226–7; Mearsheimer (2001), pp. 42–3; and the different interpretation in Steiner (2003), pp. 258–77.

[3] This has been shown convincingly by Schroeder (1994). Cf. Krüger and Schroeder (2001).

[4] Cf. Langer (1962); Baumgart (1999).

[5] Cf. Langer (1968); Taylor (1954); Schöllgen (2000).

[6] See Dülffer, Kröger and Wippich (1997).

moderate the conduct of the other powers and ever more to prevail in an eventual clash. They not only sought to fortify their state and military machineries for this purpose; they also increasingly drew on imperialist yet at the core nationalist ideologies to mobilise their populations.[7] Of course, some of the Great War's principal combatants – Britain, France and notably Austria-Hungary and Russia – had to pursue such mobilisation efforts within what were partly integrated yet for the most part highly heterogenous empires. In turn, they provoked – immediately or over time – not only defensive nationalism on the part of challenged 'new' powers like Japan but also the rise of nationalist counter-movements among the minorities these empires comprised, which ranged from reactionary to progressively anti-colonialist.

Further, while the prewar era had also witnessed the first veritable 'globalisation' of the international economy, growing capitalist interdependence did not have the effect that some observers, like Norman Angell, predicted: to make a major war unthinkable, because it threatened to destroy the web of international commerce and bring about economic collapse.[8] For economic was also a function of political rivalry as governments sought to harness dynamically growing yet also fluctuating national economies to strengthen their states' power bases and military capabilities.[9] By the end of the nineteenth century, all major European powers apart from Britain had established similar forms of 'mercantilistic', state-run economic organisation and sought to protect key industries and agricultural interests through tariff barriers. And even though Britain maintained free trade throughout the Empire till 1914, the proposal of Colonial Secretary Joseph Chamberlain in 1903 to establish a protective 'imperial preference' had sparked far-ranging discussions.[10] Yet could the old order be replaced by a 'liberal' world economic system, as demanded by its new hegemon, the United States, and British liberal internationalists like Keynes?[11] And, more importantly, could such changes indeed hold the key to Europe's pacification?

Undoubtedly, the adverse conditions for postwar stability were also determined by a collapse of trade and widespread economic *malaise*. The need for revitalising European economies and to establish an international financial system that could cope with this task, and in which the new lender of last resort, the United States, would have to play a predominant role, was imperative. What mattered even more, however, was to deal with the political consequences of the prewar era and the war itself. Yet by 1918 there was no longer any European mechanism to rely on; nor were there even basic premises of

---

[7] Cf. Joll (1992), pp. 42–108, 174–98; Nicolson (1937), pp. 40ff; Hobsbawm (1992); Benner (2001).

[8] See Angell (1913).

[9] Cf. Hobsbawm (1987); Kennedy (1988); Cain and Hopkins (2001).

[10] Cf. Steiner (2003), pp. 15–16; Thompson (1997).

[11] Wilson, 'Fourteen Points', 8 January 1918, *PWW*, XLV, pp. 537–8; Keynes (1919), pp. 9ff.

what would hence be crucial: a transatlantic international system (let alone a global one).

The war had led to the irreversible breakdown of Europe's pre-1914 pentarchy of great powers and the balance-of-power system which had caused it in the first place.[12] With the demise of two of the pentarchy's three eastern Empires, Austria-Hungary and Tsarist Russia, the war had shattered the basis for even a nominal re-establishment of the old order, or rather *disorder*. The third, the vanquished Wilhelminian Empire was in a process of transition to an as-yet inherently unstable Weimar Republic, isolated like Bolshevik Russia and in search of a new political role in European and world politics. While eastern central Europe became the structurally most unsettled region of Europe, the international centre of gravity had thus shifted to the west.

If from any power, the main impetus for re-establishing European peace had to come from the western victors of the war. At the same time, while Britain and France had achieved their costly victory only with support from overseas, the rise of the United States as 'the power that finally determined the outcome of Europe's conflicts' had widened the European into an essentially transatlantic state-system.[13] But it was still highly unclear how far Wilson would be able to convince public opinion in his own country that the United States was called upon to take on an unprecedented role in this system – that it had to become the principal guarantor of the new world order he envisaged. Most of all, it remained doubtful whether he could legitimate such a role vis-à-vis a US Congress that was dominated by a Republican opposition deeply suspicious of far-reaching global commitments.[14]

When the armistice was signed between the Allies and the Central Powers on 11 November 1918, all sides thus confronted a deeply unsettled *status quo* and an unhinged state-system. In even greater disarray, however, were the basic premises – the ground-rules and assumptions – governing international relations. By 1918, the tenets of balance-of-power politics, which had been at the core of prewar diplomacy, were widely discredited. By many they were seen as having led the powers into the abyss of 1914. Yet this was not a notion espoused by all leading policymakers in Europe, certainly not in France. Nor was it unanimously embraced in Britain. There, influential voices like the acting foreign secretary Lord Curzon and his assistant permanent under-secretary Eyre Crowe were still reluctant to discard what they regarded as a venerable tradition of British 'balancing diplomacy'. Having viewed Britain's entry into the war as a legitimate defensive act against Germany's aggression,

---

[12] See the overviews in Joll (1992), pp. 1–9, 234–40; Bell (1986), pp. 31–47.

[13] Bracher (1978), p. 19. Cf. Kennedy (1988), pp. 366ff; Duroselle (1994).

[14] This was a constant source of uncertainty in 1919. See Mantoux (1992), I, pp. 31–2; War Cabinet minutes, 28 February 1919, CAB 23/15.

both believed that Britain's role in the postwar world had to remain that of regulating Europe's balance of power. They believed that this was what British interests commanded, chiefly to prevent the re-emergence of any German threats, yet also to moderate French postwar policy.[15]

But the view that old-style power politics had caused the war and had to be overcome was certainly prevalent among liberal and leftist circles in Britain and the United States. It was advocated by such influential pressure-groups as the American League to Enforce Peace (LEP) and the British League of Nations Union (LNU).[16] And, crucially, it was a guiding aim of what the American president himself envisaged. In his widely noted speech at London's Guild Hall on 28 December 1918 Wilson declared that the critical task of peacemaking was to discard an 'old order' in which the international 'balance' had depended on 'the sword' and 'the unstable equilibrium of competitive interests'.[17] The British wartime premier Lloyd George and Lord Robert Cecil, then minister for the blockade, also took up this call, not without conviction but chiefly on grounds of *realpolitik*. Their main aim was to pave the way for close postwar co-operation with Washington.[18]

Not the only, but probably *the* principal challenge peacemakers at Versailles, and their successors in the 1920s, faced was to replace the old by a new system of international politics, which included the hence indispensable American power in efforts to reconstruct Europe. Their daunting task was to establish a security architecture that addressed French and wider European concerns; that underpinned Europe's economic recuperation; that accommodated competing national aspirations particularly in eastern Europe and that finally also created the preconditions for a more constructive *modus vivendi* with Bolshevik Russia. Yet the crucial requirement was to accommodate Germany without jeopardising the security of its neighbours, above all France and the re-established Polish state. For, as the perceptive South African prime minister, Jan Christian Smuts, impressed on those gathered at Versailles in March 1919, 'Germany will remain, despite everything, a dominant element in continental Europe, and it would be a folly to believe that we can reconstruct the world without her assistance.'[19] This was to be the yardstick for all peacemaking efforts after World War I.

---

[15] See Curzon's statements, War Cabinet meeting, 30 December 1918, *PWW*, LIII, pp. 565–6. Crowe memorandum, 7 December 1918, cited in Rothwell (1972), p. 254; Crowe minutes, 30 and 31 December 1918, FO 371/4353/f29/PC152.

[16] Cf. Knock (1992), pp. 56–7; Birn (1985); Ceadel (1980).

[17] Wilson address at Guild Hall, 28 December 1918, *PWW*, LIII, p. 532.

[18] Cecil memorandum to Imperial War Cabinet, 17 December 1918, CAB 23/42; War Cabinet minutes, 30 December 1918, *PWW*, LIII, pp. 565–6.

[19] Smuts letter, read by Lloyd George to the Council of Four, 27 March 1919, Mantoux (1992), I, p. 38.

2   Wilson, Lloyd George and the quest for a 'peace to end all wars'

How did Wilson and Lloyd George intend to cope with these wider challenges? How and how far did they perceive them and the more immediate problems of 1918, all crystallising around the German question? How precisely did they envisage forging a 'peace to end all wars'? To explore this, not only their goals and strategies must be compared. It also has to be re-assessed on what assumptions each statesman operated, against which constraints each sought to legitimate his endeavours and what lessons each had drawn from the Great War.

Towards a new world order? The aspirations and limits of Wilson's Progressivism

The alleged 'failure' of Wilson's peace policy at Versailles was already widely highlighted at the time, not least during the ratification debates in the US Senate.[1] In the eyes of Keynes and other liberal critics the problem lay not with the tenets of Wilsonianism itself but the fact that they had been compromised at Versailles, essentially by the machinations of European power politics as practised by Lloyd George and Clemenceau. Keynes' verdict was that Wilson's inability to make his interlocutors accept his laudable programme contributed decisively to the 'Carthaginian peace'.[2] More clout, though, have had subsequent 'realist' condemnations of Wilson's approach. As we have seen, Morgenthau, Lippmann and their followers claimed that Wilsonianism was not viable because it failed to appreciate that world politics was governed by the balance of power. And they have asserted that, under the circumstances of 1919, the primary US interest, which Wilson neglected, lay in aiding Britain and France in establishing a postwar order on these premises. In their eyes, he thus utterly failed to deal with the central problem of the interwar period, that of German power.[3]

---

[1] Keynes (1919), pp. 9–10.
[2] *Ibid.*, p. 35; Wilson meeting with Senate Foreign Relations Committee, 19 August 1919, *PWW*, LXII, pp. 339–411.
[3] Lippmann (1943), pp. 6–8; Morgenthau (1952), pp. 4ff. Cf. Smith (1994), pp. 103–9.

By contrast, favourable assessments of Wilson's peace policy stress that, while it could not be realised in 1919, his vision was inherently forward-looking and ultimately borne out in the twentieth century, making it a 'Wilsonian century'. All in all, thus the claim, the evolution of international relations since 1945 has borne out what Wilson predicted in 1917 – namely: that a stable, liberal world order could only flourish on the principles of collective security and national self-determination; and that the application of these principles would also harness nationalism to democratic – and peaceful – ends.[4] But in terms of the aspirations he had – not least to make Germany part of his new system – Wilson's quest to 'end all wars' failed miserably in the interwar period. The question thus remains: did it come to nought because of its inherent contradictions – or because the international constellation was such that it could not (yet) bear fruit? In fact, one question cannot be divorced from the other.

In the light of his time, it seems more appropriate to conclude that Wilson's most forward-looking impulse was his aspiration to establish novel international institutions, and an unprecedented covenant of rules, to recast the inherently war-prone 'order' of the pre-1914 era. In 1919, his was the most consistent, yet also the historically and strategically most uninformed, attempt to create a genuinely new world order. He envisaged it as a system in which the 'strong' powers co-operated in the maintenance of world peace, committed themselves to universal rules for peaceful conflict-resolution and thus also protected the interests and integrity of the 'weak' states, hence equal under international law.[5] Historically as important, his was the first attempt to commit the rising world power United States to such an order – to becoming an arbiter of peace, particularly in Europe but also the wider world. But in both respects Wilson pursued too radical an agenda. It was too radical to offer constructive answers to the specific problems of 1918, notably the future of Germany, and to make possible international bargains germane to stabilising war-ravaged Europe. Particularly his bid for a universal application of the self-determination principle failed at Versailles and *de facto* led to outcomes hindering European consolidation, especially on Germany's eastern borders. Yet, critically, Wilson's design was also too ambitious to gain sufficient legitimacy at home, in the courts of the Senate and US public opinion.[6]

On the surface, the American president's 'crusade' was directed squarely against the forces of autocracy and the 'old order', as embodied above all by the Wilhelminian Empire but also the Austro-Hungarian monarchy. Following the October revolution, it was of course also a bid to contain the forces of Bolshevism, to prevent them spreading from a civil war-torn Russia to

---

[4] See above all Link (1979); Knock (1992); Ninkovich (1999); Smith (1994), pp. 90ff.
[5] Wilson speech, San Diego, 19 September 1919, Shaw (1924), II, p. 1017.
[6] Cf. Ambrosius (1987), pp. 172–206; Stone (1970), pp. 100–27.

Germany and western Europe.[7] But Wilson sought to spur an even wider transformation. He sought to dismantle 'old-style' power politics as such, including that practised by the heretofore more or less democratic imperial powers Britain and France. Contrary to what contemporaries and later 'realist' critics have claimed, Wilson was essentially right in identifying the prewar order's fundamental problem. He highlighted it in his seminal 'peace without victory' speech before the Senate on 22 January 1917, two months before America entered the war, when demanding that '(t)here must be, not a balance of power, but a community of power; not organised rivalries, but an organised common peace'.[8] This peace, which Wilson outlined in 1917/18, was to be founded on two principles indeed never applied before: universal collective security and national self-determination. And it was to be guaranteed by an equally unprecedented 'universal association', the League of Nations. It was to bolster the global spread of democracy and, eventually, comprise only democratic nation-states.[9]

Wilson also sought to further peace through a reorganisation, and liberalisation, of the world economic system. When on 8 January 1918 he presented his famous Fourteen Points, he gave the 'removal, so far as possible, of all economic barriers and the establishment of an equality of trade conditions' among all signatories of the peace high priority.[10] Wilson thus intended to break down the 'closed' tariff systems of the Central Empires (and France), which in his view had eroded peace almost as much as their militarism. They were to be supplanted by a non-discriminatory trading system based upon the American 'open-door' principle. Wilson thus espoused a precept of US foreign economic policy first championed under his Republican predecessor William Taft to 'open up' the Chinese market in opposition to European imperial interests in 1899–1900. Making the open-door paradigm a global standard was to become one of the most constant maxims of US foreign policy in the 1920s.[11] The liberalisation of foreign trade was a core interest of an economic power rapidly rising to global predominance. But it remained to be seen how far Wilson could prevail on an increasingly protectionist Congress to apply such maxims at home and refrain from levying new tariffs.[12]

For all the weightiness of economic concerns, however, Wilson's bid for a new world order was essentially politically motivated. The prescriptions of his Fourteen Points were all distinctly political in nature, and so was the thrust of his subsequent endeavours. In turn, his peace policy had strong legalistic and

---

[7] Cf. Mayer (1967), pp. 21ff.
[8] Wilson Senate address, 22 January 1917, *PWW*, XL., pp. 536–7.
[9] Wilson address, Guild Hall, 28 December 1918, *PWW*, LIII, pp. 532ff.
[10] Wilson, 'Fourteen Points', *PWW*, XLV, p. 537.
[11] For a detailed analysis see chapter 5.
[12] Cf. Williams (1972b), pp. 12ff; Hawley (1979); Leffler (1981); Smith (1994), pp. 92–5.

moralistic components. But it was essentially unhistorical, conceived with no more than superficial consideration for any broader historical precedents or understandings not derived from the exceptional American experience. In many ways, Wilson's quest can be seen as an ambitious attempt to internationalise Progressive principles of American policy, as he interpreted them. On one level, he sought to make the US Monroe Doctrine of 1823 the world's essential charter. Defining it as befitted his purpose, Wilson in January 1917 proposed that all 'nations should with one accord adopt the doctrine of President Monroe as the doctrine of the world: that no nation should seek to extend its polity over any other nation or people . . . that all nations henceforth should avoid entangling alliances which would draw them into competitions of power'.[13]

On a deeper level, Wilson's peace policy was invigorated, and limited, by his Progressive worldview. It was Progressive in the sense that Wilson sought to apply standards from the realm of American domestic politics to the sphere of international conflict-resolution. He sought to reform world politics by drawing on liberal maxims from the domestic reform agenda that he and other American Progressives championed. Translated to world politics, these included above all 'open covenants openly arrived at' and the rule of international law, notably clear rules for adjudicating international disputes.[14]

Yet Wilson of course derived his standards from one of the most exceptionally fortunate state- and nation-building processes in modern history. In contrast to the United States, modern continental European states had for centuries evolved in close proximity to potentially and often *de facto* adversarial neighbours. The evolution of strong, armed – and often autocratic – states and their specific foreign-policy practices are incomprehensible without due regard for these essential geo-political conditions. By comparison, the American republic emerged almost entirely free from external threats (the only notable exception being the war of 1812). The claim to preserve this state of affairs, and US hegemony in the western hemisphere, informed the Monroe Doctrine.

Wilson thus was indeed a Progressive internationalist.[15] But what made his approach most distinctive was his espousal of what for lack of a better word could be called a credo of American 'exemplarism'. In many ways, it was the opposite of US exceptionalism, the notion that the American republic was a unique 'shining city on the hill', to be shielded from corrupting foreign influences. In fact, Wilson's was only the first of two 'exemplarist' designs advanced by American policymakers to recast Europe before Nazism. The second was the Republicans' Progressive design, whose contours emerged under Secretary

---

[13] Wilson speech to League to Enforce Peace, 27 May 1916, *PWW*, XXXVII, pp. 113ff; Wilson Senate address, 22 January 1917, *PWW*, XL, pp. 536–9.

[14] Wilson, 'Fourteen Points', *PWW*, XLV, pp. 534–9. See Hofstadter (1955) and (1962).

[15] Thus Knock (1992). See also Knock (1998), pp. 111–30.

of State Hughes and Commerce Secretary Hoover in the early 1920s.[16] Not unlike his Republican opponents, if more fervently than them, Wilson believed that the principles enshrined in the US constitution were universal and that the American polity could serve as a model for all mankind. Yet, in contrast to them, he also believed that Washington should take the political lead in globalising this model, or more precisely his version of it.

There was no precedent for such a momentous step in the history of international *or* American politics. To take it, Wilson had to bridge an immense gap. He not only had to persuade his European counterparts that his was the way of the future. He also had to convince US public opinion and, above all, a Congressional majority that it was not only imperative for world peace but also in America's own best interest. In retrospect, there is no doubt that Wilson faced a gigantic up-hill struggle, especially on the domestic front. It was not until the turn of 1918/19 that, on his way to Europe, he translated the Fourteen Points into a concrete peacemaking agenda, which he then presented in London, Paris and Rome. In shaping this agenda, he relied on a small entourage of advisers, most prominently his special envoy Colonel House and, for League affairs, Isaiah Bowman, while Secretary of State Robert Lansing was only marginally involved.[17] Far more than Britain's, however, American policy was essentially determined by one man.

Wilson at first contemplated preserving a modified Austria-Hungary as a stabilising anchor in central Europe but later dismissed this prospect. His ambitions pointed in a different direction: all autocratic empires had to lose their controlling influence on world politics. They had to be reformed, and if necessary broken up, to accord the different nationalities they had comprised 'the freest opportunity of autonomous development'. Most notably, Wilson demanded the creation of 'an independent Polish state' on 'the territories inhabited by indisputably Polish populations' and with 'a free and secure access to the sea'. He was convinced that the aspirations of all nations, particularly the smaller ones, could be directed to democratic ends. Like other liberal internationalists of his time, he indeed saw an intimate correlation between a state's constitution and its international behaviour. Democracies, thus his core assumption, would no longer be prone to wage war amongst each other. Yet to safeguard such democratic peace, they had to unite in what he in January 1918 called a new 'general association of nations'.[18]

Indubitably, no feature in Wilson's postwar edifice was more important than its centrepiece, or rather superstructure: the League. Yet his plans for it long remained remarkably imprecise. They were only fleshed out just before the

[16] On Republican progressivism see chapter 5.
[17] Cf. Walworth (1986); Gelfand (1998), pp. 189–203.
[18] Wilson, 'Fourteen Points', *PWW*, XLV, pp. 537–8.

opening of the peace conference in January 1919, not least influenced by proposals of the South African premier Smuts.[19] The 'general association' of nations Wilson presented to the delegates at Versailles was to found peace on universal disarmament, enabling arms reductions not only among the vanquished but also the victors. But most of all it was to establish two new mandatory standards of international politics: the commitment of all member-states to seek a peaceful resolution, and if necessary arbitration, of international disputes; and the commitment to collective security, prescribing that, in the last resort, all members would aid a victim of aggression. Thus, the League was to become 'a single overwhelming, powerful group of nations who shall be the trustee of the peace of the world'.

Most profoundly, world peace would be underpinned by what Wilson saw as the ultimate power in international affairs: 'the moral force of the public opinion of the world'. The scrutiny and civilising power of 'the public view', which he deemed inherently anti-aggressive, could hence act through the League's 'instrument'. Wilson was confident that, if properly organised, no potential aggressor would ultimately dare contravene this force – and that it would also influence the public in a belligerent state.[20] Yet, while attaching high hopes to 'open diplomacy', the American president was not a one-sided idealist. He envisaged that if public opinion failed economic sanctions could be invoked. And behind everything else stood the threat of collective sanction: the majority's military intervention against an aggressor once all arbitration efforts had failed. In short, this also was to protect France against German revisionism. It should be noted, however, that although he met Clemenceau in Paris in December 1918 Wilson never gave special consideration to French security prior to Versailles.[21]

From the outset, the American president confronted a perhaps inevitable tension inherent in his design. It was the tension between the League's ideal of equality for all its members and the need to ensure that its Covenant would actually be enforced. Wilson's thinking on this problem underwent a noteworthy evolution in 1918/19. He never abandononed his conviction that, as there could be no equality of power or territory among the world's nations, the League's central premise had to be 'equality of rights'. Yet, directly exposed to the European postwar crisis, Wilson realised that to sustain his design it was crucial to endow the more powerful states with special responsibilities. Thus, if less than Lloyd George – and still far removed from Franklin Delano

[19] See Smuts (1918).
[20] Wilson address, Guild Hall, 28 December 1918, *PWW*, LIII, p. 532; Wilson address, 14 February 1919, *PWW*, LV, p. 175; Wilson, 'Fourteen Points', *PWW*, XLV, p. 536. For Wilson's early plans see his speech to the League to Enforce Peace, 27 May 1916, *PWW*, XXXVII, pp. 113ff. Cf. Knock (1992), pp. 76–7.
[21] House diary, 19 December 1918, *PWW*, LIII, pp. 448–9.

Roosevelt's 'Four Policemen' concept of 1945 – he accepted a new emphasis. For, as he put it in September 1919, 'only the power of the strong can maintain the right of the weak'.[22]

It is important to understand that Wilson did not want America to become a quasi-European power. On 30 December 1918, he reminded his audience at London's Free Trade Hall that the United States had 'always felt from the very beginning of her history that she must keep herself separate from any kind of connection with European politics'. And the war had not changed this. Americans still had 'no interest' in European balance-of-power machinations. Instead, Wilson eventually endorsed British plans for a League Executive Council. It would include temporary representatives from among the smaller states but, at the core, the United States, the European great powers and, for Asia, Japan. As permanent members, they would underpin postwar security.[23]

As Wilson's design was universal, he sought to draw not only the newly democratic Germany but also Bolshevik Russia into the League's orbit. He thus hoped to bolster not only their acceptance of the peace but also democratisation processes drawing both countries away from reactionary or communist alternatives.[24] In his 'Fourteen Points' Wilson had offered German leaders a conciliatory settlement and 'a place of equality among the peoples of the world'.[25] In other words, to give it a stake in the new order, Germany was to be admitted to the League as swiftly as possible. This also remained the main aim of American policy at Versailles. As will be seen, it was overall compatible with British blueprints for a new international concert. But it was diametrically opposed to what Clemenceau originally sought, namely to erect a peace order around and essentially *against* Germany. In the face of French opposition, Wilson had to concede before the peace conference even opened that Germany could only join the League after 'a period of probation'. Nevertheless, he insisted that postwar stability was elusive if the victors remained pitted against the vanquished.[26]

In private, Wilson had asserted in 1917 that by the time of peacemaking Washington would be able to prevail on its allies to accept his programme because they would be 'among other things, financially in our hands'. Once in Europe, however, he recognised that to implement his 'vision' he needed one partner above all: Britain. This went beyond the rhetoric of his declaration at

---

[22] Wilson Senate address, 22 January 1917, *PWW*, XL, p. 536; Wilson speech, 19 September 1919, Shaw (1924), II, p. 1017.

[23] Wilson speech, 30 December 1918, *PWW*, LIII, p. 550; Wilson speech, 19 September 1919, Shaw (1924), II, p. 1017.

[24] Cf. Mayer (1967), pp. 361–2, 570–1.

[25] Wilson, 'Fourteen Points', 8 January 1918, *PWW*, XLV, p. 538.

[26] Diary of Dr Grayson, 6 January 1919, *PWW*, LIII, p. 622; Council of Four, 27 March 1919, Mantoux (1992), I, pp. 39–40.

Buckingham Palace that the two 'great nations' were called upon to 'organise the moral forces of the world' in accordance with 'the right and justice' they represented.[27]

Wilson remained far from envisaging a peace controlled by a kind of shared Anglo-American hegemony. On a personal level, he continued to distrust Lloyd George.[28] And he also remained cautious because, as he confided to Clemenceau, 'the American people were anti-British . . . the easiest thing in the world would be to get them to build a navy larger than the British navy'. But the more acrimonious the negotiations became, the more 'higher realism' commanded forging a common approach with the British premier – irrespective of Wilson's antipathy to him and British imperialism. In January 1919, the American president thought it 'good politics to play the British game "more or less" in formulating the league covenant . . ., thus gaining British support that would be withheld from a personal program'.[29] Indeed, Wilson's quest would be futile if it remained a personal crusade. He had to make compromises with his European interlocutors. The essential question was what kind of compromises these would be, and whether they would compromise what he really sought to achieve.

Towards a new directorate of powers – and a moderate peace? Lloyd George's peace policy between domestic, imperial and international constraints

At the end of the war, the 'mercurial' British wartime premier found himself in a harder position than the 'prophet' Wilson.[30] To a certain extent, Lloyd George had put himself in this position, or at least aggravated it, by pursuing peace aims and raising expectations that were hardly reconcilable. For he had claimed early on that he had it in his power to shape a moderate and lasting peace. And he had asserted that he could do so while fulfilling his main promise during the 'Khaki elections' of December 1918 – to make Germany pay for the hardships it had caused Britain and the Empire.[31] Lloyd George's role at Versailles and the consistency of his peace policy have remained deeply controversial. Was he, as Keynes claimed, essentially an opportunist improviser

---

[27] Wilson to House, 21 July 1917, in Stannard Baker (1927–39), VII, p. 180; Wilson remarks, 27 December 1918, *PWW*, LIII, p. 523.

[28] House diary, 31 December 1918, House Papers. Cf. Tillmann (1961), pp. 68ff.

[29] House diary, 19 December 1918, *PWW*, LIII, p. 448; Grayson diary, 6 January 1919, *PWW*, LIII, p. 622.

[30] Thus Smuts on Lloyd George and Nicolson on Wilson. See Wilson (1970), p. 357; Nicolson (1931), p. 209.

[31] Cf. Nicolson (1931), pp. 21ff. On Lloyd George's policy see Dockrill and Goold (1981); Goldstein (1991); Rothwell (1972).

too unprincipled to make an economically reasonable peace, constantly oscil-
lating between his desire for leniency and public opinion's demand for retribution?[32] Or was he rather the only 'consummate politician' at Versailles,
seeking to negotiate a balanced settlement yet having to manoeuvre between
the opposite poles of Wilson and Clemenceau?[33]

From a distance, Lloyd George's course in 1919 and thereafter seems not so
much dictated by personal whims or lack of principles. Rather, his policies
evolved in response to a twofold, and formidable, challenge not of his choosing.
He had to reconcile, and ultimately failed to reconcile, what were indeed two
inherently conflicting requirements. On the one hand, for all its physical and
economic exhaustion the British Empire emerged from the war as one of the
most powerful victors. Politically pivotal as a European power and potentially
also as mediator between Europe and America, Britain had to play a leading part
in any attempt to found a stable peace. And Lloyd George was genuinely
convinced that his government had to prevent a re-emergence of prewar patterns
of international rivalry, which had produced such disastrous consequences.[34]

Yet, on the other hand, any British leader in 1918/19 had to satisfy the
claims in Britain and the Dominions to be compensated for the deprivations of
four arduous years of war. Facing miners' and dockers' strikes during the
Versailles conference, Lloyd George had to cope with the immense adjustments of reconverting the wartime to a peacetime economy; and he had to
initiate overdue social reforms. Further, he had to consolidate what no one
among Britain's ruling elites was yet prepared to scale back, let alone relinquish: the Empire. In short, the prime minister had to make good on his
promise to create not only a 'land' but an Empire 'fit for heroes'.[35] To achieve
this, and to repay Britain's substantial war-debts to America, he was resolved to
gain 'reparations' from Germany.[36] Though generally critical of prewar imperialism he, like most War Cabinet members, had no doubt – and certainly
did not question in public – that Wilhelminian militarism had caused the
catastrophe of 1914.[37]

During the war, Lloyd George had disclaimed any British interest in general
indemnities.[38] But once it was won, and to ensure victory in the December

---

[32] See Keynes (1971), X, pp. 23–4. Cf. Skidelsky (1983), pp. 389–90.

[33] See Morgan (1979), p. 132; Lentin (1985), pp. 5–13.

[34] War Cabinet minutes, 17 December 1918, CAB 23/42, and 30 December 1918, *PWW*, LIII,
pp. 562–3.

[35] Nicolson (1931), p. 21. Cf. Goldstein (1998), pp. 276–7.

[36] Lloyd George, war-aims speech, 5 January 1918, in Temperley (1969), I, pp. 189–92. Cf. Burk
(1985).

[37] See Lloyd George's parliamentary defence of Versailles, 3 July 1919, *Hansard*, 5th series, vol.
117, cols. 1211–32.

[38] Lloyd George speech, 5 January 1918, in Temperley (1969), I, pp. 189–92.

elections of 1918, he vowed to 'make Germany pay'. It was to pay not only for the devastation its 'aggression' had caused in Belgium and northern France but also for the human and financial toll the war had taken on Britain. In an election campaign also featuring the slogan 'hang the Kaiser' Lloyd George did not shy away from capitalising on widespread anti–German sentiment. Yet, as Harold Nicolson, his private secretary at Versailles, stressed, he 'never completely lost his head' in the 'welter of democracy': he always added that Germany's capacity to pay had to be considered – and that German payments must not 'inflict injury upon our own export and international trade'.[39]

To strike this balance without rescinding any claims also became the central aim of the Treasury's peace planning. Whereas the Khaki election's outcome was unequivocal – the Lloyd George coalition won decisively – the government's stance on reparations remained ambivalent. The assumption that there was a way to safeguard British trade without substantive concessions on indemnities marked British reparations policy throughout the 1920s. At Versailles, for all their rhetoric of moderation the British delegation would not cede an inch.[40]

Preceding Wilson's Fourteen Points, yet much less noted, Lloyd George had first outlined Britain's wider war aims in a speech on 5 January 1918. He did so in response to pressures from liberal and leftist circles grouped around Labour and the League of Nations Union, yet even more importantly to build bridges to Wilson. Convinced that America had to be Britain's crucial partner in forging peace, Lloyd George was mindful of the latter's 'peace without victory' agenda. On Britain's behalf, he proposed three pillars of postwar order: a restored 'sanctity of treaties'; a territorial settlement predicated on the right of self-determination or the consent of the governed; and, notably, a newly established league of nations whose main purpose would be to 'limit the burden of armaments and diminish the probability of war'. The British premier saw the need to guarantee postwar stability, and particularly French security, against renewed German aggression. But he also saw a key British interest in offering peace terms to Germany that permitted future reconciliation. Thus, though demanding reparations Lloyd George presented a comparatively lenient peace programme. He declared that while Britain supported France's claim for Alsace-Lorraine to right 'the wrong of 1871', it was not fighting to achieve 'the break-up of the German peoples or the disintegration of their State or country'. And although denouncing its military autocracy as a 'dangerous

---

[39] Nicolson (1931), p. 23.
[40] See Keynes memorandum, 26 November 1918, Keynes (1971), XVI, pp. 348–78; War Cabinet minutes, 24 December 1918, CAB 23/42. Cf. Bunselmeyer (1975), pp. 84ff.

anachronism' he did not make destroying Germany's 'Imperial Constitution' an explicit British war aim.[41]

Nevertheless, the prime minister generally assented to building the European postwar order on the principle of self-determination, if with consideration for the Central Powers. To reach out to Wilson and placate liberal and Labour opinion at home, he pledged his support for 'an independent Poland'. Like Wilson, he originally favoured preserving an internally reformed Austro-Hungarian Empire. He thus championed 'genuine self-government', by which he meant extensive home-rule rather than the outright secession of Czechs, Slovaks and Yugoslavs. During the subsequent peace negotiations, however, Britain rejected Wilson's unmitigated espousal of self-determination – essentially for fear of the repercussions this might have for the British Empire, particularly in Ireland. Moreover, British policymakers were far warier than their American counterparts that such radical changes might undercut stability from the start, particularly in eastern Europe.[42]

How, then, did Lloyd George envisage realising Britain's war aims? And, more importantly, how did he propose to meet the underlying challenge of forging a peace that reinforced European and imperial consolidation? British policy under Lloyd George only gradually evolved into a more coherent strategy. It remained marred by contradictory assumptions, often governed by tactical considerations and short-term interests. But its guiding rationales became nonetheless discernible by late 1918.[43] And they were further concretised during the conference itself, becoming most distinct in Lloyd George's famous Fontainebleau memorandum of March 1919. It embodied his 'vision' of an integrative, 'moderate' peace ultimately guaranteed by a new directorate of great powers; yet it also stressed that Britain was unwilling to yield on its indemnity claims to further this 'grand design'.[44]

The core elements, and tensions, of Britain's agenda can be summarised as follows: a departure from prewar alliance policies and the not so 'splendid isolation' preceding them; consideration for French security demands but also the deep-seated anxiety that Britain could make too far-reaching commitments; and an adamant interest in reparations from Germany coupled with the concern to see it stabilised as a republic and integrated into the postwar order

[41] Lloyd George speech, 5 January 1918, in Temperley (1969), I, pp. 189–90. Cf. the critical assessment in Newton (1998), pp. 36ff.
[42] Lloyd George speech, 5 January 1918, in Temperley (1969), I, pp. 190–1; General Wilson to Drummond, 2 January 1919, FO 608/121.
[43] In October 1918, Lloyd George asked Smuts to prepare the British peace brief for Versailles. Later, he relied on Cecil. See Smuts to Lloyd George, 21 October 1918, CAB 24/70. Cf. Goldstein (1991), pp. 94–8.
[44] Lloyd George, Fontainebleau memorandum, 22 March 1919, in Lloyd George (1938), I, pp. 403–16.

as soon as possible.[45] As formative, however, became a new transatlantic orientation, the desire for partnership, and burden-sharing, with the United States. For only such a partnership would allow Britain to steer the new great-power directorate its prime minister envisaged and, crucially, commit America to upholding European stability.[46] By contrast, Bolshevik Russia was to remain excluded from any international agreements until its regime assumed a less 'hostile' attitude – or, even better, was toppled. Like Wilson, Lloyd George held that the Russian problem could only be addressed following a peace with Germany, and once the Russian civil war was decided.[47]

It should not be forgotten though that after the armistice the British War Cabinet by no means agreed on whether Britain should pursue a new or a 'traditional' course to prevent a recurrence of 1914. An influential minority, notable among them Lord Curzon and the Australian prime minister William Hughes, still advocated reliance on what they saw as time-honoured practices to secure the hard-won victory. What they desired to salvage, not least against Wilson's encroachments, were Britain's imperial prerogatives and a basic common interest with France in forestalling German attempts to reverse the defeat. Deeply sceptical about Wilson's aspirations, both held that the time for 'reasonable' power politics was by no means gone; Britain would fare best by forming an alliance with France to contain Germany and protect the strategic-ally vital shores of western Europe. At the same time, they hoped that this could serve to calm France, facilitating future moderation towards Germany.[48]

As noted, the Foreign Office's higher echelons, and notably Eyre Crowe, still shared this outlook at that stage. Crowe originally doubted that despite its fledgling democratisation Germany would ever alter its unsettling ways. He also argued that while America was an increasingly important 'friend', it was also 'a long way off'. France, by contrast, sat 'at [Britain's] door' and had to be treated as a vital partner in efforts to stabilise postwar Europe. Crowe warned that Britain should not rely too readily on elaborate League and disarmament schemes to guarantee the peace.[49]

A majority in cabinet, however, including Cecil, Smuts and Lloyd George himself, had reached different conclusions. Essentially, their position was that

---

[45] War Cabinet minutes, 30 December 1918, *PWW*, LIII, pp. 565–6; Treasury memorandum, 26 November 1918, in Rothwell (1972), pp. 348ff. Concretely, however, Lloyd George hardly aided German Social Democrats in establishing a republican government.

[46] War Cabinet minutes, 17 December 1918, CAB 23/4; 30 December 1918, *PWW*, LIII, pp. 565–6.

[47] Lloyd George speech, 5 January 1918, in Temperley (1969), I, pp. 191–2; Cecil memorandum, 17 December 1918, CAB 23/42.

[48] War Cabinet minutes, 17 December 1918, CAB 23/42.

[49] Crowe memorandum, 7 December 1918, cited in Rothwell (1972), p. 254; Crowe minutes, 30 December 1918, FO 371/4353/f29/PC152.

while power questions could not be eradicated from international affairs, and Britain had a right to eliminate the threat of the German fleet, balance-of-power calculations could and must no longer determine the postwar world. And they reckoned that, not an *entente* with France, but a re-orientation towards the United States held the key to reinforcing the peace and Britain's global position. Lloyd George's finessing should not conceal that his policy was guided by more fundamental conclusions he had drawn from the war's carnage and its causes. In contrast to Curzon and Hughes, and like Cecil and Smuts, he recognised that the prewar order required a decisive reform. In the run-up to Versailles, Lloyd George thus reaffirmed his support for the League.[50]

In December 1918, both Cecil and Smuts presented the War Cabinet with plans that placed the League at the centre of the postwar system yet were nonetheless distinct. What Smuts put forward in his *The League of Nations: A Practical Suggestion* dovetailed with Wilson's vision.[51] He proposed a League that was both powerful and egalitarian, envisaging it as an organisation giving the smaller powers a tangible say and only a slim majority to the great powers in its Executive Council. Further, the League, and not the colonial powers, would oversee Germany's former colonies through a mandate system. Cecil also desired to make the League the world's main decisionmaking body. He hoped to prevent future wars by establishing a tightly knit arbitration system to settle international disputes. Essentially, however, he envisaged the League as the seat of a refashioned concert of five great powers – apart from Britain and America, France, Italy and Japan. These were to be clearly in charge of the postwar system. Cecil saw this mechanism as the League's 'pivot'. Originally excluded, the vanquished Germany was to be admitted in due course – if it complied with the victors' terms.[52]

While praising Smuts' *Practical Suggestion*, Lloyd George largely followed Cecil's design. To underpin his plea for moderate settlement at Versailles, he, too, drew on the 'historical precedent' of 1815. In his interpretation, Wellington and Castlereagh, although formerly France's 'bitterest enemies', had then opposed Prussia's desire to impose 'crushing terms' on the vanquished. Instead of destroying France, both had sought incorporate a power 'whose presence was necessary for civilisation and European stability' into the congress system. The victors of 1918 were well advised to treat Germany with equal foresight.[53] More than Cecil, Lloyd George came to envisage the League essentially as a supplementary organisation. It could offer the great powers a platform for

---

[50] War Cabinet minutes, 30 December 1918, *PWW*, LIII, pp. 565–6; 17 and 31 December 1918, CAB 23/42; Lloyd George (1938), I, pp. 77ff; War Cabinet minutes, 26 October 1918, CAB 23/40.

[51] Smuts (1919). Cf. Egerton (1978), p. 83.

[52] Cecil memorandum, 17 December 1918, CAB 23/42.

[53] See Lloyd George statement, 27 March 1919, Mantoux (1992), I, p. 31.

concerting their efforts, assist them in providing what ultimately only they, not the League, could provide: security. Britain's backing for the League was thus informed by the desire to adapt a rationale of nineteenth-century British policy to post-World War I realities. It was the rationale to safeguard a European equilibrium, and core national interests, by operating through an international concert. In 1919, Lloyd George sought to establish a directorate hence not only including Europe's principal powers but also the newly crucial United States.[54]

In different guises, this aim would also shape British policy after the fall of Lloyd George. To realise it at Versailles, it was indispensable to reach an understanding with Clemenceau; yet forging a common agenda with Wilson was imperative. Indeed, Lloyd George was prepared to make numerous concessions, not least on the League, to spread the burden of maintaining postwar order on British and American shoulders. This rationale often lay behind what, at first glance, not seldom appears as opportunistic British conduct. Although abidingly sceptical of Wilson's wider aspirations, Lloyd George indeed became the first British premier pursuing a broadly transatlantic approach to Europe's pacification.[55] By the end of 1918, he regarded an *entente* with America as the cornerstone of the peace he envisaged. Having met with Wilson in December, he sought to strike strategic bargains with an American president whose prestige in Britain reached a zenith at that point, as it did all over western and central Europe. Above all, Lloyd George and Cecil supported American League schemes. As Cecil underlined to the War Cabinet on 30 December, the 'greatest guarantee' of a 'settled peace' was 'a good understanding with the United States', only to be 'secured' if Britain was prepared 'to adhere to the idea of the League of Nations'.[56]

Lloyd George did not want to see Wilson impose his will on the peace conference in the manner of a 'conquering hero'.[57] But his core assumption was that for all their differences, notably in colonial and naval affairs, there was an overriding congruence of interests between the British Empire and the United States. Wilson needed British support to implement his design; and Britain had every interest in engaging Washington in Europe's consolidation. This could underpin a kind of Anglo-American super-directorate in the postwar world, serving to re-assure France, contain the Bolshevik revolution and further Germany's eventual rehabilitation.

Lloyd George and Lord Balfour, then his foreign secretary, agreed with Wilson that 'Germany's inclusion' into the new order was not a matter 'for the

[54] War Cabinet minutes, 17 December 1918, CAB 23/42.
[55] See Lloyd George (1938), I, pp. 77–83.
[56] War Cabinet minutes, 30 December 1918, *PWW*, LIII, pp. 567–8; 31 December 1918, CAB 23/42.
[57] Willert (1952), p. 161.

immediate future' but had to be approached as early as possible. To facilitate Anglo-American agreements on matters of especial interest to Britain, such as limiting Wilson's aspirations for a 'Freedom of the Seas' for the sake of imperial defence, the War Cabinet decided to make the League the 'first subject' at Versailles. Of course, there were also core financial interests at stake. As Churchill, then secretary of state for war, reminded his colleagues, it was critical 'to induce the United States to let us off the debt we had contracted with them'. If Wilson accepted this premise, but only then, should Britain be lenient vis-à-vis Germany.[58] This nexus became a maxim of British reparations policy throughout the 1920s but, as Washington never accepted such linkage, it remained a maxim of wishful thinking.

Apart from reparations, however, what clearly prevailed was the mutual interest in focusing on what united rather than divided Britain and America clearly prevailed. This notably applied to the most tangible issue affecting both powers' strategic interests: the postwar naval regime. While agreeing that it was imperative to destroy the German fleet, British and American policymakers were deeply divided over the 'Freedom of the Seas' and the world's future naval regime. At the close of the war, its elites regarded Britain as the world's supreme military power. And Lloyd George told Wilson that Britain would 'spend her last guinea to keep a navy superior to that of the United States'. At bottom, however, the old and financially weakened hegemon found it ever harder even to maintain parity with its financially stronger competitor. Following the armistice, Lloyd George proposed that Washington should curb its planned naval construction in return for Britain's backing of the League. For his part, Wilson had an interest in curbing the power of the influential 'Big Navy' party in Washington. In short, both powers reached a preliminary naval compromise, agreeing to resolve their differences at a separate summit, which was then achieved at the 1921/2 Washington conference.[59] Subsequently, Lloyd George and Wilson used their leverage to ensure that major naval questions were never seriously broached at Versailles.[60]

Likewise, Britain and America confirmed each other's wider – self-accorded – prerogatives. After some altercations, Lloyd George supported Wilson's claim that 'nothing' in the League Covenant would 'affect the validity of . . . regional understandings like the Monroe Doctrine'. To buttress the strategic partnership, Britain eventually also underwrote a League-based mandate

---

[58] War Cabinet minutes, 30 December 1918, *PWW*, LIII, pp. 559, 567.

[59] War Cabinet minutes, 26 October 1918 and 10 November 1918, CAB 23/14; House diary, 4 November and 19 December 1918, Seymour (1926–8), IV, pp. 180–1; *PWW*, LIII, p. 448; Lloyd George, Fontainebleau memorandum, 22 March 1919, *PWW*, LVI, pp. 259–70.

[60] See e.g. their responses to Clemenceau's challenges to their naval policies, 26 March 1919, Mantoux (1992), I, pp. 20ff.

system for Germany's former colonies.[61] In return, Wilson desisted from challenging British colonialism through his self-determination agenda. And, if never explicitly, he dropped his demand for 'Feedom of the Seas', which had implicitly threatened Britain's long-standing naval security doctrine – above all the prerogative to impose naval blockades.[62]

[61] Article XXI of the Covenant, *PWW*, LVIII, p. 195. The War Cabinet had originally backed the Dominions' demand to control contiguous German colonies. See War Cabinet minutes, 30 December 1918, *PWW*, LIII, pp. 562–3.

[62] Cf. Tillmann (1961), pp. 46–54.

3   The ill-founded peace of 1919

What, then, were the central issues Lloyd George and Wilson had to tackle at Versailles? At the heart of the conference agenda lay the question what shape and place Germany was to have in the new international system. It was intricately bound up with the question of what price Germany would have to pay, both in terms of reparations and territory, for a war that in the eyes of the victors had been principally caused by its aggression. Around these questions, all wider challenges facing the peacemakers in Europe revolved – above all the paramount security question. What, if any, security architecture could bolster postwar stability? How far could Wilson's vision of a League-based world order harmonise with Lloyd George's bid for a new great-power directorate? How far, if at all, could both be reconciled with Clemenceau's aspirations? As will be seen, the French premier wanted to ban the German threat through a settlement based on force, a firm victors' alliance *and* an eastern neighbour stripped of much of its prewar territory, notably the Rhineland. Yet the German problem also underlay a second fundamental question – that of how to strike a balance between French security interests, the American championing of self-determination and the requirements of a stable international order. These particularly clashed in one area: eastern central Europe. Here, the interests of the defeated power stood against Polish, Czech and Slovak claims for nation-states of their own. That these would have to be established in part on heretofore German territories threatened to create new and acute seedbeds of international conflict.

Against this background, inter-allied controversies centred on four cardinal issues, which – unresolved at Versailles – would also remain the core issues of international politics up to the 'Great Depression': the Rhineland problem; inseparable from it, the future underpinnings of European security; the Polish–German border settlement; and the issue of reparations. Here, Wilson's call for a peace not burdened by punitive indemnities stood against British and French claims for sizeable indemnities. And these claims could never be divorced from what was not even on the Versailles agenda but always on the minds of British and French delegates: Washington's demands for a full repayment of its war loans. How to come to terms with the Russian question remained a further, and most elusive, problem, with multiple ramifications for the future European order. Apart from seeking ways to oust the Bolshevik regime the Big Three never seriously approached a 'resolution' of this question at Versailles. Yet it should be emphasised again that they simply did not have it in their power to achieve this, to accomplish more than a basic containment of what they decried as the Bolshevik menace. This was to affect any subsequent attempts to stabilise Europe and particularly to recast the western powers' relations with Germany, introducing an inherently unsettling element; but it never proved disastrously destabilising.[1]

In sum, it was all but impossible for Wilson, Lloyd George or any other peacemaker to lay solid foundations for a new world order in 1919 – immediately after a conflagration on the scale of the Great War. But it was even more inconceivable to pacify postwar Europe, at least in the short and medium term, by profoundly altering its geo-political configuration. During the peace conference, no other than Wilson himself acknowledged the immense potential for conflict arising from the fact that, in his words, the victors were 'compelled to change boundaries and national sovereignties'; for 'these changes [ran] counter to long-established customs'. He did not 'fear future wars brought about by the secret plotting of governments, but rather conflicts created by popular discontent', adding that '(i)f we ourselves are guilty of injustice, such discontent is inevitable'.[2] Wilson believed that this could be forestalled by negotiating 'with moderation and fairness', particularly vis-à-vis Germany. In fact, however, reorganising Europe's map on the basis of self-determination was bound to produce discord and competing claims, especially because it had to be accommodated with the victors' security interests, notably those of France. And satisfying these interests, and their claims for reparations, was hardly conceivable without creating even more disputes – particularly if the new order was to be thrust upon the vanquished power without negotiations.[3]

In short, given the scope of the problems and *forces profondes* they had to grapple with, the utmost Versailles could achieve was to lay the basic groundwork for a European peace order. The peacemakers' critical task was to agree on rules and mechanisms enabling them to manage the conflicts arising not only at but also *after* the conference – conflicts that were simply unavoidable. For only thus could they hope to pave the way for what was crucial but not yet achievable in 1919: to strike the essential bargain agreements with Germany that were imperative to stabilise both its republican order and the international system as a whole.[4] Yet, as will be shown, the victors failed to meet this task.

---

[1] Cf. Mayer (1967), pp. 284–343; Jacobson (1998), pp. 451ff.
[2] Council of Four, 27 March 1919, Mantoux (1992), I, p. 31. Cf. Walworth (1986), pp. 12ff.
[3] Council of Four, 20–3 April 1919, Mantoux (1992), I, pp. 290–310.
[4] Council of Four, 5–6 May 1919, Mantoux (1992), I, pp. 442–89.

What immensely complicated any attempt to settle the German question, and to agree on ground-rules to this end, was the fact that policymakers on all sides had to ensure that whatever they decided would enjoy not only international but also domestic legitimacy. As Harold Nicolson stressed in defending Lloyd George, the latter was as little a free agent at Versailles as his principal interlocutors. Being democratically 'chosen delegates', it was 'wholly impossible' for the 'plenipotentiaries' to act 'in flagrant violation' of the public opinion in their respective countries, which equally applied to those representing Germany's interests.[5] In other words, Wilson, Lloyd George and Clemenceau not only had to hammer out an agreement at the negotiating-table. They also each had to placate very different primary concerns among their domestic audiences, voiced by increasingly influential public opinion-makers and pressure-groups – be they security, reparations or the avoidance of entangling commitments. *Mutatis mutandis*, the same was of course true for the new and embattled leaders of what in January 1919 became the Republic of Weimar, who clamoured to be represented at the peace conference in the first place. Indeed, in an era of uneven yet spreading democratisation, the new relevance of domestic politics created an array of constraints unprecedented in the history of modern peacemaking. Versailles was thus far removed from the comparatively arcane proceedings of the Congress of Vienna.[6]

It is hard to understate the scale and radical nature of the changes that Wilson demanded on the basis of the Fourteen Points. The peace conference had to reveal how far European governments were prepared, after the experiences of 1914–18, to base their security and prosperity on entirely new foundations – how far they would be willing to accept, and able to justify domestically, that these should hence be guaranteed by a League regime of collective security and a new covenant of international law. And it also remained to be seen how far they would be willing to rely on guarantees that would ultimately have to be upheld not only by Britain and France but also by a power that had never taken on such commitments before, the United States.

Clemenceau and the French search for *sécurité*

While by no means posing the most radical demands within the French spectrum, what Clemenceau presented as his country's agenda at Versailles went against the grain of the British and American peace programmes. In many ways, both in his aims and the methods he proposed, Clemenceau's approach to peacemaking was even diametrically opposed to what Lloyd George and

---

[5] Nicolson (1931), pp. 89–90.
[6] Cf. Goldstein (1998), pp. 147–66; Soutou (1998), pp. 167–88; Schwabe (1998).

Wilson sought. But it also stood *pars pro toto* for the wider anxieties and interests of Germany's neighbours that the Anglo-American powers had to address. Foremost among the French premier's concerns was not revenge or retribution. Rather, it was the search for *sécurité*, the aim to ensure that France would never again be threatened by a superior German power. This governed all other French demands, and Clemenceau doubtless reckoned that it also was what French public opinion chiefly demanded.[7]

In short, Clemenceau did not believe that lasting security could be achieved either through a lenient, 'equitable' settlement with Germany or by relying on Wilson's abstract notions of collective security. The conclusions he had drawn from the war's carnage were fundamentally different from those shaping Wilson's or even Lloyd George's policy. He presented a peace programme informed by the experience of decades, if not centuries, of intermittent yet constantly widening European hostilities that, particularly since the Franco-Prussian war, had pitted France against its eastern neighbour. He also did so in view of the harsh settlement that the newly united Germany had imposed on France in 1871 and the latter's blood-letting, deeply exhausting victory in 1918. And he did so, finally, in the face of what he and other French decisionmakers perceived as a defeated power deeply resenting its capitulation and waiting to seize the first opportunity to right this wrong.[8]

On these premises, Clemenceau envisaged a peace settlement that, on one level, relied on classic balance-of-power prescriptions yet also went far beyond nineteenth-century *realpolitik* in order to contain Germany. On the one hand, he sought from Britain and America the firmest possible alliance guarantees against future German attacks. These could be supplemented, but not re-placed, by the League's collective-security provisions. When meeting Wilson in Paris in mid-December 1918, the French premier had already voiced his doubts about the prospects of making the League 'workable' as the postwar order's central security mechanism. As Colonel House put it, Clemenceau 'believe[d] in war' rather than American visions of peace. By the end of December, Clemenceau felt obliged to assure the French *Chambre* that he was still 'faithful' to an 'old system which appears to be discredited today', which he defined as a 'system of alliances'. This faith would also inform his positions at the peace conference.[9]

The second and far more radical agenda that France pursued had been hammered out following the armistice but was not fully disclosed to Wilson

---

[7] See Clemenceau (1930), pp. 3ff, 50ff. Cf. Stevenson (1982) and (1998), pp. 87–109; Soutou (1989), pp. 490ff; Duroselle (1988), pp. 720ff; Miquel (1977), pp. 141ff.

[8] Cf. Soutou (1998), pp. 168–9.

[9] House diary, 19 December 1918, *PWW*, LIII, p. 448; Clemenceau speech, 29 December 1918, in *The Times*, 31 December 1918.

and Lloyd George until the conference opened. It hinged on imposing far-reaching territorial, economic and security restrictions on Germany, designed to pre-empt its resurgence not just in the short term. Essentially, Clemenceau's was the attempt to redress the imbalance of economic and demographic potentials between France and Germany that had emerged since 1870 and was bound to grow wider unless altered by force.[10] In 1919, a French nation-state of 40 million faced a neighbour of more than 60 million inhabitants and a gross domestic product more than one-and-a-half times that of France.

Apart from insisting that Alsace-Lorraine should be returned to France without a plebiscite, Clemenceau demanded that Germany be stripped of its military might and settled with punitive indemnities. The wider French aim was to weaken Germany's economic potential, or at least its command over it.[11] Beyond this, Clemenceau and his principal advisers, André Tardieu and Léon Bourgeois, intended to dismember Germany. While not aiming to undo Bismarck's work completely, their goal was to deprive the *voisin d'outre-Rhin* of its most critical strategic assets. Although this clashed with self-determination, France thus supported Poland's claims to be reconstituted in the 'historical' frontiers of 1772, including all of Upper Silesia, what became known as the 'Polish Corridor' and Danzig. Against US opposition, Paris equally championed Czech claims for the Sudetenland.

Chiefly, however, French policymakers sought to gain control over the Rhineland. Tardieu envisaged severing all territories on the left bank of the Rhine from Germany and organising them into neutral, disarmed states. Nominally independent, these would in practice fall under French tutelage, not least as part of a 'Western European Customs Union'. Further, the Rhineland and all bridgeheads across the Rhine were to be occupied indefinitely by the Allies. At Versailles, Tardieu insisted that France required Germany's dismemberment as an essential foundation of its postwar security. Just like Britain and America, it needed a 'zone of safety'. While, as naval powers, the latter had created such a zone by wrecking Germany's fleet, France, 'unprotected by the ocean, unable to eliminate the millions of Germans trained to war', had to establish it on the Rhine.[12]

The French delegation pursued its territorial aims in part to increase its bargaining power vis-à-vis Wilson and Lloyd George and to obtain satisfactory security guarantees. Fundamentally, though, France desired both: maximal Anglo-American commitments *and* a materially reduced German threat. What

[10] Clemenceau (1930), pp. 22ff; Tardieu (1921a), pp. 768ff.
[11] Cf. Soutou (1989), pp. 780ff. This was also sought through mandatory coal-deliveries and controlling the Saar region. See the different interpretation in Trachtenberg (1980).
[12] Tardieu memorandum, 20 January 1919, in Tardieu (1921a), pp. 165–84; Tardieu (1921b), p. 165. Cf. McDougall (1978), pp. 120ff.

Clemenceau and his advisers envisaged was undoubtedly the harshest version of an intentionally defensive but effectively punitive peace advanced at Versailles. It foreshadowed what the French premier at the time, Raymond Poincaré, would later seek to achieve by invading the Ruhr area. In 1919, French policy not only threatened to undermine Wilson's vision of a 'peace to end all wars'. It also thwarted any prospects of approaching a settlement *with* Germany.

The German dilemma in 1919 – no prospects for a sustainable peace with or without Germany

De facto, though it would be raised time and again during the Versailles conference, one of the most critical procedural questions of peacemaking was thus answered before it even began: the defeated power would not be represented at the negotiating-table. Wilson had originally intended to invite not only German but also Russian representatives to Versailles. Yet neither he nor Lloyd George could overcome France's veto. At the same time, both came to espouse the view that, given the virulence of the Franco-German antagonism, it would be impossible to forge a settlement with the Germans. Instead, the 'Big Three' agreed that Berlin would merely be allowed to respond to allied proposals in written form. This the new German foreign minister Ulrich von Brockdorff-Rantzau did in March 1919, with some impact especially on British public opinion, yet to little effect at the conference itself.[13]

The new centre-left government under Philipp Scheidemann essentially argued that Germany's new western orientation and anti-Bolshevik course could only be sustained through a lenient peace settlement, essentially on the basis of Wilson's Fourteen Points.[14] The underlying aim of the *spiritus rector* behind this approach, Brockdorff-Rantzau, was that of every German foreign minister of the 1920s: to restore Germany's great-power status as swiftly as possible. Backed by Germany's provisional president Friedrich Ebert, he thus demanded Germany's immediate admission to the League's Executive Council.[15]

Brockdorff-Rantzau's tactic was to present counterproposals designed to show that the victors' peace plans were not only inconsistent with Wilson's Fourteen Points and the professed allied aim to foster German democratisation but also impracticable. He argued that their implementation would damage the

---

[13] Council of Ten, 13–23 January 1919, *FRUS 1919*, III, pp. 536ff; Council of Four, 24 April–6 May 1919, 29–30 May 1919, Mantoux (1992), I, pp. 290–489, II, pp. 251ff. Cf. Fry (1998), pp. 574–5.

[14] In 1917, Germany had imposed a harsh settlement on Russia at Brest-Litovsk. Cf. Schwabe (1998), pp. 44–52.

[15] Brockdorff-Rantzau speech, 14 February 1919, in Brockdorff-Rantzau (1920), pp. 58–9.

victors' own best interests – they would destabilise Germany, open the gates to Bolshevik infiltration and undermine Europe's economic reconstruction. Hoping to prepare the ground for actual negotiations, Brockdorff-Rantzau's appeal was especially directed at America and Britain. To start a bargaining process, the German foreign minister underscored Berlin's readiness to trade long-term financial obligations for moderate territorial provisions. On the advice of the German bankers Carl Melchior and Max Warburg, he in February 1919 made an offer of 100 billion *Goldmark* as compensation for war damages. In return, Germany was to retain its territorial integrity in the borders of 1914.[16] But there were to be no negotiations. Any German hopes finally came to nought in early May.

Dismayed, the German delegation condemned the ensuing treaty as 'the last dreadful triumph' of old-style power politics, an attempt to punish Germany betraying a 'moribund conception of the world, imperialist and capitalist in tendency'.[17] Brockdorff-Rantzau even recommended that his government should refuse to sign the treaty. Yet, rather than risk an allied occupation, Germany eventually did sign it. In a wider perspective, his futile endeavours merely highlight one fundamental dilemma marring all peacemaking efforts at Versailles. Even if Wilson and Lloyd George had been able to persuade Clemenceau to admit Germany to the talks, it would have been exceedingly difficult to agree on anything close to a mutually acceptable settlement. Conflicting peace aims and the domestic pressures weighing on all sides, yet especially on the leaders of France and a German republic whose very survival still hung in the balance, would have left very little room for compromise. Thus, not only would a participation of German representatives have produced deadlock and most likely a breakdown of the negotiations. They would also have been in far too weak a position – internationally, as the vanquished, domestically, because of unrealistic expectations – to attain a satisfactory agreement, one that, in Wilson's words, did not furnish Germany 'with powerful reasons for seeking revenge at some future time'.[18]

But it was not possible either, and certainly not achieved at Versailles, to mould without German representatives a 'moderate' and 'fair' settlement acceptable to Berlin.[19] Lloyd George's exhortations notwithstanding, it was simply beyond the victors to lay down peace terms as if they were 'impartial arbiters'; and the fact that they ultimately imposed them had to erode their legitimacy in Germany from the start.[20] Any peace decreed by the victors could

[16] Cf. Schwabe (1998), pp. 53–4.
[17] Quoted in Schwabe (1985d), p. 361; Brockdorff-Rantzau to Ebert, 9 June 1919, quoted after Wengst (1973), pp. 81–2.
[18] Council of Four, 26 March 1919, Mantoux (1992), I, p. 20. Cf. Schwabe (1998), p. 67.
[19] Council of Four, 27 March 1919, Mantoux (1992), I, p. 31.
[20] Fountainebleau memorandum, Lloyd George (1938), I, p. 408.

be presented by German propaganda as a 'dictated', 'shameful' peace. As it turned out, Versailles would indeed be perceived as such, rejected by a vast majority of Germans, including the old and new elites of what would become the Weimar Republic.

The tenuous compromises of the victors: the Rhineland settlement and the short-lived security arrangements of 1919

Thus, the Paris Peace Conference remained a gathering of the victors. All in all twenty-seven powers were called on to participate, but not the mightiest vanquished power, nor the Soviet pariah. In their absence, the Supreme Council made up of the Britain, the United States, France and Italy soon became the central decisionmaking body. There were also the Council of Five, which in addition included Japan, and the Council of Ten, which also comprised smaller powers. But all major decisions affecting Europe's future were made between the 'Big Three', Wilson, Lloyd George and Clemenceau.[21]

In fact, both the American president and the British prime minister came to act as advocates of what they perceived as German interests vis-à-vis France (with the notable exception of Britain's stance on reparations). By virtue of the political and financial leverage he commanded, Wilson was poised to become the conference's main arbiter. And this is certainly how he saw himself.[22] But, pursuing his more general priorities, he was not able to fulfil this role. Neither he nor Lloyd George could forge a peace acceptable to all sides. The longer the deliberations lasted, the more palpable it became that this was and remained an elusive prospect.

Once the conference had opened on 12 January 1919, it soon became clear that, amongst themselves, the victors faced one paramount challenge: how to square the circle between Wilson's ideals and Clemenceau's essentials. Arguably, the only power capable of mediating between French and American conceptions of peace was Britain. And Lloyd George indeed regarded himself as the 'master politician' who could achieve this, guiding the first bid to establish a Euro-Atlantic peace order.[23] Yet he was unable to accomplish his self-chosen mission, both because essential aspects of what Wilson and Clemenceau sought remained irreconcilable and because British interests, certainly those touching reparations, were incompatible with the position of an 'impartial' umpire.

---

[21] Council of Four, 24 April–6 May 1919, 29–30 May 1919, Mantoux (1992), I, pp. 290ff, II, pp. 251ff. Cf. Nicolson (1931), pp. 336ff.

[22] Bowman memorandum, 10 December 1918, *PWW*, LIII, pp. 353ff. Cf. Walworth (1986), pp. 25ff.

[23] Council of Four, 26–7 March 1919, Mantoux (1992), I, pp. 20–1. Cf. Lentin (1985), pp. 83ff.

In the conference's opening stages, inter-allied fault-lines first emerged, not surprisingly, when it came to discussing the League and foundations of post-war security. Clemenceau's key aide, Léon Bourgeois, affirmed that France would only endorse a robust *société des nations*. In his design, the League was a mechanism that enforced the peace settlement, kept Germany in check and oversaw the fulfilment of its disarmament obligations. As such, it had to be endowed with its own international forces to reinforce sanctions and act against aggressors. At the same time, it was to be a framework for the victors' continued co-operation, ensuring their postwar control and the Anglo-American commitment to French security. By contrast, Germany's accession to the League had to be ruled out, even at a later stage. France threatened to shun the League unless Britain and America met these demands.[24] Yet what Bourgeois outlined of course conflicted with core premises of both American and British League policy. Although Wilson was prepared to go to great lengths in accommodating France to realise his peace programme, he felt he had no mandate to endorse such far-reaching proposals. At bottom, French plans threatened to undercut what he envisaged the League to become: not an institution enforcing peace by military might but a 'universal association' relying on collective security and 'world opinion' – and seeking to integrate the vanquished power. Albeit remaining a less ardent believer in the League, Lloyd George strongly supported Wilson. He adhered to Cecil's rationale that this offered the only prospect for establishing a great-power concert incorporating America; and he insisted that the door for drawing Germany into the new organisation had to be kept open.[25]

When its hopes of obtaining a 'muscular' League vanished, the French delegation shifted to emphasising the more draconian side of its peace aims. Above all, it accentuated what Clemenceau had contemplated from the outset: the demand for a Rhenish buffer state. In late February, with Wilson absent from Versailles, Colonel House all but ceded to French pressure for the creation of an independent Rhenish republic *de facto* controlled by Paris. House noted that he had come 'to recognise the force and unanimity of French feeling that future invasions by Germany must be made absolutely impossible'.[26] Soon thereafter, however, French aspirations encountered staunch Anglo-American opposition. For they threatened to erode what Lloyd George and Wilson regarded as the minimal requirements for stabilising Europe on the basis of the Versailles settlement, yet also eventually *with* Germany. Back at

---

[24] For Bourgeois's proposal see Geouffre de Lapradelle (1929–36), I, pp. 169ff. Cf. Stevenson (1998), p. 93.
[25] Wilson address, 28 December 1918, *PWW*, LIII, p. 532; Wilson speech, 19 September 1919, Shaw (1924), II, p. 1017; Miller (1928), II, pp. 61ff.
[26] House acted against Wilson's instructions. See House to Wilson, 19 February 1919, Wilson to House, 20 February 1919; House diary, 27 February 1919, Seymour (1926–8), IV, pp. 332–6, 344–5.

Versailles in March, Wilson overruled his *chargé d'affaires*, re-affirming his rejection of any French schemes that blatantly contradicted his aspirations for a peace without annexations.[27]

The British position on the Rhineland was unequivocal and would remain so throughout the 1920s. British decisionmakers regarded a semi-independent Rhineland under French control as a recipe for constant instability. And as one British delegate, Philip Kerr, remarked, France's excessive claims would also counteract allied 'solidarity', undercutting the willingness of Britain and its Dominions to come to France's aid once again should another war with Germany erupt.[28] Confronted with what he saw as Clemenceau's dangerous aspirations, Lloyd George in late March withdrew to Fontainebleau, accompanied by his key advisers.[29] There, he produced his widely noted yet ambivalent call for a moderate peace. The Fontainebleau memorandum sprang from profound concerns that the British premier shared with Wilson, namely that Germany would succumb to Bolshevism, and Europe to widespread disorder, unless Britain and America could mitigate French demands. Lloyd George argued that the Allies should avoid as far as possible 'transferring' German populations to other states. And he insisted above all that there must be 'no attempt to separate the Rhenish Provinces from the rest of Germany'. Fundamentally, he declared, a stable peace depended on eliminating 'causes of exasperation constantly stirring up the spirits of patriotism' and 'fairplay' in Germany (and among the victors).[30]

During the Council of Four's subsequent deliberations Wilson endorsed Lloyd George's plea. If he ever wanted to realise his peace aims, the allies had to show 'moderation' towards Germany. And they had to ensure that its new leaders would not be swept from power either by old-guard forces or the looming Bolshevik-threat. As Wilson argued on 27 March, the 'greatest mistake' the victors could make was to 'furnish [Germany] with powerful reasons for seeking revenge at some future time' – to give 'even an impression of injustice'. But this mistake could simply not be avoided in the constellation of 1919.[31]

Predictably, Clemenceau came out strongly against what he considered Lloyd's George's 'illusory' design. In his verdict, the British premier sought to appease Germany at its neighbours' expense. As he also – rightly – remarked, Lloyd George based his call for conciliation on a distinct double-standard. He was not prepared to offer any concessions harming cardinal British interests –

---

[27] Cf. Schuker (1998), pp. 296ff.   [28] Tardieu (1921b), p. 173.

[29] These included the conference's influential secretary, Maurice Hankey, Kerr and the chief of the General Staff, Sir Henry Wilson.

[30] Fontainebleau memorandum, 22 March 1919, Lloyd George (1938), I, pp. 403–16; see also *PWW*, LVI, pp. 259–70.

[31] Council of Four, 16 and 27 March 1919, Mantoux (1992), I, pp. 20, 31.

interests that were financial and imperial. Clemenceau thus insisted that if it was indeed 'necessary' to placate Germany, 'she should be offered colonial satisfaction, naval satisfaction, or [commercial] satisfaction'.[32] It indeed seems revealing that, while warning not to overburden Germany, Lloyd George reiterated that the defeated power owed the allies 'full reparation'.[33] Similarly, Wilson, who rightly feared Congressional opposition, rejected any compromise on what affected tangible US interests, namely the repayment of French and British war-debts, to encourage a lenient treatment of Germany. At bottom, though, Clemenceau rejected the entire rationale of what Wilson and Lloyd George envisaged. In his eyes, the victors' main obligation was 'to do something to spare the world from German aggression for a long time'. And this meant enforcing the peace without half-hearted concessions that would not appease the vanquished anyway.[34]

Ultimately, these differences could not be resolved at Versailles. What the 'triumvirate' did manage, yet only after a bitter struggle in the conference's final phase (March–June 1919), was to forge – tenuous – compromises on two of the thorniest issues: the Rhineland and the Polish border. On the third, reparations, not even this proved possible. In Nicolson's judgement, it was only because of the Fontainebleau memorandum's 'fiery stimulus' that 'the rulers of the world really concentrated on making peace with Germany'.[35] In fact, however, the political skills of Lloyd George, who changed fronts between Wilson and Clemenceau, siding with the former on security and the latter on reparations, only played one part in this process. The other, essential, part was played by Wilson, even though his influence was waning towards the end.

Already before Lloyd George's retreat to Fontainebleau, he and Wilson had rallied to a common approach to counter Clemenceau's Rhineland agenda. It led to a bargain between the three principal powers that avoided dismantling Germany while seeking to address French security concerns in a new way. This bargain rested on two main pillars. One of them, however, was temporary from the start and the other would crumble when Wilson lost the 'treaty fight' in 1920. The first was a concession to French demands for a buffer zone. In return for France's abandoning its claim for a 'free Rhine state', the Rhineland was to be jointly occupied for a period of fifteen years to ensure German compliance with the peace treaty. And it was to be permanently demilitarised (i.e. Germany was prohibited from maintaining any 'military installation' not only on the Rhine's left bank but also within a zone of fifty kilometres on its right bank).[36]

[32] Lloyd George (1938), I, pp. 416–20. Cf. Dockrill and Goold (1981), p. 29.
[33] Fontainebleau memorandum, 25 March 1919, Lloyd George (1938), I, p. 415.
[34] Council of Four, 27 March 1919, Mantoux (1992), I, p. 33.
[35] Nicolson (1931), p. 51.
[36] Council of Four, 27 March 1919, Mantoux (1992), I, pp. 39–40; War Cabinet minutes, 28 February 1919, CAB 23/15.

In response to the criticism that German protests had sparked among liberal and Labour opinion in Britain, Lloyd George subsequently demanded a drastic curtailment of the occupation. He raised the stakes by insisting that unless Germany was appeased the Allies would have to invade it. Following Britain's last-minute intervention in early June, Clemenceau conceded that the Rhine-land could be evacuated before the fifteen-year deadline if Germany fulfilled its treaty obligations.[37] The second pillar of the inter-allied settlement emerged in response to French demands for more 'tangible' security guarantees. Britain and the United States finally agreed to offer Paris an explicit guarantee that, 'acting under the authority of the League', they would 'come to the immediate assistance . . . of France in case of unprovoked aggression of Germany'. Considering even these overtures insufficient, Clemenceau only accepted them for lack of better alternatives.[38]

On the basis of these understandings, France agreed to join the League, but only on condition that Germany would remain excluded for the foreseeable future. Both Wilson and Lloyd George had pressed for making Germany's admission a clear provision of the treaty. In early June, the British premier even threatened to withdraw from the conference unless this was conceded. Yet, although Wilson backed his demand, Clemenceau did not budge. The formula finally enshrined in the treaty centred on the pledge that Germany could join the organisation in the near future – if it showed good faith in fulfilling the peace terms. This left France with ample leverage to block Berlin's entry in accordance with its security interests.

The British government did not offer its commitment lightly – and made it dependent on an American ratification of the treaty. Lloyd George sought to satisfy Clemenceau's security demands precisely because London wanted to avoid having to 'rescue' France should draconian French policies provoke renewed German attacks.[39] Yet nor did Britain desire to become France's main protector and guarantor of the European *status quo*. That is why, from the British perspective, engaging the United States remained imperative. But the American attitude towards the guarantee agreement was highly ambivalent from the start. For its provisions contradicted the very principles of collective security that Wilson had sought to implement. As House noted on 27 March, the agreement would 'be looked upon as a direct blow to the League of Nations', because there was no reason for any such old-style alliances 'if the League did what it was supposed to do'. It was thus all the more remarkable,

[37] Council of Four, 2 June 1919, Mantoux (1992), II, pp. 268–72.

[38] Fontainebleau memorandum, 22 March 1919, Lloyd George (1938), I, pp. 411–15; Council of Four, 27 March 1919, Mantoux (1992), I, p. 33.

[39] War Cabinet minutes, 28 February 1919, CAB 23/15. Britain also needed French support to consolidate and expand imperial interests in the Middle East – against Wilson. Cf. Tillmann (1961), pp. 219–27.

and evidence of his willingness to strike bargains with Clemenceau, that Wilson actually agreed to the treaty.[40]

Cecil told Bourgeois that France was well advised to accept whatever guarantees Wilson had to offer, because any US commitment to European stability did not spring from strictly defined self-interest. As America could afford to 'let European affairs go and take care of her own' from the distance the ocean afforded, the treaty was a 'present to France'.[41] In fact, it would also have been a 'present' to Britain. Cecil here captured a general problem besetting transatlantic relations in the interwar period. There was no critical US security interest (yet) warranting far-reaching commitments to Wilson's new world order and European stabilisation in particular. There was no tangible threat or reason why a majority in Congress and the wider American public should have supported such commitments. Overcoming isolationist opposition in attempts to foster peaceful change abroad remained a cardinal challenge for both Wilson and his Republican successors.

The reparations 'shambles'

The dispute over reparations proved to be the most acrimonious and inconclusive of the peace conference, producing what Wilson rightly called a 'shambles'.[42] To fathom this acrimony, it is indispensable to put the reparations problem in its proper – transatlantic – context. At stake in 1919 and thereafter was not only how much and on what grounds Germany would have to pay for the war; it was also the question how and how far Britain and France would have to service their war-debt obligations to America.

Wilson had originally insisted that 'no contributions, no punitive damages' should be imposed on the vanquished. By November 1918, he had adopted the formula that Germany would have to compensate the victors 'for all damage done to the civilian population of the Allies and their property by [its] aggression'. But, to Lloyd George's dismay, the American president did not consider British indemnity claims on a par with French and Belgian demands for 'pure reparation' for war damages. And, more importantly, Wilson was adamant that there would be no American 'peace dividend' for its allies: they would have to repay their war-debts in full.[43]

---

[40] House diary, 27 March 1919, Seymour (1926–8), IV, p. 395.
[41] Cecil statement, quoted after Miller (1928), I, p. 216.
[42] Council of Four, Mantoux (1992), I, p. xxvi, II, pp. 284ff. The debate over reparations at and after Versailles remains deeply controversial. Important contributions are Keynes (1919); Krüger (1973); Kent (1989), pp. 17–102; Ferguson (1998a).
[43] Wilson speech, 11 February 1918, Wilson note, 5 November 1918, *PWW*, LIII, pp. 25–6, 456–7; *FRUS 1919*, I, pp. 340–2; War Cabinet minutes, 30 December 1918, *PWW*, LIII, p. 563; War Cabinet minutes, 31 December 1918, CAB 23/42.

Wilson never departed from these central premises at Versailles. Yet he also insisted that in settling reparations Britain and France had to consider overriding 'political necessities'; they must 'do nothing which would have the consequence of completely destroying Germany'. Wilson reminded Clemenceau that the Allies could not base their calculations on assessments of 'prewar Germany', whose government had been 'determined to lead the country to economic mastery of the world'. Postwar Germany was 'disorganised and demoralised', its 'capacity to pay' much 'reduced'. He thus argued against 'pushing' demands 'to a point which would allow no German government to sign the peace' and plunge Germany into Bolshevism.[44] To prevent this, the American president proposed fixing a definite reparations sum – $30 billion – and to make businesslike arrangements allowing Germany to transfer it without ruining its economy.[45] But, though threatening financial sanctions, he could not 'convince' Clemenceau and Lloyd George to adopt his scheme. With a common interest in avoiding a premature curtailment of reparations, the two indebted victors even joined forces against him.

As noted, Lloyd George shared Wilson's political concerns. But in practice he could not extricate himself from the constraints partly stemming from his own promises. As he reminded Wilson in late March, it would be as difficult for him as for Clemenceau 'to dispel the illusions which surround the subject of reparation'. He faced the calamity that '[f]our hundred members of the British Parliament have sworn to extract from Germany the very last penny to which we are entitled'.[46] To placate left-liberal opinion in Britain Lloyd George in June nevertheless called for a substantial reduction of German indemnities. Beyond such tactical oscillations, however, the British premier still had no doubt that Germany had to pay for a war which had originated with its prewar policies. Nor did he doubt that Britain had a just claim to its share of reparations. Deeming it impossible to reach a tenable compromise, he focused on prodding his counterparts to agree on a *modus* for settling the question *after* Versailles. He proposed establishing a reparations commission that would collaborate with German experts to determine the full reparations sum, Germany's 'capacity to pay' and a schedule of payments.[47]

The French delegation outright refuted Wilson's proposals, and it also raised numerous objections to the original British designs. But although he never fully agreed with Lloyd George Clemenceau finally accepted his overall

[44] Council of Four, 25 and 26 March 1919, Mantoux (1992), I, pp. 6, 20, 27.
[45] Wilson drew on proposals by US bankers, notably Thomas Lamont. Cf. Kent (1989), p. 72.
[46] Council of Four, 26 March 1919, Mantoux (1992), I, p. 19. See also Peace Conference, British Empire Delegation, Minutes 33ff, 1 June 1919ff, CAB 29.
[47] Fontainebleau memorandum, 22 March 1919, Loyd George (1938), I, p. 415; Lloyd George draft proposal, 29 March 1919, in Burnett (1940), I, pp. 754–5.

plan.[48] Despite this tentative accord, however, the net-result of the Big Three's altercations was that the Versailles treaty did not include anything even approaching a conclusive reparations settlement. This question thus became the thorniest issue of the immediate postwar period. The treaty's only un-equivocal provision was the declaration of Germany's war guilt in article 231 on which future payment demands were based. It is difficult to conceive of an outcome leaving more room for subsequent controversies.[49]

The creation of a new European fault-line: the Polish–German border settlement

What were the other main outcomes of the deliberations? Here it is only necessary to recapitulate those that were to be at the centre of European disputes in the 1920s and beyond. While stating that they should be the starting-point for general efforts to this end, the victors imposed drastic disarmament provisions on Germany, which were subsequently overseen by the Inter-Allied Military Commission of Control (IMCC). Losing its imperial status and fleet, the defeated power was only allowed to keep a professional army of 100,000 men. Yet while Germany was thus relegated from the ranks of military great powers, it retained all the war-making potential inherent in what remained Europe's largest and most advanced industrial economy.[50]

More conflict-prone still were the treaty's territorial provisions, those placing Germany's former colonies under a League mandate system yet above all those delineating the new *status quo* in eastern Europe. Here, the predomin-antly German-speaking Sudeten area fell to newly created Czechoslovakia. Most importantly, however, Germany had to cede the 'Polish Corridor' (with the seaport of Danzig being made a 'free city' associated with Poland) and the Posen province to the new Polish nation-state.[51]

Throughout the negotiations, France had backed Polish claims for a state in the frontiers of 1772 and, in particular, the industrial and coal resources of Upper Silesia.[52] This had also figured in early treaty drafts. In late March, however, Lloyd George had called for a readjustment of Poland's preliminary western border in favour of Germany, seeking to minimise future German grievances. And, with an increasingly concerned Wilson backing his plea, the Big Three indeed agreed on several changes to this effect. Then, in June, Lloyd George pushed through a plebiscite to determine the future status of Upper

---

[48] Allied reply to German counterproposals, 16 June 1919, in Luckau (1941), pp. 438–41.
[49] Cf. Trachtenberg (1980), pp. 62ff; Krüger (1973), pp. 187ff; Ferguson (1998a), pp. 407ff.
[50] *FRUS 1919*, IV, pp. 183ff. Cf. Jaffe (1985).
[51] In the west, Germany had to return Alsace-Lorraine and cede the Eupen and Malmédy provinces to Belgium. Its coal mines falling to France, the Saar region came under League supervision for fifteen years pending a plebiscite over its final status.
[52] Cf. Wandycz (1961), pp. 12ff, and (1998).

Silesia.[53] But in the scheme of things these were minor adjustments. They did not solve the underlying problem. The plebiscite took place on 21 March 1921, and 60 per cent of those participating favoured remaining part of Germany. But, unable to reach an agreement, the Allied Supreme Council referred the decision to the League Council which, under French pressure, decreed demarcation-lines favouring Poland.

There is no way around concluding that, as this decision and the prohibition of Austria's *Anschluß* with Germany demonstrated, the victors' power-political considerations outweighed Wilsonian notions of self-determination when both came into conflict. In Germany, this served to discredit further not only the Versailles settlement but also its main institution, the League. The chief of the British Imperial Staff, General Wilson, thus identified a fundamental problem raised by the aspiration to base the peace on national self-determination when stating that in Europe 'ethnographical claims [were] in distinct opposition to those of military security and defence'.[54]

But the problem reached even deeper. The core issue that particularly Wilson never managed to address was that on the historically evolved map of European geo-politics, so textured by centuries of international rivalry – in the widest sense – and the aforementioned nineteenth-century waves of nationalist mobilisation, there were rarely uncontested 'national' claims to a given territory. Instead, whether based on notions of ethnicity, language or political precedent, such claims were often, though not inexorably, in conflict with each other. Nowhere was this more entrenched than in central eastern Europe. Any attempt to redraw Europe's political map by victors' decree was thus prone to produce new or rekindle old conflicts. If this was nonetheless endeavoured, nothing was more imperative than the establishment of a forceful mediating agency that provided clear rules for an 'equitable' settlement of colliding interests. Required was an instrument permitting an actual negotiating-process, and all parties to make their case – the victors and the vanquished. In Wilson's design, the League was to become this instrument. But it *de facto* never received the necessary mandate, at least where it was crucial: in Germany's relations with Poland.[55]

In 1919, then, a structurally highly unstable constellation had been created. It was a constellation in which the – uneven – application of the self-determination principle clashed with the most basic requirements of European stability *and* the legitimacy of the Versailles system. For Versailles pitted continental

---

[53] Fontainebleau memorandum, 25 March 1919, Lloyd George (1938), I, p. 409; Lloyd George remarks, 19 March 1919, in Headlam-Morley (1972), pp. 60–3; Mantoux (1992), I, p. xxv, II, pp. 345ff. Cf. Goldstein (1991), pp. 260–1.

[54] Wilson to Drummond, 2 January 1919, FO 608/121, quoted after Dockrill and Goold (1981), p. 34.

[55] Wilson speech, San Diego, 19 September 1919, in Shaw (1924), II, pp. 1017ff.

Europe's potentially still most powerful state, intent on revising a 'shameful peace' against smaller states to the east that comprised not only formerly German territories but also sizeable German minorities. To prevent this constellation from sparking not only incessant disputes but renewed war was a key challenge facing Anglo–American policymakers in the postwar era. And it placed a heavy burden on decisionmakers not only in Warsaw, Prague and Paris but also in Berlin.

Versailles, the impossible peace

With a view to the German question and the prospects of Europe's stabilisation, the Rhineland compromise, the Polish–German border settlement and the reparations 'shambles' were the most consequential results of Versailles. No less important, albeit even more transient, was the Anglo-American guarantee for France and the basic inter-allied understanding establishing the League. All was enshrined in the Treaty of Versailles signed in the Hall of Mirrors on 28 June 1919. As is well documented, both Lloyd George and Wilson vigorously defended the treaty as the best outcome possible under the circumstances, one in the House of Commons, the other vis-à-vis the Congress.[56] But already in May the French commentator Jacques Bainville had (in)famously predicted that the peace would be 'too gentle for all that is in it which is harsh'.[57] And Colonel House noted on 29 June that the treaty was 'bad and should never have been made'; it would 'involve Europe in infinite difficulties in its enforcement'.[58] What does an appraisal from a distance of more than eighty years yield?

As we have seen, the Versailles settlement could be no more than an inherently brittle amalgamation of power-political interests, internationalist ideals and economic concerns. And it indeed 'failed' to establish a firm balance of power against Germany – while settling it with what, from a German perspective, had to be perceived as unjust, punitive terms. But given that any agreements reached in 1919 were premised on essentially irreconcilable conceptions of peace the outcome could hardly have been otherwise. Wilson indeed failed to 'enforce his own prophecy' of a peace to end all wars. It is in the nature of all international negotiations, yet particularly of negotiations on the scale of Versailles, that all protagonists have to compromise; and the American president indeed had to make undesirable compromises. Yet the

---

[56] Lloyd George speech in the Commons, 3 July 1919, *Hansard*, 5th series, vol. 117, cols. 1211–32; Wilson meeting with the Senate Foreign Relations Committee, 19 August 1919, *PWW*, LXII, pp. 339–411.
[57] *Action Française*, 8 May 1919, quoted after Miquel (1972), p. 404. Cf. Schuker (1998), pp. 275–6.
[58] House diary, 29 June 1919, Seymour (1926–8), IV, pp. 488–9.

same held for Clemenceau, who also obtained far less than what he had sought, a peace to end all German threats. As for Lloyd George, he may have taught the world, in Nicolson's epithet, 'that apparent opportunism was not always irreconcilable with vision'. But he could not make Versailles into a more 'just' and 'reasonable' treaty either.[59]

Yet the main 'flaw' of the Versailles settlement was not that it was either too gentle for being so harsh or too harsh for being so gentle vis-à-vis Germany. Its main, and unavoidable, shortcomings were that it was an imposed peace and that it did not lay any solid foundations for a functioning postwar system of international politics, especially not in the crucial realm of security. It is highly doubtful that a settlement further fragmenting Germany would have produced greater European stability. As will be shown, all French attempts in the early 1920s to go beyond the limits of Versailles to realise this aim had the opposite effect.[60] In fact, Europe could only be stabilised, and the peace secured, if Germany could be accommodated. And that made it imperative to open avenues of co-operation with its new republican leaders – avenues that the already existing Versailles system did not provide. This was the crux of the postwar era, precisely because one of the settlement's most 'memorable' results was, as Churchill noted, 'the preservation of united Germany'. Versailles had indeed largely preserved the Bismarckian state, and with it Germany's potentially overbearing power.[61]

All in all, the vanquished power lost seven million inhabitants and more than 25,000 square miles of its prewar territory. But, due to the Anglo–American powers' intervention, Versailles had borne out neither Germany's worst fears nor France's highest hopes. Although this was concealed to most observers in Berlin by the pressing hardships of 1919, it indeed provided Weimar Germany with a new opening. It has often been argued that it set the stage for the inevitable: Germany's bid to overthrow the peace by force as soon as it had regained the means to do so. Yet, as will be shown, Versailles could also set the stage for a wholly different process. Albeit under very unfavourable conditions, Germany could embark on the stony path of orientating itself towards the west, of seeking a *rapprochement* with the victors – and of stabilising as a democratic state. As Weimar's future foreign minister Gustav Stresemann concluded soon after the peace conference, this was in fact what Germany's political and economic interests commanded.[62]

---

[59] Nicolson (1931), pp. 209–10.   [60] See chapter 7.
[61] Churchill (1929), pp. 202–3.
[62] Stresemann statement, December 1920, Stresemann Papers, vol. 216. Cf. Hildebrand (1995), pp. 149–301; Hillgruber (1969); Krüger (1985a), pp. 14ff.

Overwhelmingly, however, the German outcry over Versailles knew no bounds. Harsh criticism came not only from right-wing extremists and communists but also those supporting the governing Weimar Coalition, including Social Democrats. Under the thrall of relentless propaganda, most Germans, who had nourished high hopes for a lenient peace following Wilson's Fourteen Points, felt betrayed when the actual settlement was revealed. To many who felt that Germany had not really been defeated but 'stabbed in the back' by left-wing revolutionaries and Weimar republicans the treaty appeared all the more unjust.[63] Casting off 'the yoke of Versailles' became the most formative premise of German postwar policy. Yet how to achieve this – through negotiations or, ultimately, through war – remained highly unclear as the Weimar Republic struggled into existence. How far such a transformation process could even begin depended on whether the republic would put down any roots. Most of all, however, it depended on the victors' policies after Versailles. And those of the Anglo-American powers held the key.

The Versailles system undermined – the consequences of Wilson's defeat

In fact, neither Wilson nor Lloyd George were oblivious to the fact that, in cardinal respects, the peace remained deplorably unfinished. In Wilson's view, the key to remedying its deficiencies – to reassure France, reconcile Germany and ensure Europe's reconstruction – lay in establishing the League as the postwar order's essential 'clearing-house'. It was to serve as the mechanism to adjudicate and settle all conflicts caused by the war and not yet resolved at the peace conference.[64] In December 1918, one of Wilson's principal advisers, Isaiah Bowman, had proposed that the League's main function should be to guarantee '*territorial integrity plus later alteration of terms and alteration of boundaries if it could be shown that injustice had been done or that conditions had changed*'. As Bowman saw it, this would become easier once the '*passion*' of the war '*subsided*'.[65] After the Paris conference, Wilson re-accentuated this message. He asserted that the League was more critical than ever to bolster the peaceful change he envisaged. But to achieve this it had to become an institution in which all 'the right-thinking nations' could 'concert their purpose and their power', not only the victors but also Germany. Likewise, the American president believed that only the League could stabilise German democracy and ultimately also lead Bolshevik Russia on this path.[66]

---

[63] Cf. Bessel (1993); Schwabe (1985d), pp. 327ff; Heinemann (1983).

[64] Wilson speech in San Diego, 19 September 1919, in Shaw (1924), II, p. 1017.

[65] Bowman memorandum, 10 December 1918, in Seymour (1926–8), IV, pp. 280–1.

[66] Wilson address, Cheyenne, Wyoming, 23 September 1919, *PWW*, LXIII, pp. 449–53.

Still no ardent believer in the League, Lloyd George by and large pursued the same post-Versailles aims as Wilson but he adopted a different approach. In his Fontainebleau memorandum Lloyd George had repeated that it was essential to establish the League 'as the effective guardian of international right and international liberty', above all in Europe. And in his defence of Versailles in parliament he stressed that it could serve to redress any 'crudities, irregularities, and injustices' the treaty still contained.[67] Essentially, though, he still pinned his hopes on the League becoming an instrument for close co-operation with the United States. To limit British commitments at a time when domestic reforms were imperative and resources scarce, the British premier was keenly interested in assuring continued US engagement in Europe. Britain's guarantee to France hinged on this. Although it still irked him to deal with a man of Wilson's worldview, Lloyd George reckoned that only American help would allow him to shape postwar politics, assuage French security concerns and, on this basis, draw Germany into the new peace order.[68]

Thus, realising Lloyd George's aspirations and Wilson's vision of 'a permanent concert of power' required more than anything else that the latter won his 'treaty fight' against the Republican Senate majority at home. This fight, and Republican opposition to the League Covenant, centred on two issues: article X and US sovereignty. It reached its climax when hearings on the treaty began in the Senate's Foreign Relations Committee in July 1919. To ensure ratification, Wilson – whose health was failing – not only sought to win over Congress. He also embarked on an unprecedented tour of the Mid-West and the western states to make his case for US engagement in his new world order.[69] But his was to be a futile endeavour.

In a widely noted speech on 28 February 1919, the chairman of the Foreign Relations Committee, Republican Senator Henry Cabot Lodge, staked out the Republican case against Wilson's design. Lodge voiced *caveats* that would remain critical for US foreign policy in the interwar period. He argued that creating a League of Nations was not necessarily harmful; but creating it in Wilson's manner, as a kind of new 'international state' would be a grave mistake. It would curtail US sovereignty and freedom of action, particularly in the western hemisphere. In his view, subscribing to the Covenant's article X would thus completely reverse US foreign policy as defined by the Monroe Doctrine. To commit Washington to guaranteeing 'the territorial integrity or political independence' of all League members, as prescribed by it, would

---

[67] Fontainebleau memorandum, 22 March 1919, Lloyd George (1938), I p. 409; Lloyd George speech in the Commons, 3 July 1919, *Hansard*, 5th series, vol. 117, cols. 1211–32. Cf. Fry (1998), pp. 582–3.

[68] Lloyd George speech in the Commons, 3 July 1919, *Hansard*, 5th series, vol. 117, cols. 1211–32.

[69] *PWW*, LXIII, pp. 180–453.

create unbearable obligations. Above all, it would sooner or later enmesh the United States in perilous inner-European rivalries. Lodge warned that League-style collective security thus threatened to replace 'Americanism' with inherently undesirable 'internationalism'.[70]

Subsequently, those soon called the 'irreconcilable' treaty opponents formulated a catalogue of fourteen reservations, which reflected Lodge's concerns. They insisted that it had to remain a Congressional prerogative to make far-reaching commitments of the kind article X denoted. The most vocal 'irreconcilable', Senator William Borah of Idaho, suspected Wilson of having made secret alliance deals with Britain and France to realise his League plans.[71]

While the common ground between Wilson and his opponents was scarce to begin with, his response to their concerns left little leeway for compromise. Wilson stressed that while America would indeed have to make 'very grave and solemn' commitments to collective security, article X entailed a 'moral, not a legal obligation'. Sanctions could only be passed by a unanimous decision of the Executive Council. And finally Congress would have to determine the practical consequences of a 'call for action'.[72] Ultimately, however, the president could not accept Lodge's core proposal, namely that the United States should ratify the treaty but not article X. He maintained that this would exempt Washington from 'all responsibility for the preservation of peace' and amount to a 'rejection of the covenant'. On 2 October, having just returned from his exhausting engagements in the American West, Wilson suffered a severe stroke. Yet even without this handicap he could not have won the 'treaty fight'. The Senate finally rejected the Versailles treaty in March 1920.[73]

The Republican veto reflected fundamental American reservations towards potentially costly commitments in Europe. This became a cardinal reference-point for all subsequent bids to fashion a US stabilisation policy in the post-World War I era. Wilson's defeat let not only his but also Lloyd George's hopes founder. It largely eroded any prospects of furthering peaceful change through the mechanisms of 1919; and it undermined the Versailles system's security framework, which hit France hardest.

It has been claimed that if America had joined the League the German problem could have been solved even without stabilising Germany as a republic – by

---

[70] Lodge, Senate speech, 28 February 1919, *Congressional Record*, 65th Record, 3rd session, 4520–30. Cf. Widenor (1980).

[71] Wilson meeting with the Senate Foreign Relations Committee, 19 August 1919, *PWW*, LXII, pp. 339–411. Cf. Bailey (1947), pp. 387–8; Stone (1970), pp. 100–27; Ambrosius (1987), pp. 172–206.

[72] Wilson meeting with the Senate Foreign Relations Committee, 19 August 1919, *PWW*, LXII, pp. 339–411. Cf. Knock (1992), p. 258.

[73] Wilson address, Cheyenne, Wyoming, 23 September 1919, *PWW*, LXIII, pp. 449–53. Cf. Ambrosius (1987), pp. 190–206.

'automatically' involving Washington in the 'European balance of power' and thus containing German ambitions.[74] This seems misleading. In all likelihood, as French anxieties at Versailles underlined, even with British and American support the League would have been too feeble and inflexible an institution to serve its central purpose: to furnish a robust security architecture for consolidating war-ravaged Europe. It would have required an extensive probationary period – to prove that its principal powers were willing to enforce its covenant – before gaining legitimacy. Moreover, critical post-Versailles questions, above all the reparations problem, did not fall under its 'jurisdiction'. Crucially, the League's key members had to pave the way for Germany's admission *and* ensure the institution's workability thereafter. As it came into being, the League could not be the postwar world's key instrument of security.

The Anglo-American guarantee for France might have compensated for some of these constraints. It may have contained German revisionism and given Paris the requisite reassurance for shifting from coercive to conciliatory policies vis-à-vis its neighbour. Yet this remains a speculative scenario. Not least, a victors' alliance would of course have been perceived as antagonistic by German leaders, whether nationalist or moderate. This in turn would have made any German *rapprochement* with the west far more difficult. Thus, an Anglo-American alliance with France might have been a precursor for, but could not replace, what was essentially required: a new regional concert integrating not only America but also, eventually, Germany. This was also a precondition for stabilising eastern European – for pacifying Polish–German relations and for eventually finding what the Big Three deemed so undesirable: a *modus* of 'peaceful coexistence' with Bolshevik Russia.

As will be shown, the successors of Wilson and Lloyd George began to create such a system – on distinctly different premises from what any of the Big Three had sought. Stabilising postwar Europe indeed required a new form of great-power co-operation. But this would gain momentum outside the League – and outside formal alliance structures. Following the Ruhr crisis, it would take more than two years of arduous negotiations between the western powers and Germany to forge the first veritable peace settlement after 1918, and recast the international system.

---

[74] Smith (1994), p. 105.

4   The escalation of Europe's post-Versailles crisis, 1920–1923

At the heart of Europe's post-Versailles crisis clearly lay the unresolved German question and the latent antagonism between German revisionism and the French bid to maintain Europe's precarious *status quo* of 1919. This also lay at the centre of the reparations conflict overshadowing international politics between 1920 and 1923. As Keynes was only the most prominent critic to expound in 1919, there were two inextricably intertwined dimensions to the imbroglio over reparations.[1] On one level, it was bound up with the question of who would ultimately bear the costs of the war and buttress Europe financially. On a second, even more important, level, it was inseparable from the question of who would command the power resources that nation-states still deemed necessary to safeguard their security, even in an era so marked by international interdependence.

After Versailles, the reparations conflict retained its distinct transatlantic dimension. There was and remained a *de facto* linkage between the reparations France and Britain demanded from Germany and their debts to America (Britain owed the United States $4.7 billion, France $4 billion – and roughly the same amount to Britain). Yet successive Republican administrations after 1920 refused to acknowledge this nexus to forestall the formation of a European debtor coalition that could ultimately force America to collect its dues from Germany. At the same time, Wilson's successor Warren Harding and even more so the Republican-dominated Congress insisted that there could not even be a partial debt-relief for America's wartime allies. Thus a *circulus vitiosus* emerged. The American creditor pressed its allied debtors to honour their obligations fully and without delay. And this led a soon almost insolvent France, and Britain, to put screws on the German reparations 'debtor', first according to the Paris payment scheme, then the London ultimatum of May 1921, which set the sum of German indemnities at 132 billion goldmark.[2]

---

[1] Keynes (1919). Cf. Ferguson (1998b), pp. 395–432.
[2] Cf. Link (1970), pp. 106ff; Leffler (1979), pp. 27ff; Artaud (1978), pp. 363–73; Silverman (1982), pp. 186–93.

Isolated and lacking any international influence, Germany at first sought to minimise payments, partly through fuelling inflation; and it desperately tried to attract American help as well as capital.[3] As this bore no fruit, the Wirth coalition governments of 1921/2 adopted a 'policy of fulfilment'. Its rationale was to prove to Britain and France that their reparations policy was self-defeating. By ostensibly struggling to meet allied demands, Berlin hoped to show that the victors were not only harming Germany but also their interest in a recuperating German democracy and trading partner.[4] Yet this tactic could not bear any fruit either so long as Britain did not moderate France's uncompromising stance and the United States kept aloof from the European maelstrom. Ever more, the reparations dispute thus became the proxy battleground on which the future of the Versailles system was fought out. Conversely, its solution held the key to reforming the postwar order.

From 1920, it became a growing American interest, and British concern, 'to render impossible that form of statesmanship' which in the eyes of the new US commerce secretary Herbert Hoover characterised French reparations policy and maintained Europe's 'whole economic and political life . . . in an atmosphere of war'.[5] What both American and British policymakers accurately perceived as Europe's regression to old-style power politics after Versailles points to a core characteristic of international relations in the 1920s. If not by a Wilsonian new beginning, postwar Europe was not to be consolidated either by relying on prewar balance-of-power prescriptions.

Following in Clemenceau's footsteps, successive French governments sought new ways of checking German revisionism. After the Anglo-American guarantee had collapsed, their foremost concern became to search for compensatory bases of security. Above all, Paris clamoured for fresh guarantees from Britain; in parallel, it began to forge *status quo* alliances with the new states of eastern Europe. But France's eastern alliance system, chiefly resting on pacts with Poland and Czechoslovakia, was only a very inadequate compensation for the abortive Anglo-American alliance or, more importantly, a less confrontational course vis-à-vis Germany.[6] And, crucially, there was little scope for reconstituting an Anglo-French *entente* on the ruins that America's withdrawal had left behind.

In fact, after the catastrophe of 1914–18 British were no more in a position than American leaders to legitimate alliance commitments to France and the European *status quo* – or that is at least what they strongly felt. This, too, was a distinctive feature of international politics in the decade after Versailles. Even

[3] Cf. Krüger (1985a), pp. 77–81.   [4] Cf. Laubach (1968); Krüger (1985a), pp. 132–73.
[5] Hoover to Hughes, 24 April 1922, NA RG 59/800.51/316. For British perceptions see Curzon to British Embassy (Washington), 12 October 1923, *DBFP*, I, XXI, pp. 563ff.
[6] Cf. Jacobson (1983b); Calier and Soutou (2001); Wandycz (1961), pp. 29ff.

at the danger of confirming the obvious it should be emphasised that Anglo-American perceptions of the German threat continued to differ widely from those prevalent in France. Having already complicated the peace negotiations, this discrepancy actually grew wider in the immediate postwar period. The more French policy was deemed unduly harsh in London and Washington, the more Germany appeared as the 'underdog' in need of protection; and the more French, not German, 'provocations' were seen as the main obstacle to Europe's stabilisation.[7] The gulf grew widest between French and American outlooks. British leaders were more concerned about a possible German drift towards armed revisionism than their American counterparts. Yet they, too, thought French invocations of *le danger allemand* increasingly exaggerated. And they struggled to control an *entente* partner whose assertiveness threatened to undermine not only Weimar Germany but also any chances of peaceful change as Europe descended into an ever deeper postwar crisis.

Towards the pinnacle of the European crisis: the failure of Lloyd George's Genoa policy and Poincaré's bid for an artificial hegemony in Europe

Growing disenchantment with the outcome of Versailles was indubitably a key precondition for Britain's re-orientation towards a definite policy of peaceful change in the early 1920s. In some Conservative circles, suspicion of Germany's allegedly unchangeable desire for revenge – and the strength of unreformed *revanchist* forces within its frail republican system – remained entrenched.[8] Very rapidly, however, the call to fortify the order of 1919 at the side of France became the cause of a minority, also in the Foreign Office.

For altering British, and American, perceptions of Versailles probably no other influence proved more pertinent than that of Keynes' *Economic Consequences of the Peace*.[9] Keynes had resigned as Treasury representative at the peace conference in protest at Lloyd George's policy. He argued that the treaty would not merely wreck fledgling Weimar Germany but also irreparably damage the western capitalist system as a whole. By shifting 'their unbearable financial burdens on to the shoulders of the defeated', the victors would provoke Germany's collapse and, with its 'pivot', destroy the delicate 'European economic system' of the prewar era. Nor had they made any arrangements to 'adjust the [financial] systems of the Old World and the New' and 'restor[e] the finances of France'. In 1920, Keynes reiterated that European stabilisation

---

[7] See the comparative analyses in chapters 5 and 6.
[8] See Crowe memorandum, 7 December 1918, cited in Rothwell (1972), p. 254. Cf. Ferris (1989), pp. 18ff.
[9] Cf. Skidelsky (1983), pp. 384–91.

required a new 'allegiance towards economic tasks', which commanded revising the 'Carthaginian peace' of 1919.[10] His claims appealed most to liberal internationalists in Lloyd George's coalition and the Labour party, but also the City's circles of high finance. It also fomented pacifist sentiment beyond pressure-groups like the Union for Democratic Control.[11]

This put tangible pressure on British policymaking. But it was not decisive. For it was Lloyd George himself who led what Keynes malignantly called the singular undertaking of 'protecting Europe from as many evil consequences of his own Treaty as it lay in his power to prevent'.[12] From 1920 onwards, the British premier advanced his own grand design for restoring Europe's security and prosperity. He sought to draw consequences from the shortcomings of the Versailles system – with the aim of maintaining it as such – and, crucially, he sought to re-adjust British policy after America's withdrawal from Europe. The Lloyd George government faced two central challenges. It had to establish a European security system on the battered edifice of 1919 while also satisfying French demands for fresh British guarantees. And it urgently needed to find a common Anglo-French approach to contain the escalating reparations crisis. The latter was a prerequisite for revitalising Europe's economies and catapulting Britain out of its postwar recession; and it was the first step to prevent Germany's economic and political disintegration. For Germany remained not merely the most important British market but, also in Lloyd George's view, the pivot of any durable European order.[13]

Following Wilson's defeat, Lloyd George and his decidedly anti-internationalist foreign secretary Curzon distanced Britain from the League. Both believed that, bereft of US support, it could no longer play a central part in stabilising Europe. Yet the option to resort to a burdensome alliance with France to keep Germany in check and direct European affairs was also soon ruled out by a majority in cabinet, notably Curzon.[14] So what could be done instead? Between 1920 and his fall in October 1922, Lloyd George pursued his own, distinctly unilateral and never really coherent 'grand design' for pacifying postwar Europe. The British premier had two main aims. First, he sought to reassure France short of concluding a formal alliance. On this basis, he intended to consolidate the Versailles system by drawing not only Germany but also Soviet Russia into its orbit. This he essentially hoped to achieve via the

---

[10] Keynes (1919), pp. 9–10, 35, 211, and (1921), pp. 70ff, 167ff.
[11] *Union for Democratic Control Policy Statement* (1919). Cf. Skidelsky (1983), pp. 396–7; Birn (1985), pp. 36ff.
[12] Keynes (1921), pp. 7–8.
[13] See notes of a conversation between Lloyd George and Poincaré, Boulogne, 25 February 1922, *DBFP*, I, XIX, no. 34, pp. 170–92. Cf. Sharp (1984), pp. 72ff; Stamm (1977), pp. 40ff.
[14] Cf. Nicolson (1937), pp. 42–3; Bennett (1989), pp. 15–33.

economic sphere – economic co-operation was to pave the way for political *rapprochement*.[15]

Lloyd George's – futile – bid to establish a postwar order along these lines first culminated in the attempt to forge a limited *entente* with France, which for all practical purposes foundered at the Cannes conference in January 1922. Then, with major consequences, it reached its peak, and limits, in the abortive scheme for European reconstruction he advanced at the subsequent Genoa conference (April 1922). At Cannes, Britain and France were unable to agree on the extent of Britain's commitment. Lloyd George was unwilling, and domestically unable, to underwrite what the French president Poincaré desired: a full-blown Anglo-French alliance guaranteeing not only France's border with Germany but also the entire French system of *status quo* alliances in eastern Europe. Not least, this conflicted with Britain's underlying interest in furthering a peaceful change of relations between Germany and its neighbours. To keep open as many political and territorial options as possible, British policy was intent on avoiding everything that cemented a *status quo* deemed untenable.[16]

At Genoa, Lloyd George aimed to implement an ambitious agenda for Europe's recuperation. And he also hoped to broach the subject of reparations, particularly with France, to prepare the ground for a scaled-down settlement – one not burdening Germany in a way detrimental to its revitalisation. Yet the British premier also pursued wider aims. He sought to bolster Germany's political rehabilitation on the international stage. And, in particular, he hoped to finalise plans for an international consortium whose main purpose was to re-open the Russian market. Eventually, he thus also hoped to prepare the ground for political relations with the Bolshevik regime, chiefly to pre-empt an undesirable *rapprochement* between the two pariah states of the Versailles system.[17]

But Lloyd George's Genoa policy foundered. It foundered not least because the failure of the Cannes talks had outright alienated Poincaré, which obstructed any solution to the intensifying Anglo-French conflict over reparations.[18] Eventually, Lloyd George had to cede to Poincaré and take

---

[15] See notes of a conversation between Lloyd George and Briand, 4 January 1922, *DBFP*, I, XIX, no. 1, pp. 1–7; notes of a conversation between Lloyd George and Poincaré, Boulogne, 25 February 1922, *DBFP*, I, XIX, no. 34, pp. 170–92. Cf. Sharp (1984), pp. 22–64; Stamm (1977), pp. 85ff.

[16] See notes of conversations between Lloyd George and Briand, 5 and 8 January 1922, *DBFP*, I, XIX, nos. 3 and 8, pp. 11–15, 56–8. Cf. Orde (1978), pp. 15–23.

[17] See notes of a conversation between British, Belgian, French, Italian and Russian representatives, Genoa, 14 April 1922; notes of a conversation between Lloyd George, Wirth and Rathenau, Genoa, 19 April 1922, *DBFP*, I, XIX, nos. 72 and 78, pp. 380–404, 452–62. Cf. Fink (1984). For the positions and perspectives of the Soviet and German 'pariahs' see Hildebrand (1980), pp. 48ff.

[18] Cf. Orde (1978), pp. 18–21.

reparations off the Genoa agenda. Crucially, however, the conference came to nothing because British policy had failed to engage the United States in its bid to cope with the intricate problems of reparations and reconstruction. While a total of thirty-four states attended, including – for the first time – Germany, the world's new main creditor refused to be present at Genoa, unwilling to fund Britain's unilateral design.[19] Not least, then, the Genoa conference came to nought because, frustrated by America's abandonment of Versailles and a new Republican administration ostensibly rejecting any political commitments, the British premier had abandoned one core premise of his policy in 1919. He no longer made any serious effort to forge an Anglo-American approach to European consolidation. Overestimating British power, he sought to solve critical European problems, namely that of reparations, which could only be addressed with America's support.

Lloyd George's credibility was severely damaged, particularly because he was also blamed for the 'diplomatic defeat' of the soon mythical, and overrated, Russo-German Rapallo agreement of 16 April 1922. At Genoa, Germany made its first appearance on the international stage since 1919; and Lloyd George impressed on Chancellor Wirth that he desired 'a settlement with Russia and with Germany' in order to accomplish his underlying aim: to 'see Europe settle down'. But Britain had failed to build bridges. There was no firm ground for substantive discussions with a German government that, against strong domestic opposition, sought to persevere with its policy of fulfilment. Germany's foreign minister, Walther Rathenau, shortly assassinated thereafter, had come to the talks not only worried that Germany's powerlessness would be confirmed. He also feared that the victors would reach a separate agreement behind German backs, unfavourably linking Russian war-indemnity claims with western reparations demands.[20] This the German delegation sought to pre-empt by coming to terms with the Soviet commissar for foreign affairs, Georgi Chicherin, first. And, essentially, this is what Germany accomplished through the Rapallo treaty.

The aims of Ago von Maltzan, the under-secretary at the *Auswärtige Amt* who was the real driving-force behind the agreement, reached further. He hoped to invigorate relations with Soviet Russia not only in order to overcome Germany's postwar isolation but also to countervail French pressures. But the

---

[19] See the US note in reply to Britain's invitation, 8 March 1922, *FRUS 1922*, I, pp. 392–4; Sir A. Geddes (British ambassador, Washington) to Curzon, 7 March 1922, *DBFP*, I, XIX, no. 39, pp. 198–9. Crucially, Britain had not yet signed war-debt accords with America. See chapter 7. Cf. Fink (1984), pp. 125–8; Petricioli (1995).

[20] See Rathenau notes of a conversation with the French ambassador Laurent, 15 March 1922, in Pogge von Strandmann (1985), pp. 292–4, cabinet minutes, 24 March 1922, *AR Wirth I und II*, pp. 636–7; notes of a conversation between Lloyd George and Wirth, 7 May 1922, *DBFP*, I, XIX, no. 118, pp. 779, 777–86. Cf. Laubach (1968), pp. 125ff.

Rapallo accords were far from constituting a sinister step in this direction. They served to settle the most important postwar issues between the two 'pariah-states'. Both parties pledged to resume diplomatic ties and renounced mutual indemnity claims for war costs and damages. In a supplementary secret exchange of notes, Germany committed itself only to participate in the consortium that Lloyd George envisaged after previous agreement with Moscow. Yet, contrary to western suspicions then and ever since, Rapallo did not prefigure the 1939 Hitler–Stalin Pact. It did not include any secret provisions about covert military co-operation between Germany and Soviet Russia.[21]

In its repercussions for Germany's relations with the west, though, Rapallo clearly backfired. It widened an already considerable gap of mutual suspicion, particularly between Paris and Berlin. This far offset whatever Berlin could gain through revived relations with Moscow.[22] And it made Lloyd George's imperious pacification efforts even harder than before. Nonetheless, Rapallo also highlighted a central problem facing British diplomacy: unless it found ways to anchor Weimar Germany to a western system, and to negotiate questions of security and reparations on an equal footing, even moderate German leaders could eventually feel compelled to explore alternative avenues. And the main alternative avenue would have led to Moscow.

His 'defeat' at Genoa severely damaged Lloyd George's international and domestic standing. Soon thereafter, he fell from power over the Chanak crisis.[23] On 7 December 1922, the new Conservative premier Bonar Law described the lesson arising from his predecessor's high-handed pursuits by noting that Britain 'cannot act alone as the policeman of the world . . . the financial and social condition of the country makes that impossible'.[24] Indeed, the collapse of Lloyd George's coalition in October 1922 had ended Britain's bid to pacify Europe 'single-handedly'.

Yet Europe's descent into crisis had not come to an end at Genoa. What eclipsed it was the failure of France's bid for an 'artificial hegemony' in continental Europe, initiated under its predominant premier of the 1920s, Raymond Poincaré, as a result of the rising frustrations of French policy on all fronts. Nothing revealed the limitations of a balance-of-power approach to European order in the decade after 1919 more strikingly than this essentially defensive measure. Having exhausted all subjective options since Versailles to bring Britain and the United States to back France's security and reparations demands, Poincaré ultimately felt compelled to achieve them unilaterally and

---

[21] Cf. Pogge von Strandmann (1981), pp. 123–46; Krüger (1985a), pp. 173–5; Zeidler (1993), pp. 82–7; Fink, Frohn and Heideking (1991).

[22] For the British perspective see Salzmann (2003).

[23] Threatening war to aid Greece against Turkish nationalists under Kemal, Lloyd George lost Conservative Unionist support. Cf. Morgan (1979), pp. 207–8.

[24] Bonar Law statement, *Times*, 7 December 1922.

in January 1923 ordered French troops to occupy the strategically vital Ruhr area.

Whatever his ultimate intentions, Poincaré's coercive course was not only soon met with German 'passive resistance'. It also sparked a conflict that by the autumn of 1923 threatened to undermine Weimar Germany's economic and political order.[25] At the same time, none of France's aims, neither Germany's 'fulfilment' of reparations obligations nor the establishment of more permanent bridgeheads across the Rhine, had been realised. Not least due to the failure or sheer absence of Anglo-American engagement in the immediate postwar era, the Franco-German problem had escalated into what became a watershed crisis of the Versailles system. The transformation of Euro-Atlantic politics it generated will be at the centre of the following analysis.

[25] See chapter 7. Cf. Keiger (1997), pp. 294f; Bariéty (1977), pp. 369ff.

Part I

The Anglo-American stabilisation of Europe, 1923–1924

The making of the 'unfinished transatlantic peace order' between 1923 and 1925 was a process initiated by decisionmakers in Whitehall and Washington. Thus, to gauge what stabilisation was achieved in Europe after World War I – and why – one has to understand first the policies developed by Britain and the United States to overcome the Ruhr crisis and recast Franco-German relations. Their impact then has to be traced in the wider context of a no longer Eurocentric but Euro-Atlantic postwar system, which was significantly altered through the 1924 London conference. The crucial question became how far leading policymakers could change the underlying rules, and conditions, of international politics – and how far they could not only reform the brittle 'order' of Versailles but also lay the foundations for a durable, and legitimate, system of international politics where none had been before.

5   Towards a Progressive transformation of European politics
The reorientation of American stabilisation policy, 1921–1923

The interpretation of America's 'futile' quest for French security, German rehabilitation and wider European stability after World War I has undergone many revisions. Early indictments of 'fatal American isolationism' have been rejected. For any less than superficial research showed that the United States never completely withdrew from Europe after 1919; and recent research has even emphasised underlying continuity between Wilson's internationalism and Republican policy in the 'Wilsonian century'.[1] Yet the nature and implications of America's selective involvement in stabilising, or destabilising, the Old World remain the subject of controversy.

Arguably, the still most substantial attempt at synthesis interprets post-Wilsonian policy as a 'corporatist' bid for American commercial expansion *and* European reconstruction. It accounts for its dynamics, and limits, by pointing to a strong consensus emerging among the 'new era's' political and commercial elites. It was the consensus that America's interest was served best by relying almost exclusively on US financial leverage, economic practices and private agents to stabilise Europe and reform the world economy. Both were to be remade after the example of the 'corporatist order' of liberal capitalism underpinning America's return to 'normalcy' – or, in fact, 'Republican restoration' – under Harding and Coolidge. Still prevalent, then, is the view that these were also the remedies Wilson's successors applied, in vain, to the Franco-German dilemma, seeking 'to revitalise Germany's productive power without restoring its prewar hegemony'.[2]

Undoubtedly, the 'corporatist synthesis' reveals *one* important dimension of interwar American foreign relations: its domestic determinants and constraints. More illuminating, however, appears an analysis that, in short, places US 'economic diplomacy' where it belongs: in a wider, essentially political context

---

[1] See Leffler (1979); Costigliola (1984); Burk (1992); Ninkovich (1999), pp. 1–11.
[2] See Hogan (1987), pp. 8, 11–12, and (1991), pp. 38–105; for an assessment of the wider 'cycles' of US politics see Schlesinger (1999), pp. 24–31.

of what in the early 1920s evolved into a more far-reaching American pacification strategy for Europe. While domestically Republican conservatism reigned supreme, this strategy became one of the most influential novel approaches to international politics – and stabilisation – in the twentieth century. Far from static, it evolved, progressed – and regressed – in the fulcrum decade after 1919. It can be characterised as the attempt, pursued under Wilson's successor at the reins of US foreign policy, Charles E. Hughes, to internationalise a model of order and peaceful change that in fact had its roots in America's 'Progressive era'. It derived from Progressive approaches to political and economic reform, advanced both by Theodore Roosevelt and Wilson early in the twentieth century to resuscitate US democracy and contain the brutally expanding capitalism of the 'Gilded Age'.[3] More precisely, it could be said that Hughes' policies were based on his 'conservative' understanding of such reform approaches.

What the new secretary of state wanted to promote was an evolutionary transformation of the international system; he sought to effect a progressive yet also pragmatic reform of what he deemed a crisis-prone order, that of Versailles. At the same time, he sought to minimise governmental interference in this process, relying as far as possible on the expertise of financiers and other informal agents. Following his lead, the underlying rationale of US diplomacy came to employ America's newly expanding, essentially financial *and* political, power efficiently, and as informally as possible, *yet under clear political supervision*. His key aim became to counter international instability, be it caused by uncontrollable revolutions – looming on the horizon since 1917 – or by a crisis-prone *status quo* such as that of 1919.

Rather than by continuity, American policy was thus marked by a complex reorientation. In a clear departure from Wilsonian principles, it crystallised into the Republican attempt to realise Wilson's aim of a new Euro-Atlantic order by distinctly different means. What rendered possible the initiation of American stabilisation policies in 1923 was a gradual learning process. Broadly speaking, it comprised two main stages. First, there was a marked change of ideas and assumptions, which only gained momentum in the face of Europe's protracted crisis following what Hughes perceived as an inherently 'flawed' peace.[4] It manifested itself in the Hughes plan, which was developed in December 1922, on the eve of the French Ruhr invasion. What Hughes proposed became not only the Republican design to 'solve' the intricate

<hr>

[3] Hughes (1925), pp. 8ff. On Progressivism see Hofstadter (1955); Link and Catton (1973); Link and McCormick (1983); Brinkley (1995), pp. 3ff.

[4] See Hughes statement in the Senate debates over Versailles, November 1919, in Danelski and Tulchin (1973), pp. 210–11.

reparations problem. In a wider sense, it encapsulated America's Progressive model of promoting stability by 'depoliticising' Europe's postwar conflicts.

Accelerated by the escalating Ruhr crisis, however, there was a second, more far-reaching departure, a recasting of the Harding administration's actual policies. It was geared to putting the power of America's informal postwar hegemony behind what until then had been mere proposals. Crucially, it was this shift that allowed Americans and Europeans to find new ways to implement Hughes' designs – and in the process begin to transform European politics. This novel mode of transatlantic co-operation would hinge on the closest informal – and formal – concertation of America and Britain since 1919.

Beyond Wilson's legacy – the origins and economic orientation of Republican foreign policy after 1919

Defining for Republican postwar policy was the rejection of the treaty system of Versailles. But that was not tantamount to the complete abandonment of Wilson's international aims. This attitude also characterised Hughes' approach. Ever since the end of the war, the former Supreme Court judge and unsuccessful Republican presidential candidate of 1916 had been a vocal opponent of what he criticised as Wilson's advocacy of a 'rigid' universal system of collective security under the League Covenant. In essence, Hughes thought it too static and *status quo* orientated to promote either US interests or durable peace. He thus explicitly rejected commitments to a system not permitting changes in the international order that might be 'advisable in the future'. As the future secretary of state emphasised early on, more perspective on the requirements of peace could only be gained with more distance from the war, and new international agreements had to be sufficiently flexible to make necessary adjustments. In Hughes' eyes, the 'peacemakers' at Versailles could not have such perspective, particularly with a view to the German problem.[5]

But it would also remain a guiding notion of Hughes' policies after 1919 that the principal threat to European and world peace was not so much over-extending Wilsonian idealism as 'disorder . . . and the tendency toward revolutions within the States'.[6] The warning example of Bolshevik Russia and Germany's volatile situation after the armistice reinforced his view that such disorder could become uncontrollable. It threatened to spread, particularly in the absence of any American engagement in Europe, to such a degree as to harm even a distant America's political and economic self-interest in stability.

---

[5] *Ibid.*
[6] Hughes statement in the 1919 Senate debates, cited in Pusey (1951), II, p. 395.

In a similar vein, Herbert Hoover, who in 1919–20 had acted as Wilson's adviser before becoming secretary of commerce under Harding, originally defended the League as the only mechanism through which 'redress can be found and . . . the good will of the world can be enforced'. In October 1919, he emphasised that America should participate in a 'world council' that would prevent the re-ascension of autocratic militarism and protect the new democratic states of eastern Europe, warning that if the League failed 'the world must readjust itself to the old balance-of-power theory and great wars will result from this realignment'.[7] Even in retrospect, Hoover would praise the Geneva organisation as the only alternative to 'chaos over the whole earth' in 1918.[8] Yet, like Hughes, he soon deemed the compromised order of Versailles in urgent need of reform to reconstruct Europe and counter both revolutionary and revisionist pressures, not least in Germany. A formative experience for Hoover had been organising the sizeable aid programme of the American Relief Administration (ARA) in central Europe immediately after the war.

The more the Franco-German antagonism over reparations escalated, the more Hoover, echoing Keynes, advocated a concentration on economic necessities in war-ravaged European countries that, in his view, lacked the requisite mechanisms of economic organisation for their revitalisation. In the commerce secretary's judgement, a radical reorientation was needed to remedy these shortcomings and contain resurgent European militarism and balance-of-power machinations. In 1922, he urged that economic diplomacy should supersede what he deplored as a regression to old-style power politics, above all France's undeclared reparations war against Germany.[9]

What thus became desirable, though not yet imperative for Republican policymakers observing the Old World's crises from their 'hemispheric fortress', and comforted by America's comparative self-sufficiency, was to devise an alternative approach to European stabilisation. Fundamentally, early Republican attempts to formulate strategies to this end indeed hinged on incorporating west and central Europe into a new economic order. It was to be based on precepts of what became the chief doctrine of US commercial diplomacy after World War I – that of the 'open door'. This doctrine's principal proponents, Hoover and the highly influential chairman of the federal Tariff Commission, William Culbertson, held that globalising the 'open door' held the key to fostering both the cardinal US interest in global commercial expansion *and* a universally beneficial consolidation of Europe.[10]

---

[7] Hoover, 'We Cannot Fiddle while Rome Burns', address, Palo Alto, 2 October 1919, in Hoover (1919).
[8] Hoover article, *New York Times*, 28 July 1919, Hoover Papers, box 164; Hoover (1961), p. 248.
[9] Hoover memorandum, Paris, July 1919, Hoover Papers, box 164; Hoover to Hughes, 24 April 1922, NA RG 59/800.51/316.
[10] See Hoover (1922).

Like Wilson, Republican decisionmakers thus tried to revive a doctrine first developed in the prewar period, namely under the Republican president Taft in the bid to 'open up' China. In its Open-Door Notes of 1899–1900, the Taft administration had demanded to end the imperial powers' carving-up of China and free access to the Chinese market.[11] Subsequently, this 'open-door policy' was adapted to US interests and economic conditions after 1919. At its core lay the promotion of a non-discriminating system of bilateral trade agreements on the basis of most-favoured-nation trade status. It was thus principally directed against any 'closed system' relying on tariff barriers, cartels and other means of barring US access to the world market through state-sanctioned protectionism.

In principle, American policy thus rejected all trade restrictions imposed by the Versailles treaty. Above all, however, it was to clash with what Americans perceived as France's attempt to create a 'closed' Franco-German economic bloc by occupying the Ruhr in 1923.[12] It should be emphasised, though, that – mainly due to Congressional pressure – America's pursuit of the 'open door' from the start featured a strong protectionist component. The president was accorded ample unilateral sanction powers, which he could exercise unilaterally. Hence, Republican commercial policy was clearly designed to benefit chiefly the world's by then leading exporter of capital and goods. This hegemonic version of the 'open-door doctrine' was enshrined in the Fordney–McCumber Tariff Act passed by Congress in 1922.[13]

Sharing Hoover's and Culbertson's assumptions, Hughes largely espoused America's new commercial policy. Consequently, he lent the State Department's support 'to apply the open-door everywhere throughout the world', particularly against the 'closed' imperial-preference systems still maintained by Britain and France.[14] With deliberate political intent, the first major bilateral trade agreement that Washington concluded after the war on new American terms was the treaty of commerce with Germany, signed at the peak of the Ruhr crisis on 8 December 1923. While France had come to be seen as its principal opponent, Germany would hence become the main 'auxiliary power' in the bid to expand the American open-door principles in Europe.[15]

Characteristically, Hoover continued to assess postwar Europe's ills from a fundamentally economic angle. On the one hand, he consistently stressed the reassuring degree of American self-sufficiency. On the other, however, he was

[11] Cf. Iriye (1977), pp. 20ff; Lake (1988).
[12] See chapter 3.
[13] See Culbertson's key memorandum, 16 July 1921; Culbertson to White, 8 January 1922, Culbertson Papers, boxes 46, 47; Hoover to Knauth, 23 December 1922, Hoover Papers, box 292. Cf. Leffler (1979), pp. 44–52.
[14] Thus Hughes in December 1923, quoted in Costigliola (1984), p. 103.
[15] Cf. Link (1970), pp. 324–37.

the first key policymaker who also warned that what he foresaw as growing transatlantic interdependence meant that America's long-term prosperity could only be sustained if that of Europe was put on a sounder footing. Significantly, the commerce secretary had early on won Hughes' support for his view that the crux of Europe's difficulties, which would also affect America's economy, lay 'in the economic relationships of France and Germany alone'. On 5 November 1923, he noted that as the German situation was 'near breakdown' France had only one of two options, either 'to support democratic government in Germany or to face implacable hate and constant danger'.[16]

In Hoover's judgement, the Franco-German problem was also amenable to an economically founded solution. Consequently, he proposed that the administration should refrain from any political interference and rely instead on financial diplomacy to attack the underlying reparations conundrum. It should enlist the co-operation of economic elites on both sides of the Atlantic, notably financial experts and bankers. These were to forge a reparations regime solely under the aspect of its financial viability – unalloyed by political considerations. At the same time, the commerce secretary asserted that it was 'the most unlikely event on the economic earth' after the experiences of the Great War that 'the United States, as a government, [would] again engage in any governmental loans' to European countries. Any 'financial assistance' had to 'arise from our private investors'.[17] Crucially, this economic approach to international consolidation, most marked between 1919 and 1922, initially reinforced the prevailing tendency of official US aloofness from Europe. It thus severely limited intergovernmental co-operation across the Atlantic – if not the emergence of a new transatlantic system of international politics as such.

The 'Hughes Doctrine' and the evolution of a US strategy for peaceful change in Europe

Gradually, however, and particularly after Lloyd George's failure at Genoa and the clearly perceived deterioration of Franco-German relations in late 1922, the almost exclusively economic character of US policy began to change. Principally under Hughes' lead, economic diplomacy became part and parcel of a genuine Republican stabilisation policy, which proved decisive for Euro-Atlantic politics in the 1920s. In short, a more far-reaching agenda emerged, clearly rooted in long-standing traditions of US domestic politics. Essentially, Hughes' main aim became to endow US informal hegemony with a Progressive impetus.

---

[16] Hoover memorandum for Harding, 23 January 1922, Hoover Papers, box 21; Hoover memorandum, 5 November 1923, in Hoover (1952a), p. 182; Hoover (1922).

[17] Hoover to Harding, 4 January 1922, Harding Papers, PCF, Box 5.

Although never formally propounded, by the end of 1922 an unspoken 'Hughes Doctrine' had evolved. At the core, it was an internationalised Monroe Doctrine. On the one hand, the United States came to act as a formal – and overall benign – hegemonic power guaranteeing stability in the American hemisphere. Within it, and in the naval sphere, the newly predominant maritime power was prepared to commit itself to international regimes and treaties serving this purpose. Outside this designated sphere of influence, however, American policy would limit itself to the informal pursuit of stability. Here, Hughes came to conceive of America's role as that of an aloof yet engaged arbiter – officially 'neutral' and unfettered yet employing both the financial leverage *and* increasingly the political influence that arose from America's new economic pre-eminence.

Where US security interests were directly at stake Hughes played a leading official role, most notably in creating the 'Washington system' of 1922.[18] He did so in close, if competitive, co-operation with Britain. Fulfilling his central aims, the Washington conference proved remarkably effective in limiting naval armament through fixed international parities and maintaining a rather stable *status quo* in the Pacific throughout the 1920s. Hughes soon considered the proceedings an exemplary approach to regionally focused intergovernmental co-operation. He would consistently urge the Europeans to emulate it to solve their 'regional problems'.[19]

The quest for stability outside the American hemisphere followed a different rationale. Europe – whence after 1919 neither Hughes nor any other key US decisionmaker perceived a serious security threat, even in the long term – clearly lay beyond America's 'mental' strategic frontier.[20] What the secretary of state envisaged as Washington's contribution to European peace and Franco-German reconciliation after Versailles never crystallised into a captivating 'vision'. A renewed Wilsonian quest, even under different auspices, remained alien to Hughes' pragmatic, if often legalistic, thinking. Rather, he sought to promote concrete co-operation with European states to tackle the deeper causes of the Old World's crisis: problems of postwar reconstruction, the accommodation of the vanquished and, especially in Germany, the adaptation to post-imperial, democratic 'realities'. Political and financial elites, formal *and* informal actors had to be engaged in this process. Thus, Hughes aimed to overcome what he deemed the greatest deficiency of European politics: that the war's adversaries were still embroiled in nationalist rivalries and 'irrational' power struggles, chiefly over reparations.[21]

---

[18] See Hughes' key memorandum, *FRUS 1921*, I, pp. 53–61. Cf. Costigliola (1984), pp. 80–1.
[19] Hughes letter to Sir Eric Drummond, 16 June 1924, *FRUS 1924*, II, pp. 80–3.
[20] See Coolidge's State of the Union Address, 6 December 1923, *FRUS 1923*, I, p. vii.
[21] Hughes memorandum, 6 November 1923, NA RG 59 462.00 R296/596.

From the turn of 1922/3, the aim of America's policy of peaceful change would be nothing less than to recast the rules of international politics on American terms. Hughes tried to foster not only economic stabilisation but also regional security co-operation. To achieve this, he saw the need both to redefine the administration's official role and to keep international involvement at a domestically acceptable minimum. In the absence of forceful presidential leadership under Harding and his successor Calvin Coolidge, this led him to strengthen the role of the State Department not only vis-à-vis Congress but also the Commerce Department. In relations with Europe, Hughes was to follow what could be called his guiding principles of informal US pre-eminence, which in June 1924 he defined as: 'Independence – that does not mean and never meant isolation. Co-operation – that does not mean and never meant alliances or political entanglements.'[22]

As former Supreme Court judge, Hughes had a Progressive outlook and marshalled a law-based rationalism not dissimilar to Wilson's; nor were the long-term aims of his foreign policy necessarily less ambitious than those of the missionary peacemaker at Versailles.[23] After the Washington conference, the Republican secretary of state declared that he sought 'to establish a *Pax Americana* maintained not by arms but by mutual respect and good will and the tranquillizing processes of reason'.[24] Overall, though, he came to espouse a more gradualist, regionally focused credo of peaceful change. In September 1923, one month before recasting America's Ruhr policy, Hughes noted that the 'way to peace [was] through agreement, not through force'. In his view, the 'question [was] not of any ambitious general scheme to prevent war'. Imperative was instead 'the constant effort. . . to diminish among people the disposition to resort to force and to find a just and reasonable basis for accord'.[25]

The 'entanglement' in ambitious general schemes – and this duality remained crucial for Hughes' policy – he not only saw as harmful to US interests and domestically undesirable, particularly in the face of Congress' stiff isolationist opposition. He also viewed it as inexpedient and even detrimental to Europe's pacification, which in his eyes required a 'neutral' US arbiter. Gradually, then, after the failure of Genoa and the escalation of Franco-German tensions in late 1922, the predominant economic orientation of Washington's European policy, largely set by Hoover, started to change. Under Hughes' lead, a broader Republican consolidation strategy for Europe

---

[22] Hughes memorandum, 1 July 1924, cited in Saueressig (1996), p. 46.
[23] See Hughes, 'The Supreme Court', in Hughes (1925).
[24] *Ibid.*, p. 259.
[25] Hughes, 'Address to the Canadian Bar Association', 4 September 1923, in Hughes (1925), p. 8; Hoover (1922).

emerged. Its *leitmotif* became to replace the order of Versailles by a new Euro-Atlantic system, a 'community of ideals, interests and purposes'. Already rooted in his thought by then was the idea that this community should comprise not only the victors of 1918, mainly France and America's most congenial partner Britain. Europe's stability also required not only the economic but also the political inclusion of Weimar Germany.[26] By contrast, though Soviet Russia remained a troubling source of instability, the Harding administration neither recognised its regime nor developed a coherent policy to deal with the Soviet question. The limited aim of Hughes' strategy remained to fortify Germany as a bulwark against Bolshevik expansion by drawing it into the western camp.[27]

'Depoliticisation' – the Progressive path to overcoming the Franco-German crisis

Prior to the turning-point of 1923, the implications of the Hughes doctrine for Anglo-American co-operation and Europe became most evident in the run-up to the Genoa conference when Republican policymakers rejected Lloyd George's 'grand design'. They opposed what they saw as his attempt to co-opt US support to build a new European order on British terms. In Hughes' eyes, the British premier aimed to 'distort' what should have been an 'economic conference' by giving it a wider political purpose. In Hoover's view, this purpose was to re-assert Britain's position as the hub of a revived world economy and to lure Germany and Russia into the British orbit.[28]

After Lloyd George's fall, Hughes put forward the closest approximation of an American 'grand design' for Europe's Progressive stabilisation in the 1920s in his 'New Haven Speech' on 29 December 1922. Speaking out against French threats to enforce unilateral reparations sanctions against Germany, the secretary of state left no doubt as to what position the US administration took on the Franco-German question. His warning to Paris, and signal to London and Berlin, centred on the declaration that Washington did 'not wish to see a prostrate Germany'.[29] He duly emphasised that there could be 'no economic recuperation in Europe unless Germany recuperates' nor 'permanent peace unless economic satisfactions are enjoyed by all' – both the victors and the

---

[26] See Hughes (1925), pp. 8ff; Harding, State of the Union Address, 12 April 1921, *FRUS 1921*, I, pp. xviii–xx.

[27] Hughes, 'Deal Only with Upright States', in Hughes (1922). Cf. Kennan (1951), pp. 24ff.

[28] For Hughes' position see *FRUS 1922*, I, p. 393; see also Hoover to Harding, 25 January 1922, Hoover Papers, box 21.

[29] *FRUS 1922*, II, p. 201; Hughes interview with Jusserand, 26 December 1922, *ibid.*, pp. 195ff.

vanquished.[30] What Hughes proposed to avert this 'disaster', and to ensure the largest possible reparation payments to America's war-debtors, was an 'expert plan', drawn up by the State Department. Its aim was the 'depoliticisation' of what he knew to be a politically highly charged conflict. Its 'solution' was to be sought outside the sphere of power politics, by financial 'experts of the highest authority'. These were to be gathered in two 'independent committees' with the mandate to assess 'objectively' Germany's 'actual capacity to pay' and to propose mechanisms for 'an efficient transfer of reparations'.[31] Hughes promised his government's support and held out the prospect that private American capital could underpin the envisaged scheme.[32] Yet he still acted on the assumption that it was not for Washington but for the European governments, particularly Paris and Berlin, to pave the political way for implementing his design, thus hoping to contain any risk for his government as far as possible.[33] As he impressed on America's interventionist ambassador in Berlin, Houghton, on 16 May 1923, 'America was the only point of stability in the world' and 'for this reason, we absolutely could not make any move unless it would surely be successful'.[34]

Hughes' informal approach, and his restraint, was also informed by what he saw as salient domestic constraints. He was highly wary of taking any step with which either Congress or US public opinion could take issue. And, at least in his perception, both remained distinctly suspicious of any intervention in the European conflict.[35] Yet the secretary of state also invoked these constraints vis-à-vis the Europeans to justify the limits of American stabilisation policy.[36] Hughes consistently emphasised that not only the war-debt issue but also strategic questions, especially possible security commitments in Europe, fell outside the 'province of the executive' in Washington. Having tried in vain to widen his freedom of action vis-à-vis the Senate in 1921–2, he thereafter largely conceded that the Senate's powerful Foreign Relations Committee and its Debt Commission had the final say in these areas. Thus, the administration was not in a position to exercise discretion on debt cancellation, let alone to become a formal 'umpire' or guarantor of European peace.

---

[30] *FRUS 1922*, II, pp. 199–202. Cf. Castle Diary, vol. 3, p. 158.

[31] *FRUS 1922*, II, pp. 199–202; Hughes memorandum, 18 December 1922, Hughes Papers.

[32] Hughes' New Haven approach drew on a confluence of interests and ideas uniting US policy-makers and financiers from mid-1922. See Lamont to Hughes, 24 November 1924, Hughes Papers. Cf. Hogan (1991), pp. 38ff.

[33] See record of Hughes' conversation with Britain's ambassador Geddes, 25 January 1923, *FRUS 1923*, II, pp. 54–5; record of Hughes' conversation with the German and Belgian ambassadors, 3 May 1923, *FRUS 1923*, II, pp. 60ff.

[34] Castle Diary, 16 May 1925, vol. 7.

[35] *Ibid.* See Lippmann (1922) and (1925).

[36] Record of Hughes' conversation with the German and Belgian ambassadors, 3 May 1923, *FRUS 1923*, II, pp. 60–1.

Heeding Congressional demarcations, the State Department continued to deny any formal connection between reparations and war-debts. But Hughes nonetheless realised that there was practically no hope of retrieving debts from Britain and France unless Germany paid sufficient reparations. Accordingly, he underscored that he had 'no desire to see Germany relieved of her responsibility for the war or her just obligations'.[37] For almost a year of crisis, however, the political conditions Washington set for considering an engagement in Europe remained unfulfilled, and the Hughes plan no more than a signal. It was only in response to the rapid escalation of the Ruhr conflict in October and November 1923 that the process of *de facto* reorientation in America's European policy, initiated in 1922, gained crucial momentum.

[37] Hughes communiqué to the British government, 16 October 1923, NA RG59 462.00 R296/16.

6   Towards transatlantic co-operation and a new European order

The reorientation of British stabilisation policy, 1922–1924

In the post-World War I era, Britain was not a *status quo* power, at least not in Europe. Yet numerous post-1945 studies on Britain's foreign relations in the 1920s have attempted to show just that: that Britain's core interest was to preserve the system of 1919, however imperfect it seemed, not least to British policymakers themselves.[1] In the 'realist' view, the litmus test for British foreign policy became how far it could revive the only possible 'axis of stability' after America's withdrawal from Versailles – a fundamentally *status quo*-orientated *entente* with France that upheld Europe's balance of power against Germany's revisionist ambitions. Chiefly for economic reasons, yet also because of a flawed notion of 'appeasement', British leaders allegedly failed this test.[2]

More recently, Britain's quest for postwar order has been placed – like America's – in an overarching continuity. Rather than forge alliances, Britain allegedly sought to 'regulate' Europe's *status quo* essentially by reviving, in key respects, the old European order of the nineteenth century.[3] Further, it has been accentuated that British 'appeasement' was shaped by a corporatist 'coalition' akin to that in the United States, comprising the ruling policy-making elite, the City and the Bank of England under its influential governor Montagu Norman. Their common priority, it was claimed, was to preserve Britain's liberal-capitalist order, based on 'free enterprise and the limited state', against revolutionary tendencies in and outside the country.[4]

Was it this set of aims, and this coalition, that shaped Britain's pursuit of European pacification from the Ruhr crisis to the Great Depression? In short, while previous approaches illuminate certain general tendencies they, on closer

---

[1] See Ferris (1989), pp. 43–4; Orde (1978) pp. 2–5; Kennedy (1988), pp. 400ff.
[2] Cf. Kennedy (1983), pp. 22–3; Marks (1976), 143–4. On economic 'appeasement' see Newton (1996), pp. 4–5, 17ff.
[3] See Grayson (1997), pp. 32–115; Ferris (1989), p. 46.
[4] See Newton (1996), pp. 4–5.

inspection, throw a distorting light on British policy in the 1920s. There was indeed a strong bond of common interest between British policymakers and financiers when, in 1923/4, the task was to protect British trade and reparations claims while keeping an undivided Germany within a liberal-capitalist western system.[5] Essentially, however, Britain's strategy for solving the Franco-German conflict was shaped by the 'classic' protagonists of foreign policymaking, above all in the Foreign Office. They had far more control over policy priorities than their counterparts in the State Department. Moreover, British 'appeasement' was certainly not an aberration, a policy that only emerged in dealing with the dictators of the 1930s. It grew out of a long tradition shaping British policy since the early nineteenth century.[6] Yet what made a tangible difference for   Europe's pacification after 1919 was the reorientation of British thought and practice, particularly after the *caesura* of 1923. Crucially, British policymakers came to reject a preservation of the *status quo* of Versailles and eventually pursued its qualitative transformation – in co-operation with, and to appease, a *democratic* Germany.

Although much attention has focused on Lloyd George, the evolution of British stabilisation policy by no means reached its limits in 1922.[7] Rather, his futile Genoa policy can be seen as the beginning of a process in which British decisionmakers tried to redress the shortcomings of 1919, providing valuable lessons for his successors. In many ways, it was only after the catalytic Ruhr crisis that Britain developed gradually more comprehensive and workable strategies of peaceful change.[8] Increasingly, policymakers not only sought to adjust the evidently crisis-prone parameters of 1919 but to forge a new international system. Crucially, they came to realise that the Franco-German question could not be solved by alliances or military means. This reorientation culminated in two complementary yet also markedly idiosyncratic approaches to European pacification, which have to be re-appraised as two stages of a wider process recasting British policy after the Great War. The first was Ramsay MacDonald's attempt to overcome the Ruhr crisis, and the Franco-German antagonism, through a policy of transatlantic co-operation and evolutionary accommodation in 1924. The second was Austen Chamberlain's attempt to forge a more durable framework for European security, a new concert of European powers, in 1925.[9]

[5] See chapters 9 and 10.   [6] Cf. Kennedy (1983), pp. 21–2.
[7] Cf. Dockrill and Goold (1981); Sharp (1984).
[8] For Curzon's Ruhr policy in 1923 see chapter 7.
[9] This will be analysed in chapter 12.

MacDonald's evolutionary approach to Europe's pacification

The short-lived government of Britain's first Labour premier in 1924 – and his direction of Britain's external relations both as premier and his own foreign secretary – undoubtedly marked a *caesura* in British foreign policy after 1918.[10] MacDonald departed both from Lloyd George's 'grand designs' and Curzon's subsequent policy of aloofness during the Ruhr crisis. Essentially, he sought to reclaim what he saw as Britain's natural role: that of an 'active agent for peace' in Europe, intervening above all to settle the Franco-German conflict over the Ruhr and reparations.[11] No less significantly, his government marked a high-point in the hitherto neglected effort to redefine Britain's postwar relationship – and burden-sharing – with America in this endeavour.

Yet the questions of what significance the changes MacDonald initiated had, and what they portended for British and European security, long remained rather obscure – before becoming part of the wider controversy over British 'appeasement'. MacDonald's reputation has undoubtedly been affected by the fact that he initially shaped British policy only for a short period – no more than nine months in 1924, then not again until 1929. On the one hand, his attempt to strengthen the League and to further reconciliation with Germany – and Soviet Russia – was interpreted as naïve.[12] On the other, his 'appeasement' policies have been viewed as driven by ideological leftist internationalism.[13] MacDonald has particularly been criticised for placing inordinate trust both in the League and Weimar Germany's embattled republican leaders. Yet how valid is the claim that he effectively cajoled France into a detrimental reparations settlement?[14] And how far did his evolutionary approach undermine a united Anglo-French front against German resurgence? Was MacDonald, finally, allowing US financial interests to gain a decisive – and detrimental – influence on European politics?

A closer look at MacDonald's policy and its contribution to invigorating Euro-Atlantic international politics in the 1920s leads to markedly different conclusions. Albeit hardly able to sustain it during his brief first premiership, MacDonald developed Britain's first comprehensive strategy for settling the Franco-German conflict, far surpassing Lloyd George's abortive 'grand design' of 1922. Crucially, it was the first approach that met the central challenge of the 1920s – to forge a *transatlantic* approach to this end. The only 'Atlanticist' among Britain's leading foreign policymakers of the 1920s,

---

[10] See Cowling (1971).
[11] MacDonald to Bonar Law, 29 January 1923, MacDonald Papers, 5/33.
[12] Cf. Orde (1978), pp. 55–75; Winkler (1956); Marquand (1977), pp. 293ff.
[13] Cf. Schuker (1976), pp. 192–204; Gilbert (1966); Kennedy (1983).
[14] Thus a core thesis of Schuker (1976), pp. 383ff.

MacDonald had a more profound understanding of the need to combine Britain's political clout and the economic means of her elusive partner, the United States. This also distinguished his course from Chamberlain's later quest for the Locarno pact. Under MacDonald's direction, British diplomacy finally broke with its previous priority of maintaining, however reluctantly, the Anglo-French *entente* and a by 1923 untenable *status quo*. Instead, it shifted to a forward engagement to consolidate postwar Europe through new ground-rules of reassurance, evolutionary change and integration – the reassurance of France, a change of relations between Britain, Europe and America and the international integration of Weimar Germany.

What, then, marked MacDonald's outlook on the challenges of Euro-Atlantic peacemaking? And what made his an 'evolutionary' policy of peaceful change? *Prima facie* most notable seems a pronounced tension between principle and practice. Both the war and subsequent crises had only reinforced MacDonald's belief in left-liberal assumptions about the requirements of peace. Yet as prime minister he came to pursue a remarkably pragmatic course. What became ever more pronounced, however, and bridged the gap between far-reaching aims and gradualist means, was his evolutionary outlook on Europe's pacification. It changed essentially through his observation of the Franco-German crisis and, crucially, the conclusions he drew from British passivity in 1923.

On a deeper level, it appears justified to characterise his path as a highly individual learning-process. This may be illustrated by the following juxtaposition. In 1918, MacDonald had seen no long-standing British traditions to build on in making peace.[15] As a committed internationalist in the Independent Labour Party (ILP), he had called for a radical new beginning after the war had finally discredited what he saw as inherently flawed precepts of power politics and secret diplomacy. MacDonald had categorically demanded that the 'whole corrupting system should be swept away'.[16] And he had rejected the 'frame of mind' that sought to rebuild Europe through a 'Holy Alliance' of the victors.[17] Consequently, MacDonald became one of the most vocal British critics of the Versailles treaty. He held that Wilson had been 'outmanoeuvred' by the 'European diplomatists' Clemenceau and Lloyd George.[18] Animated by 'the logic of war', the peace could only be a temporary 'armistice' bearing, in the 'punishment' inflicted on a republican Germany, already the seeds of the next war. Thus, Versailles had to be urgently replaced by a 'real peace' following Wilson's universalist principles. To achieve this,

---

[15] MacDonald (1918), p. 115. Cf. Gordon (1969), pp. 31ff.
[16] MacDonald (1918), p. 115.
[17] *Bulletin of the International Labour and Socialist Conference* (Berne), 7 February 1919. Cf. Marquand (1977), pp. 248–52.
[18] MacDonald (1914).

MacDonald urged that Britain should take a lead in turning the hamstrung League into a 'strengthened and democratised' agency of peace.[19]

Half a decade later, the Labour premier deemed the pursuit of high-level co-operation between the major powers, and a regional rather than a universalist approach, both a necessity and Europe's best hope for peace. More than that, he would also work closely with the heads of international capitalism on both sides of the Atlantic to forge the reparations accords of 1924.[20] These, in essence, were the lessons MacDonald had drawn from Europe's postwar imbroglio. Not without a certain historical irony, he thus greatly contributed to stabilising the embattled liberal-capitalist order of the nascent Euro-Atlantic state system.[21]

More generally, MacDonald's reorientation was informed by what, in July 1924, he called the refusal to draw 'false distinctions between idealism and practical*ism*' in foreign policy. He rejected a crude dichotomy between 'idealist' and 'realist' conceptions of international relations. Most consistently, MacDonald stressed the importance of psychological factors. And he criticised those who even after the Great War clung to traditions of national power politics, observing: 'The one thing that matters is psychology . . . Unless we change the qualities of our minds we had better arm to the teeth.' Hence, then, was also to spring the main impetus for transformation of the western powers' relations with Germany.[22] MacDonald believed that changes in mentality could only be spurred through concrete co-operation between statesmen, not by abstract covenants. As a steadfast proponent of 'open diplomacy', however, he was also keenly aware of a dimension that his predecessor Curzon had dismissed: the need for gaining domestic backing for international initiatives. In MacDonald's view, not only political leaders but also public opinion had to be educated about the requirements of an integrative peace. Characteristically, he felt that the British public had already advanced further than that in continental Europe. Here, as in other spheres, Britain could set a moral example.[23]

The conflict of 1923 did not alter but rather reinforce MacDonald's view of the crisis of the Versailles system. Yet it also reinforced his gravitation towards a more pragmatic approach to Europe's pacification. As Labour opposition leader in 1923, he had consistently criticised Curzon's Ruhr policy, or

---

[19] MacDonald (1919); Miller (1967), p. 86; *Labour Party Annual Conference Report 1922*, p. 193.

[20] MacDonald to Grahame, 29 June 1924, *DBFP*, I, XXVI, no. 493.

[21] Cf. Maier (1988), pp. 482–8.

[22] MacDonald minute, 3 July 1924, FO 371/9818; MacDonald statement, 15 August 1924, Proceedings of the London Reparations Conference, II, CAB 29/103–4, pp. 7–8; MacDonald (1923a). Cf. Ferris (1989), pp. 44–5.

[23] MacDonald speech in the Commons, March 1923, *Hansard*, 5th series, vol. 161, col. 326; MacDonald notes about deliberations with Leon Blum, March 1923, MacDonald Papers, MDP 8/1.

lack thereof, and emphasised the need to shift from a hapless 'policy of neutrality' to a more active mediation between the antagonists. For MacDonald, Poincaré's Ruhr incursion was tantamount to renewed war against Germany. He argued that, if left unchecked by Britain, French actions would spark another continental conflagration.[24] In MacDonald's judgement, France was not only undercutting Germany's economic base. It also threatened its fragile republican order, discrediting those who sought an accommodation with the west and benefiting nationalist forces. As he noted in May 1924, 'the worst form of German nationalism was the result of the way that Germany had been handled by the Allies' both in 1919 and thereafter. Ultimately, MacDonald saw the spectre of Germany's political and territorial disintegration, spelling catastrophic consequences for England's prosperity and the stability of Europe.[25]

In MacDonald's perception, the gravest threat to European stability was not a by then largely non-existent German danger but France's remaining imperialistic tendencies, its 'historical craving' for a preponderance over central Europe. He thus considered it erroneous 'to assume that events in France are in consequence of feeling insecure'.[26] As will be seen, MacDonald became more sensitive to France's *subjective* security concerns only in his 1924 negotiations with the Socialist premier Herriot.[27] While arguing that only active British arbitration could stop Poincaré, MacDonald thus deemed the Germans not blameless but clearly the 'underdogs' vis-à-vis France. He especially sympathised with politicians who – like *Reichspräsident* Ebert – were the essentially social democratic guardians of Weimar's republic, struggling to defend it against internal and external challenges.[28] Despite unquestionable Germanophile tendencies, however, his resolve to accommodate Germany did not anticipate British policy in the 1930s. Rather, he saw a tangible British interest in fostering the Weimar Republic precisely to prevent its replacement by an anti-democratic – and anti-western – regime.[29]

MacDonald thus emphasised the political case for a British intervention. But he did not lose sight of Britain's more immediate interests. Not least to win public support, and, echoing Hughes, he took up one of the main liberal themes of the era, namely that economic interdependence required Britain to act: It could simply not afford to see its most important trading

---

[24] MacDonald (1923b); MacDonald speech in the Commons, March 1923, *Hansard*, 5th series, vol. 161, col. 326.

[25] MacDonald to Knox (Berlin), 6 May 1924, MacDonald to Crewe (Paris), 26 January 1924, *DBFP*, I, XXVI, nos. 462, 344.

[26] MacDonald minute, 18 February 1924, FO 371/9813: C 2028/1346/18.

[27] See chapter 5.

[28] MacDonald statements, *Times*, 16 February 1924; MacDonald (1919).

[29] MacDonald speech in the Commons, 23 July 1923, *Hansard*, 5th series, vol. 167, col. 67.

partner – overburdened by excessive reparations claims – succumb to hyper-inflation and economic chaos. The Labour opposition leader invoked the danger of a British recession and rising unemployment. And he demanded to replace reparations with a concerted European reconstruction programme.[30]

The quest for integrative stabilisation – the departure of British foreign policy in 1924

Resolved to set British policy on a new course, the Labour premier came to espouse a markedly presidential style of policymaking. Yet he also consulted the heads of British professional diplomacy, above all the Foreign Office's *spiritus rector*, Eyre Crowe. MacDonald quickly sought to draw up a 'comprehensive policy' to resolve the Franco–German crisis, contain Poincaré and prevent a permanent French control of the Ruhr. On 5 February 1924, a Foreign Office memorandum reflecting Crowe's general line warned of France's underlying desire to go beyond Versailles and establish a permanent European predominance, ostensibly to constrain Germany; in the long run, this could pose a threat to Britain.[31]

By this time, Crowe held that Poincaré only 'meant to throw dust in the eyes of the Germans'. His 'pettifogging and ridiculous arguments' concerning the fulfilment of France's reparations demands merely served one purpose: to keep the Ruhr in French hands. Crowe thus underscored the need to increase pressure on France. He advised MacDonald to insist vis-à-vis Poincaré that the US plan for an expert inquiry into reparations was the only acceptable basis for a settlement. And he insisted that Britain should offer France a firm pledge of support in ensuring German payments and, crucially, enhanced security guarantees. Yet this was only to be 'discussed' once France had agreed to 'something definite' and evacuated the Ruhr.[32]

Ever since 1921, Crowe had held that Britain had to rely on a workable *entente* with France to uphold the treaty system. Until 1923, the main rationale of his approach – and British policy – remained that a breach between the *entente* partners had to be avoided. A guarantee pact just short of a full military alliance, however, might allow Britain to make France more conciliatory towards Germany.[33] By March 1924, though, Crowe had begun to alter his outlook, endorsing a proposal by Britain's ambassador in Berlin, Viscount D'Abernon 'to get the French out of the Rhineland [and] placate German

---

[30] *Hansard* 5th series, vol. 159, cols. 3237–45. Cf. Orde (1990), pp. 203ff; Marquand (1977), p. 293.
[31] Sterndale-Bennett memorandum, 5 February 1924, FO 371/9813: C 2028/1346/18.
[32] Crowe to Phipps (Paris), 20 March 1924, *DBFP*, I, XXVI, no. 394; Crowe minute, 25 February 1924, FO 371/9818: C2842/2048/18.
[33] *DBFP*, I, XVII, no. 38.

national feeling'. Following D'Abernon, Crowe thought that this might be achieved through a regional non-aggression pact including Germany along the lines of what the German foreign minister Stresemann had proposed on 11 February.[34] But any such scheme would not be implemented until 1925.

MacDonald endorsed Crowe's rationale but refused to contemplate an old-style guarantee pact with France, thus also considering the German proposal neither timely nor promising.[35] Yet the prime minister also had a second alternative to consider. Lord Cecil, a protagonist of the pro-League movement in Britain and since 1920 Britain's principal representative in Geneva, had proposed in 1922 that Britain subscribe to a far-reaching League scheme of disarmament and collective security.[36] Cecil envisaged a universal Treaty of Mutual Guarantee. It was to commit all signatories to provide immediate and automatic assistance against aggression. Yet, though taking up long-standing Labour demands, Cecil's plan was unanimously rejected by the Committee of Imperial Defence in April 1924. After consulting the Dominions, the MacDonald government finally informed the League in July that it no longer supported the scheme.[37] Agreeing with Crowe's diagnosis and Cecil's general aims, yet not with the remedy proposed by either of them, MacDonald felt all the more compelled to advance his own policy of peaceful change. In his words 'European in the fullest sense of the word', this policy would in fact become transatlantic in scope.[38]

Fundamentally, the prime minister remained resolved to abandon balance-of-power politics; Britain would 'have no sectional alliances' and 'give no guarantees of a special kind' to France.[39] MacDonald developed what could be termed a two-stage strategy. In the longer run, he remained committed to the ambitious goal of forging a 'society' of democratic nations inclusive of

[34] Addison to Nicolson, 1 March 1924, FO 371/9813: C 3814/1346/18; Crowe minute, 25 February 1924, German memorandum to the Foreign Office, 11 February 1924, D'Abernon to MacDonald, 19 February 1924, FO 371/9818: C 2048/2048/18.

[35] On MacDonald's attitude see Hankey to Smuts, 22 May 1924, Hankey Papers. Both MacDonald and Crowe were acutely aware that any British initiatives were limited by the need to consolidate public finances. In March 1922, urged by the Treasury to reduce expenditures, the Lloyd George cabinet had established the 'ten-year rule'. It was based on the premise that, given Germany's disarmament under Versailles, Britain did not expect to prepare for war within a ten-year period. Subsequently, the British General Staff underscored consistently that Britain's armed forces were unprepared to engage in a major European war. Resources were concentrated on imperial defence. See memorandum of the 165th CID meeting, 30 November 1922, CAB 2/3; General Staff memorandum to the CID, 29 September 1924, CAB 4/11, 516-B. Cf. Bond (1980), pp. 23ff.

[36] Under Baldwin, Cecil became lord privy seal charged with League affairs from May 1923.

[37] League resolution, September 1922, *League of Nations* (1922), pp. 24–7; Cecil statements in the CID, December 1922, CID paper 383-B, CAB 4/8; CID 183rd meeting, April 1924, CAB 2/4; FO 371/10568–9.

[38] MacDonald minute, 18 February 1924, FO 371/9813.

[39] MacDonald (1923a), pp. 19–20, and (1925).

Germany – and Soviet Russia. To this end, he continued to champion a fundamental reform of the League – a reform completing Wilson's design by integrating both the victors and the vanquished of the war into a flexible system of collective security under a reformed Covenant. MacDonald foresaw a transitional phase when for purely defensive purposes a modicum of military preparedness seemed unavoidable to secure the peace. But he also felt that Britain had to take the moral lead in an all-European effort 'to place national security on a totally different foundation'.[40] Yet what foundation was this to be?

On 26 February 1924, MacDonald informed Stresemann that he aspired to buttress European security not through 'regional combinations of individual States' conjuring up the 'old system of alliances' but through 'general and more universal arrangements for neutralisation and non-aggression'.[41] Only gradually, and not least under constant French pressure for more tangible assurances, MacDonald's security policy become more concrete. What he eventually proposed, in the autumn of 1924, to solve the European security question was an initiative empowering the League to become at last Europe's central mechanism of collective security *and* peaceful change. MacDonald hoped to achieve this through the so-called Geneva Protocol and Germany's early inclusion into the new League system. In contrast to French policymakers he sought to create a framework not cementing an untenable *status quo* but furthering an evolutionary change beyond Europe's postwar dividing-lines.[42] Yet this initiative would fail.[43]

MacDonald's short- and medium-term agenda, however, was more modestly defined and effectual. From the outset, his priority was to tackle the reparations problem. Essentially, he opted to disentangle it as far as possible from Europe's overarching security question, only resolvable *after* settling the Ruhr conflict. As he impressed upon the French government in March 1924, a comprehensive reparations agreement would already constitute a vital step towards enhancing European security.[44] In his view, the only viable approach to what was most urgently needed, a comprehensive reparations agreement, was an international negotiation-process under Anglo-American auspices that prevented a bilateral Franco-German agreement dictated by Poincaré. In this process, both French leaders and Weimar's 'moral elite' – in his view 'sincere spirits who were truly democratic' – were to participate on equal terms. By

---

[40] MacDonald, (1923a), pp. 19–24. Cf. Ceadel (1980); Schuker (1976), pp. 249ff.

[41] MacDonald to Addison (Berlin), 26 February 1924, FO 371/9801.

[42] MacDonald (1925); MacDonald speech to the League Assembly in September 1924, Cmd 2289: *League of Nations Fifth Assembly.*

[43] See chapter 12.

[44] MacDonald to Phipps, 24 March 1924, FO 371/9730.

involving both the United States and Germany, MacDonald consciously aimed at shifting postwar politics from the Versailles system to a new transatlantic concert.[45]

The British premier soon realised that an unequivocal implementation of Hughes' 'expert plan' of December 1922 offered the most promising means to the end he envisaged.[46] MacDonald was mindful of the strongest bond of common interest uniting Britain and America – at the core, the interest in ensuring a revitalisation of Germany and, consequently, the entire European market. In his judgement, an unprecedented interdependence tied the economies of Europe and the United States together, making transatlantic concertation indispensable. And, like his predecessor Stanley Baldwin, the Labour premier accepted that a clear commitment to honouring America's war-debt claims was a prerequisite for this concertation – as long as there was no new general international settlement in sight that curtailed both debts and reparations. At the same time, such a commitment of course palpably limited Britain's financial room to manoeuvre.[47] Mainly through his exchanges with Hughes, often via Britain's ambassador in Washington, Esme Howard, MacDonald developed a rather subtle understanding of US conduct. He acutely perceived the Republican administration's preference for informal diplomacy, which he put down to overriding domestic constraints, not least an uneducated American public. Thus, recognising the limits of official US engagement had to be the starting-point. More than Lloyd George, MacDonald saw that America had to be engaged on American terms.[48]

In the process, however, the prime minister's strategy came to be the reverse of Hughes'. In short, he intended to build on America's 'depoliticisation' scheme precisely to reinvigorate the stagnating or rather non-existent *political* process of peaceful accommodation in Europe. And while deeming US financial engagement critical, MacDonald was wary lest Europe might be overwhelmed by America's overbearing trade policies and *laissez-faire* capitalism. In this sphere, he thus aspired to a European platform, a 'federation of Free Trade nations'. In his eyes the American challenge gave European leaders all the more reason to overcome postwar divisions.[49]

---

[45] MacDonald statement, *Times*, 16 February 1924; MacDonald to Grahame (Rome), 29 June 1924, *DBFP*, I, XXVI, p. 733.
[46] MacDonald to D'Abernon, 29 May 1924, MacDonald Papers, MDP 30/69/94.
[47] For Baldwin's debt policy and the Anglo-American debt settlement of July 1923, see chapter 7.
[48] MacDonald to Howard (Washington), 16 June 1924, MacDonald Papers, MDP 30/69/94.
[49] MacDonald to D'Abernon, 29 May 1924, MacDonald Papers, MDP 30/69/94; MacDonald statement, in *Free Trader*, December 1925, p. 265; MacDonald statements, 8 July 1924, *DBFP*, I, XXVI, no. 507, pp. 753–6. Cf. Boyce (1987), pp. 114–15.

7 The turning-point
The Anglo-American intervention in the Ruhr crisis

It has long been contended that the – Anglo-American – policies and financial forces that 'defeated' Poincaré's Ruhr policy in the autumn of 1923 effectively eroded Europe's best chances for stability: France's bid to found it on a contained and potentially even divided Germany.[1] Can this be maintained? Or was the shift that led to the London conference rather a different turning-point? If there was a systemic sea-change in the 1920s during which the parameters of Versailles, France's defensive attempts to exceed them and the destabilisation they caused were altered, then it came in the autumn of 1923. It was also the turning-point at which previous British 'neutrality' and US aloofness in the face of the Franco-German imbroglio gave way to intervention and active pursuits of European stabilisation. This, strictly speaking, initiated the making of the nascent transatlantic peace order the 1920s.

By the end of 1923, it was becoming drastically obvious not only in London and Washington that there were not even rudiments of a functioning international system to master the new geo-political and structural challenges that the war had left in its wake. Above all, Anglo-American policymakers realised that while the resolution of the most pressing problems depended on Weimar Germany's co-operation *and survival*, no ground-rules had been found to engage it or even to preserve its integrity. As we have seen, however, France's Ruhr intervention had spurred the reorientation of both British and American assumptions about the requirements of European stability – and the strategies to achieve it. Yet only Poincaré's escalatory course in the autumn of 1923 provoked the crisis finally altering Anglo-American policies – and transatlantic politics.

More recent studies have justly accentuated that Poincaré's final aim was not to make the Ruhr occupation permanent, let alone provoke Germany's outright disintegration. Rather, he indeed sought to acquire 'productive pawns' and enter into separate agreements with Ruhr industrialists, all with the aim of securing German 'fulfilment' on the reparations front – and French

---

[1] See Schuker (1976), pp. 3ff, 383ff; Bariéty (1977), pp. 250ff; McDougall (1978), pp. 305ff.

preponderance.[2] In effect, though, the French premier's awkward combination of coercion and bureaucratic insistence on the Versailles treaty had by October 1923 sparked an escalation of the Franco-German stand-off, indeed raising the spectre of Weimar Germany's political, economic and territorial disintegration.

Crucially, it was this dimension of Poincaré's Ruhr policy – and other, more drastic designs contemplated in France – that were perceived with ever graver concern by both British and American policymakers.[3] They eventually intervened against a French incursion that, rather than foster continental stability in anticipation of the 1950s, i.e. at the expense of a sovereign German state, would most likely have had the opposite effect.[4] For Poincaré's course had encouraged those in France who favoured a European order based on a separate Rhineland and, like the French president Alexandre Millerand, long-term corporatist agreements between French steel-magnates and Ruhr industrialists to control German resources.[5] Both would almost inevitably have provoked a vehement nationalist reaction in Germany and further weakened Weimar's republican forces. They would thus have precipitated a violent reaction against the 'yoke of Versailles' far earlier than under Hitler. In fact, the frustration of France's bid for an 'artificial' hegemony in Europe manifested the limitations of any attempt to consolidate Europe nominally through Versailles, yet practically by means of a policy of coercion and division vis-à-vis Germany.

Rather, the essential impulse for achieving a modicum of European stability, which would be tangible after the 1924 London conference, was given through the combined efforts of British and American policymakers to forge a pacific settlement of the Franco-German conflict. Both were pursued by foreign-policy establishments whose penchants for non-entanglement and limited commitments had been reinforced by the Great War. After 1919, there had been limited political will – and room to manoeuvre – to commit Britain and the United States to far-reaching strategic guarantees or reconstruction programmes in continental Europe. Nor had there been a readiness to further European peace through tangible concessions, be it on security, debts or reparations. Nevertheless, once initiated around the turn of 1923/4 Anglo-American pursuits evolved into the most substantial and indeed most integrative attempts to stabilise interwar Europe – in co-operation with France *and* Germany.[6]

---

[2] For Poincaré's own justification of his Ruhr policy, see his speech before the *Chambre* on the day of the French invasion, *JOC*, 11 January 1923, pp. 14–18. Cf. Keiger (1997); Fischer (2003); and the more critical assessments in Jeannesson (1998), pp. 294ff, and Short (2000), pp. 415–52.

[3] Curzon to Saint-Aulaire, 13 June 1923, *DBFP*, I, XXI, pp. 343–4; Chamberlain to Birkenhead, 17 August 1923, Austen Chamberlain Papers, AC 35/2/25; notes of a conversation between Hughes and Jusserand, 6 November 1923, NA RG 59 462.00 R296/596.

[4] Cf. the different interpretations in Schuker (1976), pp. 336–7; McDougall (1978), pp. 16, 369.

[5] Cf. Maier (1988), pp. 408–9.   [6] See Cohrs (2003), pp. 8–14.

Most momentous was Hughes' bid to 'depoliticise' the reparations dispute. But no less significant was MacDonald's pursuit of a fully fledged political settlement ending the Franco-German antagonism, launched after Curzon's grudging abandonment of hapless 'neutrality'. Both approaches essentially sought a gradual change of the order of 1919 and to consolidate the newly republican German state by anchoring it into a western-orientated international system. And both were predicated on the notion that this could consolidate France's position as well.

That Poincaré's policy would fail was for long far from inevitable. And there were numerous internal and external reasons for its ultimate failure – from inner divisions among French policymakers to France's Ruhr-induced financial crisis and dependence on foreign – Anglo-American – capital. Yet what ultimately turned the French 'victory' of September 1923 – when Germany abandoned 'passive resistance' – into a pyrrhic victory was the political intervention of Britain and United States. Yet France's alleged 'defeat' of 1923 also created the preconditions for a new and, compared with 1923, far more sustainable international system. It was advantageous not only for Germany but also for France – basing stability on mutual *rapprochement* and accommodation. To this end, London sought to revive Britain's role as international mediator spurring *quid pro quo* bargains. Washington sought to create a framework for Progressive co-operation between policymakers and financiers to spur 'private', primarily economic stabilisation efforts.

Prompting peaceful change – the abandonment of British 'neutrality'

The first decisive impulse for an Anglo-American engagement in the Ruhr crisis was given by Britain. A still reluctant Curzon attempted to advance a British design for an international conference – only to pave the way for the subsequent implementation of the American design of defusing the conflict through an expert inquiry. By mid-October 1923, it was becoming drastically clear even to a hitherto paralysed Baldwin government that, as MacDonald had long demanded, Britain had to abandon its 'neutrality' to prevent long-term damages not only to core British interests.[7] What Poincaré pursued now seemed bound to produce further protracted crises – the erosion of stability, trade and economic chaos not only in Germany.[8]

---

[7] Cf. O'Riordan (2001), pp. 101–24.
[8] Cabinet conclusion, 9 August 1923, CAB 23/46; Curzon to British Embassy (Washington), 12 October 1923, *DBFP*, I, XXI, pp. 563ff.

Already in March, Stanley Baldwin had noted that '[i]f the English speaking peoples don't pull together now, western civilization will slide into the abyss'.[9] And as chancellor of the Exchequer under Bonar Law he had been instrumental in creating the basic preconditions for such postwar co-operation by negotiating a settlement of Britain's war-debts with the US Debt Commission, which was finally signed in July 1923. But it was not until 12 October that Curzon took constructive steps towards a common Anglo-American Ruhr policy, signalling to Washington that London would hence unequivocally support the call for an internationalised solution of the reparations problem.[10] The foreign secretary had been encouraged to this step by a Harding press statement, made after a long period of official US disinterest in the Ruhr. In it, the president had underlined that his administration still stood by the principles of Hughes' New Haven proposal of December 1922.[11] In fact, the October initiative was Curzon's second noteworthy mediation attempt. In August, he had proposed a cessation of German passive resistance and France's occupation in return for an 'impartial inquiry' into Germany's capacity to pay.[12] Yet it took two more months before he abandoned his policy of neutrality and distanced himself *openly* from French actions in the Ruhr, thereby exposing Poincaré's growing international isolation.[13] Up until then, British policy had been marred by a lack of strategic purpose. It had sought to avoid alienating France by openly criticising Poincaré – not least because Curzon deemed Britain's leverage insufficient to contain him. Yet it had also refrained from officially sanctioning France's incursion, feebly appealing to the French premier for moderation.[14]

This had been compounded by an unresolved tension between Curzon's rigidly 'neutral' course and Prime Minister Baldwin's intermittent attempts to initiate a common Anglo-French reparations policy. By October, Curzon had come to think that Poincaré played a double-game, pursuing 'definite objects' in the Ruhr and the Rhineland. Baldwin's bid to mend fences had led to a hastily convened summit with Poincaré in Paris on 19 September. The prime minister endeavoured 'to re-establish personal confidence' and 'put the Frenchman wise about the state of feeling in England'.[15] Yet his initiative merely resulted in a non-committal joint communiqué. Given both powers' persistent differences over Germany and Poincaré's unabated suspicions

[9] Baldwin to Lord Middleton, 11 March 1923, Williamson and Baldwin (2004), p. 80.
[10] See Curzon's instructions to the British Embassy (Washington), *DBFP*, I, XXI, pp. 563ff.
[11] Foreign Office memorandum, 9 January 1924, FO 371: C 702/C900/70/18.
[12] Curzon to allied ambassadors, 11 August 1923, Cmd 1943, Papers relating to British Policy during the Ruhr Conflict (1923), pp. 48–61.
[13] Curzon statement, Imperial Conference, 5 October 1923, Curzon Papers, MSS Eur. F112/312; Baldwin statement, *Times*, 26 October 1923.
[14] Cf. Bennett (1989), pp. 34–40.
[15] Curzon Papers, MSS Eur. F112/312; Neville Chamberlain diary, 24 September 1923, quoted after Bennett (1989), pp. 37–8.

vis-à-vis Britain, this was hardly surprising.[16] The US ambassador in Brussels, Henry Fletcher, cabled to Hughes that British policy had 'failed lamentably in its dealings with France'. Though 'disapproving' of French policy in the Rhineland and the Ruhr, British diplomats were 'unwilling to come to grips with France on the fundamental issue' – namely to find a *modus operandi* for recovering reparations.[17] In fact, Curzon's reluctant decision to 'come to grips with France' by turning to America was what eventually set European politics on a new, Atlantic course. But only MacDonald would sustain it.

The Conservative government felt compelled to seek the diplomatic offensive when it became obvious, not least to a ferocious Labour opposition and the British public, that by provoking Germany's collapse Poincaré threatened to unravel what postwar order Britain had sought to foster.[18] Most directly, French policy affected not only Britain's reparations claims but also what Baldwin defined as overriding peacetime concerns: 'trade and commerce' – 'essential to the life of our people'. As the prime minister impressed on his Cabinet, this in turn aggravated 'the outstanding political problem in the political life of the country': unemployment. Britain had to intervene on behalf of the 'economic recovery of Germany' to prevent a complete collapse of 'the whole economic system of Europe' so vital for British trade.[19] More specifically, the Baldwin government intervened to prevent the conglomeration of the continent's coal-and-steel resources under one authority and the emergence of a continental trading bloc 'closed' to British commerce.[20]

In the Foreign Office's view, Poincaré was no longer content with occupying the Ruhr temporarily and exploiting its industries through the *Mission Interalliée de Contrôle des Usines et des Mines* (MICUM). Rather, he seemed resolved to extend the powers of MICUM – and France – beyond the parameters of 1919, and eventually extend French control to the Rhineland, even if this ruined the French state.[21] Economic predominance was in fact sought more eagerly by the French steel-producers of the powerful *Comité des Forges*.[22] And Poincaré was unable to control those who intended to turn France's Ruhr

---

[16] Cf. Keiger (1997), pp. 300–1; Nicolson (1937), p. 372.

[17] Fletcher to Hughes, 27 October 1923, NA RG 59 462.00 R 296/70.

[18] Foreign Office memorandum, 9 January 1924, FO 371: C 702/C900/70/18.

[19] Baldwin statement, November 1923, quoted in Kennedy (1981), p. 229; Cabinet conclusions, 23 October 1923, CAB 23/45. In Baldwin's view, Britain had to pursue this policy not only to revitalise European markets essential for British trade but also to enable Germany finally to pay reparations through increased exports, even though renewed German competition could create problems for British industry. See Baldwin note, 7 October 1923, Williamson and Baldwin (2004), p. 115.

[20] Foreign Office memorandum, 24 November 1923, FO 371/8750: C21981/3/3/18; Kilmarnock to Foreign Office, 18 December 1923, FO 371/8690: C22354.

[21] Report of Crowe's conversations with Saint-Aulaire, MAE, Série Europe, 1918–29, Rive Gauche du Rhin/36.

[22] Addison report, 28 February 1924, FO 371/9763: C3419/79/18.

'pawns' into permanently occupied territories and sought to incite political separatism in the Rhineland. These included above all Paul Tirard, head of the Interallied Rhineland High Commission; General Degoutte, who headed MICUM; and the commander of the occupied zones on the Rhine's left bank, General de Metz. Thus, contrary to what Curzon concluded, Poincaré was not the *spiritus rector* behind French expansionism.[23] Yet to contain what his policy had unleashed became a salient motive for Britain's intervention. In a speech in Plymouth on 25 October 1923 Baldwin announced the new course. He underscored that Britain could not accept 'the disintegration or the disruption of [Germany], which must put back for years her powers of reparation'. Nor could he 'contemplate the breaking-off of any part of Germany into a separate state which would at once break the Treaty of Versailles'.[24]

Worth emphasising are the underlying *political* motives for Britain's intervention.[25] The Weimar Republic's acute crisis in 1923 had reinforced what Lloyd George and his Conservative successors had long neglected: Britain's interest in salvaging not only the economic but also the political integrity of Germany. London became concerned that France's escalatory policies would weaken the Stresemann government's position to such an extent that it would be domestically and internationally paralysed. The most disconcerting perspective was that Germany might become ungovernable – and that insurrection by the radical left might open the door for Soviet infiltration.[26] This was a threat never taken overly seriously in the Foreign Office yet looming until communist unrest in Saxony and Thuringia was suppressed in late October.[27]

Still more important, however, was the international sphere. Here, a strengthened Weimar Germany seemed the best counter-balance against a highly undesirable French hegemony over continental Europe. On 5 October, Curzon thundered before the Imperial Conference in London: 'The war gave [France] the opportunity, and with a defeated enemy and a distracted Europe, she aspires to attain . . . the domination of the European Continent.' Baldwin told the Canadian premier Mackenzie King that France had become 'a great militarist power' facing an 'unarmed neighbour' in the east; this constellation made the 'position' of Britain, which had 'gone very far in reducing her military and naval strength' after the war, 'really insecure'. And Crowe warned that unless Britain pursued a more aggressive course Poincaré's actions would cause chronic instability in central Europe and renewed war.[28]

---

[23] Curzon Papers, MSS Eur. F112/312. Cf. Maier (1988), pp. 392–5.
[24] *Times*, 26 October 1923.
[25] Cf. the differing emphases in Schwabe (1985b); O'Riordan (2001), pp. 101–24.
[26] Cf. Newton (1998), pp. 318ff; Carsten (1984), pp. 36ff.
[27] Foreign Office memorandum, 28 January 1924, FO 371: C 19472/1/18.
[28] Curzon Papers, MSS Eur. F112/312; Mackenzie King diary, 1 October 1923, Williamson and Baldwin (2004), p. 112: Foreign Office memorandum, 28 January 1924, FO 371: C 19472/1/18.

By mid-November, the Foreign Office even considered using Britain's short-term debt-claims vis-à-vis France as a lever to bring France to the negotiating-table; and the chancellor of the exchequer, Neville Chamberlain, thought this an option worth contemplating.[29] But like Conservative Ruhr policy as a whole this initiative remained inconclusive. Five years after the armistice, British statesmen were certainly unwilling to intervene militarily to block France. Yet nor were they any longer prepared to tolerate French provocations of Germany. Curzon had barely begun to outline a new Ruhr policy, however, when Baldwin's first government had to resign in January 1924.[30] It would fall to MacDonald to develop it into a coherent strategy and mediate between France, Germany and the United States.[31]

In mid-October 1923, the Foreign Office had drawn up two plans to de-escalate the Franco-German conflict, essentially designed to engage the American world creditor. The first was highly undesirable for Washington: the call for an international conference on both reparations and inter-allied war-debts. The second essentially reflected what Sir James Bradbury had already suggested in the Reparations Commission in January: to use America's proposal for an expert inquiry as the starting-point for an agreement. As Ambassador Fletcher noted on 27 October, the British government preferred the first alternative – it pursued the second option only because the Foreign Office hoped thus 'to enlist [Washington's] interest and influence in the reparations settlement'.[32]

Britain's overture had a catalytic effect on American policy. And very quickly Curzon's preference for a 'full-dress' conference was outweighed by Washington's option for the – informal – expert approach.[33] According to his close adviser William R. Castle, Hughes' reaction to London's proposal had been 'thoroughly cordial in tone'. He preferred to keep Anglo-American consultations secret yet was prepared to make them public if this could serve to put pressure on France.[34] Yet the secretary of state had also left no doubt what blueprint developments were to follow, underlining that Washington 'still stood in favour of the [New Haven] plan'. He made an overall European acceptance of the expert scheme the *conditio sine qua non* for any US participation in efforts to overcome the Ruhr crisis. Was there a 'confluence' of British and American reparations policies?[35] In fact, the Coolidge administration only acted once the

---

[29] Foreign Office to Treasury, 14 November 1923; Treasury to Foreign Office, 4 January 1924, FO 371: C 19472/1/18; N. Chamberlain note, 10 January 1924, CAB 24/164: C.P. 29.
[30] Cf. Bennett (1989), pp. 38–9.
[31] Cf. O'Riordan (2001), pp. 101–41.
[32] Curzon to British Embassy (Washington), 12 October 1923, *DBFP*, I, XXI, pp. 563ff; Fletcher to Hughes, 27 October 1923, NA RG 59 462.00 R 296/70.
[33] Fletcher to Hughes, 27 October 1923, NA RG 59 462.00 R 296/70.
[34] Castle Diary, 16 October 1923, vol. 4, p. 169.   [35] See Hogan (1991), p. 57.

Baldwin government fallen in line behind its design. There was no question which power was the decisive arbiter of international politics in 1923.[36]

Officially, Hughes persisted with his informal policy, safeguarding America's position as 'neutral arbiter' in the European dispute. Fundamentally, however, he remained as wary as Hoover that Britain and France would use any opportunity to renegotiate war-debts and link them with reparations to the detriment of US claims. Washington would not countenance being exposed to an Anglo-French debtor coalition seeking to manoeuvre the United States into the uncomfortable position of collecting its dues by becoming Germany's reparations creditor. Consequently, Hughes 'maintained the essential difference between the question of Germany's capacity to pay' and 'the payment by the Allies of their debts to the United States which constitute distinct obligations'.[37]

The secretary's 'drawing-of-the-line' in October reinforced a basic principle of American postwar policy towards Europe. The utmost Republican concession was to give a vague promise that European efforts to solve the reparations problem might be rewarded in future by more lenient war-debt agreements. So as to avoid a renewal of politicised disputes over reparations and debts Hughes re-asserted his New Haven design, thus setting the stage for the Dawes negotiations of 1924. He emphasised that America was 'entirely willing to take part in an economic conference' that assembled 'all the European Allies' and produced 'an appropriate financial plan' for securing reparation payments.[38] As his right hand Castle observed, 'the British gave us an opening which we very quickly took'.[39]

America's return to Europe

The United States formally 'returned' to Europe in early December 1923. It was then that Hughes gave official backing to the participation of American experts in the 'independent inquiry' that he had proposed almost one year earlier.[40] Foremost among them would be the banker Charles Dawes and the former chairman of General Electric, Owen Young. Yet the decisive shift of American policy that would set the terms for the Dawes process and the subsequent London conference had occurred more than a month earlier. It

---

[36] Hughes to Harvey, 16 October 1923, *FRUS 1923*, II, pp. 73–4. Coolidge had replaced Harding after the latter's death in August.

[37] Hughes communiqué to the British government, 16 October 1923, NA RG 59 462.00 R296/16.

[38] *Ibid.*; Castle Diary, 16 October 1923, vol. 4, pp. 168–9.

[39] Castle Diary, 26 October 1923, vol. 4, p. 177.

[40] Hughes to French government, 11 December 1923; 'The Dawes Plan', Beeritz Memorandum, Hughes Papers, box 172; *FRUS 1923*, II, pp. 87–109.

had manifested itself in Hughes' decision, announced on 25 October, that 'the time had arrived' to promote a 'constructive policy' – US policy.[41]

After more than a year of political crisis, Hughes' resolve to rely on non-governmental expertise to pursue his informal stabilisation strategy for Europe had hardened. And it had been reinforced by what he regarded as common interests uniting America's political and financial elites.[42] Yet precisely bankers like J.P. Morgan had continued to demand that politicians, not financiers, take the initiative. Hughes was to use the administration's decisive authority to hammer out the international agreement indispensable for implementing the expert scheme and sorely lacking in 1922.[43] Thus, financiers were urging policymakers to act. But they were not *shaping* international politics. Rather, it was Hughes' agreement with the new British premier MacDonald to advance the expert approach that prepared the ground for a newly intensified co-operation between key Anglo-American financiers. Both would become crucial elements of European stabilisation politics in 1924.

In the financial sphere, leading bankers of Wall Street and the City as well as, notably, the British and American central banks intensified collaboration in the pursuit of European consolidation. Foremost among the former were J.P. Morgan, his partners Dwight Morrow and Russell Leffingwell, and the London-based associates of Morgan Grenfell, above all Thomas Lamont.[44] Heading the latter and hugely influential were the governor of the Federal Reserve Bank of New York (FRBNY), Benjamin Strong, and his British counterpart, Montagu Norman.[45]

Strong and Norman fundamentally agreed that central banks had a prominent role in aiding governmental efforts to stabilise Europe. And both deemed a close Anglo-American understanding imperative. They not only shared a basic common interest in reforming continental European currency systems; they also held that British and American financiers had to co-operate in order to chart new – and lucrative – ways for channelling America's excess capital to where it was urgently needed, Europe. Undoubtedly, Britain and the United States remained competitors in all realms of postwar finance. In Strong's view, the path to stability for Germany *and* France was a path of US-style financial and political modernisation. Not surprisingly, Norman asserted Britain's interest in drawing Germany into its financial orbit.[46] Yet the systemic changes of

---

[41] Hughes' instructions to the US Embassy in Berlin, 25 October 1923, NA RG 59 462.00 R296/33b.

[42] See chapter 5. The bankers' role seems overstated in Hogan (1991), pp. 66ff, and Burk (1991).

[43] J.P. Morgan to E.C. Grenfell, 18 April 1922, J.P. Morgan Papers, box 177; Lamont to Morgan, Harjes et Cie, 25 March 1924, Lamont Papers, TWL 176/8. Cf. Schuker (1976), pp. 272ff.

[44] Cf. Burk (1991), pp. 125–8.

[45] Cf. Chandler (1958), pp. 297ff; Clay (1957), pp. 140ff.

[46] Norman to Strong, 9 August 1922, Strong to Norman, 7 September 1922, Strong to Norman correspondence, Strong Papers; Norman to Treasury, 14 December 1923, FO 371/8690: C21687/129/18. Cf. Clarke (1967), pp. 72–7.

1923/4 would manifest that the long-term rivalry between the old and the new hegemon of global finance had been decided. The American interest in stabilising Germany's new currency, the *Rentenmark*, on the gold-dollar standard would prevail over Britain's bid to include Germany in a sterling-based monetary system.[47]

Strong saw both the excessive inflation in Germany and France's deteriorating public finances as the outgrowth of political manoeuvres, on the part of Berlin to evade reparations, and on that of Paris to sustain the Ruhr occupation. Like most US policymakers and financiers, he also saw all of this as symptoms of a more structural problem – the inevitable consequence of excessive state control, misdirected public spending and mismanagement. Both France and Germany had to embark on austerity-minded public-finance reforms and efforts at currency stabilisation, which in turn could generate economic and political stabilisation.[48] Such recommendations accorded with Republican views. Like Hoover, Hughes well understood that any expert scheme could ultimately only succeed if it was underpinned by US capital. This from the start made the support of key bankers crucial. In fact, J.P. Morgan's estimation that Europe's financial stabilisation required first political foundations had remained unchanged since 1922. He posed strict conditions for aiding any reparations settlement by placing urgently needed loans in Germany *and* France.[49]

Morgan & Co. had been one of the principal French capital suppliers ever since the nadir of the war. In 1923/4, the firm was clearly interested, not only financially, in aiding France's postwar recovery, viewing this task with more sympathy than that of revitalising France's wartime antagonist.[50] J.P. Morgan himself had headed the bankers' committee attempting to assess the conditions for reparations payments in the spring of 1922. Due to lack of political coordination and France's refusal to co-operate, however, this had produced no concrete results.[51] A central obstacle that Anglo-American financiers had faced in their effort to put the reparations complex on a sounder financial footing was French resistance against lifting the Reparations Commission's restrictions on any inquiry. To eliminate such restrictions became a core condition Hughes set for US participation in the expert inquiry in November. US bankers now warned the French government that unless it altered its Ruhr policy it could not expect any loans to balance a budget burdened by occupation-costs and stabilise an ever feebler franc.[52]

---

[47] See also chapter 7. Cf. Costigliola (1977), pp. 911–34; Hogan (1991), pp. 71ff.
[48] Strong to Grissinger, Federal Reserve Board, 17 October 1924, Strong Papers.
[49] J.P. Morgan to E.C. Grenfell, 18 April 1922, J.P. Morgan Papers, box 177; Lamont to J.P. Morgan, 16 October 1922, Lamont Papers.
[50] Cf. Burk (1991), pp. 125ff.
[51] Foreign Office memorandum, 14 June 1922, FO 371 C8534/99/62.
[52] Cf. Costigliola (1973), pp. 90–101.

While Hughes unequivocally insisted on informal diplomacy in close co-operation with US financial elites, it should be noted that his approach was not unanimously favoured by American diplomats, at least not as the sole response to the Ruhr conflict. On 27 October 1923, Fletcher warned Hughes from Brussels that Europe's difficulties were 'political rather than economic and financial, and any financial plan must ultimately lead us to the political field because of the necessity of foreign control of German finance, etc.'. No less, Poincaré would first have to be induced to withdraw from the Ruhr.[53] By contrast, Fletcher's colleague in Paris, Myron Herrick, was – like Hughes – more concerned with implementing the expert plan itself. Herrick emphasised the need to secure strong domestic support for the new approach. Besides, to invoke the interests of US 'public opinion', essentially the opinion of bankers and potential investors, could become America's 'political weapon for forcing constructive results' in Europe.[54] Herrick thereby outlined a tactic that Hughes successfully employed throughout 1924.

The secretary of state took Fletcher's critique into consideration. But the pre-eminent task he saw was to initiate the expert negotiations; political talks had to follow later. Overall, Hughes espoused an outlook most succinctly expressed by Hoover in December 1923. Analysing Germany's rapidly deteri-orating 'food situation', the commerce secretary concluded that while the 'most constructive solution' lay in 'the creation of a foreign commercial credit', such measures could only have a 'temporary' effect.[55] The 'ultimate solution' lay in the 'settlement of political relations' between France and Germany and the 'rehabilitation of productive [German] industry'. Hoover predicted that this process 'would require time'. But he and Hughes agreed that it could only be initiated by Washington, which now put it weight behind the expert scheme. The Europeans, not America, would then have to make the requisite political concessions to implement it. And Britain was to act as a formal mediator.

This was the most momentous reversal in transatlantic politics since Versailles, shaping its course until 1929. Yet America's intervention was far less unavoidable than Britain's bid to resolve a Franco-German impasse tan-gibly affecting its security interests and prosperity. A closer inspection of the underlying and more immediate motives for Washington's renewed engage-ment in Europe makes this clear. Hughes had indeed hesitated considerably before taking decisive steps. He had only considered taking the initiative once both France and Germany had reached such a deadlock that they were 'ready' to accept the American solution without undue conditions. Yet when he decided to act it was by no means clear that France would accept his scheme

---

[53] Fletcher to Hughes, 27 October 1923, NA RG 59 462.00 R296/70.
[54] Herrick to Hughes, 31 October 1923, NA RG 59 462.00 R296/42.
[55] Hoover to Hamilton Fish Jr, 8 December 1923, Hoover Papers, box 75.

rather than exploit its initial 'victory'. Nor was it only the growing pressure of public and financial opinion in the United States that made Hughes act. Bankers such as J.P. Morgan did not drive US 'corporatist' policy in 1923.[56] And the fact that, as he stressed to the French chargé d'affaires André de Laboulaye in late October, US public opinion was *not* opposed to France's 'controversial' Ruhr policy even increased the secretary's caution.[57]

Rather, what led to the reorientation of American policy from cautious aloofness to cautious forward engagement was a combination of situational considerations, both domestic and external, and long-term strategic motives. Yet the latter outweighed the former. It should be clear by now that – as in Britain's case – the Ruhr crisis had begun to affect more fundamental US interests by the autumn of 1923. On one level, there was doubtless the economic interest in preserving Germany as one mainstay of a revitalised and 'open' world economy. The realities of postwar transatlantic interdependence, as perceived by US policymakers, now weighed against continued aloofness – however much less America was dependent on Europe than vice versa. Essentially, the concern that Germany could be lost as a market for US exports *and capital* began to outweigh the notion that the – temporary – elimination of the German competitor on the world market could benefit American industries.[58] US policy followed the Commerce Department's rationale, which Hoover publicly underscored on 19 October: 'Germany as a market is twice as important to this country as she is as a competitor.'[59]

US involvement was also propelled by the assessment that particularly through the MICUM agreements Poincaré aspired to establish a closed 'economic bloc', a 'strangle hold' on Rhine and Ruhr.[60] For this, and French industrialists' aspirations to control German coal and steel, clashed with America's interest in asserting the 'open door' in Europe.[61] On 8 November, Castle commented that such an outcome 'would be a disaster to England and to a less[er] extent to this country'.[62]

Essentially, however, a deeper concern spurred Hughes into action. It was the realisation that unless he abandoned aloofness, the Franco-German crisis could escalate to a point where, with Germany's integrity, not merely a pillar of

---

[56] Cf. Link (1970), pp. 201–33, and (1969), pp. 373–82.

[57] Record of conversation between Hughes and Laboulaye, 24 October 1923, NA RG 59 462.00 R296/49a.

[58] Cf. Link (1969), pp. 373ff.

[59] Hoover press release, 19 October 1923, Hoover Papers, box 74; Commerce Department memorandum, July 1923, Records of the Department of Commerce, NA RG 151, file 046.

[60] Hughes to Castle, 8 November 1923, Castle Diary, vol. 4, p. 211.

[61] Cf. Link (1969), pp. 378ff, who in my view overstates the economic case for America's intervention.

[62] Castle Diary, vol. 4, p. 211.

the world economy was jeopardised. Also the political basis of any future stability in Europe would be undermined. This threatened serious long-term repercussions not only for American commerce but also for political relations with a structurally unsettled Europe.[63] Thus, not only economic but also wider political concerns converged to form a strong common denominator of British and American policies in 1924. Irrespective of commercial rivalry, stabilising Germany and integrating it into an altered, consolidated system of international politics and finance became an underlying common aim.[64]

Beyond the limits of Versailles – towards the 'depoliticisation' of European power politics

Neither British nor American statesmen underestimated the scale of Germany's internal disorder. In their perception, in the 'fateful months' of October and November 1923 the very survival of the republic was at stake. In November, the question arose whether, wrecked by inflation and costly 'passive resistance', Weimar's frail parliamentary system would be able to cope with the crisis. From Washington's perspective, it appeared indeed on the brink of collapse through mounting pressures from German industrialists, right- and left-wing extremists – and, last but not least, the *Reichswehr* under its powerful chief of staff, General von Seeckt.[65]

In late September, US Ambassador Houghton had been approached by Hugo Stinnes, a leading Ruhr industrialist. Stinnes requested American backing for a right-wing *coup d'état* scheme that, he claimed, was supported by chief representatives of German heavy industry. The Stresemann government was to be replaced by a triumvirate comprising himself, Seeckt and the former director of Krupp, Otto Wiedfeldt; only this would allow Germany to re-emerge as Europe's leading industrial power – and pay reparations. In the ambassador's judgement, the forces that Stinnes represented desired a 'Fascist movement', similar to Mussolini's in Italy – a 'dictator seeking the abolition of parliamentary government'.[66] Houghton's reaction reflected a view shared by

---

[63] Hughes memorandum, 6 November 1923, NA RG 59 462.00 R296/596; Hughes to Castle, 8 November 1923, Castle Diary, vol. 4, p. 211.

[64] Hughes to Castle, 8 November 1923, Castle Diary, vol. 4, p. 211; Beeritz memorandum, Hughes Papers, box 172. Cf. Maier (1988), pp. 355–6.

[65] Houghton to Hughes, 7 October 1923, Houghton Papers. In November, Seeckt actually demanded dictatorial powers from President Ebert, who refused to grant them. The general did not support other authoritarian schemes to overthrow the Stresemann government that were being hatched in Bavaria at that time; and the infamous Munich *Putsch* attempt launched by Hitler and Ludendorff, *inter alia*, was repulsed by regular police forces on 9 November 1923. Cf. Kolb (1988), p. 53.

[66] Houghton Diary on conversation with Stinnes, 22 September 1923; Houghton to Hughes, 7 October 1923, Houghton Papers.

Castle but *not* by Hughes or Hoover, namely that 'Parliamentary Government in Germany has not succeeded.' He even suggested that a temporary dictatorship 'might easily be to Germany's advantage' but essentially feared it would ultimately lead to a 'Red Republic'. In the State Department's perception, this was the gravest danger. Castle hoped that through America's intervention 'the incipient revolution in Germany can be stopped'.[67]

But Hughes was not prepared to encourage an authoritarian coup to remedy the German crisis. With sober pragmatism, the secretary of state insisted that US policy had to bolster the Stresemann government. It had to support what he perceived as Stresemann's attempt to shift towards co-operation with the western powers.[68] By late October, Hughes viewed the German chancellor as a key guarantor for a calculable German policy, struggling to avert Germany's collapse through a reparations settlement along American lines. The first important step Stresemann had taken against vehement domestic opposition had been the liquidation of passive resistance on 26 September. No less, Washington welcomed the preparations for a fundamental currency reform under *Reichsbank* president Hjalmar Schacht. These culminated in the introduction of the first psychologically, then materially successful *Rentenmark* on 15 November, which drastically curbed inflation, beginning to restore German finances.[69]

Thus, Berlin's note to the Reparations Commission of 24 October could carry more weight than all previous pleas for American help. It declared Germany's readiness to accept an inquiry into its capacity to pay reparations.[70] As Hughes emphasised, it afforded the 'opportunity' to 'work out' a new policy and launch an expert inquiry. Observing Hughes' hardening determination, Castle noted: 'October 26 will certainly be one of the most important days since the war so far as a settlement in Europe is concerned.'[71]

In sum, what proved as decisive for America's intervention in 1923 as European fatigue and attrition was Hughes' perception that Britain and Germany had begun to accept the rules on which the US arbiter predicated its engagement. He only committed the administration to an implementation of the expert scheme once he felt assured that this could be realised on his terms, i.e. on no other than America's – hegemonic – terms. While Poincaré still *appeared* strongly opposed to an internationalised settlement, Hughes thus saw

[67] Houghton to Hughes, 7 October 1923, Houghton Papers. For Hughes' and Castle's attitudes see Castle Diary, 26 and 30 October 1923, vol. 4, pp. 177–8, 184–5.
[68] Hughes to Castle, 30 October 1923, Castle Diary, vol. 4, p. 185; Hughes to US Embassy (Berlin), 25 October 1923, NA RG 59 462.00 R296/33b; *FRUS 1923*, II, pp. 70–3.
[69] Cf. Link (1969), pp. 379–81; Baechler (1996), pp. 354ff, 423ff.
[70] *ADAP*, A, VIII, pp. 506ff. Cf. Krüger (1985a), pp. 226–7.
[71] Hughes to US Embassy (Berlin), 25 October 1923, NA RG 59 462.00 R296/33b; Castle Diary, 25 October 1923, vol. 4, p. 172.

improved prospects for putting pressure on France.[72] This he did from early November onwards. And London followed suit. The combined effect was felt acutely in Paris.[73]

On 6 November, Hughes impressed on the French chargé Laboulaye that as Berlin had 'capitulated' by liquidating passive resistance, 'what was needed was an economic program', adding sharply: 'Had Poincaré any program?'[74] Hughes now warned France that US 'opinion would change very quickly' if France 'having secured her victory' would resist 'working out a financial plan' and take further military measures. He stressed that Germany's 'solidarity', not its collapse, was required. Internally, the State Department – like the Foreign Office – even considered using French war-debts as a lever 'unless France will adopt a more reasonable attitude'. Castle reckoned that this 'should knock blazes out of the franc'.[75] Yet it was not pursued.

Crucially, Hughes now insisted on making the scope of the expert inquiry *unlimited*, only to be influenced by financial considerations. Should Poincaré try to impose political limits, 'the inquiry would be abortive'. Concretely, it would have to proceed unaffected by France's interest in maintaining the sanction powers invoked in January 1923 to enforce its reparation claims.[76] The thrust of the American strategy was to invoke the necessities of financial rationality against France's political resistance. Not formally, but in logical consequence of 'depoliticisation', Hughes thereby challenged the very foundations of Versailles. And he challenged Poincaré's resort to financial concerns, the need to ensure German reparations, to attain political objectives. France, which had 'over-stretched' its resources for the sake of security, could not sustain its policy under the systemic conditions of post-1918 international politics and finance, particularly not against the financial hegemon. America would 'offer' its rules and mechanisms to replace those of the French aspirant for continental predominance.[77]

To win Poincaré's approval, Hughes advanced an argumentation that would become the hallmark of US policy in and beyond 1924. He underlined to Laboulaye that his government had no intention of 'curtailing any of the French treaty rights', which Paris could still defend in the Council of Allied Ambassadors.[78] At the same time, however, he demanded Poincaré's consent to a process that, as both Anglo-American policymakers and financiers intended,

---

[72] Memorandum, Hughes conversation with Laboulaye, 18 October 1923, *FRUS 1923*, II, p. 81.
[73] Cf. Maier (1988), pp. 411–15; Miquel (1961), pp. 450ff.
[74] Castle Diary, vol. 4, p. 197.
[75] Hughes to Laboulaye, 24 October 1923, NA RG 59 462.00 R296/49a; Castle Diary, 3 November 1923, vol. 4, p. 194.
[76] Hughes to Laboulaye, 31 October 1923, NA RG 59 462.00 R296/28/1/2; Hughes to Jusserand, 6 November 1923, Castle Diary, vol. 4, p. 197.
[77] Cf. Schuker (1976), p. 172.   [78] Castle Diary, 29 October 1923, vol. 4, p. 181.

would establish 'complementary' mechanisms to supervise reparations *outside the parameters of 1919.* If this strategy succeeded the Versailles system would be superseded by a new structure in this essential area, a structure established by the United States. Only contours of this reasoning were apparent in November 1923. Yet it had crystallised into a central rationale of US stabilisation policy when the London conference opened. Poincaré eventually agreed to America's terms in early December, *de facto* endorsing an unlimited expert inquiry.[79]

[79] See Laroche (1957), p. 185.

8 From antagonism to accommodation
The reorientation of French and German postwar policies, 1923–1924

Why had Poincaré in the end effectively accepted US conditions? Had he simply ceded to America's overwhelming financial pressure? Why did he fail to capitalise on France's seemingly strong position after the cessation of German passive resistance? And why had Stresemann endorsed the Anglo-American proposal so unequivocally? Answers to these questions are more complex than is *prima facie* apparent. They are in fact inextricably linked with two further questions. Why did the Anglo-American intervention become so decisive? And why was it that between Poincaré's shift and the 1924 London conference the European constellation – and transatlantic politics – was so fundamentally altered? All of these questions can be re-appraised by focusing not only on the behaviour of national policymakers, however important their decisions and domestic constraints. A more comprehensive explanation results from shifting to a systemic analysis of the now rapidly changing international configuration. To be asked is: who shaped the ground-rules of the Dawes process and, more generally, international politics from December 1923?

The answer is twofold: obviously, the United States, and, more subtly, Britain. As Washington's indispensable 'interest and influence' was to be engaged only on American terms, there was a clearly prevalent trend in 1924. What began to transform Euro-Atlantic relations was Hughes' strategy of 'depoliticisation', not Curzon's old-style diplomacy or the Versailles-based designs that Poincaré tried to re-assert until his electoral defeat in May 1924. Nothing exposed the altered postwar constellation, the new (im)balance of power and possibilities between Britain and America, and between the old and the new world, more clearly.

The US intervention determined the 'playing-field' on which the outcome of the Franco-German crisis and the future of the international system were decided. Yet, however skilfully Hughes employed it, America's financial leverage could not by itself pave the way for the Dawes settlement. Nor could the influence of US experts and bankers. The shift from the nadir of Franco-German strife in 1923 to the reparations agreement of 1924 was markedly influenced by financial necessities.[1] But it was not economically predetermined. Rather, it resulted from changes in the international system worth considering not only from the Anglo-American but also the French and German perspectives.

In one respect, America's intervention had such a galvanising effect because by authorising US participation in the expert negotiations Washington had finally made a highly circumscribed but essential *governmental commitment* to European stabilisation. Hughes thus fulfilled the modicum of America's hegemonic role – for the first time since 1919 and on terms very distinct from Wilson's. Finally, though, the 'economic peace' of 1924 could only be achieved through London's political mediation. Under MacDonald, Britain seized the role of a pivotal power between continental Europe and the United States. And, ultimately, European politics could only be recast the Anglo-American way because, owing to different constraints and motivations, not only Germany but also France acutely desired America's *and* Britain's return to Europe. Policymakers in Whitehall and Washington held that those directing foreign policies in Berlin and Paris had to be induced, and if need be forced, to accept their designs for overcoming the reparations crisis. MacDonald believed as much as Hughes that German *and* French leaders had to accept Anglo-American principles of pacific settlement. And, essentially, they also believed that this would not only further Anglo-American interests but also be recognised as advantageous by Europe's core rivals.

The process of how, and how far, French and German policymakers came to adopt Anglo-American approaches to master their bilateral problems after five years of confrontation thus deserves particular attention. On one level, France and Germany had indeed reached what Hughes had drily forecast in the summer of 1923: a point at which both were so exhausted that they endorsed his blueprint without further resistance.[2] Poincaré and Stresemann saw that French coercion and German resistance had manoeuvred mutual relations into deadlock. The Stresemann government had been near the end of its tether. In Paris, it had by and large become clear that France could not resolve its postwar dilemmas through unilateral 'settlements' imposed against Anglo-American opposition. More salient, however, was that America's engagement and Britain's subsequent mediation began to foster different reorientation processes on *both* sides of the Versailles divide. The more drastic sea-change occurred in Germany, a power under massive external and internal pressures, inferior in terms of power and internationally ostracised since Versailles. Changes in France were more hesitant and certainly not deemed inescapable after the 'victory' over Germany in September 1923. Nevertheless, in 1924 Franco-German relations

---

[1] See Schuker (1976), pp. 3ff, 30ff.
[2] Hughes to Herrick, 5 March 1923, *FRUS 1923*, II, p. 194. Cf. Leffler (1979), pp. 83ff.

began to gravitate from enforcement and resistance to negotiation and accommodation. Hence, both powers would seek Anglo-American involvement not least because each hoped to use and steer the expert process to suit its own interests. In this hope, Poincaré was in the short term more mistaken than Stresemann.

The espousal of America's progressive design required from German and French policymaking elites fundamental changes of paradigm. They pertained not only to traditional assumptions underpinning each power's international policies but also the practices each had adopted to safeguard national interests after 1918. In the German case, this change demanded abandoning the 'revisionism syndrome' – aspirations to overthrow the Versailles system by regaining military power and a 'free hand', holding an imaginary 'balance' between east and west.[3] In a wider sense, it required a departure from Wilhelminian notions of self-reliant *Machtstaatspolitik*, the imperatives of defending the state's *raison* and interests through self-reliant, autocratic power politics.[4] In the French case, it required relinquishing the notion of preserving national security on the basis of a strained continental hegemony *against* Germany. The question was how far French leaders could depart from a policy of weakening or even dividing the 'archenemy' *outre-Rhin* whose power potential could not be matched.[5]

Postwar constraints and miscalculations – Poincaré's bid to re-assert French predominance in the Versailles system

Contrary to some studies, then, leading French policymakers were no less interested in America's participation in the reparations process than their German counterparts. Poincaré retained this interest throughout the expert deliberations in Paris as much as his successor Herriot thereafter.[6] In the spring of 1924, however, divergences among French elites persisted. Chiefly the officials overseeing France's occupation, Tirard, General de Metz and the head of MICUM, General Degoutte, continued to clamour for a permanent foothold on the Rhine's right bank.

Since November 1923, Tirard had fought for the creation of a fully recognised Rhenish state *de facto* controlled by France.[7] He had also drawn up plans for an economic penetration of the Rhineland and a Rhenish Bank, also under French control. This Poincaré expressly supported.[8] But in January France

---

[3] Cf. Krüger (1985a), pp. 13ff.
[4] Cf. Hildebrand (1995), pp. 302ff; Nipperdey (1993), pp. 621ff.
[5] Cf. Jacobson (1983b).
[6] Cf. Bariéty (1977), pp. 289ff.
[7] Tirard note, 26 November 1923, PA, 9406H/3654/269548ff. Cf. Erdmann (1966), pp. 136ff.
[8] Tirard reports to Poincaré, 30 October and 20 November 1923, Poincaré to French Embassy (London), 8 December 1923, MAE, Série Europe, 1918–29, Rive Gauche du Rhin/107, 108.

had to give up these plans. For they were not only opposed by Stresemann but also the British government and Bank of England, both aiming to forestall a French financial preponderance on the Rhine.[9]

Powerful pressure-groups, chiefly the *Comité des Forges*, claimed that precisely when Poincaré endorsed the Anglo-American scheme the prospects for extending France's influence even beyond the MICUM agreements were actually *improving*. France was to appropriate the Ruhr's coal production and, finally, make it a permanent French customs zone. Even the MICUM accords alone, concluded on 23 November, promised France up to a quarter of German production until April 1924.[10] What proved critical, however, was that by then not only the *Quai d'Orsay* and the Finance Ministry but also Poincaré himself had concluded that there were overriding financial *and* political reasons for abandoning such unilateral exploits. Though vacillating, policymakers in Paris gravitated towards the conclusion that France's *raison d'état* could best be salvaged by revitalising co-operation with Britain and the United States. In Poincaré's erroneous judgement, France could do so from a position of strength.

From the outset, the Finance Ministry had been most adamant in opposing Rhenish expansion plans. French finance ministers – Louis Loucheur and later Etienne Clémentel – thought their price too high: both for the French budget and because they undercut France's position vis-à-vis its war-debt creditors. They also feared that France would lose its credit in the essential Anglo-American financial markets.[11] More lenient war-debt conditions and fresh external capital, however, were precisely what Paris urgently required for currency stabilisation and public finance. The latter remained a chronic problem until Poincaré consolidated the franc in late 1926; and an important factor in France's relations with the Anglo-American powers and Germany. Financial constraints and 'the fall of the franc' were pressing concerns throughout the Dawes negotiations, indeed constituting 'the weakest link in France's diplomatic armour'.[12] But Poincaré was also influenced by wider political concerns.

While sharp divisions between Poincaré, senior French occupation officials and steel magnates persisted, there was a basic alteration of perceptions among French policymaking elites. What at first had been seen as a hard-won victory over Germany that furnished a new base for French security threatened to

---

[9] D'Abernon to Schubert, 22 November 1922, PA, 9409H/3654/269844; minutes of a meeting between Foreign Office and Treasury officials, 27 November 1923, FO 371/8690: C22354/129/18. Norman to Treasury, 14 December 1923, FO 371/8690: C21687/129/18. Cf. McDougall (1978), pp. 286ff.

[10] Cf. Maier (1988), pp. 393–4, 408–10; Bariéty (1977), pp. 253–81.

[11] Cf. Schuker (1976), pp. 172–3.

[12] Crewe to MacDonald, 20 February 1924, MacDonald Papers, MDP 30/69/94. Cf. Laroche (1957), p. 185; Keiger (1997), pp. 300ff; Bussière (1992).

unravel. More precisely, it would remain a pyrrhic victory unless France could instrumentalise the newly acquired pledges to gain Anglo-American support for a reparations agreement also reinforcing the Versailles system. This, however, appeared ever more elusive if France perpetuated its Ruhr policy.

Like the *Quai d'Orsay*'s political director, Emmanuel de Peretti, Poincaré now felt mounting pressure to adjust his course against internal hard-liners. Essentially, he did not desire to alienate Britain any further. For it remained – even after the series of mutual frustrations since Versailles – the sole powerful ally *and* underwriter of the Versailles system left for France. In his bid to bolster the *status quo*, Poincaré thus sought to revive an exclusive Anglo-French *entente*. Only then would France be prepared to relinquish her coercion of Germany.[13] Potentially, Britain also remained the most important partner in bargaining for more lenient debt settlements with America.[14]

As for the United States, Poincaré's decision to adhere to the expert approach was unmistakably influenced by the realisation that France depended on Washington's *official* goodwill in more than one respect. If Paris finally desired to attract sorely needed US capital, the backing of major Wall Street firms, above all J.P. Morgan, and the Republican administration was indispensable. This Poincaré understood well. And he also understood that the Coolidge administration's favour was equally vital to negotiate a bearable war-debt agreement *and* carry it through in the *Chambre*. More generally, co-operation now came to be seen as the only viable strategy to re-attract America's political support, precisely to reconsolidate the order of 1919. Underlying all was Poincaré's concern that Paris risked acute international isolation unless he reversed his course.[15] On 6 December, he had impressed on his cabinet that France had to strengthen its position for an eventual reparations settlement, mainly through fresh consultations with Britain and America. This had to take precedence over political and commercial advantages pressed from Germany. By December, the thrust of Poincaré's shift was clear: France had to return to what he deemed the letter of Versailles to safeguard its interests.[16]

By the spring of 1924, Poincaré thus no longer aimed to 'solve' France's security problem by fundamentally altering the central European 'balance'. Rather, he acted on the premise that to bolster its bargaining-power both on reparations and security, France had to become *a participant* in the expert deliberations and renew political negotiations, the latter chiefly with Britain.[17]

---

[13] Poincaré to MacDonald, 25 February 1924, *DBFP*, I, XXVI, no. 371. Cf. Jeannesson (1998).
[14] Seydoux memorandum, 4 February 1924, in Mendl to Tyrrell, 3 March 1924, FO 371/9812: C 3956/1288/18.
[15] Poincaré speech, 23 November 1923, *JOC*, pp. 3693–9.
[16] Poincaré himself would later vigorously defend his decision of December 1923. See Poincaré (1930), pp. 5–6. Cf. Keiger (1997), pp. 301ff; Calier and Soutou (2001).
[17] Cf. Laroche (1957), p. 185.

Poincaré also desired to put Franco-German relations back on a sober footing while nonetheless re-asserting the rules of 1919. That France would be strong enough to achieve this, however, had been a miscalculation in 1923 and would remain one in 1924. Through France's representative at the expert deliberations, Louis Barthou, Poincaré repeatedly sought to limit the scope of the Dawes inquiry.[18] At the same time, he strove to reinforce the power of the Reparations Commission. Yet, as we have seen, this was diametrically opposed to Hughes' policy. Poincaré would seek in vain to hold his ground as the United States succeeded in keeping the Dawes process *outside* the parameters of Versailles.[19]

Postwar constraints and the option for *Westpolitik* – Stresemann's quest for peaceful change and a return to the international system

Most predictably under the circumstances of 1923 Germany desired a British intervention even more than France; and, more fervently still, the isolated power desired America's re-entry on to the European scene. Successive German governments had implored Wilson's successors ever since 1920 to bring their weight to bear – the weight of a power outside the order of 1919, without reparations claims and with all the surplus capital Germany needed as urgently for its recovery as France.[20] This remained a crucial element of Stresemann's foreign policy in 1923/4.

Stresemann's predecessor during the Ruhr crisis, chancellor Wilhelm Cuno, had desperately tried to induce Washington – and London – to play a moderating role vis-à-vis France. Yet all of his attempts had foundered. Apart from an overall highly unfavourable international constellation, this was due to misperceptions of what formally 'neutral' British and American governments were willing to offer. Particularly in Washington, German demands were deemed excessive, which most notably doomed Cuno's Rhine pact initiative of December 1922, launched just before the Ruhr occupation. Cuno had sought to win the Harding administration as underwriter of a non-aggression pact of all powers interested in the Rhine, thus anticipating core elements of the later Locarno initiative.[21] Yet only Stresemann would, from August 1923, fulfil the preconditions Hughes set for US engagement.

The course Stresemann began to chart, his *Westpolitik*, can indeed be seen as an attempt *sui generis*, between Wilhelminian power politics and Hitler's racially motivated bid for world supremacy, to forge a 'republican foreign

---

[18] Poincaré to MacDonald, 25 February 1924, *DBFP*, I, XXVI, no. 371.
[19] See chapter 9.
[20] Cf. Krüger (1985a), pp. 77–81; Ferguson (1997).   [21] Cf. Rupieper (1979), pp. 55–66.

policy'.[22] Stresemann sought to reintegrate Germany in the international system as an 'equal' great power by pursuing accommodation with the west *and*, if less straightforwardly, with the east. And he sought to revise the Versailles system through an essentially transatlantic policy of peaceful change, seeking political-cum-economic bargains with the western powers. To analyse Stresemann's policy in a wider Euro-Atlantic context may serve to re-assess more precisely what international stabilisation the Anglo-American powers could achieve in post-Versailles Europe. And it may permit us to re-evaluate how hazardous it really was for Britain, America and the world to buttress the fortunes of Weimar Germany instead of weakening it.

The defeat of 1918 had been no clear *caesura* for those who, like Stresemann, aimed to recast Weimar's foreign policy after the war's traumatic experiences and formative decades of Wilhelminian *Machtpolitik*.[23] Stresemann had condemned the 'yoke' of 1919. And he was not alone in believing that a vast majority of Germans demanded a substantial revision of the Versailles treaty.[24] Yet, while hardly undergoing a 'Canossa experience', Stresemann, a fullhearted constitutional monarchist before 1914, had by 1922 undergone a remarkable reorientation process. A vociferous proponent of annexationist aims during the war, he attempted to adjust to what he saw as the fundamentally altered realities of power and international relations after 1918. Stresemann herein headed a vanguard of realist republican policymakers at the German Foreign Office who would set Weimar policy on a western course between 1923 and 1929.[25] He was seconded and in many ways influenced by Carl von Schubert, who became his 'right hand' and, in December 1924, undersecretary of state at the *Wilhemstraße*.[26] As early as 1920, Schubert had called Germany's principal task to return to 'the concert of powers as an equal partner'.[27]

Like Schubert, Stresemann generally favoured a restoration of Germany's military strength corresponding to its size and making it *bündnisfähig* (eligible for alliances). But he strongly opposed a return to a power-political course aiming to topple the Versailles system by force. And he equally opposed an orientation essentially aspiring to join forces with Soviet Russia to this end. In his reckoning, the postwar power-constellation meant that preparing for

---

[22] The groundbreaking work is Krüger (1985a). See also Wright (2002) and (1995); Baechler (1996); Berg (1990); Lee and Michalka (1982), pp. 350–74.

[23] Cf. Wright (2002), pp. 111–49; Hildebrand (1995), pp. 149–301, 383ff.

[24] Stresemann speech during the German National Assembly's deliberations over the Versailles treaty, 12 May 1919, *SB, Nationalversammlung*, vol. 327, pp. 1000ff; Stresemann (1919). Cf. Salewski (1980), pp. 14–25; Krüger (1985a), pp. 14ff.

[25] Krüger (1984).

[26] Cf. Baechler (1996), pp. 470–87.

[27] Schubert to Haniel, 17 June 1920, quoted after Krüger (1985a), p. 261.

another war would end in a further German defeat, greater than that of 1918.[28] It would thus defeat Stresemann's core objective: to reclaim for Germany the position of a great power with equal rights, status and possibilities within the postwar system. He sought to revise the order of 1919 accordingly, not to undermine it as such. This was one of the deepest lessons Stresemann had drawn from the cataclysm of 1914–18. Germany had to avoid alienating Moscow. And warnings regarding a Russo-German *rapprochement* could at times serve tactical purposes vis-à-vis the western powers. Yet such a *rapprochement* was not to be sought at the expense of Germany's vital interests, and in Stresemann's view these lay not in the east but in the west. In short, his path to regaining Germany's sovereignty, reviving its economic strength and achieving its international rehabilitation did not lead via Moscow. It led via London and Washington, New York and, necessarily, Paris.[29]

This was a thrust not only conflicting with the aspirations of Seeckt and *Reichswehr* minister Otto Geßler.[30] It also contradicted and, from 1923, superseded the 'eastern orientation' long favoured by influential figures in and beyond the *Auswärtige Amt*, notably Schubert's predecessor Maltzan, the architect of Rapallo. Like other proponents of orientating German policy eastward, Maltzan sought to overcome Germany's isolation by means of old-style *realpolitik*. In his calculation, linking up with Soviet Russia could countervail France's predominance, buttress German efforts to revise Versailles and, in particular, allow Berlin to tighten the screws on Poland.[31] Yet, as we have seen, Rapallo had increased rather than decreased Germany's isolation.

The Ruhr crisis – and his frontline involvement in preventing Germany's break-up as chancellor for 100 days – reinforced and furnished the requisite legitimacy for Stresemann's new course.[32] In view of the external and internal pressures of 1923, grand revisionist designs were not on the agenda. Rather, Stresemann first searched for ways to *return* to the *status quo* of 1919. He had often seen no other choice but to attempt negotiations with Poincaré. And he had been unable to prevent the MICUM agreements of November 1923. Yet he consistently sought to counter French bids to penetrate the Rhineland, fighting separatism and corporatist schemes of French and German industrialists, behind which he suspected French designs to undermine the German

[28] Stresemann speech, 30 March 1924, Stresemann (1932), II, pp. 164–93; Stresemann memorandum, 26 October 1926, *ADAP*, B, I/2, S. 375. Cf. Berg (1990), pp. 69–84.
[29] Stresemann statements, December 1920, Stresemann Papers, vol. 216.
[30] Cf. Zeidler (1993), pp. 82–7.
[31] Cf. Pogge von Strandmann (1981), pp. 123–46; Krüger (1985a), pp. 173–5. From 1924 German ambassador in Washington, Maltzan gravitated towards Stresemann's policy before dying in a plane crash.
[32] Cf. Wright (2002), pp. 203–59.

state. Domestically, he defended Berlin's authority both against communist insurgents and proponents of radical, dictatorial alternatives like Stinnes.[33]

Stresemann's unequivocal priority was to salvage Germany's economic and political unity. And, essentially, he hoped to achieve this by relying on what he called the 'interconnectedness' of world economic interests linking Germany with Britain and America. Stresemann would later describe the rationale and *telos* of his policy as 'using world economic relations in order to conduct foreign policy with the only element which still makes us a great power: our economic power'.[34] Among many, this was a crucial means distinguishing his policy from Hitler's. But it could only be used by pursuing a policy of negotiation and international bargaining. Accommodation with France was the primary necessity. Yet Britain, and even more the United States, came to play crucial roles.

Stresemann's assumptions about postwar international politics were informed by his belief in the unprecedented relevance of economic power and interdependence in the global, yet especially the transatlantic, economy. This interdependence was accentuated both by allied indebtedness to America and the reparations problem.[35] Stresemann held that in view of this a lasting impoverishment of Germany – as a key factor in this economy and Europe's largest market – would ultimately be seen as disadvantageous by the victors themselves.

Following this reasoning, and reflecting Keynes' assessment, Stresemann sought to engage the United States as Germany's 'senior partner' in the process of peaceful revision he envisaged. He deemed it a power with a natural interest in recasting the economic and political conditions of 1919. And he calculated that the more America would, in the process, become Germany's principal creditor, the more its political and financial elites would have a stake in ensuring Germany's economic *and* political rehabilitation. They would not only be interested in reviving Germany's 'power as a consumer', reintegrating it into a US-dominated economic order. They also had, more than Britain, the requisite means to foster Germany's revitalisation: debt leverage towards France and excess capital.[36]

This struck many chords with Hughes' approach to European stabilisation. At the turn of 1923/4, however, the first German task was to return to the basis of Versailles. Consequently, as we have seen, Stresemann sought to prepare the

---

[33] Stresemann statement, 17 November 1923, *AR Stresemann, I und II*, II, no. 267. Stresemann decidedly opposed the separatist course pursued by the Mayor of Cologne, Konrad Adenauer. See Rödder (1993), pp. 545–54.

[34] Stresemann *Reichstag* speech, 25 November 1922, *SB*, vol. 357, p. 9157; Stresemann speech, *Vossische Zeitung*, 17 December 1920, Stresemann interview with the *Chicago Tribune* (1920), Stresemann Papers, vol. 216; Stresemann speech, 22 November 1925, in Turner (1967), p. 434.

[35] Stresemann *Reichstag* speech, 25 November 1922, *SB*, vol. 357, p. 9157.

[36] Stresemann *Reichstag* speech, 28 April 1921, Stresemann (1926), I, p. 362.

ground for an American – and British – intervention. If he felt that 'the decisions about Europe's future [lay] essentially in the hands of the United States', this was never more true than in late 1923.[37] Only co-operation with Washington – and an agreement with France on these foundations – could set the course for 'an economically reasonable solution of the reparations question'. And only such co-operation could restore full German sovereignty over the Ruhr.[38]

Stresemann's reasoning also applied to Britain – to the hopes he attached to a weightier British role in shaping European politics. Yet Britain was sought more as a political than an economic 'senior partner'. For all its more conciliatory attitude, Britain remained one of the two principal underwriters of Versailles, reparations creditor and France's 'ally' within a somewhat amorphous *entente*. Fundamentally, however, Stresemann reckoned that a British sense of balance would sooner or later counteract French designs, even if this had long been a vain hope. In his view, the Ruhr conflict had shown Britain's 'at present limited power'; yet it remained nonetheless crucial as a power capable of exerting a moderating *political* influence on France.

Stresemann did *not* seek to drive a wedge between the *entente* powers in order to undermine Versailles. Precisely because Germany hoped to engage British influence vis-à-vis France, he considered it highly counterproductive 'if one plays off England's very *realpolitik*-orientated, economically tuned sense against French policy'.[39] In 1923 and thereafter, Stresemann consistently sought to encourage first Curzon, then MacDonald to play the role of a moderator between France and Germany. This would be even more decisive in the one crucial area where America remained aloof: European security.[40] Given MacDonald's interest in Germany's international reintegration, it would open up new prospects for Anglo-German co-operation in 1924. These premises may explain the tenacity with which Stresemann pursued his in fact highly risky policy of seeking an international settlement under Anglo-American auspices in 1923/4. And it may explain why he was prepared to make – and defend – what to many seemed excessive financial sacrifices in the expert scheme. In the spring of 1924, Stresemann argued that the German government had to do everything to secure this scheme's implementation. With the backing of London and Washington, facts had to be created before France could do its share, perpetuating its hold on the Ruhr through MICUM.[41]

[37] Stresemann to Maltzan (Washington), 7 April 1925, Stresemann Papers, H 158699.
[38] Stresemann *Reichstag* speech, 12 August 1923, *SB*, vol. 361, pp. 11839–40.
[39] Stresemann statement, 17 November 1923, *AR Stresemann I und II*, II, no. 267, pp. 1114–15; Stresemann, 'Politik und Wirtschaft, *Die Zeit*, 15 May 1923, Stresemann (1976), pp. 279–80. For a different interpretation see Kissinger (1994), pp. 271–2.
[40] Stresemann *Reichstag* speech, 25 November 1922, *SB*, vol. 357, pp. 9151–60.
[41] Stresemann memorandum, 24 February 1924, Stresemann (1932), I, pp. 302–17; Stresemann speech, 14 April 1924, *AR Marx I und II*, no. 175.

Yet, like all leaders of Weimar's coalition governments, Stresemann belonged to an elite minority. Domestic polarisation, which had reached a new climax during the Ruhr conflict, was one of the main burdens on Weimar foreign policy. To legitimate the search for external compromise, co-operation and partial acceptance of the realities of Versailles remained a critical central challenge within a national spectrum in many ways the opposite of a 'culture of compromise'.[42] The sustainability of peaceful change in the international sphere depended significantly on how far that challenge could be mastered.

As chancellor, Stresemann had seen the overriding need to foster a 'front of national unity', a 'concentration of all civic forces' to ensure Germany's 'survival as a great power'. After the 1924 elections, he had thus sought to include not only the Social Democrats but also the German Nationalists (DNVP) in the governing coalition, which also included his own party, the national liberal German People's Party (DVP). Such struggles became an integral part of his bid to legitimate *Westpolitik* domestically until 1929.[43] Besides facing corporate and separatist pressures on Rhine and Ruhr, Stresemann had to defend his course against an array of critics. These ranged from left-wing extremists seeking a new order along Soviet lines to forces, grouped round the DNVP, that fundamentally rejected any concessions to the 'victors of Versailles'. They were often indistinguishable from those rejecting the Weimar Republic as such.

As one of the most influential figures embodying traditions of militarily orientated foreign policy, General Seeckt saw Germany's future not in co-operation with the west but in regaining offensive alliance options. Thus, he sought to prepare for what he deemed an inescapably violent struggle to throw off the yoke of Versailles – in alliance with Soviet Russia.[44] This orientation went far beyond what the *Wilhelmstraße's* 'eastern faction' recommended. In fact, though, covert military co-operation between both countries only began very slowly after Rapallo. The Foreign Ministry opposed it.[45]

The inner-German tensions over Stresemann's course and Germany's relations with Soviet Russia did not escape British and American policymakers – much less those in Paris – particularly after the domestic crisis of October 1923. In contrast to France, however, given that both Whitehall and Washington held that Germany had nearly completed her disarmament in accordance with Versailles, its secret rearmament activities were rather downgraded as a serious challenge to international security. French anxieties were often considered exaggerated and detrimental to an overall consolidation of relations with

---

[42] Cf. Stürmer (1967), p. 17; Bracher (1978), p. 64; Evans (2003), pp. 78–138.

[43] Stresemann speech, 25 December 1924, Stresemann Papers, vol. 25, H 157794–95. Cf. Grathwol (1980), pp. 21–30.

[44] Cf. Zeidler (1993), pp. 82ff; Geyer (1980), pp. 31ff.   [45] Cf. Krüger (1985a), p. 175.

Germany.[46] In retrospect, however, what emerged here can be seen as a vital strategic question facing Anglo-American and French leaders. It was the question how far they could – or should – contain or tightly control any German revival if any such advance continued to rest on shaky republican foundations. What French policymakers had consistently dreaded was that such a revival could pave the way for an all the more threatening reaction – the resurgence of a more assertive Germany or even an autocratic, revisionist regime.[47] That regime could then capitalise on the advances Weimar's leaders had made.

This was a long-held majority position in France. Significantly, however, it had never found strong advocates in either Britain or the United States after 1919. There the view prevailed by the end of 1923 that a containment and even more a division of Germany could only strengthen revisionist elements. For it could only be effected at the expense of the republican policymakers who – like Stresemann – sought a peaceful accommodation with the west. And it could only be effected to the detriment of Germany's economic recovery in which London and Washington placed far-reaching hopes with a view to Berlin's acceptance of the new, western-orientated order.

Rather than being divided or dominated by corporatist arrangements under French auspices, Germany had to be consolidated as a *republican state*. The more German elites, both political and economic, could be given a stake in developing co-operative relations with the western powers – and, crucially, *on a par* with them – the greater the prospects that a majority among these elites would eventually not only embrace this westward course but also the Weimar Republic itself. And the more convincingly it could be shown to the wider German electorate that pursuing such a course was in Germany's well-understood best interest, the better Weimar's republican leaders would be able to prevail against anti-western and revisionist forces. At the same time, this would of course also serve the underlying economic and political interests of Britain and the United States best. And it would reduce not only the need for more far-reaching strategic commitments by these two powers in 1923 but also the likelihood that such commitments would ever have to be made in the future, as new German generations would appreciate the advantages of a *Pax Anglo-Americana*.

As noted, this was a common denominator of the strategies that leading policymakers in both Whitehall and Washington developed, and which both Hughes and MacDonald sought to advance in 1924. Figuratively speaking, though, central fault-lines of post-World War I international politics did not run only along the Rhine but straight through the *Reichstag* and the *Assemblée*

---

[46] MacDonald minutes, 18 April and 15 July 1924, FO 371/9750: C 6157/2977/18 and C 11050/70/18; Hughes to Allen, 17 August 1923, NA RG 59 462.00 R29/2923.

[47] Poincaré to MacDonald, 25 February 1924, *DBFP*, I, XXVI, no. 371.

Nationale. They also ran through the executive boards of industrial firms in France and the Ruhr, the headquarters of the French army and the *Reichswehr* as well as the poorhouses of those who had been decommissioned after Versailles – to name only the most important. Since 1919 'paths toward corporatist stability' had been sought both in France and Germany.[48] The core question of peaceful change and stabilisation, however, was how far policy-makers, co-operating with financial elites, could forge international, and inter-state, compromises that bridged these fault-lines. This would remain the cardinal problem in 1924 and thereafter.

[48] Cf. Maier (1988), pp. 353–4.

9   The two paths to the London conference

The Dawes process and the recasting of European international politics

The period between the Anglo-American return to Europe in late 1923 and the opening of the London reparations conference in mid-July 1924 can be seen as the first of two fulcrum periods in the history of post-World War I international politics. The second was the pre-phase of Locarno in 1925. For this period cleared not only the path for the London proceedings. It also determined the future of Germany's relations with the west and, in a wider perspective, the shape of central Europe for the remainder of the 1920s. More importantly, the shape of the international system that by the mid-1920s underpinned Europe's 'relative stabilisation' became manifest. Or did the developments of 1924 rather have a different significance? Did they rather, as has been argued, initiate the erosion of Europe's postwar order, ultimately preparing the ground for World War II?[1]

A comparison of what impact American and British policies had in 1924 sheds light on the complex process of intergovernmental and inter-elite accommodation that not merely ended the Ruhr crisis. In fact, two processes of change have to be examined to gauge how the path to London was cleared. Both were indeed mutually reinforcing. The first, economically orientated 'expert process', spurred by the United States, overcame the previous deadlock of European diplomacy. It thus spurred a second, political accommodation process, fostered by MacDonald's mediation vis-à-vis France and flanked by financial elites. It would take centre-stage after the publication of the Dawes report in early April. On new, transatlantic foundations, it transformed 'classic' international politics in Europe, reinvigorating intergovernmental efforts to negotiate a balanced settlement.

Through these twin developments the crux of postwar diplomacy, the reparations dispute and the Franco-German conflict behind it, was for the first time addressed in a concerted manner. The involvement of both German

---

[1] See Schuker (1976), pp. 171–294; Bariéty (1977), pp. 369ff; Jacobson (1983a).

policymakers and financiers on terms approaching equality became a matter of 'business rationality' *and* political common sense. This superseded the dividing-lines of Versailles. It was not a foregone conclusion that Poincaré's bid for continental preponderance would be frustrated by the Dawes negotiations and the American power projection underpinning them. But less inevitable still was that this turning-of-the-tide would bring a palpable gain in political stability. With Washington's backing, this could only be achieved by Britain's self-interested brokerage between France and Germany and between Europe's political elites and the financiers of London and New York.

The effect of the Dawes committee deliberations on Euro-Atlantic relations can hardly be overstated. On one level, they charted a way to defuse the reparations crisis, even if the inquiry in Dawes' own view was constrained by 'political necessities' and, in J.P. Morgan & Co.'s original assessment, lacked financial calibration.[2] More importantly, however, it served to galvanise European politics. It achieved this not only through its novel 'expert' approach to the long highly politicised reparations complex, as the principal US mediator Owen Young emphasised.[3] It also offered European 'high politics' and the complex interaction between governments and US financiers a new crystallisation-point. British, French – and German – policymakers hence concentrated on establishing advantageous bargaining-positions within the bounds of the Dawes process, and towards the United States.

Yet once the expert talks had commenced in Paris in December 1923, and almost until their results were published, the Coolidge administration reverted to a policy of aloofness. Hughes followed the maxim he had established since January, namely that America had 'no desire to become an arbitrator or dictator in the reparations problem'.[4] He made clear that the three US experts in Paris, Dawes, Young and Robinson, were 'not acting under instructions from this Government'. Nevertheless, he asserted through James Logan, the American representative at the Reparations Commission, that the experts would not lose sight of US interests.[5] Political 'flank manoeuvres' vis-à-vis France and Germany he essentially left to the new British government under MacDonald.[6] The State Department concentrated on refuting undesirable attempts at political interference, particularly from Poincaré, and to reiterate the credo of depoliticisation through all available channels both in Paris and Berlin.[7]

---

[2] Dawes, 'Reparations, 1924–29' file, Dawes Papers; Leffingwell to Lamont, 9 April 1924, J.P. Morgan to Morgan & Co., 26 April 1924, Lamont Papers, TWL, 176/8 and 9.
[3] Logan to State Department, 14 April 1924, NA RG 59 462.00 R 296/268.
[4] Hughes to US embassies in Europe, 6 January 1923, NA RG 50 462.00 R296/13a.
[5] Hughes to Logan, 12 January 1924, NA RG 59 462.00 R296/133.
[6] Hughes circular on US policy, 23 April 1924, NA RG 59 462.00 R296/286a.
[7] Kellogg to Hughes, 16 April 1924, NA RG 59 462.00 R296/175.

Particularly via Logan, who became an important informal agent of US policy, Hughes reminded Europeans that his administration had 'consistently urged the economic character of the problem'. Washington continued to insist that it should be settled 'by the formulation of an adequate financial plan', unhampered by 'the interjection of questions of a political character'. These notably included the terms of France's evacuation of the Ruhr.[8] American influence acted as the salient background-force of international politics in the spring of 1924. Yet political developments centred on the European stage, particularly on Britain's bid to bring France and Germany in line behind the expert scheme.

Integrative *versus* enforced stabilisation: MacDonald's pursuit of a Franco-German accommodation

Did MacDonald become a passive agent of American policy in Europe? Hughes' restraint in fact accentuated the importance of British diplomacy. Owing to the new prime minister's forward engagement, Britain's role became no less than pivotal. As we have seen, both American and German leaders looked towards London for political mediation while France sought reassurance. And both in Paris and Berlin by no means incommensurable reorientations had begun. Yet they still had to converge, and a new, political path to a reparations settlement still had to be found. The essential contribution of MacDonald's evolutionary approach in 1924 was that it catalysed and canalised peaceful change between Germany and the west. British efforts contributed greatly to converting the original American scheme to resolve the Franco-German power struggle, essentially a set of financial prescriptions, into a fully fledged – and hence more legitimate – political agreement. This was a dimension clearly underestimated from the distance of Washington, but not in France or Germany.

To be sure, MacDonald was not acting on internationalist impulses alone. Tangible British interests were at stake. And his assumption was that what was best for Britain was also in Europe's best interest: a de-escalation of the reparations conflict – providing for German payments and the recovery of French debts and thus allowing Britain to fulfil its obligations to America; a reform of the Versailles system; political consolidation, economic reconstruction and the revival of trade in continental Europe, all underpinned by American capital.[9] MacDonald's core aim remained to contain French power politics, rehabilitate Germany and, in the medium term, reinvigorate the League. His

---

[8] Hughes to Logan, 23 February 1923; Hughes to Logan, 12 January 1924, NA RG 59 462.00 R296/76 and 133.
[9] Lampson to Otto Niemeyer (Treasury), 30 June 1924, FO 371/9749: C10426/70/18; minutes of the Chequers conversations, 21–2 June 1924, FO 371/9749: C 10427/70/18.

underlying belief was that all of these objectives could be reconciled. At the core, he held that French demands for *sécurité* were compatible with Germany's international integration if only progress could be made in resolving their conflict politically.[10]

Once in office, MacDonald rapidly began to implement a two-prong strategy. On the one hand, it centred on placing Anglo-American co-operation on the reparations question on a new footing. On the other, he began to approach first France, then Germany to prepare the ground for an integrative accommodation process.[11] The Labour premier's emphasis on direct mediation soon led to his plan for a full-fledged international conference to settle the reparations problem – to be held under Anglo-American auspices. He concluded that this was the only realistic way to prevent a bilateral Franco-German 'agreement' dictated by Poincaré at German expense. It also was to pave the way for a more comprehensive settlement between the wartime allies and Germany. Though careful not to press this point in public, MacDonald privately hoped that such a settlement would spur an early French evacuation of the Ruhr and the restoration of German sovereignty in the Rhineland.[12] MacDonald's bid to realise his design of a new transatlantic concert to overcome Versailles' limitations was to shape Britain's diplomatic efforts from January 1924.

To this end, the British premier made an unequivocal implementation of the US 'expert strategy' a cardinal objective of his policy.[13] Crucially, he developed Curzon's passive pledge of support into a policy of engaging the Coolidge administration – and US high finance – while respecting American preferences and limits. Under MacDonald, British policy for the first time acknowledged the reconfiguration of the international power-constellation after 1918. If London desired an augmented American role in Europe, it could no longer 'co-opt' Washington on British terms. MacDonald's was the only approach by a leading British policymaker in the 1920s in fact furthering a novel mode of limited yet effective 'competitive' Anglo-American co-operation.[14] Seconded by Crowe, his 'iron chancellor' Philip Snowden and Montagu Norman, he endeavoured to hammer out a co-ordinated strategy with Washington.

In 1924, British diplomacy would consistently 'give particular weight' to US interests. MacDonald assured Hughes that Britain would not seek to alter the

---

[10] MacDonald statements, *Quai d'Orsay*, 8 July 1924, *DBFP*, I, XXVI, no. 507.

[11] MacDonald statement, *Times*, 16 February 1924, transmitted to Hughes, 18 February 1924, NA RG 59 462.00 R296/200; MacDonald to Phipps, 4 February 1924, *DBFP*, I, XXVI, no. 349.

[12] MacDonald to Phipps, 4 February 1924; MacDonald to Crewe, 21 May 1924, *DBFP*, I, XXVI, nos. 349, 1744.

[13] Kellogg to Hughes, 17 April 1924, NA RG 59 462.00 R296/273; MacDonald to D'Abernon, 29 May 1924, MacDonald Papers, MDP 30/69/94.

[14] Cf. the emphasis on continuity between Curzon and MacDonald in O'Riordan (2001), pp. 145ff.

'rules of the game' he had set. As Crowe underlined, London recognised that a realisation of the expert scheme and wider peaceful change in Europe were inconceivable without Washington's support and the willingness of bankers such as J.P. Morgan to underpin both with capital.[15] Instead of concrete diplomatic support, MacDonald sought Washington's decisive indirect backing. Through US ambassador Kellogg and Britain's ambassador in Washington, Esme Howard, he kept Hughes abreast of London's negotiations with Paris and Berlin.[16] Overall, US diplomats were appreciative of MacDonald's efforts, if at first wary of his socialist credentials. Coolidge himself expressed his confidence that the Labour government could foster 'a gradual adjustment of all the difficult European problems, both international and social'.[17]

Both towards France and Germany, Britain came to a policy of incentive and firmness, which essentially translated the Dawes negotiations into a political pacification process.[18] MacDonald first concentrated on fostering new, pragmatic relations with Paris. He underscored his willingness to address France's legitimate concerns over reparations and security, assuring Poincaré that Britain would back his claims – yet only if France adhered to the Dawes process. And, albeit not on terms satisfying any French leader, he held out the promise that, following a reparation deal, Britain would commit itself to a new League-based security system. Yet MacDonald also drew a clear line, emphasising that neither Britain nor the United States would tolerate France's permanent seizure of the Ruhr or continued French *diktats* to Germany.[19]

MacDonald's efforts carried more weight than Curzon's because they were based on a consistent policy, co-ordination with Washington and an expert approach that by early 1924 had gathered undeniable momentum. Characteristically, the British premier as strenuously sought an understanding with Poincaré as later with the socialist Herriot. He did, however, grow increasingly suspicious of Poincaré's agenda as French obstructionism persisted in the spring of 1924.[20] In effect, no tangible progress would be made until Herriot's electoral victory in May.

On 26 January 1924, the new prime minister, seeking to foster *rapprochement* and to put public pressure on France, sent an open letter to Poincaré. It urgently called for a renewal of Anglo-French co-operation and a negotiated

---

[15] Crowe memorandum, 24 June 1924, *DBFP*, I, XXVI, no. 493.

[16] Kellogg to Hughes, 17 April 1924, NA RG 59 462.00 R296/273; MacDonald to Howard, 16 June 1924, MacDonald Papers, MDP 30/69/94.

[17] Kellogg to Hughes, 18 February 1924, NA RG 59 462.00 R296/200; Coolidge to Kellogg, 18 February 1924, Coolidge Papers, box 203, file 712.

[18] See Saint-Aulaire (1953), pp. 694ff. Cf. Schuker (1976), pp. 245ff.

[19] MacDonald to Poincaré, 21 February 1924, *DBFP*, I, XXVI, no. 369; MacDonald to Crewe, 17 April 1924, FO 800/218/228a.

[20] Crowe to Phipps (Paris), 20 March 1924, *DBFP*, I, XXVI, no. 394.

settlement of the Ruhr conflict. MacDonald conceded that France had 'with some justification' sought 'other and more tangible safeguards' after the joint Anglo-American guarantee of 1919 had lapsed. But he also told Poincaré in no uncertain terms that it was 'widely felt in England' that, contrary to the 'provisions' of Versailles, France 'was endeavouring to create a situation which gains for it what it failed to get during the Allied peace negotiations'. British policy encouraged French leaders to assess the security problem they faced in the wider perspective of achieving European stability rather than insist on the containment of Germany.[21]

As he conveyed to MacDonald through ambassador Saint-Aulaire, Poincaré was in fact keen to re-establish a new Anglo-French *entente*.[22] Officially, however, he did so – not surprisingly – by invoking once more France's deep-seated security concerns and disappointment over Anglo-American disengagement since the war to justify the occupation. All French measures had intended 'to defend France against the temptations of a German *revanche*'. British perceptions of France as contemplating 'the political and economic eradication of Germany' were mistaken.[23] Doubtless, French policymakers never stopped seeing reparations and security as two inseparable concerns. And they sought to link both issues in the Dawes negotiations, aiming to re-assert the Versailles system. France required fresh British assurances in one field, security, to be more conciliatory in the other, reparations, and relinquish the 'legitimate' security *glacis* on the Rhine.

Yet Poincaré failed to gain Britain's agreement to new guarantees and far-reaching linkages. While seeking to revitalise relations, the underlying goal of British diplomacy remained to thwart what MacDonald and Crowe saw as Poincaré's concealed ambitions for continental supremacy.[24] For its part, the American government never considered altering the terms of either the expert negotiations or its role in order to accommodate Poincaré. Washington refused to make fresh security commitments, particularly prior to a reparations agreement.[25]

From the outset, MacDonald consistently underlined Britain's firm opposition to Poincaré's 'illegitimate' policy of supporting separatist movements in the Rhineland.[26] The British government refused to recognise the 'so-called

[21] MacDonald to Poincaré, 26 January 1924, FO 800/218/191–4; *Times*, 4 February 1924; MacDonald minute, 18 February 1924, FO 371/9813: C 2028/1346/18; MacDonald and Crowe minutes, 19 February 1924, FO 371/9825: C4760/G; MacDonald to Poincaré, 21 February 1924, *DBFP*, I, XXVI, no. 369.

[22] Crowe memorandum, 19 February 1924, FO 371/9825: C2900/G.

[23] Poincaré to MacDonald, 25 February 1924, *DBFP*, I, XXVI, no. 371; Crewe to MacDonald, 11 February 1924, MacDonald Papers, MDP 30/69/94, no. 96; Crowe memorandum, 22 February 1924, FO 371/9825: C3414/G.

[24] MacDonald minute, 18 February 1924, FO 371/9813: C 2028/1346/18.

[25] Hughes to Logan, 23 February 1923, NA RG 59 462.00 R296/76.

[26] MacDonald to Crewe, 26 January 1924, *DBFP*, I, XXVI, no. 344.

autonomous governments of the Palatinate', considering them French puppet-regimes.[27] MacDonald continued to dread the spectre of a permanently unsettled Weimar Germany. His stance was hardened by reports from D'Abernon, Britain's ambassador in Paris, the Marquess of Crewe, and the British high commissioner in the Rhineland, Lord Kilmarnock – all stressing that French policy still sought to undercut not only Germany's economic base.[28] In MacDonald's judgement, this could ultimately only benefit those nationalist forces in Germany who opposed the expert negotiations and the entire prospect of Germany's accommodation with the west. While German industrialists by then maintained that the terms France sought to impose were 'financially impossible', Berlin was still struggling to re-establish its authority. Stresemann's intention was 'to stop private negotiations between MICUM and individual firms' and open intergovernmental negotiations. To support the German government in these efforts became a constant of MacDonald's policy.[29] The Anglo-American intervention would strengthen the authority of governments in Germany *and* France against the 'international convergence' of corporate interests operating on both banks of the Rhine.[30]

In the Foreign Office, Crowe strongly supported MacDonald's policy. By mid-March 1924, he held that Poincaré was engaging in a deceptive policy of procrastination to secure whatever he could prior to the publication of the experts' report. French statements regarding 'the evacuation of the Ruhr' were 'looked upon as [not] having any relation to fact'. Crowe maintained that French security demands had to be addressed in the medium term and that a Rhine pact arrangement could be a useful device to de-escalate Franco-German tensions. Yet his primary concern was to contain Poincaré's ambitions.[31] Following Crowe's advice, MacDonald asserted firm priorities: Britain would only be willing to raise the security question *after* France had accepted a reparations settlement *and* evacuated the Ruhr.[32] British policy did not diverge from this course until the London conference.

Anglo-French relations thus remained marred by mutual suspicion in the spring of 1924. Yet there were also more fundamental differences. Each power had drawn different lessons from the developments of 1923; and there was still a legacy of mutual mistrust after years of inconclusive *entente* negotiations and

[27] MacDonald to Phipps, 2 February 1924, *DBFP*, I, XXVI, no. 348.
[28] Crewe to MacDonald, 1 March 1924, *DBFP*, I, XXVI, no. 377; D'Abernon to MacDonald, 23 March 1924, MacDonald Papers, MDP 30/69/94, no. 104.
[29] MacDonald to Knox, 6 May 1924; MacDonald to Crewe, 26 January 1924, *DBFP*, I, XXVI, nos. 462, 344; MacDonald speech in the Commons, 27 March 1924, *Hansard*, cols. 1596ff.
[30] Maier (1988), p. 414.
[31] Crowe to Phipps, 20 March 1924, *DBFP*, I, XXVI, pp. 587–8; Crowe memorandum, 19 February 1924, FO 371/9825: C2900/G; Saint-Aulaire (1953), p. 690.
[32] Crowe minute, 25 February 1924, FO 371/9818: C 2842/2048/18.

mutual alienation. Poincaré sought to win London's support for re-asserting the order of 1919 and French prerogatives vis-à-vis Germany. MacDonald sought to reorientate French diplomacy towards a different, integrative route to European stability. Against this background, it seems hardly surprising that – despite common interests – the prospects for finding a modicum of common ground only improved after Poincaré's resignation.[33]

From the outset, MacDonald's overtures to France had gone hand in hand with the attempt to turn his long-term aim of stabilising Weimar Germany and bringing her back into the 'society of nations' into a concrete policy. He essentially pursued a – somewhat paternalistic – policy of 'guardianship'. He impressed upon the Marx government that it would be well advised to leave it basically to Britain and the United States to safeguard German interests on the road to a reparations settlement.[34] In essence, British diplomacy intended to retain control over the political process of peaceful change between France and Germany. And MacDonald, not Stresemann, set its pace and rules in 1924. From early on, British policymakers saw Stresemann and the Marx government as reliable, if often overly demanding partners.[35] They held that Berlin should concentrate on preparing the domestic ground for implementing the envisaged expert report. MacDonald and Crowe urged Stresemann to accept the experts' scheme 'in its entirety'.[36] This was also what Hughes impressed upon Berlin.[37] In the international sphere, London rejected German calls for an early deadline for France's evacuation of the Ruhr, which could only complicate Anglo-French negotiations. As MacDonald confessed to D'Abernon, on 29 May, he often saw himself 'faced with the difficulty of saving Germany from herself'.[38]

In the face of Anglo-American opposition, Stresemann basically refrained from pressing German claims until Britain ensured France's participation at the London conference. Rather, to ease MacDonald's task and deprive Poincaré of arguments for prolonging the occupation, he sought to meet French security demands as far as domestically possible. Against the *Reichswehr's* opposition, Stresemann gained his government's acceptance of renewed inter-allied military control, which had been suspended in 1923.[39] MacDonald welcomed this. Overall, however, he asserted the same priorities as towards France. He discouraged German overtures to put the security question back on

---

[33] MacDonald to Crewe, 21 May 1924, *DBFP*, I, XXVI, no. 468; Poincaré *Sénat* speech, 13 March 1924, *JOC*, pp. 281ff.
[34] MacDonald to D'Abernon, 29 May 1924, MacDonald Papers, MDP 30/69/94.
[35] MacDonald to Phipps, 4 February 1924, *DBFP*, I, XXVI, no. 349; MacDonald interview, *Times*, 16 February 1924; Crowe minutes, 5 and 25 February 1924, FO 371/9813: C2028/1346/18.
[36] MacDonald to D'Abernon, 29 May 1924, MacDonald Papers, MDP 30/69/94.
[37] Hughes circular on US policy, 23 April 1924, NA RG 59 462.00 R296/286a.
[38] MacDonald to Knox, 6 May 1924, *DBFP*, I, XXVI, no. 462.
[39] Cf. Salewski (1966), pp. 240ff.

the international agenda, through fresh Rhine pact proposals, prior to a reparations settlement.[40]

Stresemann's main aim to return to international diplomacy as an 'equal' power indeed accorded with what the Labour premier sought to achieve. As he and Crowe realised, it was crucial to buttress Berlin's western-orientated course, and legitimate it through concrete results, to contain German nationalists railing against it.[41] Yet German rehabilitation was to be advanced on Anglo-American terms. Until July, Stresemann and Schubert indeed largely refrained from a self-reliant foreign policy, ceding the high-ground of negotiations with France to Britain. And they counted on the power of America's financial diplomacy to effect 'a solution of the reparations question in the spirit of reconciliatory politics'.[42]

From stagnation to compromise: what paved the way for the London settlement

The publication of the Dawes report on 9 April 1924 did not mark a watershed in transatlantic relations. Yet it gave European and Euro-Atlantic politics fresh impulses, reinforcing the transformation underway since December 1923. The report had a significant political impact insofar as it provided the basis for the London accords and, consequently, the reparations regime superseding the Franco-Belgian Ruhr regime. It thus shaped relations between the Anglo-American powers, France and Germany until the adoption of the Young plan in 1929.[43]

In the eyes of Young, who already was the pivotal 'broker' in 1924, the Dawes committee's deliberations resulted in the 'irreducible maximum' of what concessions the interested powers could make without risking renewed conflict.[44] Young had effectively prevented a split between the British and French delegations. The former, under Bradbury, had been eager to resolve the postwar reparations crisis rather than maximise reparations. The latter, headed by Barthou and seconded by Belgium and Italy, had still striven to achieve such maximisation through a settlement conforming with Versailles.[45] Chiefly US mediation produced a plan that became the only alternative to further

---

[40] German memorandum to British Foreign Office, 11 February 1924; D'Abernon to MacDonald, 19 February 1924, FO 371/9818: C 2842/2048/18. On MacDonald's attitude see Hankey to Smuts, 22 May 1924, Hankey Papers.

[41] MacDonald minute, 18 April 1924, FO 371/9825: C6157/2977/18; Addison to Nicolson, 1 March 1924; Crowe minute, 13 March 1924, FO 371/9813: C3814/1346/18.

[42] Stresemann to German embassy (London), 21 January 1924, PA, GA Abt. III, vol. 4; Schubert memorandum, 28 June 1924, *ADAP*, A, X, p. 408. Cf. Wright (2002), pp. 270–3.

[43] Cf. Schuker (1976), pp. 180ff.

[44] Logan to State Department, 14 April 1924, NA RG 59 462.00 R 296/268.

[45] Bradbury to Snowden, 12 March 1924, FO 371/9739: C4525/70/18.

economic dislocation in Europe and 'the further embittering of Franco-German and Franco-British relations'.[46]

The Dawes plan, as was clearly perceived at the time, did not provide either a conclusive scheme to solve the reparations problem or a final sum of German obligations. Formally, the decision of the 1921 London conference to fix Germany's 'theoretical debt' at 132 billion gold marks was not rescinded. Rather, the report offered a scheme to 'facilitate a final and comprehensive agreement' to be reached once a modicum of European stability consolidation had been re-established.[47] To this end, it proposed a revised schedule of annual payments. Above all, to give German recovery a 'breathing space', the first annuity, to be paid by August 1925, was effectively reduced to less than one tenth of subsequent 'normal annuities', applying from 1928/9 onwards. Germany would have to remit 200 million marks while 800 million marks were to be supplied by an international loan. A common assumption was that this could only be floated on the American market.[48]

The experts concluded that 'business and not politics' had been the measure of their deliberations. The main incentive, and guarantee, for the plan's execution was that is was deemed financially viable, *not* that governments vouched for it. This particularly corresponded with Washington's informal, economic approach to European stabilisation. Yet the Dawes Committee also emphasised that its recommendations could not be entirely free from 'political considerations'. It reckoned accurately that the plan's implementation required wider political acceptance, above all the endorsement of governments and parliaments in Germany and France.[49] Dawes himself later characterised the result as 'dominated' by financial concerns but also 'a compromise between economic principles and political necessities'.[50] Indeed, the expert compromise mattered most for its political implications.

While Paris' reaction remained lukewarm, the Dawes report was quickly endorsed in Washington, London and Berlin. Its publication reinforced the marked parallelism of interests between the Anglo-American powers and Germany already evident in 1923. The Marx government unconditionally accepted the experts' findings on 14 April.[51] As Stresemann later told his party behind closed doors: 'What is now taking place, in this report, is . . . the initiation of Anglo-American world-economic tendencies against French

---

[46] Logan to State Department, 14 April 1924, NA RG 59 462.00 R 296/268.
[47] Commission des Réparations (1924), p., 35.
[48] See FRBNY Governor Strong's reports on the Dawes plan, 23–8 April 1924, Strong Papers. Cf. Feldman (1993).
[49] Commission des Réparations (1924), p. 3.
[50] Dawes essay, 'Reparations, 1924–29' file, Dawes Papers.
[51] German note, 14 April 1924, *AR Marx I und II*, no. 175.

imperialism'.[52] Apart from the relatively lenient financial stipulations, he particularly welcomed the financiers' insistence that 'Germany's economic unity is a cardinal precondition for German payments.'[53]

For London and Washington, this soon became a key argument against the continued Ruhr occupation. This was underscored by the experts' emphasis on the need to ensure an unhampered resumption of economic activity in all of Germany to attract indispensable Anglo-American capital.[54] No less significant was the proposal for a new transfer-system ensuring a 'businesslike' flow of reparations. The question whether its control should remain under the authority of the Reparations Commission (RepCo) – and thus France – or whether, following Anglo-American preferences, an entirely new mechanism was needed became critical in subsequent negotiations.

From Poincaré's perspective, the report thus questioned both France's Ruhr regime and central pillars of the Versailles system, notably French sanction powers through the RepCo. Immediately before its publication, Poincaré had reiterated the strict political conditions he attached to the plan's endorsement. On 2 April, he underscored in the *Chambre* that France had been 'too long deceived' to 'renounce possibilities of future constraint. She will only evacuate the Ruhr in proportion to [German] payments.'[55] It was thus hardly surprising that Paris still opposed ending the MICUM agreements. Poincaré intended to prolong them to forestall Anglo-American attempts to replace France's 'wider' pledges through the Dawes plan, even threatening renewed use of force.[56] To counter this, the German government quickly invoked the recently published Dawes report, seeking more than ever to redirect negotiations to the intergovernmental level. And Stresemann successfully ensured Anglo-American support.[57] France was powerful enough to extract reparations, yet too vulnerable to sever the Ruhr industry from Germany or perpetuate the MICUM system against the will of London and Washington.[58] Poincaré finally agreed to enter into negotiations over the report, excluding Germany, on 25 April.[59]

The Coolidge administration regarded the Dawes report as precisely the 'adequate plan' that Europe's stabilisation required – and which it was now the European powers' duty to implement. In Hughes' eyes, the *modus operandi* of pacific settlement that Washington had championed had already proved superior to French power politics. He trusted that 'it may recommend itself to

---

[52] Stresemann speech, 6 July 1924, quoted after Maxelon (1972), p. 158.

[53] Stresemann statement, 20 April 1924, Stresemann (1932), I, p. 394.

[54] Commission des Réparations (1924), pp. 3–4.

[55] Phipps to MacDonald, 3 April 1924, MacDonald Papers, MDP 30/69/94, no. 272.

[56] Cf. Bariéty (1977), pp. 305ff.

[57] German Foreign Ministry to Hoesch (Paris), 10 April 1924, PA, Sonderreferat Wirtschaft, 9426H/3657/270981–7; Houghton to Hughes, 9 April 1924, NA RG 59 462.00 R 296/251.

[58] Thus Maier (1988), p. 419.   [59] Cf. McDougall (1978), pp. 323ff.

all European governments interested as a method by which, through mutual concessions, they can arrive at a stable adjustment of the intricate and vexatious problem of reparations'.[60] Following the report's publication, the State Department thus immediately began to press for its swift realisation. It did so on two fronts: the domestic and the European, where it particularly urged Berlin to accept the results without delay. America's principal lever and incentive was one and the same: capital to fund a workable reparations scheme, and European reconstruction.

The Republican administration was by then distinctly aware of the influence that the United States commanded due to its financial supremacy. Mainly addressing Poincaré, Hughes declared on 14 June: 'It is obvious that the [Dawes] plan cannot become operative except with the accord of the United States, of special importance being [the] friendly interest of this Government in the proposed loan.'[61] Precisely because his informally pursued 'grand design' had proved so successful, Hughes was resolved to maintain his course. The rules that he had proposed to 'solve' the reparations problem had been accepted; his definition of America's role as informal arbiter had preserved a large measure of domestic and international freedom of manoeuvre.

Hughes thus opted to rely on the leverage of American bankers, chiefly J.P. Morgan.[62] And he counted on their co-operation with London's high finance and the MacDonald government.[63] In his view, they were predestined to make far-reaching economic *and political* demands, notably that for an early French Ruhr evacuation, without having to offer burdensome political guarantees in return. Nor did they have to justify new obligations in Europe either to the isolationist US Congress or public. At the same time, the administration could thus also avoid being seen as dictating the terms of the European reparations settlement.[64]

On a tactical level, Washington simply insisted that, after successfully initiating its 'depoliticisation' strategy, it would not be drawn into diplomatic wrangling. Hughes impressed on the Europeans that US investors would only invest in German loan-obligations, and French bonds, if they themselves ensured safe political conditions.[65] On 1 May, he welcomed that 'the Allies' were 'looking upon [the Dawes scheme] with full sympathy' and that Germany had 'expressed a willingness to cooperate'. In practice, the State Department continued to rely on the Labour government's political brokerage, particularly

[60] Hughes to Howard, 1 May 1924, NA RG 59 462.00 R 296/262.
[61] Hughes to Logan, 14 June 1924, *FRUS 1924*, II, p. 22.
[62] Hughes statements, 9 May 1924, Hughes Papers.
[63] Hughes to Howard, 1 May 1924, NA RG 59 462.00 R 296/262.
[64] Hughes to Logan, 15 March 1924; Herrick to Hughes, 17 April 1924, NA RG 59 462.00 R296/212, 279.
[65] London welcomed this. See Kellogg to Hughes, 12 May 1924, NA RG 59 462.00 R296/352.

vis-à-vis France.[66] Only in early July Hughes finally espoused what, privately, he had gravitated towards since May: an informal presence at the European negotiations in London.

Domestically, the administration's efforts focused on legitimating or rather 'selling' the Dawes report. What Coolidge declared at the annual Associated Press luncheon on 23 April remained the official Republican credo: 'Sound business reasons exist why we should participate in the financing of works of peace in Europe.' Decisive was the prospect of expanding trade with a revitalised Europe. Taking his cue from Commerce Secretary Hoover, Coolidge called it 'notorious' that, due to shifts in global finance, 'foreign gold has been flowing into our country in great abundance'. He argued that some of it could be 'used more to our financial advantage in Europe', which remained starved of gold and capital. Confident of Wall Street's support, Republican policymakers concentrated their efforts on potential investors in German loan-obligations. Coolidge publicly emphasised his trust 'that private American capital will be willing to participate in advancing [the] loan' required to realise the Dawes scheme.[67]

Ultimately, Washington's trust in the hence ever weightier interests of US bankers was vindicated. J.P. Morgan and his partners Thomas Lamont and Dwight Morrow initially did not consider the Dawes report an appropriate recipe for solving the reparations problem. Yet the more it seemed the only alternative to continued European disarray the more they put their weight behind its implementation.[68] Much has been made of the bankers' role as a quasi higher force marginalising policymakers in international relations in 1924.[69] It was indeed important. But decisive was what policymakers could and did achieve. Washington's official reserve permitted and necessitated the prominent part that US bankers assumed in paving the final way to the London conference. Yet their perception of the European situation had hardened their and especially J.P. Morgan's conviction that it was not the financiers' responsibility to replace politicians in fulfilling their essential task. It remained to hammer out the essential political consensus allowing the financiers to act effectively within their remit.[70] Morgan had stressed this point when conferring with Bradbury and Barthou at the RepCo in Paris in late April. He would be willing to use his authority to obtain the contemplated loan, noting that this would not pose major financial problems. But the political

[66] Hughes to Howard, 1 May 1924, Kellogg to Hughes, 16 February 1924, NA RG 59 462.00 R296/262, 175.
[67] Hughes to US Embassies in Europe, NA RG 59 462.00 R296/286a; Hoover to H. Fish Jr, 8 December 1923, Hoover Papers, box 75.
[68] Cf. Schuker (1976), pp. 260ff.
[69] See Burk (1991), pp. 125–57, and (1989).
[70] J.P. Morgan to Morgan, Grenfell & Co., 2 July 1924, Lamont Papers, TWL 176/11.

representatives of all countries involved had to act first: a political had to precede the financial settlement.[71] In the summer of 1924, one was hardly separable from the other.

Paradoxically, then, while the bankers called for political solutions, Hughes, for obvious reasons, continued to stress the essentially economic character of the questions at hand. It should be noted, though, that J.P. Morgan & Co. originally refrained from specific political demands. Their chief concern remained to obtain French assurances that Germany's economic life would no longer be disrupted. But they did not insist on an unconditional withdrawal of French troops from the Ruhr.[72] By contrast, Montagu Norman, the crucial intermediary between US financiers and Europe, demanded that an end to the Ruhr occupation and firm assurances against any future French incursions be made essential preconditions for the flow of Anglo-American capital. And he knew precisely that these were highly political demands.[73]

Significantly, this strict interpretation was eventually endorsed by J.P. Morgan & Co. And their willingness to float the first essential $800 million loan under the Dawes scheme was critical to its success.[74] Were they, perhaps against their better judgement, siding with France's opponents? In fact, American bankers retained strong sympathies for France. Having already acted decisively to stabilise French currency with a $100 million loan in the acute crisis preceding Herriot's election in May, J.P. Morgan still sought to aid the recovery of French public finance as well as the franc. Like Anglo-American policymakers, financiers were refusing to engage in a zero-sum game where every gain for Germany equalled a loss for France and European stability. Yet the very 'business logic' they propounded went against all that Poincaré sought to defend in the spring of 1924. It furnished Anglo-American diplomacy with powerful political weaponry.

Transcending the politics of 1919 – the consequences and rescue of the Chequers summit

Against this background, MacDonald's role as 'arbitrator between France, Germany and the Dawes plan' became decisive in preparing the ground for the London conference. London's initial reaction to the Dawes report had not been unequivocal. While Britain's representatives Bradbury and McKenna felt that British interests had been steadfastly defended, the Treasury, particularly

---

[71] J.P. Morgan to J.P. Morgan & Co., 26 April 1924, Lamont Papers, TWL 176/9.

[72] Morrow to Lamont, 24 July 1924, Lamont file, Morrow Papers.

[73] Norman memorandum, 15 July 1924, Lamont Papers, TWL 176/12. Cf. Leffler (1979), pp. 106ff.

[74] Cf. Costigliola (1984), pp. 60ff.

under-secretary Sir Otto Niemeyer, had numerous misgivings about particular clauses, particularly the excessive height of German annuities. What quickly prevailed, however, was the Foreign Office's political evaluation. Crowe saw the report as the best possible mechanism to end France's Ruhr occupation and rehabilitate Germany. Predictably, the scheme was also endorsed by Norman, who urged Whitehall to hasten its political ratification.[75]

MacDonald himself went even further. He asserted that the plan offered the most promising 'instrument' to further his main political objectives: to settle the reparations dispute, which would also strengthen the embattled Labour government domestically, but would also alter political relations between the western powers and Germany and, ultimately, Europe's postwar order. Seconded by Crowe, MacDonald's main aim became to conclude his efforts with a 'conference in chief' where not only France – and Germany – but also 'America might be represented in some shape or form'.[76]

Given the political constellation of May 1924, British efforts once again centred on Paris. Yet they were also consistently directed at paving the way for final negotiations with Germany. Their remarkable success was undoubtedly furthered by the fact that with Herriot, the leader of the *Cartel des Gauches*, an alliance of socialists and radicals, hence (re)directed French policy. French disillusionment with Poincaré's Ruhr policy had been a key factor in his defeat. Poincaré had found it ever harder to win parliamentary backing for domestic austerity programmes; and he had struggled to sustain an occupation that brought France no obvious gains either in terms of security or in the form of reparation payments. Both factors also spurred France's further, if hesitant, reorientation towards an accommodation with the Anglo-American powers and Germany.[77] Though by a slender margin, Herriot had been given a mandate to pursue a more conciliatory course.

Was the new premier the 'untried pilot' in the intricate domain of international politics and finance?[78] Did his naïve trust in MacDonald's internationalism hasten the end of France's postwar predominance, then sealed at the London conference?[79] In his negotiations with the strategically shrewd MacDonald and Crowe, Herriot indeed often seemed hapless.[80] Yet in a wider perspective, he advanced further towards a 'realistic' reparations policy than his predecessor. For he premised his policy on the assumption that, given France's financial and international constraints, Paris could best defend its

---

[75] Bradbury to Snowden, 12 March 1924, FO 371/9739: C4525/70/18; Niemeyer memorandum, 14 April 1924, Crowe minute, 9 April 1924, FO 371/9740: C6331/70/18, C 6080/70/18.

[76] MacDonald to D'Abernon, 29 May 1924, MacDonald Papers, MDP 30/69/94.

[77] Poincaré to MacDonald, 25 February 1924, *DBFP*, I, XXVI, no. 371. Cf. Keiger (1997), pp. 294ff.

[78] Herrick to Hughes, 7 June 1924, NA RG 59 U.S. 851.002.109.

[79] See Schuker (1976), pp. 232ff.   [80] See Bariéty (1977), ch. 10.

interests by asserting them through international agreements. France was compelled to support a process that Poincaré had in the end merely attempted to block.

MacDonald soon saw Herriot as a potential ally in pursuing an integrative policy towards Germany. Herriot had declared that he was not hostile towards Germany and eager to 'dispel the shadow of Bismarck'.[81] In the *Chambre*, on 17 June, he avowed his rejection of 'the policy of isolation and force' and 'the seizure of territorial pledges'.[82] And he was prepared to depart from what he considered his predecessor's anti-British course.[83] No less, Herriot was ideologically committed to strengthening the League. Soon, however, he demanded more concrete British guarantees regarding reparations and security. This eventually crystallised in his plea for a wide-ranging bilateral pact.[84] Doubtless, Herriot had to operate under marked domestic constraints; he had to pursue international co-operation without being seen as 'selling out' cardinal French security interests.[85] This would have restricted any French statesman's room to manoeuvre in 1924. The more negotiations with Britain led to demands for French concessions the more Herriot fell back on a defensive, Poincarist course.

Conversely, it remained an abiding concern for MacDonald that France would only accept the Dawes report if Britain made political concessions first: a pledge to support sanctions in the event of German default and wider security guarantees. As ambassador Kellogg noted, such concerns hardened British support for the American scheme. This set the terms on which MacDonald sought to establish a 'new basis of friendship of co-operation' with France.[86] His 'carrot-and-stick' policy vis-à-vis Paris entered a decisive phase in the run-up to the London conference. It culminated in successive Anglo-French summit-meetings at Chequers, on 21–22 June, and at the *Quai d'Orsay* on 8 July 1924. Both have been criticised as successful British attempts to cajole a weak French leadership into accepting the British reparations agenda without offering Herriot any substantive guarantees in return. Had Herriot become 'easy prey' to the 'predator' MacDonald?[87]

In certain respects, Britain indeed tightened the screws on France. Under Snowden, who opposed reparations on principle, the Treasury stepped up its

[81] Herriot (1924), pp. 559–60.   [82] *JOC, Débats*, 17 June 1924, pp. 2305ff.
[83] Crewe to MacDonald, 25 May 1924, FO 371/9843: C 8508/8509/8510/G.
[84] Herriot statement in the *Chambre*, 19 June 1924, *JOC*, pp. 2340ff.
[85] Crewe to MacDonald, 3 June 1924; Phipps to MacDonald, 17 June 1924, MacDonald Papers, MDP 30/69/94, nos. 347, 383.
[86] MacDonald to Crewe, 17 April 1924, FO 800/218/228a; Crewe to MacDonald, 28 January 1924, MacDonald Papers, MDP 30/69/94, no. 55; Kellogg to Hughes, 16 April 1924, NA RG 59 462.00 R296/271.
[87] Cf. Schuker (1976), pp. 237ff, 256ff; Adamthwaite (1995), p. 103.

debt demands vis-à-vis Paris while downplaying its interest in reparation payments.[88] London was also less willing than ever to contemplate any alliance guarantees. But if one asks what impact MacDonald's diplomacy had not only on Anglo-French relations but also European international politics, a different picture emerges.

Given France's acute financial crisis in late spring of 1924, not inconceivable was a scenario in which Anglo-American financiers would have left the French government with no choice but to accept their conditions *without* political negotiations. Likewise, Germany might have been pressured into accepting the Dawes plan through a quasi-ultimatum. This might have rendered possible its formal implementation; yet it would hardly have made for a widely acceptable and legitimate way of ending the Franco-German crisis. In a wider perspective, it would have thwarted a transformation of European politics from coercion to negotiation. This latter path could only be cleared through an international conference between the western powers and Germany. However unsatisfactory to France, without the reassurance MacDonald gave Herriot, ensuring his participation on terms bearable for French public opinion, no reparations conference might have been convened at all. As significantly, the Chequers and *Quai d'Orsay* summits set the essential political framework for the London talks.

As Britain's ambassador in Paris, Crewe, had predicted, Herriot arrived at Chequers intent on abandoning not only Poincaré's hostility towards England but also his Ruhr policy.[89] Accompanied only by the Foreign Ministry's political director Peretti, and his *chef de cabinet* Gaston Bergery, he hoped to win British support for cardinal French demands on sanctions and political guarantees; and he thought that he had achieved this. In his interpretation, he and MacDonald had resolved to seek a reparations agreement on the basis of Versailles and without infringing France's prerogatives to determine when and on what conditions to terminate the Ruhr occupation.[90]

By contrast, MacDonald thought that he had essentially convinced Herriot to accept Britain's set of priorities and ground-rules for the envisaged conference. This optimism was premature. A further round of Anglo-French negotiations was needed to attain not only Herriot's consent but also a modicum of domestic support for his new conciliatory course. In substance, though, what MacDonald cabled to Britain's ambassador in Rome, Ronald Grahame, on 29 June, would not be altered thereafter. The main result of Chequers had been

---

[88] Lampson memorandum to Niemeyer, 30 June 1924; Niemeyer to Foreign Office, 4 July 1924, FO 371/9749: C 10426/70/18, C 10720/70/18.

[89] Crewe to MacDonald, 25 May 1924, FO 371/9843: C 8508/8509/8510/G; Herriot letter, 20 July 1924, MAE, PA-AP 89, Herriot, no. 23; Suarez (1932), pp. 18ff.

[90] 'Plan Herriot', 21 June 1924, Herriot Papers.

the agreement to convene 'a small allied conference for the sole purpose of concerting the necessary arrangements for putting into operation the Dawes Report'. Questions of 'inter-allied debts' and the 'problem of security' would be 'taken up later'. Aided by Crowe's subtlety, the British premier had also won Herriot's approval on the form of the envisaged settlement. Its 'instrument' was to be a 'protocol', not an officious treaty, 'to avoid any appearance of wishing to amend the treaty of Versailles'. Behind the diplomatic wording, however, MacDonald, Crowe and Snowden by now unanimously agreed on the need to go beyond the treaty system of 1919 in practice.[91]

The first task of the conference would be to decide the question 'who is to be the authority to declare that there has been flagrant [German] failure' to pay and to impose appropriate sanctions. Crucially, in accord with Hughes and the American bankers MacDonald held that this 'duty' could no longer 'properly be entrusted to the Reparations Commission'. Re-asserting his long-term objective to revitalise the League, the British premier had proposed that it should be entrusted to the financial committee of the League.[92]

The second conference task on which Britain had obtained Herriot's consent concerned satisfactory guarantees for the crucial Dawes loan. Here, MacDonald established an important link: that between the loan's flotation and France's withdrawal from the Ruhr. Anticipating Morgan's position, he insisted that US financiers would not give any credits unless German sovereignty over the Ruhr was restored. MacDonald told Herriot that, should Germany adamantly refuse payments, nothing short of renewed war could force it. Continuing an 'aggressive occupation', however, could only prove counterproductive, further inciting German nationalists against the Marx government. Herriot conceded that Poincaré's policy could not be upheld: France would evacuate its forces, yet only to the extent that Germany fulfilled its obligations. Although this remained a contentious issue, Chequers here set an important precedent.[93]

To ease Herriot's acceptance of this diplomatic reversal, MacDonald agreed to issue a joint communiqué stressing Germany's obligation to complete disarmament in accordance with Versailles and to accept a general allied inspection.[94] Yet Britain refused to make further concessions either on war-debts or security. MacDonald emphasised that his hands were tied domestically – he could not offer France a military pact. MacDonald's arguments

---

[91] MacDonald to Grahame, 29 June 1924, *DBFP*, I, XXVI, no. 493. For Chequers see the FO minutes, 21–2 June 1924, FO 371/9749: C 10427/70/18. For Foreign Office plans to go beyond Versailles through an 'overhead agreement' see Central Department memorandum, 19 June 1924, FO 371/9748: C 10073/70/18.

[92] MacDonald to Grahame, 29 June 1924, *DBFP*, I, XXVI, no. 493, p. 733.

[93] Foreign Office minutes of the Chequers conversations, 21–2 June 1924, FO 371/9749: C 10427/70/18.

[94] For the French and British communiqués see Glasgow (1925), pp. 134–5.

anticipated those that Chamberlain would later use vis-à-vis Briand: military guarantees would not be supported by cabinet or public opinion; binding commitments would be rejected by the Dominions; and the British service ministries could not make the requisite military preparations. MacDonald also underlined, however, that for him the era of exclusive Anglo-French *ententes* had ended. He sought a novel 'moral collaboration' between both powers, essentially joint efforts to reinvigorate the League's collective apparatus. Herriot was hard put to sell this 'moral pact of continuous collaboration', only envisaged *after* a satisfactory reparations conference, at home.[95]

The German reaction to Chequers betrayed almost the opposite anxieties to those voiced in France, namely that the Anglo-French compromise constituted the revival of *entente* politics excluding Germany. In Stresemann's view, it had raised the danger that Germany would once again face a united allied front and further reparations ultimatums. To counter such tendencies, he moved swiftly to ensure, against the opposition of the DNVP and Seeckt, Berlin's acceptance of a general disarmament inspection.[96]

Just as swiftly, however, MacDonald reassured Stresemann that German concerns were unfounded. Chequers had not altered British policy. He confirmed that Germany could 'rightly expect to feel assured' that, in implementing the Dawes report, 'the allies [were] formally pledged to the withdrawal of the sanctions'. And he impressed on Herriot that retaining sanctions until Berlin met all conditions would 'gravely imperil' the 'whole prospect of a reparation settlement'.[97] Nor had Chequers altered MacDonald's hostility to the MICUM arrangements. While Herriot maintained Poincaré's policy of step-by-step prolongation, Stresemann sought their termination by 31 July, and he could count on British support.[98] The London conference finally closed this chapter of French aspirations to control Germany.

Thus MacDonald's assertive policy towards France always had a marked German dimension. As he had 'suuggested' at Chequers, a principal purpose of the planned conference was that once inter-allied agreement had been reached 'Germany should be invited to attend, not in order to be confronted with a document definitely settled' but 'to meet the allies in . . . negotiation'.[99] In

---

[95] Foreign Office minutes of the Chequers conversations, 21–2 June 1924, FO 371/9749: C 10427/70/18; French and British communiqués, Glasgow (1925), pp. 134–5; Crewe to FO, 25 June 1924, FO 371/9818: C 100780/2048/18. For Herriot's defence of his 'concessions' at Chequers see Herriot (1948), II, pp. 138ff.

[96] Hoesch to Stresemann, 27 June 1924, *ADAP*, A, X, no. 160; Stresemann statement, 29 June 1924, *ADAP*, A, X, no. 164.

[97] MacDonald to Crewe, 2 July 1924, *DBFP*, I, XXVI, no. 500, p. 742.

[98] German note, 4 July 1924, *ADAP*, A, X, no. 175; MacDonald to German Foreign Ministry (undated), PA, 9426H/3657/271242–4.

[99] MacDonald to Grahame, 29 June 1924, *DBFP*, I, XXVI, no. 493.

fact, Chequers opened the first real window of opportunity for Germany's 'return' to the international system since the Genoa conference, and a better one at that.

In the aftermath of the Anglo-French summit, it was Crowe who transformed the concessions that Britain had wrung from Herriot into a firm conference-platform. Did the under-secretary 'overreach' himself by pressing France to accept Britain's terms without further delay?[100] Not quite. Crowe favoured using the Dawes report as a vehicle not to alter the treaty of 1919 but to supersede it in practice. He sought to seize the opportunity afforded by Herriot to wrest control over postwar politics from France, which could not be achieved without America's financial leverage. Like MacDonald, Crowe was eager to strip the Reparations Commission, the main instrument of French assertion since 1919, of its authority under the Dawes regime. Yet he also considered it politically expedient vis-à-vis Paris not to seek, in 'appearance', 'a treaty explicitly modifying the Treaty of Versailles'.[101]

In June 1924, there was doubtless a British tendency to promise all things to all sides, yet put France off on security and guarantees, to realise MacDonald's conference plan. British diplomats had become impatient following highly frustrating postwar relations with France, culminating in Poincaré's Ruhr intervention.[102] To be sure, Britain's distrust was equalled if not exceeded by persisting French *ressentiments* towards an elusive British *entente* partner. Most profoundly, however, MacDonald's and Crowe's assertiveness showed how necessary they considered, at this juncture, a fundamental change of postwar politics. Ever more pronounced became what French ambassador Saint-Aulaire described as 'a growing tendency . . . to treat France and Germany on the same footing as regards security'.[103] This applied even more to Britain's first priority – to implement the Dawes plan.

As the French ministerial crisis following Chequers revealed, MacDonald's original assessment of Herriot's domestic strength had been mistaken. He was lambasted by the conservative *Bloc National* for having given up French essentials without winning any satisfactory British guarantees.[104] Yet MacDonald drew consequences to salvage the Dawes process, which crucially depended on its legitimation in France and, more immediately, Herriot's political survival.

[100] Thus Schuker (1976), p. 257.

[101] Crowe drafts for conference invitation to France and other powers, prepared before Chequers, FO371/9748: C10070/70/18; Crowe to Kellogg, 24 June 1924, *DBFP*, I, XXVI, no. 493.

[102] See notably Crowe memorandum, 19 February 1924, FO 371/9825: C 2900/G.

[103] Saint-Aulaire to French Foreign Ministry, 24 March 1924, MAE, Série Europe, Grande-Bretagne, no. 71.

[104] Crewe to MacDonald, 4 July 1924, FO 371/9846: C 10719/10193/18; Herrick to Hughes, 5 July 1924, NA RG 59 462.00 R296/399.

His visit to Paris in early July was more than a 'rescue mission' for the French premier. It rescued the Dawes settlement as such.[105]

On 8 July, once more seconded by Crowe, MacDonald met Herriot, this time backed not only by Peretti but also the reparations specialist Jacques Seydoux. In MacDonald's words, their main purpose was to find a 'new and temporary formula' sufficient to ensure parliamentary support for Herriot 'even if both of them knew that it was not workable'.[106] The *Quai d'Orsay* had prepared conference proposals reinforcing the position of the RepCo and blocking any alterations of the Versailles treaty. These also stressed what France expected from Britain. Apart from debt relief, this was chiefly a mutual security pact akin to what Briand had vainly sought from Lloyd George at the 1922 Cannes conference.[107]

Yet MacDonald refused to cede any substantial ground on either debts or security; and Britain would essentially have its way. He insisted that a new reparations 'protocol' not altering but complementing the Versailles treaty would be indispensable, and the only way to secure America's backing, on which the conference's success depended. It was 'necessary to give the United States every satisfaction and to interest them so that they will be ready to join with us'. While acknowledging Herriot's domestic challenges, MacDonald also argued that it was in France's own interest to avoid a reparations 'ultimatum', noting that '[i]f we impose on Germany a signature . . . by *force majeure* . . . the agreement thus obtained will have little value'. For the German government would then be unable to implement accords which required a two-thirds majority in the German parliament.[108] MacDonald thus pursued what Hughes, Herriot and Stresemann practised as well. He invoked genuinely perceived, yet tactically exaggerated, domestic preoccupations of his own and other governments to accomplish his aims.

Under British pressure, Herriot avowed that he still sought an understanding with Germany, not 'an ultimatum'. Yet, in line with French policy since 1919, and seconded by Peretti, he insisted that first the Anglo-French *entente* had to be strengthened to prevent Germany from using the expert scheme to drive 'a wedge' into the Versailles sytem. For this 'might open the door' to further revisions and thus, inevitably, war.[109] For France, the reparations

---

[105] MacDonald minute, 5 July 1924, FO 371/9846: C 10657/10193/18; Lamont to Morrow, 11 July 1924, Lamont file, Morrow Papers; Crewe to MacDonald, 7 July 1924, FO 371/9849: C 10794/10794/18; *Hansard*, 5th series, cols. 1753–4.

[106] See MacDonald's confidential statements to Lamont, Lamont to Morrow, 11 July 1924, Lamont file, Morrow Papers.

[107] Minutes of Anglo-French deliberations at the *Quai d'Orsay*, 8 July 1924, *DBFP*, I, XXVI, no. 507.

[108] MacDonald to Herriot, 8 July 1924, *DBFP*, I, XXVI, no. 507.

[109] Herriot to MacDonald, 8 July 1924, *DBFP*, I, XXVI, no. 507.

question remained essentially 'as much a military as a political problem' – and only secondarily a financial question. Herriot shared MacDonald's distinction between the forces of a 'good', republican Germany and their nationalist opponents. But he was understandably more anxious lest the latter ultimately reap the benefits from concessions made to the former.[110] This – both in its French and German dimensions – remained a critical dilemma facing Anglo-American policymakers after 1923. Yet, while Washington mostly downplayed it, London by then regarded the invocation of *'le danger allemand'* increasingly as self-serving French dramatisation.[111]

MacDonald thus stuck to his guns and Labour's internationalist premises, finally suggesting the 'closest of alliances, that which is not written on a sheet of paper', nor based on bilateral guarantees. He argued that 'if Germany declared war on France in regard to reparations this would be in reality war against the Allies because we are all concerned, even the United States, in the execution of the Dawes plan'.[112] In effect, both British and American decision-makers sought to overcome European insecurity by fostering this kind of interdependence. Ultimately, MacDonald foresaw a long and arduous process of changing mentalities; and it was the duty of British and French statesmen – just like German leaders – to foster it. To find common ground it was necessary to begin 'by educating public opinion in our two countries' with regard to security.[113] The *Quai d'Orsay* meeting ended with a number of formula compromises, in Crowe's verdict 'to calm down the French', which omitted or fudged on the hardest questions awaiting resolution – notably those of sanctions and France's withdrawal from the Ruhr. But the overall framework that Britain desired was left intact.[114]

Thus, Britain and France had forged only a minimal consensus yet it was the necessary compromise to open the door to the London conference. Policies *began* to converge but were still markedly apart. Britain's emphasis on accommodation on the path to a sustainable settlement with Germany still contrasted with the French emphasis on containment and control. Significantly, Herriot no longer agreed to signing a protocol with the German government; Berlin was merely to be notified of the allied agreements. Further, the Reparations Commission was to retain its powers to declare default. MacDonald reckoned that these questions had to be resolved in the framework of multilateral rather

---

[110] Statements by Herriot and Peretti, 8 July 1924, *DBFP*, I, XXVI, no. 507.
[111] MacDonald minutes, 18 April and 15 July 1924, FO 371/9750: C 6157/2977/18, C 11050/70/18.
[112] MacDonald to Herriot, 8 July 1924, *DBFP*, I, XXVI, no. 507.
[113] Minutes of Anglo-French deliberations at the *Quai d'Orsay*, 8 July 1924, *DBFP*, I, XXVI, no. 507.
[114] Franco-British memorandum of 9 July, 1924, cabinet files, Cmd 2191; Sthamer telegram, 12 July 1924, PA, 3398/1736/D739955-8.

than bilateral negotiations. And, as he told the Commons on 10 July, he was confident that British mediation and American pressure could combine to resolve them in their favour.[115]

Britain, the United States and Germany: systemic shifts, parallel interests – and their limits

Washington welcomed the outcome of the Anglo-French negotiations. Hughes remained wary lest Britain's political concessions to France might endanger what he sought, an unimpeded realisation of the expert scheme. Nevertheless, he backed MacDonald's course. His positions were reinforced by the powerful coalition of Anglo-American financiers that, led by Norman and J.P. Morgan, were now making their harsher criteria for supporting the proposed settlement known.

In the last month preceding the London conference, Hughes acted as a distinctly detached arbiter. He had pressed the Europeans to remove all political obstacles barring an implementation his design. And he sought to bring the powerful influence of US bankers to bear on the European situation.[116] Anglo-American co-operation thus took the form of a subtle yet effective interplay between Hughes, the Morgan partners, MacDonald and Norman.[117] As MacDonald had signalled before Chequers, he realised that the United States, 'not being party in the Versailles treaty', could not assume formal responsibilities and must not be embroiled 'unnecessarily in the European matter'.[118] Yet he relied on Hughes' influence.

By July 1924, significant parallels between British and American objectives and methods regarding the Dawes process had emerged, shaping European politics. Common to both approaches was their aim to recast the postwar constellation. This hinged on satisfying French interests while relocating the power to determine the treatment of Germany from France to Britain and, 'informally', the United States. It crystallised in the common aim of depriving the Reparations Commission of its authority to declare default and decree sanctions. It was neither in Britain's nor in America's interest to retain an institution that France could use in future to challenge the Dawes regime and provoke another cycle of reparations conflicts.

The best guarantee against such an eventuality, as both sides agreed, was to transfer the RepCo's authority to a new decisionmaking body, created

---

[115] MacDonald statement in the Commons, 10 July 1924, *Hansard*, 5th series, cols. 2464–7.
[116] Hughes to Kellogg, 24 June 1924, *FRUS 1924*, II, pp. 32–3; Herrick to Hughes, 5 July 1924, NA RG 59 462.00 R296/399; Morrow memorandum, 12 July 1924; Lamont to Morrow, 11 July 1924, Lamont Papers, TWL 176/12.
[117] For a detailed account see Schuker (1976), pp. 289–94.
[118] Kellogg to Hughes, 18 June 1924, Kellogg Papers.

explicitly under the Dawes scheme. Predictably, the US secretary of state favoured using the leverage of high finance to achieve this core political aim.[119] MacDonald essentially accepted Bradbury's interpretation that the Dawes report would not merely supplement but *de facto* replace the reparations clauses of 1919.[120] On 15 July, he thus adopted Lamont's proposal that the new central authority, to be jointly controlled by British and American representatives, should be the Transfer Committee that the expert report itself recommended.[121] MacDonald wrote to Lamont that he could use this proposal to bring 'Herriot and his henchmen' to London 'in the proper attitude'.[122]

The underlying Anglo-American interest, then, was to use the London conference to set international politics on a course of peaceful change. This superseded all efforts at *status quo* preservation first pursued by Poincaré, then – after Chequers – by Herriot. It furthered Germany's agenda for a modification of Versailles, if not with the swiftness Stresemann desired. In essential points, therefore, a marked congruence of interests between America, Britain and Germany had emerged. Yet, from Hughes' standpoint, this congruence was less far-reaching than either MacDonald or Stresemann anticipated. And it did not pre-ordain the outcome of London. To begin with, even by early July Hughes was still reluctant to pledge even informal US participation at the envisaged conference. And to a considerable extent Hughes had to be prodded by Anglo-American financiers, notably Morgan, Lamont and Norman, to step up his support for a comprehensive international summit. J.P. Morgan refused to step into the breach that Washington's refusal to mediate left. He pressed European statesmen finally to prepare the political ground for the reparations settlement. Morgan & Co. would not enter 'into the breach between England and France and Germany, before they agree among themselves concerning fundamental questions'.[123]

Hughes essentially shared this view. He simply refused to commit the Republican administration, even informally, until Anglo-French negotiations had established that the conference would have genuine prospects of success. At the same time, though, he had long planned to dispatch Kellogg as America's 'unofficial representative' once this had been ensured.[124] The State Department thus in fact prepared for diplomatic engagement in London.

---

[119] Morrow memorandum, 12 July 1924; Lamont to Morrow, 11 July 1924, Lamont Papers, TWL 176/12.

[120] Bradbury to Crowe, 8 July 1924, FO 371/9750: C 11050/70/18.

[121] MacDonald minute, 15 July 1924, FO 371/9750: C 11050/70/18.

[122] For MacDonald's statement see Lamont & Grenfell to Morgan and Morrow, 10 July 1924, Lamont Papers, TWL 176/12.

[123] J.P. Morgan & Co. to Morgan, Grenfell & Co., 2 July 1924, Lamont Papers, TWL 176/11.

[124] See Beerits memoranda, 'The Dawes Plan', Hughes Papers, 172/27; *FRUS 1924*, II, pp. 24–32; Grew Diary, 14 July 1924, Grew Papers.

Already on 24 June Hughes had laconically characterised the main 'object-ive' for 'forthcoming conference' as 'the promotion of economic recuperation and recovery of just claims against Germany in such a manner as will render unnecessary imposition of sanctions as have been imposed in the past'. Funda-mentally, the secretary agreed with Morrow and Morgan that a successful implementation of the Dawes plan could only be assured if France and Britain committed themselves to guarantee 'the political independence, the territorial integrity, and the sovereignty' of Germany. Hughes thus regarded an early termination of France's Ruhr occupation as desirable.[125] Nevertheless, as long as an end to the MICUM contracts was assured, resolving the larger Ruhr question was only a secondary priority for Washington. Until the opening of the London conference, it was clearly subordinated to the desire for a swift implementation of the expert plan.

Like Hoover, and more than US bankers, Hughes counted on the dynamics of depoliticisation. Once the Dawes plan was put into effect, political obstacles could be removed under improved conditions – or they would fall to the wayside by the sheer force of economic momentum. Against this background, America's interest in supporting Stresemann's second cardinal aim, and MacDonald's underlying objective, was even less pronounced.[126] Washington sought to foster Germany's political rehabilitation, not least to legitimate the Dawes regime in Germany. Yet in view of Herriot's embattled position, the State Department favoured opening the conference as an inter-allied meeting. To be avoided at all cost was its immediate breakdown due to a Franco-German éclat. Instead, Hughes authorised Logan to assure Stresemann that he and Anglo-American bankers would act as 'guardians of German interests', essentially by implementing America's 'terms of reference'.[127] In this sense, in marked contrast to British policy, the American approach only indirectly buttressed a more integrative process of European stabilisation 'with the participation and thus equal treatment' of a heretofore isolated Germany.[128] The decisive impetus in this direction would have to be given by MacDonald.

---

[125] Hughes to Kellogg, 24 June 1924, *FRUS 1924*, II, p. 32; Hughes to Howard, 1 May 1924, NA RG 59 462.00 R296/262; Morrow to Hughes, 12 July 1924, Lamont Papers, TWL 176/13; Hughes to Laboulaye, 9 May 1924, Hughes Papers.

[126] Hughes to Laboulaye, 9 May 1924, Hughes Papers; Robinson to Hughes, 8 July 1924, NA RG 59 462.00 R296/407.

[127] Logan statements, 4 June 1924, Stresemann (1932), I, p. 415.

[128] Link (1970), p. 262.

10 The first 'real' peace settlement after World War I

The London agreement of 1924 and the consequences of the 'economic peace'

The outcome of the London conference was already widely perceived in the summer of 1924 as a veritable *caesura* both in European and transatlantic relations. Yet the question as to precisely what kind of *caesura* it constituted has remained decidedly controversial. Previous accounts have uncovered countless nuances, conflicts and reversals marking the intense negotiations between the 'anodyne' opening speeches of 16 July and invocations of a new international spirit on 16 August 1924.[1] Yet they have also drawn a markedly polarised picture of what shifts in the post-Versailles constellation the conference brought about.

Most influentially, London has been interpreted as the first high-point of short-sighted Anglo-American appeasement after 1919 that, with the pursuit of narrow financial interests, eroded the Versailles system. Anglo-American policymakers and financiers allegedly forced a settlement on France that undermined not only French but all western possibilities to prevent a perilous resurgence of Germany. Accordingly, the agreement has been termed an unquestionable 'victory' for German revisionist policy – the stepping-stone for its attempts to alter not only the reparations clauses but also the wider *status quo* of Versailles.[2] Yet the London conference has also been called critical for a continued 'republican' policy of peaceful revision under Stresemann.[3] Can the outcome of London thus essentially be gauged in terms of Europe's balance of power – where Germany's position clearly improved? Or did it have a different, positive impact on Europe's stabilisation in the 1920s?

In 1924, midway through the negotiations, Herriot – alluding to Bismarck's victory of 1871 – indeed dreaded a second 'Treaty of Frankfurt' for France.[4]

---

[1] The most detailed accounts, especially from the French perspective, are Schuker (1976), pp. 295–382; Bariéty (1977), pp. 602–732. See also Link (1970), pp. 260–306.
[2] See Schuker (1976), pp. 295ff, 383–4.
[3] Cf. Baechler (1996), pp. 518–41.
[4] Phipps to FO, 31 July 1924, FO 371/9863: C 12256/11642/18.

He betrayed a sentiment then still shared above all by the Poincarist right. Yet he would thereafter defend the accords as an inescapable compromise with Germany and the Anglo-American powers.[5] In fact, particularly in Britain, the United States and Germany, yet also in many French quarters, the London settlement soon came to be seen as marking not only the end of the crisis-ridden postwar years and the onset of a period of international, and domestic, consolidation. In a larger sense, it also appeared to bring the – belated – dawning of a distinctly 'American peace' in Europe.[6] Hughes indeed claimed the 'peace of London' as a success of US foreign policy.[7] In Snowden's verdict, by contrast, it was Britain that had essentially brokered what marked nothing less than a 'new deal' for Europe. The Labour government had managed to 'co-opt' the financial prowess of the new world to redress the instability of the old.[8] Is this a more apposite appraisal? Or was the London conference a different *caesura* altogether?

The London settlement indeed marked an end-point, yet *not* the end of prospective attempts to bolster French security after 1919. Rather, the conference was the end-point of the first formative process of systemic change in postwar international relations – and the starting-point for the emergence of a viable Euro-Atlantic peace system. This development had originated with the Ruhr crisis and the Anglo-American return to Europe in the autumn of 1923. Thus refocused, an analysis placing the London conference in a wider historical perspective can re-assess the critical changes in the rules and practices of Euro-Atlantic politics that occurred in the summer of 1924.

Not least, the conference revealed how far British and American policymakers were willing, and able, to shape the process of European consolidation politically. It showed how far they could assert political priorities, such as an even-handed Ruhr compromise, not only vis-à-vis France and Germany but also Anglo-American high finance. Essentially, this permits a re-appraisal of the question: what mode of international negotiations made the outcome of 1924 possible – and what this portended for European stability. Did the turning-of-the-tide ultimately result from financial pressures exerted by Anglo-American bankers? Or did a different, more far-reaching, reconfiguration take place?

The London settlement did not signify a second 'Treaty of Frankfurt' for France. In many ways, it represented a tactical defeat for French policy, which had to make difficult adjustments under immense domestic and international pressure. And it was doubtless originally regarded as a defeat in France – yet in

---

[5] Herriot speech in the *Sénat*, 26 August 1924, *JOS*, pp. 1314–23.

[6] Kellogg to State Department, 16 August 1924; 'America's Part in the "Peace of London"', *Literary Digest*, 30 August 1924; *Le Matin*, 7 August 1924; *München-Augsburger Abendzeitung*, 7 July 1924, NA RG 59 420.00 R296/508, 507, 488.

[7] Hughes to Kellogg; Kellogg, to Coolidge, 16 August 1924, NA RG 59 462.00 R296/507, 509.

[8] Snowden statement, Imperial Conference, 15 August 1924, CAB 29/105.

fact neither Herriot nor Poincaré but only a minority of nationalist elites and public opinion-makers took this line.[9] The London accords were, inescapably, a set of complex compromises. More importantly, however, they indeed marked a 'new deal' in a forward-looking sense, a lease of life for Europe's reconstruction in the 1920s. This 'deal' was precisely *not* the product of zero-sum diplomacy. German gains did not equal French losses, even though this only became more obvious over time, notably with the Locarno pact. Hence, not only French security and reparations politics but also Europe's financial and political consolidation were predicated no longer on Germany's containment but on its inclusion into a new international system. In its – 'nascent'– framework, settlements were reached, under Anglo-American auspices, through mutual compromise rather than decree. London was thus seminal in laying the international groundwork for Weimar Germany's accommodation with the west.

What was the specific contribution of British policymakers to this momentous development? What part did their American counterparts play? The settlement of 1924 was inherently a co-operative rather than a unilateral achievement. It was not shaped by one decisive force, neither the financial leverage of US financiers nor the informal power wielded by Washington. Rather, it was the initiation of an *Anglo-American* peace, essentially achieved through an intensification of what had already propelled change since October 1923: the novel interplay between Britain, the politically pivotal power, and America, the not only in financial but also in political terms indispensable underwriter of European peaceful change. This co-operation would not again reach such intensity in shaping the international system until the 1940s. It prepared the ground, and created the need, for the Locarno pact. Yet the London talks also highlighted essential limits of British and American policies. Neither London nor Washington was prepared, or in a position, to extend formal political guarantees to buttress the new reparations regime. Further, it was still unclear to what extent British and American policymakers had the means to 'solve' Europe's underlying, and still unsettled, security question: how far they could create a security architecture for Europe's fledgling peace.

London saw innumerable tactical manoeuvres and hard choices for both France and Germany. Yet it was not a juncture where such tactics or power-political manoeuvres proved decisive. More formative were Anglo-American reorientations. Essentially political, they set the rules and created the conditions under which French and German leaders could finally be brought to the post-World War I negotiating-table. The London negotiations were thus not least significant because they witnessed, as if under a magnifying glass, the shift

---

[9] See the French parliamentary debates on London, *JOC*, 21–3 August 1924, pp. 2953ff.

from a postwar period of enforcement and fragmentation to a period of bargaining and accommodation – above all the international accommodation of Germany.

Long prevalent has been the view that the London accords were primarily determined by the leverage of Anglo-American bankers, its decisive figures being 'non-political' actors like J.P. Morgan, Lamont and Norman.[10] By contrast, the role that official policymakers played has been rated rather low.[11] But it should be the focus of a balanced assessment. Hughes – as 'informal arbiter' on the essential margins of the negotiations – Kellogg, who headed the American delegation, MacDonald and Snowden – all had to perform one essential political task: the mediation between agendas that often were only painfully compatible: their own, those of France and Germany and the financial interests of the Anglo-American bankers.

Undoubtedly, financial pressure weighed heavily in London, but its effect was primarily catalytic. More substantive change stemmed from a more general shift: the establishment of new rules of international politics. Ultimately, MacDonald, Hughes and Kellogg were the only actors who could forge a comprehensive settlement. It not only had to be sustainable in financial terms. It also had to be politically acceptable not only in France but also in Germany, strengthening the domestic standing of *both* conciliatory governments, Marx's and Herriot's. At one point, Lamont felt obliged to remind Morgan that the governments had not primarily convened in London 'for the purpose of "getting the new money"' essential for the Dawes scheme. Rather, their task was to make complex political trade-offs.[12] In fact, more than anything else the London agreements became an accumulation of such trade-offs.

The principal questions of London

The sea-change of July–August 1924 will be traced by examining how, and how far, what had emerged as the three main questions of London, and Germany's relations with the west, could be settled. The first was the sanction question. It overshadowed the conference's first, inter-allied phase between 15 July and 2 August. Concretely, the dispute centred on the future authority of the Reparations Commission and the way in which Germany's creditors would in future sanction German default. In a larger sense, it pertained to the future of the Versailles system, France's leverage within it and the transatlantic

[10] Kellogg to Hughes, 30 July 1924, NA RG 59 462.00 R296/463.
[11] In part, this echoes the verdict of contemporary financiers. See Lamont to J.P. Morgan & Co., 15 July 1924, Lamont Papers, TWL 176/14. Cf. Hogan (1991), p. 69; Burk (1991), pp. 145–6.
[12] Lamont to J.P. Morgan & Co., 21 July 1924, Lamont Papers, TWL 176/17.

power configuration. To be decided was who would become the main arbiter in the core question of postwar politics – reparations.[13]

The second was the question of Germany's participation at the conference and, more broadly, its reintegration and *recognition* as an 'equal power' within the international system. To be decided was whether the allies would merely solve concrete 'technical' problems amongst themselves or whether London would usher in qualitative change. This question remained contentious until the very end of the first conference phase. Its resolution paved the way for the presence of a German delegation during the second, 'integrative' phase between 6 and 16 August.

What dominated this last phase and tested Franco-German readiness to compromise for the first time since 1918 was the third principal question of London. It was the question when and under what conditions France would evacuate the Ruhr as part of a reparations agreement. At stake was the territorial *status quo* in central Europe and, with it, the future Franco-German power constellation. Essentially, though, not only a realisation of the Dawes scheme but also the peaceful transformation of the Versailles system hinged on settling all three of these questions.

Dramatis personae – the protagonists and their principal aims

It seems noteworthy that the balance of influence and means to shape outcomes was somewhat distorted in London. Due to Hughes' decision to direct the American delegation from 'afar', MacDonald assumed not only the conference's formal presidency but also its overall supervision. With the help of the American bankers, the Coolidge administration could still exert a strong influence. The indispensability of America's financial-cum-political power remained unaltered, and was never far from the consciousness of all conference delegates. Nevertheless, British diplomacy capitalised on its home advantage.

The British perspective

The British delegation was best positioned to play a weighty role in determining concrete results during the London proceedings, in fact a weightier role than Britain's political-cum-financial clout had warranted in the earlier stages of the Dawes process. For MacDonald, the very fact that the conference could be convened was already a success. The very dynamics afforded by Britain's direction and America's presence, he reckoned, would greatly expedite the desired moderation of French policy and recasting of relations with Germany.

---

[13] Cf. Link (1978), p. 75.

This desire was in effect shared by all major parties and pressure-groups in Britain.[14] Aided by Crowe, the prime minister could rely on the Foreign Office's meticulous preparations and he closely consulted the Treasury, where Niemeyer offered his expertise.[15]

MacDonald's strategic aim was not merely the political endorsement of a financial programme. He sought, with the termination of France's sanction regime, a political breakthrough not only in the reparations question but also spurring a substantive change in postwar politics.[16] As its end, he envisaged a settlement backed by the United States and reached *with* Germany, which required inviting Berlin to 'meet the allies' for 'negotiation'.[17] Thus, he ultimately sought to foster a political compromise on the most contentious issue: the Ruhr evacuation. In the words of Maurice Hankey, who became MacDonald's 'right hand' during the proceedings, Britain's primary *tactical* task was once more 'to get a real concession' from France on all important questions but 'to save Herriot's face'.[18] Yet MacDonald equally strove to assure Germany through French concessions. The Marx cabinet also had to 'save its face' against nationalist opposition and, most importantly, to carry all Dawes legislation through the *Reichstag*.[19]

In his bid to 'put the plan through' in a balanced manner, the British premier was often more hindered than helped by his chancellor Snowden and Montagu Norman. Both came to play forceful roles. Yet, in Kellogg's view, they were 'prematurely interjecting the loan question and the so called bankers' position into the general political discussions'.[20] In the final phase, both openly challenged MacDonald's search for a Franco-German Ruhr agreement because they strongly leaned towards Germany and put harsh pressure on Herriot.[21]

In favour of abolishing reparations altogether, Snowden fundamentally resisted French claims. He insisted on ending all French encroachments on Germany to revive Euro-Atlantic trade.[22] Norman steadfastly maintained that a loan would only be forthcoming once investors were assured that the

---

[14] See 'London Conference: Notes of Meetings of the British Empire Delegation, 11 July – 15 August', CAB 29/105.

[15] See Foreign Office memoranda during the conference, FO 371/9751–5.

[16] MacDonald, opening speech, 15 July 1924, NA RG 59 R296/465.

[17] MacDonald to Grahame, 23 June 1924, *DBFP*, I, XXVI, no. 493; MacDonald to Crewe, 1 July 1924, MacDonald Papers, MDP 30/69/94, no. 179.

[18] Hankey to Smuts, 17 July 1924, Hankey Papers.

[19] D'Abernon to MacDonald, 4 August 1924, MacDonald Papers, MDP 30/69/94, no. 346.

[20] Kellogg to Hughes, 30 July 1924, NA RG 59 462.00 R296/463.

[21] See also for the following, 'Notes of Meetings of the British Empire Delegation, 11 July – 15 August', CAB 29/105.

[22] Snowden (1934), pp. 528–9, 778–9; Stresemann note, 12 August 1924, Stresemann (1932), I, p. 488.

Reparations Commission no longer served as an instrument of French policy and that the Ruhr occupation would be terminated immediately.[23] He exerted a palpable influence on J.P. Morgan and, ultimately, the American conference agenda as a whole.

Washington's perspective

The London conference saw the first formal representation of the United States in Europe since the Paris peace talks. As we have seen, this was not an *ad hoc* measure. Originally, Hughes and Coolidge had envisaged merely sending unofficial observers, both because they deemed the financial pressure on France to accept the Dawes plan overwhelming and because they desired to avoid having to justify fresh 'entanglements' in Europe vis-à-vis Congress. The difficult Anglo-French negotiations of early July and MacDonald's prodding, however, spurred the realisation that a more direct diplomatic impetus from Washington would be required to reach a sustainable settlement.

Hughes dispatched a delegation well instructed to fulfil the task of aloof mediation that he had assigned to it.[24] Apart from Kellogg, it comprised two key agents of US policy in Europe, Young and, notably, Logan. Tacitly, however, the Coolidge administration sought to leave the difficult task of political brokerage largely to the British government. While not overly bothered with technical nuances, Kellogg acted as a valuable moderating influence, notably on the Ruhr question.[25] At first, however, Logan became the spokesman of US policy, particularly on the thorny sanctions question.[26] He was flanked by Young, who essentially continued the search for compromise he had already pursued during the Dawes deliberations. Striving to see a way out for France in the sanctions question, he ultimately had to cede to the bankers' intransigence.[27]

Essentially, Hughes had not changed his view that Washington's aims could be achieved most effectively by persisting with the informal statesmanship he had so successfully practised thus far. He set out by overseeing American strategy from Washington. From late July, however, he became a more engaged arbiter, first travelling to London, officially to address the annual convention of

---

[23] Norman memorandum, 15 July 1924, Lamont Papers, TWL 176/12.

[24] For the final decisionmaking process before London see *FRUS 1924*, II, pp. 24–32. Cf. Schuker (1976), p. 295.

[25] See Kellogg's reports, 16 July – 16 August 1924, NA RG 59 R296/428–507.

[26] Logan memorandum, 'The London Conference', 5 September 1924, Logan Papers.

[27] Young to Lamont, 22 July 1924, Lamont Papers, TWL 176/18; Young to Morgan, 4 August 1924, Young Papers, box R-16. Treasury Secretary Mellon provided further intermittent support.

the American Bar Association, then to Berlin.[28] As such, he made American influence felt through three channels: the official delegation; US bankers, above all J.P. Morgan and Lamont; and Ambassador Alanson Houghton, who was sent to Berlin to reassure a German government waiting to be called to London. Finally, in the decisive days of late July and early August, the secretary himself took up the task of mediation.[29]

The overriding purpose Hughes saw for the conference remained what he had outlined to Kellogg on 24 June.[30] He sought to ensure the finalisation of his 'depoliticisation' strategy. France had to guarantee that the Dawes plan could be implemented without *any* undesirable political interference and 'measures of compulsion'. Any political advances the negotiations might bring, whether Germany's international rehabilitation or Franco-German *rapprochement*, were secondary and a function of the plan's implementation.[31] As Hughes had told Laboulaye on 5 July, he deemed a German presence in London generally desirable, as it would help ensure that the Dawes scheme would be accepted by *all* sides. And he assured Stresemann that the American delegation would only endorse a settlement that Berlin 'would be willing to sign' as well. But Washington would support Germany's invitation only once the inter-allied differences had been settled.[32]

That Washington would officially underwrite the desired intergovernmental agreement was out of the question. Nor would the administration extend guarantees for the proposed Dawes loan. Nor, finally, would it *formally* accept to become the 'umpire' in the reparations question. Crucially, though, Hughes sought to alter the previous sanction mechanism under Versailles – even though, as will be seen, he did not make a complete replacement of the Reparations Commission a *conditio sine qua non*.

As a consequence of Hughes' informal approach, the Anglo-American bankers were granted the highest measure of direct influence on shaping an international settlement since the war – and to a degree unprecedented in European history. Yet their leverage was also used by MacDonald and Hughes to further their political objectives. In this respect, then, London marked a culmination of the interlocking processes of 'depoliticisation' and political accommodation that were altering the international system. This would prevail over France's attempts to uphold the order of Versailles in every critical aspect.

---

[28] See Beerits memoranda, 'The Dawes Plan', 'The European Trip of 1924', Hughes Papers, 172/27, 173/54.
[29] In the US press, this was clearly viewed as an official support for the Dawes settlement. See 'Hughes Tells Europe How Far We Can Go', *Literary Digest*, 2 August 1924.
[30] See *FRUS 1924*, II, pp. 32–5.
[31] Hughes instructions to Kellogg, 24 June 1924, *FRUS 1924*, II, pp. 32–3.
[32] Hughes memorandum, 5 July 1924, Hughes Papers.

The aims of the Anglo-American bankers

Significantly, while both the British and American governments were ready to countenance rather flexible compromises with France, the stance of key US financiers had become uncompromising by the time the conference opened. Their intransigence had a particular impact on the critical sanctions and evacuation questions. In early July, all Morgan partners had reached the consensus that the prospects for floating a German loan on the US financial market had greatly improved. What policymakers now had to achieve, and what bankers could only 'assist with', was to guarantee political stability and, notably, protection against any future French interference in the German economy.[33]

Morgan and Lamont had criticised MacDonald's concessions to Herriot in Paris, for they could revive French resistance against their demand to dethrone the Reparations Commission. Morgan still sought to further a lucrative reparations arrangement that would improve the European environment for future investments. But he feared that MacDonald might sacrifice the bankers' interests to achieve political accommodation with France.[34] Thus, he also remained even warier than Hughes of a German participation in the negotiations, fearing their breakdown through renewed Franco-German skirmishes. Like Norman, the Morgan partners argued that they could push through German interests far more effectively in the latter's absence.[35]

Lamont had on 12 July summarised J.P. Morgan's 'fundamentals' in a way that basically foreclosed any trade-offs with Paris. No loan under the Dawes plan would be 'acceptable to the American markets' if the Reparations Commission retained 'the power to declare default'. Instead, the Dawes plan's proposed Transfer Committee was to 'hold sole power of declaration as to German default'.[36]

Morgan himself still relied on Norman's political acumen. He thus quickly endorsed two essential demands the latter made on the eve of the negotiations. The first corresponded with Lamont's aim of shifting all sanction power to the Transfer Committee.[37] The second, however, extended the bankers' non-negotiable conditions significantly: France had to pledge to evacuate the Ruhr as soon as the Dawes plan was put into effect. All previous control mechanisms such as the Rhineland Commission and the Rhenish railway authority were to

[33] J.P. Morgan & Co. to Morgan, Grenfell & Co., 2 July 1924, Lamont Papers, TWL 176/11.
[34] Lamont to J.P. Morgan, 15 July 1924; J.P. Morgan to Grenfell, 15 July 1924, and 16 July 1924, Lamont Papers, TWL 176/14, 15.
[35] Bergmann report to German Foreign Ministry, 19 July 1924, PA, RM 5, vol. 1, II, no. 432.
[36] Lamont memorandum to MacDonald, 12 July 1924, Kellogg Papers.
[37] Norman memorandum, 15 July 1924, Lamont Papers, TWL 176/12.

be dismantled. Confidentially, Norman and Young had already informed *Reichsbank* president Schacht about these conditions on 15 July.[38]

The French position

Standing *pars pro toto* for France, Herriot has been portrayed as the almost 'tragic figure' of the London conference.[39] At the time, Kellogg held that the Herriot's 'personal inclination [was] to make a wide departure in his policy from the Poincaré thesis and practically accept the Dawes report'. Yet he was 'vacillating', 'timid concerning possible reaction in the French chamber'. The ambassador stressed that both he and MacDonald 'fully appreciate[d] the futility of pushing Herriot so far as to cause his being thrown out of office'. For this would '[wreck] the whole agreement because of its subsequent repudiation by the French Parliament'.[40]

Herriot was indeed unable to defend previous essentials of France's postwar policy. Yet, in view of the hardening Anglo-American pressure it has to be asked whether any French leader, however sophisticated his tactics, could have obtained a settlement strengthening France's status and security on the basis of Versailles. Could any have reinforced the RepCo's prerogatives, prolonged French control over the Ruhr – and Germany's isolation? This seems doubtful indeed. In short, France's positions were no longer tenable. By the very act of agreeing to the international conference, Herriot had embarked on a path of substantive change.

Herriot entered into negotiations on the assumption that, in the initial inter-allied framework, France could still redirect developments and reinforce the Versailles treaty.[41] In return for accepting the Dawes plan, France hoped to wring concessions from the Anglo-American governments and bankers – essentially in the form of loans, debt-relief and security commitments.[42] But Herriot had to realise that he was as mistaken in such hopes as Poincaré before him. Since Chequers, France's bargaining-position on all core questions – sanctions, evacuation and Germany's participation – had grown decidedly weaker. Nevertheless, France did not leave London 'defeated' but as signatory of a more than just face-saving compromise.

French dilemmas were aggravated by the fact that the delegation, always in close touch with the domestic expectations, was deeply divided over which course could save France from ignominy. More than once, the French premier

[38] Schacht to German Foreign Office, 15 July 1924, PA, RM 5, vol. 19, II, no. 411.
[39] Cf. Schuker (1976), pp. 298–300; Bariéty (1977), pp. 602ff. See against this Herriot's memoirs (1948), II, pp. 154ff.
[40] Kellogg to Hughes, 30 July 1924, NA RG 59 462.00 R296/463.
[41] Herriot opening statements, 15 July, NA RG 59 462.00 R296/462.
[42] Record of talks between MacDonald and Herriot, 24 July 1924, *DBFP*, I, XXVI, no. 517; Kellogg to Hughes, 30 July 1924, NA RG 59 462.00 R296/463.

was caught between the representatives of two fundamentally divergent responses to Anglo-American pressure: his finance minister, Clémentel, and his war minister, General Charles Nollet, the latter in Kellogg's judgement a 'reactionary' whose desertion would nonetheless be 'disastrous'.[43]

In short, Nollet invoked the overriding importance of national security. He thus strongly opposed the evacuation of the Ruhr, anticipating later French debates over the Rhineland. Nollet advocated a strategy of deceleration, using every conceivable leverage to retain control over the Ruhr. In particular, he wanted to make French concessions dependent not only on prompt German payments but also on Berlin's compliance regarding disarmament and military control. MacDonald had considerable difficulty in keeping French demands to this effect at bay.

Less popular in France, yet ultimately more influential, was Clémentel's sober, economically orientated approach. He assured Lamont in private that the Herriot government realised how 'disastrous' the impact of Poincaré's coercive policy had been not only for Germany but also for France. Clémentel underlined Paris' underlying desire to co-operate with Britain and America in reinstating Germany's economic and political integrity. He also stressed the French self-interest in creating safe conditions for Anglo-American investments under the Dawes scheme, as this was France's only hope of attracting its share of urgently needed capital.[44]

Overall, France faced an arduous re-adjustment process during the 1924 negotiations, an unavoidable struggle to adapt to the new ground-rules of peaceful change that London and Washington sought to introduce. This demanded a complete alteration of the bases of French security and self-assertion after the war: the abandonment of artificial hegemony and treaty 'execution' vis-à-vis Germany. This became the only way to improve relations with those powers that alone could provide the craved-for security – Britain – and indispensable resources – America.[45]

The German position

For Germany, the stakes at the London conference were at least as high as for France. This was reflected in Stresemann's open threat to resign should Germany be barred from attending.[46] For the outcome had to show whether

---

[43] Kellogg to Hughes, 30 July 1924, NA RG 59 462.00 R296/463. Cf. Saint-Aulaire (1953), pp. 718ff.

[44] Lamont obviously welcomed this. See Lamont to J.P. Morgan & Co., 20 July 1924, Lamont Papers, TWL 176/17.

[45] Herriot (1948), II, p. 154.

[46] Stresemann to Hoesch, 7 July 1924, PA, RM 5, vol. 19, II, no. 565; Phipps to MacDonald, 25 July 1924, *DBFP*, I, XXVI, no. 519. For the German perspective on the London conference see the documents on 'Die Londoner Konferenz', PA, Büro des Staatssekretärs, vols. 9–10, app. II.

the entire western orientation that he had steadfastly pursued since the autumn of 1923 had borne fruit. The Marx coalition stood or fell with the political results of London. In a narrower sense, the negotiations had to lead to a reparations settlement that could be presented as not stifling the nascent recovery initiated with the currency reform of November 1923.[47]

Stresemann's 'fundamentals' remained unchanged. They were confirmed by Schubert just after the German delegation's eventual arrival in London on 6 August. As Schubert informed the head of the Foreign Office's Central Department, Miles Lampson, the 'present German Government cannot hope to get their two-thirds majority in the *Reichstag* unless the questions of (a) the military occupation of the Ruhr' and '(b) allied railwaymen in the Rhineland are settled'. Both Stresemann and Marx were domestically 'committed' on these points. The Ruhr question 'was in fact the most vital question of all'.[48]

During the conference's opening-stages, Stresemann was compelled to rely on Anglo-American diplomats and bankers to represent these German interests vis-à-vis France. Yet he was not content with such guardianship alone. Overarching all specific demands was the foreign minister's long-standing objective to seize on the conference to effect Germany's return to the comity of great powers.[49] Such political goals clearly outweighed more narrowly defined reparations concerns. Stresemann was indeed prepared to pay a considerable economic 'price' to attain his political aims.[50] This was to become a hallmark of Weimar foreign policy.

To prepare the ground for this, the foreign minister had prevailed on the Marx government to recognise that, prior to a new diplomatic opening, their main task lay on the home front. They had to rally support for the Dawes plan in the *Reichstag*, especially against German Nationalist opposition.[51] This went hand in hand with the struggle to keep the strained coalition government itself in power.[52]

The politics of the London Conference I – the sanctions question

Rather than in the conference's plenary meetings, its core decisionmaking evolved in a council comprising MacDonald, Kellogg, Herriot and two further heads of delegation. And they had centred on three main committees of which

---

[47] Cf. Wright (2002), pp. 286–90; James (1985).
[48] Stresemann memorandum, 5 August 1924, *ADAP*, A, XI, no. 1; Lampson record of a conversation with Schubert, 6 August 1924, *DBFP*, I, XXVI, no. 530.
[49] Stresemann memorandum, 5 August 1924, *ADAP*, A, XI, no. 1.
[50] Finlayson report, 12 August 1924, *DBFP*, I, XXVI, no. 537.
[51] D'Abernon to MacDonald, 27 July 1924, *DBFP*, I, XXVI, no. 520.
[52] Cf. Baechler (1996), pp. 532–6.

the first and most important one dealt with the 'default question'. Further, there were numerous, often more conclusive, informal meetings. On 1 August, after two weeks of intense negotiations, Kellogg informed Hughes that while the conference was 'not yet out of the woods' on the cardinal 'question of default' a 'serious deadlock' was no longer to be expected. In Kellogg's assessment, the most serious problem remained France's demands for arbitration in the case of disagreements in the Transfer Committee on what sanctions were appropriate in the event of 'flagrant' German default on reparations. In essence, Paris was 'very much afraid of the Transfer Committee' and thus seeking to retain an 'arbitral' body still constituted under Versailles: either the League's Financial Committee or the Reparations Commission itself.[53]

In the crucial last week of July, the first committee produced a first compromise proposal that constrained the Reparations Commission's authority yet still left it in power. This basically built on an original proposal by Hughes, which Young had then developed further. The committee proposed a new sanction mechanism whereby in case of 'flagrant default' the decision would still be made by the RepCo, yet only with the participation of a US representative and after hearing the newly appointed agent-general for reparations.[54] Moreover, not one but *all* allied governments ultimately had to agree on a unanimous course. The security of the envisaged loan would be given 'absolute priority'.[55]

From the bankers' vantage-point, however, this did not alter the basic fact that the Reparations Commission still occupied a decisive position. As Norman maintained, France thus retained power beyond Anglo-American control.[56] This seemed particularly problematic as there was the acute danger that Herriot's government might fall. Any successor not honouring the agreement could then fall back on the old machinery to turn back the clock of international accommodation. It should be noted again that the bankers were not bent on beating France into submission to further their expansionist aims in Europe. They did recognise Herriot's domestic difficulties. Nevertheless, core financial interests prevailed.[57]

---

[53] Kellogg to Hughes, 1 August 1924, Kellogg Papers.
[54] Logan proposal, 19 July 1924, minutes of the First Committee, CAB 29/103–4: Proceedings of the London Reparations Conference, I, pp. 268–96; Fischer report, 15 July 1924, PA, St. S C, vol. 7, no. 409; Young to Lamont, 22 July 1924, Lamont Papers, TWL 176/18.
[55] Fischer report, 15 July 1924, PA, St. S C, vol. 7, no. 409.
[56] Report of the First Committee, CAB 29/103–4: Proceedings of the London Reparations Conference, I, pp. 66ff; for the bankers' reaction see Lamont to Morgan, 20 July 1924, Lamont Papers, TWL 176/17; J.P. Morgan press statement, 26 July 1924, Morgan Papers, box 195; Morgan, Morrow and Leffingwell to Lamont, 18 July 1924 and 19 July 1924, Lamont Papers, TWL 176/16.
[57] Morgan, Morrow and Leffingwell to Lamont, 18 July 1924 and 19 July 1924, Lamont Papers, TWL 176/16; Lamont to Morrow, 28 July 1924, Lamont Papers, TWL 176/20.

What instilled 'fear' in the French delegation and made Herriot seek MacDonald's last-minute backing was that the bankers had presented him with a *de facto* ultimatum in the last days of July. In fact, backed by his associates Morrow and the even more adamant Leffingwell, Morgan simply insisted on his previous requirements. Their interest still lay in establishing a new mechanism – the Transfer Committee – that France could no longer usurp for political purposes.[58] On 25 July, Lamont had pointed out the one possible alternative financiers would countenance. He stated that if 'the Allied Governments, because of considerations of high policy, find it impossible to arrange the safeguards required' US investments had to be 'protected by the joint and several guarantee of the Allied Governments'.[59]

This left policymakers with a tough choice. Either they had to establish a regime of formal guarantees underpinning the reparations regime; or they had to accept the bankers' conditions. That they finally opted for the latter did not so much stem from British preferences. MacDonald envisaged an arbitration regime conforming with the League Covenant that would have left the final decision on sanctions to governments – and accorded Britain a veto against France.[60] Rather, it followed from Hughes' unremitting pursuit of a 'progressive' path minimising state interference and guarantees. Under these self-imposed constraints, MacDonald, Kellogg and Hughes faced the task of preventing an '*unrefined* conclusion of the conference'. They had to forge an agreement that satisfied the bankers and permitted Herriot to salvage a modicum of domestic standing.[61]

Seeing the risk of impending deadlock, Hughes in the last week of July proceeded to resume his role as unofficial 'umpire'. He came to pursue an effective two-pronged strategy that now clearly focused on obtaining Herriot's acceptance of a sanction regime beyond Versailles. The secretary of state brought to bear Washington's influence directly and through trusted informal agents, in this case Lamont. While carefully guarding his unofficial status in London, Hughes met Herriot outside the conference and impressed on him the need, and the advantages, of reaching an agreement.[62] Through his intermediary Lamont, he painted the consequences of French obstinacy in bleak colours – a breakdown of the talks would provoke a renewed French financial crisis and depreciation of the franc. France would have to choose between preserving

---

[58] Lamont to MacDonald, 25 July 1924, Kellogg Papers; Morgan, Morrow, Leffingwell to Lamont, 18 July 1924 and 19 July 1924, Lamont to J.P. Morgan & Co., 20 July 1924, Lamont Papers, TWL 176/16, 17; Young to J.P. Morgan, 4 August 1924, J.P. Morgan & Co. Files, Morrow Papers.
[59] Lamont to MacDonald, 25 July 1924, Kellogg Papers.
[60] MacDonald minute, 24 July 1924, FO 371/9751/C 11924/70/18.
[61] Kellogg to Hughes, 30 July 1924, NA RG 59 462.00 R296/463.
[62] Kellogg to Olds, 5 August 1924, Kellogg Papers.

its – tenuous – prerogatives under Versailles and restoring public finance.[63] Again through Lamont, Hughes impressed on the Belgian premier Georges Theunis that Herriot's 'best chance of handling his parliament was to grasp the nettle, make his adjustments with the British and then go to Paris and tell them to take it or leave it'.[64] In a parallel move to prevent the conference's collapse, Coolidge on 29 July proposed the Supreme Court's chief justice as final arbiter in the default question.[65]

While following Hughes' intervention British and French representatives still negotiated over ways to retain a role for the Reparations Commission, Kellogg rejected all further initiatives 'to change the Dawes Plan' in order to buttress Versailles. This remained America's official position, powerfully joining Washington's political interest with the banker's financial 'fundamentals'. And MacDonald finally agreed.[66] Pursuing his evolutionary approach, he had made securing a *political* result in London his first priority. Originally, MacDonald had thought it sufficient to obtain French guarantees to refrain from an unreasonable use of sanctions.[67] Facing the bankers' unremitting opposition, however, he finally drew on a plan prepared by Sir John Fischer-Williams of the Treasury. Fischer-Williams suggested empowering the World Court at The Hague to decide in case of divergences on German default. In MacDonald's view, this offered an 'iron' bridge of compromise for France.[68]

Yet, following Hughes' guidelines, Kellogg instructed Logan 'as far as possible to keep away from the League' in finding a highest 'arbitral body'. In fact, neither the World Court nor the League's Financial Committee were finally chosen. Rather, as Kellogg reported on 1 August, a 'substantial change' had been made, which accorded with Hughes' and the bankers' essentials.[69] If no unanimity could be reached in the Reparations Commission the ultimate decision would lie with a new panel established under the Dawes scheme, the Transfer Committee. Crucially, reflecting the shift in the postwar power-constellation, it would be headed by a US representative.[70] Hughes had already informed MacDonald on 11 July that he would not object to 'summoning' an

[63] Beerits memorandum, 'The Dawes Plan', pp. 27–8, Hughes Papers, container 172/27.
[64] Lamont to Morrow, 28 July 1924, Lamont Papers, TWL 176/20. Cf. Schuker (1976), pp. 312–13.
[65] Grew to Kellogg, 29 July 1924, NA RG 59 462.00 R296/460a; Castle Diary, 7 August 1924, vol. 6, p. 234.
[66] Kellogg to Hughes, 1 August 1924, Kellogg Papers.
[67] MacDonald statement, Imperial Conference, 18 July 1924, CAB 29/105.
[68] MacDonald minute, 24 July 1924, FO 371/9751/C 11924/70/18; Fischer-Williams memorandum, 21 July 1924, FO 371/9752: C12395/70/18.
[69] Kellogg to Hughes (Brussels), 1 August 1924, Kellogg Papers.
[70] CAB 29/103–4: Proceedings of the London Reparations Conference, I, pp. 298–301.

American 'agent-general' for reparations for this task. This task would fall to the young financier Parker Gilbert.[71]

The final compromise was confirmed on 2 August. Somewhat ironically, it was prompted by a French proposal.[72] Fundamentally, though, it derived from MacDonald's preparatory mediation, Washington's insistence on the Dawes mechanism and the blueprint of the Anglo-American financiers. This first seminal result of London manifested the prevalence of American political-cum-financial might over French means to uphold the mainstays of Versailles. It also manifested the bond of common interest uniting America, Britain and, naturally, Germany in advancing beyond the system of 1919. At the same time, it cleared the way for Germany's return to world politics.

The politics of the London conference II – the German question

On 2 August, those assembled in London made the watershed announcement 'to send an invitation to Germany to attend the conference to discuss the best methods of applying the Dawes Report'.[73] The German delegation, led by chancellor Wilhelm Marx and Stresemann, arrived in London on 5 August. Much as it has been taken for granted in retrospect, till the very end Germany's participation was by no means a foregone conclusion.

That the Marx government finally received the keenly awaited signal was not due to the influence of the bankers. For they still insisted that they could 'fight' for German demands more effectively than Berlin, notably that for an immediate Ruhr evacuation.[74] Norman told Schacht on 5 August that Morgan sought to settle this question by force of financial preponderance rather than risk a reversion to Franco-German back-stabbing.[75] Rather, the path to Germany's political rehabilitation was opened by three factors: first, the dynamics of the conference itself, which produced the successful default compromise; second, and most importantly, the culmination of MacDonald's consistent bid to promote Germany's political reintegration; and third, once again acting as a salient background force, Hughes' eventual espousal of this bid.

Crucially, without MacDonald's effort to stay his course when there was pressure both from the bankers and Herriot to exclude Germany after all to secure swift allied agreement, there might not have been a politically

---

[71] Brooks to MacDonald, 11 July 1924, MacDonald Papers, MDP 30/69/94, no. 237.

[72] CAB 29/103–4: Proceedings of the London Reparations Conference, I, pp. 298–9.

[73] Foreign Office memorandum, 4 August 1924, *DBFP*, I, XXVI, no. 526.

[74] See Norman memorandum, 5 August 1924, Lamont Papers, TWL 176/22; German attaché Dufour Feronce to German Foreign Ministry, 24 July 1924, PA, St. S C, vol. 9.

[75] Norman memorandum, 5 August 1924, Lamont Papers, TWL 176/22.

sustainable London agreement at all.[76] By forestalling a further allied 'decree' imposed on Germany, the British premier secured the essential sea-change of London and postwar international politics. As he had earlier told Herriot, this would make for a settlement with 'greater moral value than the [German] acceptance of the Treaty of Versailles'.[77]

Both MacDonald's and Hughes' views on what a sustainable agreement required were unquestionably influenced by what each perceived as the specific domestic constellations in France and Germany. If, in their eyes, Herriot exaggerated his obstacles on the home front, the German government missed no opportunity either to emphasise theirs. On 15 July, US diplomat Robbins cabled from Berlin that 'the situation as regards the acceptance of the Dawes report' was 'extremely serious'.[78] Above all, Robbins stressed that unless Herriot consented to 'a definite date for the economic evacuation of the Ruhr' the German parliament would never pass 'the necessary laws'. Britain's ambassador D'Abernon conveyed a more optimistic picture. Commenting on the *Reichstag* debate of 26 July, he told MacDonald that there was 'general anxiety among parties to reach a settlement on [the] basis of the Dawes plan' – with the exception of the German Nationals and the communists. The chief demand made by DNVP spokesman Otto Hoetzsch was that the Marx government 'should not go to London except on a footing of complete equality'. And Stresemann had endorsed this demand.[79]

Stresemann conveyed to Herriot and MacDonald that 'he would unhesitatingly resign if the Germans were not invited to the Conference'.[80] But the British premier needed no such reminder, reassuring Berlin that he remained the strongest proponent of such a step. Yet he made his support contigent on German pledges of co-operative behaviour. Through Crowe, MacDonald asked to be handed in advance 'some authoritative indication' of what the German government planned to implement the Dawes plan. On 29 July, Crowe told the German ambassador, Sthamer, that the 'political situation in France was such that the longer a final settlement is postponed the greater will be the danger of parliamentary and newspaper influence placing obstacles in the way'. In this light, he insisted, any German 'spinning out' of controversies would only be counterproductive.[81]

As the British minister in Paris, Eric Phipps, had earlier commented, letting Herriot 'fall' would indeed be easier than 'to maintain him in power'; but it would also be a 'great mistake'. For his likely successor, Briand, would be

[76] *Ibid.* Cf. Herriot (1948), II, pp. 161–6.
[77] MacDonald to Herriot (Paris), 8 July 1924, *DBFP*, I, XXVI, no. 507.
[78] Robbins to Hughes, 15 July 1924, NA RG 59 462.00 R296/426.
[79] D'Abernon to MacDonald, 27 July 1924, *DBFP*, I, XXVI, no. 521.
[80] Phipps to MacDonald, 25 July 1924, *DBFP*, I, XXVI, no. 519.
[81] Crowe record of a conversation with Sthamer, 29 July 1924, *DBFP*, I, XXVI, no. 524.

obliged to form a 'ministry of "concentration"' and thus become a 'prisoner' of the nationalist 'Right Centre'.[82] This corresponded with MacDonald's main motive for allowing Herriot to save his face. The British premier still feared that a Franco-German showdown in London could entail a French reversion to coercion.[83] Hughes shared this preoccupation.[84] Predictably, though, Stresemann strove to meet British demands. Sthamer promised Crowe that 'everything' required to implement the Dawes plan would be in place by 15 August.[85]

MacDonald could not have ensured Germany's invitation had he not been backed by a concomitant shift in Washington's official attitude, which cast America's weight in the same scale. In early August, Hughes gave the most distinct signal yet that Washington wished to involve the German government and financiers like Schacht in the negotiations and wider diplomatic process of implementing the Dawes plan. He decided to pay his first ever – semi-official – visit to Berlin where he held talks with Stresemann, Marx and president Ebert on 3 August. His visit served two main purposes: to reassure the Germans of US support in realising the reparations scheme and to put pressure on them to comply with it.

Motivating Hughes was a growing sense that the London conference had acquired an unforeseen significance for Republican foreign policy. And he feared that any agreement would soon be invalidated if it could not gain acceptance in France *and* Germany. As he realised by then, however, a pre-requisite for this was to elevate the German government's international standing by backing its formal representation in London.[86] On 4 August, Hughes told Kellogg that 'the importance of creating confidence by giving German labour a new incentive is obvious'.[87] This, then, was a crucial departure in America's semi-informal yet forward engagement in the 1920s. And it came, not only for Germany, at a crucial time.

Closer to home, Hughes mainly sought to contain the risk that the Dawes strategy, on which the administration had staked considerable political capital, would not bring any concrete results. For this threatened to undermine his entire informal approach from two sides. Either its failure would be grist to the mill of those advocating complete US isolation from Europe; or it could oblige Hughes to advance an alternative, more official strategy – a formal US stabilisation policy for Europe. Yet the latter was plainly not on the cards in 1924.

---

[82] Phipps to MacDonald, 25 July 1924, *DBFP*, I, XXVI, no. 519.
[83] Lampson memorandum, 24 July 1924, FO 371/9751: C 11924/70/18.
[84] Hughes to Kellogg, 4 August 1924, NA RG 59 462.00 R296/503.
[85] Crowe record of a conversation Sthamer, 1 August 1924 *DBFP*, I, XXVI, no. 525.
[86] Beerits memorandum on Hughes' talks in Berlin, 3 August 1924, Hughes Papers.
[87] Hughes to Kellogg, 4 August 1924, NA RG 59 462.00 R296/503.

On 4 August, D'Abernon reported to MacDonald that Hughes' 'general judgement' was 'distinctly optimistic as to [the] probability of a rapid solution' in London. Accordingly, Stresemann and Marx had been 'extremely gratified' with his 'guarded' but 'friendly' attitude on all core questions. Yet Hughes had not lost his sense of effective restraint. Eager to tone down German expectations on the issue of France's military evacuation, he emphasised the 'difficulty of [the] French President's parliamentary position'.[88] Ultimately, though, the overriding US interest was neither to save the German nor the French government but to induce both to implement the Dawes plan. As Hughes impressed upon his interlocutors in Berlin, this was 'the American policy. If you turn this down, America is through.' It was Germany's 'last chance'; should there be a 'rupture' at this point, Berlin would be 'held responsible'.[89]

Fundamentally, however, one subtle yet notable change in Hughes' outlook had occurred, reinforced through his direct exposure to the European situation. He no longer regarded a political agreement, and its legitimation, as a secondary concern.[90] This did not inaugurate a complete shift in America's depoliticisation strategy. But it brought Hughes closer to grasping – like MacDonald – the multiple dimensions of the compromise to be hammered out in London. A balance had to be struck. Required was a workable international agreement to which all delegations, and the bankers, could subscribe. At the same time, the settlement had to be so calibrated in such a way that both Herriot and Stresemann could present it at home, each in his own terms, as a hard-won victory worth ratifying.

The politics of the London Conference III – the Ruhr question: the first Franco-German compromise after 1918

Overall, Hughes was confident after his Berlin talks that, once in London, the Marx government would support a swift conclusion of the proceedings without introducing irksome political demands.[91] As Castle noted on 6 August, the German delegation would be 'crazy' to risk a rupture.[92] In fact, American optimism would eventually be borne out. Yet it was premature. Kellogg had stressed on 1 August that he apprehended 'considerable trouble with the German Delegation over some points'. These included mainly the precise conditions of France's withdrawal from the Ruhr and, bound up with this, the future of 5,000 French and Belgian officials overseeing the Rhenish

---

[88] D'Abernon to MacDonald, 4 August 1924, MacDonald Papers, MDP 30/69/94, no. 346.
[89] Beerits memorandum on Hughes' talks in Berlin, 3 August 1924, Hughes Papers; Hughes statements, 3 August, reported in *Le Matin*, 7 August 1924, NA RG 59 462.00 R296/507.
[90] Hughes to Kellogg, 4 August 1924, NA RG 59 462.00 R296/503.
[91] *Ibid.* Hughes to Kellogg, Southampton, 6 August 1924, Kellogg Papers.
[92] Castle Diary, 6 August 1924, vol. 6, p. 230ff.

railways. Before the German delegation even arrived, a combined Anglo-American effort had 'succeeded' in obtaining French and Belgian consent to fixing a 'definite time' for the 'complete evacuation'. But the 'maximum time' which Paris had accepted still amounted to two years. Only if Germany carried out all Dawes provisions with utmost promptness could it be reduced to one year.[93]

At the same time, Stresemann had underscored on 25 July that Germany's acceptance of the reparations settlement would hinge on an early and definite deadline for the withdrawal of French troops.[94] What remained unresolved was the core symbolical and power-political question whether Weimar Germany's integrity could be restored, first to the status of December 1922. In effect, and hardly surprisingly, it would take more than ten days of heated negotiations to forge a compromise that even then both Paris and Berlin only accepted with great difficulty. The first litmus test after 1918 for direct Franco-German negotiations and integrative politics under Anglo-American auspices indeed became indeed one of the hardest. For, like the sanction question, the Ruhr negotiations challenged the very foundations on which France had sought to rely until 1923. Besides the Rhineland occupation and Germany's isolation, France's control over the Ruhr constituted a central pillar of the compensatory predominance it had established 'beyond' the Versailles treaty.

Thus, the Ruhr settlement had to reveal how far not only German but also French policymakers had advanced, or been compelled, to accept new international bargaining-rules. No less, it had to show how far the Anglo-American mediators, chiefly MacDonald and Kellogg, could not only exert pressure but also provide such rules to expedite this difficult process. For France, the aim of re-asserting control over the Ruhr, which Nollet called non-negotiable from the outset, became even more importance once Herriot had lost the 'fight' over the sanction regime. Much as the Socialist premier personally favoured a swift evacuation, concerns of power and domestic standing markedly collided with this in August 1924.[95]

Herriot had told Kellogg 'very confidentially' on 30 July that 'he would be willing to fix in the date for [a] complete evacuation of the Ruhr with progressive evacuation as Germany showed its disposition to carry out [the] report'.[96] Yet, once he faced the German delegation this was a concession he could no longer afford to make, at least not without extracting a high price. As Nollet insisted, this included German fulfilment of the disarmament clauses of Versailles and long transitional arrangements that France could hope to prolong even further

---

[93] Kellogg to Hughes, 1 August 1924, Kellogg Papers.
[94] Robbins to State Department, 25 July 1924, NA RG 59 462.00 R296/449.
[95] Cf. Schuker (1976), pp. 325–34.
[96] Kellogg to Hughes, 30 July 1924, NA RG 59 462.00 R296/463.

once the immediate Anglo-American pressure had abated. Herriot thus sought to postpone the hard decisions of a *do ut des* accommodation with Germany to avoid losing further credibility in France.[97]

As we have seen, the German government faced in many ways exactly the reverse scenario.[98] Stresemann came to London resolved to demand a military evacuation and the withdrawal of allied railwaymen from the Ruhr significantly before the one-year deadline still favoured by Whitehall and Washington. As Schubert conveyed to MacDonald, Stresemann remained domestically compelled to make this the essential condition for signing the London protocol.[99]

How far, if at all, could these conflicting sets of claims be reconciled? At the outset, while Herriot sought to dig in his heels and solicit MacDonald's support, Stresemann's insistence on an early 'liberation' of the Ruhr was undoubtedly hardened by the Anglo-American financiers' refusal to drop their harsh political conditions. In the conference's final phase, a powerful bloc led by Norman and the Morgan partners and supported by Snowden adhered adamantly to the 'essential' of immediate evacuation. On 9 August, Lamont presented Herriot with an 'ultimatum', which he once again conveyed via Theunis. He stressed that because the 'Allied Governments' were unwilling to 'guarantee the Loan', they now had to provide other 'safeguards' for 'a tranquilised state in Central Europe'. And this could only be achieved by fulfilling two core requirements: the 'withdrawal of French and Belgian Railwaymen' and the 'military evacuation of the Ruhr'.[100] Subsequently, Snowden and Norman encouraged Stresemann to demand a progressive evacuation scheme forcing France to withdraw in three-month stages.[101]

In London, then, 'accustoming' themselves to Anglo-American business reasoning meant for the Germans and more brutally for the French to bow to non-negotiable economic requirements as interpreted by Anglo-American high finance. These remained a key factor for international politics. Yet it would not be the critical factor for the final Ruhr settlement. Rather, American and British policymakers came to use financial pressure as a strategic lever in their decisive attempt *not* to enforce the bankers' conditions. Both Kellog and MacDonald were determined not to impose a domestically unacceptable Ruhr settlement on Herriot, as this would have undermined the Dawes plan. Indeed, what hence propelled the negotiations towards a new postwar settlement, and

---

[97] Hoesch memorandum, 11 August 1924, PA, General Files, 3398/1736/D740329–331; Finlayson report, 12 August 1924, *DBFP*, I, XXVI, no. 537.

[98] D'Abernon to MacDonald, 27 July 1924, *DBFP*, I, XXVI, no. 521.

[99] Stresemann to Maltzan, 6 August 1924, PA, St. S C, vol. 9, no. 8; Stresemann to Herriot and Kellogg, 6 August 1924, Stresemann (1932), I, p. 481; Lampson memorandum, 6 August 1924, *DBFP*, I, XXVI, no. 530.

[100] Lamont to Theunis, 9 August 1924, Kellogg Papers.

[101] Dufour Feronce memorandum, 13 August 1924, PA, St. S C, vol. 9, no 10.

fostered Franco-German accommodation, was the combined impetus of official US power and MacDonald's mediation.

The new 'spirit' crystallising at London manifested itself in Kellogg's observation that the terms of France's Ruhr evacuation were to be negotiated through the politics of '*quid pro quo*'. Following Hughes' instructions, Kellogg had consistently opposed any French attempts to retain a last lever of control in the Ruhr. On 1 August, he underscored that this was liable to provoke renewed Franco-German 'jealousies and animosities'. Yet the American delegates also urged the Germans to ease France's acceptance through economic concessions. They were to offer purchasing a certain percentage of the Dawes scheme's railroad bonds and subscribe to part of the envisaged loan. Stresemann was also advised not to press for an immediate evacuation, which he would not 'get'. Kellogg concluded that 'unless Germany is too stiff' all could be settled.[102]

From Hughes' vantage-point, a swift end of France's Ruhr occupation was as desirable as Germany's return to international negotiations. But his interest in accelerating the implementation of the Dawes plan still took precedence.[103] He had instructed Kellogg from Berlin that 'possibly [an] accommodation may be found in the suggestion' that 'if Germany promptly carried out the Dawes plan the time allowed for evacuation could be considerably reduced', preferably to one year.[104] Kellogg was to pursue this solution through 'informal' negotiations with the German delegates, MacDonald and Herriot – i.e. without the bankers. Fundamentally, Hughes had more faith than Morgan & Co. in the inherent dynamism of 'progressive' stabilisation once the expert scheme was put in operation. He held that political obstacles like settling the withdrawal of France's remaining troops would be swept aside in due course. The key lay in preventing a premature breakdown of the conference.

MacDonald's efforts on Germany's behalf were less conspicuous than those of Snowden and Norman. Yet in effect they were more constructive because he sought to further a tenable compromise, building narrow yet passable bridges for Herriot as well. Like Hughes, he saw clearly that the Germans could only be brought back into the 'game' of international politics on terms tolerable for France. MacDonald's brokerage on the Ruhr issue was hardly a resort to last-minute improvisation. It built on a consistent approach, a strategy combining face-saving mediation and political pressure. It was geared to inducing Herriot to concede an early evacuation without appearing to have 'sold out' French interests to Germany and Anglo-American high finance. But MacDonald also drew on the full leverage of political-cum-financial power that Britain and America had assembled in London.

---

[102] Kellogg memorandum to Hughes, 1 August 1924, Kellogg Papers.
[103] Beerits memorandum, 3 August 1924, Hughes Papers.
[104] Hughes to Kellogg, 4 August 1924, NA RG 59 462.00 R296/503.

Already on 24 July, MacDonald told Herriot that the question of France's evacuation of territories 'outside the limits' set by the Versailles treaty would have to be resolved on a basis of reciprocity with Germany. France had repeatedly declared that the occupation was 'in no way bound up with the question of security'. This, then, could no longer be invoked. In short, MacDonald demanded that Herriot abandon a course whose 'declared object-ive' was 'to create in Germany by the seizure of pledges and by coercion the will to pay'. MacDonald told Herriot that he could count on his support, not least in preventing further ultimatums of Anglo-American financiers, only if he agreed to a fundamental shift in the treatment of Germany − essentially, a negotiated settlement with the power that had been excluded from Versailles. The Labour premier thus continued to act as patron of German interests.[105] Yet, to forge an agreement that Herriot could legitimate in France, he also came to back − in league with Kellogg − a compromise that upheld a one-year deadline for France's withdrawal. Snowden's criticism notwithstanding, this would remain Britain's official position until the close of the conference.[106]

Urged on by Kellogg and MacDonald, Stresemann and Herriot discussed the conditions of military evacuation on 10 and 11 August. At this point, the French premier had endorsed the Anglo-American one-year deadline. In an attempt to placate Nollet, however, he sought to link evacuation with the finalisation of German disarmament under Versailles. Further, he demanded the signing of a Franco-German commercial treaty 'giving France the most-favoured-nation clause' and granting the same to Germany. Finally, he re-asserted France's MICUM agenda on a new basis, proposing 'French participation in German heavy industries in the Ruhr' and a new 'community of interests' between German and French industrialists.[107]

It was highly characteristic of Stresemann's approach that, despite the opposition of Rhenish-Westphalian heavy industry, he was willing to discuss such commercial concessions.[108] Like MacDonald, Stresemann feared that Herriot might be replaced by a reactionary government, noting on 11 August that 'economic concessions of limited scope' were thus 'of secondary import-ance'. Clearly central was the political aim: to fix a date for military evacuation. After a long period of isolation, German leaders were keen to work towards a *do ut des* agreement with France. Neither Stresemann nor Marx wanted to risk a breakdown of the talks and Germany's return to international isolation.[109]

---

[105] MacDonald to Herriot, 24 July 1924, *DBFP*, I, XXVI, no. 517.
[106] *AR Marx I und II*, annex 7, note 7.
[107] Finlayson report, 12 August 1924, *DBFP*, I, XXVI, no. 537.
[108] Stresemann to AA, 11 August 1924, *ADAP*, A, XI, no. 18.
[109] On the German perspective see Baechler (1996), pp. 537–43; on the French see Bariéty (1977), pp. 635–711.

Significantly, then, for the first time since 1918 French and German policy-makers discussed how best to implement, and legitimate, a compromise that could work to their mutual advantage. As the British financial attaché in Berlin, H.C.F. Finlayson, observed, Herriot had not directly linked the 'question of the price to be paid' by Germany for the 'evacuation' with French economic 'counter conditions'. Yet it was precisely on this plane of bargaining that both sides envisaged a *rapprochement*.[110] London thus indeed prefigured a central form of Franco-German accommodation in the Locarno era. A commercial treaty, however, would only be concluded in August 1927.[111]

Initially, the German side felt unable to accept Herriot's first offer. Stresemann underlined that 'German opinion would not understand that we adopt the plan' and 'accord commercial advantages' to France yet 'the evacuation of the Ruhr will be postponed so far', i.e. by one year. He now proposed the Anglo-American 'stage formula' for France's successive withdrawal; a final date had to be 'definitely fixed' – preferably 10 January 1925. As a 'beau geste', France was to commence on 15 August to retreat from the 'bottle-neck' it occupied to protect its Rhenish bridgeheads.[112] Yet Germany did not accept any linkage with the disarmament clauses of Versailles.

Herriot's penultimate concession was to propose a formula centred on a *maximum* of one year.[113] Deeming this still too vague a proposition, Stresemann asked MacDonald to intervene on Germany's behalf. The British premier strove to lead a final round of talks to compromise. Though sympathetic towards German demands, he remained determined to avoid a one-sided settlement. Towards both Marx and Stresemann he emphasised Herriot's predicament, the requirements laid down by Versailles and the need for Germany to assure France on disarmament. Late on 13 August, he strongly advised the German delegation finally to accept the French proposal, viewing it as the limit of what concessions Herriot could make. He anticipated that France's withdrawal could actually be accelerated later on, should Franco-German relations thaw further.[114]

On 14 August, MacDonald finally minuted that he saw 'no prospects of getting the French out of the Ruhr short of a year' and was not 'inclined to break the Conference on that point'.[115] In the critical final days, it was Kellogg who decisively increased pressure on Germany, unequivocally backing the

---

[110] Finlayson report, 12 August 1924, *DBFP*, I, XXVI, no. 537.
[111] Cf. Krüger (1985a), pp. 368–9.
[112] Stresemann to Herriot, 11 August 1924, *ADAP*, A, XI, no. 27; Finlayson report, 12 August 1924, *DBFP*, I, XXVI, no. 537.
[113] *AR Marx I und II*, annex 1, note 43.
[114] MacDonald to Stresemann, 12 August 1924; MacDonald note, 13 August 1924, *AR Marx I und II*, annex 2. See *ibid.*, annex 7, note 7.
[115] MacDonald minute to the Board of Trade, 14 August 1924, *DBFP*, I, XXVI, p. 830, fn. 5.

British line. He even – and effectively – hinted at the option of an ultimatum should Germany refuse to accept the one-year deadline. After consulting with *Reichspräsident* Ebert in Berlin, the German delegation on 15 August finally accepted it.[116]

Nevertheless, Marx demanded last-minute concessions, notably a more precise French commitment to evacuate within ten months of the Dawes plan's ratification. On the last day of the negotiations, MacDonald thus again urged Herriot to 'take every possible step to hasten the evacuation' as its continuation could only 'jeopardise the arrangements agreed upon at the London Conference'. Yet the utmost Herriot countenanced was to assure the German delegation in private that French troops would withdraw immediately from Dortmund and that the overall deadline would come into force on the day the settlement was signed, 16 August.[117] In effect, this corresponded closely with Stresemann's final demands.

Thus, a hard-won compromise had been forged that at the time satisfied no side completely. Very soon, however, it prepared the ground for what became a swift and irreversible development: France's withdrawal from the *glacis* of the Ruhr, then *de facto* concluded – less than a year after the London conference – on 1 August 1925. For all the financiers' influence, the final 'deal' struck at London was thus essentially political. Given the accumulation of odds against it, it appears all the more remarkable that, though only after a near breakdown of the proceedings, France and Germany found a compromise formula. In the final analysis, this outcome would have remained elusive without MacDonald's brokerage, Kellogg's steadfastness and the political groundwork laid by Hughes.

The consequences of the 'economic peace' of 1924 – a re-appraisal

What made the London settlement significant and formative for the evolution of Europe's stabilisation between 1924 and 1929 was that it reflected, and altered, the political-cum-financial configuration of postwar transatlantic relations. Essentially, the outcome of 1924 could have a momentous impact because, on the deepest level, it mirrored the actual distribution of power and possibilities after 1918; and it changed the asymmetrical Euro-Atlantic system accordingly. The lion's share of financial leverage, and political power,

---

[116] Record of talks between Kellogg, MacDonald and the German delegation, 14 August 1924, Marx cable to Ebert and the German cabinet, 14 August 1924, *AR Marx I und II*, annex 8, no. 275; Stresemann to Maltzan, 15 August 1924, PA, St. S C, vol. 10, no. 68.
[117] *AR Marx I und II*, no. 276; MacDonald to Herriot, *DBFP*, I, XXVI, no. 546; German memorandum, 14 August 1924, Stresemann (1932), I, pp. 494ff.

no longer lay in French or European hands. It was wielded by US policymakers and bankers. British diplomacy could be effective because at this juncture it operated in league with them.

This throws into relief the structurally hegemonic character of the Euro-Atlantic international system after World War I. London showed the extent to which policymakers in Washington and Whitehall were prepared to use the leverage they had vis-à-vis France and Germany after the nadir of 1923. Both powers could limit their own engagement at the conference while impelling France and Germany to make the concessions on which the success of London depended. Neither felt that it had to offer more substantial incentives to expedite Franco-German 'reconciliation', particularly in terms of formal political guarantees regarding loans or security. London thus also revealed the limits of what commitments Anglo-American decisionmakers were willing to make *up to this point* to further peaceful change in Europe.

Nevertheless, after five years of frustration and aloofness, Britain and America now – finally – *de facto* underpinned the first postwar settlement including Germany. Both powers, and particularly the United States, had long appeared aloof after the failures of 1919 and 1922. Yet only their policies could, and now did, have a decisive stabilising impact on European politics. In their combined effect, America's quest for 'progressive' reform and Britain's bid for political accommodation prompted a renaissance of international politics in Europe on new foundations, essentially intergovernmental politics with a strong financial component. This began to transform western Europe's most critical relationship after 1918, that between France and Germany. And it could also set the stage for a new beginning in relations between Europe and the United States, potentially even the emergence of something unprecedented: a transatlantic international system.

The American strategy of resolving political conflicts by administering economic means lent itself to clearing the thorny path towards a reparations settlement on 'rational' business terms, thus giving the decisive initial impetus. Overall, this depoliticisation strategy was subtly orchestrated by Hughes and upheld by the US delegation at the conference. But it was also enforced by the financial clout of US financiers, notably J.P. Morgan and Lamont.[118]

The bankers' insistence on a set of non-negotiable political conditions for floating the Dawes loan influenced the outcome of London significantly, hastening in particular the end of French sanctions against Germany. Yet, crucially, their impetus would not have sufficed. It could only have an impact because Hughes' informal approach had prepared the political ground. Person-ally, Hughes believed that the Dawes plan could indeed lay the foundations for

---

[118] Cf. Burk (1991), pp. 146–7.

replacing long-standing power-political rivalries in Europe with tough but peaceful economic competition.[119] To be sure, its ground-rules were largely to be determined by, and benefit most, the newly pre-eminent American power. To this end, and concurring with Morgan's preferences, the Coolidge administration unequivocally backed Parker Gilbert as new agent-general for reparations.[120]

Yet, on balance, Britain's contribution to the London settlement, hitherto underrated, was in many ways equally critical. For MacDonald's diplomacy essentially turned the American 'depoliticisation' scheme into a comprehensive political settlement. His mediation strategies ensured that not merely the will of the market was executed but instead a tenable political compromise could be hammered out – first among the Allies, then with the Germans. Notably, MacDonald fostered a mutually acceptable scheme for France's evacuation of the Ruhr. As the aftermath of London revealed, only such agreements could set Euro-Atlantic politics on a course of reform. For, crucially, they could be legitimated not just in financial circles but also, if with difficulty, in French and German domestic politics.

The Labour government thus rightly welcomed the London accords as more than a financial 'new deal' for Europe. While privately still critical of the Ruhr settlement, Snowden emphasised in public that the economic peace inaugurated at London would also buttress Europe's political pacification.[121] MacDonald stressed the common interest of the victors and the vanquished of the Great War in a 'comprehensive reconstruction' of Europe, boosting 'political reconciliation' between Germany and the western powers.[122] This accorded with British interests in promoting a European consolidation that rendered alliance guarantees unnecessary and revived both transatlantic trade and the flow of US capital to an invigorated German reparations debtor.

From the moment the conference closed, both policymakers and financiers anticipated almost unanimously that the Dawes scheme had not yet completely disentangled the reparations conundrum; that it would at best be a temporary solution and, sooner or later, need revision. This was a prospect indeed welcomed by the Germans and the British, viewed as inevitable by the Americans and accepted as the lesser of several evils by the French. In a larger sense, as its makers clearly perceived as well, the London agreement had of course not yet 'solved' the Franco-German problem. Yet the agreements signed in mid-August and implemented in the autumn of 1924 furnished a rather effective

---

[119] Hughes to Morrow, 19 September 1924, quoted after Feis (1950), p. 42.
[120] Hughes to Coolidge, 23 August 1924, NA RG 59 462.00 R296/532. Cf. Link (1970), pp. 322–3.
[121] Snowden declaration, Imperial Conference, 15 August 1924, CAB 29/105.
[122] MacDonald statement, *Times*, 18 August 1924; MacDonald statement in cabinet, 5 August 1924, CAB 23/48.

mechanism for managing, with the reparations dispute, what had been at the epicentre of Europe's postwar crisis. The new *modus operandi* reduced Germany's obligations in accordance with its 'actual capacity to pay' and allowed for the decisive transfer of American capital to Germany. This would thereafter fuel the 'Dawes system', the transatlantic cycle of US loans, German reparation payments and, in turn, French and British war-debt payments to the world's new lender of last resort.[123]

A pivotal question of Euro-Atlantic stabilisation after London remained whether this cycle would be controlled, and if need be buttressed, through political guarantees. As will be seen, after Hughes had ruled out Washington's support for such guarantees throughout the conference, this question would be answered negatively in the autumn of 1924.[124] Ultimately, this would have grave consequences in 1929. From the perspective of the mid-1920s, however, it should be underlined that without the advances of London and the Dawes regime not even a 'relative' consolidation of the Weimar Republic, and Europe, would have been attainable after World War I.

Measured solely in its impact on Europe's 'balance of power', the 'economic peace' of 1924, not rescinded until the Great Depression, had recast the constellation of power and possibilities between Germany and France. At the same time, it had altered the very foundations for a stable peace order in Europe. One definite answer to the Franco-German question had been given: European, and particularly French, security could hence no longer be founded on a containment of a more or less fragmented Germany. Rather, the defeated power of 1918 was set to retain, or rather regain, its political and economic unity – with still disputed borders in the west as well as the east. And it was presented with an opening for restoring its potentially predominant capabilities. Besides, bypassing the then economically ailing France, Berlin had intertwined its economic and financial interests very effectively with those of America and Britain.[125]

The most tangible systemic shift in the international power configuration was indeed that from August 1924 onwards France had *de facto* lost its sanction prerogatives under Versailles. This accorded with Hughes' cardinal conference objective.[126] Henceforth, sanctions against Germany would be economic in character and their imposition no longer controlled by France – or Britain – but the United States. Concretely, decisions would lie in the hands of a steering committee created under the new regime and headed by the American 'King of the Dawes Plan', Parker Gilbert.[127]

---

[123] For a critical analysis see Kent (1989), pp. 103ff.   [124] See chapter 11.
[125] Cf. Link (1970), p. 587; Orde (1990), pp. 253–4.
[126] Hughes instructions to Kellogg, 24 June 1924, *FRUS 1924*, II, pp. 32–3.
[127] Hughes to Coolidge, 16 August 1924, NA RG 59 462.00 R296/504.

Thus, Paris had been deprived of a critical lever for controlling Germany's crucial strategic resources on the Ruhr. With it, also the French hold on the strategic *glacis* of the Rhineland, and its power to maintain the Versailles system, had been weakened. Thus, the Anglo-American pacification of Europe initiated in 1924 had by no means removed the structural imbalance between France's existing preponderance of power and Germany's significantly superior potential. But, crucially, any international system that was to consolidate European peace without breaking up Germany and provoking a reversal to the crisis of 1923 had to cope with this disequilibrium. It had to establish rules and underlying principles to manage its unsettling effect. This would be the central challenge for Euro-Atlantic security politics after the London conference.

It was precisely in this respect, however, that the London accords also already constituted a veritable watershed in postwar international politics. For, systemically most significant, the 'new deal' of 1924 was the first agreement after 1918 not imposed by the victors on the vanquished. Rather, it was reached on terms in principle acceptable to both France and Germany – in essence, Anglo-American terms. International consolidation through multilateral compromise and an integrative process would determine the course of Euro-Atlantic relations until the onset of the World Economic Crisis in 1929. This opened the perspective of Weimar Germany becoming, through a peaceful change of the Versailles system, a power with equitable international status, possibilities *and obligations*.

The London settlement thus marked the beginning of a more complex process of international accommodation, first between Germany and the west, yet not limited to this part of Europe. In this sense, MacDonald's verdict on the achievement of London can be upheld: 'This agreement may be regarded as the first Peace Treaty, because we sign it with a feeling that we have turned our backs on the terrible years of war and war mentality.'[128] While formally leaving the treaty of 1919 unaltered, it can thus justly be called the first pillar of the 'unfinished transatlantic peace order' superseding Versailles in the 1920s.[129]

What marked a departure in London was the very fact that, admittedly under Anglo-American pressure, French and German leaders had accepted as the very basis of their relations that a solution to the outstanding problems dividing them could only be found through an actual bargaining-process. France could no longer rely on the victor's prerogative to decree terms, Germany no longer on the rationale to elude the consequences of such impositions by *raison du vaincu*, inflation and obstruction. Ultimately both sides considered a compromise more important than an – unattainable – 'complete'

---

[128] MacDonald statement, 15 August 1924, CAB 29/103–4: Proceedings of the London Reparations Conference, II, pp. 7–8.
[129] See Cohrs (2003), pp. 15–20.

national victory.[130] This obviously involved sacrifices for the French and Germans, not for the mediating Anglo-American powers. The new mode of politics inaugurated in 1924 shaped Franco-German relations until the decline of 1929–32.

Despite disappointments over details and, particularly, the Ruhr compromise, Stresemann could see the London accords as a considerable success of his policy. The Anglo-American intervention he had sought to further and his own insistence on Germany's 'fundamentals' had produced a result that, based on the 'interconnectedness of world-economic interests', ended Germany's postwar isolation.[131] A difficult challenge that still had to be met before the Dawes plan could be implemented, however, was to ensure its domestic approval in Germany and France.

In Berlin, this meant passing the necessary Dawes legislation against virulent opposition both from communist and, above all, nationalist-*völkisch* circles. As they affected the constitution, the Dawes laws changing the status of the German railways required a two-thirds majority in the *Reichstag*, impossible without the partial support of the DNVP. The parliamentary debates showed the entire array of forces aligned not only against the Dawes settlement but also against Germany's western orientation as such.[132] Nationalists decried the Dawes plan as a conspiracy hatched by American financiers and Jewish international capitalists to penetrate the German economy.[133] That there was a suprisingly clear margin in the decisive vote on 29 August 1924 could be put down to a coalition of interests bringing together the Marx government, US diplomats and, decisively, American high finance.[134] Both Houghton and the Morgan partners acted vigorously behind the political scenes, impressing upon the DNVP that the consequence of refusal would be a blockage of any US loans to Germany.[135]

The public and parliamentary debates about the London agreement in France were on the surface no less controversial than in Germany. They also manifested a wide range of criticism, particularly of Herriot's lack of leadership during the negotiations. Significantly, though, as has been pointed out, no further Anglo-American pressure was required to ensure the accords' ratification. No French politicians either of the left or, notably, the right could

[130] Marx to Ebert, 14 August 1924, *AR Marx I und II*, no. 275.
[131] Stresemann *Reichstag* speech, 23 August 1924, Stresemann (1932), I, pp. 505ff; German Foreign Ministry, official résumé, 19 August 1924, *AR Marx I und II*, no. 283.
[132] Cf. Baechler (1996), pp. 552–6; Stürmer (1967), pp. 63ff; Krüger (1985a), pp. 246–7; Holz (1977), pp. 58–113.
[133] Thus most acidly the communist spokesman Rosenberg, 26 August 1924, *SB*, vol. 381, pp. 944ff.
[134] Cf. Link (1970), pp. 306–11.
[135] Hughes to Coolidge, 23 August 1924, NA RG 59 462.00 R296/532.

advance a serious alternative to the path Herriot was pursuing, not even Poincaré himself.[136] Yet the latter voiced his deep distrust in the 'good faith of Germany', warning that as the 'scaffolding of London' depended on the compliance of not only the present but also future German governments it had been built on 'quicksand'.[137] In the last week of August, Herriot defended the London settlement both in the *Sénat* and in the *Chambre*, praising it as 'the beginning of real peace' between France and Germany. Essentially, however, he argued that France simply could not afford a return to coercive policies or the financial dislocation that a failure at London would have entailed, including the spectre of Anglo-American sanctions.[138] The French parliament clearly endorsed the Dawes settlement.

In retrospect, not only Clémentel but also Herriot thus acknowledged that the outcome of London amounted to a substantive gain for France's prospects of recovering prosperity and improving postwar security.[139] The Socialist premier can be seen as the first of successive French leaders, including Briand and later Poincaré, who saw no alternative to an 'arrangement' with Germany and the Anglo-American powers. This went hand in hand with a new domestic emphasis on financial consolidation.[140] All of this corresponded with MacDonald's and Hughes' 'essentials'. It underscored the influence of reorientated Anglo-American stabilisation policies on the recasting of French policy in the mid-1920s, which was only surpassed by their impact on Weimar Germany.

---

[136] Cf. Schuker (1976), pp. 392–3. See *Sénat* debates, 26 August 1924, *JOS*, pp. 1295ff.

[137] Poincaré statement in the *Sénat* debates, 26 August 1924, *JOS*, p. 1313.

[138] Herriot statement in the *Chambre* debates, 21 and 23 August 1924, *JOC*, pp. 2959, 3076ff.

[139] On France's arduous political and financial consolidation between 1924 and 1926 see Maier (1988), pp. 494–510.

[140] Herriot statement in the *Chambre* debates, 23 August 1924, *JOC*, p. 3084.

Part II

Europe's nascent *Pax Anglo-Americana*, 1924–1925

As the aftermath of the London conference revealed, the Anglo-American settlement had opened new perspectives, yet also created a new urgency, for attempts to address what it could not resolve, at least in the short term: Europe's underlying security problem of the 1920s. British policymakers came to perceive this far more acutely than their American counterparts. From the end of the war until the climax of the Ruhr crisis, the problem had been the absence of international security *per se* and the lack of any effective international system to cope with endemic European instability. After London, the problem was essentially the lack of a security framework for Europe's incipient 'economic' stabilisation as well as Germany's resurgence and transition towards a stable republican order. Could this framework be created through the League? Would it be predicated on an Anglo-French *entente* after all? Or would it be founded on different, new premises?

Unmistakably, what contemporary observers simply referred to as the European security question both overshadowed and prompted the further reorientation of British policy under MacDonald in 1924 and later Chamberlain's quest for a new international equilibrium at Locarno. By contrast, the American administration and US high finance did not significantly depart from the precedent of 1924 and persevered with their 'Progressive' pursuit of European stability. More precisely, however, European and American policymakers faced two questions of security in the autumn of 1924. The second, not entirely settled at London, was the question what, if any, political guarantees would buttress the new Dawes system of loans and reparation transfers. What degree of political control and transfer security would be provided by the American government when US financiers had to furnish most of the essential capital? Further steps towards a transatlantic peace order after London depended on how far policymakers on both sides of the Atlantic could master these problems. The overarching question was to what extent it would be possible to consolidate Europe's nascent 'economic peace' of 1924.

As will be shown, this 'economic peace' could not be secured through a reversion to – Anglo-French – alliance politics, backed by America and upholding Europe's 'balance' of power against a revitalising Germany. Nor could it be achieved by finally turning the League into Europe's long-sought superstructure of universal collective security and checking German ambitions through the Geneva Protocol of 1924. What consolidated European stability was, rather, a second stage in the transformation of Euro-Atlantic international politics in the 1920s, this time chiefly fostered by Britain, yet also, more broadly, under the *aegis* of the United States. This transformation hinged on advances towards a *regional* security system in Europe. Its nucleus emerged, with the Locarno pact, from the triangular concert including Britain, France and a reintegrated Germany. But its impact was not limited to western Europe. It also created the first realistic prospects for stabilising eastern Europe after the Great War.

The core negotiations leading to Locarno were an inner-European process, mediated by a British broker and centring on a new security bargain between Britain, France and Germany. Yet they evolved within a changing Euro-Atlantic system whose really pre-eminent power was America. In this sense, while on one level a distinctly – west – European endeavour, the making of the Locarno accords also always had a marked transatlantic dimension. Its springs, nature and scope can only be fully understood when analysed in this wider context. Under the geo-political and geo-economic conditions of the mid-1920s, it became the second formative stage in the wider consolidation process beginning in 1924.

Yet in the aftermath of the London settlement, the nascent *Pax Anglo-Americana* did not, or at least not yet, evolve into a coherent transatlantic system, or concert. Rather, what emerged was a two-level system. More precisely, the Locarno pact and the political stabilisation it brought Europe in 1925 were the result of two – parallel and essentially interlocking – developments. Britain's new security policy, reorientated under Chamberlain, propelled one, the most conspicuous, process: the diplomatic deliberations leading to Locarno. But the other, underlying process of political-cum-financial revitalisation in and beyond Germany was chiefly determined by American power, wielded by Hughes and those who, like Kellogg and FRBNY Governor Strong, sought to continue America's Progressive pursuit of European consolidation after him. Once again, both processes were shaped by distinct British and American approaches to peaceful change. Both fostered further integrative accommodation between the western powers and Germany. Thus, they also created the necessary, if as yet far from sufficient, preconditions for transforming relations between Germany and its eastern neighbours.

11   The dawning of a Progressive *Pax Americana* in Europe?

In a narrower sense, the pre-history of Locarno began with the implementation of the Dawes plan in the autumn of 1924. For it changed the wider international 'playing-field' on which the reorganisation of European security politics in the mid-1920s took place. To a considerable extent, it became a 'playing-field' determined, and delimited, by the American endeavour to make the Dawes system into a cornerstone of what in Republican thinking emerged as a Progressive *Pax Americana* for Europe.

In concrete terms, once the German parliament had passed the requisite laws, two agreements remained to be finalised to launch the new reparations regime. First, the European allies and the United States, as 'associated power', had to agree on the division of German payments under the Dawes scheme. This was accomplished at the Paris conference of September 1924. The Coolidge administration's core interest was to be reimbursed for army costs that Germany 'was obligated to pay' under the 1921 Treaty of Berlin.[1] In short, the Paris agreement fixed inter-allied reparations shares without much controversy and US army-cost payments to Washington's satisfaction. At the same time, the United States remained a power unbridled by the provisions of 1919, not 'committed morally or legally' to enforce 'the collection of reparations from Germany'.[2] Further, and more importantly, the western governments and Anglo-American bankers had to reach a consensus on the final modalities of the Dawes loan to Germany. This eventually emerged at a meeting in London in mid-October.

These settlements can indeed be characterised as further steps in the realisation of American designs to foster Europe's recuperation through informal or 'private' stabilisation programmes.[3] They could only be achieved through further Anglo-American co-operation, both official and private. Yet they also underscored further the shift of the international centre of gravity not only in terms of finance. America's Progressive approach prevailed. And rather than even consider formal, politically controlled recovery programmes, anything

---

[1] Kellogg memorandum on 'The Dawes Report', March 1925, Kellogg Papers.
[2] *Ibid.*; Hughes to Herrick, 29 November 1924, *FRUS 1924*, II, p. 94.
[3] See Hogan (1991), p. 71.

even remotely anticipating the Marshall plan, the Coolidge administration relied on private investment channels and controls.[4] This confirmed what the London conference had already shown, namely the essential limits of British and American stabilisation policies. While Whitehall did not have the means, Washington was simply not prepared to extend formal political guarantees underpinning the new reparations regime – and Europe's 'economic peace'.

British constraints

American thus superseded British concepts, which envisaged a higher degree of governmental steering. MacDonald still favoured establishing an intergovernmental framework not only to deal with Europe's broader security problems but also to regulate the new loan-and-reparations cycle. Yet, acknowledging US predominance, his short-lived government could not advance any coherent plans. In principle, then, the British approach to both financial and political security differed considerably from the American. As the Treasury underscored, however, given its indebtedness and need for internal retrenchment, Britain was no more in a position than France or Germany to recast the Dawes process, or Anglo-American debt policy, the 'European way'.[5]

Fundamentally, the Labour government followed a continuity of British policy in seeking to further the reconstruction of a 'liberal' world economy under the *leitmotif* of 'peace through free trade'. Within it, not only French finances and Germany's economy were to be stabilised. A prospering Germany would also again be a competitor; but chiefly it would be a potent reparations debtor and, once again, Britain's most important market in Europe.[6] British diplomacy thus focused on accelerating negotiations over an Anglo-German Commercial Treaty, according both sides unconditional most-favoured-nation status. It was signed on 2 December 1924.[7] Politically, Britain sought to channel the energies of a reinvigorated republican Germany towards pacific economic competition. Yet MacDonald realised that, essentially, this could only be propelled by America and through US loans.[8] As noted, the new distribution of power in international finance also manifested itself in the fact that, after a lengthy tug-of-war between the Bank of England and the Federal Reserve Bank of New York, Germany was incorporated in the gold-dollar system.[9]

---

[4] Cf. Hogan (1987), pp. 4–12.

[5] MacDonald to Auriol, 15 September 1924, FO 371/9761: C 12851/75/18; Kellogg to Hughes, 12 August 1924, NA RG 59 462.00 R296/491; Niemeyer to Crowe, 14 August 1924, FO 371/9863: C 13040/11/62. Cf. Orde (1990), pp. 203ff.

[6] Sterndale–Bennett memorandum, 10 January 1926, *DBFP*, IA, I, pp. 9–12. Cf. Kennedy (1975).

[7] Cf. Krüger (1985a), pp. 257–8.

[8] See MacDonald to Norman, 24 September 1924, T 194/281, Bank of England Files, BE OV 34/105, quoted after Orde (1990), p. 265.

[9] See chapter 7. Cf. Dayer (1991), pp. 162–73; Costigliola (1977).

But Britain's political and financial elites never lost sight of their underlying aim: to re-establish the *status quo ante bellum* as far as possible, with the City still seeking to regain pre-eminence from Wall Street. MacDonald, Snowden and their Conservative successors, notably Baldwin and his chancellor Churchill, shared premises from which no British government would depart before the Slump and subsequent introduction of the protectionist imperial-preference system. All held that Britain's chief interest lay in reforming yet preserving a liberal-capitalist system at home and abroad. All sought to bolster free trade while also trying to cope with the war's repercussions through new, but still very circumscribed, state interventionism. A particular challenge was rising unemployment, which stabilised at mostly over 10 per cent throughout the 1920s. In the view of its leaders, then, Britain's prosperity critically depended on reinvigorating a liberal world economy in which British exports were unimpeded by high tariff barriers like those America imposed from 1921.[10]

This orientation was of course also espoused by Norman and the Bank of England. And it went hand in hand with the long-standing desire of re-introducing the prewar gold standard. Both Norman and Churchill deemed this a prerequisite for returning to the Empire's golden age. And from the autumn of 1924, it became the main aim of Conservative economic policy. FRBNY Governor Strong had in fact also long pressed Britain to take this step. Like Hoover, Strong was mainly concerned about the negative effects of disorderly currency relations and the repercussions of possible British inflation. Yet he also sought to expand US foreign lending, expecting that rising British interest-rates after the return to gold would make the City a less potent competitor.[11] With Morgan & Co.'s senior partners in London, Strong thus supported Norman's efforts significantly.[12]

Churchill had originally been sceptical about this gold-standard policy, fearing that the Americans pursued a hidden agenda. He also anticipated, correctly, that returning to the gold standard would be detrimental for British exports because it would overvalue sterling vis-à-vis the dollar. This threatened to aggravate the cardinal postwar problem of unemployment.[13] In January 1925, Churchill thus still advocated postponing a return to gold for fear that it would have 'very serious' consequences.[14] Eventually, however, the chancellor followed the recommendation of under-secretary Niemeyer. Niemeyer considered returning to gold essential for consolidating Britain's standing in the

---

[10] Cf. Newton (1996), pp. 30–1; Pollard (1992), pp. 109–11; Boyce (1987), pp. 71ff.
[11] Strong to Norman, 4 November 1924, Strong Papers, 1116.4. Cf. Chandler (1958), pp. 300ff.
[12] Strong minute, 11 January 1925, Lamont Papers, TWL 103–13.
[13] Quoted after Kindleberger (1973), p. 30.
[14] Churchill memorandum, 29 January 1925, Treasury Papers, T175/9; Gilbert (1976), pp. 300–5.

world economy.[15] And Norman vigorously supported his line.[16] The decision to re-establish the gold standard was finally taken in mid-March and announced by Churchill on 28 April. As it turned out, however, doing so on the detrimentally high prewar parity of $4.86 indeed spelled very negative consequences for Britain's recovery in the period of 'normalcy' between 1925 and 1929. It would limit the Baldwin government's ability to boost British prosperity and reduce unemployment. And it would limit its ability to pursue bolder approaches to international reconstruction and the reparations issue.[17]

Disputes among the ex-allied powers over the allocation of Dawes annuities – and war-debts – also placed considerable strains on the newly invigorated Anglo-American co-operation of 1924, both official and private. But at least in the decisive years between 1924 and 1929, rivalry between the old and the newly predominant power in the world financial system was clearly submerged by overall concurrent interests, notably that in consolidating Franco-German relations.[18] Essentially, however, those who had a decisive say in promoting European recovery by economic means sat in Washington and New York. And they sought to achieve it the American way. How, then, was the complex of Europe's still unsettled problems perceived from the vantage-points of US policymakers and financiers? What precisely did the success of London mean for the further evolution of US policy?

US policy and the paradigm of the Dawes settlement

What had a marked impact on the – superficially – Eurocentric development of European international politics, particularly security politics, in the mid-1920s was the fact that for US decisionmakers, notably Hughes, the London settlement quickly acquired a paradigmatic character. From the autumn of 1924, an underlying elite consensus emerged, uniting the Coolidge administration and Wall Street. In short, the Dawes approach held such an appeal because it essentially furthered the stabilisation objectives of informal hegemony. America's financial prowess and concomitant political influence had been used, and could be used further, to refashion European politics without entangling the United States in the formal guarantee of either the reparations regime or Franco-German pacification at large. This set the stage for, and constrained, the further evolution of transatlantic politics. But Washington did not completely retreat from its role as a powerful *informal* arbiter in European affairs. Most notably, it would decisively buttress the process leading to the Locarno pact.

---

[15] Niemeyer memorandum, 2 February 1925, Treasury Papers, T175/9.

[16] Norman memorandum, 2 February 1925, Treasury Papers, T175/9. Cf. Kindleberger (1973), pp. 30–1.

[17] Cf. Boyce (1987), pp. 71–8; Eichengreen (1992).

[18] Cf. Costigliola (1977); Hogan (1991), pp. 70ff.

The restrictions Washington imposed on further official engagement stemmed not only from the cherished Republican maxim of non-entanglement in Europe, which eased the administration's interaction with Congress. They were also informed by a profound confidence in the Progressive approach to European consolidation, as exemplified by the success of London. Ever more, and especially after Hughes' departure in January 1925, US policy was driven by a pronounced faith in the blessings of minimal governmental interference and a staunch belief in the self-invigorating dynamism of peaceful change via the economic sphere.[19] Carefully delimited co-operation with Britain to safeguard the Dawes scheme continued. Yet there was also, expressed most succinctly by Hoover, the increasingly assertive notion that on the premises of 1924 the old *Pax Britannica*, already severely challenged by the late nineteenth century and collapsing thereafter, could be replaced by a new *Pax Americana*. Hoover envisaged the latter as a system of co-operating and economically competing liberal-capitalist states, undergirded by America's financial power and evolving under the informal control of the US government.[20] Within it, and in accordance with Washington's directives, semi-private agents like Young and Parker Gilbert were to occupy key positions in the process of Europe's rationalisation and modernisation, all following the Progressive model of America's 'New Era'.[21]

Hoover remained the most influential proponent of unhampered economic diplomacy as the key to securing vital US interests *and* Europe's further consolidation in an interdependent yet asymmetrical transatlantic system. As the commerce secretary never failed to stress, while the United States had tangible financial and political interests across the Atlantic, it was Europe that depended on America, not vice versa. In Hoover's view, the outcome of London and America's success in stabilising European currencies, notably sterling, bore out the strategy he had advocated ever since 1920. In a speech on 1 December 1924, he emphasised that 'there were economic issues born of the war for which no solution was possible until time and bitter experience' had

---

[19] See Hoover's address on 'Government Ownership', 29 September 1924, Hoover (1924). There, the secretary of commerce concluded that European governments 'have much more concentrated power and responsibility than we have ever been willing to grant to our Government', which 'necessarily leaves to private enterprise many things which other nations can, if they prefer, do through Government'. Yet Hoover of course maintained that America's 'model' was that of the future, asserting that European 'Socialism' had 'no place with us' and preferably should not have a place with 'the nations of Europe' either. *Ibid.*

[20] Hoover address, 14 December 1924, Hoover Papers, box 75. See also Hoover (1924).

[21] From the expert's vantage-point, Owen Young argued after the success of the Dawes settlement that the time had come to supersede the outmoded 'science of war' and 'industry of foreign relations' with a new 'science of peace'. International 'misunderstanding' could be overcome by hence fully relying on the 'impartial authority' of experts that were 'free from the handicaps of domestic politics' afflicting politicians on all sides of a given dispute. Young (1925).

allowed for a settlement 'founded solely upon economic ground' and untarnished by 'political considerations'. Hoover recognised that the administration's part in bringing it about had been important. But its main contribution had been to set an example in 'disinterested statesmanship'. What had really advanced European recovery was the 'unofficial mission of disinterested private citizens', notably Young. Hoover concluded that the pursuit of US economic diplomacy had turned into 'a peace mission without parallel in international history', and that there was every reason to believe that it could be sustained.[22]

Hoover's views were widely shared by the leaders of US high finance, notably FRBNY Governor Strong, who became a key agent of America's continued stabilisation efforts in the Dawes plan era, especially in recasting the international currency system.[23] Chiefly co-operating with the heads of the British and German central banks, Norman and Schacht, Strong's ultimate aim was to consolidate New York's new predominance as hub of global finance. This he undoubtedly realised. Yet, with Hughes' backing, Strong also sought to foster monetary stability in Britain, Germany and France, viewing it as an essential precondition for Europe's economic rehabilitation.[24] While he saw Britain's return to gold and Germany's currency reform as first notable successes, both had to be sustained, and France yet had to overcome its financial crisis.

What Hoover delineated and Strong backed indeed became guiding principles of America's bid to effect a pacific transformation of Europe after 1924. The renewed emphasis on informal, economic pacification was also endorsed fundamentally by Hughes. While not excluding further engagement the secretary of state had come to regard America's intervention on behalf of the Dawes plan as the maximal extent to which the administration could throw its weight into Europe's political balance, at least for the foreseeable future. Essentially, this would demarcate the boundaries of America's 'formal' role in fostering European consolidation – boundaries not transgressed under his successor, Kellogg, in the latter 1920s.[25]

A prevalent notion among principal US decisionmakers became that the Dawes settlement, resulting from carefully circumscribed co-operation with Britain, constituted not merely as a preliminary advance, inherently at risk without stronger political underpinnings. Rather, it was seen as a solid foundation of European stability, and conflict-resolution, in its own right.[26] In

---

[22] Hoover address, 14 December 1924, Hoover Papers, box 75. Cf. Hawley (1974).
[23] Strong to Young, 16 July 1924, Young Papers, box R-14.
[24] Cf. Clarke (1967), pp. 60–6; Hogan (1991), pp. 71–2.
[25] See chapter 13.
[26] Kellogg memorandum on 'The Dawes Report', March 1925, Kellogg Papers.

Hughes' eyes, the London accords had by no means produced a new European security dilemma by fostering Germany's recuperation. Rather, they offered the key to transcending this dilemma: as the best guarantee for France's security, the creation of interdependent interests with a capitalist, republican Germany. Its new political and economic elites would hence have a stake in maintaining their western orientation – and their commitment to peaceful ways of changing the postwar *status quo*.[27]

More generally, the Ruhr crisis and the concrete difficulties arising from the Dawes plan's implementation had further reinforced the American perception that the Versailles system as such was a crucial obstacle to Europe's stabilisation. US policymakers thus favoured its further revision, a reform that eliminated all discriminations hampering Germany's western integration, and US commercial expansion.[28] A cardinal maxim of Republican policy remained, however, that any change had to be gradual, effected only with Washington's consent and commensurable with America's core economic interests.

On 29 November 1924, Hughes established a cardinal premise of America's further pursuits of peaceful change in Europe, valid until the 1930s. He underscored that the Coolidge administration offered 'no objection to the modification of the Treaty of Versailles not deemed incompatible with our interests'. But it could not 'admit that any rights acquired by this government by treaty or otherwise can in any way be diminished or altered by an agreement between the Allies and Germany' to which the US government was 'not a party' and on 'terms to which it has not consented'.[29] While formally remaining outside Europe's postwar order, the semi-hegemonic American power thus claimed the right to retain a decisive voice in shaping the ground-rules of treaty revision and, more broadly, the desired transformation of international politics.

In the autumn of 1924, US policymakers, and financiers, were originally not so much worried about a recurrent Franco-German conflict stemming from unresolved security issues. Their apprehensions were more concrete, and essentially economic. They concerned a 'transfer crisis' of the Dawes regime and the repercussions it could have not only in Germany and Europe but also the United States. The Morgan partner Dwight Morrow was not the only banker voicing such concerns to the State Department. His foreboding was that Europe's fledgling economic recovery might founder if the expert plan was undermined because US financiers would then be unable to advance

---

[27] Hughes to Kellogg, 20 September 1924; Hughes circular to US embassies in Europe, 23 April 1924, NA RG 59 462.00 R296/607, 286a.

[28] See Castle's comments, 7 October 1924, Castle Diary, vol. 6.

[29] Hughes to Herrick, 29 November 1924, *FRUS 1924*, II, p. 94.

the promised loan under stable conditions. Not least, Morrow pointed to a potentially critical factor: the reaction of German nationalist parties to the far-reaching external regulations that the Dawes regime imposed.[30]

By contrast, Hughes saw no acute danger of a political backlash in Germany. Having come to regard both Stresemann and Marx as reliable negotiating-partners in the making of the Dawes plan, he deemed them well capable of implementing it further. Castle, who met both protagonists in Berlin on 22 October, confirmed the increasingly favourable US impression of Weimar German leaders. He considered Marx 'a man of integrity' and 'moderate power' and Stresemann an efficient 'politician rather than a statesman', albeit lacking a 'straight-forward face'.[31]

By and large, Hughes and Castle trusted German leaders to realise that they were bearing a temporary burden redounding to Germany's advantage in the longer term. And, as Hughes told Morrow, he foresaw no violent German reaction against the unprecedented external interference. Backing London's appraisal, he stressed his belief that following the war and the turmoil of 1923 'the great masses of the people want peace' and 'the people of Germany' were no 'exception'. Reiterating maxims of his Progressive approach, Hughes impressed on the Morgan partners that 'there must be a basis for hope' and a 'fair degree of economic stability to maintain this peaceable disposition'. The 'execution' of the Dawes plan was 'necessary to meet these conditions'. Hughes warned that its failure could have 'disastrous' economic consequences not only in Europe but also in America. More than Hoover, he thus emphasised the 'reality' of transatlantic interdependence. Yet he also used this argument to spur the American bankers into action where the administration rejected an official role.[32]

In September, J.P. Morgan & Co. had approached the State Department on the matter of possible governmental guarantees for the German loan.[33] But Hughes affirmed unequivocally that he had 'no right to pledge' the government's support 'either legally or morally' on this issue. He expected that US bankers, acting on behalf of their own and wider US interests, would 'undertake the participation which the world expects and which is believed to be essential to the success of the [Dawes] plan'.[34] In this vital aspect, the Coolidge administration thus again primarily counted on informal agents. No strategies were contemplated to provide official securities and controls. What emerged

---

[30] Morrow to Hughes, 18 September 1924, NA RG 59 462.00 R296/604.

[31] Castle Diary, 22 October 1924, vol. 6.

[32] Hughes to Morrow, 19 September 1924, repeated to Kellogg, 20 September 1924, NA RG 59 462.00 R296/607.

[33] Morrow to Hughes, 18 September 1924, NA RG 59 462.00 R296/604; Lamont memorandum, 16 September 1924, Lamont Papers, TWL 177/12.

[34] Hughes to Morrow, 19 September 1924, NA RG 59 462.00 R296/611.

instead, and soon, was an understanding with the House of Morgan. The administration would informally endorse the initial private loans; Morgan oversaw the actual transactions. As Treasury Secretary Andrew W. Mellon argued, the 'leadership' on loans had to be 'conceded to Morgan's' because otherwise 'loan possibilities would be in danger as Morgan's co-operation was essential'.[35]

In the end, Hughes fell back on a course adopted ever since his futile attempt in 1921–2 to win Congressional support for a more tightly controlled foreign commercial policy. Then, Hoover's *laissez-faire* approach had prevailed.[36] And then, as in 1924, governmental loan supervision would have required Congressional authorisation. But Congress remained unwilling to provide it, let alone fund bail-out schemes for failing private loans. In Hughes' view, his informal strategy of 1923/4 had proved too effective to be jeopardised by re-opening old battles. Fundamentally, neither the administration nor a Republican-dominated Congress desired to be manoeuvred into a position where the United States would ultimately have to 'liquidate' the war's consequences.[37]

If for different reasons MacDonald also ceded the leadership in floating the loan and establishing the Dawes regime to the Anglo-American financiers. He did so in view of America's incontestable preponderance and his own concentration on security politics while also struggling for his government's survival. MacDonald gave Norman free rein to organise the international loan-syndicate with Morgan & Co., only reining in his relentless attempts to force more political concessions on France.[38] Essentially, he and Hughes blocked all bankers' demands for still firmer French guarantees concerning the Ruhr evacuation.[39]

In effect, Morgan & Co. swiftly organised the syndicate for floating the German loan on Wall Street. On 10 October, the State Department assured, at Morgan's request, that it had 'no objections' to the loan.[40] On the same day, the agreement providing for an 800-million-goldmark loan to Germany was concluded in London. On 11 October, Schacht transmitted Stresemann's 'sincere thanks' to J.P. Morgan and Lamont for their efforts, expressing his 'hopes that

---

[35] Hughes to Coolidge, 23 August 1924, NA RG 59 4620.00 R296/532.
[36] Hoover memorandum, 23 January 1922, Hoover Papers, box 21.
[37] Hughes to Coolidge, 23 August 1924, NA RG 59 462.00 R296/532; Hughes to Herrick, 6 February 1925, Kellogg Papers. Cf. Schuker (1987), p. 15.
[38] MacDonald to Lamont, 4 September 1924, Kellogg Papers; MacDonald to Norman, 24 September 1924, quoted after Orde (1990), p. 265.
[39] Lamont memorandum, 16 September 1924, Lamont Papers, TWL 177/12; MacDonald to Norman, 24 September 1924, quoted after Orde (1990), p. 265; Kellogg to Lamont, 24 September 1924, Kellogg Papers.
[40] J.P. Morgan & Co. to Hughes, 10 October 1924, Harrison to J.P. Morgan & Co., 10 October 1924, NA RG 59 462.00 R296/604, 611.

Europe has turned the corner and takes the way for peace'. Though mindful of the 'difficulties' still lying ahead, Morgan shared the hope that the 'transaction' marked 'a turning point in the business currents of Europe'.[41]

On 15 October, Kellogg expressed his satisfaction about the 'complete success of the German loan' and 'the splendid work done by Morgan and Lamont', a satisfaction that Hughes shared.[42] It should be noted, however, that immediately after this success Morgan announced that his firm would hence no longer extend any loans to Germany.[43] This remained Morgan & Co.'s policy until the Great Depression. J.P. Morgan essentially never altered his suspicion of the wider intentions of German politicians and business elites. He considered most, and notably Stresemann, monarchists at heart who might seek to reinstate the emperor and prepare for a revisionist war.[44]

Morgan's decision notwithstanding, it was in Germany, rather than in France, that the United States *de facto* came to create a 'penetrated system' as the new chief creditor also controlling the new reparations regime.[45] While US capital began to flow, the Dawes regime entailed significant encroachments on German sovereignty, especially placing the control of reparation transfers largely in American hands. Following Hoover's approach, this unprecedented, highly dynamic process was overseen, in consultation with Washington, by the informally operating agent-general Parker Gilbert.[46]

Stresemann deliberately accepted 'Germany's penetration with American capital' and a high degree of US interference in German economic and political life.[47] He did so ultimately to extricate Germany from the constraints of Versailles through a close co-operation with the international system's strongest power. Stresemann anticipated correctly that the American creditor's growing engagement would also augment its interest in the well-being of its principal debtor. He not least hoped to seize on this to reduce German obligations once the reparations settlement was up for revision.[48]

It is worth emphasising again that the Dawes regime, as operating from October 1924, was not merely a mechanism to ensure the transfer of reparations. It also constituted the financial backbone for what German and wider

---

[41] Schacht to J.P. Morgan, 11 October 1924, J.P. Morgan to Schacht, 12 October 1924, Morgan Papers, box 195.

[42] Kellogg to Hughes, 15 October 1924, Kellogg Papers.

[43] *Journal of Commerce*, 17 October 1924. Cf. McNeil (1986), pp. 82–3.

[44] Thus Morgan to Wiedfeldt. See Wiedfeldt to German Foreign Ministry, 15 December 1924, PA, RM 27, vol. 4; Lamont statements before the Senate Investigating Committee in 1931, cited in McNeil (1986), p. 82.

[45] While US banks subscribed to half of the first 800-million-goldmark loan, Britain still took roughly a quarter.

[46] Kellogg to Wiedfeldt, 5 January 1925, *FRUS 1925*, I, pp. 16–17; Gilbert (1925–30) and (1925–6).

[47] Cf. Link (1970), pp. 322ff, and (1974), pp. 488, 496.

[48] Stresemann speech, 14 December 1925, *ADAP*, B, I, 1, annex II, p. 729; Stresemann *Reichstag* speech, 23 August 1924, Stresemann (1932), I, p. 519.

European recovery occurred in the 1920s. More precisely, the decisive initial flow of US capital to Germany engendered a transatlantic cycle of *unregulated* financial stabilisation: Germany received funds to revive its economy and pay reparations, which France and Britain in turn could use to reduce their debts to America. In view of these debts, Britain's influence on changing what eventually became a highly problematic 'system' was highly limited.[49] Rather, this system was the most ostensible manifestation of the Progressive *Pax Americana* in Europe. Crucially, it was in this constellation, and amid the structural changes it engendered, that European policymakers could hence seek to recast security relations, first between the western powers and Germany.

Left without political guarantees or concerted mechanisms for crisis management, and the bail-out of US loans, the Dawes regime remained highly susceptible to crisis. And it remained so beyond its modest revision through the 1929 Young plan. It was thus clearly distinct from, and a negative example for, the Bretton Woods system after World War II. In the 1920s, no institutions akin to a transatlantic monetary fund or a potent world bank were envisaged. What could be called their precursor, the Bank for International Settlements, was only established in 1930 and never received what would have been critical: America's full backing.[50]

More broadly, then, the Dawes regime remained less than robust because it emerged in a period when there was as yet no transatlantic financial order with robust underpinnings, nor a set of mutually accepted rules governing trade. As taking shape by the mid-1920s, the reigning gold-standard system was premised on a quasi-religious belief in the indispensability of gold as the commodity not merely stabilising but also automatically regulating transatlantic flows of capital and trade.[51]

The belief in the 'automaticity' of this system, and its key relevance for international stability, became even more entrenched in France than in Britain and America.[52] All key economies had tied their currencies to a fixed gold ratio; and the gold-dollar ratio became the leading standard. The more gold a country possessed the wider its monetary base was meant to be, which in turn supposedly enabled it to stimulate the domestic economy through lower interest-rates. By contrast, a country 'losing' gold was supposed to deflate its economy yet thereby also 'lower prices so as to stimulate exports, and to raise interest rates so as to reverse the outflow of capital'.[53] Supposedly, gold thus not only bound the world economy together but also ensured a financial equilibrium by

[49] Cf. Orde (1990), pp. 3–4, 203ff.
[50] See chapter 26. Cf. Costigliola (1972), pp. 602–20; Hogan (1987), pp. 17, 30–1.
[51] See Eichengreen (1992), pp. 304ff.
[52] See Mouré (2002), pp. 181–99, 259–67.
[53] See Kennedy (1999), p. 75.

balancing out any fluctuations within the system. In reality, however, even under the still rather fair economic conditions of the latter 1920s the gold-dollar system soon exhibited a marked imbalance: the American world creditor accumulated most gold and surplus capital.[54] And would a system of this kind cope with a serious crisis?

With the benefit of hindsight, there can be little doubt that it was exceedingly difficult, if not impossible, to halt the disintegration of the postwar financial order after the 1929 Wall Street crash. And it has been unhistorically claimed that these were inevitable consequences. Arguably, it was all but impossible for either policymakers or financial experts to anticipate, from the vantage-point of late 1924, the magnitude of the crisis unleashed in 1929.[55] But there is no way around concluding that the gold–dollar system of the 1920s was a fair-weather system. It was not designed to absorb more than minor disturbances, and there were (as yet) no international mechanisms, either political or financial, to remedy major problems. The key question was whether emerging deficiencies of the Euro-Atlantic sphere's financial architecture would lead decisionmakers to strengthen its pillars pre-emptively, *before* a major crisis occurred. The same applied to the new reparations regime. Yet in the prevailing atmosphere of pronounced, if not dogmatic, confidence in this architecture, particularly in Washington and New York, the prospects for timely re-assessments of this kind were dim in both cases. And this became a liability for Europe's political stabilisation.

In fact, after only a few months of accelerating American lending to Germany, the US Commerce Department began to acknowledge that the sheer volume of private – and short-term – loans began to spin out of control.[56] By the spring of 1925, even Hoover contemplated the need for governmental checks. Very quickly, however, both the Republican non-interference paradigm and the federal government's weakness as financial regulator were confirmed. Particularly the Commerce Department came to consider official loan supervision not only impracticable but also potentially too burdensome for the administration.[57] And the State Department's outlook on Germany's consolidation and the working of the Dawes plan remained optimistic. Summarising prevalent assumptions in March 1925, Kellogg stressed that 'Germany intends to and can carry out the payments provided for' in the Dawes scheme. It owed 'no large external or internal

---

[54] See the Epilogue.
[55] See Schuker (1987), pp. 15–38.
[56] Commerce Department records on 'German Foreign Loans, January 1925 – April 1926', NA RG 39, box 85.
[57] See chapter 18. Cf. Hawley (1974).

debt', and its currency had been reformed 'on a gold basis', within the US gold-dollar system.[58]

Undoubtedly, then, the Dawes system originally rested on less than solid foundations. Yet it is well worth underlining again that without it not even a 'relative' consolidation of Weimar Germany, and Europe, would have been attainable after 1923. As Stresemann had hoped, the Dawes plan and the capital flow it triggered gave the German economy the boost it urgently needed. However misplaced many funds were, at least in American eyes – going as they did into subsidies and wage-rises, allowing Germany to live 'beyond its means' rather than foster structural reforms – they laid the groundwork for the Weimar Republic's stabilisation between 1925 and 1929.[59] How far this could be sustained was an open question, certainly in 1924.

That similar loans to France were not equally forthcoming had many, not only political, reasons. Rather than underlying anti-French attitudes on the part of US policymakers, a principal factor accounting for America's concentration on Germany was the unresolved war-debt question. Hughes did not shy away from using France's need for US capital, whose allocation had to be authorised, as a political instrument to pressure Paris into complying with Washington's demands.

After Coolidge's re-election in November 1924, the Republican administration maintained its policy to block further private loans to France until Paris had followed London in signing, and ratifying, a war-debt settlement on US terms. Consequently, when Morgan & Co. consulted the State Department concerning a proposed $100,000,000 loan to the Herriot government, Hughes underscored that he 'should certainly oppose the flotation in the United States of a French loan' as long as this remained doubtful.[60] The Morgan partners complied. A change of this axiom only drew closer with the conclusion of the Mellon–Bérenger debt agreement in 1926. Pending French ratification, however, there was no turning-of-the-tide.[61] The pattern that US power projection in the form of capital bypassed France and centred on Germany persisted throughout the 'era of London and Locarno'.

Thus, the Republican administration continued to guard jealously all prerogatives accruing from the financial outcome of the Great War and America's new position as war-debt creditor and lender of last resort. In a memorandum for Coolidge, transmitted on 23 August 1924, Hughes underlined his main 'fear' arising from this constellation: the formation of

---

[58] Kellogg memorandum, 'The Dawes Report', March 1925, Kellogg Papers.
[59] See also chapter 18. For the long-standing controversy over Germany's 'relative stabilisation' see Borchardt (1982), pp. 165–82; Holtferich (1984), pp. 122–41; Ferguson (1997).
[60] Hughes to Logan, 11 November 1924, NA RG 59 462.00 R296/694a.
[61] Cf. Costigliola (1984), pp. 134–8.

European debtor coalition against the United States. He did not waver from the Republicans' bilateral approach to the debt issue, intent on setting the terms, first vis-à-vis Britain, then France.[62] As will be shown, the decisions the US government made in the autumn of 1924 had significant repercussions for European security negotiations in 1925 and thereafter. They widened, respectively constrained, their protagonists' freedom of action – giving Stresemann new opportunities and restricting those of Herriot and Briand to act against Anglo-American preferences.

---

[62] Hughes to Coolidge, 23 August 1924, Kellogg to Hughes, 12 August 1924, NA RG 59 462.00 R296/532, 491; Grew Diary, 14 August 1924, vol. 1924/5, p. 222, Grew Papers; Kellogg memorandum, 'The Dawes Report', March 1925, Kellogg Papers.

12   Towards the Locarno pact
Britain's quest for a new European concert, 1924–1925

From an Anglo-American perspective, the making of the Locarno accords can be analysed as a process comprising four distinct stages after the – limited – foundations of the Dawes system had been laid: (1) 'gestation' – the failure of the Geneva Protocol's universalist, League-based approach to security and the search for alternative models (September 1924 – mid-January 1925); (2) 'germination' – the recasting of British security policy towards the pursuit of a pact as nucleus of a new European concert, not least under the impact of Stresemann's 'security initiative' and America's endorsement of this approach (late January – March 1925); (3) 'crisis and perseverance' – Britain's promotion of newly integrative negotiations over the Rhine pact with France and Germany, spurred by American pressure (culminating between June and August 1925); and finally (4) 'resolution' – the finalisation of the security accords and actual emergence of the new European concert at the Locarno conference (October 1925).

The limits of the Geneva Protocol and the pre-Locarno constellation

After the London conference, the Coolidge administration re-affirmed its anti-Wilsonian creed, and the Hughes doctrine, in the domain of 'classic' security politics. In the autumn of 1924, Hughes reverted to what he regarded as a proven and advantageous policy of strategic non-entanglement outside the American hemisphere. Both he and his designated successor Kellogg thought that they could foster European security most effectively, and without provoking Congressional opposition, if they guarded their 'neutrality'. Both thus excluded a partisan involvement in the League or European politics.[1] Hughes maintained that even if 'we may not always exert our influence when we should', the crucial 'fact' was that 'a large part of our influence is due to the fact of our independence'.[2] Formally, America thus remained an unbridled

---

[1] Hughes to Drummond, 16 June 1924, *FRUS 1924*, II, pp. 80–3; Hughes résumé to Castle, 7 December 1925, Kellogg Papers; Kellogg to Coolidge, 7 October 1924, Kellogg Papers.

[2] Hughes to Castle, Castle Diary, 5 February 1924, vol. 5, pp. 44–5.

arbiter outside the Versailles system. This made Britain's role in seeking a security framework for Europe's economic pacification pivotal.

The policy that MacDonald came to pursue to 'solve' Europe's new security question and reassure France without direct US support centred on the League of Nations; it culminated in an initiative to empower the League to become at last Europe's central mechanism of collective security *and* peaceful change. He hoped to achieve this through his version of the Geneva Protocol and a swift inclusion of Germany into the League.[3] After the bid for a shricter regime of collective security, the Cecil-Requin Treaty of Mutual Assistance, had collapsed, not least through Britain's veto, MacDonald endeavoured to forge a common security platform with Herriot and the Czechoslovak prime minister Edouard Beneš at the League Assembly in September 1924. Yet, in short, his policy did not succeed.

Formally, the Protocol was destined to 'close' the gap remaining in the Covenant ever since its establishment, namely that League members regained the freedom to pursue independent action if the council failed to reach a unanimous decision on how to counter an aggressor.[4] MacDonald sought to fill this gap through 'an elaborate system of universal reconciliation and arbitration as essential link between disarmament and collective security'.[5] Crucially, he hoped to integrate Germany, and eventually Soviet Russia, into this reformed security system.[6] On 4 September, MacDonald declared in Geneva: 'The London Conference created a new relationship between Germany and the other European states, and the relationship should be sealed and sanctified by Germany's appearance on the floor of this Assembly.' Through the Protocol, the Labour premier also sought to offer an alternative commitment to France. Throughout the Geneva negotiations, however, his misgivings about Herriot's underlying motives grew.[7] The French premier had at this point resigned himself to accepting the impossibility of bilateral British guarantees. Consequently, he and the *Quai d'Orsay* hoped to commit Britain, and fortify the European *status quo*, by means of the Protocol.[8]

But MacDonald soon distanced himself from French attempts to turn the Protocol into the covenant of a rigid regime of collective security, including 'automatic sanctions' against aggressors and geared to cementing the postwar

---

[3] MacDonald (1925) and (1923a), pp. 19–24.
[4] Cf. Steiner (1993), pp. 47f; Orde (1978), pp. 68–9; Noel Baker (1925), pp. 18ff; Walters (1952), I, pp. 269ff.
[5] MacDonald speech before the League Assembly, 4 September 1924, *UF*, VI, no. 1370a. Cf. Gordon (1969), p. 51.
[6] MacDonald (1925). For the Protocol see *Société des Nations* (1924), pp. 502–6.
[7] *UF*, VI, no. 1370a; Cmd 2289: *League of Nations Fifth Assembly*, Report of the British Delegates (September–October 1924).
[8] Cf. Bariéty (1977), pp. 664–82, and (2000), p. 126.

order.[9] On 22 September, the prime minister reassured his cabinet and the Dominions that he would never support Protocol provisions that went beyond the previous Covenant.[10] He resisted obliging Britain, as the hub of a global empire, to make advance commitments to enforcing the Protocol's regime. For this not only threatened to take vital strategic decisions out of the hands of the British government. It also threatened to place an unprecedented burden on Britain, requiring a degree of military preparedness clearly at odds with MacDonald's disarmament aims.

It was with these marked reservations that the British cabinet in principle supported the version of the Protocol that the League Assembly passed on 2 October. Yet MacDonald instructed Britain's delegates in Geneva, Parmoor and Henderson, not to sign it. Before any final decision could be made, the Labour government fell over the Zinoviev letter, made public by the Foreign Office on 22 October and alleging Soviet machinations to stir revolution in Britain.[11] To the very end, MacDonald had fought, in vain, for recognising the Soviet Union and for concluding general peace and commercial treaties with Moscow.

Washington criticised MacDonald's security policy and categorically rejected the Geneva Protocol. Essentially, the State Department suspected the emergence of a 'new holy alliance' under the guise of the Protocol's 'tightened' regime of obligatory sanctions and arbitration. What came to be regarded as a predominantly French initiative collided with 'fixed policies' to which Washington had 'an avowed attachment', above all the Monroe Doctrine. The Protocol not only threatened to limit American 'independence' in dealing with Latin American states that belonged to the League,[12] US policymakers also suspected that behind it lay French designs to entrench the European *status quo*, ultimately by military means, and thus obstructing American efforts at peaceful change. As Kellogg told Coolidge on 7 October, he was glad that Washington was 'not bound by any obligations to maintain the political integrity and independence of all the turbulent nations of Europe'.[13]

To vindicate Washington's opposition to the Protocol, Hughes repeatedly took recourse to the 'model' of the 1921/2 Washington conference. Addressing

[9] MacDonald memorandum, 3 July 1924, FO 371/9818: C 10067/2048/18; Crowe memorandum, 17 November 1924, FO 371/10571, W 9974/134/98; Foreign Office memorandum, 9 November 1924, CAB 24/168, CP 481 (24).
[10] Minutes of the British Empire Delegation meetings, 22 September 1924, FO 371/10570: W 8073/134/98.
[11] 183rd session of the CID, 3 April 1924, CAB 2/4; Foreign Office memorandum, 9 November 1924, CAB 24/168, CP 481 (24); *Société des Nations* (1924), pp. 502–6. Cf. Marquand (1977), pp. 381–8.
[12] Kellogg to Hughes, 15 October 1924, Kellogg Papers; Fletcher (Rome) to Hughes, 15 December 1924, NA RG 59 511.3131/263; State Department memorandum, 20 November 1924, NA RG 59 511.3131/246.
[13] Kellogg to Coolidge, 7 October 1924, Kellogg Papers. Cf. Burks (1959), pp. 891–905.

the League's secretary general, Sir Eric Drummond, he praised it as an example of how specific security problems – here: security in the Pacific and naval disarmament – could be settled through the co-operation of regional 'associations of nations'. And he advised the Europeans to seek similarly flexible solutions, essentially by developing their own regional system, based on principles of international arbitration and peaceful conflict-resolution. He held that this would suffice to pacify the Franco-German conflict and buttress European security. By implication, it would relieve the United States of any responsibilities to intervene as the 'world's policeman' in Europe.[14]

Berlin welcomed MacDonald's proposal for German membership in the League and, on 29 September, the Marx government declared its general willingness to join the Geneva organisation. Yet Stresemann posed two core conditions. First, Germany was to be assured of a 'permanent seat in the Council' and a 'participation on equal footing with the other nations'; and second, as 'a disarmed people surrounded by strongly armed neighbours', Germany was to be exempted from supporting compulsory sanctions. Essentially, Berlin sought to preserve neutrality should the League impose sanctions on Soviet Russia. These would remain contentious issues throughout 1925. In principle, however, the perspective of Germany's entry into the League accorded with Stresemann's desire to regain international influence *and* responsibilities.[15]

Yet German League policy in late 1924 was indeed mainly 'a function of the policy towards England'.[16] Ever more, in Stresemann's – and Schubert's – thinking, Britain was assigned the 'key role' as the only potential arbiter of a new European security order that desired to promote peaceful change. Fundamentally, though, Germany sought a regional pact rather than a League-based system. Berlin was relieved when the Protocol came to nothing after MacDonald's resignation. In Stresemann's eyes, it was hardly in Germany's interest to back a scheme that strengthened French prerogatives under Versailles and France's eastern alliance system.[17]

Confronted with the volatile European security constellation at the end of 1924, the new foreign secretary in Baldwin's second cabinet, Austen Chamberlain, opted to abandon MacDonald's quest for a flexible protocol. It was finally rejected both by the cabinet and the influential Committee of Imperial Defence

---

[14] Hughes to Drummond, 16 June 1924, *FRUS 1924*, II, pp. 80–3; Hughes memorandum, 12 July 1921, *FRUS 1921*, I, pp. 53–61.

[15] Robbins to Hughes, 30 September 1924, NA RG 59 462.00 R296/397. Cf. Krüger (1985a), pp. 262–5, and against it Kimmich (1976), pp. 44–8.

[16] Krüger (1985a), p. 262.

[17] Schubert note, 29 August 1923, *ADAP*, A, VIII, p. 311; Stresemann to D'Abernon, 11 February 1924, *ADAP*, A, IX, no. 146; Robbins to Hughes, 30 September 1924, NA RG 59 462.00 R296/397.

on 16 December – on grounds reflecting MacDonald's misgivings. The prevalent view was that the Protocol could not be reconciled with vital British interests because it would have obliged Britain to enforce its 'automatic sanction clauses' around the globe, thus impinging on national sovereignty in cardinal questions of imperial defence. No less, the Baldwin government refused to commit itself to what Chamberlain deemed a 'rigid' order of collective security reinforcing the *status quo* of 1919 in Europe as a whole. This hardly concurred with Britain's desire to advance European stabilisation by promoting further pacific changes in the sphere of international security.[18]

By the end of 1924, then, one cardinal feature of postwar politics had become unmistakable. Neither the League nor, more specifically, the Geneva Protocol provided the platform for reorganising European security relations. No general, universal schemes would serve this purpose, not least because of British and American reservations. There was a strong and growing pressure on Britain to seek alternative remedies for French and continental insecurity. Also evident, or rather confirmed, was the fact that any alternative security system would have to be forged by the Europeans themselves; Washington would assume no formal responsibilities. This set the stage for the subsequent Locarno process. It could be called the pre-Locarno constellation.

The Baldwin cabinet's decision to discard the Protocol triggered the first tangible crisis of European *détente* since the London conference. What arose was the danger that, without new means of accommodating France's search for *sécurité*, the incipient accommodation process between the western powers and Germany might not only be halted but reversed. In London, there were acute concerns that France would revert to enforcing Germany's containment, thus jeopardising its international reintegration.[19]

For Herriot, by contrast, the recurrent predicament of French postwar policy resurfaced. On the one hand, aided by US capital, the *voisin d'outre-Rhin* was to all appearances regaining the strength that its economic and demographic potential warranted, while bilateral relations remained tense and unregulated. On the other, France was not only in the grips of a widening financial crisis, and set to lose in the foreseeable future its main security pillars under Versailles: military control and the occupied Rhineland. It also found itself once more without any tangible British security guarantees.[20]

The newly rising tension was reflected in the allied disarmament note of 10 January 1925. At the behest of the French government, it stated that due to

---

[18] CID Minutes, 16 December 1924, CAB 16/56/4657; Chamberlain statement before the League Assembly, 12 March 1925, Cmd 2368: Papers relating to the Protocol for the Peaceful Settlement of International Disputes (1925).

[19] Nicolson memorandum, 26 January 1925, FO 371/11065, W 2035/9/98.

[20] Seydoux memorandum, 22 February 1925, MAE, Série Europe, Grande-Bretagne, vol. 73, pp. 7ff.

Germany's failure to comply with the disarmament clauses of Versailles the promised evacuation of the Cologne zone would be postponed indefinitely. Herriot indeed threatened to perpetuate not only the operations of the IMCC but also the Rhineland occupation.[21] In the perception of Stresemann and Schubert, this highlighted the danger that Germany would again be relegated to the status of an 'object' of international politics.[22] Hence, in the narrowest sense, the active British – and German – quests for what became the Locarno pact originated. France – and the United States – reacted to their initiatives.

The reorientation of British foreign policy under Chamberlain and Britain's subsequent 'brokerage' between France and Germany would prove decisive in paving the way to Locarno. Without the British commitment, Stresemann's security initiative, Briand's reactive pursuits and America's financial-cum-political power alone would not have achieved significant results. No new European security regime would have emerged in the mid-1920s.[23] Systemically, however, it should be noted that Chamberlain benefited tangibly from US engagement in Europe since the Ruhr crisis; and he constantly had to reckon with Washington's interest in a 'political insurance' of US loans and Europe's 'Progressive' stabilisation. Britain could not only build on the advances, and precedent, of 1924 – unthinkable without the forceful American intervention – British efforts could also seize on the significant, if not indispensable, support that the Coolidge administration and American high finance provided throughout the protracted pact negotiations of 1925.

The reorientation of British stabilisation policy in 1925

After Lloyd George's frustrated quest for European reconstruction in 1922 and MacDonald's bid for a society of democratic nations in 1924, Chamberlain's 'new course' marked the third British attempt after the Great War to establish a new international concert, and stable order, in Europe. Like the Locarno accords themselves, Chamberlain's Locarno policy has been the subject of markedly divergent evaluations. What could be called the 'idealist' critique has asserted that by favouring security accords with Europe's remaining great powers British policy essentially weakened the League. Thus, it ultimately undermined all prospects of reviving Protocol-style collective security in the interwar period.[24]

---

[21] Cf. Wurm (1979), pp. 200ff; Salewski (1966), pp. 42–51.
[22] Schubert to Hoesch, 8 December 1924, PA, St. S, vol. 24.
[23] This was certainly also Chamberlain's view. See Chamberlain to D'Abernon, 2 April 1925, *DBFP*, I, XXVII, no. 283.
[24] Cf. Steiner (1993).

Far more influential, the 'realist' critique has placed Chamberlain's efforts in the pre-history of Munich-style appeasement.[25] It has criticised them as the pursuit of a hybrid compromise between regional and collective security – at the expense of joining France in fortifying Europe's balance of power against Germany. Did Chamberlain thus merely seal France's 'defeat' of London?[26] Allegedly, Britain furthered a deceptive truce in western Europe and borders of different, inferior validity in the east, undermining Polish and Czech security and setting the stage for the demise of the Versailles order in the 1930s.[27] By contrast, more recent accounts have viewed Chamberlain's policy more benignly, describing it essentially as the painful attempt to return to the best of the pre-1914 system and to revive the Anglo-French *entente* as its central axis.[28]

In fact, Chamberlain's policy of peaceful change was *neither* a flawed attempt to escape the realities of postwar Europe's balance-of-power politics *nor* a laudable return to its prewar roots. Rather, it was an idiosyncratic, and peculiarly Eurocentric, attempt to draw lessons from the war and subsequent frustrations of British policy, particularly Curzon's failure to prevent a Franco-German escalation during the Ruhr crisis.[29] At the same time, it was a conscious quest to build on traditions of British foreign policy that had shaped the Vienna system of 1814/15 in fostering a new international equilibrium in Europe. Its nucleus was to be a new concert system integrating Germany on conditions satisfactory for France.[30]

As noted, those who recast the course of British foreign policy between December 1924 and March 1925 *de facto* premised their pursuits on Europe's initial consolidation through the Dawes process, propelled by Anglo-American co-operation. In retrospect, however, one of the most striking features of Chamberlain's Locarno policy was its almost exclusively European, and not transatlantic, orientation. For British decisionmakers, there was no doubt that the most critical issue of the time, the Franco-German security problem, demanded not an economic but a political answer – and it demanded not an Anglo-American but essentially a *British* answer.

Chamberlain's learning process

By January 1925, in Chamberlain's, and Crowe's, perception, the pivotal Franco-German question posed itself in four key facets. How, on the one

---

[25] See Marks (1976), p. 63; Kissinger (1994), pp. 264–5; Jacobson (1972b), pp. 12–17; Schroeder (1976), pp. 223–43.
[26] Thus Schuker (1976), pp. 385–93.
[27] See Wandycz (1961), pp. 332ff; Jacobson (1972b), p. 29.
[28] See Grayson (1997), pp. 32–115; Magee (1995); Goldstein (1996), pp. 122–35.
[29] Chamberlain minute, 21 February 1925, FO 371/11064/W1252/9/98.
[30] See Cohrs (2003), pp. 22–6. Cf. Jacobson (2004), pp. 11–32.

hand, could Britain satisfy France's demands for security guarantees, more acute precisely because of the relative *détente* initiated in 1924? And how could this be achieved to such a degree that Germany's detrimental exclusion from the concert of powers could be ended? How, on the other hand, could Germany be reconciled with a less than radically modified post-World War I order? And how could Germany be tied to a 'western system' to such an extent that, even in the long term, it would refrain from aspiring to regain supremacy in continental Europe through a violent overthrow of the postwar *status quo*?[31]

Britain's eventual pursuit of the Locarno pact as a way to answer these questions was not simply the outgrowth of an overarching continuity of British appeasement. Rather, it was propelled by Chamberlain's personal commitment and the Foreign Office's resurgent influence under his permanent under-secretary, and *eminence grise*, Eyre Crowe (until his death in April 1925). To appreciate Chamberlain's influence, it should be underlined that the Baldwin cabinet was markedly divided on the issue of what responsibilities Britain was to assume as a power facing not only European but also domestic and imperial obligations. One imperialist school of thought, represented most forcefully by Colonial and Dominions secretary Leopold Amery and Churchill, clearly regarded the Empire as Britain's pre-eminent concern and advocated an imperial 'policy of aloofness' from Europea's postwar squabbles. They held that Britain could only resume its traditional balancing-role once a 'natural balance of forces' had re-established itself between France and Germany, peacefully or by force.[32] Another school of thought, aptly characterised as 'little Englander' and represented by cabinet secretary Hankey, favoured neither a focus on imperial concerns nor any binding commitments in Europe. Instead, it stressed the priority of domestic reform and retrenchment.[33] In May 1924, Hankey had told the South African premier Smuts that though Britain could not 'disinterest' itself 'in European affairs' – for 'geographical' and 'commercial' reasons – the best attitude was 'one of aloofness, rather on the lines of the United States'.[34]

It was against these dominant tides of Conservative opinion, and the Labour opposition's League preferences, that following Baldwin's call for 'an alternative policy' Chamberlain developed, and finally prevailed with, his definition of Britain's role as a European power. He thus ensured Britain's new commitment to Europe in the 1920s.[35] Consequently, having been marginalised under Lloyd

---

[31] Chamberlain to Grahame, 26 February 1925, FO 371/10727; Nicolson memorandum, prepared under Crowe's supervision, 26 January 1925, FO 371/11065, W 2035/9/98; 195th CID meeting, 13 February 1925, CAB 2/4. Cf. Crowe (1972), pp. 49–74; Otte (1998).

[32] 195th CID meeting, 13 February 1925, CAB 24/172, CP 105 (25).

[33] See Goldstein (1996), p. 135.

[34] Hankey to Smuts, 22 May 1924, Hankey Papers.

[35] This is rightly stressed, albeit on different grounds, in Grayson (1997), p. 32.

George, the Foreign Office again became the centre of gravity of British foreign policy. In the early stages, its new course, the pursuit of an integrative European concert, was propelled by Crowe. Long portrayed as favouring an exclusive pact with France, Crowe had actually, as noted, favoured a policy including Germany as early as June 1924.[36] The key memorandum of 26 January 1925 he co-authored with Nicolson proposed an Anglo-French pact *as nucleus* for a wider European concert.[37]

Ultimately, however, Chamberlain would assert his own, idiosyncratic approach to European stabilisation. What, then, spurred his 'learning process' in 1925? And what characterised the policies he would pursue on the path to Locarno – and indeed until he left office in 1929? Chamberlain's reorientation hardly resembled a linear process. At the outset, it was characterised by hesitancy in the face of cabinet opposition to what he had originally favoured – to regain European security by first allying with France. Nor was it a radical departure from British traditions of minimising the 'continental commitment'. And yet it transcended mere contingency-planning. Effectively, Chamberlain contributed to a marked change in the principles of British policy and Britain's role in European politics after 1918.

This change can roughly be delineated as follows. In December 1924, Chamberlain had still favoured an approach predicated on a return to prewar balance-of-power premises and the primacy of containing German revisionism. He strongly advocated the conclusion of an Anglo-French alliance, which could also include Belgium. It was to replace the Protocol as a 'nucleus of certainty, of stability, and of security' in western Europe – and might *eventually* draw Germany into the western orbit.[38] By March 1925, when Chamberlain had re-assessed the 'Ruhr fiasco' and fathomed his international and domestic constraints, his approach had not only tactically changed. It had indeed been transformed. He now espoused a policy of reviving the 'concert of Europe', which was to crystallise in a quadrilateral pact that enclosed Germany from the beginning and guaranteed the inviolability of the Franco-German border on the Rhine.[39]

Stresemann's Rhine pact proposal of late January undoubtedly provided Chamberlain with a crystallisation-point for this shift. Encouraged by D'Abernon, the German foreign minister had taken the initiative with a memorandum first sent to London on 20 January, then to Paris on 9 February.[40]

---

[36] Crowe to Kellogg, 24 June 1924, *DBFP*, I, XXVI, no. 493, p. 734.
[37] Nicolson memorandum, 26 January 1925, FO 371/11065, W 2035/9/98.
[38] 192nd CID meeting, 16 December 1924, CAB 24/172, CP 125 (25).
[39] Chamberlain to D'Abernon, 18 March 1925, *DBFP*, I, XXVII, no. 255; Chamberlain minute, 19 March 1925, FO 371/10756, C 3539/3539/18.
[40] *AR Luther I and II*, I, p. XVII; *ADAP*, A, XII, nos. 37, 81. Cf. Krüger (1985a), pp. 217–18; Johnson (2000).

Stresemann's proposal hinged on the pledge to recognise the present territorial *status quo* on the Rhine, renounce war and solve disputes with Germany's neighbours 'only through peaceful conciliation'.[41] Britain was envisaged as the pact's main guarantor.

But Chamberlain's original reaction to Berlin's overture was ambivalent. It was marked by suspicion and the will to recast the German initiative to his own ends. On 30 January, he was still distinctly wary of Stresemann's ulterior motives, suspecting the intention to divide the *entente*. Characteristically, he retorted that such manoeuvres would only 'destroy any influence which the British Government might have with the Government of France'. Yet, these caveats notwithstanding, the foreign secretary soon recommended the pact initiative to Herriot as 'the most hopeful sign' yet from Germany.[42] And the new course he now charted was not only compatible with Stresemann's plans; in fact, it developed them further. Crowe had immediately favoured seizing upon the German initiative, calling it on 22 January, 'a move in the right direction'. Subsequently, Crowe's persistence was instrumental in convincing Baldwin's cabinet to endorse the pact.[43]

While Crowe stood behind it, Chamberlain's reorientation was accelerated by the constraining powers of the cabinet and public opinion. As he informed the French ambassador Fleuriau on 19 March, though until 'very recently' still 'partisan of an Anglo-French-Belgian arrangement', he had become convinced of 'the impossibility [of] making the mass of the English people accept accords to which Germany was not a party'.[44] Yet when Chamberlain defended his new approach in parliament, he also faced different charges. Conservative backbenchers echoed both Churchill's brand of imperial aloofness and Hankey's isolationism. All invoked the danger of excessive British commitments under the proposed pact, arguing that Britain should not interfere in Europe unless in an acute conflict. By contrast, MacDonald and some Liberals argued for a revised Geneva Protocol instead.[45]

Crucially, though, the balance of forces within Baldwin's government had by early March shifted towards espousing the German offer as a welcome starting-point. In its decisive resolution of 4 March, the cabinet declared that it was in Britain's interest to encourage France and Belgium to enter into quadruple accords including Germany. The resolution underscored that a rejection of Stresemann's overture could drive Berlin into the arms of Moscow.[46]

---

[41] Cf. Krüger (1980), pp. 582ff.

[42] Chamberlain to D'Abernon, 30 January 1925; Chamberlain to Crewe, 16 February 1925, *DBFP*, I, XXVII, nos. 195, 200.

[43] Cf. Crowe (1972), p. 51.

[44] Fleuriau to Herriot, 19 March 1925, MAE, Série Europe, Grande-Bretagne, vol. 74, p. 84.

[45] *Hansard*, 5th series, vol. 182, cols. 307–22; vol. 185, cols. 1584–1668.

[46] CAB 23/49, CC 14 (25).

Significantly, the new course was by then also supported by the makers of British defence policy, particularly most of the chiefs of staff. During the CID meeting of 19 February, only the secretary for war, Laming Worthington-Evans, had argued that it would be impractical to accept a still occupied Germany into a pact. But Samuel Hoare, the secretary for air, had warned against an exclusive arrangement with France, maintaining that this would only exacerbate Europe's most precarious problem: its division into two 'camps', the victors and the vanquished.[47] In early July, the chiefs of staff argued that the proposed 'Quadruple Pact' comprising Germany 'fulfil[led] the requirements of a sound national defence' by keeping any future war 'as far as possible from the English Channel'. This would allow Britain to avoid costly rearmament required to honour alternative alliance commitments to France so that it could instead concentrate scarce resources on imperial defence.[48]

Reinforcing Chamberlain's reorientation on the international level was his attempt to forge a common Anglo-French response to Germany. In essence, he increasingly saw the need to limit and redirect Herriot's *entente* and *status quo* orientated policy. The French government's initial reaction to the German proposals was one of profound caution. It chiefly sought to arrest the momentum of Stresemann's 'security offensive', attaching stringent conditions to even beginning negotiations over the German note of 9 February.[49]

Herriot demanded that Germany first recognise all French occupation rights in the Rhineland and sign treaties with Poland and Czechoslovakia guaranteeing their territorial *status quo*. The *Quai d'Orsay* knew that these were unacceptable conditions. Herriot's key adviser Seydoux surmised that Berlin's underlying aim was to erode the Versailles treaty and prepare the ground for revision, both regarding the Rhineland and Germany's eastern borders. This France had to check. As the French premier told Chamberlain during bilateral consultations on 16 March, London and Paris must not leave Germany 'a "free hand" in the East'.[50] At least, Berlin should be required to sign obligatory arbitration treaties with its eastern neighbours and enter the League unconditionally. This would be tantamount to Germany's voluntary recognition of the Versailles treaty; and it was to be an 'essential condition for a pact'.[51]

---

[47] 196th CID meeting, 19 February 1925, cabinet session, 2 March 1925, CAB 24/172, CP 105 (25).

[48] CID paper 625–B, 3 July 1925, CAB 4/13. Britain subsequently refused to hold bilateral staff talks with France on how to counter a German aggression via the Rhineland. Cf. Howard (1972), pp. 77–95.

[49] Herriot Papers, PA-AP 89; Bariéty (2000), p. 127; Chamberlain to Crowe, 7 March 1925, *DBFP*, I, XXVII, no. 225.

[50] Chamberlain to Crowe, 7 March 1925, *DBFP*, I, XXVII, no. 225.

[51] Seydoux memorandum, 22 February 1925, MAE, Série Europe, Grande-Bretagne, vol. 73, p. 7.

Why, given all these caveats, had Herriot not outright rejected Stresemann's offer? In short, because he could not 'discard' it without provoking 'all kinds of suspicions'. In Seydoux's judgement, France would be accused of 'bad faith' by Anglo-American politicians, who could eventually 'oblige' Paris to abandon its hold on Germany 'without any compensations'. Essentially, though, French policymakers came to see the pact as an opening for more substantial British guarantees. Initially, Herriot thus proposed two separate treaties: the Rhine pact and an Anglo-French 'treaty of security'.[52] French thus gravitated towards British policy. But Herriot still procrastinated. From April 1925, it would fall to Briand to take French policy to a new level.

The need for a new European concert and the legacy of Castlereagh

While understanding Herriot's concerns, Chamberlain rejected his proposal of two separate pacts. Like Lloyd George and MacDonald before him, he invoked the constraints imposed not only by the cabinet but also by British 'public opinion' and the Dominions against a bilateral alliance. Overall, Chamberlain agreed with Herriot that Britain and France had to seize the initiative from Stresemann. Until Locarno, he championed 'the procedure that consists in reaching an agreement, preliminarily, among Allies, prior to the signing' of any accords with Germany.[53] But to achieve such accords was by now his clear priority.

In response to Herriot and domestic pressures, Chamberlain began to chart what he later termed his 'noble work of appeasement in Europe'. The foreign secretary's guiding notion was that Britain could, and should, once again become Europe's 'honest broker'.[54] On 19 March, he affirmed his belief 'that Great Britain has it in her power at this moment to bring peace to Europe. To achieve this end two things are indispensable: 1. that we should remove or allay French fears; 2. that we should bring Germany back into the concert of Europe.'[55] By this time, it had become an axiom of his policy that neither was sufficient by itself yet that, clearly, the latter step was inconceivable without the former.

---

[52] Herriot to Fleuriau (London), 16 March 1925, Seydoux memorandum, 28 February 1925, Laroche memorandum, 23 February 1924, Herriot notes, 16 March 1925, MAE, Série Europe, Grande-Bretagne, vols. 73, 74.

[53] Chamberlain to Crowe, 7 March 1925, *DBFP*, I, XXVII, no. 225; Herriot notes, 16 March 1925, MAE, Série Europe, Grande-Bretagne, vol. 74.

[54] Austen to Ida Chamberlain, 28 November 1925, Austen Chamberlain Papers, AC 5/1/370; Chamberlain to Crewe, 2 April 1925, FO 800/257/483.

[55] Chamberlain minute, 19 March 1925, FO 371/10756: C 3539/3539/18.

What, then, were the long-standing, and what were the new assumptions underlying Chamberlain's departure of 1925? Not least, he had altered his assessment of how far the Paris peace order could be sustained. In 1919, Chamberlain had judged that, chiefly because of the unresolved German problem, Versailles fell short of a 'real peace'.[56] Yet not even after the Ruhr crisis had he seen any overriding strategic necessity for a major adjustment of the Versailles treaty. Shortly before becoming foreign secretary in November 1924, he still held that it had to be preserved as 'the basis – and only possible basis of – Europe's law'.[57] But Chamberlain's subsequent re-assessment of both the shortcomings of Versailles and the wider causes of the Ruhr conflict changed this stance. He came to espouse a proposition first advocated by Crowe and Nicolson, namely that a modification of Versailles would be desirable 'if the concert of Europe [could] thus gradually be recreated'.[58] Essentially, like Crowe Chamberlain came to believe that only this way could Britain act as a 'moral force' in stabilising the European state-system.

What spurred this shift was the foreign secretary's changing perception of the Franco-German question. Vis-à-vis Germany, his actions were motivated by an abiding concern about the 'colossus' in the heart of Europe, only temporarily weakened, beset with a persistent 'authoritarian legacy' and with a demographic and economic potential far superior to that of France.[59] As Germany's latent revisionism remained the gravest challenge to peace, British policy had to pursue two parallel aims: to control Germany *and* to reintegrate it into the comity of nations.

In Chamberlain's view, German revisionism stemmed not least from the victors having ostracised the vanquished power from the postwar order since Versailles. If they could not accommodate it, Germany would sooner or later challenge the *status quo* by force and, even if this possibility seemed remote in 1925, seek an alliance with Soviet Russia.[60] Casting an uneasy shadow westward, Soviet behaviour remained a highly uncertain 'factor' for British policy. The Foreign Office considered Soviet Russia a potentially dangerous power

---

[56] Austen to Hilda Chamberlain, 19 July 1919, Austen Chamberlain Papers, AC 5/1/126.

[57] Chamberlain statement in the Commons, 14 July 1924, *Hansard*, 5th series, vol. 176, cols. 109–10.

[58] Nicolson memorandum, 26 January 1925, FO 371 /11065: W 2035/9/98.

[59] Already in 1919 Chamberlain noted: 'Even the old Germany would not . . . rashly challenge a new war in the West, but the chaos on their eastern frontier, and their hatred . . . must be a dangerous temptation . . . But if Germany remains or becomes democratic, they cannot repeat the folly of Frederick the Great and Bismarck and his later followers. No democracy can or will make aggressive war its year-long study and business, though it may flare up in sudden passion. But think of Germany with its 60 or 70 millions of people and France with its dwindling 40!' Austen to Hilda Chamberlain, 29 June 1919, Austen Chamberlain Papers, AC 5/1/132.

[60] Chamberlain note, 25 January 1925, FO 371/11064: W 362/9/98; cabinet session, 14 April 1925, CAB 23/52/15.

intent on exploiting German discontent to topple the international order. Although Soviet policy was deemed too preoccupied with internal problems to pose such risks in the near future, there was thus an overriding British interest to 'link Germany with the system of the west'.[61]

The general conclusion that the Foreign Office drew from all this was that although Berlin's 'unappeased' ambitions constituted no immediate danger for Britain its security remained inextricably linked with that of Europe. For all his lingering suspicion about German trustworthiness, however, Chamberlain did not rule out that Weimar Germany could adopt a western-style foreign policy. By this he essentially meant British 'rules' of diplomacy and *do ut des* compromise. Thus, it was in Britain's vital national interest to promote not a containment of Germany but its orientation towards peaceful accommodation. Yet this could only proceed if German decisionmakers proved their willingness to abide by the rules of the envisaged concert system – and to fulfil Germany's basic obligations under Versailles, including disarmament. For Chamberlain, this meant that Germany had to join the League, which he saw as a platform for the new concert diplomacy, and acted there 'in a friendly and conciliatory spirit'. In return, Britain could prevail upon France to recognise Germany's special geographic position and military status after Versailles.[62]

Chamberlain's general attitude towards France was markedly more accommodating and supportive. As his evaluation of the German problem reveals, he continued to believe that there were legitimate grounds for French anxieties. Consequently, the preservation of a close Anglo-French *entente* remained an imperative of British policy. It could be based on shared strategic interests and what the foreign secretary, who described himself as the cabinet's most Francophile member, saw as strong bonds between the French- and English-speaking cultures.[63] His central motive for reassuring Britain's wartime ally, however, was more pragmatic – and essentially defensive. It was the conviction that, without British support and moderating influence, French leaders would feel compelled to repeat Poincaré's provocations of Germany during the Ruhr conflict. Britain would then risk being 'dragged along, unwilling, impotent, in the wake of France towards the new Armageddon', another continental war.[64]

Making the Rhine frontier inviolable was and remained a cardinal concern for Chamberlain, and the core purpose of the envisaged pact. Yet he also saw the pact as an instrument for promoting peaceful change, transcending

---

[61] Chamberlain to Grahame, 26 February 1925; Foreign Office memorandum, 20 February 1925, *DBFP*, I, XXVII, nos. 212, 205.

[62] Chamberlain note, 25 January 1925, FO 371/11064: W 362/9/98; Chamberlain to D'Abernon, 18 March 1925, *DBFP*, I, XXVII, no. 255; Chamberlain to Grahame, 26 February 1925, *DBFP*, I, XXVII, no. 212.

[63] Cf. Grayson (1997), pp. 32–3.

[64] Chamberlain minute, 4 January 1925, FO 371/11064/W362/2/98.

Versailles to foster Franco-German accommodation. As Seydoux had anticipated, this 'threatened' France's two remaining strategic *atouts* under the
Versailles treaty: military control through the IMCC and, crucially, the military occupation of the Rhineland.[65] Chamberlain reassured Herriot on 16
March that Britain would not push France to relinquish either. But he also
underscored that 'if France insisted upon maintaining the occupation of
Cologne on grounds which appeared to British public opinion frivolous' that
could make it 'impossible' for him to remain 'alongside France', which would
be a 'disaster' for both powers.[66]

There was indeed all the more reason, then, to make the evacuation of the
Rhineland part and parcel, if not of the Rhine pact itself then of the wider
conciliation process with Germany. France had to find new bases of security; in
Chamberlain's judgement, it could find these in the new guarantees the pact
afforded. As will be seen, this indeed concurred with Stresemann's aims. The
key for Chamberlain, however, was to foster change in a controlled manner,
overseen by Britain and France – and essentially on British terms. Put in
perspective, his 'noble work of appeasement' thus did not spring from internationalist naïveté. It rested on the premise that by fulfilling the strategic role
as Europe's main mediator Britain was most aptly positioned to limit the extent
of further, undesirable commitments in terms of military power and economic
resources. Moreover, Whitehall could thus hope to restrict even this limited
guarantee to what was considered the geo-strategically vital area of 'western
Europe', under which at this critical juncture Germany was subsumed.

By contrast, eastern Europe, and particularly Poland and Czechoslovakia,
clearly lay beyond this strategic frontier. As Chamberlain put it (in)famously
on 16 February 1925: 'No British Government would ever risk the bones of a
single British grenadier' to defend the Polish Corridor. His views reflected a
widely held attitude in the Conservative government.[67] Whereas the desired
'nucleus of certainty, of stability and of security' in western Europe was to be
solidified, the political – and territorial – *status quo* in the east was potentially
negotiable.

It is important to note, however, that for Chamberlain and Crowe this was
closely connected with the idea that the envisaged western nucleus could
'gradually be enlarged in expanding circles'. On their horizons, it was not in
Britain's interest to confine the desired process of peaceful change to Franco-
German relations. It could also extend to what both regarded as the continent's

[65] Seydoux memorandum, 22 February 1925, MAE, Série Europe, Grande-Bretagne, vol. 73.
[66] Herriot notes, 16 March 1925, MAE, Série Europe, Grande-Bretagne, vol. 74; Chamberlain to
Crowe, 7 March 1925, *DBFP*, I, XXVII, no. 225.
[67] Chamberlain to Crewe, 16 February 1925, *DBFP*, I, XXVII, no. 200. Cf. Bátonyi (1999), pp.
222ff.

most unsettled region: that beyond Germany's eastern borders.[68] Thus, creating a west European concert *with* Germany could also buttress the stability of Poland and Czechoslovakia. On British 'mental maps', an 'adjustment' of Germany's eastern frontiers was indeed desirable in the longer-term process of European consolidation.[69] But it was crucial to commit Germany to change by peaceful means.

On 7 March, Chamberlain maintained vis-à-vis Herriot and the French president Gaston Doumergue that 'the undertaking to avoid recourse to war for the realisation of any hopes which Germany might cherish, even in regard to the eastern frontier, was in itself a new security for Poland'. The 'general appeasement that would follow an accord between ourselves and Germany would tend to render more secure the situation everywhere'.[70] On 24 March, the foreign secretary again underscored, in the Commons, that the German offer made 'perfectly clear that in the years to come she may try by diplomacy' and other 'peaceful ways' to 'effect changes in the Eastern frontier'.[71] Yet the overriding fact was that, by offering arbitration treaties with Poland and Czechoslovakia, Germany 'renounce[d] . . . any attempt to change the frontier by military force'.[72] This was the limit of what conditions Britain would pose in the east.[73]

Chamberlain's reasoning also revealed a second formative premise, his 'generational' rationale of peaceful change. As he told Herriot, Britain and France could not 'hold Germany down forever'. Their 'object' had to be to foster such substantial changes that 'by the time that Germany might really have become dangerous again she should enjoy sufficient well-being and have travelled too far' to 'care to risk what she then possessed on the chance that she might recover what she had lost in 1914'. As a consequence, Britain had a fundamental interest in preventing the creation of a European security order too 'rigid' to permit successive 'adjustments' over time – in western and eastern Europe. Thus, Britain could not give 'any guarantees for the Eastern frontiers', not least because there was no prospect of gaining cabinet or public support for them at home.[74]

In this vital respect, then, British diplomacy indeed pursued *realpolitik*. All in all, the British outlook revealed a prudent sense of priority. Yet this was

---

[68] Foreign Office memorandum, 20 February 1925, *DBFP*, I, XXVII, no. 205; Chamberlain minute, 26 March 1924, FO 371/10729, C3975/459/18.

[69] Cf. Orde (1978), pp. 196ff.

[70] Chamberlain to Crowe, 7 March 1925, *DBFP*, I, XXVII, no. 225.

[71] *Hansard*, 5th series, vol. 185, cols. 1584ff.

[72] Chamberlain to D'Abernon, 25 March 1925, *DBFP*, I, XXVII, no. 269.

[73] For the overall positive Czech reaction to British policy see Bátonyi (1999), pp. 206–8. On Polish concerns see Cienciala and Kormanicki (1984), pp. 223–76.

[74] Chamberlain to Crowe, 7 March 1925, *DBFP*, I, XXVII, no. 225; Herriot notes, 16 March 1925, MAE, Série Europe, Grande-Bretagne, vol. 74.

coupled with two – rather complacent – hopes: first, that the thorniest issue of European diplomacy could be relegated to an unspecified future and, second, that if necessary there would be a way to make peaceful 'adjustments' at the expense of Poland and Czechoslovakia.

This was Chamberlain's case for Locarno. In principle and practice he had begun to transcend the 'logic' of Versailles. Yet in order to understand what endowed his bid to 'solve' the Franco-German question with a keener sense of direction, and wider significance, one has to explore it in a wider context. Worth tracing is his interpretation of guiding precedents and analogies. In essence, Chamberlain sought to apply after 1918 what he regarded as exemplary practices of British foreign policy in the nineteenth century. He was herein influenced by the historian James W. Headlam-Morley, then a special adviser to the Foreign Office.[75]

Two weeks after receiving the initial German pact proposal, Chamberlain described what became his core rationale until 1929. In late February 1925, he acknowledged that he was 'much struck' with Headlam-Morley's observation 'that the first thought of Castlereagh after 1815 was to restore the Concert of Europe'. And he would maintain that 'the more ambitious peacemakers of Versailles, when they framed the Covenant, still left a gap which only a new Concert of Europe could fill'. On 14 March, Chamberlain confirmed: 'Britain's part now is the same as in 1815 and *mutatis mutandis* Castlereagh's policy is the right one today.'[76]

In fact, the historical that precedent that the foreign secretary invoked had marked a significant departure in British foreign policy. Essentially, Chamberlain would endeavour to emulate Castlereagh's approach of 1815 in abandoning balance-of-power doctrines and adopting a policy of forward engagement in Europe.[77] It was to be premised on a consistent British commitment to shaping Europe's international system and fostering an international equilibrium, a balance of status and rights between powers of markedly disparate power capabilities, above all Britain, France and Germany. He thus opted against intervening only, as in 1914, to readjust a 'mechanical' balance of power and for pre-empting Europe's regression into crisis and, possibly, another war.

With this rationale in mind, Chamberlain saw himself in 'a continuity of British foreign policy' that had culminated in the early nineteenth century.[78] Yet how far had he – like MacDonald – devised a policy that met the stabilisation requirements of the widened Euro-Atlantic system after 1918? As the

[75] See Headlam-Morley (1930).
[76] Chamberlain minute, 21 February 1925; Chamberlain note, 14 March 1925, FO 371/11064: W1252/9/98, FO 10756: C 3539/3539/18.
[77] Cf. Schroeder (1987).
[78] Austen to Ida Chamberlain, 28 November 1925, Austen Chamberlain Papers, AC 5/1/30.

Dawes process had manifested, in an era when security and international finance were inextricably linked one newly pertinent criterion here was Britain's capacity to co-operate with the United States.

Towards a European equilibrium, the British way – Chamberlain's Eurocentric vision of Locarno

In fact, Chamberlain's new outlook did not extend to a new readiness to revive the Anglo-American approach to European stabilisation of 1924. Essentially, he saw no need for such an approach in 1925 – admittedly in a phase when Hughes' successor Kellogg was seemingly reverting to pronounced US aloofness in international security. Nevertheless, Chamberlain's pursuits marked a regression from MacDonald's bid to join forces with Washington. On one level, his was a return to more traditional patterns of British strategic policy, distancing a long-established foreign-policymaking elite from one regarded as 'arriviste'.[79]

More profoundly, though, Chamberlain's attitude reflected the Conservative elite's reaction to the momentous change already described: the change in the distribution of power and responsibility between the international system's old and future hegemonic powers. Even if a latent naval competition had been moderated by the Anglo-American agreement shaping the Washington naval system of 1922, a subterranean rivalry persisted. It affected policymakers more than the closely co-operating financial elites.[80] This change was to be of enduring significance in the history of twentieth-century international politics. As already indicated, it can best be described as a transition-process: the long-term transition from British international pre-eminence, at its height underpinning a *Pax Britannica* in and beyond Europe, to an economically potent but still politically constrained American predominance after 1918. This process continued to have a marked impact on the extent of peaceful change in the post-World War I international system.

While stressing that it was essential for 'mutual understanding' between the British and the Americans to 'realise' what they 'have not got in common', Baldwin continued to invoke 'Anglo-American friendship' and its critical importance for world peace. But Chamberlain, like many Conservatives, saw post-Wilsonian US foreign policy as little more than the pursuit of narrow economic interests, lacking the political will and wherewithal to buttress international security. In March 1925, he summarised his underlying assumption: 'With America withdrawn, or taking part only where her interests are

---

[79] Cf. McKercher (1991b), pp. 225–6, and (1999), pp. 1–31.
[80] Cf. McKercher (1984), pp. 3ff; Hogan (1991), pp. 212–27.

directly concerned in the collection of money, Great Britain is the only possible influence for peace and stabilisation.'[81] In marked contrast to his future Locarno partners, Briand and Stresemann, Chamberlain thus made a clear distinction between the 'heights of grand policy' – essentially European professional diplomacy – and the more mundane sphere of transatlantic finance. Seeing no benefit in seizing on America's political-cum-financial power to further the security pact, the foreign secretary rarely alluded to financial factors and constraints, and did so mainly to put pressure on France. In general, the Foreign Office strikingly neglected the financial dimension of European security.[82]

Consequently, at the dawn of what for Chamberlain became the 'Locarno era' no political strategy was seriously contemplated, nor any serious effort made, to build a transatlantic concert of powers and bring America into the guarantee of European stability. It also has to be stressed, however, that given the succession of American refusals since Versailles to engage in this field, probably no European leader could have convinced Washington to underwrite the European pact. Nor was there an imminent crisis requiring US intervention.

---

[81] Baldwin, 'Anglo-American Friendship', Address at the Annual Reunion Dinner of the British War Missions to the United States', 29 April 1925, in Baldwin (1937), pp. 230-3. Chamberlain to Howard, 18 March 1925, *DBFP*, I, XXVII, no. 256.

[82] Chamberlain to Crewe, 27 June 1925; 7 July 1925, Austen Chamberlain Papers, AC 52/221, 224; Foreign Office memorandum, 20 February 1925, *DBFP*, I, XXVII, no. 205.

13 Regression?
US policy and the 'political insurance' of Europe's 'economic peace'

After the London settlement there was indeed an underlying continuity in the 'Progressive' approach to European stabilisation that Wilson's successors championed.[1] Yet there was also a marked reorientation, or more precisely a regression, in the State Department's efforts to develop strategies to secure Europe's economically underpinned *Pax Americana*. Continuity was accentuated by the fact that Ambassador Kellogg, designated to succeed Hughes in January 1925, unequivocally endorsed the principles laid down by his predecessor.[2]

On 7 October 1924, Kellogg had outlined to Coolidge what was to become the credo of his policy. He stressed that he realised 'how much more influence we will have if we maintain our freedom of action, at the same time co-operating in the friendliest spirit with a desire to help' the Europeans. He did not believe that the administration 'could have accomplished so much in the Dawes Plan settlement if we had been parties in the League, the sanctions, and tied up in European politics'.[3] To the detriment of further advances in transatlantic co-operation, Kellogg felt that Europe's consolidation had progressed so far that he could exercise even more restraint than Hughes in fostering peaceful change. In his judgement, there was no structural or pressing security problem demanding US attention, neither in 1925 nor thereafter.[4]

Heeding the advice of his mentor, Senator Borah, who vehemently opposed any US entanglements in Europe, Kellogg never even tried to develop, and legitimate vis-à-vis Congress, a more engaged European policy.[5] At the same time, he reckoned that he was simply not in a position to do so.[6] Having

---

[1] See chapter 11.
[2] The impact of Kellogg's policy on the Locarno process has never been systematically analysed. Studies have concentrated on the Kellogg–Briand pact. See Ferrell (1969); Ellis (1967); Costigliola (1984), pp. 190–2.
[3] Kellogg to Coolidge, 7 October 1924, Kellogg Papers.
[4] Kellogg to Coolidge, 30 April 1925, Kellogg Papers.
[5] Castle Diary, 20 November 1925, vol. 8, p. 125.
[6] *Ibid.*, 11 December 1924, 20 March 1925, vol. 7, pp. 10, 88–9.

been a Republican senator from 1916 until 1922, he especially viewed the Senate as an overwhelming counterweight to any strategic ambitions of this kind. No less, he dreaded Congressional influence on what he saw as America's fickle public opinion.[7] Kellogg's timidity vis-à-vis Congress, and his unwillingness to take risks in advocating further US commitments in Europe, indeed constrained his influence. Ultimately, however, he merely accentuated a tendency that Hughes had initiated after the London settlement. He fell back on a *restrictive* pursuit of informal diplomacy vis-à-vis Europe, relying on US financial power and 'self-regulating' economic stabilisation.[8]

Precisely because the Dawes regime triggered a soon torrential flow of US capital to Germany and created an ever tighter web of financial interests, there was a growing American interest in a 'political insurance' of Europe's economic peace. Yet this interest only grew gradually. In the spring of 1925, neither the State Department nor American financiers and diplomats in Europe saw cause for imminent concern. Even less did they see the need for a new American stabilisation initiative akin to the Hughes plan of 1922. Yet there was a heightened sense that the Dawes regime as such might eventually be jeopardised should the still volatile political relations between France and Germany deteriorate once again.

As Kellogg and his key adviser Castle realised, economic pacification could not take root in the short term. A modicum of political stabilisation had to be achieved to create safe conditions for private US investment, particularly in Germany, and to re-open France for US capital.[9] Like Hughes, however, they also felt that to pave the way for enhanced security was a task falling squarely into the responsibility of the European governments.[10] In mid-February 1925, Kellogg told Chamberlain that he considered 'French security' the 'hub of the whole situation', and he enquired whether London could 'do anything to reassure' Paris.[11]

The new secretary of state's assessment of the main obstacle to further progress towards regional co-operation in Europe was not different from his conclusions following the Dawes negotiations. As he put it in April 1925, France would not abandon its military orientation and 'cut down her army until she feels that she has security against Germany'. Against this background, Kellogg had welcomed Berlin's 'Rhine pact initiative' when first

[7] See Kellogg's numerous exchanges with Borah in 1925 and 1926, Kellogg Papers.
[8] Kellogg to Lamont, 19 August 1924, Lamont Papers, 4-C, 177–2; Kellogg to Coolidge, 30 April 1925, Kellogg Papers.
[9] Kellogg memorandum, 16 March 1925, *FRUS 1925*, I, pp. 20–1; Castle Diary, 16 March 1925, vol. 7, pp. 84–5; Kellogg address, 14 December 1925, Kellogg Papers.
[10] Cf. Link (1970), pp. 344ff.
[11] Chamberlain to Howard, 17 February 1925, *DBFP*, I, XXVII, no. 201.

officially notified by Ambassador Maltzan on 16 March, more than a month after Britain and France. At the core, he saw the pact as a means 'to guarantee French security'.[12]

Following Cuno's proposal of 1922, Stresemann had originally considered inviting the Coolidge administration to act as underwriter or guardian of a Rhine pact.[13] Yet he soon acknowledged that Washington would not depart from its 'non-entanglement' doctrine. When approached by Stresemann in January 1925 Ambassador Houghton underlined that US participation was out of the question.[14] This Kellogg confirmed in March. Essentially, the secretary quickly came to regard the German initiative as a welcome alternative both to the Geneva Protocol and a re-emergence of European alliance politics under the influence of France. It seemed the most promising way to foster European security without entangling Washington.[15] Kellogg also knew of course that influential senators like Borah still fervently opposed any *rapprochement* with the League. In 1925, Borah decried the Protocol as envisaging 'the most ambitious military autocracy' ever known.[16]

Consequently, when Maltzan, contravening Stresemann's instructions, sounded out the State Department as to whether America could contemplate a 'special relationship' with Germany outside the League as a possible alternative to the pact, Kellogg strongly rejected this overture. Castle lectured Maltzan that while he understood that Germany would rather have the 'most powerful nation in the world' as a 'friend' than 'the nations represented at Geneva', this interest was not reciprocated in Washington. On the contrary, what the United States desired was conciliation between the Europeans, and here 'the League might be very useful'.[17]

On these premises, US policy endorsed the security pact. The German security initiative and Britain's willingness to promote the pact suited not only the administration but also American financiers. Rapidly, a consensus emerged that, while avoiding fresh formal US commitments, it promised tangible gains in political stability and the safety of US investment in Europe. Yet the United States would not become a 'guardian of European peace' by acting as the pact's 'trustee'.[18] Even less, however, was Kellogg willing to

---

[12] Kellogg to Coolidge, 30 April 1925, Kellogg Papers; Kellogg memorandum, 16 March 1925, *FRUS 1925*, I, pp. 20–1.

[13] See Stresemann's press declaration, 7 March 1925, Stresemann (1932), II, pp. 64–5; Stresemann notes, 3 September 1923, *ADAP*, A, VIII, pp. 317–22. Cf. Berg (1990), pp. 349–50.

[14] Houghton to Hughes, 12 January 1925, Hughes Papers.

[15] Kellogg to Maltzan, 16 March 1925, *FRUS 1925*, I, p. 20; Kellogg to Hughes, 19 June 1925, Kellogg Papers.

[16] Borah to T.Q. Harrison, 30 March 1925, quoted after Maddox (1970), p. 168.

[17] Kellogg memorandum, 16 March 1925, *FRUS 1925*, I, pp. 20–1; Castle Diary, 16 March 1925, vol. 7, pp. 84–5.

[18] Houghton to Hughes, 12 January 1925, Hughes Papers. Cf. Link (1970), pp. 342–4.

support schemes that excluded Germany. On 30 April 1925, he categorically rejected Herriot's counterproposals: Washington would 'not join in any pact of security to France or guarantee against Germany'. Kellogg adhered to the premise that the United States had nothing 'to offer as an inducement' to France in terms of formal strategic commitments. Echoing British views, he refused to promote any schemes that smacked of alliance politics and could re-accentuate Europe's old and detrimental divisions.[19]

In short, the Coolidge administration would at no point see a vital interest in departing from the position of a 'disinterested' arbiter. Rather, once the European powers had embarked on the Locarno process, US diplomacy and high finance came to buttress it with the 'proven' means at their disposal: political-cum-economic influence and capital. What evolved in the spring of 1925 could be termed a 'carrots-and-sticks' strategy under the *leitmotif* of informal hegemony. On the one hand, Kellogg authorised US diplomats in Europe to underscore America's interest in the success of the Rhine pact.[20] This was notably pursued by Ambassador Houghton in London, his successor in Berlin, the Germanophile Jacob Schurman, and his long-serving counterpart in Paris, Herrick.[21] All put pressure on European governments, notably the French, and offered – vague – incentives for the pact's swift conclusion, particularly a more benign war-debt and loan policy.[22] On the other hand, and to greater effect, the State Department again relied on informal agents. The most powerful agent of US interests in Europe in 1925 was FRBNY Governor Strong. The reparations agent Parker Gilbert, by contrast, clearly concentrated on ensuring the operation of the Dawes plan.[23]

With Kellogg retaining a detached position throughout the European negotiations, Houghton became the key diplomatic spokesman of US policy, at times pursuing his own private foreign policy. Overall in line with the State Department, he on 4 May delivered what became widely publicised as 'America's Peace Ultimatum to Europe'.[24] Houghton called on 'the peoples of Europe' to lay the foundations for 'permanent peace' if they wanted to continue to benefit from US loans.[25] For his part, Strong repeatedly travelled to Germany, providing the new government under Hans Luther with crucial

---

[19] Kellogg to Coolidge, 30 April 1925, Kellogg Papers.
[20] Chamberlain to Howard, 26 May 1925, *DBFP*, I, XXVII, no. 344.
[21] *Ibid.*; Schurman to State Department, 13 April 1925, NA RG 59 862.002/163–4. Cf. Berg (1990), pp. 350–5; Gottwald (1965), pp. 52–3; Herrick report, 17 December 1926, NA RG 59 751.62/95.
[22] Castle Diary, 22 June 1925, vol. 7, p. 183.
[23] Cf. Chandler (1958), pp. 297–307; Castle notes of a conversation with Gilbert, 4 January 1926, NA RG 59 862.51/1925.
[24] *Literary Digest*, 16 May 1925.
[25] Houghton speech to the Pilgrim Society, London, 4 May 1925, Houghton Papers.

support in the critical phase of July–August 1925. He, too, stated in no uncertain terms what he had earlier impressed on French authorities as well:
a failure of the security pact would entail the curtailment or even withdrawal
of American investment.[26]

In most respects, US diplomacy thus effectively built on the precedent
of the Dawes process. In a departure from 1924, however, American agents
never engaged in direct mediation between London, Paris and Berlin. This
time, they 'merely' placed America's financial weight into the scales of postwar
stabilisation – coming down forcefully on the side of the regional European
pact. In a further contrast to 1924, the administration also abandoned its
advocacy of 'depoliticisation'. It acknowledged the need for a political process,
initiated by European leaders and fostering Germany's integration into a
western 'community of ideals, interests, and purposes'.

This also meant that Kellogg not only acknowledged but also welcomed that
Britain would play a crucial part in the ensuing negotiating-process. As he told
Coolidge in late April, 'England . . . may succeed in entering into a security
pact' which would make it the main guarantor of political *détente* between
France and Germany. Kellogg saw a strong bond of common interest between
Britain and the United States in the promotion of a political stabilisation
process that complemented and secured the Dawes regime. Thus, by fostering
the Locarno process, Britain effectively became the guardian of what Republican elites envisaged as Europe's *Pax Americana* – and US financial interests.[27]
By early June, Washington noted that Britain's engagement 'laid foundations of
real importance for an improvement in the European situation'.[28] In 1925,
then, the suspicion which subsequently was to inform American attitudes, and
policies, towards Europe was markedly muted. US decisionmakers did not yet
suspect that European initiatives for political and economic co-operation
'beyond Versailles' could advance to such a degree that they led to agreements
'behind America's back', directed against the world creditor. After Locarno,
however, Castle would point to precisely this danger and, eventually, such
concerns would spur a marked tension and ambivalence in US stabilisation
policy.[29]

What kind of pacification did America's political and financial leaders expect
the pact to further – one limited to Germany and western Europe or one
reaching beyond this region? Did such regional categories matter at all from the
distance of Washington and New York? In short, American expectations were

---

[26] Strong memorandum of conversations with Luther, Stresemann and Schacht in Berlin, 11 July
1925, Strong Papers.
[27] Kellogg to Coolidge, 30 April 1925, Kellogg Papers; Chamberlain to Howard, 26 May 1925,
DBFP, I, XXVII, no. 344.
[28] Chamberlain to Howard, 3 June 1925, *DBFP*, I, XXVII, no. 357.
[29] Castle to Houghton, 3 November 1925, Houghton Papers. Cf. Link (1970), pp. 350–1.

sweeping and general. Fundamentally, Kellogg considered the proposed west European pact a sufficient basis for overall European security and the inclusion of Germany. Like Chamberlain, he judged, with self-serving optimism, that it could not only consolidate Germany's relations with the west but also further eastern Europe's pacification.[30] For there, as in the west, it could serve above all to promote the peaceful change of an untenable *status quo*. More sceptical voices among US diplomats were rare in 1925. Only Houghton, overall still a fervent proponent of the pact, voiced the concern that Germany's proposals, by restricting guarantees to western Europe, threatened to create borders of inferior status in the east and thus 'fix the point where the next great war will begin', namely the Polish–German frontier.[31]

There is no indication, though, that the higher echelons of the State Department or the administration shared Houghton's – temporary – apprehensions. On the contrary, most leading US policymakers, and financiers, deemed not only the western but also the eastern *status quo* in need of peaceful 'adjustment'.[32] On 22 July Strong noted after meeting Stresemann, Luther and Schacht in Berlin that while they were willing to 'enter into definite obligations' on their western frontier, the Germans also 'definitely' desired two 'principal things' in return: 'the immediate evacuation of the Cologne Area' and an accelerated evacuation of the remaining Rhenish zones; and, in future, the 'rectification of the frontier with Poland', especially the elimination of the '"Corridor"'. In private, Strong noted that German claims in the west were justified and that there was 'room for great improvement in the situation as to the Eastern Frontier'.[33]

The Americans thus promoted the pact to bolster pacific changes in Europe in the longer term – of course without involving the United States directly.[34] Houghton himself had told Chamberlain in June that neither the 'Silesian settlement' nor the 'Polish corridor' could 'endure permanently'. Yet he agreed with Chamberlain that it would not serve 'interests of peace' if these issues were placed on the agenda prematurely. They should be resolved in a 'better atmosphere than is now possible so soon after the close of the Great War'.[35]

Following this rationale, US diplomats and financiers never discouraged Stresemann's political and economically orientated revisionism. Crucially, however, they never explicitly encouraged German ambitions either, let alone pledged direct support for them. Basically, the legalistic rationale of official US

[30] Kellogg address, 14 December 1925, Kellogg Papers. Cf. Costigliola (1979), pp. 85–105.
[31] Houghton to Coolidge, 19 August 1925, Houghton Papers.
[32] Castle Diary, 22 June 1925, vol. 7, pp. 183–4.
[33] Strong memorandum, 'Politics in Germany', 22 July 1925, Strong memorandum, 11 July 1925, Strong Papers.
[34] Kellogg to Coolidge, 8 November 1925, Hughes to Castle, 7 December 1925, Kellogg Papers.
[35] Chamberlain to Howard, 3 June 1925, *DBFP*, I, XXVII, no. 357.

policy remained that peaceful change could be achieved through conciliation and arbitration – the gradual espousal of mutually recognised rules for the pacific settlement of regional problems. More generally, it could be achieved through what the Rhine pact was to foster: the shift of European politics from atavistic rivalry over territory to concentration on economic reconstruction.[36]

American preferences and pressure were also registered in Poland. As Foreign Minister Skrzyński confided to Chamberlain on his return from a trip to Washington on 9 September 1925, his impression was that 'the Government and public of the United States . . . approved of the policy of the Mutual Pact, and were inclined to regard Poland as the obstacle to peace'.[37]

---

[36] Kellogg address, 14 December 1925, Kellogg Papers. Cf. Berg (1990), pp. 380–405.
[37] Chamberlain memorandum, 11 September 1925, *DBFP*, I, XXVII, no. 470.

14   Beyond irreconcilable differences?

New German and French approaches to European security

How perceptive were British and American assessments of the Franco-German problem and the aims of French and German policymakers? Undoubtedly, Stresemann and Briand, who directed French foreign policy from April 1925, pursued different interests and agendas through the Rhine pact. Each had different ideas about what kind of security order and what wider consequences it was to engender. Apart from the British and the American, there were distinct French and German rationales for what became the Locarno system.[1] Were these differences so fundamental that any pact could only conceal but not overcome them?

As will be shown, the *status quo* power France and the revisionist power Germany came to pursue different but not irreconcilable aims and strategies in the era of London and Locarno. There certainly was a tension between what Briand and Stresemann sought; but there was also a remarkable degree of common ground. A critical question became how far British diplomacy could propel a peace process that helped to maximise such common ground. And what part could US policy play under its self-imposed restraints? Re-appraising these questions requires, first, a further systematic comparison of French and German postwar policies, which centres on each power's approach to the Locarno pact.

Accommodation with the west and peaceful revision – Stresemann's Locarno policy

The unsettled security question and the need to counter what Berlin regarded as the danger of a reconstituted Anglo-French *entente* that again cemented the *status quo* and isolated Germany – these concerns lay behind the German Rhine pact initiative evolving, with D'Abernon's prodding, around the turn of 1924/5.[2] Most immediately, Stresemann reacted to the allied declaration

---

[1] See Jacobson (1972b), pp. 35–44.
[2] Schubert memorandum, 29 December 1924, PA, St. S FS, vol. 1, 4509/E 124 822ff. Cf. Krüger (1985a), pp. 269–70; Wright (1995), pp. 109–27.

to postpone the evacuation of the Cologne occupation zone. Rather than undermine the *entente* or destabilise European order, Stresemann's new security policy had different, if no less ambitious, goals. Its basic premise was that only if Germany could satisfy France's need for security (*Sicherheitsbedürfnis*) in a new way – essentially by recognising the territorial *status quo* of 1919 in the west – could he hope to realise his main aim: Germany's return to the status of an equal great power.[3] Inseparable from this, however, was the aim to improve the conditions for a peaceful revision, a 'gradual softening', of the Versailles system itself.[4]

Thus, the German foreign minister doubtless also hoped to open new avenues of *pacific* territorial revision in the east. Yet this was a secondary aim. Contrary to some accounts, his policy was always based on the rationale that any pact in the west had to be accompanied by new security arrangements in the east – not least to meet French demands. To this end, Germany proposed *separate* arbitration agreements with Poland and Czechoslovakia, stipulating that all bilateral disputes were to be resolved by peaceful means.[5]

The range of revisionist priorities Stresemann pursued may be summarised as follows: first, and foremost, came an early evacuation of the Cologne zone and, further, the occupied Rhineland as a whole.[6] This would never be an explicit demand but became Germany's essential *quid pro quo* condition for signing the pact; it was crucial for legitimating the German Foreign Office's *Westpolitik* as such. By the same token, Stresemann desired a swift termination of military control. Then, second, came a 'bearable' resolution of the reparations question and the long-term aim of 'armaments parity' with the other powers. Only the last, precarious, step was to be territorial revision, above all in eastern Europe but also comprising the newly Belgian territories of Eupen–Malmédy and the Saar. Exercising restraint in pursuing this last agenda would be the hardest test of Weimar foreign policy, particularly because not only fervent nationalists espoused the notion that Germany could not renounce 'rightful' claims for its eastern territories. It was shared by nearly the entire German spectrum including the Social Democrats.[7] Yet,

---

[3] Schubert memorandum, 4 June 1925, Stresemann Papers, H 159103–109. Cf. Wright (2002), pp. 200–1.

[4] Krüger (1985a), p. 212. This rationale also informed Stresemann's often misquoted letter to the German crown prince of 7 September 1924, written to gain the German Nationals' support. See *UF*, VI, pp. 486–7.

[5] Stresemann to Rauscher (Warsaw), 8 March 1924, *ADAP*, A, XI, no. 189. Cf. Baechler (1996), p. 501.

[6] Stresemann to Houghton, January 1925, Stresemann (1932), II, pp. 261–2.

[7] Cf. Krüger (1985a), p. 214, and (1980), pp. 577ff; Enssle (1980). Stresemann also held that, in the longer term, a rehabilitated Germany should be able to re-assume colonial activities, i.e. be granted League mandates. But Britain blocked such German aspirations. See Luther notes of talks with Stresemann and Chamberlain in London on 2 December 1925, Stresemann Papers, vol. 272, H148062–70.

crucially, Stresemann only envisaged territorial changes if they could be achieved in 'agreement' with Germany's neighbours and did not jeopardise its accommodation with the western powers.

The German blueprint for a 'Rhine pact' sprang from core concepts developed by Stresemann and Schubert since late 1922.[8] As noted, similar proposals had already been made to Britain in 1924.[9] The planning of the *Auswärtige Amt* was revived after the London conference when from Berlin's vantage-point the danger emerged that Germany's return to world politics via the world economy could be impeded by French security concerns.

What mattered most for Stresemann – apart from Herriot's response – was Chamberlain's willingness to co-operate. For even more than in 1924, Britain was cast to assume the crucial role of not only guaranteeing the pact but also acting as indispensable mediator between Germany and France. As America remained off-stage, Britain was the only power that could use its political leverage vis-à-vis Paris to promote a conclusion of the pact – and Germany's further international reintegration. Domestically, Stresemann could argue that, through the accords, Germany would obtain a British guarantee against further French incursions across the Rhine. His main 'defensive' objective was and remained to regain German unity and sovereignty over the Rhineland.[10] Thus, contrary to Chamberlain's and Briand's original suspicions, it was never Stresemann's intention, and would have been highly counterproductive, to drive a wedge between London and Paris. In fact, then, German policy was largely compatible with Chamberlain's re-calibrated strategy of drawing Germany into a new European concert. This goes a long way towards explaining why all crises of the Locarno process in 1925 could be mastered.

Instead of persisting with seeking an American guarantee as well, the German foreign minister counted on Washington's interest in using US power to promote the pact behind the scenes of European diplomacy, and in German domestic politics. By contrast, he discarded Maltzan's idea of privileging a German–American 'special relationship' outside the League over accommodation with France and Britain.[11] In the larger picture, however, Stresemann's security strategy was intimately connected with his rationale to develop a new kind of German foreign policy. That rationale was to create a political framework for pursuing 'global policy' by *economic* means – an economically

[8] Stresemann press statement, 2 September 1923, Stresemann (1932), I, pp. 100–2; Stresemann notes, 3 September 1923, *ADAP*, A, VIII, pp. 317–22. For the Rhine pact plan that Schubert had been asked to draft see *AR Stresemann I und II*, I, no. 134.

[9] Stresemann to D'Abernon, 11 February 1924, *ADAP*, A, IX, no. 146.

[10] Stresemann statement, 7 March 1925, Stresemann Papers, General Files, vol. 21, 7310/H 158 405–15; Stresemann statements before the *Reichstag*'s Foreign Affairs Committee, 11 March 1925, Stresemann Papers, Political Files, vol. 277, 7135/H 148981f.

[11] Stresemann to Maltzan, 7 April 1925, Stresemann (1932), I, p. 78.

orientated approach to peaceful revision.[12] Yet in view of Germany's persisting financial weakness this could only be realised with the support of Berlin's *de facto* senior partner in world politics: the United States. The expansion of US capital export and the interdependence it engendered were not only indispensable for Germany's recovery. They were equally critical for this novel approach to international politics after the Great War.

Stresemann was only too aware of the fact that, in the spring of 1925, Germany again passed through an extended phase of recession, suffering from acute capital shortages and recurrent budget crises. Although the Luther government struggled to persevere with deflationary policies to attract capital after half a decade of inflation, this state of affairs would continue throughout the summer.[13] To overcome it, Berlin sought to widen economic co-operation and remove tariff barriers vis-à-vis Britain and America, while also completing a provisional trade agreement with Paris on 28 February.[14] Beyond this, Stresemann intended to create the preconditions for using economic means to attain specific revisionist aims, both towards France and Poland. He saw no realistic alternative to this course, not only because the road to renewed power politics was barred under the circumstances. More fundamentally, Stresemann rejected the use of force as a viable option for Germany after the war.[15]

The foreign minister held on to his 'economic' approach not least to accelerate the dynamism of the European revision processes he sought. Like Schubert, he was motivated by the constant fear that he might lose the necessary parliamentary base and support of the most important German interest-groups for a continuation of his western-orientated course. It had to yield results, and quickly, to quieten calls for more assertive and radical alternatives.[16] German foreign policy indeed had to draw a 'fine line' between the willingness to further *détente* with the west and revisionist *caveats*. The latter were amplified by strong domestic pressures against any kind of *status quo* concessions to the western powers and, even more so, to Poland and Czechoslovakia.

The greatest domestic challenge for Stresemann and Chancellor Luther remained to find a *modus vivendi* with the DNVP. Luther's so-called *Bürgerblock* government, formed in January 1925, tried to corral the nationalists in a coalition to strengthen their moderate wing. This was to ensure their support for Stresemann's security policy but also threatened to make the government

---

[12] Stresemann *Reichstag* speech, 16 April 1925, Stresemann Papers, General Files, vol. 23, 7312/H 158741–65.

[13] Stresemann *Reichstag* speech, 18 May 1925, Stresemann Papers, General Files, vol. 24, 7313/H 158976ff. Cf. Winkler (1985), pp. 729ff; Feldman (1985a); Kruedener (1990).

[14] Cf. Krüger (1985a), pp. 288–9. For the challenges to liberal economic policies in Weimar Germany see Nicholls (1994), pp. 15–31.

[15] See chapter 8.

[16] Stresemann *Reichstag* speech, 16 April 1925, Stresemann Papers, General Files, vol. 23, 7312/H 158741–65.

hostage to the concessions – especially regarding protectionist tariff policies – that the Nationalists demanded in return.[17] The phalanx of more radical forces calling for a return to a 'policy of the free hand' was still strong in 1925. Particularly the *Reichswehr* chief of staff, General Seeckt, and the *Reichswehr* minister, Otto Geßler, maintained their resistance to Stresemann's pact policy.[18] They denounced his offer to France – especially the voluntary recognition of the Rhine border of 1919, entailing the renunciation of Alsace-Lorraine – as a 'betrayal' of German national interests. What manifested itself was rampant anti-western nationalism, the same that had rallied against the 'enslaving' dependence on America and foreign control under the Dawes plan. It was stirred up further by the influential right-wing press.[19]

Briand's Locarno policy: The search for new foundations of French security and the European *status quo*

Briand's espousal of the security pact was indeed a 'deliberate choice'. It was the deliberate choice to place France's relations with Germany, and Britain, on new foundations, made soon after he began to direct foreign policy under Herriot's successor Paul Painlevé in April 1925.[20] Against the background of France's protracted financial-cum-political *malaise*, however, it was also inescapably connected with the realisation that, given the Anglo-American espousal of the pact there was hardly a promising alternative road to enhanced French security.

As in the German case, the attitudes of Chamberlain and America's political and financial leaders were thus critical. Briand would in fact claim that the pact idea had originated with none other than himself: that he had first 'had' it in 1921 when negotiating with Lloyd George. Following the collapse of the Anglo-American guarantee of 1919, he had long held that not an alliance 'forged against one state' but 'a guarantee pact that proceeded from a spirit of mutual aid' was required for the 'reconstitution of Europe'.[21] Significantly, before and after Locarno Briand stressed that France chiefly sought not merely a guarantee of the Rhine frontier but a new British commitment to French

---

[17] Cf. Grathwol (1980), pp. 94ff; Stürmer (1967), pp. 107ff.

[18] Cf. Zeidler (1993), pp. 82–7, 303.

[19] Cf. Koszyk (1972), pp. 274–6.

[20] Thus Bariéty (2000), p. 127. On Briand's policy see his statements to the *Assemblée*'s Foreign Affairs Committee, 19 December 1925, 23 February 1926, Procès verbaux, C14763–64, C14763, no. 46, pp. 6ff, no. 51, pp. 13ff; Briand instructions to French diplomats, 4 November 1925, MAE, Z 1, Pacte de sécurité, 284–6, vol. 86, pp. 202ff. Cf. Bariéty (2000), pp. 117–34; Keeton (1987), pp. 24ff; Jacobson (1972b), pp. 12ff; Wurm (1979); Unger (2005), pp. 417–544.

[21] Briand to the Foreign Affairs Committee, 19 December 1925, Procès verbaux, C14763, no. 46, pp. 6ff.

security, however limited. For only such a commitment would permit the 'improvement' of Franco-German relations.[22]

At first, though, the new foreign minister harboured considerable suspicions, fearing that Germany's 'original proposals' had been 'actuated by a desire to divide France from Great Britain'. In his view, this could be countered, and the Germans 'caught in their own trap', if Paris and London closed ranks and revived their *entente*.[23] Originally, Briand forestalled progress both on the pact negotiations and the termination of military control. He also espoused Herriot's catalogue of tough conditions. Already in mid-March, while still French representative in Geneva, he had proposed 'making Germany enter the League' a key premise for 'any further negotiation'.[24]

But Briand soon transcended Herriot's reticent approach, subordinating all concrete doubts over Stresemann's intentions to the core aim of achieving a breakthrough in France's *rapprochement* with Germany – and the Anglo-American powers. Nevertheless, not least due to the Third Republic's drawn-out political and financial crisis, his policy always remained reactive. In contrast to what Chamberlain and Stresemann pursued, its hallmarks were 'control through deceleration' and tit-for-tat concessions. Only gradually, Briand developed a coherent strategy to shift from 'execution' to substantial negotiations.[25]

Underlying this new approach, Briand's Locarno policy, was a genuine reorientation: that from seeking French security through coercion and eastern alliances *against* Germany to integrating the latter into a mutual system of security and, in his version, *status quo preservation*. Crucially, this system was to be guaranteed by Britain. From the start, Briand's deepest anxiety was that France could be left with non-binding British commitments after it had already proved 'impossible' to 'realise a particular Anglo-French accord for the security of the Rhine'.[26] Ultimately, Briand felt he had no choice but to scale down French expectations in view of the limits Britain set. There was to be neither an Anglo-French 'pact within the pact' with bilateral staff talks on how to repel a German invasion via the Rhineland nor a guarantee of Germany's eastern frontiers.[27] This affected fundamentals of previous French alliance policy

---

[22] Briand instructions to French diplomats, 4 November 1925, MAE, Z 1, Pacte de sécurité, 284–6, vol. 86, p. 203.

[23] Crewe to Chamberlain, 30 May 1925, *DBFP*, I, XXVII, no. 353.

[24] Herriot memorandum, 16 March 1925, MAE, Série Europe, Grande-Bretagne, vol. 74, pp. 23–4. Cf. Bariéty (2000), pp. 127–8.

[25] Briand to the Foreign Affairs Commission, 19 December 1925, Procès verbaux, C14763, no. 46, pp. 6ff.

[26] Briand instructions, 4 November 1925, MAE, Z 1, Pacte de sécurité, 284–6, vol. 85, p. 202; Briand to the Foreign Affairs Commission, 19 December 1925, Procès verbaux, C14763, no. 46, pp. 10–11.

[27] Cf. Howard (1972), pp. 93ff.

vis-à-vis Poland and Czechoslovakia. Did Briand in fact pursue *rapprochement* with Germany at the expense of their stability?[28] This was undoubtedly a prevalent perception in Warsaw at the time – yet not of the Czechoslovak premier Beneš.[29] In the analysis of the British Foreign Office, the cardinal French concern was that 'the proposed pact should result in the Rhineland becoming a barrier which would stop the French from going to the help of Poland in the event of a German attack'. Accordingly, British diplomacy backed Briand's demand that 'France should retain the right to guarantee arbitration treaties between Germany and her eastern neighbours.' Yet, crucially, Paris had to do so without Britain's support.[30]

Fundamentally, Briand reckoned like Chamberlain and Beneš that the security pact, and a Germany more reconciled with the postwar order, would not weaken France's guarantees to Poland and Czechoslovakia but rather improve their security.[31] But the core problem for France remained the pact's implications in the west. Eastern concerns became a *pars pro toto* for French security, and one of France's main levers in negotiations with Britain and Germany. By June, Briand's priority was to oblige Germany only to guarantee the *status quo* of 1919 in the west and to renounce forcible revision in the east instead. And France no longer sought a British commitment in western *and* eastern Europe but only London's assurance to come to France's aid in the event of direct German aggression. For Briand, the Rhine pact thus became less an instrument against invasion than a mechanism to control the international system in collaboration with the British *entente* partner.[32]

De facto, then, French policymakers gravitated towards Britain's approach to the German problem. Yet there was indubitably still a different emphasis. Briand's rationale was to build French security on new foundations *with* Germany. But he sought to achieve this by tying Berlin into a pact system not only steered by a revitalised *entente* but also reinforcing the Versailles system. He hoped that this would check Germany's revisionist ambitions and convince German elites to adjust to the order of 1919. This was of course a highly problematic assumption. Moreover, eliminating Germany's core grievance would strike at the heart of French strategic interests: the hold on the Rhineland. This dilemma would overshadow 'Locarno politics' between 1926

---

[28] Cf. Wandycz (1961), pp. 157ff, 368ff, and (1988), pp. 25ff.

[29] Chamberlain to Crowe on conversations with the Polish foreign minister Skrzyński, 14 March 1925, *DBFP*, I, XXVII, no. 247; Beneš to Berthelot, 20 September 1925, MAE, Série Europe, Grande-Bretagne, vol. 82. Cf. Cienciala and Kormanicki (1984), pp. 223ff.

[30] Sterndale-Bennett memorandum, 7 April 1925; Hurst memorandum, 18 June 1925, *DBFP*, I, XXVII, nos. 291, 385.

[31] Cf. Wandycz (1961), pp. 368–9.

[32] French note, 16 June 1925, *Locarno-Konferenz*, no. 14. Cf. Bariéty (1977), p. 664; Jacobson (1972b), pp. 38ff; Suarez (1938–41), IV, pp. 161ff.

and 1929, permitting less, and above all less rapid, change than Germany and Britain desired.

Most of Briand's moves can thus be explained as endeavours to maximise Britain's commitment to France and to buttress the European *status quo*.[33] But, like Stresemann's policy, his re-oriented strategy was also motivated by the need to improve relations with the American creditor. Particularly in Washington, France had to lose the stigma of being Europe's chief 'trouble-maker' after the war, forcibly holding down its eastern neighbour. Ultimately, Briand's intention was to regain control over the process of postwar readjust-ment in order to decelerate it and to preserve as much of France's pre-eminence as possible.[34] To achieve this, however, France would in fact have to alter its political and economic relations with Germany and the Anglo-American powers far beyond the parameters of 1919.

More profoundly, then, Briand's journey to Locarno was no less the result of a learning process than Chamberlain's or Stresemann's. And it can be placed in the continuity of a more general reorientation of French policy since 1923 – the search for more sustainable ways of safeguarding France's position, and the order of Versailles, in a changing international constellation. This process had in some ways been initiated by Poincaré, though he had not actually 'embarked' France on the road to Locarno.[35] It gained ground only under Herriot, then becoming ever more unavoidable after the London conference. It was Briand, however, who took it to a logical conclusion. His was a departure in form more than in substance and aim. Yet the mode of international politics France adopted mattered substantially in 1925. Briand's up-hill struggle on the inter-national and the domestic fronts was backed by his trusted aide, the *Quai d'Orsay*'s *secrétaire général* Philippe Berthelot, who ensured consistency in French policy.[36]

What were the deeper reasons for this change of paradigm in French postwar policy? In short, Briand's was the most far-reaching attempt to draw consequences from France's 'eroding bargaining power' in international politics after the Ruhr crisis. On one level, he had to reckon that France's *atouts* under Versailles would sooner or later be lost even without any revision of the treaty. France's withdrawal from the Rhineland was to be completed in stages between 1925 and 1935. This could not be postponed indefinitely, and nor could the end of military control, once Germany had basically fulfilled its

---

[33] Briand instructions, 4 November 1925, MAE, Z 1, Pacte de sécurité, 284–6, vol. 86, pp. 202–3.
[34] See Briand's statements to the Foreign Affairs Commission, 19 December 1925, Procès verbaux, C14763, no. 46, pp. 10–11. Cf. Adamthwaite (1995), pp. 116–17.
[35] Keiger (1997), p. 311.
[36] *Quai d'Orsay* memorandum to Fleuriau, 13 May 1925, MAE, Série Europe, Grande-Bretagne, vol. 75.

obligations. Briand distinctly felt Britain's pressure to eliminate such sources of irritation in the treaty powers' relations with Germany.[37] At the same time, he and Berthelot clearly saw the deeper problem that should Germany recover, the 'natural' structural imbalance between France and its eastern neighbour would resurface. It was thus all the more urgent to win Britain's backing in the attempt to control the extent of Germany's re-acquisition of power – and to impose strict limits on German armament and ambitions for territorial revision.[38]

In the constellation of 1925, Briand realised that France had no longer either the political or financial clout to enforce the Versailles system unilaterally. French policy had to chart a new course of controlled peaceful change in relations with Germany and *rapprochement* with the Anglo-American powers.[39] France could no longer afford to build its security on costly armed preponderance. The shift towards defensiveness would later become in every sense concrete in the so-called Maginot Line, authorised in 1928. More profoundly still, Briand's policy was shaped by France's growing financial and political difficulties. Throughout the pact negotiations, he was in fact more constrained by these problems than by a disunited, mainly nationalist and Poincarist opposition.[40] Herriot's Cartel had been unable to address France's worsening financial problems through austerity measures. His successors faced the same predicament. Successive attempts by Finance Minister Joseph Caillaux to initiate reform legislation were to no avail. France passed through more than a year of not just 'parliamentary agony'.[41]

Crucially, such concerns heightened Caillaux's, and Briand's, awareness that Paris needed to regain the support of its principal creditor. In the spring of 1925, this was still a closed avenue as America's *de facto* loan embargo persisted. The main US demand remained that France conclude a debt settlement. Yet the *Quai d'Orsay* also stressed that France had to improve overall relations with the Coolidge administration.[42] In the end, as Briand argued in the domestic debate, this could not be achieved without heeding America's espousal of the security pact. The French foreign minister underlined that his was the painful attempt to safeguard France without antagonising 'the present

---

[37] Crewe to Chamberlain, 13 May 1925, Austen Chamberlain Papers, AC 52/212; *Quai d'Orsay* memorandum, 13 May 1925, MAE, Série Europe, Grande-Bretagne, vol. 75.

[38] Briand to the Foreign Affairs Commission, 19 December 1925, Procès verbaux, C14763, no. 46, pp. 10–12.

[39] According to Bariéty, Briand never acknowledged this underlying aim. See Bariéty (2000), p. 127.

[40] Chamberlain to Crewe, 14 May 1925, *DBFP*, I, XXVII, no. 322.

[41] *JOS*, 10 April 1925, pp. 836–59; *JOC*, 19–22 November 1925, pp. 3801–913; Suarez (1928), pp. 45ff. Cf. Maier (1988), pp. 498–501.

[42] Seydoux memorandum, 28 February, MAE, Z 1, Série Europe, Grande-Bretagne, vol. 73, pp. 77–8.

force which dominates Europe' – the 'power of the City of London and of Wall Street'. Nonetheless, he adhered to his belief that security questions had to be settled by political means. This remained a core premise for Briand as much as for Chamberlain and Stresemann.[43]

Domestically, Briand had to proceed as cautiously as his German counterpart, remaining caught in a marked tension.[44] He constantly had to contemplate concessions affecting domestically neuralgic concerns, notably over the Rhineland and Germany's eastern borders.[45] The growing realisation that French security required new foundations ultimately provided Briand's Locarno policy with strong parliamentary approval in October 1925. But until then its volatile base in the *Chambre* made him vulnerable to nationalist opposition. The challenge that Briand faced, and saw, was twofold: how much change was possible while retaining sufficient guarantees vis-à-vis Germany; and how decisive a change could be made acceptable to 'French opinion'? Most influential among his critics were those who, like Poincaré, at first strictly opposed basing France's safety on voluntary German assurances and very limited British guarantees. Aided by the nationalist press, they accentuated the danger of losing control over the Rhineland and, with it, the very base for France's military preponderance.[46] Remarkable, though, was how little Briand's opponents had to offer in terms of an alternative policy – except for coercive recipes that had proved ineffective ever since 1919. In fact, Poincaré eventually came to back Briand's general orientation.[47]

---

[43] D'Abernon to Chamberlain, 15 May 1925, *DBFP*, I, XXVII, no. 324.
[44] Briand instructions, 4 November 1925, MAE, Z 1, Pacte de sécurité, 284–6, vol. 86, pp. 202–3.
[45] Laroche memorandum, 26 February 1924, MAE, Série Europe, Grande-Bretagne, vol. 73, pp. 56–7.
[46] Chamberlain to Crewe, 14 May 1925, *DBFP*, I, XXVII, no. 322; Suarez (1928), pp. 45–6.
[47] Cf. Laroche (1957), pp. 214–15; Keiger (1997), pp. 318–19, and (2004), pp. 95–108.

15   The path to Locarno – and its transatlantic dimension

As Chamberlain realised acutely in his consultations with Briand and diplomatic exchanges with Stresemann, each of them pursued specific interests and harboured different assumptions on what the Rhine pact was to achieve.[1] In particular, each had his own rationale as to how dynamic or restrained a transformation of European politics the pact was to inaugurate, and what this portended for the order of 1919. In sum, Briand's main aim in the protracted negotiations with Britain and Germany between April and October 1925 remained to retain the upper hand in upholding the Versailles system, and French pre-eminence. He sought to decelerate and minimise inescapable changes; and he sought to conciliate *and* rein in a resurgent Germany, both through the pact and by closing ranks with Britain and the United States.

Stresemann's main rationale was in some ways the opposite: to accelerate Germany's return to the concert of great powers, which was to yield new possibilities for peaceful revisions. His was to be a path towards 'liberating' the Rhineland and forging new ground-rules for modifying the Versailles system politically, economically and, in a more distant future, territorially. He hoped to achieve all of this in a co-operative manner, recognising French, and British, interests while also enhancing Germany's standing with the US creditor.

Thus, both sides were beginning to pursue their aims on the shared assumption that neither could reach them without a consolidation of their bilateral relations, which had to go hand in hand with a consolidation of Germany's position in Europe. As Briand *de facto* accepted, and as Anglo-American policymakers had seriously acknowledged since 1923, this could not be achieved on the premises of 1919. Complicating international consensus, however, was the fact that both Briand and Stresemann felt compelled to overstate conflicting demands to legitimate their conciliatory policies in the polarised domestic spectra they faced. Throughout 1925 all policymakers involved, and especially French and German leaders, were at times severely

---

[1] Chamberlain to Crewe, 14 May 1925, Chamberlain to D'Abernon, 30 July 1925, *DBFP*, I, XXVII, nos. 322, 431.

constrained by internal opposition. Yet, as in 1924, all sides also seized on domestic constraints to limit concessions to the other powers.

Even if siding more with Briand than Stresemann, Chamberlain had in fact recognised one of the gravest challenges for European politics after the Great War: the need to forge compromises that could not only be sustained in international diplomacy but also legitimated domestically.[2] After London, Locarno was to be the second pacific settlement between Germany and the west that resulted from a negotiating-process between – more or less stable – democratic states. Its protagonists were obliged to win approval within three distinctly different parliamentary systems and national fields of forces: the French, the German and, albeit more favourable, the British. And they also had to produce an outcome satisfying the preponderant American power – concretely, not only Republican policymakers but also, and essentially, US financiers. Finally, if of secondary importance to the protagonists of Locarno, there was the need, particularly for France, to take into account Polish and Czech interests.

These complexities notwithstanding, British and American decisionmakers were not naïvely mistaken in assuming that, against often strong oppositional currents, Stresemann and Briand were approaching a modicum of common ground – at least one sufficient for the pact's conclusion.[3] Spurred by the Anglo-American powers, and to a remarkable extent, French and German policies had begun to converge since the Ruhr crisis. In a wider perspective, it is worth emphasising that such simultaneity of convergence and persisting divergences is the norm rather than the exception in the history of international politics. Nor is it necessarily the *prima causa* for the disintegration of peace orders, as long as there is a mechanism making it possible to balance and, as far as possible, reconcile different aims – or else to subordinate them to greater common interests.[4] The central question of pact diplomacy in 1925, and Locarno politics thereafter, was and remained how far the new European concert that Chamberlain envisaged could become such a mechanism.

The fundamental challenge facing British more than US diplomacy was to initiate and buttress a complex process of Franco-German accommodation. The pact negotiations had to bear different kinds of fruit. They had to yield results that Briand could vindicate as a success of his policy of control and deceleration and that Stresemann could 'sell' as decisive steps on the path of

---

[2] Chamberlain to Addison (Berlin) and Max Muller (Warsaw), 16 June 1925, *DBFP*, I, XXVII, no. 383, p. 614; Austen to Hilda Chamberlain, 28 November 1925, Austen Chamberlain Papers, AC 5/1/370.

[3] Chamberlain minute, 19 March 1925, FO 371/10756, C 3539/3539/18.

[4] On the nineteenth-century system see Schroeder (1994) and (1987). Cf. Ikenberry (2001), pp. 11–18.

Germany's re-ascendance and 'liberation'.[5] To be sustainable, the outcome had to give both Weimar's embattled political elite and the Third Republic's Briandist camp a stake, and a platform, in advancing what essentially was a Franco-German peace process.[6] It fell to Britain to foster this process without pressing ahead too fast or too little.

At the height of the pre-Locarno crisis, FRBNY Governor Strong observed on 22 July that a peculiar dichotomy had come to mark German and European politics. Unsurprisingly, it was the dichotomy between what he considered the private, genuine attitudes of politicians and the official positions they assumed to justify their policies. Privately, Anglo-American financiers were told that 'Germany was sparing no effort to observe the terms of the treaty of Versailles' and 'the Dawes Plan'. But the 'official correspondence' conveyed that 'Germany was seeking by subterfuge and otherwise to escape the obligations imposed upon her.' For Strong, the explanation for this lay in the fact that away from the public's gaze and expectations Luther and Stresemann had 'a theory of their future which is quite different from that which they exhibit officially'. Essentially, they desired 'to live in peace' with their neighbours, 'to develop industrially, and to repay and build up' what they could. Officially, however, German policy was 'characterised by distrust'.[7] What Kellogg had concluded from negotiating with Herriot in 1924 was that the same applied to French policymakers and their excessive security demands vis-à-vis Germany.[8]

Overall, US observers considered this publicly imposed distrust, not the clash of fundamental interests, 'possibly the worst feature of the European situation today'. Yet it was also on this level that they saw their essential, and necessarily informal, task. It was because of the still prevailing mutual suspicions in postwar Europe that American, and British, decisionmakers had to act as mediators between French and German leaders to further a sober reconciliation of material interests, first behind closed doors.[9] In 1925 and thereafter, this remained the self-chosen 'mission' of America's informal diplomacy, pursued in accordance with the interests of Republican and Wall Street elites.[10]

The nature and dynamics of the Locarno process

What shaped the process culminating in the Locarno pact? Was Chamberlain finally outmanoeuvred by shrewd German moves to loosen the bonds of

---

[5] On the British perception see Chamberlain to D'Abernon, 2 April 1925, *DBFP*, I, XXVII, no. 283.
[6] Cf. Krüger (1985a), p. 297; Hagspiel (1987), pp. 319ff; and against this Knipping (1987).
[7] Strong memorandum, 'Politics in Germany', 22 July 1925, Strong Papers.
[8] Kellogg to White, 19 September 1924, Kellogg to Coolidge, 30 April 1925, Kellogg Papers.
[9] Strong memorandum, 22 July 1925, Strong Papers; Kellogg to Coolidge, 30 April 1925, Kellogg Papers.
[10] Castle Diary, 5–7 July 1925, vol. 8; Castle to Houghton, 3 November 1925, Houghton Papers.

Versailles, not least because Britain lacked a consistent strategy?[11] Or was British policy rather usurped by French plans to cement the malfunctioning order of 1919?[12] And were American policymakers after all merely standing on the sidelines, ready to condone one or the other outcome?

In fact, it was in many ways British diplomacy that effected, and US influence that catalysed, the essential shift to what became known as 'Locarno politics': concerted accommodation between the western powers and Germany. Undoubtedly, conflicting interests and particular aims persisted. Yet between April and October 1925 all sides began to realise that a new mechanism or indeed system of international politics was required to come to terms with national agendas that necessarily diverged after the havoc that the Great War had wrought. In the Euro-Atlantic constellation of the mid-1920s, these agendas indeed comprised not only strategic and political but also, closely bound up with them, financial interests that did or could collide with each other.

To gauge the dynamics of the Locarno process it is helpful to ask, in analogy to 1923/4, if the Locarno pact was inevitable – and, if so, when and why it became inevitable, or at least compelling. The answer seems to be threefold. On one level, the pact doubtless drew closer when it became apparent in the summer of 1925 that, despite acute crises, both Briand and Stresemann managed to adhere to the common goal of forging an agreement and reconciling their different agendas. Both avoided maximal demands that satisfied national audiences yet threatened to wreck the negotiations. This applied to all the critical fields: disarmament control, the guarantee of Germany's eastern frontiers and eventually also the central issue of the Rhineland. Yet, as can hardly be overstated, it would not have occurred without the impact of British – and American – efforts to ensure that the incipient Franco-German peace process did not collapse. A settlement of the kind realised at Locarno – a regional, western-orientated security regime including Germany – became very probable once Chamberlain had resolved to pursue an integrative pact on British terms. And it became even more likely once Washington and US financiers had concluded that such a regime offered the best safeguards for Europe's economic pacification. Both had become clear by March 1925. This was when, fundamentally, the path to Locarno was opened up.

Following Britain's lead, the security negotiations essentially proceeded along European lines. They were driven forward, not by a completely new postwar diplomacy but rather by a revival and, on the European side, intensification of the politics that had forged the London settlement. This *modus procedendi* was now brought to bear on the pivotal security question. This time, the process gained momentum without any *direct* American participation.

[11] See Kissinger (1994), pp. 267–88; and against this Grayson (1997), pp. 66–7.
[12] Cf. Jacobson (1983a).

Especially at the height of the pre-Locarno crisis in June and July, however, US initiatives to promote the pact had a tangible effect. Heeded even more in Paris and Berlin were signals that US decision-makers were prepared to tighten the financial screws on Germany, and keep them on France, if the accords fell through.

Not only the protagonists of European diplomacy but all important interest-groups in France and Germany desiring a new or uninterrupted flow of American capital had to reckon with the American interest in political safe-guards for these loans – and America's wider stabilisation efforts.[13] Overall, US influence – incentives, pressure and financial leverage – expedited the Locarno process not decisively but significantly. As a still effective 'background force', it was particularly important in overcoming domestic obstacles both in France and Germany.

In the final analysis, however, it was Chamberlain's commitment and resili-ence as mediator between Stresemann and Briand that proved pivotal for Locarno. The British foreign secretary self-confidently defined his role as that of an 'honest broker', who was acting 'perhaps even a little more honestly than the author of that famous phrase', Bismarck.[14] In practice, though, he hardly came to act as an entirely even-handed arbiter in the negotiations preceding Locarno – as little as Bismarck during the 1878 Congress of Berlin. Aided by Crowe's successor as permanent under-secretary, William Tyrrell, Chamberlain in fact defined his agenda much as MacDonald had done in 1924. In his view, Britain had to shape the diplomatic process to forestall 'the constant risk that either France or Germany may upset the apple-cart'. And, without Britain's intervention, the German initiative 'would have fallen still-born as did the Cuno proposition' of 1922. Left to their own devices, French and German policymakers would have 'shatter[ed]' all hopes of obtaining an agreement. Chamberlain's maxim became that unless the British 'broker' came to 'hold the balance & use [its] influence on both sides to the full', Franco-German tensions would persist 'till Armageddon breaks out again'.[15] This was not an entirely inaccurate assessment.

Despite the distinct limits of Britain's commitment, Chamberlain was the only actor who could offer France essential reassurance. And only this allowed him, Briand and Stresemann to transform the German pact initiative into the core of a novel European peace system.[16] Likewise, only British diplomacy

---

[13] Thus Kellogg's résumé before the Council on Foreign Relations, New York, 14 December 1925, Kellogg Papers.

[14] Chamberlain to Crewe, 2 April 1925, FO 800/257/483.

[15] Chamberlain to D'Abernon, 2 April 1925, *DBFP*, I, XXVII, no. 283; Chamberlain note, 14 March 1925, FO 371/10756: C 3539/3539/18.

[16] For his own appraisal see Austen to Ida Chamberlain, 28 November 1925, Austen Chamberlain Papers, AC 5/1/370.

could bring sufficient weight to bear on Briand to move Paris towards accepting Berlin as an equal negotiating-partner. Ultimately, however, it was only at Locarno itself that Chamberlain, Briand and Stresemann became something akin to a new 'triumvirate' of European politics. That this did not happen earlier was chiefly due to Briand's veto. But it can also be attributed to Chamberlain's very understanding of his mediating role between Paris and Berlin. Essentially, he came to act on the assumption that in order to create a new European concert Britain could not yet pursue actual concert diplomacy. Rather, it had to privilege consultations with France precisely to draw Germany into the diplomatic process and ensure the pact's implementation.

Based on the cabinet resolutions of mid-March, Chamberlain translated this rationale into a two-pronged policy. From April, he first embarked upon separate negotiations with Briand while at the same time urging Stresemann to accept Britain's lead and refrain from posing further conditions that complicated his task. Britain and France were to begin 'by agreeing among [themselves]' on the pact terms to be proposed to Germany.[17] French preferences were then communicated to Berlin through informal diplomatic channels and, eventually, official French notes. Germany was only to participate in actual negotiations once an Anglo-French consensus had emerged.

Trying to forge a common platform with Briand, Chamberlain made concessions on some points, notably on separating the evacuation of the Cologne zone from the pact negotiations.[18] Yet he ultimately aimed for a pact largely determined by Britain. It has been asserted that the foreign secretary dramatised differences between British and German positions while overemphasising parallel interests with France.[19] He in fact did so because Stresemann refused to follow his lead without resistance and because it corresponded with his role-definition. Chamberlain left no doubt that his 'sympathies' were 'French'. But he intended to make a virtue of this penchant. He argued that if he was not seen as 'pro-French' he could 'never get them to move on the lines of Cabinet policy' and he 'could not afford to say or do as much to help Germany'. Yet Britain would not defend 'all the vagaries of French policy'. It had to prevent France from 'committing suicide under the influence of her fears'.[20]

Parallel, Crowe had instructed D'Abernon on 9 March that unless he moved to 'press at least as much as we are pressing France, we must fail'. Only 'with German assistance' could British diplomacy 'persuade France to treat German overtures seriously'. With Berlin's help, Britain was to take charge of the pact

---

[17] Chamberlain to Crowe, 7 March 1925, *DBFP*, I, XXVII, no. 225.
[18] Chamberlain memorandum, 2 October 1925, *DBFP*, I, XXVII, no. 509.
[19] For the German perspective see Krüger (1985a), p. 293.
[20] Chamberlain note to Lampson, 14 March 1925, FO 371/10756: C 3539/3539/18.

process, and Chamberlain indeed seized the initiative from Stresemann.[21] What thus propelled pre-Locarno politics were not as yet trilateral negotiations on an equal footing. Rather, like that of London, the Locarno conference was made possible through Britain's consultations with France, and its subsequent brokerage between Paris and Berlin.

Chamberlain's insistence on this strategy was reinforced by the fact that his perceptions of Briand's and Stresemann's domestic challenges contrasted starkly. Unlike D'Abernon, he ranked the complexities that Stresemann faced decidedly lower than those facing Briand. The foreign secretary essentially underestimated the difficulties besetting Luther's *Bürgerblock* coalition because he long thought that it instrumentalised its constraints, thus exacerbating Briand's problems. He did not accept that this could apply vice versa. Too often, in his view, Luther and Stresemann endangered international comprom-ise through concessions to the German nationalists.[22] But there was also an overriding British interest in circumnavigating domestic cliffs in Germany to keep the security negotiations on track. As Chamberlain told Ambassador Sthamer, the new president's election on 26 April had produced a 'very unfavourable impression upon public opinion in this country as well as in France'. Given the new president's expression of support for Stresemann's policy, however, he 'saw no reason' to change his policy. Yet Berlin had to prove that it was prepared to 'adhere scrupulously' to its security proposal. Overall, the onus in the pact negotiations thus clearly lay on German rather than on French leaders. They had to allay 'the uneasy suspicions' with which Germany was still 'watched' in the west and the east.[23]

By contrast, Chamberlain never failed to stress that Briand could not afford to 'rouse French Nationalist opinion by appearing to yield too much or too readily'.[24] He indeed saw Briand as the only politician capable of delivering the shift in French policy that Britain desired, at this stage in fact deeming him far more indispensable than Stresemann. For Briand seemed to be the only French leader who not merely sought genuine conciliation with Germany but could also overcome the Poincarist right's opposition to the pact.[25]

---

[21] Crowe to D'Abernon *DBFP*, I, XXVII, no. 231; Chamberlain to Crewe, 2 April 1925, FO 800/257/483.

[22] Chamberlain to Addison, 21 June 1925; Chamberlain to D'Abernon, 30 July 1925, *DBFP*, I, XXVII, nos. 388, 431.

[23] Chamberlain to Addison, 30 April 1925; Chamberlain to Max Muller, 16 June 1925, *DBFP*, I, XXVII, nos. 300, 383.

[24] Chamberlain to Crewe, 14 May 1925, *DBFP*, I, XXVII, no. 322.

[25] Chamberlain memoranda to the cabinet, 9 March 1925 and 2 October 1925, *DBFP*, I, XXVII, nos. 232, 509.

The crisis of 1925 – and its resolution

The obstacles to Franco-German *détente*, and the indispensability of British mediation and US influence, were strikingly revealed by the gravest yet hardly unpredictable crisis of the pact process. What turned into a protracted stand-off between the treaty powers and Germany started with a controversy over the allied note on German disarmament of 4 June and escalated after the publication of France's first official reply to Stresemann's 'security initiative' on 16 June. In Germany, the impasse was only overcome through Stresemann's long struggle to win support for an affirmative response to the French note, finally transmitted on 20 July. In the sphere of international politics, it did not end until France and Britain agreed on a draft treaty of the pact following Chamberlain's meeting with Briand in London on 11–12 August.

In all likelihood, the pact process could no longer have been entirely derailed by this stage. But the conflicts that it revealed were substantial. As British and American policymakers realised, the underlying danger was that Germany's relations with the west would once again collapse into the previous postwar pattern of victors seeking to impose conditions on the vanquished and the latter seeking to counter or elude this. Indeed, both Briand and Stresemann felt the need to strengthen their domestic – and international – bargaining positions *on old terms*. Both tried to refashion the scope of the security pact to make it palatable to nationalist opposition in their countries. But they did not stop there.

A first conflict arose over the IMCC's report on the completion of German disarmament, belatedly transmitted in an official note on 4 June.[26] Not least, Briand used the report to stress once again the extent of French security concerns in the French *Assemblée*. This put further pressure on Britain.[27] The note highlighted more long-term problems, such as the reorganisation of German police forces and the *Reichswehr*'s intent to re-forge a 'people in arms' around such nuclei. Yet while containing new stipulations, it also concluded that Germany had basically fulfilled allied disarmament demands. This *de facto* prepared the end of military control, even though the IMCC was not formally withdrawn until January 1927. But the note's tone was that of an allied decree commanding the execution of the Treaty of Versailles and threatening sanctions in case of non-compliance. To compound difficulties, it arrived in Berlin before the first official Anglo-French response to the German security initiative, causing considerable dismay for the Luther government.[28] Yet, significantly, it did not jeopardise Stresemann's pursuit of the Rhine pact.

---

[26] Cf. Salewski (1966), p. 289.
[27] Chamberlain to Grahame, 11 June 1925, *DBFP*, I, XXVII, p. 602.
[28] Cf. Salewski (1966), pp. 294–305; Fox (1969), pp. 143–64.

For his part, Chamberlain felt all the more reason to refocus negotiations on the security accords. He had already urged Briand in May not to resort to coercive policies.[29] But the latter nonetheless attempted to continue Herriot's defensive policy of linkage on disarmament, evacuation and security. Briand sought to establish the principle that ending disarmament inspections and, crucially, an early termination of the Rhineland occupation were contingent on enhanced assurances of security – in fact Germany's, and Britain's, agreement to a pact on French terms.[30] But Chamberlain insisted that the exchanges over German disarmament should quickly be eliminated as an irritant in the pact negotiations, which he sought to keep separate from them. Having reached the conclusion that Germany had basically fulfilled its obligations under Versailles, London was 'prepared to stretch a point here and there in favour of Germany, provided she shows a reasonable spirit'.[31] In fact, the disarmament controversy quickly abated after Berlin assured the ex-allied powers that it would address all 'justified' complaints. In return, France proceeded in July to complete not only the evacuation of the Ruhr but also that of the 'sanction cities', Düsseldorf, Duisburg and Ruhrort, occupied since 1921. This underscored both the short reach of French stalling manoeuvres against British opposition and the evolving new quality of pre-Locarno diplomacy.

A more profound crisis of the incipient peace process was triggered by France's official reply to the German 'security memorandum' on 16 June. Endorsed by Chamberlain, it was finally sent after a long period of internal quarrels and consultations with London.[32] The French note generally accepted the proposal of a Mutual Security Pact but demanded a reinforcement of the guarantees it would contain.[33] It put German and British diplomacy to the test, particularly because of the domestic turmoil it fomented in Germany, which temporarily cast doubt on the continuation of Stresemann's policy. Yet the inner-German altercations also led to renewed US efforts on behalf of the pact.

The conditions France posed concerned above all the eastern arbitration treaties. They were to become an obligatory part of the pact and, after London's refusal, to be guaranteed by France.[34] Briand's insistence on this last point, which ultimately implied that France would become the arbiter in Polish–German disputes, met with Stresemann's counter-claim that this was a condition impossible to fulfil for any German government. The same applied

[29] Chamberlain to Crewe, 28 May 1925; Chamberlain to D'Abernon, 7 May 1925, Austen Chamberlain Papers, AC 52/214, 269.
[30] Crewe to Chamberlain, 5 and 22 February 1925, Austen Chamberlain Papers, AC 52/184, 190.
[31] Crewe to Chamberlain, 13 May 1925, Austen Chamberlain Papers, AC 52/212; Chamberlain memorandum, 16 July 1925, DBFP, I, XXVII, no. 414.
[32] Chamberlain to Briand, 8 June 1925, DBFP, I, XXVII, no. 363.
[33] Locarno-Konferenz, no. 14.   [34] Ibid.

to the final French demand that Germany was to enter the League without setting any preconditions. Above all, Paris desired to foreclose any exception regarding article 16 of the Covenant, regulating the participation in collective sanctions against aggressors.[35] Briand's note underscored that the crux remained the 'wider' question of French security. For German and British policymakers, it underlined the fundamental problem of what guarantees would suffice to make France abandon its coercive postwar policies.[36]

What contributed, and what contributed most, to overcoming this perhaps unavoidable impasse? Fundamentally, as in the decisive stages of the Dawes negotiations, the bargaining-process over the pact had by that time begun to acquire a momentum of its own. Different aims notwithstanding, particularly between British and German policies, a parallelism of interests had emerged, which Briand ultimately shared. It hinged on a sense that the gains of salvaging the overall agreement increasingly outweighed any conceivable gains made by insisting on particular interests at the risk of undermining the overall process. On the basis of this rationale, the crisis was resolved through a combination of four main factors.

(1) Undoubtedly, Stresemann's readiness to allay French anxieties and build bridges against entrenched DNVP opposition mattered considerably. While Germany did not relinquish the option of peacefully altering the *status quo* in eastern Europe, the Luther government's perseverance played an important part in salvaging the pact. All of this crystallised in the German note of 20 July.[37]

(2) Arguably most important in the international realm, and so far insufficiently appreciated, was that Chamberlain, though criticising Stresemann's subservience to nationalist demands, did most in concrete terms to forge the framework for a pact *conducive to peaceful change*. He thus effectively strengthened Stresemann's case – and the prospects of realising the pact. Britain could prevail on France to accept two basic premises. On the one hand, Chamberlain 'convinced' Briand that only successful negotiations offered a realistic chance of addressing France's overriding problem of insecurity *with* British support. Should they fail, no alternative British commitment could be expected. On the other hand, he impressed on the French foreign minister that to master the security problem, and preserve a close *entente*, France had to make concessions to Germany. It had to espouse a pact furthering international arbitration and obliging Germany to accept controlled peaceful change. This, however, could not be achieved by making the envisaged treaty a 'legalistic'

---

[35] Stresemann statements to the *Reichstag*'s Foreign Affairs Committee, 17 July 1925, Stresemann (1932), II, pp. 146–51.

[36] Hurst memorandum, June 18 1925, *DBFP*, I, XXVII, no. 385.

[37] *Locarno-Konferenz*, no. 16. Cf. Krüger (1985a), pp. 292ff.

document enshrining the *status quo* in western *and* eastern Europe.[38] Only the intervention of Britain allowed German efforts to meet French demands, and to put forward enhanced arbitration treaties, to have any effect.

(3) More in reaction to Chamberlain's prodding than by seizing the initiative himself, Briand moved towards adopting these premises. More concretely, he recognised the need for a more co-operative approach not only to the arbitration question; and he realised that to be successful the pact agreement had to be directly negotiated with Germany and take into account German concerns.[39] Further, he now began to make this case more persistently on the home front.

(4) Finally, the ground for the Locarno pact was prepared because, as in 1924, the Americans intensified their informal efforts to rescue a European agreement including Germany. Notably Houghton and Strong intervened more directly. They brought to bear political influence and financial pressure both behind the scenes of European politics and in public, here particularly vis-à-vis the domestic critics of Briand's and Stresemann's policies. The longer the political-cum-financial calamities in France and Germany persisted the more tangible could be the effect of American 'threats' that aborting the security negotiations would entail a continued embargo or withdrawal of US capital and support. The Coolidge administration did not have to pursue a far-reaching diplomatic offensive to underscore this. For all sides understood that US 'sanctions' could only aggravate the economic *malaise* east and west of the Rhine. This influenced political behaviour both in Paris and Berlin throughout the summer and autumn of 1925.

Franco-German controversies and the impact of American influence

The inner-German controversies over Stresemann's new security policy reached a climax in the wake of the French note. He and Luther continued their efforts to keep the DNVP tied to the government to moderate its radical wing. Yet the Nationalists' aversion to the entire course of *rapprochement* with the victors remained unchanged.[40] As before the London conference, Stresemann had to threaten his resignation to salvage his course.[41]

What was perceived as an acute crisis in Paris and London caused no major stir in American politics. Nor did it lead Kellogg to reconsider the wisdom of his non-entanglement policy. But from late June US efforts under the *leitmotif*

---

[38] Hurst memorandum, 18 June 1925, *DBFP*, I, XXVII, no. 385.
[39] Phipps to Chamberlain, 27 July 1925, FO 371/10737: C 9984/459/18; Briand statement to Chamberlain, 11 August 1925, FO 371/10738: C 10609/459/18.
[40] Cf. Grathwol (1980), pp. 70ff; Baechler (1996), pp. 599–611.
[41] *AR Luther I und II*, I, no. 110.

of 'carrots and sticks' were nonetheless amplified, albeit on a minor scale. Following the first controversies over the French note, Coolidge himself impressed on Britain's Ambassador Howard that new American loans to France would only, if at all, be authorised by his administration if France concluded the pact. This Chamberlain subsequently used to prod Briand.[42] Authorised by Kellogg, Houghton reiterated Coolidge's simple yet effective equation – and so did Herrick in Paris and Schurman in Berlin: 'Americans would not lend their money unless they thought peace was firmly established and the safety of their investments thus ensured.'[43] Strong underscored on 11 July that every time Paris made a decision like postponing the evacuation of the Cologne zone, this 'sent a chill over the financial community' in New York.[44] A continuation of such policies would make it 'exceedingly difficult indeed for any of the affected parties to place loans in America'. What Strong, like Kellogg, emphasised was dreaded by Briand but accorded well with the rationales of German and British policy. Hand in hand with an enhancement of security through the pact had to go the elimination of sources of irritation and insecurity for US investors. Rather than cement the *status quo*, regional stabilisation had to spur peaceful change.[45]

In contrast to Chamberlain, US diplomats and bankers underestimated rather than overestimated the internal constraints on Briand's foreign policy. Particularly in the State Department, there was no sense that the future of the Painlevé government – or the Third Republic – was at stake because of the contemplated security concessions to Germany. On the contrary, France was still seen as the troublemaker of postwar politics that was now well advised to reciprocate the offers of Weimar policymakers, who were deemed ever more trustworthy. As Houghton informed Chamberlain on 3 June, the 'American public . . . had recently come to regard France as being a disturbing element in Europe'. On the other hand, a moderation of French policy that avoided 'unnecessarily provocative . . . phraseology' vis-à-vis Germany and sought to place relations with Berlin on a new basis could also have beneficial consequences for France's standing with America.[46]

American pressure on Paris thus exceeded that exerted on Berlin. And the Coolidge administration upheld the loan 'embargo' pending a debt agreement.[47]

---

[42] Chamberlain to Crewe, 27 June 1925, 7 July 1925, Austen Chamberlain Papers, AC 52/221, 224.

[43] Chamberlain to Howard, 3 June 1925, *DBFP*, I, XXVII, no. 357; Schurman report, 29 October 1925, NA RG 59 862.00/2060; Herrick report, 17 December 1926, NA RG 59 751.62/95.

[44] Strong memorandum on conversations with Luther, Stresemann and Schacht in Berlin, 11 July 1925, Strong Papers.

[45] Kellogg address, 14 December 1925, Kellogg Papers.

[46] Kellogg to Coolidge, 30 April 1925, Kellogg Papers; Castle Diary, 5–6 July 1925, vol. 8; Chamberlain to Howard, 3 June 1925, *DBFP*, I, XXVII, no. 357.

[47] Cf. Maier (1988), p. 502.

In view of what he saw as Caillaux's inability to implement structural reforms stabilising the budget and the franc, Strong unequivocally backed this policy. Even after Locarno, the FRBNY governor rejected French requests finally to grant the $100,000,000 loan already discussed in 1924. J.P. Morgan's main concern remained financial rather than connected with wider Franco-German *détente*. While his firm desired to aid French consolidation efforts, Morgan criticised the French Treasury and the Bank of France under its governor Emile Moreau for disregarding the 'laws' of responsible public finance.[48]

In the State Department Kellogg endorsed the administration's tough stance vis-à-vis France. Like Hoover, he maintained that the main 'inducement' Washington had to offer to bolster French and German pact efforts was an unrestricted flow of US capital and America's continued support for an economically underpinned stabilisation.[49] Apart from tentative suggestions that Houghton conveyed to Chamberlain, the secretary gave no signal to the Europeans that he was prepared to play a more active, if unofficial, role in overcoming the deadlock in their negotiations.[50]

By contrast, Castle, who had travelled to London for a first-hand impression of the European situation, saw the pact in serious jeopardy and, in early July, recommended to step up US engagement. In his view, it still ultimately fell to the Europeans to settle their differences in the realm of security. Yet he also held that there were two major obstacles US diplomacy could help to overcome: on the one hand, the note of 16 June seemed to indicate that Paris was intent on burying the entire pact project; on the other, there was the danger that the German government, caving in to DNVP pressure, would give France the pretext for doing just that by linking the pact with the evacuation of the Rhineland.[51]

Against this background, Castle suggested that Houghton should resume what he had so successfully practised to push through the Dawes plan, namely to return to Berlin to 'have a quiet talk' with the Luther government and impress US views on the German Nationals. Yet, as it proved impossible to co-ordinate such a mission with Kellogg, it never materialised. Having returned to Washington, the most Castle could do was to remind Ambassador Maltzan that Washington would have to re-evaluate its friendly relations with Berlin if Germany abandoned the pact.[52] Parallel, US diplomacy demonstratively backed Chamberlain's mediation efforts throughout the summer of 1925, while

---

[48] Strong to Parmentier (Paris), 8 May 1926, Strong Papers; J.P. Morgan & Co. to H.H. Harjes, 18 December 1925, quoted after Burk (1991), p. 138.

[49] Hoover to Kellogg, 16 April 1925; Kellogg to Hoover, 7 May 1925, NA RG 59 862.51/1925.

[50] Houghton note, 3 July 1925; Castle to Houghton, 14 July 1925, Houghton Papers; Kellogg to Coolidge, 30 April 1925, Kellogg Papers.

[51] Castle Diary, 5 July 1925, vol. 8.

[52] Castle Diary, 6, 7, 15 July 1925, vol. 8; Castle to Houghton, 14 July 1925, Houghton Papers.

the British foreign secretary kept Houghton scrupulously informed about their progress. Even more explicitly than in 1924, Washington thus relied on Britain's political brokerage, counting on Chamberlain's effectiveness as a *de facto* agent of US interests in Europe.[53]

While the Coolidge administration consequently restricted its informal pursuits, the most important, and direct, US intervention in Germany was Strong's visit to Berlin at the height of the crisis. Meeting Luther, Stresemann and Schacht in mid-July, Strong reiterated what he had earlier declared to French authorities – namely that the 'basic condition for loans' was America's 'confidence in a peaceful evolution of Europe'. To ensure this, America had welcomed the German pact proposal and urgently wished its success. In Strong's view, all German politicians realised 'that the future of Germany rests very largely upon the wisdom with which decisions are made by [the Dawes regime's] Transfer Committee' – and thus ultimately in the hands of Gilbert and the United States. Gilbert had acquired an 'almost unassailable position' in wielding a degree of foreign control over the country's economic life that, in Strong's opinion, the American people would never have accepted.[54]

As we have seen, American interventions could be all the more effective at this juncture because both Germany and France suffered from acute capital shortages. The domestic debates over the security pact fell in a period of economic stagnation in Germany and severe budgetary and currency crisis in France.[55] Consequently, while also sparking resentment America's financial arguments for the pact were not lost on either side. In the inner-French debates, Briand stressed ever more urgently that it was a matter of French *raison d'état* to depart from a course that, like Poincaré's, openly conflicted with the preferences of London and Washington – and that went against the newly pre-eminent '[w]eight of money' wielded by Anglo-American financiers.[56]

In Germany, Stresemann also eagerly seized upon American exhortations to master domestic–political controversies. On 20 July, he declared in the *Reichstag*'s Foreign Affairs Committee that if Germany did 'not come to a co-operation with the financially powerful states, with America' he 'foresaw an economic breakdown' that 'would have uncontrollable repercussions' for Germany.[57] As he impressed on more moderate DNVP representatives, there was thus no alternative to persisting with Germany's western orientation and

---

[53] Chamberlain to Howard, 26 May 1925, Chamberlain to Chilton, 11 June 1925, *DBFP*, I, XXVII, nos. 344, 376.

[54] Strong memoranda, 13 and 22 July 1925, Strong Papers.

[55] For a comparative analysis see Maier (1988), pp. 488–501. Cf. Suarez (1928) pp. 45ff; Kolb (1988), pp. 71–82.

[56] D'Abernon to Chamberlain, 15 May 1925; on Briand's worries over the US embargo see Crewe to Chamberlain, 27 May 1925, *DBFP*, I, XXVII, nos. 324, 346.

[57] Stresemann (1932), II, p. 149. Cf. Stürmer (1967), pp. 119, 130.

the long-winded pact negotiations. Yet Stresemann also stressed that his policy, precisely by stabilising Germany's relations with the west, not only secured the Rhineland against renewed French 'persecution' but also created 'new possibilities in the east'.[58] Backing his position, Luther told Strong on 11 July that his government could therefore 'never' countenance a reinforcement of the eastern *status quo*, particularly through a French guarantee of the eastern arbitration treaties.[59]

Ultimately, Stresemann was not to be deterred from his course. The Luther government eventually ensured DNVP support by making specific domestic concessions on tariff policy, raising tariffs to protect the special agricultural interests that the DNVP represented. On 23 July, D'Abernon reported that the German National leader Count Kuno Westarp would now 'support the Government'. The only remaining opposition to Stresemann's policy came from the right-wing 'extremists' and 'the Communists', who opposed Germany's entry into 'an anti-Soviet League of the Western Powers'.[60]

The German note of 20 July indeed manifested Stresemann's intent to go to great lengths to salvage the security pact. Chamberlain had warned Berlin in advance not to 'frustrate [its] own initiative and bring the mutual pact proposals to nought' by 'making . . . difficulties' over the French note. Essentially, he still sought to prescribe the course of German pact policy, strongly suggesting to Stresemann that the proper way to proceed would be to acknowledge the 'spirit of conciliation' of Briand's note, 'avoid all petty discussion of detail' and 'accept without cavil the broad general principles which it enumerates'. In fact, the German note did insist that the French guarantee of Germany's arbitration accords with its eastern neighbours and article 16 remained contentious points. Here Germany again invoked its special geographic position and disarmed status after the war. Behind this, as Chamberlain privately acknowledged, lay German *raison d'état* – the desire not to burden relations with Moscow and to weaken Poland's diplomatic position.[61] To the German public, Stresemann underscored, not for the last time, that Germany did not want to become the site of the next European war.[62]

In substance, however, the German government made conciliatory proposals. These hinged on an extension of the 'system of arbitration treaties'

---

[58] Stresemann to Maltzan, 7 April 1925, Stresemann Papers, vol. 23, H150698; Stresemann statement to the Foreign Affairs Committee, 17 July 1925, Stresemann (1932), II, pp. 146–51.

[59] Strong memorandum, 11 July 1925, Strong Papers.

[60] D'Abernon to Chamberlain, 23 July 1925, *DBFP*, I, XXVII, no. 422. Cf. Stürmer (1980), pp. 237ff.

[61] Chamberlain to Addison, 21 June 1925, Chamberlain to Tyrrell, 8 October 1925, *DBFP*, I, XXVII, no. 388, pp. 832–6.

[62] Stresemann statements to the Foreign Affairs Committee, 17 July 1925, Stresemann (1932), II, pp. 146–51.

developed by Schubert with the assistance of the German Foreign Office's legal expert Friedrich Gaus. In essence, Germany offered to enshrine in the pact the renunciation of war as a means of territorial revision – and to give Warsaw an informal assurance that a modification of Germany's eastern border was not 'acute'. Further, to placate Paris, an explicit linkage of the pact and the Rhineland evacuation was avoided. Finally, Stresemann now suggested settling the outstanding difficulties 'in direct consultation', opening up the perspective of an international conference to finalise the pact. US Ambassador Jacob Schurman celebrated the foreign minister's vigorous defence of his proposals in the *Reichstag* as a 'victory'.[63]

Crisis management and the net-effect of British brokerage

While Kellogg and Strong were content with Germany's willingness to compromise, Chamberlain was at first exasperated by what he called the Luther government's 'blindness'. He denounced the German note as an 'election manifesto' sabotaging his mediation efforts with Briand. He held that Luther and Stresemann had thought 'only of the party position in Germany' and of placating the DNVP. Now they were 'begging that the allied governments will show a patience' and 'statesmanship' in the 'face of public opinion', of which 'they avow themselves incapable'.[64] This perception changed only gradually. Only after Locarno did Chamberlain give Stresemann and Luther more credit for their balancing of international and internal demands. Of greater consequence, however, was the policy that he actually pursued, both before and in response to the German proposals. For it was in this phase, between late May and mid-August 1925, that Britain's diplomacy of firmness and incentive played a crucial part in inducing Briand to alter the premises of French security policy.

In short, Briand *began* to accept controlled peaceful change. He was not yet willing or able to recast previous French policy completely or to 'abandon' the alliances with Poland and Czechoslovakia. Yet he came to subordinate this to the primary goals of clinching the pact, spurring *rapprochement* with Germany and gaining the greatest *possible* British commitments.[65]

This process was spurred by Chamberlain, who, seconded by Tyrrell and the Foreign Office's legal expert Cecil Hurst, persevered in upholding two maxims of British pact policy. First, he re-asserted that Britain would not guarantee the eastern arbitration treaties.[66] Britain originally supported Briand's demand that 'France should retain the right to guarantee arbitration

---

[63] Stresemann (1932), II, pp. 161ff. Cf. Krüger (1980).
[64] Chamberlain to D'Abernon, 30 July 1925, *DBFP*, I, XXVII, no. 431.
[65] Cf. Bariéty (2000), p. 128.
[66] Chamberlain to Briand, 28 May 1925; Crewe to Chamberlain, 30 May, 1925, *DBFP*, I, XVII, nos. 349, 353.

treaties between Germany and her eastern neighbours.' But France had to do so without London's backing.[67] This diminished Paris' prospects of establishing effective controls enforcing the *status quo* as part of the Locarno agreements. More generally, and even more defining for the eventual accords, Chamberlain insisted on making the pact an instrument for stabilising Europe's postwar order by facilitating its peaceful reform – in co-operation with Germany. In other words, Britain rejected all French attempts to turn the pact primarily into an instrument facilitating intervention against Germany and, ultimately, a bulwark of the *status quo* in western *and* eastern Europe. To this end, decisively furthering German interests, British diplomacy promoted a new arbitration regime not controllable by individual powers like France.

On these premises, not unlike MacDonald after the 1924 Chequers summit, Chamberlain pursued his two-pronged strategy of closing ranks with France and saving Briand's face while pursuing British aims that *de facto* – and more than he sometimes realised – concurred with those of Stresemann. The British foreign secretary took pains to maintain a common front with Briand. And he took pains to explain, not least to the Baldwin cabinet, that in attaching strict conditions to his espousal of the pact Briand 'had to consider French opinion'. He could not afford any appearance of being outmanoeuvred by Stresemann.[68] Yet despite his penchant for a revived *entente*, Chamberlain ceded no substantial ground in limiting Britain's commitment to the continental *status quo*. He warned Briand time and again against undermining the pact by demanding excessive British guarantees. A chief Foreign Office concern was that Britain might be called upon to come to France's aid should German troops cross the Rhineland in repelling a French attack after Paris had honoured its alliance obligations towards Poland. Chamberlain acknowledged that this could politically compel Britain to intervene. But it would not accept to be bound to do so by its pact guarantees – as long as Germany's actions were in self-defence and thus involved no breach of the envisaged accords.

British policymakers maintained successfully that the negotiations' emphasis should not be on modalities of military sanctions but the conclusion of arbitration treaties between Germany and France as well as between Germany and its eastern neighbours. All possibilities of arbitration and pacific settlement in conformity with the League Covenant should be exhausted first. Compulsory arbitration, however, such as the Geneva Protocol had envisaged, was to be excluded.[69] Thus, it would finally be at London's discretion to decide what

---

[67] Hurst memorandum, 18 June 1925, *DBFP*, I, XXVII, no. 385.
[68] Chamberlain to Crewe, 14 May 1925, *DBFP*, I , XXVII, no. 322.
[69] Chamberlain to Briand, 8 June 1925; Hurst memorandum, 18 June 1925, *DBFP*, I, XXVII, nos. 363, 385.

constituted a sufficient case for military intervention. There was to be no automatism, nor any pledge to defend France pre-emptively.

The case Chamberlain and Tyrrell made vis-à-vis Briand drew on the precedent of July 1914. Both essentially argued that there would be no direct threat of aggression through a German mobilisation without a preceding period of tension. This would give the League Council time to deliberate the case and prepare immediate sanctions.[70] Chamberlain told Briand that Britain sought to close every 'loophole for war', the only exception being 'self-defence against aggression'.[71] British obligations to France and Belgium had to be limited to averting an acute danger of German aggression, in essence to 'repel invasion'.[72] As Hurst argued on 11 July, all disputes concerning the Rhineland's demilitarised zones, such as troop concentrations and the establishment of fortifications, should be submitted to the League Council for arbitration.[73] Likewise, all other disputes between Germany and its neighbours in west *and* in the east should be made subject to the Council's procedures of pacific settlement prior to any military sanctions.

Both issues remained contentious. But in the end Briand had to content himself with the British concession that there should be a distinction between flagrant and non-flagrant violations of the demilitarised Rhineland. While the former, now including a concentration of (German) troops, were classified as unprovoked acts of aggression that would result in Britain's immediate intervention, any non-flagrant breaches would not. They were to be examined first by the League Council.[74] Essentially, Chamberlain thus asserted that, under the Rhine pact, Britain would render immediate military assistance to France 'only in the event of some serious threat of an aggressive character which would confer some distinct advantage on the aggressor'. In short, London had to be convinced that Germany reoccupied the Rhineland militarily with the intention of waging a full-scale war against France before making the *political* decision to intervene. Not least, Chamberlain insisted that this would be the only way of ratifying the pact in the British parliament. This was the understanding reached when he and Briand finally succeeded in forging a common platform during closed-door meetings in London on 11–12 August.[75] Disputes over article 16 and the final status of the eastern arbitration treaties had still not been resolved. Overall, though, the parameters that British diplomacy had set largely prevailed.

---

[70] Cf. Jacobson (1972b), p. 32.

[71] Chamberlain to Crewe, 27 June 1925, Austen Chamberlain Papers, AC 52/221.

[72] Chamberlain statements in cabinet, 22 June 1925, CAB 23/50/30.

[73] Hurst memorandum, 11 July 1925, Cecil Papers, 51090.

[74] Chamberlain to D'Abernon, 11 August 1925, Austen Chamberlain Papers, AC 52/291.

[75] Cabinet minutes, 5 August 1925, CAB 23/50/43; notes of a conversation between Chamberlain and Briand, 11 August 1925, FO 371/10738: C 10609/459/18.

What both foreign ministers agreed on effectively brought an answer to the question that had beset Anglo-French relations ever since 1919. It fixed the modalities and limits of Britain's strategic 'continental commitment' to underpin French security in the 1920s. At the same time, it was an Anglo-French 'compromise' on terms which corresponded far more with British – and German – interests in establishing new ground-rules of peaceful change for a nascent European concert than with France's original essentials.[76] Viewed in the context of Anglo-French relations after 1923, Briand had begun to cede ground on most of France's long-held *conditiones sine qua non* vis-à-vis London and Berlin. He had done so essentially to retain British support, and in the hope that France would still be in a position to redirect, and arrest, the momentum of European developments at a later stage.[77]

The Anglo-French draft treaty for the Rhine pact of 11 August paved the way for meetings of the three powers' legal experts Hurst, Henri Fromageot and Gaus in London in early September. They forged the legal foundations of the Locarno agreements. On the basis of the jurists' recommendations, the Allies invited Germany on 15 September to negotiate the final treaty at a conference to be convened in Locarno.[78]

As Strong had predicted in July, despite professions of allied unity, the common Anglo-German interest in finalising the pact through an – integrative – international conference finally superseded French interests. For Briand had long sought to insist on completing the negotiations by way of diplomatic notes, intent on maintaining the appearance of two *entente* powers pursuing a concerted policy vis-à-vis Germany.[79] Washington did not interfere with the Anglo-French deliberations, officially or unofficially. In private, however, Houghton had already told Tyrrell in June that 'sooner rather than later' a 'conference would be necessary' to bring the negotiations to a successful conclusion. Like Kellogg, he favoured the calling of an international conference, not least because of the 'German susceptibility to be treated on a footing of equality'. Houghton invoked the precedent of the London conference 'as a case in point, in which the presence of German ministers had largely contributed towards the success of the scheme'.[80]

Before the Locarno proceedings could be opened, however, another – minor – turn for the worse occurred when, under considerable domestic pressure, both

---

[76] *Quai d'Orsay* to Fleuriau, 29 July 1925, MAE, Série Europe, Grande-Bretagne, vol. 80.
[77] Notes of a conversation between Chamberlain and Briand, 11 August 1925, FO 371/10738: C 10609/459/18.
[78] Hurst report, 4 September 1925, FO 371/10739: C 11425/459/18; Foreign Office to Addison, 12 September 1925; Chamberlain to D'Abernon, 24 September 1925, *DBFP*, I, XXVII, nos. 471, 488.
[79] Strong memorandum, 22 July 1925, Strong Papers.
[80] Chamberlain to Chilton, 11 June 1925, *DBFP*, I, XXVII, no. 376.

French and German policymakers launched last-ditch attempts to maximise their bargaining-power for the conference. This in turn led Chamberlain to re-affirm his conference agenda and aims. As he recorded after meeting Briand in Geneva on 9 September, both agreed that the jurists' conversations in London had been 'broadly satisfactory'. Yet it was also precisely then that, facing the rather unwelcome perspective of a conference, Briand again underscored his suspicions vis-à-vis Germany. He now reiterated the need for enhanced safeguards for France and its eastern allies, warning that the eastern frontiers still 'formed the great stumbling block'. As the French foreign minister told Chamberlain, his chief anxiety remained that through the special conditions Berlin sought, also regarding article 16, it could conjure up two dangerous scenarios – if Germany 'contemplated war': first, to 'water down' the eastern treaties to such an extent that 'the possibility of war in Eastern Europe' was not 'excluded'; and, second, 'a return to the Bismarckian policy of a Russian alliance which would expose all European civilisation to the perils of Bolshevism'.[81]

For all sides, but particularly for Berlin, the virulence of these problems was thrown into relief by Chicherin's spectacular visits to Berlin and Paris in early October. On 2 October, just before departing for Locarno, Stresemann had to assure the Soviet commissar for foreign affairs that he would uphold Germany's demands for exemptions from article 16 and refuse any guarantee of the Polish–German frontier.[82] Chamberlain had long emphasised that Moscow was 'doing all it could for dissuading Germany from entering into any pact'. In contrast to Briand, he thus insisted that Germany's interest in avoiding tensions with Soviet Russia while pursuing the western pact should be taken seriously. Yet, under Briand's influence, he also began to suspect that Germany was retreating from earlier assurances to 'put in black and white' that 'she renounces recourse to war as a method of changing the eastern frontiers'. Gaus had in fact explained that his government could not sign a document explicitly renouncing war with respect to the eastern frontiers because Berlin regarded this as tantamount to recognising them. But he had also stressed that the Germans were 'willing to tie themselves up with such conditions that recourse to war would in fact be impossible'.[83]

As Chamberlain concluded on 2 October, there was all the more reason in view of these complexities to tie Germany to a western system through the pact and its obligations. The key to a success of this policy, however, lay more than

---

[81] Chamberlain memorandum, 9 September 1925, *DBFP*, I, XXVII, no. 468.
[82] Stresemann diary, 30 September 1925, Stresemann Papers, vol. 272, H147979–91. Cf. Walsdorff (1971), pp. 137ff.
[83] Chamberlain memorandum, 9 September 1925; Chamberlain to Tyrrell, 8 October 1925, *DBFP*, I, XXVII, nos. 521, 468; Chamberlain to D'Abernon, 30 September 1925, Austen Chamberlain Papers, AC 52/297.

ever in preserving 'the union existing among the Allies'. Britain and France had to steer the envisaged conference. This way, the foreign secretary also hoped to cope with the fresh and in his eyes untimely demand that Stresemann had made, namely that for an evacuation of the Cologne zone in return for Germany's signature under the pact.[84] Essentially, Chamberlain feared that negotiations with the Luther government could 'prove troublesome' because it again 'yield[ed] unduly to Nationalist pressure', thus increasing 'the difficulties of the French Government with French public opinion'. On balance, he calculated that the Germans 'still desire[d] the success of a proposal which originated with them'. And he was confident that Briand would 'do everything in his power' to secure the negotiations' 'success'. All in all, then, Chamberlain's assumptions on how Anglo-French solidarity and Germany's controlled inclusion had to converge to realise the pact, and a new European concert, had been reinforced. He went to Locarno 'in a spirit of sober hopefulness'.[85]

What occurred between the spring and autumn of 1925, advanced by British mediation and spurred by American pressure and incentive, was a second phase in the underlying process of peaceful change in the western powers' relations with Germany in the mid-1920s. As it occurred in the most critical sphere of international security, it was all the harder to sustain but also became all the more remarkable. It gave rise to a further formative shift, a further recasting of European and Euro-Atlantic postwar politics.

At the outset, mutual suspicions and misperceptions had still been prevalent. Endeavours to revive exclusive allied 'politics of the *entente*' had stood against alleged German aspirations to divide Britain and France to prepare the ground for a radical revision of Versailles. But in the subsequent stages of this process, which progressed intermittently, but tended to gain new momentum in overcoming setbacks, a new mode of international diplomacy had gained contours. Particularly the resolution of the 'July crisis' manifested the remarkable degree to which, prodded by the Anglo-American powers, European policymakers pursued new ways to master postwar problems – to overcome what were in effect reconcilable differences between France and Germany. Above all, this threw into relief how far a success of the Rhine pact had by that time become an overriding interest on *all sides*. This common interest prevailed over French *and* German tendencies to fall back into old-style acrimony and the exploitation of frictions for domestic gains.

Even though they had not yet acquired any coherent form, what *in practice*, and backed by America, had gained decisive ground were the practices and politics of a new European concert. It was within these new parameters that statesmen began to forge new rules of resolving international conflicts, in many

---

[84] *Ibid.*
[85] Chamberlain memorandum, 2 October 1925, *DBFP*, I, XXVII, no. 509.

ways comparable to those that had underpinned the London settlement. These were chiefly rules of international arbitration and peaceful settlement, premised on renunciation of force as a means of upholding or revising what was an untenable *status quo*. On a deeper level, what came to prevail was the espousal of gradualism and multilateral *quid pro quo* bargains – all geared to furthering and legitimating international accommodation.

This development in fact preceded, and it alone rendered possible, the actual Locarno conference. But it only culminated at this conference itself. As in 1924, British diplomacy managed to keep Britain's strategic commitment to Europe at a minimum. But it also again made a crucial *political* commitment. Once again Germany and above all France had to make the most trenchant departures and concessions. The United States on the other hand wagered even less than in 1924 and still stood to gain as much as Britain, without any further commitments to Europe.

16   The second 'real' peace settlement after World War I

The Locarno conference and the emergence of a new European concert

Europe's second 'real' peace conference after the Great War opened on 5 October 1925, attended by delegates from Britain, France, Germany, Belgium and Italy. Following the British recommendation, the foreign ministers of Poland and Czechoslovakia, Skrzyński and Beneš, only joined the conference for the final deliberations on the eastern arbitration treaties.[1] In contrast to the London conference, America was not represented, not even through unofficial observers. On 25 May, Houghton had still 'hint[ed]' to Chamberlain that the United States 'might be prepared to participate in such a conference in the same way as they had done in the Reparation Conference'. Yet this remained an isolated overture. As Locarno centred on resolving what from Washington's perspective seemed intricate questions of European security, Kellogg never considered offering US mediation. And Chamberlain confided to Ambassador Howard that he could 'not see how, in negotiations for a political pact of this character where no American co-operation can be expected, the presence of American unofficial or semi-official participants could really help us to a solution'.[2]

Unlike London, Locarno was not a critical turning-point where the entire outcome was still at stake when the proceedings opened – or indeed the progress of postwar pacification as such. It was not a juncture where fundamental issues pertaining to the envisaged agreement still had to be resolved. Nor did it as yet furnish the occasion to resolve wider problems which then overshadowed European politics after 1925, notably the Rhineland question. In contrast to that of 1924, the Locarno settlement was not so much brought about or qualitatively altered by the final conference. Rather, it was the result of a nine-month process of negotiations which then culminated in mid-October

---

[1] On the Locarno conference see the British documents under FO 371/10741–4 and *DBFP*, I, XXVII; the official protocols and further materials, *AR Luther I and II*, I, pp. 669ff; the collected documents on the *Locarno-Konferenz*; MAE, Série Europe, Grande-Bretagne, vol. 85. Cf. Orde (1978), pp. 131–45; Jacobson (1972b), pp. 60–7; Krüger (1985a), pp. 295–301; Johnson (2004b).

[2] Chamberlain to Howard, 26 May 1925, *DBFP*, I, XXVII, no. 344.

1925, a process on which the 'external' force of American power had had a marked impact.

At the forefront of the Locarno summit itself were precisely the two core issues that the separate diplomatic exchanges between the ex-allied powers and Germany had not been able to settle: Germany's special status under article 16; and the question of what guarantees there would be, no longer for the *status quo* on Germany's eastern borders but for the commitment of all parties to peaceful means in settling disputes about them.[3] To be defined, then, were not only the obligations Germany would assume once it joined the League. More fundamentally, Locarno had to define what precisely were to be the ground-rules governing the evolution of Europe's international system – and stabilisation. Yet given the Luther government's persistent demands for linking the pact with an evacuation of the Cologne zone and, on the other hand, France's core security concerns, the underlying problem, at this conference, was the future of the Rhineland occupation. In turn, this remained connected with Germany's fulfilment of postwar disarmament obligations and the future of military control.[4]

It was thus revealing that the only notable disputes in Locarno were not sparked by the pact treaties themselves but by the different French, German and British expectations about their immediate and wider consequences. That controversy would centre on these dimensions seems hardly surprising. For even more than article 16 and the eastern treaties, which partly clouded it, they unmistakably pointed to what was really on the agenda in Locarno. It was the old and new question of how far a new underlying balance between French security – or rather reassurance – and German rehabilitation, between control and change could be struck while integrating Germany into a new European security system.[5]

Essentially, then, the Locarno summit, being the first occasion where Chamberlain entered into direct negotiations with Briand *and* Stresemann, had to confirm how far a more than transient new quality had emerged in European politics. It had to reveal whether concerted European diplomacy could operate in practice to produce concrete results – or whether there would be another backlash, another return to patterns of *entente* politics *vs* Germany. The compromises that had taken shape over the summer of 1925 had to be consolidated; in the process, certain outstanding issues had to be resolved. As all records indicate, the negotiations in Locarno indeed evolved in a remarkably

---

[3] Chamberlain to Tyrrell, 8 October 1925, *DBFP*, I, XXVII, no. 521.
[4] See Luther (1960), pp. 368–85.
[5] Chamberlain to Foreign Office, 13 October 1925, FO 371/10742: C 13004/459/18; Chamberlain to Tyrrell, 16 October 1925, FO 371/10742: C 13091/459/18; Schubert memorandum, 14 October 1925, PA, St. S, 4509/E129612–21.

constructive atmosphere. Ten days of concerted search for compromise ended without any significant crisis or near-complete breakdown similar to those that had marked the London proceedings.[6] As early as 8 October, *The Times*, commenting on the first private talks between Briand and Luther, could thus praise the 'spirit of Locarno'.[7] One day after the close of the summit, on 17 October, Chamberlain would write of the 'extraordinary' quality of his negotiations with Briand and Stresemann, though more than one impasse had had to be overcome.[8]

It fact, it was not until Locarno that Chamberlain could actually endeavour to execute what he had set out to achieve in a Castlereaghean spirit: to appease French anxieties *and* integrate Germany into a recast European order. The British foreign secretary retained his predilection for manning a steering-committee of two with Briand. Yet what gave the summit its underlying significance for the further evolution not only of European politics but also of transatlantic relations was something else. Considering the sea-changes that were debated, and that it took place a mere two years after the nadir of the Ruhr crisis, the first real test of a twentieth-century version of 'Congress of Vienna' diplomacy proved remarkably successful. In a narrower sense, it was the Locarno conference that actually founded the new European concert. This concert would be the dominant, if constantly challenged framework, and mode, of politics governing the relations between Britain, France and Germany throughout the period of Europe's 'relative' stabilisation, and it only disintegrated after, not before, 1929. In a wider sense, the Locarno pact also became the core of the new European security regime that consolidated what had been initiated in 1924. As such, it was the central European building-block of a budding wider Euro-Atlantic system dominated, albeit financially more than politically, by the United States.

The settled and the unsettled questions of Locarno

Briand opened the conference's second meeting on 6 October by highlighting once more that France, while intent on the western pact, could not neglect its alliance commitments in the east. He made a cardinal condition for his approval that the pact treaties had to include, *and that France had to guarantee*, the eastern arbitration treaties in one form or another.[9] Gravitating towards the British position, Briand had already on 9 September proposed to Chamberlain

---

[6] See Foreign Office memoranda under FO 371/10741–4.
[7] *Times*, 8 October 1925.
[8] Chamberlain to Tyrrell, 17 October 1925, Austen Chamberlain Papers, AC 6/1/623.
[9] Chamberlain to Foreign Office, 7 October 1925, FO 371/10741: C 1746/459/18; French notes, 6–10 October 1925, MAE, Série Europe, Grande-Bretagne, vol. 85.

that the 'eastern treaties' could be placed under a League guarantee, with France then 'acting as some sort of agent of the League'. And the Polish foreign minister Skrzyński had not been 'altogether unfavourable' to this idea. *De facto*, however, in contrast to the more affirmative position espoused by Beneš, Warsaw's attitude to the pact had become more of a liability than an asset in the French perception. As Chamberlain noted, Briand had described Poland as "'the rheumatism of Europe'" at a luncheon in Geneva.[10]

Weightier, though, were France's wider concerns. Briand stressed that, while he did not doubt the peaceful intentions of Germany's present leaders, France required safeguards against the eventuality of a turning-of-the-tide, the reversal to a more aggressive German policy in the future.[11] Stresemann was not oblivious to such concerns. But the German delegation stubbornly insisted that, for domestic reasons, they could not accept any guarantee of the eastern arbitration treaties.[12] Stresemann underscored that he recognised France's special obligations to Poland. Yet in his view Germany had already taken these into consideration by the very act of proposing the arbitration treaties. Chamberlain at first merely reiterated the position he had maintained vis-à-vis Briand since April, namely that Britain was not prepared to make any fresh commitments regarding the eastern treaties. But he also urged Luther and Stresemann – in vain – that Germany should accept some kind of French guarantee as a *quid pro quo* for Briand's agreement to the pact. He argued that, in view of the treaties' emphasis on arbitration, this could actually redound to Germany's advantage as it would also constrain France's alliance guarantees to Poland and Czechoslovakia.[13]

Yet, as is well known, what the British delegation finally proposed, and what both Stresemann and Briand endorsed, was a different compromise distinctly favourable to German interests. France's guarantee to Poland and Czechoslovakia against German incursions was formally dissociated from the actual pact, making the latter acceptable for Germany. But article 2 of the Locarno accords stated that France had the right to intervene against Germany under article 16 of the League Covenant – if its Council had declared Germany the aggressor in a conflict with its easten neighbours. The British legal expert Hurst argued successfully that this provision rendered a formal French guarantee of the eastern accords in the pact itself superfluous.

---

[10] Chamberlain memorandum, 9 September 1925; Chamberlain memorandum on a conversation with Beneš, 12 September 1925, *DBFP*, I, XXVII, nos. 468, 473.

[11] Notes of the second conference meeting, 6 October 1925, FO 371/10742; French notes, 6–10 October 1925, MAE, Série Europe, Grande-Bretagne, vol. 85. Cf. Bariéty (2000), pp. 129–31.

[12] See German delegation to German Foreign Ministry, 9 October 1925, PA, St. S, 4509/E128590–2.

[13] Notes of the second conference meeting, 6 October 1925, FO 371/10742; Chamberlain to Foreign Office, 7 October 1925, FO 371/10741 C 12476/459/18.

This was grudgingly accepted by Briand and Beneš. And it came to supersede Skrzyński's counterproposal of an additional tripartite guarantee treaty between France, Germany and Poland, which the Luther government could not have signed. France thus had to be content with signing separate guarantee treaties with Poland and Czechoslovakia on the very day of the Locarno pact; these were then also mentioned in the final conference protocol.[14]

The ensuing controversy over article 16 was first broached during Luther's memorable encounter with Briand on 7 October. The German chancellor set out by reiterating Stresemann's core argument, by then common currency in the German debate: France's insistence on the article's strict application raised the danger of making Germany the battleground of the next European war should there be a conflict between the League powers and Soviet Russia. For it would permit the transit of foreign troops through German territory, whereas Germany lacked the armed power to enforce any sanctions in the first place. While thus highlighting postwar armament disparities, Luther also stressed that not only military but also economic sanctions could provoke such a scenario.[15] Stresemann backed his chancellor by defending these positions vis-à-vis Briand on 8 October.[16] The French foreign minister acknowledged the German objections in the end but simply countered that the League, and Germany's unreserved acceptance of its obligations, remained 'the pivot on which the whole guarantee pact turned'.[17]

Unlike his French counterpart, Chamberlain was not overly concerned about the German demand for a special status under article 16.[18] He deemed it natural that Stresemann had to take into consideration Germany's geopolitical position as well as Soviet interests. Moreover, in his view the League's sanction regime had already been so decisively weakened through postwar developments that a conflict over the article's 'strict interpretation' was beside the point. Crucially, he could not allow it to become the stumbling-block wrecking the pact negotiations. Consequently, Chamberlain stressed that the Covenant's framers had still 'contemplated that America would be a member of the League' and that 'Germany would be admitted in a short time.' Thus, the core assumption had been that the force of any Council decision would be so overwhelming that any potential aggressor would be deterred from the start. With American support, economic sanctions would have been equally deterring. The power of both types of sanction, then, had been 'greatly weakened' by

---

[14] Chamberlain memorandum of a conversation with Skrzyński, 9 October 1925, FO 840/1/6.
[15] Luther memorandum, 7 October 1925, Stresemann Papers, ministerial office files, 3123/ D645137–8; Luther (1960), pp. 368ff.
[16] *AR Luther I und II*, no. 179.
[17] Chamberlain to Tyrrell, 8 October 1925, *DBFP*, I, XXVII, no. 523.
[18] Chamberlain to Foreign Office, 8 October 1925, FO 371/10742: C 12881/459/18; Chamberlain memorandum, 2 October 1925, *DBFP*, I, XXVII, no. 509.

Washington's 'abstention'. And, for Britain, the 'greatest sea Power in the League', the application of sanctions also carried the risk of bringing it 'into direct conflict' with the non-League power, the United States.[19]

On these premises, the foreign secretary maintained that Germany, like Britain, should retain a 'certain liberty', yet not a free hand, to make the final decision on how far it would participate in military or economic sanctions imposed by the League. Already during the second conference session on 6 October, Chamberlain had emphasised that what mattered more than obligations under article 16, which would always be subject to different interpretations, was the clear commitment of all pact signatories in one specific area: on the Rhine. Chamberlain underscored that his government now extended to Germany what it had earlier only contemplated to reassure France: on the basis of its new pact guarantee, and previous League obligations, Britain would come to the defence of either power should one party commit a *flagrant* aggression against the other.[20]

The eventual compromise on article 16 crystallised in the so-called 'supplement F'. Largely following Stresemann's arguments and Chamberlain's intervention, it recognised Germany's special status in the 'comity of nations' under the circumstances of 1925, marked by its low level of armament and its *Mittellage* ('middle-position') between the western powers and Soviet Russia. Contrary to Briand's original demand, the supplement stated that Germany only had to enforce the League Covenant insofar as it 'is commensurable with her military situation and . . . her geographic position'.[21] Ultimately, the British and, indirectly, the American interest in preventing the widening of compulsory sanction regimes in Europe again weighed in favour of the German position – and forced France to adapt.

During a private interview with Stresemann on 8 October, Chamberlain was briefed exhaustively on Chicherin's visit to Berlin. In return, he stressed that Britain had no ambitions to '"detach"' Germany from Russia but 'a very real desire not to throw Germany into the arms of Russia by closing to her every opportunity of friendship or even of normal relations'. In other words, Chamberlain sought to further Germany's detachment from what he called a 'Bismarckian tradition of friendship with Russia' and of retaining a 'free hand', which conflicted with Berlin's adherence to the rules of the 'comity of nations'. It was a tradition that the foreign secretary identified with the new *Reichspräsident* Hindenburg. As he told Tyrrell, he sought to prevent Moscow and those 'Prussian Conservatives' who intended to undermine the Rhine pact

---

[19] Chamberlain to Tyrrell, 8 October 1925, *DBFP*, I, XXVII, no. 522.
[20] *Ibid.*; notes of the second conference meeting, 6 October 1925, FO 371/10741; Chamberlain to Foreign Office, 7 October 1925, FO 371/10741: C 12746/459/18.
[21] *UF*, VI, p. 637; *Locarno-Konferenz*, no. 25. Cf. Krüger (1980), pp. 607ff.

from gaining undue influence on German policymaking.[22] Here, and in the aim of widening western and German trade with Russia, Chamberlain and Stresemann could in fact reach a basic understanding.

As indicated, the dispute over the Rhine pact's wider scope and meaning, which was to shape 'Locarno politics' from 1926, already began during the negotiations in October 1925. It escalated during the informal meetings between Chamberlain, Briand, Stresemann and Luther in the final phase of the conference. On 12 October, Stresemann opened deliberations by pleading not only for allied concessions on military control. He also returned to his earlier, and cardinal, demand: a fixed date for the evacuation of the Cologne zone. Supported by Luther, the German foreign minister's rationale was and would remain that this was to be an immediate consequence of the Locarno accords.[23] Both Luther and Stresemann emphasised that, more than the end of disarmament control, it was the Rhineland question with which the acceptance of their policy in Germany stood or fell. They could not return to Berlin 'empty-handed' on this vital issue. Stresemann thus relied on precisely the same arguments that he had used, at the London conference, to hasten the end of the Ruhr occupation.

But Briand could not simply espouse this logic. He underlined that while the nature of the Locarno pact should make such changes conceivable at a later stage – if it was adhered to – it was not within his remit to agree to them at the conference itself. In principle, the evacuation of the Rhineland depended on Germany's execution of the Versailles treaty. The utmost concession the French foreign minister made was that, once back in Paris, he would declare in parliament that the pact warranted a review of France's occupation system and could require certain modifications. More would be impossible. Overall, however, Briand stood firm, urging Stresemann and Luther to acknowledge that what Germany 'got out of' Locarno was considerable as it was: its rehabilitation within the European order as an equal member of the *Société des Nations*.[24]

Contrary to MacDonald in 1924, and certainly lacking the leverage of Anglo-American high finance that the Labour premier had used then, Chamberlain did not side with Germany on this critical issue. Rather, he backed Briand, seizing this opportunity to reinforce his policy of a privileged Anglo-French 'union' that controlled the outcome of Locarno. His insistence that the German demands could not be made a condition of the security pact itself

---

[22] Chamberlain to Tyrrell, 8 October 1925, *DBFP*, I, XXVII, no. 521.

[23] Schubert memorandum, 12 October 1925, Stresemann Papers, ministerial office files, 3123/ D645168ff; Chamberlain minute, 14 October 1925, FO 840/1/8.

[24] Chamberlain to Foreign Office, 13 October 1925, FO 371/10742: C 13004/459/18.

was unequivocal.[25] Through D'Abernon, Chamberlain had already tried before Locarno to keep complications of this kind off the conference agenda, impressing on Stresemann that the only 'reasonable' position for Germany was to accept the pact 'without conditions'. Yet although, according to D'Abernon, Stresemann fully realised this, the Luther government had been unwilling to 'recede from its previously declared attitude' that it would only endorse the pact if the occupying troops left Cologne.[26] This had 'strengthened' Chamberlain's resolve to 'deal firmly with the Germans' to forestall a series of further demands at the envisaged summit, merely 'made to please the German Nationalists'.[27]

Consequently, when Stresemann persisted in his attempt to bargain behind the scenes of Locarno for a last-minute agreement on the Cologne zone, indicating that Berlin could only then sign the pact, Chamberlain rejected this as an 'attempt at blackmail'. He deplored that the German manoeuvres had 'introduced a discordant note' into negotiations that he had managed to maintain on a 'high level of good faith'. The British foreign secretary had by then internalised his role as 'honest broker', setting and safeguarding the standards of the diplomatic game between the western powers and Germany. Revealingly, the concert politics he envisaged were to be marked by the 'noteworthy absence of any sort of bargaining' – at least when this appeared detrimental to cardinal British, and French, interests.[28]

In short, the combined leverage of Britain and France did succeed in limiting the conference's scope. Although Chamberlain overall desired to accelerate the end of the Rhineland occupation, his official line remained that the evacuation of the Cologne zone depended 'solely on the fulfilment of Germany's disarmament obligations'.[29] Significantly, however, on 15 October he and Briand agreed to a compromise: an agreement comprising the Rhineland occupation and German disarmament would be made shortly *after* the pact settlement. And, following earlier British preferences, French and German representatives reached a consensus that the date for commencing the Cologne evacuation was to be specified in the near future. This Briand promised to push through domestically on the threat of his resignation.[30]

---

[25] Chamberlain to Foreign Office, 14 October 1925, FO 371/10742: C 13093/459/18; Chamberlain memorandum, 2 October 1925, *DBFP*, I, XXVII, no. 509.
[26] D'Abernon to Chamberlain, 22 September 1925, *DBFP*, I, XXVII, no. 485.
[27] Chamberlain to D'Abernon, 24 September 1925, *DBFP*, I, XXVII, no. 488.
[28] Chamberlain to Tyrrell, 16 October 1925, FO 840/1/9.
[29] Chamberlain to Foreign Office, 13 October 1925, FO 371/10742: C 13004/459/18; Chamberlain to Sthamer, 29 September 1925, *DBFP*, I, XXVII, no. 502.
[30] Chamberlain to Tyrrell, 16 October 1925, FO 840/1/9; Chamberlain to Foreign Office, 16 October 1925; Chamberlain to Foreign Office, 13 October 1925, FO371/10742: C 13091/459/18.

In the aftermath of Locarno, Chamberlain would characteristically 'resign leadership' in this matter to France. And, aided by Berthelot, Briand kept his promise. In consultation with Crewe, and against some opposition by the chief of the French High Command, Marshal Foch, this was achieved by 16 November.[31] In a goodwill gesture, France did not await the official fulfilment of Germany's respective disarmament obligations.[32] The evacuation of the Cologne zone finally began on 1 December, the day the Locarno accords were signed in London. It was completed in January 1926. The more intricate problem on what terms France would agree to evacuate the entire Rhineland remained part and parcel of the Franco-German question, and a core concern of concert diplomacy, for the remainder of the era of London and Locarno.

The Locarno system, the European pillar of the unfinished transatlantic peace order – a re-appraisal

What, then, was the concrete significance of Locarno and the wider importance of what became known as 'Locarno politics'? Did the Locarno 'bargain' accord with Chamberlain's broader aims and what US decisionmakers had sought to foster? Or did the 'spirit' of Locarno merely aggravate, with Washington's blessing, what the London settlement had inaugurated: the erosion of France's postwar preponderance vis-à-vis Germany and, with it, the Versailles system's demise? Was it indeed (only) by the end of 1925 that all Anglo-French prospects for reforging a balance-of-power system to check German ambitions had been undercut?[33] Did the outcome of Locarno thus undercut even more the security of France's thereafter neglected allies Poland and Czechoslovakia?[34] Or did it buttress quite a different, more stabilising development in post-World War I international politics?[35] Did it rather improve the chances of overcoming European instability by opening up new ways of 'solving' the pivotal Franco-German question of the 1920s? And could it thus also pave the way for an as yet distant settlement of disputes between Germany and Poland – as well as Czechoslovakia?

In concrete terms, Britain had fostered, and now underwrote – with Italy – a second complex compromise between the western powers and Germany forged after the Ruhr crisis of 1923. Germany had indeed renounced all further

---

[31] Chamberlain to Müller, Austen Chamberlain Papers, 4 November 1925, AC 50/135; Crewe to Chamberlain, 15 November 1925, Austen Chamberlain Papers, AC 52/232. Cf. Jacobson (1972b), pp. 63–4.

[32] Briand to de Margerie (Berlin), 3 November 1925, MAE, Série Europe, Grande-Bretagne, vol. 86.

[33] Cf. Schuker (1976), pp. 383–90; Kissinger (1994), pp. 273ff; Jacobson (1983a).

[34] See Wandycz (1961), pp. 27ff; Cienciala and Kormanicki (1984), pp. 223ff.; Schattkowsky (1994b).

[35] Cf. Krüger (1985a), pp. 297–8; Wright (1995), pp. 121–31.

attempts to alter the *status quo* of Versailles by force. Above all, to allay French security concerns, it had recognised the existing Franco-German border on the Rhine – while only, yet unequivocally, renouncing a violent revision of its eastern borders, not their alteration *per se*.[36] Making a commitment to the peaceful resolution of all regional conflicts, the German government concluded bilateral arbitration treaties not only with France and Belgium but also, as noted, with Poland and Czechoslovakia.[37] In return, at least in Briand's view, France had recognised the German claim to re-attain, albeit gradually, the position of a European great power.[38] This was certainly also the German, and the British, interpretation of the Locarno pact's consequenses.

In 1925, Germany was of course still far from being an 'equal' power in the postwar international system. Yet, while formally unaltered, the Versailles treaty had *de facto* been significantly complemented. As one of Locarno's central provisions was that Germany would join the League, and expect to join its Council, the following year, all of the treaties, and Germany's new status, were interlocked with the League's Covenant and premises of collective security. After some altercations, the German entry was only realised in September 1926. Thence, however, the League would become not the central supranational mechanism of European security but, essentially, a platform for the concert diplomacy of Britain, France and Germany.[39] This fully accorded with the thrust of British policy.

In the final analysis, the second major breakthrough in the stabilisation of post-World War I Europe could indeed be achieved the European way. Spurring Franco-German *rapprochement*, Chamberlain's political clout as mediator between Paris and Berlin proved sufficient, and pivotal, for concluding the Locarno pact. In turn, Locarno diplomacy proved sufficient for establishing a regional, essentially west European security mechanism, whose consolidating effect was not limited to relations between the Locarno powers. This marked the most important qualitative advance in European politics since the war – indeed a change of paradigm. A beginning had been made in settling a first range of problems subsumed under Europe's central security question. This had been achieved neither by force nor universal schemes but through regionally specific compromises that took into account the interests of all – great – powers involved, including Germany. These compromises enhanced French, and European, security significantly. To be sure, the interests and aims of the smaller powers, particularly Poland, had only been a secondary

---

[36] See Stresemann speech, 14 December 1925, *ADAP*, B, I, 1, pp. 740–3.
[37] Further, France concluded compensatory guarantee treaties with Poland and Czechoslovakia. Cf. Bariéty (2000), p. 129.
[38] See Briand's appraisal, 4 November 1925, MAE, Z.1, Pacte de sécurité, 284–6, vol. 85, pp. 202–3.
[39] Chamberlain minute, 21 February 1925, FO 371/11064: W 1252/9/98.

consideration at Locarno.[40] Yet, difficult though it was to accept for Polish leaders, Locarno's stabilising effect, and Germany's new commitments, also redounded to their advantage.

Disencumbered from layers of Eurocentric interpretations, advanced mostly through the prism of the 1930s, what can be discerned is a settlement that derived its significance from two main sources. On one level, for the first time after the upheaval of Great War, a systemic *modus operandi* had been developed to settle the Franco-German question in its most critical dimension: the security dimension. In the 1920s, this pivotal question could not be solved by military alliances and deterrence but only, if at all, through intergovernmental negotiation and political accommodation. Under British auspices, 'Locarno politics' had proved to be effective in forging the indispensable ground-rules to this end – rules of international *do ut des* compromise between the continent's main western and newly western-orientated powers.

On a second level, Locarno constituted the best possible security framework for consolidating Europe's incipient 'economic peace' of 1923/4. In many ways, the accords complemented what the London conference had inaugurated. They thus continued one underlying process: the making of Europe's 'real' peace order, or its closest approximation, in the interwar period. After the Dawes settlement, that of Locarno became its second pillar. Crucially, with the consent of France it fostered Germany's further integration into 'the west' as a power of increasingly equal status, possibilities *and* obligations – yet also as a power increasingly adopting 'western' norms and rules of international politics. Chamberlain could justly claim that his 'real contribution' to Locarno had been that when this opportunity arose 'he had seized it & knew how to use it', following in MacDonald's footsteps in remaking European politics, with America's consent, the British way.[41]

The new concert system was only a nucleus. Yet it had the potential to effect a more profound transformation of Europe's postwar order, hinging on Weimar Germany's stabilisation. It was not inherently flawed, its disintegration far from inevitable from the start. Nevertheless, the Locarno pact was 'merely' the main political, and European, foundation-stone of a wider international system emerging in the mid-1920s. Albeit still in many respects disjointed, what gained contours was a Euro-Atlantic peace system whose *de facto* pre-eminent power was the United States. The latter would become a tacit, often elusive, yet not only financially crucial player in Locarno politics until the Great Depression.

---

[40] Cf. Wandycz (1961), pp. 27ff.

[41] Austen to Ida Chamberlain, 28 November 1925, Austen Chamberlain Papers, AC 5/1/370. See Cohrs (2003), pp. 27–8.

The question of how, if at all, these western advances could also further the consolidation of eastern central Europe was far from resolved in late 1925. The new Locarno concert and the stabilisation process it was to engender still had to prove that they could effectively protect Poland and Czechoslovakia from a return to more aggressive German revisionism in the future. Particularly precarious remained the Polish–German dispute over the contested border of 1919 and the future status of German minorities in Poland. But it should be stressed again that what the recasting of international politics since 1923 had initiated, and what Locarno underpinned, was *not* a process by nature confined to western Europe. Rather, it also created new chances for setting Germany's relations with its eastern neighbours on a better footing: renunciation of force, peaceful change if, and only if, it was reconcilable with the overall consolidation of Europe's nascent peace order. This created the most favourable, if still far from auspicious, preconditions for an eastern Locarno, a pacific settlement of the Polish–German question, in the interwar period.

In this light, it seems worth re-appraising whether the best safeguard for Polish and Czechoslovak stability in the 1920s was a reinforcement of France's alliances with them, particularly if this was pursued at the expense of finding a *modus vivendi* with Germany, as it had been after 1919. For such alliance politics threatened to provoke German countermoves in league with Soviet Russia that followed the same 'logic', overall heightening, not diminishing, the danger of assertive German revisionism at the expense of Poland and Czechoslovakia. Arguably, the key to French security *and* east European consolidation lay in something else. It lay in anchoring Weimar Germany to a western system and engaging it in the arduous process of developing mutually acceptable rules of peaceful change – ground-rules for extending Europe's fledgling political and economic stabilisation to and beyond the Polish–German border. Under the conditions of the 1920s, this was a stony yet the only realistic path to forestall the emergence of a new dividing-line, that between a functioning peace system in the west and a destabilised *Zwischeneuropa* in the east. Only the further evolution of Locarno politics could reveal how far policymakers on both sides of the Polish–German frontier were willing to make headway on this path.

The British appraisal of Locarno

At Locarno, Chamberlain had in effect made the most substantial British guarantee to European security since World War I. At the same time, it was probably the most far-reaching commitment possible under the constraints imposed by the need for retrenchment and his government's unwillingness to extend formal guarantees beyond Britain's west European security *glacis*. Yet, as noted, this commitment was made on the clear assumption that the nature of the pact was such that Britain would not be obliged, in the foreseeable future, to honour it militarily. Rather, it would be called upon to fulfil it politically.[42]

Ever since the Cannes conference, a majority of British policymakers had not considered an exclusive Anglo–French alliance a desirable option. To Chamberlain's initial dismay, this rejection of balance-of-power approaches had been confirmed in the debates over the security pact in 1925. Resistance to such an approach united, on different premises, Conservative imperialists, Labour and Liberal internationalists and Foreign Office professionals. More importantly, however, not only Crowe but eventually also Chamberlain had espoused the premise that a one-sided pursuit of balance-of-power politics threatened to have a destabilising effect in postwar Europe because it would antagonise Germany.[43] At the same time, such a pursuit could not have been sustained in the light of the international power configuration and America's abstention from European alliances after Versailles. Even combined Anglo–French power would not have sufficed to 'balance' an antagonistic Germany once it recovered. At least, this could not have been achieved short of perpetuating tight military control, possibly Germany's economic containment and a continued occupation of the heartlands of German potential, notably the Ruhr and the Rhineland. Yet Britain had from the outset been unwilling to adopt such a coercive approach. And the Ruhr occupation had been the watershed clearly revealing how limited its prospects were in the decade after 1919.

In his speech before the Commons on 18 November 1925, Chamberlain could thus claim with some justification: 'I do not think that the obligations of this country could be more narrowly circumscribed to [Britain's] vital national interests than they are in the Treaty of Locarno.'[44] For this reason, yet also for the 'hopes of peace' it had raised for Europe, the conference's success was celebrated in the British press and, with few exceptions, by all parties as a personal triumph for the Conservative foreign secretary.[45] In the Commons, there was some criticism from Conservative and Liberal benches concerning the treaty's compatibility with Britain's imperial obligations and its acceptability for the Dominions. Yet this could be assuaged. On the left, MacDonald generally welcomed the agreement as a step towards realising the collective-security aims of the Geneva Protocol. The only misgiving he voiced was that the western powers had excluded Soviet Russia from the negotiations.[46] Chamberlain himself reckoned that he had played his role as Europe's 'honest broker' quite convincingly. As he confided to his sister Ida on 28 November, he

---

[42] The British General Staff shared this assumption. Cf. Howard (1972), pp. 72–95.
[43] Nicolson/Crowe memorandum, 26 January 1925, FO 371 /11065: W 2035/9/98; Austen to Ida Chamberlain, 28 November 1925, Austen Chamberlain Papers, AC 5/1/30.
[44] *Hansard*, 5th series, vol. 188, col. 429.
[45] See *Times*, 17 and 18 October 1925.
[46] *Hansard*, 5th series, vol. 188, cols. 450ff, 437ff.

had endeavoured to follow Castlereagh – 'adapted to the XXth century' – and succeeded in reforging a European concert as anchor of European stability.[47] The Foreign Office's evaluation, which would inform British policy – and limit further British engagement – thereafter, concluded: '*détente* has certainly been achieved . . . No longer is Western Europe divided into two camps – the victors and the vanquished.'[48]

The American appraisal of Locarno

The Coolidge administration rated the Locarno settlement very highly. And so did American high finance. Essentially, Kellogg and Coolidge saw the Rhine pact as a logical complement, and indeed a convincing political guarantee, of the Dawes settlement.[49] This view was also adopted by Strong, the Morgan partners and Owen Young.[50] In a wider perspective, the pact was claimed as a success, or at least direct consequence, of the administration's policy of peaceful change, which had ended Europe's postwar crisis in 1924. Hoover praised Locarno on 17 October as 'a most hopeful step toward world peace'. It promised the 'dissipation of fear and the substitution of confidence as the dominating force in the conduct of international relations' in Europe.[51] In his message to Congress on 8 December, Coolidge concluded that the 'Locarno agreements represent the success of this policy which we have been adopting, of having European countries settle their own political problems without involving this country.'[52]

Kellogg publicly confirmed Coolidge's pronouncement on 14 December. Echoing British appraisals, he called Locarno the high-point of Europe's efforts after the war to 'free itself from the old system of balance of power supported by military alliances'.[53] And he stressed that it followed 'naturally and completed the work of the Dawes Committee' and the London conference. The pact thus supplemented US efforts to overcome Europe's post-Versailles divisions. While containing 'military guarantees', it was in Kellogg's view no longer 'conceived on the basis of the old balance of power which divided Europe into military camps ever jealous of each other and striving for additional armament and power'. Rather, its impetus was that of 'uniting the

---

[47] Chamberlain to Crewe, 17 November 1925, *DBFP*, IA, I, p. 345; Austen to Ida Chamberlain, 28 November 1925, Austen Chamberlain Papers, AC 5/1/30.

[48] Sterndale-Bennett memorandum, 10 January 1926, *DBFP*, IA, I, p. 9. Cf. Steed (1925).

[49] Maltzan to Stresemann, 17 October 1925, Stresemann Papers, RM 27, no. 422; Kellogg to Coolidge, 8 November 1925, Kellogg Papers. Cf. Link (1970), pp. 264–5.

[50] Young to Stresemann, 21 October 1925, Stresemann Papers, vol. 31; Schurman to Morrow, 22 October 1925, Schurman Papers, box 6.

[51] Hoover 'radiogram', 17 October 1925, Hoover Papers.

[52] *FRUS 1925*, I, p. xii.

[53] Kellogg speech, 14 December 1925; Kellogg to Coolidge, 8 November 1925, Kellogg Papers.

European nations in a common pact of security', following American principles of 'conciliation, arbitration, and judicial settlements' and indeed extendable beyond the scope of the Rhine Pact.

Castle backed Kellogg's conclusion that the expedience of Washington's rationale of remaining an informal arbiter and relying on financial leverage had thus been demonstrated. Yet his outlook was distinctly more sober. He held that European statesmen had only just begun to surmount postwar antagonisms and power politics, judging that Europe's stabilisation on new premises was as yet far from assured.[54] Officially, however, the administration had every reason to underline its support for the pact because, as Young told Stresemann, the accord's reception in US publicised opinion was overwhelmingly positive.[55] The *Literary Digest* of 31 October claimed that Locarno had seen the birth of 'the United States of Europe'. To celebrate this, there was even a thanksgiving service in New York's Cathedral of St John the Divine.[56]

In the optimistic and self-satisfied Republican outlook of late 1925, then, Locarno was most welcome because it consolidated the '*Pax Americana*' of 1924 while relieving the administration of any need to consider further strategic commitments in Europe. In particular, there seemed no further danger that Washington would be called upon to defend the *status quo* of Versailles and take sides in a new European 'system of alliances and counter-alliances'.[57] On the contrary, the regional security pact of Locarno could spur further disarmament – and US disengagement. Castle advised that the 'conclusion of the Locarno Pact with growing plans to call a disarmament conference' in Europe made it 'imperative' for Coolidge to give up his designs to hold such a conference in Washington. Instead, 'sentimental though it may be', America should support League disarmament efforts.[58]

At the same time, though rarely acknowledged, there was the notion that, through Locarno, Britain had committed itself to overseeing European security as well as Franco-German accommodation.[59] Indirectly, London thus secured US interests in Europe. While Britain played this undesirable part, the Republican administration could adhere to its policy of aloofness and more lucrative efforts of financial consolidation. Despite the prestige German policymakers had gained through Locarno, and in view of France's persistent recalcitrance concerning war-debts, Castle even went so far as to call Britain, on 6 November, 'our only remaining friend in Europe'.[60]

[54] Kellogg speech, 14 December 1925; Kellogg Papers.
[55] Young to Stresemann, 21 October 1925, Stresemann Papers, vol. 31.
[56] *Literary Digest*, 31 October 1925. Cf. Berg (1990), p. 255.
[57] Kellogg to Fletcher, 11 June 1925, Kellogg Papers.
[58] Castle Diary, 6 November 1925, vol. 8.
[59] State Department memorandum, 5 November 1925, Kellogg Papers.
[60] Castle Diary, 6 November 1925, vol. 8. Cf. Costigliola (1984), pp. 30–1.

A more far-reaching concern voiced by Castle, but with wider resonance in Washington, was that the security pact marked 'another step toward uniting Europe as against the United States'. Indeed, from late 1925 a new pattern informing American attitudes and eventually US policies in Europe emerged. The administration's general outlook on European reconciliation efforts remained supportive. Yet there were also growing suspicions regarding further, more ambitious initiatives to 'unite' Europe politically and economically. In particular, these concerned French designs to advance separate agreements with Germany that were seen as harmful to US loan and trade policies, notably any attempt to forge a debtor coalition or to revive schemes for a Franco-German trading bloc in continental Europe.[61] Such aversions had only minor short-term consequences but underlay a central and detrimental tension marking America's informal hegemony in the latter 1920s.

The Locarno part – a starting-point for further Franco-German *rapprochement*

As Chamberlain perceived more acutely than optimistic US observers, there were still numerous obstacles on the road to a pacified, let alone a united Europe when the Locarno conference closed. And he also saw more directly that Briand and Stresemann still had very divergent expectations as to what kind, and what dynamics, of *détente* that the Locarno pact was to engender. These divergences were accentuated as both foreign ministers still had to win approval for the accords in overall adverse domestic constellations. Facing a far more severe struggle on the home front than his French counterpart, Stresemann interpreted the settlement as the starting-point for a more fundamental revision of the Versailles system. Concretely, once the Cologne zone had been 'liberated', he sought above all a rapid termination of the entire Rhineland occupation.[62] By contrast, Briand saw, and vindicated, Locarno as a pact that had finally settled the postwar *status quo* and thus strengthened the foundations of 1919. Fundamentally, also the crucial Rhineland question was to be resolved on this basis. While intent on proving his goodwill vis-à-vis Berlin, Briand's maxim remained to check or at least postpone any further revisions.[63]

The French foreign minister gained overwhelming parliamentary approval for Locarno in the *Chambre*. While sixty deputies abstained, the agreement was accepted by 413 to 71 votes. This clearly indicated a change in the prevalent attitude of France's political establishment towards 'peacemaking'

---

[61] Castle to Houghton, 3 November 1925, Houghton Papers. Cf. Link (1970), pp. 350–1.

[62] Stresemann speech, 22 November 1925, in Turner (1967), pp. 418ff.

[63] Briand statements to the Foreign Affairs Commission, 19 December 1925, Procès verbaux, C14763, no. 46, pp. 6ff.

with Germany.[64] Yet it also underscored how few alternatives French decisionmakers saw under the political and financial duress of 1925. There was an
evident interest in escaping not only from a period of domestic *malaise* but
also from relative international isolation as the troublemaker in European
politics after the war, particularly vis-à-vis the Anglo-American powers.
French publicised opinion mostly hailed the security pact as the dawning of
a new era of peace and reconciliation.[65]

Yet there were also still lingering scepticism and suspicion. As during
the summer debates, it was again Poincaré who put his finger on what
some regarded as Locarno's basic flaws. Poincaré also saw the need for a
rapprochement with Germany and more cordial relations with the Anglo-
American powers to strengthen France's postwar position. But he upheld his
opposition to the specific platform of the Locarno accords as an adequate
means to this end. He clung to his opinion that Germany's acceptance of the
western *status quo* did not suffice to ensure French safety. And he warned that
Britain's commitment was too limited to guard against possible backlashes in
Germany. In Poincaré's view, Locarno also acutely challenged France's hold
on the Rhineland.[66]

Dissent also manifested itself during subsequent debates in the *Chambre*'s
Foreign Affairs Committee where Briand defended his policy, not for the first
time, in February 1926. Those who did not follow the majority argued that
Germany's Locarno promises were only backed by a minority east of the
Rhine. While France had no choice but to accept the treaty, it could not rely
on Berlin keeping its side of the bargain; Paris had effectively abandoned not
only its eastern allies but also stood to lose its Rhenish *glacis*. Other voices
bemoaned that France was not only 'oppressed by political and financial
pressures' but had also 'negotiated at Locarno under the pressure of English
policy', which was dominated by a 'lack of foresight'.[67]

The French High Command at first opposed a rapid French fulfilment of
German demands for evacuation of the Cologne zone as long as Germany had
not fulfilled the disarmament conditions posed by the Conference of Allied
Ambassadors. But by mid-November, Marshal Foch deferred to Briand's
political authority and his priority to settle this problem in the new 'spirit' of
Locarno. As Ambassador Crewe reported, the general attitude of the French
generals towards Locarno was distinctly calm and affirmative at this stage.[68]

---

[64] Cf. Laroche (1957), pp. 214–15; Suarez (1938–41), IV, pp. 137–8.
[65] This was reflected in the Foreign Affairs Commission, 19 December 1925, 12 February 1926,
Procès verbaux, C14763–4, C14763, nos. 46, 51. Cf. Adamthwaite (1995), pp. 121–2.
[66] Cf. Keiger (1997), p. 319.
[67] 12 February 1926, Procès verbaux, C14763, no. 51, pp. 13ff.
[68] Crewe to Chamberlain, 15 November 1925; Chamberlain to Müller, 4 November 1925, Austen
Chamberlain Papers, AC 52/232, AC 50/135.

But the French army would subsequently represent one of the main factors of 'hindrance' for Briand in implementing 'Locarno politics', both in resisting an evacuation of the Rhineland and by reducing troop-levels less rapidly than the government had promised.[69]

Against this background, Briand had all the more reason to praise the agreements as France's contribution to a new European peace order, which effectively strengthened its power to uphold Versailles, and thus France's standing in Europe. In his appraisal of Locarno for the French diplomatic corps on 4 November, he emphasised that Locarno had brought the 'voluntary adherence of Germany to the territorial clauses of the Treaty of Versailles'. At Locarno, the German government had 'understood the necessity' of embarking on a 'new policy' vis-à-vis France. At the same time, France had been 'assured' of the Rhine frontier's inviolability through the 'British guarantee, which, since the abandonment of the treaties of 1919, had not been obtained'. This gave France 'an opportunity to practise between ourselves and our neighbours politics of real *détente*'. Germany was now tied to the League, and the French government had retained 'every liberty' to maintain its 'defensive alliances' with Poland and Czechoslovakia.[70]

In sum, Briand concluded that France was set to resume control of European politics at Britain's side, as the dominant power in negotiations with a partly appeased, in part newly constrained Germany. The French foreign minister would later also defend his Locarno approach by stating that it responded to the 'necessity' of organising the 'diverse European states' in a 'union' to 'organise the continent economically'. He sought to achieve this through European 'solidarity', i.e. essentially under French control. This policy would give rise to the chiefly Franco-German steel-cartel agreement of 1926 and the Franco-German commercial treaty of 1927.[71] As became clear at Thoiry and thereafter, however, no French designs of this nature could be advanced against Anglo-American financial interests.[72]

What did the outcome of the pact negotiations signify for Stresemann's foreign policy? As the German foreign minister stressed in a speech on 25 November, the primary, concrete goal he claimed to have attained, particularly through Britain's guarantee, was a lasting protection of the Rhineland against renewed French encroachments. He recognised that what collided with a further 'strengthening' of Germany's international position after Locarno were

---

[69] See Jacobson (1972b), p. 370.

[70] Briand instructions, 4 November 1925, MAE, Pacte de sécurité, Z 284–6, vol. 86; Briand's statements to the Foreign Affairs Commission on 19 December 1925, Procès verbaux, C14763–64, C14763, no. 46.

[71] Cf. Wurm (1989).

[72] Briand's statement to the Foreign Affairs Commission, 19 December 1925, Procès verbaux, C14763, no. 46.

French anxieties concerning its neighbour's 'demographic preponderance' and unrestricted economic recovery. Yet, as Stresemann underlined, precisely to surmount this difficulty his rationale would remain exactly that which had proved so successful since 1923: to draw Britain away from a one-sided *entente* policy and activate it as 'the umpire of Europe', which had 'an interest in containing French hegemony'.[73]

Following his experiences in Locarno, Stresemann thus re-accentuated the 'English orientation' of his policy because he thought that in all principal questions awaiting a resolution – notably the Rhineland question and the termination of military control – German were in conformity with English interests. Essentially, he hoped that, with Chamberlain's support and Briand's reciprocity, the new modus of concert diplomacy could be effective – and produce rapid results.[74] As he summarised on 15 November, the long-term aim that Stresemann thus sought to achieve was 'the recovery of German sovereignty on German soil and within the borders of the German *Reich*'. In a wider context, the *détente* of Locarno created the conditions for Germany's continued revitalisation and access to US capital.[75] In a narrower sense, only the agreements with Britain and France had really set the stage for Stresemann's core strategy – an *active* pursuit of peaceful revision premised on using Germany's only remaining 'great weapon', its economic power. But the foreign minister was of course acutely aware of the fact that, in view of German dependence on American loans, one of the primary tools of his policy remained largely under the control of the United States.[76]

What thus informed Stresemann's outlook despite all immediate disappointments was that, following the London settlement, Locarno marked the second successful test, a precedent confirming his policy of peaceful accommodation with the western powers. Crucially, this accommodation entailed forging new rules of international politics in co-operation with these powers. As the security initiative had shown, German policymakers like Stresemann and Schubert had begun to advance their own rules and strategies. The methods of their *Westpolitik* had indeed begun to shape the ends of German policy, not only because it was the policy of a largely disarmed country. On balance, to escape postwar isolation, and since he was unable to solve conflicts bilaterally with France, Stresemann had come to espouse a 'western', in many ways liberal,

---

[73] Stresemann speech, 22 November 1925, in Turner (1967), p. 418; Stresemann speech, 14 December 1925, *ADAP*, B, I, 1, pp. 740–8.

[74] Stresemann speech, 1 December 1925, Stresemann (1926), II, pp. 220ff.

[75] Stresemann speech, 15 November 1925, Stresemann Papers, vol. 32; Stresemann *Reichstag* statements, Stresemann (1932), II, p. 160.

[76] Stresemann speech, 14 December 1925, *ADAP*, B, I, 1, p. 729; Stresemann speech, 19 December 1925, Stresemann Papers, vol. 274. On Germany's economic situation in 1925 see Borchardt (1982), pp. 704–5.

mode of international politics. This meant, however, that he, and even more strikingly Schubert, had in effect adopted key elements of British and American approaches.[77]

To persist with such a course, and possibly also to settle Germany's relations with its eastern neighbours at a later stage, Stresemann not only had to widen the party and parliamentary base for his policy. He also had to increase its general domestic legitimacy. Even more than in Briand's case, this struggle did not stop but in many ways only intensified after Locarno. Thus, as in 1924, Stresemann constantly required short-term successes – or what was domestically perceived as such. And he also had to convince domestic opponents that he was not betraying long-standing German interests. The German foreign minister was indeed resourceful in mastering this challenge, not least by using nationalist language to placate exercised home audiences.[78] What caused a backlash for his policy after Locarno, however, was precisely that Stresemann had felt compelled to raise expectations as to the pacts likely consequences – or *Rückwirkungen* – for Germany, especially regarding the Rhineland. These he could not immediately fulfil, and consequently the outcome of Locarno was greeted with less enthusiasm in Germany than in Britain, America and even France.

How frail the domestic basis for Stresemann's policy remained became obvious when the DNVP ministers within Luther's coalition government resigned in protest over the security accords on 23 October. But Luther's torso cabinet was resolved to see through the treaties' ratification in the *Reichstag*. Ultimately, this could only be achieved, on 27 November, with the – expected – backing of the opposition Social Democrats and the liberal German Democratic Party (DDP).[79] In Chamberlain's verdict, the Germans showed themselves ungrateful – to them no concession seemed 'of any value from the moment it has been made'.[80] Apart from nationalist opposition, the most serious resistance to Stresemann's course came from the *Reichswehr*. Seeckt continued to oppose the general orientation of *rapprochement* with the west, seeking to maintain avenues of covert co-operation with Soviet Russia, never losing sight of forcibly overthrowing the postwar order.[81] Concretely, the *Reichswehr* leadership would obstruct meeting Germany's remaining disarmament obligations. While neither British nor American policymakers deemed the *Reichswehr's* activities a cause for major concern, their control through Weimar's governments absorbed considerable energy and could never be quite

---

[77] Cf. Krüger (1984), pp. 105ff; Wright (1995), pp. 126–7.
[78] Stresemann letter to Crown Prince Wilhelm, 7 September 1925, *UF*, VI, pp. 486–7.
[79] Cf. Stürmer (1967), pp. 17ff; Grathwol (1980).
[80] Chamberlain to D'Abernon, 23 November 1925, *DBFP*, IA, I, no. 120.
[81] Cf. Zeidler (1993), pp. 82–7, 303.

achieved.[82] Throughout the 1920s, political authority all in all prevailed; the *Reichswehr* did not turn into an overbearing 'state within the state' of Weimar. The consolidation of this latter *republican* state, however, remained a key condition for Europe's further pacification and, in turn, inextricably bound up with the consolidation of the system of London and Locarno.

In vital respects, like that of London, Locarno thus was not a settlement drawing a thick line under Europe's postwar turmoil and eliminating the underlying causes of European instability, particularly Franco-German asymmetry. The ultimate proof of how durable the accords of the mid-1920s were would have to be made by sustaining the new framework they had created. Essentially, to be regulated, and stabilised, were the dynamism and extent of further peaceful change in Europe, which Germany sought to hasten and France sought to slow down. This was to be the central task for British and American policymakers after 1925.

Obvious though it may seem, that all sides had *begun* to see, and tackle, the underlying challenge of reconciling Germany's international rehabilitation with European stability captures the essence of what new quality had emerged in European and transatlantic politics in the fulcrum years 1924 and 1925. In this sense, not the Locarno pact alone, as Chamberlain argued, but the combined achievements of London and Locarno marked 'the real dividing line between the years of war and the years of peace' in post-World War I Europe.[83]

---

[82] Cf. Jacobson (1972b), pp. 370–1.
[83] Chamberlain press statement, 23 October 1925, cited in Toynbee and Macartney (1924–30), 1926, p. 56.

Part III

The unfinished transatlantic peace order: the system of London and Locarno, 1926–1929

How far could the nascent transatlantic peace order after World War I be consolidated? What made it so susceptible to collapse under the impact of the World Economic Crisis? These are far-ranging questions on which the final part of this study, and its epilogue, nonetheless seek to shed some new light.

Focusing on the European stage, some earlier studies have claimed that the Locarno treaty system overall functioned well until succumbing to the Great Depression's overwhelming pressures. Others have asserted that the clash between French and German aims became even more pronounced after Locarno – yet that neither British, German nor French policies evolved further. Allegedly, the 'edifice' of Locarno thus eventually collapsed because Chamberlain, Briand and Stresemann missed opportunities.[1] There has also been the view that they simply could not overcome what proved critical: towering domestic obstacles to international conciliation, chiefly in France and Germany.[2]

Most resonant, however, remains the 'realist' condemnation of Locarno-style 'tea-party' diplomacy, asserting that it had to fail because it rested on false premises. Its deepest flaw was, allegedly, that it continued to disregard, and erode, what alone could have contained Germany's unchangeable revisionism: balance-of-power prescriptions. By a similar token, Anglo-American efforts to complete Germany's rehabilitation allegedly went ever further in compromising eastern Europe's, and particularly Poland's, consolidation prospects. This was also a widely held, yet not the only, Polish view after Locarno.[3] If that view was accurate, then the settlements of London and Locarno would have created new, hazardous fault-lines in Europe. They would have created not only borders of different validity but also areas of differing stability, security and prosperity in western and eastern Europe. In sum: had Anglo-American stabilisation efforts merely instituted a 'ceasefire' before the inevitable resumption of the Franco-German 'duel' for European predominance – which purportedly entered its decisive phase as early as 1928? If so, then

---

[1] See Jacobson (1972b), pp. 367–73; Jacobson (2004), pp. 11–32.
[2] See Knipping (1987), pp. 21ff; Jacobson (1983a).
[3] See Wandycz (1961), pp. 32ff, and (1988); Schattkowsky (1994b); Bátonyi (1999).

the 'cease-fire' of the mid-1920s would merely have given Europe a short, rather deceptive 'breathing space'. And it would have allowed Germany to consolidate its re-ascension as Europe's predominant power and to threaten peace once again.[4] Was the 'spirit' of Locarno already dissipating well before the Great Depression?[5] Or was indeed the catastrophe of 1929 the decisive *caesura* destroying whatever had been established and on a rather promising trajectory before?[6]

Some scholars have described the depression essentially as a result of economic problems, hardly to be influenced by leading foreign-policymakers.[7] Others, however, have sought to establish an incriminatory cause-and-effect relationship between Anglo-American pursuits of European stability before 1929 and the all-encompassing crisis thereafter.[8] Following this approach, the critical shortcomings of the 1920s could be discovered by analysing how far US (and British) foreign economic policy was indeed apt to foster Europe's financial stabilisation; by assessing how far the Dawes regime and America's financial engagement in Germany rested on solid foundations; and by examining how far Anglo-American efforts to promote European prosperity by re-introducing the prewar gold standard and pressing for budgetary discipline proved successful.[9]

Undoubtedly, continued British yet above all American engagement in all of these areas had an important part in sustaining Europe's reconstruction after the Great War. And Weimar Germany's financial consolidation was as critical for sustaining the Franco-German peace process as a termination of France's financial crisis. Not least, both were critical for keeping in power those moderate leaders who drove this process forward. Yet financial duress could also become a catalyst for stepped-up efforts at political accommodation. As the perceptive permanent under-secretary at the Foreign Office, Tyrrell, pointed out in July 1926, both in Germany and France there was a 'very serious economic situation which demands peremptorily the adoption of a sane foreign policy aiming at the stabilisation of European conditions'.[10]

That economics mattered most continued to be a deeply held conviction not only of financiers like Strong and Norman but also of key policymakers in Washington, notably Hoover.[11] Fundamentally, however, neither financial

---

[4] Cf. Marks (1976), pp. 143–6; Kissinger (1994), pp. 266ff.
[5] See Knipping (1987), p. 41, and against this Krüger (1985a), pp. 372ff.
[6] Cf. Bell (1986), pp. 31–47.
[7] See Kindleberger (1973), pp. 1–13; Silverman (1982).
[8] Cf. Kent (1989), pp. 373–90; Friedmann and Schwartz (1963).
[9] See Eichengreen (1992); Burk (1981).
[10] Tyrrell memorandum, 26 July 1926, *DBFP*, IA, I, no. 103.
[11] Hoover address, 15 October 1928, Hoover Papers, Commerce, 1928; Strong to Gilbert, 29 October and 7 November 1925, Strong Papers, 1012.1; Norman to Strong, 2 February 1926, Strong Papers, 1116.6/2.

stability nor economic hardship were essential for fortifying the fledgling peace order of the mid-1920s. Neither the gold standard nor loans or, more broadly, rising prosperity and a 'rational' restructuring of the French and German political economies held the key to durable peace. Illuminating what did prove crucial, and why in the end no lasting stability could be achieved, requires us once again to go beyond one-sided studies of European diplomacy on the one hand and American policies on the other. And what has to be re-assessed are two different central questions. First, what accounts for the remarkable yet also in many ways constrained consolidation not merely of the 'Locarno system' but of the wider Euro-Atlantic system of London *and* Locarno between 1926 and 1929? And second, why did western and German policymakers ultimately fail to transform the settlements of the mid-1920s into a more permanent, a more than unfinished peace order? Put bluntly: did British and American approaches fail because they sought to achieve mutually irreconcilable aims: to strengthen Weimar Germany *and* to constrain German power, to accommodate it *and* to build European peace? Or did they fail because they did not do enough to buttress the newly republican Germany and those who, like Stresemann, struggled to pursue peaceful change and a *rapprochement* with the western powers?

To begin with, it is imperative to understand that Britain's pursuit of Locarno politics and America's intensified, yet once again more economically orientated stabilisation efforts continued to shape the European situation in the latter 1920s. Yet both powers abstained from further 'grand initiatives' to further Franco-German accommodation; and they did even less to initiate accommodation between Germany and Poland. Still less did they embark on anything approaching a concerted stabilisation of what remained the continent's least consolidated geo-political area, that comprising the smaller states between Germany and the Soviet Union in eastern and south-eastern Europe. Thus, the impact of what Anglo-American policymakers did and notably *what they did not* do was less conspicuous after 1925, harder to trace than in the fulcrum years after the Ruhr crisis. But it was no less critical. Both powers continued to set the key international parameters for Franco-German reconciliation and European pacification in the era of London and Locarno.

By the end of 1925, the system of London and Locarno was necessarily still unconsolidated. Arguably, it was not prone to collapse sooner or later because it concealed an underlying Franco-German antagonism. Nor was it frail because it rested on illusory premises about the reconcilability of German power and European security. The main danger was instead that the nascent peace order of the mid-1920s would not be sustained by those who had founded it. More precisely, the consolidation of Europe's hard-won peace depended on how far, in co-operation with their European counterparts, Anglo-American policymakers could build on the precedents of London and Locarno. It depended on how far they could forge further strategic bargains between the western powers and Germany, and eventually also between these powers and Germany's eastern neighbours, especially Poland. For this remained the only way to promote a more durable reform of the Versailles order, a reform that deepened Weimar Germany's international integration and, as far as possible, made its revitalisation as a great power compatible with European stability.

As will be shown, tangible progress on all of these fronts could only be made through further complex settlements comprising not only political but also financial elements. As all protagonists knew, such settlements had to be approached first in what remained the three critical, and inseparable, areas of postwar politics: European (in)security, reparations and war-debt politics. Eventually, yet only when – in retrospect – it was too late to prevent the outbreak of a gathering storm, the most significant advances of the latter 1920s were indeed made through one further 'grand' bargain. It was to be the final such agreement in the interwar period. First, came the 'final' settlement of reparations through the 1929 Young plan, once again largely effected on American terms. Then, and only possible on its basis, followed the settlement of the Rhineland question in its core aspect, the termination of the French occupation. Both could only be finalised after acrimonious diplomatic wrangling at the first Hague conference.

The changes between 1923 and 1925 manifested that, if the United States used its power and policymakers and financiers on both sides of the Atlantic co-operated, 'depoliticisation' and financial consolidation could buttress political accommodation; and the latter could in turn underpin European reconstruction. Yet quite the opposite scenario was possible as well. There was the distinct danger that if one of these processes lost momentum, the other could also be severely affected. Not only American financiers like Strong warned that a backlash in resolving outstanding Franco-German security problems could have repercussions on the willingness of US investors to advance further loans to Germany or, pending a debt settlement, to France. And this could severely limit the ability of Stresemann or Briand to persevere with their policies.[12]

Conversely, a crisis of the Dawes system, which no side excluded after 1925, could also entail a resurfacing of Franco-German tensions. For it could limit the options of pursuing – and legitimating – moderate, step-by-step approaches to reconciliation and, in the end, the politics of the European concert and transatlantic co-operation as such. In other words, it could lead to a 'renationalisation' of international politics, with all sides falling back on the pursuit of narrower national interests. Thus, finally, the stability of the international system *per se* could be at stake. As will be shown, precisely this

---

[12] Strong memorandum, 22 July 1925, Strong Papers.

would occur when the World Economic Crisis escalated. By 1926, it was still not foreseeable how far Anglo-American prescriptions of peaceful accommodation and liberal-capitalist reform would generate results legitimating these prescriptions not only to elites but also the wider electorates in Germany, France and eastern Europe. How far could the system of London and Locarno produce such results, which at best would require a long period of unhampered development to materialise?

Weighty financial constraints, not least those attributable to war-debts and reparations, continued to preoccupy political leaders, especially those in Paris and Berlin. But there was also a growing readiness to resolve international differences through a European version of 'the American way': to use financial means to achieve political aims, to strike 'deals'. Most notably, Briand and Stresemann attempted this with their Thoiry initiative for a 'final postwar settlement', launched in September 1926. Yet it was also envisaged by German policymakers, and Anglo-American financiers, to spur a peaceful revision of the east European *status quo*. Both of these endeavours, however, would be effectively vetoed by Whitehall and Washington.[13]

Ultimately, though, Europe's gravest problem remained the security question. Even if significant advances towards 'resolving' it had been made in the mid-1920s, it was still paramount. Not least, further reducing the high level of postwar insecurity remained essential for propelling the Franco-German peace process. And a critical condition for achieving this was further advances in the practices and rules of international politics. Above all, the concerted co-operation not only between the Locarno powers but also between them and America had to evolve further. And in the changing international constellation of the latter 1920s, one constant remained unchanged: only Britain and the United States could give a decisive impetus to this process. Or they *at least* had to support European efforts in this direction if they were to bear any fruit.

In this context, the need to placate domestic opposition indeed remained a constant constraint for all policymakers, especially imposing limits on French and German leaders. Yet no less a constant – and salient – characteristic of the era of London and Locarno was the very limited potential for a bilateral Franco-German 'reconciliation'. It remained limited because of both powers' dependence on British and American goodwill, and interests, on all major issues, from security to war-debts and reparations. Nor, for that matter, could any Polish–German accommodation or wider consolidation of eastern Europe be envisaged without Anglo-American support.

Against this background, perhaps all too obvious but still worth underlining is the following. The system of London and Locarno could only prove

[13] See chapters 21 and 22.

mutually advantageous and extend European stability as long as all participating powers were committed to maintaining *and fortifying* it. But what mattered in particular, and often most, was that Anglo–American policymakers made this commitment – and could legitimate it in predominantly 'isolationist' domestic environments not only in America but also in Britain. Essentially, the consolidation of the emergent transatlantic peace system depended on their engagement at least as much as its foundation in the mid-1920s. To make it durable, both powers had to continue fostering the transformation of European politics underway since the Ruhr crisis.

The British government had to persevere with its commitment to the European concert. The US administration had to decide whether it would make more tangible commitments to safeguard America's rapidly expanding financial interests, particularly in Germany. If they were unwilling or unable to achieve this, the principal 'danger' on the horizon of the latter 1920s was that the new order for which both powers had laid the groundwork would subsequently not be sustained; and that it might eventually dissolve when exposed to strong international or national pressures. In a wider context, Anglo–American decisionmakers had to buttress an even more long-term transformation. What their efforts had established was essentially (only) the *western core* of a potentially more far-reaching system of security and financial consolidation. Even if British and American policies varied considerably, their common premise was that Europe's stabilisation hinged on extending a 'western' or 'liberal' mode of international politics, finance and government. In fact, it had to be extended from the west to the east, above all to Germany, yet also to its eastern neighbours and, ultimately, Soviet Russia.

What has to be examined in greater depth, then, is how far these processes could be advanced during the 'golden' years of Euro-Atlantic stability after the Great War. First, however, a closer look at the main challenges of international politics in the era of Locarno and Locarno is indispensable.

17 Sustaining stability, legitimating peaceful change
The challenges of the latter 1920s

Undoubtedly, as both Chamberlain and Kellogg perceived distinctly in the aftermath of the security pact negotiations, Briand and Stresemann harboured different, partly conflicting ideas about what kind of new order was to emerge in 'the spirit of Locarno'. In particular, they disagreed on how rapidly any further changes of the European *status quo* ought to proceed, how substantial they were to be and according to what understandings of *quid pro quo* they were to be brought about. Their 'visions' were not least influenced by the struggle that each of them faced in legitimating the accords in their respective countries.[1]

Stresemann saw Germany's 'security initiative' and signature under the Locarno pact as a substantial German advance to meet the postwar security concerns of the ex-allied powers and especially those of France. He expected them to be rewarded by stepped-up peaceful change or what he called *Rückwirkungen* ('consequences'). Most urgently, the German foreign minister sought a swift and complete French withdrawal from the Rhineland. Likewise, he hoped for a greater understanding of the western powers for German demands to end military control. Eventually, even if this became an ever more distant objective, he also sought to create conditions that might permit a peaceful, in his outlook economically 'rational' revision of Germany's eastern borders. In his calculation, however, such changes could only be achieved with the consent of the western powers, including France, and they could only materialise if Warsaw could be 'convinced', politically and through economic pressure, that such an arrangement was also in Poland's best interest.[2]

Briand was originally inclined to interpret Locarno as a pact that principally reinforced the newly settled *status quo* in the west, essentially on the basis of Versailles. From early 1926, the underlying rationale of his policy became that any further revisions, particularly regarding the strategically sensitive Rhineland, had to be deferred as far as possible. Officially, they were made conditional on further German fulfilment of the Versailles treaty, especially its

---

[1] Chamberlain to D'Abernon, 1 February 1926, *DBFP*, IA, I, no. 231; Kellogg to Davies, 4 January 1926, Kellogg Papers.
[2] Stresemann speech, 14 December 1925, *ADAP*, B, I/I, pp. 740–3.

disarmament clauses. In private, Briand and his key advisers Berthelot and Seydoux increasingly envisaged a new, politically advantageous *quid pro quo* agreement with Berlin on this issue. In times of unabated financial *malaise*, the key became to extract an appropriate financial price for any further French concessions. In the east, Briand actually deemed the *status quo* between Germany and Poland untenable in the long run; and – like Chamberlain and the Americans – he was to a certain extent amenable to Stresemann's economic arguments. But he did not see any room to manoeuvre, either internationally or domestically (in France and Poland), to achieve a peaceful revision of the precarious borders in the near future.[3]

Unquestionably, then, divergent interpretations of the meaning and desirable consequences of the Locarno pact emerged soon after its conclusion. Yet such divergences over an international settlement are the norm rather than the exception in the history of international politics, particularly if they are heightened by the need to persuade suspicious domestic audiences. And they are not necessarily the root cause of a peace order's eventual breakdown. What has to be in place to prevent such a breakdown, however, are rules and mechanisms through which the key powers' different aims, interests and expectations can be balanced and as far as possible accommodated. In turn, this can only be achieved as long as all relevant powers remain committed to sustaining, and if necessary improving, such rules and mechanisms.

Like his European counterparts, and unlike most US decisionmakers, Chamberlain had recognised what remained one of the most daunting challenges in this respect after the Great War: the need to broker compromises that could be legitimated not only in the international sphere but also in domestic politics. This was especially daunting in the still very polarised national environments of Germany and France. No less, however, it was a cardinal, if often insufficiently acknowledged challenge for British and American foreign policymakers. For Chamberlain and Kellogg, a critical task after 1925 was to win approval in their own countries – not only in the Commons, Congress and the wider publics but also in their own governments – for any fresh commitments, or even active involvement, to advance Europe's pacification. As will be noted, both sought to circumvent this as far as possible.

Those in London and Washington who desired to back Briand's efforts were not mistaken in reckoning that he genuinely sought reconciliation with Germany. Nor were they mistaken in concluding that Stresemann desired to effect a pacific revision of the postwar order: that he sought to regain political equality and economic clout in the international sphere, not armed

---

[3] Briand instructions, 4 November 1925, MAE, Pacte de sécurité, Z 284–6, vol. 86, 202–3.
[4] Austen to Hilda Chamberlain, 28 November 1925, Austen Chamberlain Papers, AC 5/1/370.

preponderance to re-establish a German 'semi-hegemony' in Europe. With respect to the international distribution of power, however, Locarno invariably continued a development that the London conference had initiated. The crux of Euro-Atlantic politics remained that the more relations between Germany and the western powers 'normalised', and the more it re-acquired the capabilities of an 'equal' great power, the more the natural *imbalance* of potential power between Germany and France resurfaced. This was only thinly veiled by the fact that under the circumstances of 1925 France of course retained a massive military preponderance in real terms. And it was viewed with deep concern by Germany's eastern neighbours, especially Poland.[5] This constellation lay at the heart of Europe's altered but still paramount security question of the latter 1920s. And this question remained at the core of Locarno politics, also profoundly influencing transatlantic relations.

Moreover, the perhaps unavoidable 'price' all sides paid for forging the Locarno settlement was *not* that France's position had been severely weakened but that some of the thorniest issues of European politics had been left unsettled. They had not fallen into the pact's immediate scope. Yet not only Chamberlain but also Stresemann and Briand hoped that they could be resolved through the new mode of Locarno politics.[6] Overshadowing everything else was the litmus issue in Franco-German relations until 1929: the Rhineland question, or more precisely the modalities and timing of French troop reductions and ultimately their withdrawal from the remaining occupation zones. This issue was in many ways connected with the still unsettled dispute over the termination of military control. Further, Locarno placed on to the agenda of Euro-Atlantic relations the far-ranging, yet hitherto unapproachable problem of European disarmament.

Finally, as noted, there was still the question of how far the politics of London and Locarno would foster a 'resolution' of an even thornier problem: the German question in the east. In other words, how far, if at all, could western stabilisation prepare the ground for a settlement of the Polish–German stand-off over the disputed frontier of 1919 and the ensuing minority problems on both sides of that frontier? This question had for the first time been addressed, but also sidelined, at Locarno. It thus continued to be at the heart of central European instability – and a constant concern in Germany's relations with the western powers.[7] What all of these questions had in common was that

---

[5] Castle notes on a conversation with the Polish chargé d'affaires Ciechanowski, Castle Diary, 10 February 1926, vol. 8, p. 33.

[6] Chamberlain to Briand, 29 July 1926, FO 800/259/668; Stresemann speech, 22 November 1925, in Turner (1967), pp. 418ff; Briand statements to the Foreign Affairs Commission, 19 December 1925, Procès verbaux, C14763, no. 46, pp. 6ff, 23–4.

[7] By comparison, the future of the German minority in the *Sudetenland* and general revisionist concerns in relations with Czechoslovakia were regarded as long-term issues and ranked low on

they were intricately bound up with the problem of Germany's re-emerging power. Any further changes in the European constellation would directly affect the foundations on which France and Britain had sought to safeguard their security since the Ruhr crisis. While aiming to anchor Germany to a modified postwar order, particularly Paris thus insisted on maintaining, as long as possible, a controlling politico-military primacy in Europe.

At the same time, impinging on Locarno politics in numerous ways, there was of course still the question of when, and on what terms, a 'final' reparations settlement could be forged. More precisely, it remained to be seen when the decisive American power would deem the time ripe for the anticipated revision of the Dawes plan – and what would be the political consequences of this revision. This was interwoven with two further critical strands of transatlantic relations in the latter 1920s: on the one hand, the working of the Dawes regime itself, the continued flow of US capital to underpin it, and German recuperation; on the other, the continued debt-settlement controversy between the United States and France. Resolving the latter was critical for French prospects to overcome its persistent financial and political hardship of the postwar period. Would America reward Briand's conciliatory policy and Caillaux's consolidation efforts? Would Washington, and London, agree to lenient debt settlements and re-open the supply of capital? Or could the French government itself take the necessary steps to overcome the French crisis?

It is of course difficult to identify the *underlying* challenges of European consolidation from the vantage-point of the mid-1920s without seeing them through the prism of what happened after 1929. Nevertheless, it seems fair to conclude that three central challenges arose after Locarno. The first was how far it would be possible to propel and deepen Franco-German *détente*, which remained the overriding task. How far could European concert politics be driven forward by an – active – British peace broker and Britain's strategic reassurance alone? Or could the concert only become truly effective if, as for example Schubert envisaged, it was gradually widened into a transatlantic mechanism?[8] And was there any prospect of achieving this in view of Washington's heretofore very limited political will to become Europe's 'offshore balancer'? What appeared more elusive still, and had until then received only scant, defensive attention in the Foreign Office and the State Department,

---

the agenda of Weimar German foreign policy in the latter 1920s. While they did not register on the American list of concerns vis-à-vis Europe, British policymakers deemed the unresolved postwar disputes between Berlin and Prague rather peripheral. After 1925, the Foreign Office essentially reckoned that they could eventually be settled, or at least contained, either through bilateral agreements or through the League – once the Locarno concert had further moderated German policy and improved the general international climate in Europe.

[8] Schubert memorandum, 12 January 1928, *ADAP*, B, VIII, pp. 34ff.

was the second central challenge: how far, if at all, could the European concert, and economic stabilisation, be extended to the east?

The third central challenge was at the core of *transatlantic* relations after Locarno. Essentially, it remained to be seen how far policymakers and financiers could find ways to buttress economic, and thus also political, stabilisation in France, Germany and beyond. To what degree would they persevere with the efforts launched in 1923? And, crucially, to what degree would they be able – and willing – to place these efforts on a more solid footing, essentially by establishing political mechanisms for oversight, loan and bail-out guarantees and, above all, crisis management? Would the United States become the Dawes regime's underwriter after all? Would it become the last-resort guarantor for Europe's Progressive *Pax Americana*?[9] As noted, the precedent of the Dawes plan did not augur well for significant advances in this direction; yet nor did it rule them out. Finally, an open question was to what extent the United States, yet also Britain, could promote what they and Germany desired more than France: to dynamise peaceful change by financial means.

In sum, even less than other postwar settlements in modern history could the agreements of London and Locarno enshrine a new *status quo* in Europe that was already balanced and stable. More importantly still, while significant advances towards a more durable peace order had been made – compared with the state of affairs in 1919, in 1923 and even at the turn of 1924/5 – there was still no coherent Euro-Atlantic international system underpinning both European security and financial stabilisation. This is why the effectiveness of the new understandings and ground-rules that had generated the London accords and the Rhine pact, and the extent to which British and American policymakers could reinforce them, were crucial. In many ways, both became even more critical than before Locarno. Essentially, Britain and the United States had to keep on track a peace process that, as noted, Stresemann tried his utmost to push forward and Briand aimed to control. What thus became imperative was to fortify the two-tier system of London and Locarno – to fortify it to such an extent that it could, if not suspend then as far as possible manage this straining constellation – and the imbalance of French power and German power potential.

The new system had to render possible, and equilibrate, a complex dynamism. Cardinal objectives of Anglo-American stabilisation policies after the war had already been met. But Locarno politics and transatlantic co-operation had to yield further results that gave both the Third Republic's struggling proponents of conciliation and Weimar Germany's embattled elite of moderates an

---

[9] Notably the reparations agent voiced this concern. See Gilbert to Strong, 5 November 1925, Strong Papers, 1012.1.

interest in sustaining an as yet nascent Franco-German reconciliation process. Further, to widen the legitimacy of this process, it had to produce outcomes that both the German and the French side could present as corresponding with their still conflicting definitions of national interest. Similar advances had to be made on a wider scale if there were to be any prospects for a peaceful settlement of the Polish–German conflict and the consolidation of eastern Europe. It is worth emphasising that international politics in the Locarno period here prefigured a host of peace processes between more or less democratic, or democratising, states in the twentieth century.

While all sides could build on their success of Locarno, the challenges they faced were thus hardly different from what had given rise to the security pact of October 1925. Crucially, Euro-Atlantic stabilisation efforts had to create such a solid framework, and strengthen the position of Weimar's conciliatory leaders to such a degree as to prevent, also in the longer term, nationalist forces from gaining power in Berlin. For such forces could indeed abuse the power advantages that Germany's revitalisation through peaceful change had accrued. In other words, European security remained at risk as long as major German grievances were still unsettled and a 'Versailles syndrome' nourishing nationalist revisionism persisted in many quarters. What had to be stabilised in Germany to forestall a relapse to forcible revisionism was, fundamentally, a longer and more far-reaching transition process – a process of 'westernisation'.

It is thus understandable that French security concerns persisted after Locarno. It had not yet been proved that Britain's Locarno commitment, German restraint and the Locarno system as a whole would be effective and bind more than a small elite of German moderates should a real crisis break out. Nor had it yet been proved that adhering to Anglo-American prescriptions of international accommodation, 'open' economic competition and austere domestic reform programmes would redound to France's strategic and financial advantage. Arguably, however, under the conditions of the later 1920s, not bilateral diplomacy between France and Germany but only efforts to build on the approaches of London and Locarno opened up the best, if not the only, 'realistic' paths towards solving both countries' core problems. Nevertheless, it is hard to imagine a taller order.

All of these factors and forces also diminished any short-term hopes of pacifying what remained a deeply strained relationship between Germany and Poland. As the border and minority questions dividing both countries remained among the most precarious problems still besetting Europe, none but piecemeal progress was achievable in the latter 1920s. But no prospects whatsoever of peaceful change in eastern Europe – and vis-à-vis Soviet Russia – could be opened up unless British and American policymakers pursued more substantive efforts to mediate, first and foremost between Berlin and Warsaw. Yet it remained highly questionable whether either Whitehall or Washington would see a sufficient national interest in assuming commitments in this process littered with thick boards awaiting patient and persistent drilling.

More generally, then, a cardinal feature of the postwar period had not changed in the aftermath of Locarno. In view of the transatlantic system's asymmetric power configuration, progress on any front was hardly conceivable without the support of Britain and the United States. Above all, Germany and France continued to depend not only on Anglo-American capital but also on both powers' political co-operation. Thus, the extent to which those directing British and American policies still saw the need for maintaining, or even broadening, their engagement in Europe, what strategies they devised and how far they could legitimate them, domestically and abroad – all this would have a decisive bearing on how durable the Euro-Atlantic peace of the mid-1920s could be made.

London and Locarno – the greatest extent of Anglo-American engagement in the 1920s?

In some ways, and of course only in hindsight, it can indeed be said that from an Anglo-American perspective the achievements of London and Locarno were too far-reaching for their own good. They did not carry the seeds of their own destruction. But despite pronouncements to the contrary they led British as well as American policymakers to conclude that they had already made their decisive contributions to reforming the Versailles system and setting Europe on a path of stability. With few exceptions, they came to assume that with the Dawes regime and the Locarno concert they had by and large created the essential, and sufficient, mechanisms to achieve Franco-German *rapprochement* and Europe's wider pacification. A further, no less important conclusion that decisionmakers in London and Washington drew was that they could hence use, and thus did not have to enhance, the very strategies that had just proved so effective in stabilising Europe after the Ruhr crisis. At the same time, these were strategies entailing comparatively limited, or in the American case minimal, formal commitments to European security and peaceful change. And precisely because of the successes of 1924 and 1925, the line that both Chamberlain and Kellogg had to tow between internal opposition to costly commitments abroad and the pursuit of vital strategic interests in Europe became even thinner than before.

Of course, Anglo-American efforts to stabilise Europe did not cease in the latter 1920s. In some ways, British engagement in the Locarno concert as well as US engagement through the Dawes regime and financial pressure on France were more extensive after Locarno than before. But in one central respect, the efforts of the mid-1920s did mark the greatest extent of the commitment of both powers to post-World War I Europe's stabilisation. Essentially, neither

British nor American policies to sustain the fledgling system of London and Locarno were *developed further* after 1925. The Anglo-American powers remained determined to set the international ground-rules. And they indeed continued to determine the scope of further Franco-German accommodation in accordance with their core interests. Britain did so through the European concert and with a view to reparations and French debts, America through the Dawes regime and likewise as war-debt creditor of France. In the larger picture, neither power reneged from its *basic* commitment to promote further European consolidation, more or less officially. Yet both in London and in Washington there was a sense that French and German leaders were hence called upon to resolve the outstanding postwar disputes between them within the parameters, and limits, set at London at Locarno. And the same held true for German and Polish leaders. Crucially, between 1926 and late 1928, neither the United States nor Britain launched any further major initiatives – or even supported Franco-German initiatives – to propel peaceful change in Europe. As a consequence, no further 'breakthroughs' could be made. There were no further decisive advances that could have conferred significantly greater legitimacy on the new international order.

While many similar lessons had been drawn, the evolution of British and American policies after Locarno was also shaped by distinctly different conclusions about what was fostering Europe's pacification. Chamberlain concluded that European diplomacy and in essence the Locarno concert held the key. He thus overestimated both. In principle, concert diplomacy could also provide a model for conflict resolution in eastern Europe, particularly between Berlin and Warsaw, without requiring any further British guarantees. Britain remained the pivotal 'broker' in European international politics. Yet, with core national interests having been secured, it no longer shaped either the European concert or the wider Locarno process in a decisive manner.

By contrast, Washington's approach was marked by a lingering mistrust of European 'high politics'. For all the success of Locarno, the Dawes process had reinforced the conviction that outmoded forms of international politics, compromise and bargaining had to be superseded to found a more permanent peace. US policy, now shaped less by Kellogg and ever more by Hoover, completed the reorientation that had already set in after the London settlement. Reverting almost entirely to 'unpolitical' economic strategies, and confident that these would produce results deemed legitimate in Germany and France, it hence pursued the Progressive recasting of Europe in an ever more unilateral fashion.[10] The core aim, however, remained the same: to induce all

---

[10] C.S. Maier's formulation also aptly describes the US rationale, though it was Progressive rather than bourgeois. See Maier (1988).

European states to disarm, restructure their political economies – and espouse the American model of government, peaceful change and *laissez-faire* capitalism. This was to be America's mission in the latter 1920s. It would place renewed limits on Washington's political involvement in Europe; and it hardly served to buttress the new European concert. Towering above the interest in advancing Franco-German 'reconciliation', not to speak of a 'reconciliation' between Germany and its eastern neighbours, Washington's clear priority became to guard its official aloofness while at the same time controlling the terms of Europe's nascent *Pax Americana*. The latter interest especially applied to the still outstanding war-debt settlement with France, capital export to Germany and, crucially, the eventual revision of the Dawes regime.

18 Progressive visions and limited commitments
American stabilisation efforts in the era of London and Locarno

Undoubtedly, if any power then the United States had the resources to play a leading role in buttressing European security and the continent's further political and financial stabilisation in the latter half of the 1920s. The critical years following the nadir of the Ruhr crisis had shown that as a rising, financially dominating world power distanced from old European rivalries and competition America was in an ideal position to take on a more extensive mediating role in the Franco-German dispute – in some ways in a better position than Britain. More precisely, however, though America retained a critical role in the postwar international system, it was still hardly suited, and prepared, to reach beyond the limited role that Hughes had defined and fulfilled in 1924; for US policymaking remained constrained not only by prevailing domestic isolationism but also by foreign-policy traditions, and premises, that were only slowly adapted to the new reach of American power after the Great War. Nevertheless, each on their terms, French and German leaders continued to seek wider US engagement in Europe, be it to impede further alterations of the *status quo* or to accelerate peaceful change wherever possible. *Mutatis mutandis*, the same held true for Polish and Czechoslovak policymakers.

Crucially, apart from Britain's Locarno guarantees only broader American security commitments could reassure France and its eastern alliance partners further, even if these commitments fell short of full alliance guarantees, which the US Congress would never have sanctioned after the 'treaty fight' following Versailles. And they could thus potentially facilitate a more rapid completion of Franco-German arrangements requiring France's shift from territorial security bases – especially the Rhineland – to regional security agreements. From 1926 onwards, however, and indeed throughout the later 1920s, US stabilisation efforts became marked by an inherent limit, if not inconsistency. Even though the Dawes system led to a rapid expansion of financial involvement in and beyond Germany, and although it ceaselessly advocated further European reforms, the Coolidge administration declined more consistent political responsibilities in stabilising the process of peaceful change it desired. Washington continued to rely on private agents like Parker Gilbert, and it continued to encourage private financiers to step up investments in Germany. Officially, however, the administration returned to a more pronounced semi-detachment from European affairs, not only in security politics but also, and crucially, with a view to the Dawes system.

What exactly lay behind this inconsistency? It has long been maintained that it either sprang from misguided semi-isolationist policies vis-à-vis Europe or was simply the outgrowth of complacency.[1] Could one even conclude that US policymakers had all along merely done the necessary minimum to avert threats to American interests once the Ruhr crisis had escalated? Did the Coolidge administration thus merely return to earlier postwar isolationism as soon as the 'Old World's' most acute turmoil seemed contained?[2] And could any American government have pursued a more active course if it had seen the need for it?

It is important to understand that Washington's self-imposed aloofness and inconsistencies in the latter 1920s were not only, or mainly, the administration's response to the obvious domestic, and especially Congressional, constraints it faced. They can also, and chiefly, be attributed to a reinforcement of core assumptions of 'Progressive' foreign policy through the successes of 1924 and 1925. There was indeed a considerable degree of self-satisfied confidence among Republican policymakers in a 'new era' with seemingly few limits to America's prosperity, global economic expansion and attractiveness as the 'model of the future'. Yet US efforts to bolster pacifying reforms in France and Germany were not so much informed by complacency. Nor, at least in the State Department, were they marked by a myopic disregard for the fact that, while markedly improved, the European situation was still overshadowed by insecurity. Instead, what shaped American policy was a deliberate decision to rely on the highly convincing results of the mid-1920s and the inherent dynamism of their expected consequences.

Some decisionmakers, among them Kellogg, indeed came to interpret the political engagement since 1923 as the greatest necessary extent of desirable US involvement in Europe's postwar stabilisation.[3] In their view, by seeing through the Dawes plan and subsequently backing the Locarno pact, the Republican administration had played its essential part in founding (west) European peace after Wilson's failure. They thought it advisable to maintain essentially informal consolidation efforts, but these could become more restrained; and becoming enmeshed in European security politics had to be avoided at all cost. A majority of key figures, however, and notably Hoover,

---

[1] See Leffler (1979), pp. 158ff, and (1981), pp. 165–71; McNeil (1986), pp. 278–80; Link (1970), pp. 344ff; Costigliola (1984), pp. 262–7; Ferrell (1969).
[2] See Ferrell (1963), pp. 82–104.
[3] Kellogg address, 14 December 1925, Kellogg Papers.

drew markedly different conclusions – conclusions that were to determine the course of US policy until the climax of the Great Depression. In short, they insisted that London and Locarno had manifested the superiority of their definition of a Progressive approach to international affairs. In Hoover's view, as noted, European peace had been salvaged by replacing 'Old World' international politics by 'unpolitical' expert solutions and by using financial power to press for Locarno-style agreements. A degree of governmental interference in the early stages of this process had been unavoidable. Yet Washington's official role was hence to be strictly limited, while pressure on Europeans to accept American terms and prescriptions had to be stepped up.

The Coolidge administration followed the commerce secretary's lead and largely returned to what he had envisaged in the early 1920s. While also pushing for disarmament – not least on financial grounds – it essentially pursued foreign policy vis-à-vis Europe once again as foreign economic policy. Dominating it was the promotion of foreign trade, capital export and the economically driven reorganisation of European countries regardless of their power and geo-political positions. This thrust remained most obvious in America's engagement in Germany but was not confined to it. Washington essentially concentrated on using US financial leverage to spur the Europeans into accepting the new American ground-rules. As Hoover saw it, adopting these ground-rules would permit all European states to tackle their underlying, in his estimation largely economic, postwar problems with unprecedented efficiency. Thus, in a period of relative stability, a new reigning consensus emerged in Washington – by and large in an old guise.

This consensus was largely supported by leading New York bankers, particularly Strong. But it was not shared by all private financiers, who increasingly demanded governmental protection for their loans to Germany. The administration, however, practically abdicated responsibility in this critical field. Refusing to contemplate any major changes in its policies, it did not establish guarantees or bail-out mechanisms for private US loans; and, in a broader perspective, it did not use its power to make the Dawes regime more robust instead of merely keeping it operable.

In sum, it was on grounds of expedience *and* principle that the Republican administration refrained from building on Hughes' first steps and laying out a more comprehensive policy for Europe – a policy apt to solidify not only Europe's economic reconstruction but also the nascent security framework of Locarno. Republican elites relied on the force of economic necessity and what was taken to be a well-understood all-European interest to be included in a US-led zone of prosperity. They did not expand on Hughes' efforts and promote what would become essential for making the nascent *Pax (Anglo-) Americana* endure: further changes in Franco-German relations and in eastern Europe, to be achieved also via the economic sphere yet mainly through political co-operation. What thus grew even stronger in Washington than in the early 1920s was the belief in the superiority of Progressive remedies to Europe's problems, remedies that in the view of most Republican policy-makers were indeed universally applicable while requiring no unwelcome American concessions, notably war-debt relief. Intimately connected with this was an aforementioned core assumption that now resurfaced: the as yet deep-seated distrust of European-style politics, already familiar from the early postwar years. For all the advances of the mid-1920s, the very nature of such politics – the Europeans' secretive summit diplomacy and hidden agendas, mainly to shed their debt obligations and to entangle America in harmful multilateral agreements – remained suspect.

Surveying what thorny problems the European powers still had to grapple with, especially in the areas of security and disarmament, Castle concluded in March 1926: 'Human nature has not changed and Europe has changed mighty little since the War.'[4] Encapsulating Kellogg's maxim, he later added that Washington did 'not want to be expedited by anyone for any purpose' and would 'be careful to avoid getting fooled by British intrigue' or any French or German power-political machinations.[5] Hoover was even more categorical in his condemnation of antiquated European ways. In his judgement, Locarno had been a step in the right direction. Yet it had not gone far enough in making the transition from power politics to American-style reforms.[6] Somewhat paradoxically, the more the ability of European policymakers to manage their conflicts grew, the more such aversions seemed to regain ground on the western side of the Atlantic.

Strengthened by Locarno, the Dawes settlement came to be viewed as a groundwork on which the Europeans now had to build. And it was a base on which, essentially, a once more economically orientated and privately driven American quest for Europe's consolidation could progress, hand in hand with a further extension of open-door trading rules and US commercial expansion. This set of assumptions again largely informed Republican policy. Within the administration, a reflection of this trend was the State Department's hence diminished role vis-à-vis the Commerce and Treasury Departments. And it was compounded by Kellogg's relative weakness as secretary of state, which further limited the State Department's, and the administration's, already small room to manoeuvre vis-à-vis an unremittingly isolationist Congress. Neither Kellogg nor Hoover sought to widen their freedom of action to bolster peaceful

---

[4] Castle Diary, 19 March 1926, vol. 8, p. 51.
[5] Castle notes after meeting with M. Knecht in Paris, Castle Diary, 22 September 1926, vol. 10, pp. 231–2.
[6] Hoover memoranda on France and the debt settlement talks, 25 September – 1 October 1925, Hoover Papers, Commerce, box 20. Commerce Department, 'Reform in Fiscal Policies Begun in Europe', 8 June 1926, NA RG 151: 640.

change in Europe. Expanding the executive's role was simply thought neither salutary nor domestically opportune.

As we have seen, the penchant for economic diplomacy had always been strong within the administration, particularly of course inside the Commerce Department. Part of a wider stabilisation approach between 1923 and 1925, it hence regained supremacy in a purer, Hooverian form. Kellogg fell in line with this course. Above all, he continued to decline any part in addressing Europe's underlying security problem. In the sphere of security, the Coolidge administration's attention mainly centred on a limited drive for disarmament, which it deemed a highly popular cause. Eventually, driven by French overtures as much as by domestic pressures, it also came to espouse the outlawry of war, which ultimately led to the Kellogg–Briand Pact of 1928. That neither initiative became part and parcel of a more consistent US security policy diminished their effectiveness from the start.

From the perspective of early 1926, then, the main limitation of US policy was not that it pursued contradictory objectives, namely to enhance European security and rehabilitate Germany at the same time.[7] It was rather that the administration minimised America's political engagement in Europe. It erroneously expected that its goal to foster stability through economic reconstruction and disarmament could be achieved without concomitant political commitments, especially in the field of security. What limited the salutary impact of US efforts still further was a growing tendency to pursue bilateral policies vis-à-vis France and Germany. This followed quite naturally from the long-standing US interest in keeping the contentious issues of reparations and war-debts separate while pursuing specific foreign-loan agendas. It essentially allowed Washington to employ America's financial leverage most forcefully while forestalling a Franco-German coalition on debts, reparations and trade. But it also meant that no comprehensive approach to European stabilisation could be developed, an approach considering the specific requirements of Franco-German accommodation and Europe's changing power constellation as a whole.

The final ascendancy of Hooverian Progressivism

There was no unanimity among Republican decisionmakers on why the administration should eschew political involvement in Europe. Rather, two different outlooks can be distinguished – or, more precisely, one predominating and one minority position. The former was chiefly espoused by Hoover, yet also by Treasury Secretary Mellon and Coolidge himself, largely in unison with FRBNY Governor Strong and most US financiers. The latter was mainly

---

[7] Cf. Leffler (1979), pp. 362–8.

adopted by Kellogg and Castle, who as assistant secretary of state became a formative influence on State Department policy towards Europe.

Decisive was that the London and Locarno settlements stimulated – nowhere more than in Hoover's Commerce Department – a high degree of confidence in, and overestimation of, what unofficial strategies of financial stabilisation alone could achieve. The success of the Locarno accords re-inforced the notion that informal US pressures and incentives could prompt the Europeans to create the basic security structures for unimpeded economic stabilisation. This in turn nurtured the conviction that the Progressive *Pax Americana* could be expanded; and that it could be extended without requiring any major assurances or 'sacrifices' on Washington's part – be they security commitments, governmental guarantees for private loans or, eventually, a comprehensive debt and reparations settlement reducing or even cancelling most obligations. In Republican eyes, any such concessions would not only meet stiff Congressional opposition. They would also ultimately fall back on the American taxpayer. And, as importantly, they would contradict the basic premises of Hooverian Progressive policy and the restraints they imposed on governmental engagement in international politics.[8]

Precisely because of the achievements of the mid-1920s, there was hence even less incentive than before to envisage a domestically irksome extension of political, let alone military responsibilities. Vital security interests had already been satisfied in 1919 and through the Washington conference. By 1925, a navy-fortified American fortress appeared even less threatened by the possible resurgence of an antagonistic Germany.[9] There was a fundamental consensus that the US government would hence be free to pursue particular interests in Europe, especially that in collecting French debts. At the same time, it could rely on informal agents like Parker Gilbert to oversee the Dawes regime and on private bankers to advance not only capital but also the financial consolidation of Germany. This attitude prevailed although Hoover and Mellon as much as Strong and, at first hand, Parker Gilbert saw the considerable financial problems still confronting German and French policymakers in the 'Dawes plan era'.[10]

The State Department, by contrast, drew distinctly more cautious, and in retrospect more 'realistic', conclusions from assessing the European situation after Locarno. Kellogg and Castle, who offered the most piercing assessments, recognised quite clearly that Locarno had not yet solved either the Franco-

---

[8] Hoover to Hughes, 20 November 1924, NA RG 59, 800.51/499; Cross to Allport, 12 September 1925, NA RG 151/640. Cf. Brandes (1962), pp. 174–5.

[9] Kellogg address, 20 April 1926, *FRUS 1926*, I, p. 78.

[10] Hoover memoranda, 23 September 1925ff, Hoover Papers, Commerce, box 20; Mellon to Senator Edwards, 4 February 1926, NA RG 39, box 149; Gilbert to Strong, 5 November 1925, Strong Papers, 1012.1.

German question or Europe's gravest security problems. They were aware that these problems lay not least in Germany's unsettled relations with Poland.[11] And they also perceived the threat that emanated from a still rampant nationalism that kept alive the postwar antagonism between Germany and France as well as the new east European states.[12] Though not discounting the benefits of US-induced economic stabilisation, the State Department thus reckoned that European stabilisation would at best remain a more drawn-out process. At worst, gradual, businesslike reconciliation could face serious obstacles or even founder, particularly if France or Germany abandoned their Locarno policies under domestic pressure.

Kellogg and Castle thus concluded that Europe's consolidation would be far more difficult to sustain than Hoover anticipated. For this very reason, however, both reckoned that while it was in America's interest to promote further changes, and to press France to allow them, Washington had an even more pronounced interest in avoiding embroilment in European quarrels. A core State Department rationale remained to eschew all French efforts to block further alterations of the *status quo* – politically, financially or concerning disarmament. At the same time, though, Kellogg shied away from any confrontations with Congress to expand Washington's official engagement for peaceful change. In sum, then, at the dawn of what Europeans called the 'Locarno period' no leading US policymaker advocated more ambitious stabilisation policies in Europe. Some key financiers, notably Young and Parker Gilbert, came to assume different positions, especially demanding more political safeguards for the Dawes regime. Yet they lacked the leverage to alter US policy.[13]

More fundamentally, Republican attitudes reflected the reality that America was indeed the only power in the Euro-Atlantic system after World War I that could afford to steer clear of all strategic commitments in Europe, both because of its high degree of self-sufficiency and because of its favourable geo-political position. Seemingly without neglecting any even long-term threat to US national security, Washington could continue a strategic policy of selective engagement, notably through naval control regimes. Where US interests were not directly affected, it could largely persevere with a 'policy of the free hand'. And this was definitely what America's Republican elites thought in the mid-1920s.[14]

---

[11] Grew to Herrick, 20 April 1926, *FRUS 1926*, I, p. 78; Castle Diary, 19 March 1926, vol. 8, p. 51.

[12] Castle Diary, 29 January 1927, vol. 10, pp. 34–5. MID Reports, 'Intelligence Summary', 21 August – 3 September 1926, 13–21 September 1926, Records of the Military Intelligence Division, NA RG 165. Cf. Leffler (1979), pp. 164–5.

[13] Young to Hoover, 25 January 1926, Young Papers, I-73; Hoover to Gilbert, 5 August 1925, Hoover Papers, Commerce, Gilbert file.

[14] Kellogg speech, 14 December 1925, Kellogg Papers; Castle Diary, 29 January 1927, vol. 10, pp. 34–5.

In a speech on 20 April 1926, Kellogg underlined that Americans had to 'recognise the peculiarly fortunate situation' of their country. With its 'geographic isolation from those areas of the world where conflicting territorial or political issues have led to the maintenance of large standing armies', the United States had been able to reduce its land forces to a 'regular army of about 118,000' after the war. And after Locarno any German threat to the international order, which had already been deemed small after Versailles, appeared distinctly remote. Even if the Franco-German reconciliation process were to unravel, this still was unlikely to affect American security even in the more distant future. It was particularly distant as long as American – and British – naval superiority remained overwhelming. Thus the assessment of both the State and the War Departments in 1926.[15]

Against this background, rather than formulate a coherent *political* strategy to sustain Europe's pacification, the administration followed Hoover's lead. During Coolidge's second term, it restricted itself to the pursuit of three more narrowly defined priorities. Paramount remained the aim to bolster America's financial expansion hand in hand with the Dawes regime and, more broadly, Europe's Progressive reconstruction. Yet, as US financial interests commanded a continued separation of war-debt, reparations and foreign-loan issues, the administration did not develop an integrated policy – one addressing the *de facto* hardly separable requirements of French and German stabilisation. Re-asserting Hooverian ground-rules of maximal governmental restraint, Washington came to pursue two distinct, essentially bilateral, approaches towards France and Germany. This did not quite amount to the enforcement of crude *divide et impera* strategies. But it tended to keep the Europeans divided and control in American hands.

Vis-à-vis Paris, Washington stepped up its pressure for the conclusion, and ratification, of a war-debt settlement, largely on what the creditor considered 'lenient' US terms. This outweighed all other concerns after drawn-out negotiations between Mellon and Caillaux had remained fruitless in 1925. Not least, it also remained the precondition for reopening France for American capital. As the interests of US taxpayers were directly at stake, the administration and Congress assumed commanding roles through the powerful War Debt Commission, which Treasury Secretary Mellon headed. At the same time, Mellon and Hoover pushed for French austerity programmes to balance the budget and the franc, all to enable the debtor to meet its obligations without sinking further into financial *malaise*.[16]

---

[15] Grew to Herrick, 20 April 1926, *FRUS 1926*, I, p. 78; Kellogg to Davies, 4 January 1926, Kellogg Papers.

[16] Mellon to Olney, 26 August 1925, NA RG 39, box 220; Hoover memoranda, 23 September – 1 October 1925, Hoover Papers, Commerce, box 20; Commerce Department, *Annual Report*, 1925, pp. 31ff. Cf. Brandes (1962), pp. 170–80.

Towards Germany, the central US priority remained to see to the unhampered operation of the Dawes regime and to control the terms and timing of its eventual revision. No less a predominant concern remained a 'productive' flow of private loans. At the same time, however, the administration still adamantly refuted calls by Parker Gilbert, private US lenders and the German government to become an official underwriter of these processes. Instead, it left it to US financiers to ensure that their loans were 'safe' and extended for 'productive purposes'. And it left the Dawes plan's operation essentially in the hands of the reparations agent, who from the autumn of 1925 came to deplore what he saw as Washington's shirking of responsibility.[17] While retaining discretion to make US power felt whenever necessary, the administration desired to avoid political liabilities at all cost.

Distinctly less vigorous, yet not entirely passive was the Republican attempt to encourage Europeans to pursue further peaceful accommodation of their postwar disputes. Demanding more change but ruling out any direct US initiatives to further it remained the hallmark of US policy. The Coolidge administration's final priority after Locarno was the promotion of both naval and land disarmament. For domestic reasons as much as for reasons of ideological principle, this became the one area of security politics in which Washington brought its financial weight more directly to bear on the European situation. Yet the preference for bilateralism also extended to this field – and Anglo-American relations. Vis-à-vis Paris, Washington pressed for arms reduction on land. Vis-à-vis London, the central concern became extending the Washington naval system of 1922. Ultimately, however, the Republican case for limiting armaments remained half-hearted without a concerted security policy.

Abdication of responsibility? The 'uncontrolled revitalisation' of Germany

By the end of 1925, Hoover deemed the European situation riper than ever for a systematic application of Progressive methods to buttress peace along with the 'Old World's' modernisation. The commerce secretary argued with renewed vigour that America's mission was to expand a liberal-capitalist world order. All political impediments to this process, and particularly all French treaty prerogatives still barring Germany's inclusion within the order he envisaged, now had to be removed. In the eyes of Hoover and most Republican decision-makers, the continued revitalisation of Germany as an economic great power seemed not inimical but indeed conducive to Europe's further consolidation. Even more importantly, it seemed compatible with a further expansion of America's financial pre-eminence.[18]

---

[17] Gilbert to Strong, 5 November 1925, Strong Papers, 1012.1. Cf. McNeil (1986), pp. 90–1.
[18] Cf. Link (1970), pp. 344, 620ff.

Reinforcing such notions was the perception that German elites seemed willing to bear considerable burdens to anchor their country to a western community of interests. As noted, in contrast to Hughes, Hoover had all along considered the Dawes settlement as a success of 'pure' economic diplomacy. And he continued to champion it as an exemplary approach to settle Europe's quarrels, not through political compromises, but by economic means.[19] Now that a modicum of European stability had been secured, the stage seemed set for redoubling the activities of those best qualified to deepen it: US financiers and businessmen. They could expand capital export while also creating efficient transnational networks to reform ossified economic, and political, structures in Europe. The role of the Republican administration, and that of European governments, was to be maximally circumscribed. In Hoover's judgement, this 'method' also avoided any impression of Washington formally imposing its will on the European countries. Private financiers could operate behind the political scenes on which public attention focused.[20]

The commerce secretary identified two central areas where such operations were most urgently needed: currency stabilisation and general economic reform. The former was to be fostered through central bank co-operation, overseen by FRBNY Governor Strong. The main aim here was to anchor Britain and other European economies to a US-dominated gold-standard system. Hoover considered the collaboration between central banks and a concomitant reduction of undue governmental influence essential for an unhampered development of the global financial order. Ideally, all relations between economies and currencies on both sides of the Atlantic (and beyond) had to be self-regulated.[21] In January 1925, Hoover had thus backed what he deemed successful efforts by Mellon and Strong to hasten Britain's return to the gold standard. In his view, Strong's co-operation with Norman, and their previous successes in mastering Germany's inflation, could also serve as a model for stabilising the franc. Naturally, this tallied with Strong's own agenda. The FRBNY governor continued to see joint central bank strategies for stabilising currencies as a prerequisite for revitalising world trade, because they ended monetary fluctuations and misguided governmental interventions, particularly in France.[22]

For his part, Hoover used his influence to make commercial policy the unchallenged centrepiece of American foreign policy, also vis-à-vis Europe. To this end, he built on his successful efforts in the Commerce Department to

---

[19] Commerce Department, *Annual Report*, 1924, p. 7.
[20] Hoover to Harrison, 28 August 1925, NA RG 59 862.51.
[21] Commerce Department, *Annual Report*, 1925, pp. 35ff, 1926, p. 50. Cf. Leffler (1981), pp. 156–7.
[22] Strong reports to the Treasury and Commerce Departments on talks with the heads of the British, French and German central banks in 1925 and 1926, Strong Papers, 1000.5/6/7/8/9. Cf. Clarke (1967), p. 72.

develop new 'strategic plans for expanding our foreign trade with all nations'. That governmental policies were critical for the 'expansion of foreign trade' remained a cornerstone of Hoover's philosophy. Yet nor did he alter his conviction that, due to its large domestic base, the United States was less dependent on global trade than Europe. If necessary, it could 'survive as a nation' without it, albeit 'on lower living standards'. Fundamentally, Hoover held that 'every nation gains by the prosperity of another', and America thus had an interest in raising the prosperity of its trading partners. But he also argued that the government had a legitimate right to use tariffs to protect domestic industries and agriculture.[23]

At the same time, the commerce secretary still demanded that other countries reduce tariffs and other trade barriers. With particular vigour, he continued to attack Franco-German bids to forge cartels, especially steel, coal and pot-ash cartels. In Hoover's view, then, protective tariffs at home and open-door expansion abroad were 'not inconsistent'.[24] He thus rebuked criticisms of Republican tariff policy, as enshrined in the Fordney–McCumber Act of 1921. Democrats who opposed this policy argued that by blocking European exports to the US market, the administration and Congress effectively reduced their debtors' ability to pay their obligations. This was a position shared by Young, who in January 1926 told Hoover about his growing concerns. But Hoover argued that adequate protective tariffs actually benefited European exporters because they strengthened US purchasing power for their goods. According to the Commerce Department, despite US tariffs the exports of Europe's five leading economies to the United States had actually risen by 75 per cent between 1920 and 1928, compared with the export levels of 1913.[25]

More generally, Hoover sought to place the government's relations with business on what he called an entirely 'new basis' of 'organised co-operation'. The 'trained specialists' who worked for the administration were to collaborate with 'committees of business men' to promote reforms. Hoover was convinced that this 'method' could also be applied to set European states on a course of Progressive reorganisation. And the best way to achieve this was to use America's financial leverage to press governments in Paris and Berlin to implement US-style reforms while consolidating their budgets. In the French case, this had to be accompanied by a drastic reduction of wasteful spending on armaments. Economic interests and necessity would induce European elites to settle their political differences. Rising prosperity would bolster moderate

[23] Hoover address, 15 October 1928, Hoover Papers, Commerce, 1928; Hoover (1926).

[24] Commerce Department, *Annual Report*, 1926, pp. 34–7; Hoover address, 15 October 1928, Hoover Papers, Commerce, 1928. See also Chang (2002).

[25] Hoover address, 15 October 1928, Hoover Papers, Commerce, 1928; Young to Hoover, 25 January 1926, Young Papers, I-73; Commerce Department, *Commerce Yearbook* (Washington, 1921–9). Cf. Leffler (1981), pp. 165–6.

centre governments and help marginalise extremist and nationalist forces. This was not only Hoover's agenda but also one that his colleague Mellon espoused.[26] It will have to be examined how far the Republican administration's foreign economic policy, (double-)standards on tariffs and unwillingness to underpin Europe's reconstruction politically in fact undermined the *Pax Americana* it desired.[27]

What further constrained US *policy* was that from late 1925 Kellogg largely adopted Hoover's economic definition of its priorities. He did so out of conviction yet also to cater to Republican interests. In December 1925, the secretary of state declared that, following the achievements of London and Locarno, Washington could hence concentrate on lending 'assistance in the economic restoration of the world'. This mainly applied to Europe. While also striving to 'minimise international friction' as the 'Department of Peace', the State Department thus focused on 'commercial treaties, foreign tariff matters, trade discriminations and restriction questions of the open door'. Also under the 'heading of financial questions' fell 'matters relating to reparations, war debts and foreign loans'.[28]

Perhaps the gravest consequences for the system of London and Locarno spelled a further facet marking the entrenchment of Republican aloofness. In the autumn of 1925, the administration confirmed that neither the Dawes regime nor the flow of private US loans to Germany that fuelled it would be regulated, controlled or fortified through political bail-out guarantees. Not only Hoover remained confident that all of these functions could essentially best be overseen by financial experts, private investors and, if necessary, the German government. Critical, though, remained the role of Parker Gilbert, the reparations agent.[29] One effect of Locarno was undoubtedly that it removed many political hindrances that had still deterred US investors during the first year of the Dawes plan. While J.P. Morgan & Co. upheld its *de facto* loan boycott, this led to yet another upsurge in the flow of private short-term loans from the autumn of 1925. Overall US lending to Europe, which centred on these credits, surged from $527 million in 1924 to $629 in 1925.[30] Not only among US bankers but also among Republican decisionmakers, this raised concerns about the dangers of excessive capital export.

---

[26] Hoover address, 15 October 1928; Hoover memorandum, 23 September 1925, Hoover Papers, Commerce, 1928.

[27] See the epilogue.

[28] Kellogg speech, 14 December 1925, Kellogg Papers; Kellogg (1928a), p. 6.

[29] Commerce Department, *Annual Report*, 1924, pp. 7–8; Hoover to Gilbert, 5 August 1925, Hoover Papers, Commerce, Gilbert file.

[30] Lamont statement, minutes of the Senate investigating committee, 1931, in *Senate Committee on Finance: Hearings on the Sale of Foreign Bonds etc.* (Washington DC, 1932), p. 32. Cf. McNeil (1986), pp. 82–133; Kindleberger (1973), pp. 39–41.

Both the State and Commerce Departments had first been alerted by disconcerting reports of Ambassador Schurman, his commercial attaché Charles Herring and Parker Gilbert himself.[31] The common anxiety expressed in all of their reports was that US loans, especially those extended to German municipalities, were not secure if put to 'unproductive' uses such as politically motivated spending on unemployment assistance. If left unattended, Germany's structural economic problems, in American eyes chiefly due to the fact that the country maintained an excessive welfare state, which caused chronic budget deficits, might eventually provoke a transfer crisis. And such a crisis could have dangerous repercussions for US investors. As early as September 1925, Schurman had thus strongly recommended that Kellogg 'discourage the further placing of German municipal loans in America'. In subsequent exchanges, Parker Gilbert argued forcefully that the administration should assume responsibility. Above all, it was to use its authority to ensure that American loans were 'productive' and, if necessary, also guarantee them.[32]

Following Herring's analysis, the Commerce Department concluded correctly that the German government was interested in expanding America's financial involvement in order to draw Washington to its side once a 'final' reparations settlement was approached. Yet this was deemed not so much a sinister Germany ploy as a natural consequence of the world creditor's growing engagement.[33] It was another eventuality that struck Republican decision-makers as far more problematic. Hoover, Mellon and Kellogg feared that misplaced private loans could eventually affect reparations transfers under the Dawes regime. In the event of a crisis, German default could provoke an unwelcome clash of public and private interests – pitting those of the US government against those of Wall Street. From Washington's standpoint, the first concern was to ensure that Germany continued its payments to France and Britain so that they could service their obligations to America. This had to take clear precedence over the servicing of private loans.

Much to Parker Gilbert's dismay, however, the administration was no more prepared now than in 1924 to make any commitments involving it in the regulation of loans.[34] More importantly still, it refused to support any mechanisms apt to master a transfer crisis – or to prevent such a crisis in the first

---

[31] Schurman to State Department, 15 and 23 September 1925, *FRUS 1925*, II, pp. 172–5; 12 February and 5 June 1926, *FRUS 1926*, II, pp. 202–3; A. Young memorandum, 2 April 1925, NA RG 59 800.51/509 1/2; State Department to Hoover, 19 October 1925, Commerce Official, Foreign Loans, Hoover Papers.

[32] Schurman to Kellogg, 15 September 1925, *FRUS 1925*, II, p. 174; Gilbert to Strong, 5 November 1925, Strong Papers, 1012.1.

[33] Hoover to Kellogg, 8 October 1925, NA RG 59 862.51. Cf. McNeil (1986), p. 93.

[34] Kellogg to Mellon, 20 October 1925, NA RG 59 800.51/518; A. Young memorandum, 2 April 1925, NA RG59 800.51/509 1/2; Gilbert to Strong, 5 November 1925, Strong Papers, 1012.1.

place. This attitude would still be adopted by the Hoover administration during the Young plan negotiations of 1929. Undoubtedly, it nipped in the bud any tangible efforts in the latter 1920s to consolidate the reparations regime and, more broadly, Europe's financial stabilisation.[35]

In principle, it was actually Hoover who was most inclined to envisage a more active, if strictly limited role for the administration in restricting the capital flow to Germany. Yet he, too, soon came to back the official line, opposing any governmental guarantees. The commerce secretary still considered the Dawes plan the ideal instrument allowing the administration to pursue its stabilisation objectives while avoiding unwelcome liabilities.[36] Ultimately, he shared Kellogg's – and Mellon's – abiding fear that the extension of any guarantees threatened to manoeuvre Washington into a position where, should a crisis occur, it would be obliged not only to bail out American investors. In the final consequence, it would also have to rescue the Dawes regime itself and collect Anglo-French debts directly from Germany. This, however, could only be done at the expense of the US taxpayer, and Republican voter; and it would spark major confrontations with Congress.[37]

Essentially, instead of placing the Dawes regime on more solid foundations, Washington desired first the German government and the reparations agent, then the investors themselves, to assume responsibility. The utmost adjustment Washington made took the form of warnings issued by Kellogg to US bankers from October 1925. He essentially exhorted them only to place loans that would be used for 'productive' purposes and 'improve, directly or indirectly, the economic conditions in Germany', thus aiding it 'in meeting its financial obligations' under the Dawes plan.[38] This remained the State Department's formula in response to all bankers' queries, such as that by Harris, Forbes & Company, which contemplated a loan to the city of Duisburg in November 1925.[39] Kellogg's course was also influenced by Strong's adamant opposition to governmental regulations in the field of loan control or indeed the banking sector at large. Strong eventually came to co-operate with Hjalmar Schacht in pressing the German government to extend its control over foreign

[35] See chapters 25 and 26.
[36] Hoover to Harrison, 28 August 1925, NA RG 59 862.51; Hoover to Gilbert, 5 August 1925, Hoover Papers, Commerce, box 'Gilbert'. Cf. Leffler (1981), p. 159.
[37] Hoover to Mellon, 6 November 1925; Mellon to Kellogg and Hoover, 3 November 1925, NA RG 39, box 85, file G743.2; Hoover to Robinson, 23 October 1925, Commerce Official, Foreign Loans, Hoover Papers; Kellogg to Mellon, 20 November 1925, FRUS 1925, II, pp. 184–5.
[38] Kellogg to Schurman, 17 October 1925; Kellogg to Mellon, 20 November 1925, FRUS 1925, II, pp. 177–8, 184–5; Hoover to Hughes, 29 April 1922, NA RG 59, 800.51/316; Hoover (1952b), pp. 13–14.
[39] Harrison to Harris, Forbes & Company, 21 November 1925, FRUS 1925, II, pp. 186–7.

borrowing.[40] But, in contrast to Washington, neither the German authorities nor Parker Gilbert were capable of exerting such control.

As has been pointed out, the net-effect of Washington's aloofness was that in the latter 1920s the economic revitalisation of Germany, and Europe, was largely left in the hands of those – mainly private US investors – whose primary interest had to be the maximisation of profits. They could not provide what was imperative: a robust political framework underpinning more durable stability, both in the financial and in the political realm.[41] Left largely to his own devices, and operating as international financier rather than US official, Parker Gilbert sought to make the most of his limited room to manoeuvre to compensate for this. For the time being, though, he could only continue to draw attention to disconcerting developments. From 1927, the reparations agent indeed came to act as the sole 'enforcer of the Dawes Plan' and fiscal responsibility in Berlin.[42]

Limited prospects – US debt policy and the Mellon–Bérenger agreement

By contrast, all leading Republican policymakers supported a very active governmental role in setting the terms of US war-debt policy. Here, they considered an effective co-operation with Congress through the instrument of the War Debt Commission indispensable.[43] As head of the commission, Mellon took charge in reviving the negotiations to settle French debts, left in disarray following Caillaux's inconclusive mission to Washington in 1925. And it was Mellon who finally brought them to a conclusion with Ambassador Bérenger in April 1926.

Those assembled in the War Debt Commission shared the view that, despite its current financial difficulties France very much had the potential to prosper and repay debts if only its leaders set the right priorities. They had to espouse stringent fiscal policies; and they had to limit 'unproductive' military spending. After Locarno, not only the administration but also a majority in Congress came to view France's remaining security concerns as highly exaggerated – or even as a pretext for gaining more lenient debt terms. Resurfacing here was the characteristic American underestimation of Europe's underlying security problems.[44] No Republican policymaker thus saw convincing reasons for

---

[40] Strong to Gilbert, 29 October and 7 November 1925, Strong Papers, 1012.1.
[41] McNeil's verdict can indeed be confirmed. See McNeil (1986), p. 279.
[42] Finlayson report, 12 February 1927, FO 371/12140; *Report of the Agent General*, 10 June 1927, pp. 47–51.
[43] For Hoover's harsher yet still comparatively lenient line see his numerous memoranda, 23 September 1925 – 1 October 1925, Hoover Papers, Commerce, box 20.
[44] Cf. Leffler (1979), pp. 133–4.

significantly reducing, let alone cancelling French obligations. And by early 1926 there was mounting pressure on Paris not to postpone a settlement any further. Nor did Washington countenance any further attempts to link debts with reparations, as again made by France's new finance minister Raoul Peret in March.[45] Different views emerged, however, over the question of what kind of debt agreement would best ensure maximal payments and foster the desired French reforms at the same time. Both Mellon and Strong consistently favoured exploring the possibility of a lenient and permanent settlement, which would not stifle the French government's efforts. But Hoover long insisted on a harsher and only preliminary five-year settlement, which would essentially allow Washington to retain vis-à-vis Paris the levers of French indebtedness and the US loan embargo.[46]

From early on, Hoover had advocated an expert-driven approach that based US demands not on excessive Congressional claims but a capacity-to-pay formula not unlike that of the Dawes plan.[47] But ultimately he never departed from his core premise that America should not be left in a situation of having to 'fund' overly generous debt settlements and thus, *de facto*, European recovery. Further tax cuts at home, which he advocated, must not be jeopardised by dealing with the fall-out of a war that the Europeans had brought upon themselves and the world. During the final round of debt negotiations in 1926, Hoover did not hesitate to abandon his 'depoliticisation' maxims, seeking to use economic means to further political ends. He was adamant that America's power as creditor should be used to force Paris into concessions on disarmament. He went much further than Mellon in contending that Paris could consolidate French finances and serve its obligations as soon as French elites departed from fiscal irresponsibility and power politics, be it towards Germany or in what was chastised as hapless colonial pursuits in Morocco.[48]

Significantly, the view that France hardly deserved American generosity had powerful adherents in the Senate, particularly Borah and the protectionist Republican senator Smoot. They were also wary of bankers' attempts to abolish allied debts at the expense of their constituents to further their own loan interests. Borah's influence was especially dreaded by Coolidge, who constantly

[45] Kellogg to Herrick, 5 May 1925, *FRUS 1925*, II, p. 151; Kellogg to Whitehouse, 31 March 1926, *FRUS 1926*, II, p. 91.
[46] Mellon to Olney, 26 August 1925, NA RG 39, box 220; Strong memorandum, 8 May 1926, Strong Papers, 1000.7; Hoover memoranda, 30 September and 1 October 1925, Hoover Papers, Commerce, box 20.
[47] Hoover to Mellon, 6 January 1923, Hoover to Coffman, 27 April 1926, Hoover Papers, Commerce, Foreign Debts.
[48] Hoover, 'The French Debt', 30 September 1925, Hoover Papers, Commerce, Debts – France; Hoover memorandum, 23 September 1925, Hoover Papers, Commerce, box 20.

sought to deflect Congressional opposition to his own tax-reduction agenda.[49] Only a few Democrats like Senator Newton Baker advocated debt cancellation. Most, above all conservative southern Democrats, were as opposed to it as the Republican majority.

Hoover's influence and Congressional constraints indeed limited the scope for leniency vis-à-vis France. Yet they did not prevent Mellon from eventually gaining ground with his more constructive agenda. It hinged on the argument that it was more profitable for the American creditor to ensure that the French debtor remained 'solvent' than to force France into 'bankruptcy'. More unequivocally than Hoover, the Treasury secretary maintained that US prosperity depended on 'Europe as a customer' to such an extent that acceptable debt accords with France, 'essential' for European stabilisation, mattered as much to America as to Europe.[50] As the financial situation in France still deteriorated while a growing budget surplus even allowed his administration to reduce the national debt, Coolidge finally backed Mellon's line in early 1926. On these premises, yet only following drawn-out negotiations, the rather lenient Mellon–Bérenger agreement was finally signed on 29 April. It comprised a payment schedule covering sixty-two years in which the total French debt of $4,025,000,000 was to be repaid. Like the Dawes plan, the settlement considered France's capacity to pay, reducing the first five annuities.[51]

But the ratification of the agreement soon had to be postponed – with major repercussions for transatlantic and Franco-German relations. In view of France's unabated *malaise* and what Ambassador Herrick called a parliamentary opposition 'assuming formidable proportions' by the summer, Briand deemed it impossible to win a majority for the settlement in the *Chambre*.[52] Thus, deadlock ensued, even though Mellon and Kellogg took pains to stress that France had received a 'generous treatment'.[53] The French government had hoped that signing the agreement would be a vital step towards regaining access to the American financial market. And both Strong and the partners of Morgan & Co. aspired to make it the starting-point for renewed consolidation efforts. In mid-May, Leffingwell even proposed a 'financial Locarno' not only for France but also for Belgium and Italy,

---

[49] See Borah's letters in the autumn of 1925, Borah Papers, box 251, 264; Castle to Houghton, 12 November 1925, Castle Papers, box 2.

[50] Mellon to senator Edwards, 4 February 1926, NA RG 39, box 149.

[51] Yet the settlement did not include the safeguard clause that France had sought. See Kellogg to Herrick, 29 April 1926 Kellogg to Whitehouse, 31 March 1926, Whitehouse to Kellogg, 1 April 1926, *FRUS 1926*, I, pp. 91–2.

[52] Herrick to Kellogg, 8 June 1926, *FRUS 1926*, II, pp. 95–6; Kellogg to Herrick, 2 June 1926, *FRUS 1926*, I, p. 93; Mellon to Kellogg, 12 June 1926, NA RG 39, box 61; Castle to Houghton, 12 May 1926, Castle Papers, box 2.

[53] Not only Kellogg contrasted the American terms with what he considered the more severe Franco-British debt settlement. See Kellogg to Herrick, 7 June 1926, *FRUS 1926*, II, p. 97.

supported by US high finance and centring on a 'thorough plan of stability' for the three currencies, above all the franc. If Paris implemented a 'comprehensive plan', including debt-settlement ratification, then Morgan & Co. envisaged lending $100 million. Yet Washington had different priorities. It hence became a central premise of the administration's policy that the ratification of the Mellon–Bérenger agreement constituted a 'prerequisite' to any change in its stance on loan authorisation. As Lamont told Peret, nothing could be done before that had been accomplished. In fact, this fixed condition, and cardinal political obstacle, would only be removed in early 1928, roughly a year before the French parliament finally endorsed the debt settlement. But as US financiers were reluctant to invest in France anyway, the lifting of the loan embargo had no tangible impact.[54]

The encouragement of further peaceful change – but not its political pursuit

It is essential to understand, then, to what a remarkable degree the pursuit of financial interests and Hooverian economic diplomacy again became the chief determinants of US stabilisation policy in Europe – from 1926 all the way through to 1929, and beyond. This was a marked departure from the approach adopted after the Ruhr crisis when America's financial power had been used to spur political settlements in Europe. Now that the Franco-German crisis appeared fundamentally settled, the rationale of separating debt, loan, trade and reparations questions came to be strictly enforced. This took precedence over any wider political or security considerations. In particular, it largely eclipsed the State Department's far less concrete agenda of promoting further Franco-German accommodation as well as wider political changes in Europe, and of exploring avenues of co-operation with Britain to implement this agenda.

Shortly after the conclusion of Locarno pact, Kellogg publicly affirmed on 14 December 1925 that he placed 'as much store upon the spirit of Locarno as upon the treaties of Locarno'. He reassured the Europeans that Washington would continue to support their efforts to overcome 'the old balance of power sustained by alliances' through 'a regional pact'. In principle, the secretary of state held that it was also in America's interest to persevere with efforts to modify the untenable *status quo* of 1919 further. To his domestic audience, he outlined a process that led France to abandon all further attempts at treaty enforcement while reinforcing Germany's ties with the former Allies – financially through US loans, trade and the Dawes regime, politically through the European pact.[55]

---

[54] Strong to Harrison, 15 May 1926, Strong Papers, 1000.7; Kellogg to Herrick, 7 June 1926, *FRUS 1926*, II, p. 97; Strong to Mellon, 1 August 1926, Strong Papers, 1000.7.

[55] Kellogg speech, 14 December 1925, Kellogg Papers; Kellogg address, 20 April 1926, *FRUS 1926*, I, p. 78.

Initially, Kellogg seemed to see the potential for more far-reaching changes in Europe, a turning-away from power politics for the sake of regional *quid pro quo* agreements. In private, however, he soon came to share Castle's more sceptical assessment, viewing Locarno as less than a breakthrough on the road to durable stability. By April 1926, amidst burgeoning disputes over Germany's League entry, the secretary had based the department's policies on a distinctly sober outlook. He expected Franco–German conciliation to remain a long and burdensome process with hardly a definite resolution in sight. Kellogg recognised the intractability of what still divided Paris and Berlin, chiefly the Rhineland question, yet also the high level of insecurity and nationalism still pervasive on both sides.[56]

Yet it was precisely because of these uncertainties that Kellogg insisted all the more on a course of calculated detachment and highly selective involvement. Even more than before Locarno, Washington's weight was only to be used informally and at the administration's discretion. In the realm of security, the government's sole, limited focus was to be on disarmament. At the same time, Kellogg agreed with Hoover that progress in Franco–German *détente* must not be achieved at the expense of US commercial interests. Washington would not accept any bilateral agreements that might jeopardise the Dawes regime.[57] Essentially, unless directly challenged to pursue causes that influential US interest-groups supported as well – such as the outlawry of war in 1927 – Kellogg never left the path of aloofness.[58] He stayed on it because of what he still regarded as venerable traditions and enduring US interests. But he also heeded ever more scrupulously what to him seemed the unchangeable checks of Congressional isolationism. Both mattered more in this respect than any other global problems that could potentially deflect America's attention from Europe. For neither the Chinese civil war nor threats to US oil interests in Mexico and Nicaragua turned into absorbing crises in the latter 1920s, at least in the State Department's perception.[59]

By the spring of 1926, Castle had arrived at an even less optimistic assessment of how far Europeans had travelled since 1923 and what could be expected from the Locarno pact. His scepticism derived less from his analysis of the towering obstacles to long-term stability still to be mastered. It derived more from what he deemed the inability of European leaders on all sides to

---

[56] Grew to Herrick, 20 April 1926, *FRUS 1926*, I, p. 78; Castle Diary, 22–3 March 1926, vol. 8, pp. 52–4.

[57] Kellogg to Davies, 4 January 1926, Kellogg Papers, roll 17; Kellogg memorandum, 22 January 1926, *FRUS 1926*, I, pp. 210–11.

[58] See chapter 24.

[59] Kellogg speech, 14 December 1925, Kellogg Papers; Castle Diary, 24 December 1926, vol. 10, p. 310. See the US records on comparatively tranquil relations with Latin America and China in *FRUS 1926*, I – *FRUS 1929*, II.

undergo genuine changes in mentality. Principally for this reason, Castle backed Kellogg's policy of detachment unequivocally, and in fact reinforced it. Interestingly, however, he rather pointed to Briand and Chamberlain than to Stresemann when criticising Europe's deplorable penchant for 'old diplomacy'. His sceptical outlook hardened through the deepening French crisis, which he considered more disconcerting than the volatility of the German situation. On 12 April, Castle noted that the Briand government would likely be followed by a more radical alternative, an 'attempt at fascism, with a dictator . . . perhaps communism'.[60]

Castle thus warned against premature US complacency. Highly critical of the way in which Britain and France had thwarted Germany's attempt to enter the League, of which more later, he on 19 March commended Ambassador Houghton's remarks to international correspondents in London. He thought it healthy 'that people should be told how things are, not fed up on "the beauties of Locarno"'. Houghton's statements had been 'like a breath of east wind blowing across the warm over-optimism of [the American public] with regard to disarmament and European peace'.[61] In a report to Coolidge, deliberately leaked to the press, Houghton had also declared that 'Europe, so far as its statesmen are concerned, has learned nothing from the war.' And he had particularly lambasted Britain and France for 'moving toward a revival of the alliance of 1815 with the tremendous difference that it cannot hope to guarantee 40 years' tranquillity in Europe'. As Coolidge was 'furious' about Houghton's remarks, Kellogg recommended that the president should publicly 'repudiate' them.[62] But Coolidge declined.

Characteristically, Kellogg's main concern was to preserve appearances and to avoid conveying the impression that Washington, disillusioned with Locarno, was preparing to move 'towards greater isolation' vis-à-vis Europe.[63] In substance, however, the secretary of state confirmed that the United States would not 'interfere in purely European questions', especially not 'questions involving regional guarantees'. Only within these limits – and while opposing all attempts at reinforcing the Versailles *status quo* – would the US government continue to co-operate 'in solving the grave problems confronting Europe'. This re-affirmation of Hughes' doctrine of 'co-operation and independence' would remain a 'settled policy' of Republican administrations until the Great Depression.[64]

---

[60] Castle Diary, 19 March, 12 April 1926, vol. 8, pp. 51, 81.
[61] Castle Diary, 19 March 1926, vol. 8, p. 51. Castle became assistant secretary on 14 January 1927.
[62] Sterling (Britain) to Kellogg, 20 March 1926, *FRUS 1926*, I, p. 60; Castle Diary, 22–3 March 1926, vol. 8, pp. 52–4.
[63] See excerpts from *Times*, 19 March 1926, *Manchester Guardian*, 20 March 1926, in Sterling to Kellogg, 20 March 1926, *FRUS 1926*, I, p. 60.
[64] Kellogg speech, 14 December 1925, Kellogg Papers.

Neither Kellogg nor Castle thus thought that Europeans were completely weary of war and that there was 'little or no danger of a flare up'. By contrast, Dawes, who in 1925 had become Coolidge's vice president, promulgated a distinctly more confident worldview, which Hoover essentially shared. In early 1927, Dawes drew an analogy between Europe's new American peace and the 'pax romana which followed a hundred years of fighting' and when although 'the state was rotten life and property outside of Rome was safe and the world was tired of war'. Castle contradicted Dawes, observing that European conditions were still 'difficult' and neither life nor property 'safe'. To make things worse, 'nationalism in the new little nations' was still 'rampant', and America had to grapple with the 'dreadful phenomenon of communism'. Castle's further conclusions capture a key problem of international order and a still constrained US hegemony after 1919: 'Rome had put the civilised world under one overlordship. We have broken it to bits [at Versailles] and erected thereby innumerable centres of unrest. And against communism we have fascism, which certainly does not add to the chances of peace.'[65]

Yet what could the United States do if its leaders were neither willing nor able to put the 'civilised world' under one 'overlordship', at least formally? As we have seen, what stewardship Washington established in the 1920s remained informal and, following Hooverian notions, mainly tended to rely on financial power, particularly after the London settlement of 1924. As US wariness of European politics persisted, stabilisation was ultimately to be achieved by the forces of economic advantage and necessity. It was to be achieved through the well-understood self-interest of all European countries in becoming part of a liberal-capitalist world order. Most US decisionmakers were confident that what was best for America would also serve Europe best. At the same time, this would allow Washington to determine the postwar system's ground-rules without having to emulate the Romans in creating a formal empire, and peace system, to which it would then have to dedicate considerable political and financial resources.[66]

Despite criticism of Chamberlain's kow-towing to Briand, the tacit assumption of American policymakers was still that Britain had to remain the political guarantor of peaceful change in Europe instead. The State Department thus saw in the maintenance of cordial Anglo-American relations a cornerstone of US policy. But its outlook was clouded by persistent suspicions that Britain was still plotting to shed its war-debt burdens in the process of a final

---

[65] Castle Diary, 29 January 1927, vol. 10, pp. 34–5.
[66] The administration was also reluctant to support other international institutions. In January 1926, the Senate endorsed a proposal to join the World Court. But to avoid antagonising Borah, who opposed any concessions to Europe in this matter, Coolidge subsequently decided not to pursue the proposal further. See *Congressional Record*, 69th Congress, 2656–7.

reparations settlement.[67] And from 1927 Anglo-American cordiality would indeed be put to the test by the rising tensions between the two maritime powers over naval arms control.[68] Nevertheless, commenting on the drawn-out dispute over US blockade claims from the war, Castle noted on 30 March 1926 that the 'main thing' was to 'keep our friendship, such as it is, with England'. Washington and London should be able 'to establish the principle that in case of dispute representatives of the two Anglo-Saxon nations should be able to get together and settle things without bitterness and without recourse to arbitrations which always leave a sting'.[69] Though a less ardent proponent of Anglo-Saxon ties, Kellogg also continued to see Britain as a power with largely parallel interests, certainly in Europe. In Castle's perception, 'beneath the appearance of things' British leaders were no less keen on preserving a privileged relationship with America.[70]

The State Department clearly acknowledged Germany's revitalisation in the wake of London and Locarno. Castle concluded on 7 September 1926 that Germany was 'certainly getting enormous strength in all but the military sense'. And an official of the US Army's Military Intelligence Division (MID) reported that the revitalised power could be likened to 'a young giant in chains'.[71] Generally, the expectation in Washington was that Germany was bound to widen its zone of influence at the expense of France. But there was no sense that this was threatening to undermine European stability.

By the spring of 1926, US policymakers regarded the domestic situation in Weimar Germany as clearly much improved since 1924 yet still fraught with uncertainties. As Ambassador Schurman's reports documented, these arose from an as yet unstable parliamentary system and a still shaky recovery. Nor were American observers oblivious of those nationalists who continued to advocate a more aggressive revisionism, notably the DNVP and militarist organisations like the *Stahlhelm*.[72] At the same time, the Commerce Department continued to deplore that Weimar's governing parties persisted with irresponsible spending to satisfy different interest-groups ranging from steel industrialists to trade unions.[73] Crucially, however, no tendencies in Germany seemed to point to developments that could prove seriously harmful to US

[67] Castle Diary, 6 and 9 November 1925, vol. 8, pp. 109–10, 113.
[68] See chapter 23.
[69] Castle wished to 'throw the blockade claims overboard' because 'morally' they had 'no standing' Castle Diary, 30 March 1926, vol. 8, pp. 64–5. Cf. McKercher (1984), pp. 34–55.
[70] Kellogg to Davies, 4 January 1926, Kellogg Papers, roll 17; Castle Diary, 22 September 1926, vol. 10, pp. 231–2.
[71] Castle Diary, 7 September 1926, vol. 10, pp. 224; MID Reports, 'Intelligence Summary', 21 August–3 September 1926, 13–21 September 1926, 30 October – 12 November 1926, Records of the MID, NA RG 165.
[72] Schurman note, 29 December 1925, NA RG 59 751.62/43.
[73] Hoover to Harrison, 28 August 1925, NA RG 59 862.51.

interests, let alone national security. As long as Germany depended on US capital, had an ever growing interest in economic exchanges with the western powers and played by the rules of the Dawes regime, a firm basis of intertwined interests seemed assured. As long as Berlin remained committed to the pacific settlement of disputes, there appeared no reason for concern. And by 1926 the Weimar coalition governments, and Stresemann in particular, were by and large seen as pursuing just such policies. Not only in Hoover's view but also in Kellogg's estimation, over time this was bound to prove advantageous to a majority of Germans, and marginalise extremists.

Such notions were overall confirmed by what Schurman cabled from Berlin, though neither Kellogg nor Castle placed too much store on what in their perception were often embellished reports from the American embassy in Berlin. The new ambassador was convinced that German leaders had turned the corner from considering war a viable option to regain a great-power status. Interestingly, and in contrast to Schurman's appraisal, a 1926 MID report noted that the 'common insecurity' still prevailing between France and Germany could have a positive effect, namely to deepen their co-operation along the lines of Locarno, even if there was still 'extreme nationalism' in both countries.[74]

Seeking to encourage Stresemann, Washington signalled to Berlin after Locarno that it was willing to support, yet not actively promote, further changes of the postwar order where German demands seemed justified. As Coolidge himself had assured Stresemann's aide Werner von Rheinbaben on 17 October 1925, there was now 'an even greater understanding' for German arguments that in consequence of the security pact a swift Rhineland evacuation and other modifications of the Versailles settlement were desirable.[75] In principle, his administration would welcome any further political changes that served to remove impediments to economic recuperation and US expansion in Europe, particularly further advances towards Franco-German *détente*.

Between 1926 and 1928, US diplomats consistently reported to the administration in Washington that a swift 'liberation' of the Rhineland remained Germany's foremost goal. Republican policymakers were in favour of this, and they also favoured an early termination of military control, chiefly to avoid further Franco-German quarrels over it.[76] The State Department endorsed such calls for change although it received continual MID reports on German transgressions of the Versailles treaty throughout the latter 1920s. They stated what was obvious for any US diplomat in Germany: that there were still

---

[74] Schurman minute, 29 December 1925, NA RG 59 751.62/43; MID Reports, 'Intelligence Summary', 21 August – 3 September 1926, Records of the MID, NA RG 165.

[75] Maltzan to Stresemann, 17 October 1925, Stresemann Papers, RM 27, no. 422.

[76] Poole (Berlin) to State Department, 2 October 1926, NA RG 59 751.62/64; Schurman to Kellogg, 11 May 1927; Grew to Schurman, 28 April 1927; Schurman to Kellogg, 15 December 1926, NA RG 59 862.20/462, 453, 405.

numerous violations of the disarmament clauses, if on a small scale. American observers also stressed that a revision of the *status quo* on Germany's eastern borders – claims for a return of the 'Polish Corridor', Danzig and Upper Silesia – remained an official, if downplayed aim of Weinar foreign policy before Stresemann. They correctly portrayed them as demands not only kept alive by the right-wing nationalist press but embraced by a majority in postwar Germany, from the Social Democrats to DNVP adherents. MID reports also suggested that Germany particularly sought economic pre-eminence, especially in central and eastern Europe.[77]

Unquestionably, US decisionmakers had sympathies for Stresemann's argument that there should be an economically 'rational' reorganisation of the 'Polish Corridor' as the current *status quo* impeded European stabilisation. But Washington lacked the interest and political will to make a settlement of the German question in its most sensitive – eastern – dimension a concrete aim of American policy. More than Hoover, Kellogg clearly had drawn negative lessons from Wilson's attempts at drastically altering the European map in 1919. In the relative calm of the latter 1920s, neither the administration nor financiers like Strong ever encouraged Berlin to entertain hopes that America would assertively promote territorial revisions, neither vis-à-vis Poland nor vis-à-vis Czechoslovakia. The scale of tensions between Berlin and Prague, and their possible ramifications for European stability, never seemed sufficiently disconcerting to warrant much US attention in the first place.[78]

Following his experiences as head of the American Relief Administration, Hoover – who sidelined Czechoslovakia – did not consider postwar Poland a viable state. As he told Castle on 14 May 1926, 'the Poles had never yet been able to govern themselves'. Like Kellogg, he thus generally saw the need for an economic consolidation of eastern Europe. But prior to 1929 the commerce secretary never seriously considered relying on diplomacy and political pressure to effect such changes. Instead, and unsurprisingly, he thought that economic stabilisation could eventually create a climate in which Germans and Poles could settle their differences.[79] It was only under the impact of the Great Depression, and the deterioration of relations with Germany it entailed, that Hoover, by then president, would come to contemplate more ambitious revisionist designs at Poland's expense. Yet they would never be executed.

The State Department held that at least in the near future the politically destabilising effect of any territorial revision would outweigh any possible

[77] MID Reports, 'Intelligence Summary', 13 – 21 September 1926, 30 October – 12 November 1926, Records of the MID, NA RG 165.
[78] Maltzan to Stresemann, 17 October 1925, Stresemann Papers, RM 27, no. 422; Castle Diary, 14 May 1926, vol. 8, pp. 113–14; Strong to Harrison, 3 August 1926, Strong Papers, 1000.7.
[79] Castle Diary, 14 May 1926, vol. 8, p. 114.

economic gains. Nor was there a keen interest in empowering German competition for east European markets.[80] Castle essentially desired to insulate Germany from Poland's even more fervent nationalism. Yet most Republican policymakers simply reckoned that even if Germany's revisionist demands were problematic they would eventually be submerged by its overriding interest in remaining an accepted partner within the nascent Euro-Atlantic 'community'.[81]

It should be noted here that, beyond non-recognition and plans to encourage business contacts, the Coolidge administration in essence had no policy to deal with Soviet Russia. Ever since the immediate Bolshevik threat had seemed contained, any serious debate about the aims and direction of such a policy had ceased. As Kellogg still maintained in 1928, it was 'both futile and unwise to enter into relations with the Soviet Government' as long as it flatly refused to accept US principles of international relations. More generally, US strategies to extend the desired European zone of liberal-capitalist stabilisation further eastwards, beyond Germany, remained rudimentary.[82]

Ever tighter reins – the Congressional constraints on US policymaking in the latter 1920s

These, then, were basic rationales determining US policy, or the lack thereof, in post-Locarno Europe. On balance, they were more formative than domestic restraints. Yet of course Republican pursuits were also still tangibly influenced by close attention to what decisionmakers saw as a groundswell of isolationist 'public opinion' in the United States of the 'New Era'. And, more than that, they continued to be shaped by the ever-present, and in fact growing, limitations that the Republican-controlled Congress enforced. Particularly the Senate insisted ever more adamantly on wielding its prerogatives vis-à-vis the administration. It was led in this largely successful endeavour by the 'irreconcilable' William Borah, who in 1925 became chairman of the influential Foreign Relations Committee.[83]

From 1926, the Senate re-affirmed what it had established ever since the debates over Versailles: clear, and in the 1920s unalterable, limits on what the administration could pursue. Hughes had operated successfully under these constraints in 1923/4. Nor had they prevented the Coolidge administration from informally backing the security pact negotiations in 1925. After Locarno,

---

[80] Cf. Costigliola (1979), pp. 85–105.

[81] Castle Diary, 17 and 29 January 1927, vol. 10, pp. 20, 34–5; Kellogg speech, 14 December 1925, Kellogg Papers.

[82] Kellogg (1928a), pp. 47–50; Castle Diary, 12 April 1926, vol. 8, pp. 79–80.

[83] Castle Diary, 20 November 1925, vol. 8, p. 125.

however, Kellogg lacked the authority to widen his freedom of action; and he saw no need to take any political risks to do so.[84] By that time, leading members of the administration held that the prevailing Congressional tides allowed them even less room to manoeuvre. For there were no longer any immediate crises calling for US involvement in Europe. Republican politicians were not quite as swayed by Congressional – and public – opinion as Chamberlain deplored in 1926.[85] For restraint in international politics corresponded with their own aims and interests. But the attention particularly Kellogg and Coolidge paid to the possible repercussions of any contemplated measure on relations with the Senate was indeed remarkable. As a rule, it far outweighed any attempts on their part to shape the foreign-policy agenda. First and foremost, the administration always had to consider the interests of the most influential senators, above all the often uncontrollable Borah.[86]

Even in the aftermath of the Locarno accords, which he had welcomed, Borah remained ever suspicious of the League and the Europeans' duplicitous attempts at embroiling America in their rivalries.[87] And he probably stood for a majority in the Senate when reverting to an even more unequivocal 'America first' isolationism in the mid-1920s. Borah insisted that the 'first and highest obligation' the administration and Congress had was 'here in America'. In his view, this obligation chiefly lay in spurring prosperity through further tax cuts and reduced governmental spending; and it lay in keeping harm from the American people by foregoing 'lethal internationalism'.[88] As will be shown, the only exception to this rule was the senator's support for the outlawry of war, one of his long-standing personal concerns. Unaltered throughout the 1920s remained Borah's conviction that, while the American public cared little for what was happening beyond US shores, Europe had become so 'decadent' that its demise was unstoppable. As he saw it, the United States could and should keep out of this inevitable process.[89]

More often than not, Congressional opinion of this kind was powerful because it constrained governmental actions in advance. Rather than face a controversy with Congress, which would then be amplified by the press, the Coolidge administration refrained from launching potentially irksome initiatives in the first place. Or it modified international commitments in order to pre-empt

---

[84] Kellogg memorandum, 22 January 1926, *FRUS 1926*, I, pp. 210–11.
[85] Austen to Ida Chamberlain, 19 June 1926, Austen Chamberlain Papers, AC 5/1/386.
[86] Castle Diary, 20 November 1925, vol. 8, p. 125; 24 December 1926, vol. 10, p. 310.
[87] Borah to Harrison, 30 March 1925, quoted after Maddox (1970), p. 168; Borah speech in St Louis, reported in the *New York Times*, 19 May 1925. Cf. McKenna (1961), pp. 217–25.
[88] See Lippmann (1925), pp. 211ff; *Chicago Tribune*, 5 April 1925.
[89] Borah to Levinson, 12 July 1927, Borah Papers; Borah speech, in the *New York Times*, 19 May 1925; Borah Senate statements, 18 December 1925, *Congressional Record*, 69th Congress. Cf. Maddox (1970), pp. 171–80.

Senate interference. This would especially mark Kellogg's counterproposals to the French war-renunciation initiative in 1927.[90] Privately, Castle maintained his criticism of the secretary of state's timidity vis-à-vis Congress.[91] But Kellogg would indeed have run into major, perhaps insurmountable, obstacles if he had desired to pursue a more active American role in Europe. As it was, though, he did not even see the need to define, let alone take on, such a role to begin with.

The Republican case for disarmament – and its limits

There was only one field where the administration actually sought to set the international security agenda: disarmament. Here, Coolidge himself sought to seize the initiative. Yet what informed American pursuits was, no less than in other foreign-policy spheres, a mixture of caution vis-à-vis commitments and far-reaching long-term aims. As for the long term, Washington mainly desired to extend naval arms control, essentially by expanding the Washington treaty system of 1922. And it pressed for sizeable cuts in all European armies, yet especially French forces, which were deemed widely oversized. Ever since pledging to promote disarmament during the 1924 presidential campaign, Coolidge espoused what he considered a popular cause to boost both his domestic standing and his tax-cut agenda.[92]

Asked to formulate a concrete policy, Kellogg and senior State Department officials like Castle and Joseph Grew adopted a cautious attitude. In view of an undiminished sense of insecurity in many European quarters, they had very low expectations of what an American call for disarmament could achieve. In a memorandum of 20 April 1926, Kellogg acknowledged that while the 'desire for further limitation of armaments is universal' there was also 'a most natural demand for security', particularly in war-ravaged Europe.[93] Prevalent within the administration, however, was the notion that reducing arms and military spending was not only beneficial to America but also in the interest of European countries, including France. As Coolidge and, most categorically, Hoover insisted, Paris was well advised after Locarno to follow the American example and set new priorities: to redirect spending from wasteful armaments to productive peacetime use. The president shared Hoover's conviction that, with economic recovery, universal disarmament would be a far more effective means of guaranteeing French security than costly military preponderance and alliances.[94]

---

[90] See chapter 24.
[91] Castle Diary, 20 November 1925, vol. 8, p. 125.
[92] Coolidge message to Congress, 8 December 1925, *FRUS 1925*, I, pp. xii–xiii.
[93] Grew to Herrick, 20 April 1926, *FRUS 1926*, I, p. 78.
[94] Hoover memorandum, 30 September and 1 October 1925, Hoover Papers, Commerce, box 20; Coolidge address, 4 January 1926, *FRUS 1926*, I, pp. x–xi.

From December 1925, the Coolidge administration stepped up its pressure to complement the Locarno pact with far-reaching disarmament agreements. Like the British Foreign Office, however, the State Department only prepared a more concrete programme when faced with the League's invitation to join the Preparatory Disarmament Commission in Geneva. And Kellogg soon advised Coolidge to limit the scope of any American initiative. Although the secretary of state had originally supported holding a naval conference in Washington, which had been Coolidge's intention since 1924, he in January advised the president against pursuing this plan. Essentially, Kellogg – like Castle – feared that such a conference might well miscarry, not least on account of emerging Anglo-American differences over how to widen the Washington system. A critical issue for Anglo-American relations became the 'cruiser question' – the problem of agreeing on the precise criteria for regulating and curbing the construction of smaller battleships, which for different reasons both sides deemed vital for their naval defence.[95]

Coolidge finally followed the State Department's advice that his administration should rather participate in the non-binding negotiations of the League's Preparatory Commission.[96] This became, and limited, US disarmament policy. The 'Coolidge conference' on naval disarmament would eventually convene in Geneva, but only in June 1927, and by that time a deadlock in the cruiser question had been reached.[97]

In a message to Congress of 4 January 1926, Coolidge called disarmament the 'natural corollary' to the Locarno agreements, proposing to send a US delegation to Geneva to advance 'a work that was so successfully begun at the Washington conference'. Congress supported this mission, which was then led by the American ambassador in Switzerland, Hugh Gibson.[98] Also in early January, Kellogg outlined what would become the guiding principles of US disarmament policy for the remainder of the 1920s. In a letter to Secretary of War Dwight Davies, he asserted, first, that all negotiations should be limited to 'visible armament', i.e. not take into account a country's resource potential; and second, that land and naval disarmament should be kept separate. Kellogg also noted that, as the limitation of land forces principally concerned Europe, efforts to boost it 'should be confined to this region'.[99]

Clearly, despite Coolidge's exhortations vis-à-vis Paris, the United States had relatively little stake in land disarmament, which was the key issue for the European powers. Kellogg advised Gibson that, as a maritime power, America's

---

[95] Kellogg to Davies, 4 January 1926, Kellogg Papers, roll 17. Cf. McKercher (1984), pp. 55ff.

[96] Castle Diary, 6 November 1925, vol. 8, pp. 108–9.

[97] See chapter 23.

[98] Coolidge address, 4 January 1926, *FRUS 1926*, I, p. xii; *ibid.*, pp. 42–4, 51–6, 81–120.

[99] Kellogg to Davies, 4 January 1926, Kellogg Papers, roll 17.

interest was comparatively 'academic'.[100] What remained critical was the naval sphere. Here, Washington's main aim was to forestall renewed competition with Britain yet also the other principal naval powers – France, Italy and Japan – on the level of smaller, cruiser-class ships. Essentially, the State Department hoped to achieve this by broadening the Washington five-power regime. Following in Hughes' footsteps, Kellogg saw this regime as the greatest successes of Republican postwar policy and a model for regional arms reductions in Europe.[101] In his judgement, any attempt to link or mix up issues of land and naval disarmament 'would only lead to confusion and trading and render almost certain failure in both'. The State Department thus rejected more comprehensive schemes for arms reduction as envisaged by the League.[102]

Overall, US policy thus offered little scope, and from Kellogg's perspective there were indeed only limited prospects, for establishing effective disarmament regimes in Europe. The crux was that while Kellogg acknowledged that progress on this issue was hardly conceivable without further fortifying Europe's nascent security system, Washington was not prepared to underpin any measures that could strengthen this system. Confidentially, Kellogg assured War Secretary Davies that the administration would not be willing to 'buy' advances on disarmament with any new political or military guarantees. Nor would it become involved in international mechanisms to supervise arms control. Kellogg noted that the concerned powers essentially had to rely on 'the good faith of nations in carrying out their treaties'.[103]

Beyond this, only Hoover's approach seemed to present an alternative. The commerce secretary continued to make the case for using America's leverage as war-debt creditor to curb and contain French militarism.[104] And between 1926 and 1928, the administration, increasingly frustrated with the multilateral negotiations at Geneva, gravitated towards his strategy of tightening the financial screws on France. But although warnings to Paris abounded, it was never systematically pursued. Fundamentally, however, Republican policymakers believed strongly, and never more strongly than in the mid-1920s, that Europe's ills could not be cured by making American stabilisation efforts more European – i.e. by 'politicising' them. They could only be cured by pressing the Europeans to follow the American example of economic and as it were legally based conflict-resolution, executed by experts with minimal political interference. How did this compare with the British outlook on the challenges of European stabilisation after Locarno?

---

[100] *FRUS 1926*, I, pp. 78–9, 80–4. Cf. Leffler (1979), p. 160.

[101] Grew to Herrick, 20 April 1926, *FRUS 1926*, I, p. 79.

[102] Kellogg to Davies, 4 January 1926, Kellogg Papers, roll 17; Grew to Herrick, 20 April 1926, *FRUS 1926*, I, pp. 78–9.

[103] Kellogg to Davies, 4 January 1926, Kellogg Papers, roll 17; *FRUS 1926*, I, pp. 51–6, 80–100.

[104] Hoover memoranda, 23–5 September 1925, Hoover Papers, Commerce, box 20.

19   'Reciprocity'?

Britain as 'honest broker' in the Locarno system

In the Commons debate on the treaty on 18 November 1925, Chamberlain called Locarno 'the beginning, and not the end, of the noble work of appeasement in Europe'.[1] Would his emphatic prediction be borne out not only by his own actions but also the general evolution of international politics in the latter 1920s? Can British policy after Locarno indeed be characterised as an overall successful bid to promote further Franco-German *détente* and European tranquillity, pursued until overtaken by the Great Depression?[2] Or was it as flawed and futile as the original promotion of the security pact?[3] Did Chamberlain ultimately fail to fulfil his mission as 'honest broker', especially in the critical fields of collective security and disarmament?[4]

This analysis seeks to illuminate Britain's post-Locarno policy both from a different angle and through a wider lens. To gauge the extent of what Chamberlain's 'noble' policy of appeasement could achieve after Locarno, and what it could not achieve, it is not only imperative to re-assess which aims or strategies he pursued. At least as important is to explore whether, without America's political support, Britain indeed had the power – and, as Chamberlain claimed, the wherewithal – to fulfil his chosen mission: to become the main arbiter propelling Franco-German accommodation and expanding European stability to the east.

As in the American case, the domestic dimension of British foreign policy-making became increasingly important in the latter 1920s. Here, the crucial question was to what extent the Conservative foreign secretary could legitimate a consistent commitment to, and leadership within, the new European concert. For after his acclaimed success at Locarno he had to operate amid growing pressures on, and within, the second Baldwin government to concentrate on domestic reform and imperial consolidation. With Europe having ostensibly been set on a course of stability, not only Churchill demanded that Britain

---

[1] Chamberlain speech in the Commons, 18 November 1925, *Hansard*, 5th series, vol. 188, col. 420.
[2] See Grayson (1997), pp. 116–39, 282–5.
[3] See Marks (1976), pp. 74ff; Kissinger (1994), pp. 274–87.
[4] See Jacobson (1972b), pp. 119–28, 372–88.

focus squarely on these tasks.[5] How far did Chamberlain himself see the need for a continued or even expanded European role for Britain? How did he assess the domestic and imperial backdrop to the European stage of his diplomacy?

Essentially, at the very time when he impressed on the Commons that Britain's 'work of appeasement' had only begun, the foreign secretary had in private begun to gravitate towards a different outlook. It concerned not only Britain's part in the Locarno system but also the requirements of fortifying Europe's newly founded peace.[6] His new outlook was based on the assumption that Locarno had marked the greatest extent of what commitment Britain could make to European security after the Great War.

Even though Chamberlain did not admit it publicly, or even to himself, the establishment of the new European concert had been the essence of what he could contribute as a leading, *active* 'honest broker' of peaceful change. He had seized the initiative in laying the cornerstones of a system in which Britain's diplomatic weight could be used to moderate, and steer, French and German policies. Thus, he deemed Britain ideally placed hence to oversee a process through which France and Germany could settle their outstanding differences. This was to be achieved, not through further British guarantees, nor by way of complex political-cum-financial bargains, but with due recourse to the ground-rules of co-operative diplomacy so successfully inaugurated at Locarno. Chamberlain would term it the diplomacy of 'reciprocity'.[7]

In a marked contrast to US policymakers, the British foreign secretary thus had distinctly high expectations of what Locarno politics could achieve. These were perhaps never higher than in the spring of 1926, before years of ever more acrimonious negotiations with Briand and Stresemann. In retrospect, Chamberlain's optimism undoubtedly seems exaggerated. What mattered more, however, was his changing definition of Britain's role in Europe, which from late 1925 became increasingly restrained. In his judgement, Britain remained the essential mediator in all Franco-German disputes and would continue to lend its political support if the need arose.[8] He would in fact seek to control the very meaning of what constituted Locarno politics, appropriate concessions and desirable outcomes. But he saw no pressing need for, nor indeed any core national interest in, the pursuit of further major offensives in European

---

[5] Churchill memorandum, 7 February 1925, CAB 24/71(25); Niemeyer memorandum, 27 September 1926, FO 371/11331: C 10930/10060/18.

[6] Austen to Ida Chamberlain, 31 October 1925, 28 November 1925, Austen Chamberlain Papers, AC 5/1/367, 370. In the letter of 28 November, Chamberlain augured that the 'worries & difficulties' lying ahead could soon make the 'fruit' of Locarno 'seem all ashes in the mouth'. He also contemplated that he might 'willingly sing my *Nunc dimittis* and retire'.

[7] Chamberlain to D'Abernon, 1 February 1926, *DBFP*, IA, I, no. 231; Chamberlain to Briand, 29 July 1926, FO 800/259/668.

[8] Austen to Hilda Chamberlain, 25 April 1926, Austen Chamberlain Papers, AC 5/1/380.

diplomacy, in the east even less than in the west of a continent that in his eyes had finally, if gradually, begun to recover from the war.

The central premise of British policy – that a consolidation of Europe remained unachieved without Germany's further 'rehabilitation' – in principle opened up numerous avenues of common interest with Stresemann's policy of peaceful revision.[9] Above all, there was a common interest in the successive removal of what hindrances remained on the path of Franco-German 'reconciliation' and a pacific change of Germany's relations with its eastern neighbours after Locarno. Personally, Chamberlain favoured an early French withdrawal from the Rhineland. Like a majority in Baldwin's second cabinet, he originally considered the continued occupation an 'anomaly' incommensurate with the spirit of Locarno and its termination a natural consequence of the accords. From late January 1926, he thus advocated both timely reductions and, ultimately, a swift removal of all allied occupation troops.[10]

Likewise, as German disarmament under the Versailles treaty appeared by and large completed, the British government saw intrinsically no good reason for prolonging the activities of the IMCC. As Chamberlain underscored to D'Abernon on 7 February 1926, it had 'long been our policy to get military control wound up with all possible speed'. To re-assure France, the Foreign Office proposed to replace it with a League-based monitoring scheme.[11] Eventually, the Locarno concert was to remove all remaining impediments to Germany's *rapprochement* with the western powers.

More profoundly, Chamberlain's belief in the validity of integrative concert politics and the wisdom of building bridges to Germany's moderate leaders had been strengthened by the results of Locarno.[12] Though not oblivious of Weimar Germany's persistent domestic crises, neither he nor any other member of the Conservative cabinet feared that there could be, even in the longer term, a serious backlash against Stresemann's policy. Nor was there any senior official in the Foreign Office who shared the deep-seated anxieties of some in the *Quai d'Orsay* that sooner or later more assertive forces would seize upon the advances of Locarno to mount an all-out attack on Versailles. Rather, by January 1926 basically all principal British policymakers acted on the premise that, for all the problems that still had to be addressed, the essential groundwork for stabilising Germany, and Europe, had been laid.[13]

---

[9] Sterndale-Bennett memorandum, 10 January 1926, *DBFP*, IA, I, pp. 9ff.

[10] Chamberlain memorandum, 28 January 1926, *DBFP*, IA, I, pp. 231ff; Chamberlain to Crewe, 16 August 1926, *DBFP*, IA, II, no. 153; Chamberlain minute, 11 August 1926, FO 371/11298: C8807/44/18.

[11] Chamberlain to D'Abernon, 7 February 1926, *DBFP*, IA, I, no. 250. Cf. Fox (1969).

[12] Chamberlain to D'Abernon, 1 February 1926, *DBFP*, IA, I, no. 231.

[13] Sterndale-Bennett memorandum, 10 January 1926, *DBFP*, IA, I, pp. 9ff; Chamberlain to Tyrrell, 16 March 1926, *DBFP*, IA, I, no. 361.

Indeed, as soon became clear in the spring of 1926, Britain would not pursue any forward engagement in setting the post-Locarno agenda of peaceful accommodation, either in western or in eastern Europe. Fundamentally, Chamberlain thought it unwise to put pressure on France to hasten further substantive changes in the *status quo*. He soon came to believe that these could not be achieved in the short term, at least not without undermining Briand's domestic standing. Instead, the foreign secretary time and again impressed upon Stresemann that further progress could only be made if Berlin first convincingly proved its adherence to the *do ut des* rules of Locarno diplomacy, as defined by him and Briand. To placate France, Germany in particular had to fulfil its disarmament obligations under Versailles meticulously. This interpretation of the Locarno process, putting the onus squarely on the German government, became a key constant informing Chamberlain's diplomacy in the latter 1920s. Rather than advance further 'grand designs' and raise illusory hopes that could damage the Locarno concert's legitimacy, he thus adopted a cautious, essentially reactive approach. In this sense, he was correct when retrospectively concluding, in 1930, that Britain had assumed a 'semi-detached position' vis-à-vis Europe after Locarno.[14]

Underlying the relative restraint of British policy, and mostly unspoken, was another equally fundamental rationale: Although its security seemed not even in the medium term threatened by Germany's newly rising power, Britain had a clear interest in keeping this power in check. It desired to maintain all processes spurring the re-ascension of Weimar Germany as a 'normal' great power, which even if formally 'equal' had the inherent potential to dominate Europe, as gradual as possible. Ultimately, Britain and France had to control the recasting and consolidating of Europe's equilibrium at every stage. As Chamberlain told D'Abernon on 15 February 1926, like Britain, 'a nation like Germany was a Great Power even on the morrow of defeat and would always be a Great Power in whatever assembly she took a part.'[15] Yet in his calculation the former *entente* powers would oversee how quickly and on what conditions Germany would once again participate in the 'comity of nations'.

A maxim of Chamberlain's policy became that he and Briand thus had a common interest in establishing what was tantamount to an informal central axis within the new European concert.[16] While neither power would abandon the concert's integrative politics, this axis could serve to counter undesirable German attempts to hasten changes, especially 'universal disarmament' or 'armament parity' in Europe and territorial revisions in the east. Yet it could

---

[14] Chamberlain to D'Abernon, 2 February 1926; Chamberlain to Crewe, 27 April 1926, *DBFP*, IA, I, nos. 236, 468; Chamberlain (1930), p. 188.

[15] Chamberlain to D'Abernon, 15 February 1926, *DBFP*, IA, I, no. 275, p. 436.

[16] Chamberlain to Briand, 29 July 1926, FO 800/259/668. Cf. Jacobson (1972b), pp. 44ff.

equally serve to postpone alterations in the Rhineland's *status quo*. This re-orientation of Chamberlain's policy *after* Locarno often conflicted with the no less pronounced British aim to achieve Germany's full integration into the Locarno system. Such tensions not only mirrored different preferences within the Foreign Office, where Tyrrell favoured a more far-reaching agenda of peaceful change also addressing the Polish–German dispute.[17] Ultimately, they also reflected a conflict in Chamberlain's own thinking that was never quite resolved – and perhaps could not be resolved under the circumstances. Yet this new duality made British policy more one-sided and disengaged than before Locarno.

From 1926, the Foreign Office's restraint and the cabinet's lack of political will converged to arrest the further evolution of British stabilisation policy. Apart from the core sphere of security, this was most notable in London's approach to the financial 'underbelly' of Locarno diplomacy. Essentially, in contrast to the Coolidge administration, the Baldwin government placed too much emphasis on classic international politics, neglecting the newly vital and inseparable sphere of international finance. Yet, like Washington, if for different reasons, it largely failed to devise more comprehensive consolidation strategies for post-Locarno Europe, strategies apt to produce further, urgently required 'grand bargains' in the highly interdependent areas of security and financial stabilisation.[18]

As Tyrrell suggested in July, the need to overcome their financial crises through 'sane' political measures could be invoked to push for further advances in Franco-German accommodation. Alternatively, financial levers could be used to further political agreements. But Chamberlain simply did not believe that such operations could benefit Locarno politics. And, as the chancellor of the exchequer Churchill insisted, they must never be allowed to harm fundamental British interests, notably the interest to link a 'final' reparations settlement with a significant reduction of Britain's debts to America.[19] The prevalent perception remained that, in view of this indebtedness, Britain lacked the means – *and there was no need* – to pursue an ambitious agenda of financial reconstruction and political reform in Europe. One clear symptom of this was the auspiciously low level of co-operation between the Foreign Office and the Treasury on such issues. Under Churchill, the Treasury indeed became again more influential after 1925, solely controlling British reparations and war-debt policy while opposing any plans that could entail burdensome commitments in Europe.[20]

---

[17] Tyrrell memorandum, 26 July 1926, *DBFP*, IA, II, no. 103.

[18] Tyrrell developed strategies to this end but could not convince Chamberlain to implement them. See *ibid.*; Tyrrell to Phipps and D'Abernon, 29 September 1926, *DBFP*, IA, II, no. 229; Sargent memorandum, 9 October 1926, FO 371/11331: C 10930/10060/18.

[19] Tyrrell memorandum, 26 July 1926, *DBFP*, IA, II, no. 103; Churchill memorandum, 7 February 1925, CAB 24/71(25).

[20] Niemeyer memorandum, 27 September 1926; Sargent memorandum, 9 October 1926, FO 371/11331: C 10930/10060/18.

In the larger picture, then, Chamberlain's reliance on 'pure' diplomacy was reinforced by the fact that it corresponded with the Baldwin cabinet's overall priorities in the later 1920s. For these priorities were to minimise further 'costly' involvement and to collect Britain's dues from Germany and France, to advance domestic retrenchment, the reinvigoration of trade and, finally, imperial reform – all against the backdrop of a looming general strike.[21] The Conservative government's penchant for a 'Britain first' agenda was less pronounced than what the Republican administration in Washington pursued. But it often became a more important impediment to the evolution of Locarno politics than any particular feature of Chamberlain's 'honest brokerage'.

'Guiding' the Franco-German peace process – the mission and limits of British Locarno policy

Anchoring Germany to the new European concert thus became one maxim of Chamberlain's pursuits after 1925. Yet his *leitmotif* was that he could only promote this process in accordance with overriding French security concerns. Following the pact negotiations, the foreign secretary at first considered Stresemann ungrateful, criticising him for making unduly far-reaching demands for further troop reductions in the Rhineland. Over the spring and summer of 1926, however, he came to regard the German foreign minister as a pragmatic and overall trustworthy politician who was well worth backing against his opponents on the nationalist right.[22]

While sometimes still deemed too pro-German, D'Abernon's reports reinforced this perception; and so did those of his successor, Ronald Lindsay, between 1926 and 1928. The Foreign Office clearly saw that Stresemann continued to face an up-hill struggle to win support for his course in the *Reichstag*, among German pressure groups like the '*Reich* Association of the German Industry' and, not least, from *Reichspräsident* Hindenburg.[23] Stresemann's domestic calamities thus 'trouble[d]' Chamberlain. Unlike Briand, however, he saw him – and for that matter Kellogg – as both deplorably swayed by the tides of 'public opinion' and instrumentalising these tides to win concessions. Revealingly, the foreign secretary wondered on one occasion why 'other nations [could not] keep foreign affairs outside of & above domestic party politics' like Britain.[24]

[21] Cf. Taylor (1965), pp. 227–61.

[22] Chamberlain to D'Abernon, 1 February and 8 May 1926, *DBFP*, IA, I, nos. 231, 510.

[23] D'Abernon to Chamberlain, 4 February 1926, D'Abernon to Chamberlain, 5 February 1926, *DBFP*, IA, I, nos. 242, 247; Lindsay to Chamberlain, 7 December 1926, FO 371/11281: C 12969/234/18.

[24] Austen to Ida Chamberlain, 31 October 1925, Austen Chamberlain Papers, AC 5/1/367.

Chamberlain's belief in the exemplary nature of British international policy, filtered through his essentially Edwardian understanding of it, was deeply embedded. Throughout the Locarno era, he remained convinced that if only French and German politicians could emulate Britain's reasonable example the effect on European politics would be most salutary.[25] The British foreign secretary assumed quite realistically that only deeper changes of mentality in Germany and France could ultimately sustain European peace; and that these changes would require longer-term stability and international co-operation. Even more time would be needed to alter mindsets in order to pacify the relations between Germany and its eastern neighbours.

As early as 9 February 1925, Chamberlain had written to King George V that he thought such developments would not culminate until the 1960s or 1970s. The factor of time, then, was a key determinant of British Locarno policy. In the short term, British policymakers realised that especially the Rhineland issue was of more than symbolic import for the survival of the Luther government. But Chamberlain's understanding of the desirable dynamics of further peaceful change in Europe only permitted very gradual 'advances'. He never encouraged a stepped-up pursuit of Stresemann's revisionist aims.[26] What took precedence was to ensure the continuation of Locarno politics as such. And in Chamberlain's view this meant that he first and foremost had to consider Briand's vital interests, which he deemed largely identical with those of Britain.

The foreign secretary increasingly considered Briand's domestic position highly precarious, and ultimately more threatened than Stresemann's – as 'French ministries' were in his view 'inherently unstable'.[27] Fundamentally, however, this concern corresponded with the underlying aim to prevent too rapid a German resurgence. Both Chamberlain and Tyrrell were distinctly aware of the fact that, in the process of Europe's undisturbed consolidation it desired, Germany's economic and demographic preponderance was bound to re-emerge. And they of course knew that Paris deemed this deeply alarming.[28]

On one level, Britain's answer to this problem remained the same as before Locarno: German ambitions could be more effectively moderated the more Germany was anchored to the Locarno concert and the League. But Chamberlain's unchangeably paternalistic policy also still sought to 'guide' Germany and 'keep' its leaders 'in the path of their own real interests'. In his judgement,

---

[25] The Foreign Office also conveyed this through Britain's ambassadors. See D'Abernon to Chamberlain, 25 April 1926; Crewe to Chamberlain, 5 May 1926, *DBFP*, IA, I, nos. 460, 497.

[26] Chamberlain to King George V, 9 February 1925, Austen Chamberlain Papers, AC 52/378. Cf. Chamberlain to D'Abernon, 1 February 1926, *DBFP*, IA, I, no. 231. Cf. Jacobson (1972b), pp. 124ff.

[27] Chamberlain to D'Abernon, 1 February 1926, *DBFP*, IA, I, no. 232.

[28] Chamberlain also drew Washington's attention to this. See Houghton to Kellogg, 27 February 1926, *FRUS 1926*, I, p. 57.

a gradual alleviation of outstanding German grievances was imperative. Yet Germany's 'real' interest lay in re-ascending as an economically orientated great power that pursued its aims through the European concert. And it lay in avoiding French backlashes against Briand's conciliatory course, which could be the consequence of excessive German demands. For the sake of European peace, nothing was thus more critical for the British foreign secretary than that Briand stayed in power.

But time and again, Chamberlain found the Germans 'prodigiously difficult to guide' after Locarno.[29] In January 1927, he complained to Ambassador Lindsay about the 'fatal inability of the Germans to appreciate the psychology of other nations' and to 'foresee the results of their action'.[30] This especially concerned Germany's incessant pressure for ever swifter revisions, notably in the Rhineland, and the effect of continued German transgressions of Versailles' disarmament clauses on France. In private, Chamberlain highlighted a grave burden besetting Stresemann's policy when noting that there was 'bound before long to be a reaction from the present exaggerated expectations', especially hopes for a 'liberation' of the Rhineland and the end of military control. In his interpretation, neither could follow directly from the Locarno pact; it could only be accomplished through further *do ut des* compromises. And to foster such compromises through the mechanism of the European concert was to be Britain's mission.

But Chamberlain came to develop his very own definition of what principles were to guide the concert. On 1 February 1926, he characterised the basic principle of Locarno politics as that of 'reciprocity'. 'Reciprocity' was to inform a process whereby, through mutual concessions, not only Franco-German reconciliation but also a new European equilibrium could be achieved.[31] Essentially, though, Chamberlain soon established a reigning interpretation of 'reciprocity' clearly tilted in France's favour. Any further French concessions on the Rhineland occupation and military control had to be preceded by further decisive steps on the path of Germany's fulfilment of the Versailles treaty – *as defined and judged by London and Paris*. This chiefly pertained to complete German compliance on disarmament.

In practice, Chamberlain's interest in bolstering the new European concert thus came to be subordinated to another, ever more central aim. Though cognisant of Stresemann's domestic difficulties, his priority became to strengthen Briand's position, and reassure France, by establishing a new *entente* as the concert's informal directorate. In July 1926, the foreign secretary defined the second maxim of his post-Locarno diplomacy as follows: 'Working

---

[29] Austen to Hilda Chamberlain, 25 April 1926, Austen Chamberlain Papers, AC 5/1/380.
[30] Chamberlain to Lindsay, 13 January 1927, *DBFP*, IA, II, no. 395.
[31] Austen to Ida Chamberlain, 28 November 1925, Austen Chamberlain Papers, AC 5/1/370; Chamberlain to D'Abernon, 1 February 1926, *DBFP*, IA, I, no. 231.

together, France and England can do about anything. If we are once separated, the whole edifice [of Locarno] is endangered.'[32]

Significantly, though, the Foreign Office deemed any guarantees beyond those given at Locarno to compensate France for its Rhenish security *glacis* both unnecessary *and* impossible. The cabinet's 'drawing-of-the-line' at Locarno had been unequivocal, and neither Chamberlain nor Tyrrell saw any room to manoeuvre in view of overwhelming parliamentary and public aversion to fresh international commitments.[33] At the same time, the British General Staff maintained that Britain did not have the military means to fulfil even its limited Locarno guarantees in the event of an aggression. Yet both its Imperial Defence Review and the Committee of Imperial Defence (CID) concluded in July 1926 that no further strategic planning, nor a costly expansion of military capabilities for a major European war, was necessary for the foreseeable future. The Locarno accords thus reinforced the ten-year rule. In fact, Chamberlain's influence and Churchill's interest in retrenchment prompted its extension in 1928. Locarno appeared to solidify European stability to such an extent that Britain could hence concentrate scarce resources on imperial defence.[34] And it could rely on diplomacy and the promotion of disarmament to guard national security. This was more than merely a 'triumph of Treasury control'.[35] It constrained any attempt to widen Britain's strategic commitments in Europe even if Chamberlain had considered such an extension of responsibilities desirable, which he did not. Instead, the foreign secretary would concentrate on his political brokerage, confident that he could buttress an Anglo-French *entente* and anchor Germany to the Locarno concert at the same time, for the benefit of all postwar Europe.

Chamberlain tended to personalise Locarno politics. He came to see its fate intricately bound up with that of Briand and Stresemann. Tyrrell agreed that the 'happy personal relations' between the Locarno protagonists were one of the key factors 'working in favour of our policy'. More than his superior, the under-secretary thought that this was precisely why Britain should press ahead and make the most of this constellation before it might dissolve.[36] To Chamberlain, however, Briand's role ultimately appeared more essential. In his eyes, the main danger lay in overstretching the readiness of France's military and public opinion for *rapprochement*. He was convinced that if Briand fell no

---

[32] Chamberlain to Briand, 29 July 1926, FO 800/259/668; Chamberlain to D'Abernon, 30 April 1926, *DBFP*, IA, I, no. 487.

[33] Cabinet minutes, 17 and 24 February 1926, CAB 23/52, CC 5, 7 (26).

[34] Chiefs of Staff, Imperial Defence Review, 22 July 1926, CAB 4/15, 701-B; 215th CID meeting, 22 July 1926, CAB 2/4. Cf. Ferris (1989), pp. 158–78.

[35] Ferris (1989), p. 178.

[36] Chamberlain to D'Abernon, 1 February 1926; Tyrrell memorandum, 26 July 1926, *DBFP*, IA, I, nos. 232, 103.

other 'Frenchman would have both the strength and the wish' to pursue his 'policy of conciliation'. Any French movement either 'to the Right' or 'further left' would be harmful, because Poincarists would resist conciliation while Herriot would lack the necessary clout, always suspected of betraying vital national interests.[37]

These concerns were undoubtedly justified. Yet the German scenario was no less disconcerting, and the need for genuine 'reciprocity' in the Franco-German peace process paramount. Essentially, unless readjusted, Chamberlain's *entente* penchant and above all his unwillingness to lead in *shaping* the Locarno process threatened to deprive it, and Germany's international integration, of crucial momentum. And this could be most detrimental when the new order's legitimisation required such momentum most: in the formative first years after Locarno. As will be shown, these tendencies first appeared at the time of Germany's obstructed bid to join the League in the spring of 1926. And, crucially, they came to inform Britain's Rhineland policy.[38]

British restraint in the latter 1920s was even more pronounced with a view to eastern Europe's lingering postwar problems. Though generally favouring both, Chamberlain deemed it unwise to take charge in widening the European concert geographically and addressing the core of the unresolved German question in the east: the Polish–German problem. In a memorandum of 26 July 1926, Tyrrell emphasised what in principle also was Chamberlain's view, namely that 'the object of the Locarno policy' remained 'to reconcile Germany and France, and, above all, Poland and Germany'. For until friendly relations between all of these powers were 're-established, the wound in Europe cannot heal' and no continental peace – 'so vital for the resumption of our trade' – would be possible.[39]

A major British motive for fostering Germany's western orientation remained to counter what Tyrrell still called the 'Russian danger'. Anglo-Soviet relations had been deteriorating following the affair surrounding the 'Zinoviev letter', through the publication of which the Conservative party, and press, had sought to stir up a 'red scare' campaign against MacDonald and the Labour party during the elections of 1924, alleging Soviet ploys to infiltrate Britain. With influential anti-Bolshevik imperialists like Churchill and Amery in its ranks, the Baldwin cabinet subsequently abandoned MacDonald's policy of recognition and *rapprochement* towards the Soviet Union.[40] Instead, British

---

[37] Chamberlain minute, 12 October 1926, FO 371/11331; Chamberlain to D'Abernon, 2 February 1926, *DBFP*, IA, I, no. 236.

[38] Kilmarnock to Chamberlain, 3 February 1926, Chamberlain to D'Abernon, 30 April 1926, *DBFP*, IA, I, nos. 241, 487.

[39] Tyrrell memorandum, 26 July 1926, *DBFP*, IA, I, no. 103.

[40] Amery memorandum, 27 November 1924, CAB 24/169, CP 511 (24); Churchill to Chamberlain, 22 November, FO 800/256/139. Cf. Grayson (1997), pp. 255–9.

diplomacy adopted a course of 'patience, expectancy and non-interference', i.e. it *de facto* pursued a passive policy aiming to keep Moscow isolated. Nevertheless, a general interest remained the containment of Soviet encroachments on eastern Europe, which Tyrrell described as the 'next field for Russian Bolshevik attack'. And in the assessment of the Foreign Office the Locarno system offered 'the best prospects' for protecting Europe 'against the common danger from the East'.[41]

British policymakers thus upheld the maxim of 'gradually widening circles' of European stability. But in practice they had little interest in placing a resolution of the Polish–German dispute, let alone an 'eastern Locarno', on the European concert's agenda. Chamberlain had no doubt that Europe would remain unsettled unless an agreement on the 'Polish Corridor' and Danzig could be forged that accommodated German grievances while respecting Polish interests as much as possible.[42] But the latter was clearly less important. And the same held true for a settlement of German – and Polish – minority concerns. The foreign secretary demanded that Berlin stop treating Poland as the 'pariah' of European politics. Yet he also understood that German claims would not be rescinded by any major German party.[43] At the same time, though, Chamberlain had called the Poles, with the Germans, 'the restless elements in Europe north of the Balkans'. And while deeming Czechoslovakia rather adept at adapting to Locarno's new rules he considered Poland the power still least attuned to these rules. As he noted following Marshal Piłsudski's coup in May 1926, he feared that Germany's troublesome eastern neighbour could 'be on the top of a revolutionary movement' challenging Europe's 'stability and financial recovery'.[44]

Against this background, Chanberlain's main anxiety was that any British initiative in the east could spur the call for extending Britain's responsibilities in the remaining minefield of postwar Europe. This the Baldwin cabinet would have rejected from the start.[45] Non-engagement in the east thus remained a constant of British policy in the 1920s. It was reinforced by Chamberlain's rationale that it was only realistic to push the 'eastern question' of the post-World War I era as far back as possible on the European agenda. As he saw it, the most sensitive issue of territorial revision could only be resolved, with some

---

[41] Orde memorandum, 10 February 1926, FO 371/11789: N 640/640/38; Austen to Ida Chamberlain, 18 April 1926, Austen Chamberlain Papers, AC 5/1/379; Tyrrell memorandum, 26 July 1926, *DBFP*, IA, I, no. 103. Cf. Gorodetsky (1977).

[42] Foreign Office memorandum, 20 February 1925, *DBFP*, I, XXVII, no. 205; Chamberlain memorandum, 1 February 1926, *DBFP*, IA, I, no. 233.

[43] Chamberlain to D'Abernon, 24 April 1926, *DBFP*, IA, I, no. 459.

[44] Austen to Hilda Chamberlain, 22 September 1925, 28 May 1926, Austen Chamberlain Papers, AC 5/1/365, 385.

[45] Sterndale-Bennett memorandum, 10 January 1926, *DBFP*, IA, I, pp. 9ff. Cf. Bátonyi (1999), pp. 222ff.

outside help, through bilateral agreements between Germany, Poland and Czechoslovakia respectively. Chamberlain's hope was that the longer German elites operated within the Locarno framework, the more moderate, perhaps muted, their demands for border changes would become, and the easier eventual compromises.[46] In the meantime, his priority had to be to prevent eastern developments from complicating relations between the Locarno powers. And the focus of these relations was to remain the western, more precisely the Rhenish, theatre.

Chamberlain thus impressed on the German ambassador Sthamer that his expectation was that, once in the League, Berlin would 'proceed with great caution' in the east. It had to avoid treating German minorities as an 'instrument' to 'create a feeling of uncertainty about the political settlement' of 1919.[47] Like Washington, London would consistently pour cold water on any attempts by Stresemann to move towards a more assertive approach to peaceful revision in eastern Europe – be it through political negotiations or by means of economic pressures and incentives.[48] Instead, Chamberlain argued that Locarno politics could serve as a model for regional security agreements that should be emulated by Germany and its eastern neighbours. There was a sense that, rather than in brokering such agreements directly, Britain's main responsibility lay in maintaining the wider framework of the Locarno concert in order to provide a conducive environment for peaceful change. Chamberlain saw Germany's entry into the League as a further helpful step on this arduous path. But while Briand made numerous proposals for an 'eastern Locarno', the British arbiter did not envisage superintending or underwriting a more ambitious further 'grand bargain' of this kind.[49]

European engagement *versus* financial, domestic and imperial constraints

In the final analysis, then, what could prove more detrimental to the Locarno system than any pro-French bias on the part of Chamberlain was that Britain's commitment to further peaceful change and concrete European settlements would slacken. At the same time, however, there were not only strategic reasons but also growing financial, domestic and imperial pressures on British policy in the mid-1920s to gravitate exactly in that direction – to fall back on a course of limited engagement. Or this was at least how it seemed to the

---

[46] Chamberlain to D'Abernon, 4 February 1926, *DBFP*, IA, I, no. 245.
[47] *Ibid.*
[48] Chamberlain to Max Muller, 8 February 1926; Orde to D'Abernon, 9 February 1926; D'Abernon to Chamberlain, 29 July 1926, *DBFP*, IA, I, nos. 252, 254, pp. 196–7. See chapter 22.
[49] Austen to Ida Chamberlain, 18 April 1926, Austen Chamberlain Papers, AC 5/1/379.

Baldwin government.[50] In many ways, it was only now, after the exertions of the Great War's aftermath and the emphasis on European affairs until 1925, that policymakers confronted the full scale of two unresolved postwar challenges: domestic retrenchment and reform, and the consolidation of what was still by and large regarded as Britain's rightful domain: the Empire. From 1926, these dominated the cabinet's agenda more often than European concerns.[51] And the Baldwin government indeed turned its attention to the home front, where stimulating the depressed economy and fighting rising unemployment proved most urgent. Besides, it was not only the Treasury that insisted that a tight budget made both German reparations and French debt payments imperative.[52]

On the imperial front, Britain had to place relations with the Dominions on new foundations, a task begun by the Imperial Conference of 1926, which paved the way for the Westminster Statute and significantly widened the Dominions' autonomy. Chamberlain's attention was also increasingly diverted by other legacies of British imperialism, particularly in China and Egypt.[53] Although it was not yet high on his agenda, as it would be from 1927, he noted on 19 June 1926 that 'China [was] a constant source of anxiety.' He had to safeguard British interests during the recently flared-up Chinese civil war in which Britain came to back the Nationalist Kuomintang under General Chiang Kai-shek against communist forces. Likewise, the foreign secretary noted in May 1926 that 'trouble [was] brewing in Egypt'. Here, protecting Britain's 'special interests' called for a military presence to defend the Suez Canal against nationalist insurgents in an Egyptian state formally independent since 1922.[54]

With hindsight, it can thus be said that 1926 was the last year before the Great Depression when Britain was not considerably preoccupied by contingencies beyond Europe. Yet, contrary to what has sometimes been claimed, these did not tangibly interfere with Britain's management of European developments. While there was sometimes an unavoidable trade-off, the decisive determinant was and remained Chamberlain's restrictive interpretation of Britain's European policy. Hardly less constraining, though, was the Baldwin government's unquestionable preoccupation with restructuring Britain's depressed postwar economy and addressing the social consequences of retrenchment. Although less obvious, this provided the essential subtext to Chamberlain's pursuits in the sphere of European diplomacy. Britain's economy

---

[50] Cabinet minutes, 4 February 1925, CAB 23/49, C 6(25); 3 July 1925, CAB 23/50, C 33(25).
[51] Cabinet minutes, February 1926ff, CAB 23/52ff. Cf. Boyce (1987), pp. 79–185; Taylor (1965), pp. 238ff.
[52] Churchill to Clémentel, 6 February 1925, FO 371/10680: C 1786/4/62; Niemeyer to Churchill, 6 February 1925, Treasury Papers, T172/1499B. Cf. Orde (1990), pp. 292–5.
[53] Cf. Beloff (1989), pp. 44–5; Darwin (1980).
[54] Austen to Ida Chamberlain, 19 June 1926, Austen to Hilda Chamberlain, 28 May 1926, Austen Chamberlain Papers, AC 5/1/386, 385. Cf. Grayson (1997), pp. 170–211.

was affected by structural changes stemming from the war, notably what soon became superior US competition, uncertainty in traditional European markets and the weakness of the franc, which made British exports more expensive.[55] But, as noted, the Conservatives' decision to return to the gold standard clearly aggravated the situation, worsening Britain's sluggish recovery in the period of 'normalcy' between 1925 and 1929. Churchill's original premonitions were thus borne out.[56]

Reintroducing the prewar parity of $4.86 meant that sterling was overvalued and made Britain's already depressed export industries less competitive on the world market. Both the economy and exports actually grew in the 1920s. Yet they did so only very slowly, reaching a high-point in 1929 that was still well below the prewar level. These developments converged with the unbending austerity policies of the Treasury and the Bank of England to keep unemployment at well over 10 per cent, or 1 million, throughout the latter 1920s. While there was as yet no welfare system to speak of in place, or desired, by the Baldwin government, unemployment remained the cardinal problem in British domestic politics. This again confirmed Churchill's sceptical outlook of 1925.[57]

Not only for British industry but also for the City's financiers, the latter half of the 1920s became 'a period of almost unrelieved crisis'.[58] In its foreign economic policy, however, the Baldwin cabinet and the Bank of England resolutely adhered to the basic tenets of free trade and liberal internationalism which had underpinned the commercial treaty with Germany in 1925.[59] At no point did the government seriously contemplate protectionist measures. An imperial-preference system would only be introduced following the peak of the Slump in 1931. Britain thus remained a chief proponent of a liberal world economic system, criticising America's protectionist policies, which shaped that system.[60] On the other hand, London was less opposed than Washington to continental European efforts to boost postwar recovery through cartels. Empire-minded cabinet members like Churchill and Amery could not conceive of Britain as a European power in economic terms; nor could they envisage Britain actually entering into cartel agreements like the Franco–German *Entente Internationale de l'Acier* (*EIA*) of 1926. But Whitehall assumed a benign attitude.[61] To revitalise European markets, Britain increased efforts to build on

---

[55] Cf. Moggridge (1972), pp. 68ff.

[56] Churchill memorandum, 29 January 1925, Treasury Papers, T175/9.

[57] Churchill to Niemeyer, 6 February 1925, Treasury Papers, T172/1499B. Cf. Newton (1996), pp. 30–1; Pollard (1992).

[58] Boyce (1987), p. 78. Cf. Williamson (1992).

[59] Tyrrell to Sthamer, 7 June 1926, *DBFP*, IA, II, no. 51.

[60] Cf. Boyce (1987), pp. 78–185; Newton (1996), pp. 31–6.

[61] Lampson memorandum, 13 December 1923, Treasury Papers, T160/174/F6731/1; Churchill (1929). Cf. Wurm (1993), pp. 14–48.

the German example and promote currency and financial stabilisation in France and Poland. Yet, like those pursued by the United States, such endeavours were not overseen by the government but, semi-formally, by Norman, who intensified his collaboration with Strong, Moreau and Schacht.[62]

Beset by financial problems, Britain could not regain a leading role in Europe's financial consolidation; nor could it be effected on a pound-sterling basis. And even less did it have the power to reconstitute a world economic system based on free trade. As noted, by 1926 the United States had cemented its predominance in setting the rules of global trade and finance. Likewise, the ability of Baldwin's and later MacDonald's second government to pursue a bolder or more conciliatory reparations policy was very limited. A logical consequence of all this was that British policy in Europe became all the more focused on what was both an important and less costly endeavour: the pursuit of Locarno diplomacy, largely divorced from unwelcome financial ramifications. That was Chamberlain's approach. He was *almost* correct in concluding that Europe's fundamental woes were not amenable to financial remedies, as the Americans suggested. They essentially had to be addressed through international politics. Yet, as will be shown, political solutions depended critically on financial means, which were part and parcel of the bargaining-power of those policymakers who sought to advance Franco–German accommodation and peaceful change in eastern Europe.

The Foreign Office was by no means oblivious to the difficulties arising from the need to make economic and social readjustments after the Great War. Sterndale-Bennett's incisive memorandum of 10 January 1926 highlighted precisely that there was an intimate connection between the success of Locarno and reducing British unemployment. As he outlined, Locarno diplomacy could serve to improve the political conditions for a revitalisation of British trade with Europe. No less, it allowed Britain to eschew further expensive commitments.[63] The Conservative government in fact sought to master the novel domestic problems it faced through cuts in military spending.[64] And Chamberlain, who characterised himself as an 'outsider' in domestic affairs, was not the man to argue either in cabinet, the Commons or the British public at large for expanding Britain's role in Europe beyond the parameters of Locarno. Even during the escalating crisis amidst calls for a general strike in May 1926, he maintained his detachment. While the coal miners' protests

---

[62] Norman to Strong, 2 February 1926, Strong Papers, 1116.6/2; Lampson memoranda, 11 and 12 August 1926, *DBFP*, IA, II, nos. 142, 143. Cf. Orde (1990), pp. 304–5.

[63] Sterndale-Bennett memorandum, 10 January 1926, *DBFP*, IA, I, p. 9; 215th CID meeting, 22 July 1926, CAB 2/4; MacDonald statements in the Commons, 18 November 1925, *Hansard*, 5th series, vol. 188, cols. 433–4.

[64] Cf. Middlemas and Barnes (1969), pp. 343ff.

continued, Chamberlain was 'struck by the great confidence' Baldwin inspired 'in ending the [general] strike'. Nonetheless, the prime minister himself noted roughly a year later, and with some trepidation, that '[d]emocracy has arrived at a gallop in England, and I feel all the time that it is a race for life: can we educate [the people] before the crash comes?'[65] Concentrating on this task, Baldwin staunchly backed Chamberlain's foreign policy, and the foreign secretary in turn refrained from burdening the prime minister's agenda with fresh demands for more engagement in Europe.

In Chamberlain's judgement, Britain had little to gain from taking the lead in broadening the scope of the European concert either geographically or in substance. He saw no convincing rationale for contemplating a wider stabilisation agenda and devising a policy that also gave serious consideration to the financial dimension of Locarno politics. Generally, the foreign secretary thought that Locarno's pacification efforts could both buttress and benefit from economic stability and rising prosperity in France and Germany.[66] This struck a chord not only with Stresemann's and Briand's reasoning but also, naturally, with American ideas. In contrast to US decisionmakers, however, Chamberlain maintained that only the Locarno powers could propel further pacific change, essentially by accomplishing their political 'work of appeasement'. He thus continued to discount attempts to use financial instruments to advance this work.

Like Stresemann and Briand, Tyrrell was less oblivious to the interconnections between Europe's security and economic problems, between the Rhineland question and the outstanding final reparations settlement.[67] But it was Chamberlain who set the course of British policy. And he guarded his reserve towards international agreements that – like the 1924 reparations settlement – involved an array of complex political-cum-financial trade-offs. In particular, he considered it counterproductive to link the reparations problem with questions of 'high politics'. This was a further, and hitherto mostly overlooked, characteristic of Chamberlain's approach. It limited the effectiveness of British policy in the era of London and Locarno considerably.[68]

Yet there was one further reason for the Foreign Office's reticence in financial matters. In short, it was due to the fact that under Churchill the Treasury re-asserted its authority in all political matters connected with the

---

[65] Austen to Ida Chamberlain, 26 May 1926, Austen Chamberlain Papers, AC 5/1/383. Cf. Lloyd (1993), pp. 141–5; Baldwin to Lord Irwin, 26 June 1927, in Williamson (2004), p. 196.

[66] Chamberlain memorandum, 6 October 1926, FO 371/11331: C 10700/10060/18.

[67] Tyrrell to Phipps and D'Abernon, 29 September 1926, *DBFP*, IA, II, no. 229; Perowne memorandum, 29 September 1926, *DBFP*, IA, II, no. 232.

[68] Chamberlain to Max Muller, 8 February 1926, *DBFP*, IA, I, no. 252; Chamberlain note, 15 October 1926, FO 371/11331: C 11024/10060/18. This is only briefly considered in Jacobson (1972b), pp. 119ff; Grayson (1997), pp. 116–39.

domains of international finance, debts and, notably, reparations policy. This doubtless curtailed Chamberlain's room to manoeuvre from the start, leading to a pronounced demarcation of spheres of influence between the Foreign Office and the Treasury up until the Great Depression.[69] With Churchill at the helm, and with Niemeyer usually formulating policies, the Treasury followed Washington in pressing France to conclude a debt settlement. Though much less controversial in Paris, the resulting Churchill–Caillaux accords of 12 July 1926 were in fact hardly less stringent than the Mellon–Bérenger agreement.[70] Vis-à-vis Germany, the Treasury uncompromisingly protected British reparations claims. It still hoped for a final settlement allowing Britain to shed its debts to America; and it remained wary of any Franco-German plans that could jeopardise this aim.[71]

Consequently, the Baldwin government made no serious attempt to set forth British aims in the fields of European security, reconstruction and financial consolidation in one common framework. In a marked parallel to the evolution of US policy, albeit with an emphasis on political rather than economic strategies, Britain did not develop a comprehensive stabilisation policy after Locarno. As will be shown, this limited any contributions Britain could make to further 'grand bargains' between the western powers and Germany. Yet precisely such efforts would spawn the most significant developments in Euro-Atlantic politics after Locarno – from the Thoiry project of 1926 to the later negotiations over the Young plan and the Hague settlement of 1929.

Britain's limited case for disarmament – and Anglo-American co-operation

In contrast to Briand and Stresemann, Chamberlain did not consider it any more beneficial after than before Locarno to bring the United States into European international politics. He never thoroughly gauged the significance of America's financial power and involvement in the Dawes regime for Locarno diplomacy, only considering their implications when directly confronted with them, as after the Franco-German Thoiry initiative of September 1926.[72] Fundamentally, the foreign secretary continued to believe that US interference only complicated his task as arbiter of the European concert. Never far beneath the surface remained his disdain for American politics and politicians. From

---

[69] Churchill memorandum, 29 January 1925, Treasury Papers, T175/9; Churchill to Chamberlain, 1 September 1925, Treasury Papers, T172/1498; Niemeyer memorandum, 27 September 1926, FO 371/11331: C 10930/10060/18.

[70] Cmd 2692 (1926): *Agreement of the Settlement of the War Debt of France to Great Britain*; Kellogg to Herrick, 16 July 1926, *FRUS 1926*, II, pp. 99–100. Cf. Artaud (1978), pp. 798ff.

[71] Niemeyer memorandum, 27 September 1926, FO 371/11331: C 10930/10060/18.

[72] Chamberlain memorandum, 6 October 1926, FO 371/11331: C 10700/10060/18.

his experience in dealing with Kellogg and Coolidge in the later 1920s, notably on disarmament, he concluded that they were pandering to narrow financial interests and Congressional opinion. They could thus not be considered serious partners in European security affairs. On 19 June 1926, Chamberlain noted that the United States were 'as difficult to deal with as they always have been because the Administration chops & changes its policy to catch a favouring breeze or avoid a squall in the Senate'.[73]

The one field where Chamberlain deemed a limited Anglo-American co-operation desirable was that of disarmament. But his assessment changed against the backdrop of growing Anglo-American discord and tensions over naval arms control. These reached their first peak in the so-called cruiser controversy and the failure of the 1927 Geneva conference before culminating after the Anglo-French disarmament compromise of July 1928.[74] There was an overriding Anglo-American interest in maintaining the Washington system; and originally British seemed reconcilable with American views on how to widen this system to include new classes of warships, particularly lighter cruisers. Further, like Washington, London generally saw the promotion of land force reductions in Europe as an important complement to the Locarno pact, both to further European stability and to reduce economic burdens.[75]

Yet although Chamberlain was convinced that 'treaty or no treaty, no power on earth can keep Germany so disarmed indefinitely unless a measure of general disarmament follows', Whitehall remained reserved towards far-reaching schemes to this end. Under pressure from Paris, and on account of a muted but existing concern over the imbalance between French and German re-sources, Britain consistently rejected Berlin's rationale of 'armaments parity'. This would also mark Britain's position in the League's Preparatory Commission from February 1926. Fundamentally, Chamberlain maintained that no sizeable 'reduction' in armaments could be achieved 'without security', i.e. without strengthening the security system of the Locarno pact first.[76] That rationale remained the main premise of British disarmament policy after Locarno.

As the British foreign secretary told Ambassador Houghton on 26 February 1926, he in principle agreed with the American view that disarmament should be based on 'visible armament' and 'peace strength'. Yet he also subsequently impressed on Kellogg that the European situation was more complex, stating

---

[73] Austen to Ida Chamberlain, 19 June 1926, Austen Chamberlain Papers, AC 5/1/386.

[74] Cf. McKercher (1984), pp. 55ff. See chapters 23 and 24.

[75] Chamberlain memorandum, 31 October 1925, CAB 24/175, CP 454 (25); 205th and 206th sessions of the CID, 17 and 30 November 1925, CAB 2/4: cabinet minutes, 3 December 1925, CAB 23/51, CC 57(25).

[76] Chamberlain to Crewe, 12 April 1926, *DBFP*, IA, 1, no. 264; Chamberlain memorandum, 16 July 1925, CAB 24/174, CP357(25).

that 'industrial strength may be considered as a factor in land disarmament'. Behind this lay of course the realisation that no compromise could be forged with France unless Britain acknowledged Germany's overbearing potential. Chamberlain's priority remained to 'carry on a common policy with Briand'. In his calculation, to do this 'in matters which are really serious', such as the Rhineland question, Britain had to be 'ready to compromise, if necessary even to sacrifice, matters of less immediate importance'. And these undoubtedly included League-based disarmament efforts where no immediate results could be expected anyway.[77]

During the cabinet's deliberations over disarmament policy in November and December 1925, Chamberlain had conceded that, not least for financial reasons, Britain had an interest in curbing naval armament; and it had to play a constructive part in the Preparatory Commission. Like his American counterpart, the foreign secretary originally favoured separating land disarmament, which he too deemed an essentially European problem, and naval matters, which were to be addressed through the Washington system. At the outset, Chamberlain backed the idea of a new naval conference, if Washington was prepared to organise it.[78] But the foreign secretary's preference was contested by Cecil, who remained the driving force behind British disarmament policy. Eventually leading the British delegation at Geneva, Cecil not only maintained that disarmament constituted the central problem on the road to a lasting peace, to be tackled immediately, not attendant to further advances in international security. He also proposed that it should be considered in one League-based forum. On 3 December 1925, the cabinet endorsed the compromise that while a Washington-style naval conference appeared most desirable, the British delegation should also place naval matters on the Preparatory Commission's agenda, all in the hope of striking bargains with France and America.[79]

From 1927, British disarmament policy would be dominated by disagreements with the other great naval power, the United States. Yet it would also be influenced by one basic reality. As the inner cabinet disputes over the 1925/6 naval estimates and the Admiralty's request for new cruisers had manifested, the British interest in arms reduction sprang from the overriding need to check military spending. In Churchill's estimate, funds had to be concentrated on domestic and imperial affairs; and Britain had far more to gain by cutting taxes than by spending money on excessive naval programmes, however strongly he was drawn to them in principle. Although Baldwin eventually backed the

---

[77] Houghton to Kellogg, 27 February 1926, *FRUS 1926*, I, p. 57.
[78] 205th CID, 17 November 1925, CAB 2/4.
[79] Cecil statements, 206th CID, 30 November 1925, CAB 2/4; cabinet minutes, 3 December 1925, CAB 23/51, CC 57 (25).

Admiralty's demands, and although they superseded all army claims, Britiain's capacity for maintaining large naval forces was palpably challenged after the Great War.[80]

Overall, however, disarmament in fact became one of the lesser priorities of British policy in the latter 1920s. Following Chamberlain's, not Cecil's, lead, progress was *de facto* made dependent on further improvements in Europe's general security situation. Chamberlain concentrated on cultivating 'mutual confidence' between the Locarno powers, seeking to isolate his dealings with Stresemann and Briand from the potential minefield of Franco-German disarmament disputes.[81] To be examined, then, is how far he could succeed with this endeavour. And to be examined, too, is what impact 'unwelcome' American involvement in European affairs, or lack thereof, actually had on the consolidation of what even after Locarno still remained an unfinished peace.

---

[80] Churchill memorandum, 7 February 1925, CAB 24/171, CP 71 (25); cabinet minutes, 22 July 1925, CAB 23/50, CC 39 (25).
[81] Chamberlain to D'Abernon, 1 February 1926, *DBFP*, IA, I, no. 231.

20   The new European concert – and its limits

1926 became a pivotal year not only for Locarno politics but also for the evolution of the Dawes system and more generally America's relations with the European powers. For that year revealed what dynamism was possible in sustaining the nascent Euro-Atlantic peace system. Above all, however, it threw into relief what obstacles – divergent interests, lack of political will and multiple constraints – still hampered its solidification. Was Locarno politics beginning to unravel before it had even really begun, because Chamberlain, Briand and Stresemann did not or could not address the underlying Franco-German problem?[1] Was there just a semblance of Franco-German reconciliation, because Germany's growing power could ultimately not be accommodated?[2]

In fact, it was now, in the aftermath of the security pact, that the two developments characterising international relations in the era of London and Locarno emerged. And, essentially, it was now that the politics of London *and* Locarno began to take root. To an equally remarkable extent, British ground-rules of political accommodation and American terms of financial consolidation came to prevail, if more so in Weimar Germany than in France or among Germany's eastern neighbours. As a result, progress in European politics and, to a lesser degree, progress in transatlantic consolidation efforts was indeed possible; and it was achieved. Yet it could only be achieved gradually and painfully. Neither European concert diplomacy nor the US-induced stabilisation of Germany, and pressure on France, produced further outcomes as groundbreaking as those of the mid-1920s. There were no further great leaps. And – because of the outstanding problems' intractability and, not least, the Anglo-American departure from forward engagement in Europe – there simply *could* be no further great leaps.

Apart from minor French concessions on troop-level reductions, the 'just' rewards Stresemann expected for his signature under the Locarno pact remained elusive, at least in the short term. In particular, he could not hasten

---

[1] See Jacobson (1972b), pp. 80ff.   [2] See Knipping (1987), pp. 21–2.

the 'liberation' of the Rhineland.[3] From the French perspective, further reassurance was imperative. More time, consistent British support and reliable German conduct were indispensable to convince not only Briand but also a majority among French elites that further substantial changes in the *status quo* could actually be in their own interest. Underlying this was the fact that while both Germany and France eventually managed to overcome drawn-out financial *malaise* and each achieved 'relative' stability by early 1927, there was no real turning-of-the-tide in either country. Recovery remained less than robust; and it remained to be seen how far Briand and Stresemann could persevere with their conciliatory policies under these circumstances.

In France, there was still widespread resistance to America's Progressive remedies – and as yet no evidence that they would not only benefit US interests but also the French economy. Frustrated with Washington's insistence on making loans dependent on debt-settlement ratification, Poincaré eventually sought to stabilise French finances and the franc 'from within'. And he would accomplish both in the spring of 1927.[5] In Germany, there was also still considerable opposition to US demands for welfare-cuts to restore public finances and spur productivity. But, as Stresemann never failed to underline, America's continued financial engagement was critical in every respect, far more so than in France.[6]

British and American policies thus continued to have a marked influence on the on-going reorientation of French and German policies in the era of London and Locarno. They did so both positively, setting standards, and negatively – if a lack of Anglo-American leadership left Briand and Stresemann to their own devices, with no option but to seek bilateral agreements.[7] Overall, though, German and French leaders adapted to what London and Washington desired. They saw deepened co-operation with the Anglo-American powers as a prerequisite for solving the cardinal political and economic problems with which they had to grapple. Particularly under Stresemann, methods that were developed to foster peaceful change increasingly shaped the ends of German

---

[3] Stresemann speech, 22 November 1925, in Turner (1967), pp. 418ff; Stresemann *Reichstag* speech, 28 January 1926, Stresemann (1932), II, pp. 435–8.

[4] Briand statements to the Foreign Affairs Committee, 19 December 1925, Procès verbaux, C14763, no. 46, pp. 6ff, 23–4; for opposition to further concessions, especially from the French General Staff, see Hoesch to Stresemann, 21 January 1926, no. 68, PA, 3058H: D 605896–7.

[5] Cf. Wurm (1979), pp. 421–69. See chapter 25.

[6] Stresemann speech, 19 December 1925, Stresemann Papers, vol. 274; Stresemann statements to the Foreign Affairs Commission, July 1925, Stresemann (1932), II, p. 149.

[7] By contrast, the influence of Anglo-American policies on those of Poland, Czechoslovakia and the Soviet Union as well as other, smaller east European states was far less pronounced in the latter 1920s, and essentially more indirect than direct. Yet all of these powers too had to adapt to, and on balance benefited from, the new ways and 'realities' of the emerging system of London and Locarno. Essentially, though, this system continued to evolve around the western powers' transformed relations with Weimar Germany.

policy. Essentially, Stresemann's basic conviction had hardened: it was only through co-operative diplomacy within the Locarno concert and with the support of the United States that Berlin could again become a great power of equal standing. Demands for unsettling territorial revisions in the east could not be allowed to jeopardise this broader agenda and, consequently, became more and more muted.[8]

In essence, though divisions among leading policymakers were more entrenched than in Berlin, much the same trends came to mark French policy. While Poincaré continued to prefer a more assertive and self-reliant course, he did not fundamentally disagree with Briand's assessment that France could enhance its security best by controlling the *voisin d'outre-Rhin* through the Locarno system. To achieve this, unflagging British support and a *rapprochement* with the United States were and remained critical. Thus, limited though they became, Anglo–American stabilisation polices retained a decisive impact on European developments after 1925. Time and again, they shaped outcomes, and blocked advances, more than any other power or force.

Germany's return to the 'comity of nations' – a stony path

How stony the path of Germany's return to the 'comity of nations' remained was thrown into relief by the wrangling over the former pariah's entry into the League of Nations in the spring of 1926. This became the first conspicuous test for the new European concert. Similarly, the soon stalling negotiations of the League-sponsored Preparatory Commission in Geneva cast a sobering light both on Europe's persistent security dilemmas and the limits of transatlantic co-operation.[9]

But the most important developments were less conspicuous. To all members of the Locarno triumvirate, it soon became clear that only piecemeal advances could be made towards a settlement of the crucial Rhineland issue. This remained the litmus test for Locarno politics, and its legitimacy, yet also inseparable from European (in)security. After Locarno, Berlin's plea for reducing French garrisons in the second and third occupation zones sparked acrimonious disputes.[10] In Locarno diplomacy, as defined by Chamberlain and Briand, the evacuation question soon became intricately connected with that of German disarmament and the end of military control.[11]

---

[8] Stresemann report to the cabinet, 18 March 1926, *AR Luther I und II*, no. 317; Schubert to Hoesch, 20 January 1926, *ADAP*, B, II/I, no. 41; Schubert memorandum, 25 March 1927, *ADAP*, B, V, no. 29. Cf. Wright (2002), pp. 373–408.

[9] Cf. Kitching (2004), pp. 161–77.

[10] *ADAP*, B, I/I, nos. 36, 60; Stresemann *Reichstag* speech, 28 January 1926, Stresemann (1932), II, pp. 435–6; Berthelot to Laroche, 12 January 1926, MAE, Série Europe, Allemagne, vol. 144.

[11] Briand statements to the Foreign Affairs Commission, 23 February 1926, Procès verbaux, C14763, no. 51, p. 22; Chamberlain to D'Abernon, 2 February 1926, *DBFP*, IA, I, no. 236.

Essentially, the developments of 1926 highlighted that, still a mere seven years after the Great War, further progress towards 'solving' Europe's underlying security question had to be necessarily measured, if not piecemeal. And they also underscored that further significant advances in Franco-German reconciliation, or indeed Germany's international integration as such, could not be achieved through the European concert alone. In effect, because the domestic and security constraints of European diplomacy were as stifling as they were, the only real alternative for propelling the fledgling European peace process lay in widening the scope of Locarno politics. What had to be envisaged was further 'strategic bargains' akin to those of 1924 and 1925 – bargains that comprised not only political but also financial elements. In eastern Europe, whose future and stability remained inseparably linked with Franco-German *rapprochement*, such agreements were even more urgent. But they also were far more difficult to realise, because east of Germany's borders of 1919 neither the territorial nor the security situation had been settled.

Frustrations over Locarno diplomacy in fact soon led policymakers to explore new *do ut des* agreements, not only between Germany and France but also between Germany and Poland. But, characteristically, this was done not by Kellogg or Chamberlain, who eschewed further grand initiatives, but by Stresemann and Briand – from as early as November 1925.[12] Yet, given the undiminished, if unequal, Franco-German dependence on Anglo-American goodwill and capital, any endeavours of this kind could only be realised with their support, if at all.

The League Council crisis of 1926, which centred on the terms of Germany's accession, came to a head in March. It could not be resolved during the League's spring session and shaped public and elite perceptions of Locarno diplomacy for some time thereafter. Stresemann had to wait till September before he could address the Geneva assembly. As noted, it had been agreed in October 1925 that Germany's League entry was to be a direct consequence of the Locarno agreements. Yet the accession process soon stalled not least because it again raised the fundamental question of Germany's position in the changing European order. In some French quarters, concerns re-emerged that should Germany be granted a permanent seat on the League Council this would weaken Poland's position and augur badly for France's eastern alliance system.[13] Eventually, Briand backed Warsaw's demand for compensation – namely that Poland be granted a permanent Council membership, too.[14] What thus arose at the very start of the Locarno period was not merely a conflict over

---

[12] Hoesch to AA, 1 December 1925, Stresemann to Hoesch, 8 December 1925, *ADAP*, B, I/I, pp. 10–11, 46–7.

[13] Hoesch to Stresemann, 29 January 1926, *ADAP*, B, I/I, no. 70. Cf. Spenz (1966), pp. 25ff.

[14] Crewe to Chamberlain, 22 February 1926, *DBFP*, IA, I, no. 289. Cf. Pitts (1987), pp. 110ff.

status and influence at Geneva. It was the danger that old patterns of European division and rivalry would re-emerge, corroding the fledgling European concert. Yet that this crisis could be overcome within one month also manifested that the Locarno process had already acquired a remarkable momentum of its own.

Similarly, the conclusion of the Soviet–German Neutrality treaty in April 1926, hard on the heels of the League disputes, raised some eyebrows in Paris and London. But it never came close to derailing Germany's accommodation with the west. This, too, was a measure of how far European politics had progressed since Rapallo. Yet all of these developments merely underscored that Germany could not hope to achieve further dynamic changes in Europe. As noted, neither London nor Washington desired more than incremental progress. And Stresemann had to acknowledge that the Anglo-American powers espoused policies of limited liability and gradualism. Faced with a growing financial crisis and opposition to speedy concessions at home, Briand welcomed this. And Polish leaders looked for French yet also British and American backing in their bid to maintain Poland's prominent, if artificially elevated, postwar position.[15]

The League Council crisis was in many ways a transitional crisis from the Versailles to a post-Versailles order, and as such hardly surprising. Germany had signed the Locarno treaties on the premise that, when entering the League, it would join the Council as a permanent member, which corresponded with its new great-power status. It was with this expectation that Stresemann sent the entry application to Geneva on 8 February 1926.[16] What triggered subsequent altercations was Briand's attempt to use the League's special session in March, convened expressly for Germany's admission, to secure the same position for France's Polish ally.[17] He thus tried both to assuage Foreign Minister Skrzyński's concerns and to reassure adherents of the eastern alliances in France.[18] But his move also led Spain and Brazil, former temporary Council members, to claim the same status as Poland. Soon an impasse was reached.

As France could only hope to achieve its aims with Britain's backing, the attitude of Chamberlain became critical. Setting the tone for all further concert

---

[15] Briand statements to the Foreign Affairs Commission, 23 February 1926, Procès verbaux, C14763, no. 51, pp. 13ff; *Quai d'Orsay* memorandum, 27 January 1926, MAE, Série Europe, Grande-Bretagne, 284–6, vol. 58. Cf. Wandycz (1988), pp. 22ff; Pease (1986).

[16] Cabinet minutes, 8 February 1926, *AR Luther I und II*, II, no. 284. Cf. Baechler (1996), pp. 664–6.

[17] Minutes of a meeting of the Locarno powers, Geneva, 8 March 1926, *ADAP*, B, I/I, no. 145. Cf. Kimmich (1976), pp. 78ff.

[18] Briand statements to the Foreign Affairs Commission, 19 December 1925, Procès verbaux, C14763, no. 46, pp. 12–13; *Quai d'Orsay* memorandum, 27 January 1926, MAE, Série Europe, Grande-Bretagne, 284–6, vol. 58.

diplomacy, the British foreign secretary sought to break the deadlock, not through negotiations within the Locarno triangle, but by reaching a bilateral understanding with Briand first. He agreed to support French policy, and Poland's candidature, when meeting Briand for informal talks in Paris on 28 January.[19] While not oblivious to Polish concerns, Chamberlain did so mainly to strengthen Briand domestically and to revive the *entente* under Locarno's new auspices. Even though he was criticised for his too narrowly pro-French stance not only in the cabinet and in the Commons but also from the ranks of the League of Nations Union (LNU), Chamberlain refused to divert from his chosen course.[20]

In Stresemann's view, the attitude of the western powers was unacceptable. By widening the League Council they would force Berlin to legitimate what he deemed Poland's 'artificial' claim for recognition as a great power.[21] This, he told Chamberlain, threatened to discredit his entire Locarno policy in Germany where particularly the DNVP yet also *Reichspräsident* Hindenburg fundamentally opposed a German membership in the 'club of the victors'. Moreover, Stresemann's perception was that Berlin had been presented with a *fait accompli* and was facing once again, only months after Locarno, a common front of the ex-allied powers.[22]

But the upshot of the League Council crisis was not a resurfacing of European divisions. When it ended, in mid-March, what many had hoped would be Germany's solemn accession to the League had not yet materialised. More importantly, however, the Locarno powers had prevented the dispute from eroding the foundations of their new diplomacy. They had forged a compromise that, as all sides confidently predicted, would finally pave Germany's way to Geneva in September. It centred on the proposal not to give Poland the same status as Germany after all but to make it a non-permanent Council member.[23] This agreement emerged from the first round of direct informal negotiations between Chamberlain, Briand and Stresemann after Locarno, pursued at Geneva. From the autumn of 1926, such trilateral negotiations were to become the preferred mode of concerted co-operation permitting all sides to accommodate their interests as far as possible, and often behind closed doors rather than under the scrutiny of 'world

[19] Chamberlain memorandum, 1 February 1926, *DBFP*, IA, I, no. 233. Cf. Carlton (1968), pp. 354ff.

[20] Chamberlain to Baldwin, 18 March 1926, in Petrie (1939/40), II, pp. 297ff; Austen to Ida Chamberlain, 5 March 1926, Austen Chamberlain Papers, AC 5/1/375.

[21] Stresemann to German legation, Stockholm, 6 February 1926, *ADAP*, B, I/I, no. 83. Cf. Wright (2002), p. 351–2.

[22] Stresemann note, 28 February 1926, Stresemann Papers, vol. 36; Stresemann to Sthamer, 11 February 1926, *ADAP*, B, I/I, no. 95.

[23] London to Tyrrell, 16 March 1926, Chamberlain to FO, 12 March 1926, *DBFP*, IA, I, nos. 359, 336.

opinion'. Following a series of confidential meetings, during which Chamberlain again assumed a valuable mediating role, he, Briand and Stresemann reaffirmed in a communiqué on 16 March that they considered a continuation of Locarno politics paramount.[24]

At first, the British foreign secretary had urged the German side to accept Briand's original plan to avoid discrediting him and also publicly harming Skrzyński's position. But the British cabinet opposed the creation of any further permanent seats; and, for reasons of overall policy, it pressed for a swift resolution of the conflict.[25] In the end, neither Chamberlain nor Briand were prepared to risk compromising Locarno's 'works of peace' for the sake of supporting Warsaw, at least not beyond face-saving concessions. Chamberlain put his weight behind the proposal to give Poland an 'additional temporary seat' and delay its accession until after Germany entered the Council.[26] Behind the scenes, he had impressed on Briand that if Germany were prevented from entering the League 'and the Treaty of Locarno were thereby to fall through', France would 'never get from us guarantees similar to those we gave her at Locarno'. He had 'already put as great a strain on British public opinion' to reach a settlement 'as he dared do'. Should France prove 'too unyielding', it would 'inevitably' run 'perils' and 'weaken the position' of their 'best friend', himself.[27] British pressure had an effect on Briand.

Albeit inconsistent and only readjusted at the last minute, Chamberlain's actions had not damaged the League.[28] And, if with difficulty, Locarno politics had passed its first test. In September 1926, Germany would indeed return to the *Société des Nations* in a manner reconcilable with its 'special middle position' in Europe and consistent with its new, peculiar great-power status. Locarno politics was and remained great-power politics. The interests of smaller powers, notably those of eastern Europe, were considered yet ultimately viewed as secondary. Nevertheless, a functioning European concert ultimately enhanced their security, and it strengthened rather than weakened the League of Nations itself. For the League would have remained marginalised had it not become a forum for the Locarno powers and, above all, had it continued to exclude Germany.

As Stresemann declared in the *Reichstag* after his return from Geneva on 21 March, despite the temporary setback that Germany had suffered he had no

---

[24] Minutes of a meeting of the Locarno powers, 8 March 1926, *ADAP*, B, I/I, no. 145; Chamberlain to FO, 12 March 1926, *DBFP*, IA, I, no. 336; *ADAP*, B, I/I, appendix 1.

[25] Tyrrell to London, 15 March 1925, *DBFP*, IA, I, no. 351.

[26] Minutes of a conversation between Chamberlain and Luther, *ADAP*, B I/I1, no. 147; Chamberlain to D'Abernon, 28 February 1926, London to Tyrrell, 12 March, *DBFP*, IA, I, nos. 236, 336, 337.

[27] Chamberlain to Tyrrell, 16 March 1926, *DBFP*, IA, I, no. 361.

[28] Cf. against this Carlton (1968), pp. 363–4.

intention of renouncing the aim of co-operating within the League 'as a great power with equal rights'. Nor would he abandon a policy recognising that 'the global economic interconnections between peoples' required 'political understanding' and 'reconciliation'.[29] This was a declaration not least directed at Washington's address. Within the Coolidge administration, the League crisis initially aroused concerns that Britain and France might return to unbridled power politics. Washington's reaction confirmed that the United States had a pronounced interest in seeing Germany's international integration progress. But it also confirmed that Washington was not prepared to wield more than public pressure and financial threats to press the Locarno powers to settle what was theirs to settle. Houghton publicly scolded Chamberlain and Briand for their old-style *entente* manoeuvres. In his assessment, France had taken the lead while Chamberlain had dragged Britain along, if 'reluctantly because the tide of British feeling sets strongly in the opposite direction'. The US ambassador held that keeping Germany out of the League would thwart any attempts to make it a 'truly international instrument for the organization of peace'.[30]

Kellogg even displayed a certain measure of '*Schadenfreude*' about Anglo-French troubles at the League.[31] In his eyes, and in Castle's judgement, the quarrels over Germany's entry had reinforced the perception that Washington was well advised to keep a distance from Geneva.[32] Castle thought it 'absurd' that 'Brazil should be able to veto a matter that was primarily of European concern.' In his assessment the crisis showed 'the danger of attempting to make the League universal'. It appeared 'nonsensical to try to ignore the necessarily regional character of the world' – a world where, in Washington's perspective, no shared security threats linked Europe and America.[33] The League, then, was essentially seen as a useful mechanism to improve security relations in Europe.

Like Houghton, Kellogg did not hold Germany but France and Britain responsible for the impasse reached at Geneva. The State Department came out strongly in favour of Germany's inclusion into the League. In the aftermath of the crisis, Castle told the Polish representative Ciechanowski that 'Poland would probably be very foolish to keep Germany out of the League.' Echoing Chamberlain, he argued that otherwise Germany 'will and must align herself with Russia, which is the worst thing Poland can look forward to'.[34]

---

[29] *SB*, vol. 389, pp. 6451–2.
[30] Sterling (London) to Kellogg, 20 March 1926, *FRUS 1926*, I, p. 60; Castle Diary, 19 March 1926, vol. 8, p. 51.
[31] Howard to Chamberlain, 26 February 1926, *DBFP*, IA, I, no. 303.
[32] *Ibid.*
[33] Castle Diary, 29 May 1926, vol. 8, pp. 130–1.
[34] *Ibid.*, 7 May 1926, vol. 8, pp. 102–3.

More noteworthy than this warning, however, was the extent to which Republican policymakers had come to trust in Stresemann's 'policy of reconciliation'. They trusted his, and the German, interest in playing by the rules of peaceful conflict-resolution that a German League membership symbolised. While debt-settlement negotiations with France were entering an acrimonious phase, Germany was even regarded as an ever more valuable partner in Europe.[35]

As a consequence, even President Coolidge himself joined in criticism of France's 'reversion' to 'the old politics of the *balance of power*'. And he underlined that the problems which had arisen at Geneva had proved how much Europe still needed 'the support of the United States'.[36] To this end, the president explicitly proposed broadening the 'co-operation between Germany, America and England' in order to pre-empt further setbacks. Yet, as already noted, he and Kellogg were far from following this up with any concrete new strategies or initiatives, except on disarmament. The emphasis of American policy continued to lie on financial engagement in Germany and pressure on the French debtor. Ultimately, relief prevailed that the Locarno powers' overall co-operation seemed not in jeopardy.[37]

Thus far then, no side had abandoned the course of 1925. The new (west) European concert eventually proved effective. Yet, significantly, while America maintained its detachment from security affairs, Britain no longer steered European developments in the way it had done a year earlier. Although Chamberlain intervened in urgent cases, it was increasingly Briand who, with his backing, could regulate the pace and scope of Locarno politics. The French foreign minister did so with consideration for Stresemann's position but mainly, and quite naturally, in accordance with what French elite opinion appeared to permit.

This role-distribution came to mark the new Anglo-French *entente* that, following Chamberlain's preferences, soon indeed became an essential feature of the Locarno concert.[38] It sometimes served to strengthen this mechanism, but was overall detrimental to its further evolution. In the short term, however, both the concert and the prospects for Germany's further alignment with the emerging western system had not been eroded but invigorated by the Council crisis.[39] This was all the more important because it was precisely at this juncture that more substantive problems began to put strains on Locarno

---

[35] Cf. Link (1970), pp. 347–8. For US press reactions see Berg (1990), p. 357.
[36] Maltzan report, 23 March 1926, *ADAP*, B, I/I, no. 96.
[37] Castle Diary, 22–23 March 1926, vol. 8, pp. 52–4.
[38] Chamberlain to Briand, 29 July 1926, FO 800/259/668; Chamberlain to Grahame, 19 November 1926, *DBFP*, IA, II, no. 264.
[39] Cf. Krüger (1985a), p. 315; Spenz (1966), pp. 152–3.

diplomacy: problems revolving around the Rhineland – and raising questions about the future of Germany's western orientation as such.

The crux of Locarno politics – the Rhineland question and the meaning of 'reciprocity'

Since January 1926, there had been mounting indications that the momentum generated by the Locarno agreements themselves did not allow for tangible further changes in the European *status quo*, at least not in the short term. There were growing signs, too, that the 'pure' diplomacy Chamberlain envisaged would not suffice either. Essentially, the pact system had not yet provided safeguards that French policymakers deemed sufficient to enter into rapid follow-up agreements with Germany. Nor had there as yet been a sufficiently long period of reliable stability.[40]

That Franco-German accommodation would remain a drawn-out process was thrown into relief by the again hardening disputes over military control.[41] It was no coincidence, however, that tensions centred on the Rhineland where the French troop reductions from the second and third occupation zones lagged far behind Stresemann's initial hopes. This led to an outcry against his Locarno policy in the *Reichstag* and Germany's nationalist press.[42] It confirmed Chamberlain's premonitions about the backlash that 'exaggerated expectations' could provoke.[43]

From the time the Locarno treaties were signed, and the more vocally the longer they failed to materialise, Stresemann demanded concrete *Rückwirkungen*. He constantly maintained that he could not gain further domestic support for his Locarno policy unless the western powers made further concessions. After the first German hopes regarding the Rhineland had dissipated, what Stresemann essentially meant by such *Rückwirkungen* were sizeable reductions in troop levels, as promised by Britain and France in their note of 14 November 1925. The German foreign minister repeatedly recurred to resignation threats to underscore the urgency of his demands, insisting that the maintenance of large occupation forces, actually increased after Locarno, was incommensurate with the spirit of the pact.[44] Chamberlain by and large agreed with this assessment.

---

[40] Chamberlain memorandum, 28 January 1926, Crewe to Chamberlain, 3 February 1926, *DBFP*, IA, I, nos. 239, 240.

[41] Cf. Salewski (1966), pp. 328ff.

[42] Stresemann *Reichstag* speech, 28 January 1926, Stresemann (1932), II, pp. 435–6; minutes of a conversation between Stresemann and de Margerie, 4 February 1926, *ADAP*, B, I/I, no. 80.

[43] Austen to Ida Chamberlain, 28 November 1925, Austen Chamberlain Papers, AC 5/1/370.

[44] Stresemann speech, 22 November 1925, in Turner (1967), pp. 418ff; minutes of a conversation between Stresemann and D'Abernon, 3 February 1926, *ADAP*, B, I/I, no. 76.

On 5 February 1926, D'Abernon reported that the French evacuation of Cologne on 31 January had been an 'immense success' for Stresemann. Yet during the *Reichstag* debate on Locarno, Luther and Stresemann 'only got their majority on the vote of confidence by a bare margin'. In the eyes of the British ambassador, this lent credibility to Stresemann's claim that Germany's 'slackness' in meeting its disarmament obligations was essentially attributable to an as yet strong inner-German opposition to his entire Locarno policy, which made him tread carefully. Here, Chamberlain disagreed.[45]

Having made minor troop reductions possible in November 1925, Briand insisted that any further French concessions depended on Germany's compliance with the disarmament provisions of 1919. Essentially, he endeavoured to fortify what he domestically defended as Europe's new, and improved, *status quo*: the security pact agreements as the complement and new basis of Versailles. While contemplating that Germany might have to pay a considerable financial price for further revisions, the French foreign minister overall sought to forestall them. In particular, no swift moves regarding the strategically sensitive 'demilitarised zone' in the Rhineland would be countenanced.[46] The fact that none of his domestic critics could present a convincing counter-model to his course indeed constituted a considerable *atout* for Briand.[47] Yet, as he told Chamberlain on 28 January, his volatile parliamentary base and, especially, the French military's opposition to further troop withdrawals restricted his room to manoeuvre for further concessions severely.[48] Albeit with a sizeable majority, the *Chambre* only ratified the Locarno treaties on 2 March. Up until then, securing this ratification remained the *Quai d'Orsay*'s principal concern; and the numerous German disarmament violations that Paris registered only aggravated Briand's difficulties.[49]

As the British ambassador Crewe noted, Briand was generally sceptical that French concessions in the Rhineland would strengthen the Locarno spirit in Germany.[50] Yet even if he had been more optimistic, he would not have carried a majority on this issue at that point. In December, only President Painlevé had backed Briand's plea for a goodwill gesture with regard to troop

[45] D'Abernon to Chamberlain, 5 February 1926, Chamberlain to D'Abernon, 4 February 1926, *DBFP*, IA, I, nos. 247, 245.

[46] Briand statements to the Foreign Affairs Commission, 19 December 1925, Procès verbaux, C14763, no. 46, pp. 6ff, 23–4; MAE, Série Europe, Grande-Bretagne, 284–6, 86/209–10; Chamberlain to D'Abernon, 2 February 1926, *DBFP*, IA, I, no. 236, pp. 398–90.

[47] Cf. Pitts (1987), p. 112.

[48] Briand twice had to form new governments between January and July 1926. Cf. Keeton (1987), pp. 124–70.

[49] Chamberlain to D'Abernon, *DBFP*, IA, I, no. 232; Briand to Fleuriau, 11 January 1926, *DBFP*, IA, I, pp. 306–10. This Hoesch also impressed on Stresemann. See Hoesch to Stresemann, 12 December 1925, no. 962, PA, 3058H: D605778–9.

[50] Crewe to Chamberlain, December 1925, *DBFP*, IA, I, no. 161. Cf. Jacobson (1972b), pp. 78–9.

levels, arguing that such a gesture was required to prevent a resurgence of nationalism in Germany. But Painlevé had also told the German ambassador Hoesch that Briand's most formidable task remained to convince a General Staff that had won the Great War only at a heavy price to yield France's *glacis* on the Rhine.[51]

Indeed, in the eyes of Poincaré, and even more so in the eyes of Marshal Foch, maintaining control over the Rhineland was a vital French interest in a time of flux. The Rhineland remained the core strategic pawn not only for ensuring continued German payments but also an advantageous final settlement of reparations. Above all, however, in view of what many, like the chairman of the *Chambre*'s Foreign Affairs Commission, Henry Franklin-Bouillon, regarded as Britain's still insufficient Locarno guarantees, it remained France's core strategic base. While supporting their ratification – for lack of better alternatives – Franklin-Bouillon considered the Locarno accords too weak, arguing that France ultimately had to rely too much on Germany's good faith.[52] And Poincaré originally even denounced Locarno as a British ploy, aiming to divide France from its eastern allies while only offering vague guarantees as a compensation.[53] By the same token, not only *Bloc National* parliamentarians but also *Quai d'Orsay* officials like Berthelot remained suspicious of what they deemed persistent German attempts to evade Versailles' disarmament stipulations. They thus sought to keep the control instrument of the IMCC as long as possible to forestall what France dreaded most: that Germany would do everything in its power to prepare the ground for its future re-ascension as a military great power.[54]

If not for Briand, then certainly for Poincaré and Foch, two cardinal questions surfaced with new urgency in 1926. How could France regain the financial strength prerequisite for maintaining its armoured superiority vis-à-vis Germany? And how could it prevent a recasting of power relations with its eastern neighbour that threatened France's existing, yet burdensome politico-military preponderance? For it was such a continued preponderance that France still *de facto* maintained after Locarno – with British acquiescence – on the basis of the Versailles treaty, superior armed forces and an overall still intact eastern alliance system.[55] Briand sought to counter the array of domestic criticism he faced by arguing that Locarno was an 'application' of the Versailles

---

[51] Hoesch to Stresemann, 9 December 1925, 21 January 1926, nos. 952, 68, PA, 3058H: D 605771–897.

[52] Minutes of the Foreign Affairs Commission, 23 February 1926; *JOC*, 2 March 1926, cols. 1121–34.

[53] Cf. Pitts (1987), pp. 110–12.

[54] Berthelot minute, 12 January 1926, MAE, Série Europe, Allemagne, vol. 144. Cf. Salewski (1966), p. 328.

[55] Cf. Knipping (1987), pp. 21–2.

treaty. More importantly, he argued that it offered the very means to cope with unalterable postwar realities, chiefly that of a 'people of 40 million inhabitants' facing a neighbouring 'nation of 70 million inhabitants', which was also growing faster than France.[56]

Arguably, Briand did not shift the emphasis of his policy after Locarno in any dramatic way. Rather than revert to obstructionism, he still sought to enhance French security in co-operation with Germany and to help consolidate Stresemann's domestic position. He continued to see Locarno as 'a germ, which had to be developed' in 'conformity with the security of France'. This would require further political accords with Germany and, in the longer run, common steps towards Europe's 'economic organisation'. Most of all, though, while wider British guarantees seemed impossible to obtain, fortifying a common front with Chamberlain remained a cornerstone of Briand's Locarno policy.[57]

More profoundly, then, what still shaped this policy both for domestic and strategic reasons was the quest for further, more solid bases of French security.[58] French policymakers were undoubtedly intent on improving the financial foundations of French security. To this end, they sought to put relations with Washington on a better footing. A first step in this direction had been the Mellon–Bérenger agreement. Essentially, however, Briand sought security with British help – and both with and in containment of Germany. Ideally, France was looking for complementary assurances from both powers for any sizeable military reductions in the Rhineland. As for the future of military control, Paris favoured a transition from allied to some kind of League control mechanisms.[59] But deepening the co-operation with Chamberlain – and Stresemann – remained crucial.

By March 1926, Stresemann had begun to resign himself to the fact that Locarno's original impetus would not suffice to realise wider German aims.[60] Indeed, any other outcome would have been highly surprising at this stage because, essentially, Germany had nothing to offer to France in return for the political changes it sought, or at least had not offered anything yet, except for the pledge to adhere to the ground-rules of Locarno. France, on the other hand, was the power called upon to cede its most important, if volatile, security bases under Versailles – especially the Rhenish base. From a French perspective, it also remained uncertain whether Stresemann's policy would be more

[56] Briand statements to the Foreign Affairs Commission, 19 December 1925, C14763, no. 46, pp. 12–3.
[57] *Ibid.*, 23 February 1926, 19 December 1925, Procès verbaux, C14763, no. 51, p. 13–22; no. 46, pp. 22–3.
[58] Cf. Soutou (2001).
[59] *Quai d'Orsay* memorandum, 27 January 1926, MAE, Série Europe, Grande-Bretagne, vol. 58.
[60] Stresemann *Reichstag* speech, 22 March 1926, *SB*, vol. 389, p. 6451.

than a passing phenomenon. The German foreign minister acknowledged that allaying French security concerns, which in his view were also instrumentalised to stall further advances, would remain a core requirement for German diplomacy. To achieve this, thus his abiding premise, Britain had to be engaged as an intermediary between Berlin and Paris. Yet, like Briand, Stresemann had also begun to contemplate offering financial concessions to France to achieve political gains. He began to gauge whether the time had come, and how far the Dawes regime permitted, to use Germany's 'one remaining weapon', its economic power, within the Locarno concert.[61] But this would only become an acute concern in the autumn of 1926.

It is important to note that until then, in its initial, formative phase, Locarno politics did not evolve as concert politics in the strictest sense. Rather, whenever salient issues were broached, it took the form of the ex-allied powers seeking a common response to German demands, and Stresemann seeking to win Chamberlain's backing in convincing Briand that, 'in the spirit of Locarno', further revisions of the *status quo* of Versailles were overdue. It has been claimed that it was Briand who largely controlled, and arrested, peaceful change in the Locarno period.[62] In fact, though, he could only seize control to the extent that Chamberlain's policies allowed him to do so. As will be shown, Chamberlain's influence on European politics remained pivotal. He remained the only potent mediator between Paris and Berlin. And, though often overly passive and cautious, the British foreign secretary was indeed still instrumental in framing the agenda of Locarno diplomacy between 1926 and 1929, even if Briand's efforts to evade concessions or strike bargains with Stresemann were more conspicuous.

Britain's approach to the Rhineland question and military control in the spring and summer of 1926 revealed succinctly what course Chamberlain decided to chart as 'honest broker' for the remainder of the Locarno period. He never abandoned his axiom that it was possible to continue fostering French security and Germany's further western integration at the same time. This he set out to achieve by ensuring that what he and Briand defined as 'reciprocity' shaped relations between the Locarno powers. What leverage did Britain really have after Locarno? Essentially, Chamberlain had two options. Either he could seek to cast his weight on the French *or* the German side of the diplomatic scales. This he could do affirmatively, through more reassurance for France, or through stepped-up pressure, be it by threatening to withdraw this reassurance, be it by threatening to block any further German demands. Or he could seek to use Britain's political leverage vis-à-vis both Paris *and* Berlin to go beyond such limited balancing diplomacy: to promote mutually beneficial *quid pro quo* agreements that served to strengthen the European concert and buttress European peace as a whole.

Withdrawing support from Briand or backing German claims against France was out of the question for Chamberlain. Yet, as noted, his scope for providing additional reassurance through wider guarantees was distinctly constrained, too, because Chamberlain, Tyrrell and a majority in Baldwin's cabinet deemed the self-imposed limits of British Locarno policy very appropriate in this respect. They saw no sense in envisaging wider continental commitments while, at least in their views, a majority in the Commons and the British public remained deeply averse to them and demanded that the government focus instead on – crisis-ridden – domestic politics.[63]

What course did Chamberlain pursue instead? In essence, based on the conclusions that he had drawn from Locarno and the consequences he drew from Stresemann's 'ever-growing demands' thereafter, he came to adjust his strategy.[64] He now implemented his policy of reviving the Anglo-French *entente* on new premises, increasingly following the maxim that France had to be reassured first, and Briand domestically bolstered, if Locarno diplomacy was to achieve any further results. And by these the British foreign secretary still meant results acceptable to both the French and the Germans. This did not lead Britain to rescind any kind of leadership role in Europe. Crucially, however, it led Chamberlain to limit rather than shape the agenda of Locarno politics. In practice, he would never again put forward more than minor initiatives for settling Europe's outstanding postwar problems.

After Locarno, Britain had even less of a strategic interest in a continued Rhineland occupation than before.[65] And Chamberlain personally encouraged Briand to hasten troop reductions. While siding against precipitated alterations in the overall *status quo*, he thought that timely withdrawals would manifest that the Locarno agreements could indeed lead to tangible, visible improvements. Further, as both he and Briand knew, French concessions only commanded real bargaining-power if they were made significantly ahead of the 1935 deadline set at Versailles. Chamberlain informally met his French counterpart in Paris on 28 January 1926 to co-ordinate their future co-operation. He convinced him that a troop reduction of 15,000 from a then total of 75,000 would be desirable, if only to avoid being seen as reneging on the promises that both powers had made in November 1925. Likewise, London pressed for

---

[63] Cabinet minutes, 17 and 24 February 1926, CAB 23/52, CC 5, 7 (26); Tyrrell memorandum, 26 July 1926, *DBFP*, IA, I, no. 103.

[64] Chamberlain to D'Abernon, 1 February 1926; Kilmarnock report to FO, 3 February 1925, *DBFP*, IA, I, nos. 231, 241.

[65] Sterndale-Bennett memorandum, 10 April 1926, *DBFP*, IA, I, p. 857.

a compromise permitting a swift withdrawal of the IMCC. For the perception by then prevailing in the Foreign Office was that Germany had effectively met Versailles' disarmament clauses. The known breaches of the treaty that still occurred, especially the *Reichswehr*'s covert co-operation with the Red Army, were considered minor; they were not seen as a serious threat to European security.[66]

One main thrust of British policy was thus to eliminate the major remaining sources of irritation in postwar relations with Germany. In principle, this seemed to tally more with Stresemann's aims than with Briand's concerns. In practice, however, Chamberlain's European policy did not depart from the different, less than finely calibrated course already described. Forging an Anglo-French 'axis' of common interests has been described as the 'greatest virtue' of British Locarno policy.[67] Undoubtedly, any French policymaker seeking to maintain a conciliatory policy vis-à-vis Berlin required continued British assurances. And that Britain and France should have a common interest in retaining the reins of the Locarno process, and avoid too rapid a revision of the postwar *status quo* in Germany's favour, is equally understandable. Yet the greatest challenge for British policy in the latter 1920s was to avoid a degree of one-sidedness and passivity that allowed one of the Locarno system's protagonists, Briand, to set the rules vis-à-vis another, Stresemann, while not permitting sufficient recourse to the *common* rules and understandings of Locarno, which had been established on a footing of equality. But this is essentially what occurred. Concretely, it often put Briand in a position to steer, and constrain, Locarno politics in accordance with French interests – while invoking the doubtless significant constraints of French 'public opinion'.[68]

It was after the Anglo-French tête-à-tête in January 1926 that Chamberlain declared that the spirit of Locarno was one of 'reciprocity'.[69] But it soon became clear that it was up to Britain and France to determine what constituted 'reciprocity' in any given case. And as the British foreign secretary pursued an essentially reactive policy for the remainder of the 1920s, Briand was by and large empowered to block Stresemann's pursuits of peaceful change when he deemed this necessary. Although the French foreign minister desired further reconciliation with Germany, he could time and again plead that his leeway for further concessions was exhausted, and gain

---

[66] Chamberlain to D'Abernon, 2 February, *DBFP*, IA, I, no. 236; Lindsay to Chamberlain, 7 December 1926, Huxley memorandum, 13 December 1926, FO 371/11281: C 12969/234/18. Cf. Fox (1969), pp. 121ff.

[67] Cf. Jacobson (1972b), pp. 44–5.

[68] Berthelot to Fleuriau, January 1926, MAE, Série Europe, Grande-Bretagne/Fleuriau 3/35–6. Cf. Keeton (1987), pp. 209–16.

[69] Chamberlain to D'Abernon, 1 February 1926, *DBFP*, IA, I, no. 231.

Chamberlain's support.[70] Yet, in short, genuine 'reciprocity' would have required that Stresemann's interests and domestic necessities were given equal weight in the Locarno process. To ensure this as far as possible, and to promote not only a more balanced but also a more dynamic process, would have been the British 'broker's' essential role, difficult as it was under the circumstances. But Chamberlain fulfilled this role in a less than effective fashion. As a consequence, his bid to reforge an Anglo–French axis of stability did not serve to sustain the new European concert. Rather, it impeded its solidification, especially because it went hand in hand with an even more significant reorientation of British policy: the aforementioned reversion to a 'semi-detachment' from European affairs. This weakened the very ground-rules of 'reciprocity' that Chamberlain sought to advance, and it thus ultimately acted against a further fortification of the Locarno concert and a more robust development of the wider peace order emerging in post-world War I Europe.[71]

On 1 February, Chamberlain conveyed to Stresemann 'with the utmost gravity' that while Britain's policy of nurturing 'mutual confidence and co-operation' between the Locarno powers remained 'unchanged', the further 'development' of the Locarno edifice required 'mutual concessions', above all from Germany. London did not 'underestimate the difficult position and indeed the weakness' of the Luther government. But the foreign secretary accused Stresemann of 'deliberately' using this weakness to 'squeeze concessions out of the western powers'. He maintained that the 'ex-allied powers' had already modified the 'whole régime of occupation in the Rhineland'. They had thus 'fulfilled [their] part of the bargain' struck at Locarno. Having received negative reports from Britain's high commissioner in the Rhineland, Lord Kilmarnock, Chamberlain thus underscored that the time was not ripe for further adjustments. It had been Germany's turn to act. But Berlin had answered allied goodwill not by reciprocal steps, notably on disarmament, but by 'threats' and ever more far-reaching demands.[72]

Chamberlain scolded Stresemann not least because he had by that time come to view Briand's domestic standing as highly precarious. If for no concrete reason, he deemed Stresemann's position in Germany less insecure. The British foreign secretary thus agreed with Briand on the formula that it was not yet 'opportune' to broach 'large issues' like the Rhineland question. And he posited two main preconditions for any further discussion: Germany had

[70] Briand statements to the Foreign Affairs Commission, 23 February 1926, Procès verbaux, C14763, no. 51, pp. 13–22.
[71] Chamberlain to D'Abernon, 30 April 1926, Chamberlain to Grahame, 19 November 1926, *DBFP*, IA, II, nos. 487, 264; Austen to Ida Chamberlain, 28 November 1925, Austen Chamberlain Papers, AC 5/1/370.
[72] Chamberlain to D'Abernon, 1, 4 and 7 February 1926, *DBFP*, IA, II, nos. 231, 245, 250; Kilmarnock report to FO, 3 February 1925, *DBFP*, IA, I, no. 241.

to enter the League; and it finally had to fulfil its disarmament commitments.[73] As Chamberlain told Stresemann, France's not easily refutable claim that Germany had still not complied with all disarmament requirements left him no room to bring either the Rhineland or the withdrawal of the IMCC on the agenda of Locarno politics. Essentially, though, any British action was to be predicated on what he and Briand decided was good German behaviour.[74] The net-effect of this was that the Franco-German peace process stalled in the spring of 1926. Thereafter, it would progress again, yet progress very slowly. Often, it would only be invigorated by – unsuccessful – initiatives that were always launched by Stresemann or Briand, not by Chamberlain. It would never quite turn into what all three protagonists of Locarno had originally hoped for: a robust, ever more legitimate process. Even less, though, would it fulfil Stresemann's early expectations and become a dynamic process of peaceful change.

The Treaty of Berlin and the challenge of fostering Germany's western orientation

Hard on the heels of the League Council crisis, and with tensions over the Rhineland still lingering, the workings of the European concert and German–American relations were taxed further by the Soviet–German neutrality treaty. Signed on 24 April 1926, the Berlin treaty originally raised suspicions not only in Paris but also in London and Washington. After Locarno, Stresemann and Schubert had faced the challenge of reconciling the ever more clearly predominating western orientation of German policy with the less important, yet still vital, German interest to place relations with Soviet Russia on a pragmatic, calculable basis. Yet they were also acutely aware that their parallel task was no smaller: to avoid compromising German trustworthiness in London, Washington and, particularly, Paris.[75]

Not only formally but also in substance, the Berlin treaty was indeed compatible with Germany's Locarno commitments, also regarding the League. It centred on a limited pledge of mutual neutrality, which also included the promise of each party not to participate in any 'economic or financial boycott' should the other party be involved in a conflict. Thus, Stresemann went to the limits of what Locarno allowed regarding article 16 of the League

---

[73] Chamberlain to D'Abernon, 2 February 1926, Chamberlain to Crewe, 5 February 1926, *DBFP*, IA, I, nos. 236, 246.

[74] Chamberlain to D'Abernon, 7 February 1926, Chamberlain to Crewe, 16 February 1926, *DBFP*, IA, I, nos. 250, 277.

[75] Schubert to Hoesch, 20 January 1926, Schubert memorandum, 20 January 1926, *ADAP*, B, II/I, no. 41, pp. 124–5; Stresemann statements in cabinet, 24 February 1926, *AR Luther I und II*, II, no. 299. Cf. Wright (2002), pp. 354–9.

Covenant to assure Moscow benign neutrality in the event of a war between the Soviet Union and the League member Poland. And he did so to almost unanimous acclaim in the *Reichstag*, including that of DNVP foreign-affairs spokesman Hoetzsch.[76]

Before concluding it, Stresemann had anticipated that the envisaged treaty could have negative repercussions on Berlin's relations with its Locarno partners and the United States, particularly as it followed the failed German League entry. While conducting protracted negotiations with Chicherin, and aided by Schubert, he thus took pains to reassure Briand, Chamberlain and Kellogg that Germany was not pursuing 'an ambiguous policy'. From late March, the *Auswärtige Amt* argued that the planned agreement with the Soviets was to be seen as a complement to Germany's western commitments under Locarno. Berlin had to respect Moscow's demand for compensation. And facilitating a *rapprochement* between the western powers, Germany and Soviet Russia would be in the interest of all three Locarno partners. Here, Germany could serve as a 'bridgehead'.[77] Particularly towards Washington, Stresemann also used economic arguments: Germany could not 'afford the luxury of leaving the Russian market unused' and had to create the 'political foundations' to open it.[78]

In the German political spectrum, and even the Foreign Ministry, there were still proponents of a far more accentuated 'eastern policy', among them Hindenburg and DNVP representatives yet also the German ambassador to Moscow, Brockdorff-Rantzau. Criticising the Locarno pact because it involved too many concessions to the western powers, Brockdorff-Rantzau fell back on 'classic' German balance-of-power thinking. In his view, Berlin should aspire to widen its options, and perhaps even regain the status of an independent great power, by gravitating towards Moscow.[79] Even Stresemann and Schubert believed that a certain accommodation of interests between east and west was 'unavoidably forced on' Germany because of its difficult geo-political position at the centre of continental Europe. But Weimar German policy had clearly departed from the fatal prewar course of keeping a 'free hand' while pursuing a balancing-act between eastern and western alliance options. The way in which Stresemann and Schubert conducted the Berlin treaty negotiations indeed underscored how far the western orientation had come to prevail since Rapallo.

---

[76] *ADAP*, B, II, 1, pp. 403ff; cabinet minutes, 24 February 1926, *AR Luther I and II*, II, no. 299. Walsdorff (1971), pp. 157–83.

[77] Schubert to Hoesch, 10 April 1926, Schubert to D'Abernon, 31 March 1926, Schubert to German Embassy (London), 14 April 1926, *ADAP*, B, II, 1, pp. 307, 289, 335.

[78] Schubert to German embassy (Washington), 14 April 1926, *ADAP*, B, II/I, pp. 338–9.

[79] Brockdorff-Rantzau memorandum, 23 January 1926, *ADAP*, B, II/I, no. 45.

This was not least a consequence of Germany's ever more intertwined interests with the Anglo-American powers and France.

Stresemann's definition of Germany as a western-orientated power also acting as a 'broker between east and west' was most unreservedly accepted by American decisionmakers and observers. Not quite hitting the mark, Ambassador Schurman underlined Washington's understanding for Stresemann's effort to attend to Russo-German relations 'in the tradition of Bismarck's policy of balance'.[80] In line with the State Department, he considered the German interest in opening up the Russian market, which was also a long-term US interest, as unquestionably legitimate. In Washington, Kellogg and Castle were mainly concerned that no doubt was cast on Germany's primary alignment with the west. Yet, though somewhat suspicious of Stresemann's wider intentions, both came to view the Russo-German negotiations in a pragmatic light.

When briefed in advance about the agreement by Ambassador Maltzan on 12 April, Castle pointed out that some stipulations 'seemed in contradiction to the Covenant of the League'. But he seemed content with Maltzan's reply that 'the defenceless condition of Germany' required Berlin to seek a special status under article 16. Berlin had to 'calm Russian feelings'. Castle later observed to the Polish representative Ciechanowski that while the treaty contradicted the letter of the Covenant the primary aim of Poland and America had to remain that of ensuring that Germany entered the League and continued its westward course. In private, Castle wondered whether Stresemann's actions might be an attempt to placate the national 'Right' in Germany by seeking to 'play off a Russian alliance against the former enemies to the west', which was 'an extraordinarily dangerous game'. But he concluded that it would go too far to see Germany's negotiations as 'the beginning of an orientation toward Russia as against Western Europe'.[81] Essentially, neither he nor Kellogg believed that Berlin would risk jeopardising its vital financial and political links with the United States by turning to an eastern partner that had far less to offer.[82]

Understandably, once they became known the Soviet–German negotiations caused a far greater stir in Paris. As Ambassador Fleuriau told Chamberlain on 28 April, the Berlin treaty had 'produced considerable anxiety in France' and would thus 'certainly increase the difficulties of M. Briand's position'. Briand himself, however, had from early on espoused the view that what Stresemann deliberated with Chicherin was not inherently troublesome. If at a stretch, he even deemed the proposed Soviet–German treaty reconcilable

[80] Schubert memorandum, 14 April 1926, *ADAP*, B, II/I, p. 333.
[81] Castle Diary, 12 April and 7 May 1926, vol. 8, pp. 79–80, 102.
[82] Kellogg speech, 14 December 1925, Kellogg Papers.

with the Locarno treaties and article 16. His real problem was to cope with the adverse reactions of French 'public opinion'.[83] In fact, Briand not only confronted criticism in parliament and from military circles but also a harsh reaction within the *Quai d'Orsay*. Not only Berthelot deemed the agreement incompatible with Germany's obligations under article 16. At one point, the French foreign minister thus even sought Chamberlain's backing for a '*démarche*' to Berlin demanding a modification of the treaty.[84]

It was mainly due to British pressure that Paris eventually refrained from deliberating formal sanctions and adopted a more conciliatory course.[85] On 23 April, Briand reminded the *Assemblée*'s Foreign Affairs Commission of the 'desperate gestures' that Chicherin had made to prevent Germany from signing Locarno. Now, Moscow demanded a compensatory agreement with Berlin, about which Ambassador Hoesch had kept the *Quai d'Orsay* informed all along. Fundamentally, the French foreign minister now stressed that 'the accords do not contain anything at odds with the Covenant or with the obligations for Germany resulting from the Locarno accords'.[86]

In London, too, the Soviet–German negotiations had at first raised marked suspicion. Chamberlain speculated that Berlin intended to reach beyond the scope of a mere neutrality agreement – that it would enter into further secret accords with Moscow regarding Poland that conflicted with Germany's prospective League obligations. By mid-April, however, he privately noted that, if Stresemann had been up-front with D'Abernon in outlining the treaty's scope, he could find 'nothing intrinsically wrong in it'. Essentially, the foreign secretary was not so much concerned about a fundamental shift of German policy as about the consequences that Stresemann's move could spell for Germany's relations with the western powers, especially France.[87]

Because of Britain's overriding interest in continuing the Locarno process, Chamberlain thus quickly resorted to pragmatic damage-control. Like Briand, he acknowledged Stresemann's interest in a 'complement and completion of Locarno'.[88] He adopted a conciliatory tone, because any sanctions of the '*entente* powers', such as Briand's then quickly dropped idea of further blocking

[83] Chamberlain to Crewe, 18 April 1926, *DBFP*, IA, I, no. 475.

[84] Fleuriau to Chamberlain, 3 May 1926, *DBFP*, IA, I, no. 494; Grahame to Chamberlain, 30 April 1926, no. 48, FO 408/44.

[85] Crewe to Chamberlain, 5 May 1926, Chamberlain to D'Abernon, 8 May 1926, *DBFP*, IA, I, nos. 487, 510.

[86] Hoesch to AA, 11 April 1926, *ADAP*, B, II/I, no. 114; Briand statements to the Foreign Affairs Commission, 23 April 1926, C14763, no. 56, pp. 110–11, 113–14.

[87] Chamberlain memorandum, 9 April 1926; D'Abernon to Schubert, 6 April 1926, *ADAP*, B, II/I, nos. 117, 108. Austen to Ida Chamberlain, 18 April 1926, Austen Chamberlain Papers, AC 5/1/379. Chamberlain also noted that Berlin 'seems about as frightened of Warsaw as Warsaw is of Berlin'.

[88] Chamberlain minute, 10 April 1926, *DBFP*, IA, I, no. 412.

Germany's League entry, would only 'drive Germany further into the arms of Moscow'.[89] Chamberlain thus re-affirmed the rationale of British Locarno policy: buttressing Berlin's western orientation would keep Germany at a safe distance from Soviet temptations; and this aim could only be realised by keeping Germany anchored to the European concert.

In the final analysis, Stresemann's bid to safeguard German interests in relations with Moscow could indeed be reconciled with what all sides saw as the primary aim: the continued reinforcement of the Locarno edifice. Nevertheless, the Locarno triumvirate could not prevent the Soviet–German negotiations from complicating dealings between them, at least for a certain period. For the fall-out of these negotiations limited the room to manoeuvre of all three protagonists to make progress on core Locarno issues. To a certain extent, the Berlin treaty did provide Briand with reasons, and a pretext, for postponing further concessions. Especially France's attitude towards easing the Rhineland occupation became distinctly more unyielding. Chamberlain still considered the 'present situation' in the occupied zones, where nearly 10,000 more French and Belgian troops were stationed than before Locarno, untenable. But in view of 'the present state of French public opinion', he saw even less prospect than before in forcing this issue. On 28 April, the British foreign secretary thus conveyed to Stresemann that due to the 'perturbation' the Berlin treaty had caused in France, his hands were tied. Accordingly, Germany would have to pay a price for the accords: further 'changes which Locarno had rendered possible', particularly the withdrawal of French garrisons, would be out of the question for the foreseeable future.[90]

Indeed, what followed in this respect was an all but fruitless summer for Locarno diplomacy. In mid-August, Chamberlain confidentially reassured Stresemann that the principles of British Locarno policy had not lost their validity. If Berlin showed 'good faith' in honouring the security agreements, and if it finally completed disarmament to France's satisfaction, he was still prepared to use his influence with Briand to foster 'reciprocity' and hasten the end of the Rhineland occupation. He would then also renew his efforts to wind up military control. Essential for Chamberlain's balancing diplomacy, however, remained the 'close and continuous co-operation with France'.[91]

Since no German disarmament overtures were forthcoming, the foreign secretary refrained from putting any pressure on Paris either behind closed doors or within the Locarno concert. It is only a slight exaggeration to conclude

[89] Thus Chamberlain in cabinet, 14 April 1926, CAB 23/52/15.
[90] Chamberlain to Crewe, 27 April 1926; Chamberlain to D'Abernon, 28 April 1926, *DBFP*, IA, I, nos. 468, 486. Cf. Pitts (1987), pp. 115–16.
[91] Chamberlain to Stresemann, 14 August 1926, *ADAP*, B, I/II, no. 32; Chamberlain to D'Abernon, 2 February 1926, *DBFP*, IA, I, no. 236; Chamberlain to Fleuriau, 10 August 1926, *DBFP*, IA, II, no. 137.

that not only throughout 1926, but basically until 1929, Britain did not pursue a Rhineland policy of its own. Chamberlain maintained a position of wait-and-see even though, as he had underlined on 30 April, 'all British opinion' including the House of Commons and a majority in cabinet considered the continued French occupation 'radically indefensible'.[92] Briand could thus command Locarno's essential levers where it mattered most.

It was only because of Chamberlain's concern that Germany might raise the contentious issue at the League meeting in September, and thereby expose Anglo-French discord, that he on 29 July sent Briand a more urgent plea for troop reductions. By this time, he had begun to fear the negative repercussions that Anglo-French inaction on this question would have on public opinion not only in Britain but also in Germany. Here, Hindenburg's veto even threatened a key symbolic achievement: that of finally securing that Germany joined the League. The upshot of Chamberlain's 'offensive' was that, though the Locarno powers reached no understanding, France withdrew some troops in August, yet a mere 6,000. This fell far short of German expectations.[93]

The more lasting consequence of these developments was that in the initial, and indeed formative, phase of Locarno politics a distinction had been introduced – or perhaps rather: a distinction of earlier postwar politics resurfaced in a new way. It was the distinction between the *entente* powers and Germany. Chamberlain also acted as guardian of German interests. But above all he acted as umpire over German 'behaviour', defining the standards of *quid pro quo* as he – and his French counterpart – saw fit. A retrospective analysis can thus confirm the contemporary German perception: two different sets of rules began to apply within the Locarno concert.[94] This was perhaps unavoidable given what still distinguished France's from Germany's status in the changing international system so shortly after the war, and with the Treaty of Versailles of course still formally in place. Yet it also made comprehensive compromises between all three powers harder to achieve when these compromises would have been most important: at the outset, when the scope of Locarno politics had to be determined, and when the base of its legitimacy had to be widened, time and again. Combined with British passivity, these trends stifled some of the dynamism that the Locarno process could potentially gain. Significantly, however, neither Chamberlain nor Stresemann, nor even Briand, came to view Locarno diplomacy as a misguided approach. Rather, all three – and especially

[92] Chamberlain minute, 13 October 1926, FO 371/11331; Chamberlain to D'Abernon, 30 April 1926, *DBFP*, IA, I, no. 487; Chamberlain to Grahame, 19 November 1926, *DBFP*, IA, II, no. 264.
[93] Chamberlain to Briand, 29 July 1926, Austen Chamberlain Papers. AC 53/81.
[94] Stresemann statements to D'Abernon and de Margerie, 3 and 4 February 1926, *ADAP*, B, I/I, nos. 76, 80.

the German foreign minister – had to adapt to the emerging new realities of European international politics; and to a larger or lesser extent they did adapt to these realities. Nonetheless, each in his way, both Stresemann and Briand continued to seek more British engagement.[95]

By contrast, it can be seen as evidence of how far the self-limitations of US policy had by then been taken to heart, at least in Berlin, that German diplomacy made no serious attempt after Locarno to enlist Washington's support in European security affairs. The one exception concerned disarmament. Stresemann did not actively seek to encourage the Coolidge administration to use its financial might to force French concessions on the Rhineland question. Instead, he concentrated more generally on further strengthening relations with America as the key sponsor of peaceful change and, possibly, future postwar bargains in Europe. At the same time, he tried to widen the financial bases of his foreign policy by attracting further US capital to Germany. A more concrete – and constant – concern for the German Foreign Office was to cultivate American goodwill in order to create favourable alignments for an eventual 'final' reparations settlement.[96]

Acutely aware of American opposition to most aspects of French security policy, including the maintenance of French garrisons in the Rhineland and military control, the *Quai d'Orsay* also basically refrained from trying to influence Washington in France's favour. At least in this phase, it did not seek to pull the US administration towards finally buttressing the European *status quo*.[97] In fact, France had a natural interest in avoiding a scenario in which America's overbearing financial pressure would also extend to the sensitive sphere of security. For successive French governments, re-establishing financial stability was a paramount necessity; and this preoccupation also largely determined relations with the United States. Following the strenuous debt-settlement negotiations, there was a growing desire to escape what not only Poincaré but also Seydoux perceived as 'the Anglo-American financial yoke' of the postwar era.[98] But prevalent was the political will, certainly on Briand's part, to mend fences and thus finally open the door for US capital. Briand's efforts to pave the way for this by securing the ratification of the Mellon–Bérenger agreement continued throughout 1926, yet to no avail.

[95] Briand statements to the Foreign Affairs Commission, 23 April 1926, C14763, no. 56, pp. 111–12; Stresemann statements in cabinet, 13 October 1926, *AR Marx III uand IV*, no. 89.
[96] Schurman report, 7 January 1926, NA RG 59 462.00 R296/1213; Stresemann statements to the Foreign Affairs Commission, 7 October 1926, Stresemann (1932), III, pp. 37ff.
[97] Hoesch to AA, 1 December 1925, *ADAP*, B, I/I, pp. 10–11; Briand statements to the Foreign Affairs Commission, 26 April 1926, p. 101.
[98] Thus Pitts (1987), p. 121. See Seydoux memorandum, 15 June 1926, no. 56–26, MAE, Série Europe, Allemagne, vol. 389.

The Coolidge administration remained generally sympathetic to Stresemann's pleas for a rapid termination of the Rhineland occupation and military control, sharing Britain's interest in eliminating sources of friction that could interfere with America's financial engagement in Germany. As noted, one central premise of US policy had by then been reinforced. It was the premise that neither from Germany's moderate leaders nor their more nationalist – and seemingly marginalised – critics emanated any longer a serious risk for European peace.[99] Consequently, while Kellogg and Castle remained sceptical about the virtues of Locarno diplomacy, the State Department saw no insurmountable security obstacles in the way of resolving the issues still dividing France and Germany. As Kellogg impressed on Ambassador Bérenger, Washington no longer accepted French invocations of le danger allemand to justify old-style power politics.[100] Nor could France any longer justify keeping garrisons and IMCC officials east of the Rhine. Yet the American secretary of state saw no urgency warranting direct US involvement in accelerating their withdrawal.

But despite the absence of acute crises, particularly Castle yet also Kellogg had come to view the European situation in distinctly bleak colours by April 1926. Domestic conditions in Germany seemed to be improving under the Dawes regime. Yet the volatile political situation in France appeared unfavourable to a conciliatory policy.[101] Kellogg's main concern was and remained to stay above the fray, not to get enmeshed in European diplomacy. While officially denying it, he and Castle were appalled at what they saw as Anglo-French manoeuvres to revive the entente cordiale. Any secret understandings between Briand and Chamberlain at Berlin's expense jeopardised what remained Washington's cardinal aim: to tie Germany ever more firmly to a western 'community of interests'.[102] In practice, however, the secretary of state merely confirmed his 'settled policy'. Because of doctrinal principles and domestic constraints, he would not contemplate underwriting any 'regional guarantees' in Europe.[103] As Kellogg instructed the head of the US disarmament delegation at Geneva, Gibson, on 23 April, the administration would simply decline to 'become involved in such questions as those relating to the application of European security pacts'. This was and remained the Locarno powers' responsibility.[104]

[99] Castle Diary, 10 February 1926, vol. 8, p. 33; Schurman minute, 29 December 1925, NA RG 59 751.62/43.
[100] Kellogg memorandum, 25 March 1926, FRUS 1926, I, pp. 62–3; Kellogg speech, 14 December 1925, Kellogg Papers.
[101] Castle Diary, 12 April 1926, vol. 8, p. 81.
[102] Kellogg memorandum, 25 March 1926, FRUS 1926, I, pp. 62–3; Castle Diary, 19 March 1926, vol. 8, p. 51.
[103] Kellogg speech, 14 December 1925, Kellogg Papers.
[104] Kellogg instructions to Gibson, 23 April 1926, FRUS 1926, I, p. 82.

Significantly, after Locarno no influential US decisionmaker any longer considered pursuing the strategy so successfully employed between 1923 and 1925, namely to use financial power for the purpose of promoting political accommodation between Germany and its neighbours. As – for all the remaining skirmishes between the two countries – Franco-German relations had fundamentally turned the corner, or so it seemed in Washington, the emphasis shifted. Immediate incentives to operate with specific 'carrots' or 'sticks' no longer existed.

Instead, the new criteria for US benevolence were domestic, financial and more narrowly defined. Vis-à-vis Germany, continued US loans were made dependent, not on co-operative German behaviour vis-à-vis France, but – as noted – on assurances that American capital was used for efficient purposes and the Dawes regime was not jeopardised.[105] Vis-à-vis France, Washington focused on pressuring successive governments to hasten the ratification of the Mellon–Bérenger agreement. While FRBNY Governor Strong favoured rewarding domestic reform efforts in France, lifting the loan embargo was at no point linked with French concessions to Germany.[106] It remained to be seen whether US financial interests could eventually even conflict with further advances in Franco-German reconciliation. On balance, a more immediate US engagement would probably not have made a decisive difference in settling key issues of European postwar diplomacy, such as military control or the Rhineland problem. In general terms, however, a firmer US commitment to European security could have contributed significantly to reassuring France, and Germany's eastern neighbours, thus widening international avenues of peaceful change.

Foreseeable failure? The quest for disarmament after Locarno

How heavily insecurity still weighed on the European situation became nowhere more evident than in the soon all but deadlocked negotiations of the League's Preparatory Disarmament Commission. These had got underway in Geneva in January 1926. Following their first suspension in February, they would intermittently continue, over five sessions, until indefinitely adjourned in March 1928 without any concrete results.[107]

For the Locarno powers, which deliberately never made disarmament a core item on the European concert's agenda, the challenge was not so much to effect

---

[105] A.N. Young memorandum, 2 April 1925, NA RG 59 800.51/509 1/2; State Department to Hoover, 19 October 1925, Commerce Official, Foreign Loans, Hoover Papers; Gilbert to Strong, 5 November 1925, Strong Papers, 1012.1.
[106] Kellogg to Herrick, 7 June 1926, *FRUS 1926*, II, p. 97; Mellon to Kellogg, 12 June 1926, NA RG 39, box 61; Castle to Houghton, 12 May 1926, Castle Papers, box 2.
[107] Cf. Hall (1987).

real breakthroughs in this area, which no side expected. Rather, it was to prevent the unavoidable tensions arising over the thorny subject from impinging on the evolution of Locarno politics in other areas, notably the Rhineland negotiations. Moreover, all European leaders sought to minimise negative repercussions of the Genera talks on transatlantic relations. Like the even more taxing issue of territorial revision, disarmament thus pointed to the limits of what international politics could achieve under the circumstances of the post-World War I era. With hindsight, the expectations that some contemporary proponents of substantive disarmament, like Cecil, attached to it seem distinctly unrealistic, such was the degree of still prevailing insecurity in postwar Europe – and so marked the need for first strengthening security mechanisms like the Locarno concert further.

What concretely hampered the progress of the Geneva negotiations from the start were, on one level, growing Anglo-American differences over specific maritime issues such as the cruiser problem. What mattered most, however, and ultimately could not be resolved, were fundamental disagreements between the French and the American delegation, one generally backed by Britain, the other by Germany. These centred on two questions already familiar from the internal British and American discussions: first, whether naval and land disarmament issues could and should be combined; and second, and more importantly, what was to constitute the basis of any disarmament schemes – really existing armament levels like France's, or a country's (i.e. Germany's) entire weapon-making potential.

If the first point of discord was already troublesome, yet mainly procedural, the latter threw into relief the core problem. For what surfaced at Geneva was the fundamental consequence arising from the post-Versailles imbalance of power and potential between France and Germany. In an international constellation in flux, with Britain's new guarantees, yet still lacking a wider security framework that included a reliable German partner and was backed by both Anglo-American powers, the French goverment stalled. It was not prepared to countenance weakening France's final reassurance vis-à-vis Germany, namely its superior military might. Yet this was precisely what Washington ultimately demanded. From the outset, then, the aims of US, and German, disarmament policy clearly ran counter to what French policy-makers regarded as core security requirements. This was and remained the crux, and Britain could not resolve it.

The State Department was aware that Germany's neighbours regarded its revitalisation as highly disconcerting. On Kellogg's behalf, Under-Secretary Grew eventually conveyed to Briand the department's view that there was a 'natural demand for security' in Europe. In early February, the Polish chargé Ciechanowski had told Castle that Poland was 'much troubled over the question of potential resources'. Germany 'might be disarmed on paper and yet [would be] capable of rapidly turning its peace factories into munition factories'. This precisely reflected French anxieties. To Castle, however, the danger of Germany's war-making potential seemed remote. He told Ciechanowski that America 'could hardly ask the Krupp factories to go out of the business of making ploughs because, in war, they might make guns'.[108] In the same vein, neither Kellogg nor Hoover saw any sense in limiting Germany's economic development. In Kellogg's view, any attempt to 'equalise the military power of nations' or to limit it according to population or resources was an 'artificial effort to equalise that which is not and cannot be made equal'. And Hoover had of course no desire to constrain what appeared to serve both European peace and US interests: redirecting Germany towards the pursuit of peaceful, economically driven competition.[109] Ultimately, financial clearly outweighed security concerns.

As the State Department unfailingly emphasised to all European powers, the United States desired 'a real reduction of the crushing burden of armament'.[110] Effectively, though, it put little store by the League-based disarmament efforts. Following his 'principles' and pointing to the Washington regime of 1922, Kellogg insisted on drawing clear lines between naval and 'land armaments', the latter being 'primarily of interest to Europe'. And the leader of the US delegation at Geneva, Gibson, followed his instructions closely. He thus also insisted on concentrating the negotiations on 'visible, tangible armaments and to peace strength', rejecting any criteria that would have made the talks' scope unmanageable. In Kellogg's view, it was 'not possible to limit [the] ultimate war strength of any country'. Likewise, Gibson was instructed to reject any international control or sanction mechanisms that could serve to verify disarmament and punish transgressors.[111] On 23 April 1926, the American secretary of state confirmed that there was to be 'No International Supervision of the Limitations of Armaments' either by the League or by another international body.[112] Washington thus refused to give disarmament regimes any teeth. In practice, the rigid criteria and self-imposed limits of the Coolidge administration's approach would not only limit the American delegation's freedom of action. They would also limit the effectiveness of US disarmament policy as such.

---

[108] Grew to Herrick, 20 April 1926, *FRUS 1926*, I, pp. 78–9; Castle Diary, 10 February 1926, vol. 8, p. 33.

[109] Kellogg to Gibson, 23 April 1926, *FRUS 1926*, I, pp. 80–9; Hoover memoranda, 23–30 September 1925, Hoover Papers, Commerce, box 20.

[110] Castle to Ciechanowski, Castle Diary, 10 February 1926, vol. 8, p. 34.

[111] Kellogg to MacVeagh, 2 March 1926, *FRUS 1926*, I, p. 59; Grew to Herrick, 20 April 1926, *FRUS 1926*, I, pp. 59, 79; Kellogg to Davies, 4 January 1926, Kellogg Papers, roll 17; *FRUS 1926*, I, pp. 80–100.

[112] Kellogg memorandum to Gibson, 23 April 1926, *FRUS 1926*, I, pp. 87–8.

Surveying the meagre progress of the Geneva talks up to their first suspension, Ambassador Houghton had in late February expressed what had
become common currency in Washington. He concluded that however strongly
France, and Britain, professed their desire to disarm, 'until financial need
actually forces them to reduce their armies and navies' there was 'little reason to hope for any substantial reduction of either'. Washington came to
view the Geneva talks at best as a vehicle for pressing France to lower what
were deemed absurdly high armament levels against a practically disarmed
Germany. Yet while US policymakers generally hoped that they could eventually tighten the debt screws on France, no concerted effort to this end was
ever made. And, in effect, that France would unilaterally diminish its superiority in arms for the sake of economising would remain a vain hope in the
latter 1920s.[113]

Precisely because he regarded disarmament in Europe as an up-hill struggle
from the start, Houghton had argued that Washington should make tactical
concessions to deepen co-operation with Britain. Essentially, he feared that
otherwise the US delegates at Geneva were 'likely to find themselves standing
alone and thus responsible for making an agreement impossible'. Subsequently,
Kellogg made some attempts to ascertain Chamberlain's views on 'how the
Preparatory Commission is to function'. But in view of rising Anglo-American
tensions over how to adjust the Washington naval regime, no sufficient
common ground could be found. Instead, hardly wary of ulterior German
motives, the Coolidge administration soon regarded Berlin as a valuable partner in preventing a premature failure of US efforts at Geneva. As noted,
Kellogg had always harboured suspicions about France's real willingness to
cut its land forces and Britain's naval agenda. As the only continental European
power already substantially disarmed, Germany thus became a 'natural ally' of
the United States.[114]

For his part, Stresemann was even more eager to foster parallel interests
with the US delegation. Berlin sought to achieve 'a reduction of overall
armament levels' in general and a treaty-based reduction of French land
armament in particular. While this clearly remained a more long-term and
subordinate aim on Stresemann's agenda of peaceful change, German policymakers speculated on 'perhaps [opening up] an opportunity for at least modest
rearmament' at a later stage. But no one at the *Auswärtige Amt* expected any
immediate breakthroughs.[115] What German hopes there were indeed centred

---

[113] Houghton to Kellogg, 27 February 1926, Grew to Herrick, 20 April 1926, *FRUS 1926*, I, pp. 59, 78–9.

[114] Houghton to Kellogg, 27 February 1926; Kellogg to Houghton, 8 April and 11 February 1926, *FRUS 1926*, I, pp. 51ff, 58, 72–4.

[115] Stresemann instructions to the German delegation, Geneva, 26 December 1925, Köpke to Maltzan, *ADAP*, B, I/1, pp. 88, 325–6.

on the financial pressure that the American creditor could exert upon its excessively armed French debtor – even if it was well known that Washington's main interest lay in advancing naval arms control. Yet the German delegation nonetheless intended to prove itself as a reliable partner of the Americans in this area of superficial common interests to prepare the ground for extended co-operation on more vital issues in the future, chiefly the 'final' settlement of reparations.[116]

As American aims and French interests remained irreconcilable, and German representatives naturally backed US positions while Britain ultimately sided with France, this became a recipe for stalemate. As early as mid-February, Castle voiced his foreboding that the Geneva talks would soon 'degenerate into a debating society of theoretical questions'.[117] That is indeed what largely happened. French leaders operated on a markedly different set of assumptions. The principal concern of Briand as much as of Poincaré was to pre-empt anything even approaching the acceptance of 'armament parity' in any final agreement. The French delegation thus rejected all US proposals threatening France's preponderance in arms. For Briand, this preponderance constituted – with Britain's Locarno guarantees – the necessary reinsurance for further 'reconciliation' with Germany. And there was genuine anxiety in Paris that Germany's economic recovery would before too long restore its inherently superior war-making capabilities. This extended to all factors that could aid Germany in preparing for a mobilisation. French representatives in Geneva thus constantly demanded that a country's capacity for training armed forces and converting peacetime into armament production should be considered in any disarmament scheme.[118]

For tactical reasons, France insisted on avoiding a one-sided focus on land forces. Briand argued that the Preparatory Commission's negotiations had to ensure that a state could not keep a 'physical force' allowing it to 'oppress other states', but he also argued that this force could be equally 'on land as on the sea'. France used such argumentation quite effectively to control Germany and ward off US pressure. The latter was felt acutely. As Briand told the *Chambre*'s Foreign Affairs Commission in April, he had reminded Washington that there was a second, 'less apparent' form of armament in the postwar international order – 'capitalist armament, which can weigh on the freedom of peoples'. In effect, the French foreign minister thus demanded that America

---

[116] Cf. Link (1970), pp. 346ff.

[117] Castle to Ciechanowski, Castle Diary, 10 February 1926, vol. 8, p. 34.

[118] For Marshal Foch, not Germany's transgressions of the Versailles treaty but the extent of its war-making potential was the crux. See Foch's memorandum for Briand, 4 March 1926, MAE, Série Europe, Allemagne, 117. See also MAE, Série Europe, Grande-Bretagne, 58/80ff. Cf. Keeton (1987), pp. 210–11.

'disarm' as well. If the US government desired military cuts, it had to lessen its pressure on 'French finance'.[119]

Not publicly, but in substance, the British government soon tended to support France's overall position. The Foreign Office fundamentally agreed that, for the foreseeable future, disarmament was the one field where a distinction between the victors and the vanquished of the war had to be maintained. On the premise that Britain had already reduced its land and air forces to a minimum of what was acceptable, the British delegation, and Cecil in particular, was keen to promote tangible disarmament.[120] Yet, while not always steering a clear course, the Baldwin cabinet remained distinctly reserved towards any more sweeping schemes in continental Europe, such as those the United States had placed on the agenda, if in vague terms. As we have seen, this was essentially due to the British concern to preserve a certain European equilibrium and bolster French security. In view of what the Foreign Office saw as an overriding need to canalise Germany's resurgent power, any changes in Europe's balance of forces had to be measured and gradual – even if British policymakers still considered French anxieties vis-à-vis 'the German danger' exaggerated.[121]

As Chamberlain signalled to Houghton on 26 February, he in principle agreed with the American view that disarmament should be based on 'visible armaments' and 'peace strength'. And the British foreign secretary later told Gibson in Geneva that he had tried to convince the French to 'get down to realities' and 'leave such questions as security, national resources, etc., to be handled later'. But Chamberlain had no desire to press Briand on this issue. Accordingly, his bottom-line vis-à-vis Kellogg became that in practice – and essentially because of Germany's overbearing potential – the European situation was more complex and it was therefore unavoidable that a country's 'industrial strength' had to 'be considered as a factor in land disarmament'. Chamberlain thus declined to endorse Kellogg's proposal for an Anglo-American 'declaration' of disarmament principles.[122]

At the same time, London had a tangible, not least financial, interest in controlling naval competition, both from the United States and Japan. Like his American counterpart, Chamberlain had originally preferred to address this question separately, in a sequel to the Washington conference.[123] Yet the

---

[119] Briand statements to the Foreign Affairs Commission, 23 April 1926, C14763, no. 56, 117–18.
[120] See Cecil statements, 206th CID meeting, 30 November 1925, CAB 2/4; Cecil memorandum, 4 May 1926, *DBFP*, IA, I, no. 495.
[121] Chamberlain to Crewe, 12 April 1926, *DBFP*, IA, 1, no. 264; Chamberlain memorandum, 16 July 1925, CAB 24/174, CP357(25).
[122] Houghton to Kellogg, 27 February 1926, Gibson to Kellogg, 11 June 1926, *FRUS 1926*, I, pp. 57, 109.
[123] 205th CID meeting, 17 November 1925, CAB 2/4.

Baldwin government did not want Washington to dictate the terms of naval arms control. At Briand's request, the British thus eventually sided with the French delegation in proposing that land and naval armaments be considered together. Ostensibly, this was to open the door towards compromise solutions linking both areas. In fact, though, it served to contain American and German pressures on the land power, France.

In view of the Coolidge administration's refusal to consider such linkage, this confounded complications at Geneva. Decisive for Chamberlain's reticent attitude towards disarmament, however, was something else. He remained convinced that only tangible progress on the security question, i.e. further confidence-building within the European concert, would over time make serious arms reductions in Europe possible. For only thus could France feel sufficiently reassured to reduce its armed forces. Consequently, Chamberlain's unequivocal priority remained unchanged – it was that of pursuing a common policy with Briand. And equally unaltered remained his rationale that to be able to do so 'in matters which are really serious' – core Locarno issues – he had 'to compromise, if necessary even to sacrifice, matters of less immediate importance', namely disarmament.[124] For all of Cecil's verve, Britain therefore never took the lead in advancing far-reaching proposals at Geneva.

When cabling to Kellogg on 27 February, Houghton stated that the 'real importance' of the Preparatory Commission lay no longer in 'working out' a 'standard by which a measure of disarmament may be obtained', but rather in avoiding a publicly damaging breakdown of the proceedings. In the ambassador's assessment, there was no one, certainly not in Britain, who 'believe[d] for a moment' that France was 'ready to decrease its military strength'.[125] Ultimately, Chamberlain's verdict would be borne out. Disarmament could not be achieved before Europe's newly emerging security architecture had been solidified, which necessarily required time. In this sense, both French preoccupations and British caution were not groundless. Given their narrow scope and overall furtiveness, it is thus hardly surprising that the disarmament efforts of the United States remained as inconclusive as those of Britain in the decade after World War I. The gap between American – and German – objectives on the one hand and French – and British – fundamentals on the other was still too wide, and proved unbridgeable in the short or even medium term. After the Great Depression, and in a different constellation, it would become completely unbridgeable.

Not so much bolder disarmament initiatives as broader security commitments of *both* Anglo-American powers would have been required to master a problem that sooner or later had to be addressed: how to provide Weimar

---

[124] Chamberlain to Fleuriau, 10 August 1926, *DBFP*, IA, II, no. 137.
[125] Houghton to Kellogg, 27 February 1926, *FRUS 1926*, I, p. 57.

Germany gradually, yet in a controlled manner, with armed forces that were commensurate with its new status as an 'equal' European great power; and how to achieve this without undermining Europe's fledgling security system. Essentially, a solution to this problem had to be approached before other forces could seize on the unsatisfactory *status quo*, forces disregarding any international agreements and limitations. But there was no solution in sight. Perhaps the disarmament dilemma was indeed so intractable that it could not (yet) be resolved less than ten years after the end of the Great War. Alas, there would be no time to compensate later for what was neglected in the latter 1920s.[126]

---

[126] See also chapter 24.

21   Thoiry – the failed quest for a 'final postwar agreement'

In Chamberlain's words, a 'breeze from Locarno blew through the stuffy hall of the Assembly' when on 10 September 1926 the German delegation was received into the *Société des Nations*, 'well . . . but not too boisterously'.[1] With its successful accession to the League, an important first stage in Germany's reintegration into the international system after 1918 had been concluded. At the same time, this reintegration had found its publicly most recognisable expression. It was more than a symbolic moment in post-World War I international history. Yet it was by no means an end-point to the underlying processes of European stabilisation underway since the Ruhr crisis.

Concretely, the study commission charged with proposing a way out of the Council crisis in March had completed its task in time. The League Council followed its recommendation that only Germany be granted a permanent seat while the number of non-permanent seats was increased from six to nine. Of these, one was to fall to Poland, *de facto* with a guarantee of eligibility for re-election after three years.[2] Up to the last minute, Chamberlain, Cecil and their continental counterparts had been 'involved in petty jealousies and squabbles' to secure this outcome. The British foreign secretary had finally impressed on Briand and Skrzyński that Poland was in danger 'of losing everything by asking too much'. But the 'bargain' had ultimately been carried through.[3] After London and Locarno, a third, albeit less momentous step on the path of rehabilitating Germany and including it in the postwar order on terms transcending Versailles had been taken.

That Weimar Germany had ostensibly resumed its rightful international place was also welcomed in the United States, both in official circles and, even more effusively, in the press.[4] While the administration could not welcome the

---

[1] Chamberlain to Tyrrell, 10 September 1926, *DBFP*, IA, I, no. 203.
[2] Cf. Kimmich (1976), pp. 88–96.
[3] Chamberlain considered Skrzyński 'more sensible' than Pilsudski and Polish nationalists who in his eyes opposed the League as much as German nationalists. See Chamberlain to Tyrrell, 10 September 1926, *DBFP*, IA, I, no. 203.
[4] 'Germany in the League', *Literary Digest*, 18 September 1926.

accession officially – as its formal distance to the Geneva organisation remained unaltered – Under-Secretary Grew assured Berlin that the State Department was content with what was considered an 'essential step for the stabilisation of Europe'.[5]

In the autumn of 1926, and in fact throughout the so-called 'Stresemann era', leading German policymakers were resolved, not to use the League to subvert the Versailles system, but essentially to pursue German interests and enhance German credibility through co-operative diplomacy. The League was thus regarded as a forum in which Berlin could hope to make its regained international influence felt. The focus was on security, where disarmament dominated the agenda, and the international economy, where liberalising international trade for the sake of expanding German exports mattered most. Minority questions were a further priority. But the thesis that Stresemann merely intended to instrumentalise the League for pursuing a narrowly revisionist minority agenda seems unfounded.[6] Doubtless, German representatives sought to make what they deemed a discriminatory treatment of German minorities in Poland and Czechoslovakia a League concern. Yet there was never a concerted campaign to invoke the protection of these minorities as a pretext for altering Germany's eastern borders.

Rather, the road leading Stresemann and Schubert to Geneva had already spurred one promising development, and German League membership could reinforce it – if domestic politics permitted this. The principles and practices of peaceful change marking German *Westpolitik* were indeed beginning to inform its underlying aims.[7] In other words, if German decisionmakers aspired to territorial and other revisions of the Versailles order only as far as they were reconcilable with Germany's Locarno and League commitments – and otherwise refrained from pursuing these aims – the net-gain for European stability could be immense. At the very least, German revisionism would be moderated and lose much of its inherently destabilising impact, and nowhere was such restraint more critical than in eastern Europe.

In short, this is essentially what had happened in the latter 1920s; the new approaches adopted since 1924 now took root not only in London and Paris but also in Berlin. That was no small shift in postwar international politics. And it accorded largely with what British and American policymakers had

---

[5] Dieckhoff to AA, 20 September 1926, PA, Politische Abteilung III, Vereinigte Staaten, Politik 2, vol. 8, no. 594.

[6] Stresemann instructions to German embassies, 18 October 1926, *ADAP*, B, I/II, no. 152. It is instructive to juxtapose these instructions and the conclusions drawn in Fink (1979), pp. 403–22.

[7] This has been shown most convincingly by Krüger (1974), p. 241, and (1985a), pp. 355ff; and Wright (2002), pp. 393ff. See Stresemann *Reichstag* speech, 23 June 1927, in Zwoch (1972), pp. 250–5.

sought to foster: Weimar Germany's ambitions to topple the postwar order by force were more and more submerged by its co-operative relations with the western powers. To sustain this shift, two factors remained crucial: the effectiveness of the Locarno concert, as a mechanism for managing relations between Europe's larger powers as well as between them and the smaller powers within the League; and the policies of Germany's 'senior partner', the United States. Most valuable for the further evolution of Locarno politics was that the regular League Council meetings, held every three months, offered a quasi-institutionalised platform for the European concert. These meetings also provided ample opportunities to intensify the decisive personal relations within the uneven 'triumvirate' Chamberlain–Briand–Stresemann.[8]

This mode of concert diplomacy particularly corresponded with what the British foreign secretary envisaged. It seemed an ideal framework for forging 'rational compromises' by way of aloof cabinet politics, as removed as possible from the public attention of the League Assembly.[9] Thus, British diplomacy had also achieved a more general aim which it had already pursued, if on different premises, under MacDonald. It had transformed the League from an instrument of French *status quo* policies into an instrument serving Britain's integrative policy of peaceful change. Germany's inclusion was an essential advance towards making the League no longer an institution of Versailles but a kind of 'clearing agency' for settling the 'big questions' of postwar European politics within the Locarno concert. This concert took the interests of smaller powers, notably those of Belgium, Poland and Czechoslovakia, seriously. But it continued to centre, also at Geneva, on what Chamberlain had always considered the core of European politics: the strategic triangle between London, Paris and Berlin.[10]

It should be stressed again, though, that the new European concert of the decade after World War I has to be understood as a system of international politics in a wider sense. It did not exhaust itself in hence regular 'tea-party meetings' between Briand, Chamberlain and Stresemann at Geneva, which became a regular feature of international diplomacy in the era of London and Locarno. Rather, it in essence evolved into a European system of ground-rules for settling international disputes without recourse to nationalist competition or war, with an impact far beyond the Locarno triangle. This was quite far from what the drafters of the League's original Covenant had aspired to. Arguably, however, it represented the only effective way of reinvigorating the League and making it relevant for addressing Europe's core problems in

---

[8] Chamberlain memoranda, Geneva, 5–12 December 1926, *DBFP*, IA, II, nos. 323–33. Cf. the German records, *ADAP*, B, I/II, nos. 237, 258, 260.
[9] Chamberlain minute, 21 December 1926, FO 371/12125/144.
[10] Cf. Jacobson (1972b), pp. 67ff; Walters (1952), pp. 341–2.

the aftermath of the Great War. Chamberlain could quite rightly conclude that 'British policy is fully justified by the results it has produced.'[11]

Yet the 'euphoria' of Geneva could not dispel the more fundamental problems still besetting Europe. While praising the Locarnites' achievements, Chamberlain on 10 September also warned German press representatives at Geneva once more against 'exaggerated expectations' arising from Germany's new status. He emphasised that the road the Locarno powers still had to travel was 'long' and 'difficulties' still manifold.[12] Indeed, all major decisionmakers present at Geneva recognised that, on salient issues, Locarno politics and the pact's own scope and momentum had not sufficed to produce the rapid and publicly convincing changes that especially Stresemann had sought. The summer's recriminations over troop reductions had made this abundantly clear. And in early September, Briand told Stresemann that, on account of the checks that Poincaré, who once again led the French government, placed on his policy vis-à-vis Germany, his domestic leeway remained distinctly limited.[13]

Stagnation was not due to mere French obstructionism. What had proved insurmountable thus far were structural constraints, both on the international level and on that of domestic politics, all deriving from the basic search for greater security, above all in France. In fact, no other intermediate results of Locarno politics could be expected. In a wider context, the European international system had just begun to be recast, and it had just begun to emerge not only from a cataclysmic war but also from far more than half a century of military competition and imperial rivalry. By necessity, any qualitative transformation towards a stable, peace-enforcing system of international politics had to be a long-term process. 'Classic' cabinet diplomacy in Chamberlain's definition could not yield any results that were both quickly achieved *and* acceptable for all sides, because the new foundations of European security were only starting to solidify. An additional, serious complication was that in the Dawes plan era European security issues could be even less dissociated from questions of international finance than before the Ruhr crisis. And in this novel international matrix nothing of enduring significance could be achieved without the support, or at least consent, of the United States.

De facto, Germany had so far only offered France its acceptance of the rules and commitments of Locarno – and a less than complete fulfilment of its disarmament obligations. Having to act under Premier Poincaré's critical gaze

---

[11] Chamberlain to Tyrrell, 10 September 1926, *DBFP*, IA, II, no. 203.

[12] *Ibid*. For comparison, see Stresemann's statements in cabinet, 13 October 1926, *AR Marx III und IV*, no. 89.

[13] Stresemann *Reichstag* speech, 22 March 1926, *SB*, vol. 389, p. 6451; Chamberlain to Stresemann, 14 August 1926, *ADAP*, B, I/II, no. 32; Chamberlain to Fleuriau, 10 August 1926, *DBFP*, IA, II, no. 137; Schubert memorandum, 3 September 1926, *ADAP*, B, I/II, p. 157.

from late July 1926 onwards, Briand continued his policy of reconciliation. But he also re-asserted vis-à-vis Chamberlain that the achievements of Locarno could only endure if Britain and France further strengthened their *entente* and held Berlin to its promises. Both powers had to pursue a tough line towards a German government showing bad faith. And they had to establish as the essential *modus procedendi* of Locarno politics that any further western concessions depended on German goodwill in fulfilling the Versailles treaty and containing the nationalist 'patriotic societies' whose activities caused much unease in France.[14] Stresemann was disappointed. Yet neither he nor Schubert ever came to doubt that the further allayment of French security concerns remained a critical necessity for German diplomacy. This had to be part and parcel of any new Franco-German agreements.[15]

Like Briand, Stresemann persevered with his efforts to engage Britain. But Chamberlain persisted with his policy of restraint. As the British foreign secretary told both Locarno partners over the summer of 1926, the time was not yet ripe for further concrete agreements.[16] London could have taken the lead in forging further settlements, seizing on the initial dynamism that the Locarno pact had generated. Yet following an inevitable teething-phase of differences over the meaning of Locarno and readjustment to its new ground-rules, the British broker only held the reins of the European concert loosely.

That both Anglo-American powers thus disengaged from European politics and from the task of providing international leadership had tangible consequences. It made it all the harder to accomplish more than piecemeal advances towards fortifying Europe's security architecture, which in turn made negotiations over the Rhineland occupation and military control grind to a halt. Crucially, though, one determinant of Euro-Atlantic politics remained unchanged. For all their passivity, Britain and America retained a commanding influence on widening or narrowing the room for manoeuvre available to Stresemann and Briand. Both continued to have the power to enable or prevent agreements between Paris and Berlin. They continued to shape and delimit the international playing-field, also for Franco-German relations.

At no point after Locarno did this become more obvious than immediately following Germany's League entry when a core connex of postwar transatlantic relations again came to the forefront: the interdependence of international politics and finance. In view of the international and domestic constraints under which the protagonists of Locarno diplomacy had to operate, the only

---

[14] Briand to Chamberlain, 6 August 1926, 7 August 1926, FO 425.398.

[15] Stresemann memorandum, 4 February 1926, *ADAP*, B, I/I, no. 80; Stresemann speech, 28 June 1926, Stresemann (1932), II, pp. 449–51.

[16] Chamberlain to Crewe, 2 June 1926, *DBFP*, IA, I, no. 103; Dufour-Feronce to AA, 14 August 1926, *ADAP*, B, I/II, no. 32.

real alternative for regaining momentum in Europe's peace process lay in making creative use of this interdependence. In other words, it lay in reviving the approach pursued in 1924 in order to foster comprehensive international settlements. In fact, not Chamberlain or Kellogg, but Stresemann and Briand had explored this alternative ever more concretely since the autumn of 1925. This culminated in their plan for a 'final' postwar settlement between France and Germany which, after extensive preparations, emerged from their soon mythical tête-à-tête summit at Thoiry on 17 September 1926.

As envisaged by Briand and Stresemann, the Thoiry design turned on a rather simple formula: France would cede occupied land back to Germany, and Germany would pay for this by mobilising funds allocated for its reparations payments under the Dawes regime.[17] Both statesmen pursued this plan not least because of what they saw as a lack of forceful Anglo-American support for each power's interests. Particularly for Stresemann, seeking a bilateral 'deal' with Paris thus seemed the only road available to achieve the breakthrough that he so urgently needed to contain inner-German opposition to his policy. But the crux of postwar politics was that Germany and France could not settle their differences *entre deux*, neither in 1926 nor thereafter. If at all amenable to eventual bilateral solutions, all outstanding Franco-German problems – especially the Rhineland question – required a wider political-cum-financial framework. In other words, they required a constellation and wherewithal similar to those which had led to the Dawes accords. Yet only the Anglo-American powers could provide such a framework and wherewithal. In the light of the experiences gained since the Ruhr crisis, all sides were acutely aware of this.

Economic policies of peaceful change after 1925: necessity and limits

Each in his own fashion, decisionmakers not only in London and Washington but also in Paris and Berlin assumed that there was a constitutive correlation between economic revitalisation, rises in national prosperity and the enhancement of political stability in Europe, both internationally and domestically. Financial means, the 'solution' of the reparations imbroglio and the expansion of economic prosperity were also supposed to widen political avenues for resolving conflicts in other areas; they were to permit compromise solutions benefiting both the victors and the vanquished of the war. Not least, as noted, stable economic conditions also remained critical for the political survival of the Locarno protagonists, at least in France and Germany.

---

[17] Hesnard minutes of the Thoiry meeting, 17 September 1926, MAE, Série Europe, Allemagne, Thoiry, vol. 398, Z 35–12; Stresemann notes, 17 and 20 September 1926, *ADAP*, B, I/II, nos. 88, 94.

After Locarno, Briand and Stresemann each sought to develop their particular form of economic diplomacy, adapting to their needs what US policymakers had been pursuing on a grander scale since 1923. Especially the German foreign minister had made it a hallmark of his strategy ever since the Ruhr crisis to use economic means to political ends. This was one of the most 'modern' and innovative strands of international politics in the 1920s, not only in the German context.[18] At the very least, however, it remained uncertain how far French demands to preserve the *status quo* of 1925 and German demands for its peaceful modification could be balanced through economic, and concomitant political, advances. Likewise, it remained uncertain whether Weimar Germany would ultimately settle for the status of a predominantly economic great power. Increasingly, a central question thus became if, and how, further 'new deals' between the western powers and Germany could be struck – deals further enhancing the effectiveness, and legitimacy, of co-operative international politics in the fashion of London and Locarno. Yet any designs for further comprehensive bargains could only bring material gains if all sides considered their ramifications for European security; and if all relevant powers, above all the United States, had a stake in them.

How far could British and American decisionmakers foster such new deals? And, crucially, what incentives did they have in using their critical leverage? As noted, after Locarno neither Chamberlain nor Kellogg saw compelling reasons for promoting major accommodation schemes in Europe, particularly if they threatened core interests of British reparations and American debt and loan policies. Even less did they desire to become enmeshed in complex, politically sensitive manoeuvres to hasten pacific change in eastern Europe. As a consequence, neither the Foreign Office nor the State Department – or any other government agency – even began developing coherent strategies to this end. From late 1925 – and for a formative period of nearly three years – neither London nor Washington launched any noteworthy stabilisation initiatives in either western or eastern Europe.

British policymakers still counted on the pacifying effects of Europe's economic reconstruction. But in contrast to what their US counterparts pursued, 'economic appeasement' was always only one, and never the dominant, strand of British policy both under Labour and the Conservatives. Chamberlain remained convinced that any further meaningful steps towards Franco-German reconciliation could only be made through the Locarno concert. In his view, all problems still causing tensions between Paris and Berlin were

---

[18] *Ibid.*; Stresemann statements to the Foreign Affairs Commission, 7 October 1926, Stresemann (1932), III, pp. 37–8. Cf. the plans of Briand, Berthelot and Seydoux for a Thoiry-style agreement: Seydoux memorandum, 14 August 1926; Briand to Poincaré, 20 August 1926, MAE, Série Europe, Allemagne, Thoiry, vol. 398, Z 35–12,1–3. Cf. Keeton (1987), pp. 211–12.

essentially political and only amenable to carefully crafted diplomatic solutions. Britain's part remained that of promoting such solutions. While Tyrrell remained more open-minded about using economic levers, Chamberlain maintained that the admixture of financial considerations would only complicate his task.[19] Not least, ambitious schemes for Franco-German reconciliation could harm British financial, and especially reparations, interests. The Treasury impressed on the Foreign Office that Britain should not support any proposals that could jeopardise an advantageous 'final' reparations settlement or the ratification of the Churchill–Caillaux debt agreement.[20]

For Washington and Wall Street, France's ratification of the Mellon–Bérenger agreement remained the essential condition for a wider financial engagement. Generally, however, the American faith in applying economic remedies to Europe's political ills of course far exceeded that of British diplomats. By the autumn of 1926, the Coolidge administration, and key financiers, deemed the prospects for pursuing Europe's economic consolidation hand in hand with US financial expansion better than ever.[21] Yet it was also precisely at that juncture that a new phase in Euro-Atlantic postwar politics dawned. It was a phase in which, after Germany's initial recovery, there was no longer an 'automatic' parallelism between the requirements of Franco-German *rapprochement* and the political-cum-financial objectives of Britain and, especially, the United States. One set of interests and expectations could indeed conflict with the other. Nothing manifested this more strikingly than the failure of the Thoiry initiative.[22]

The Thoiry initiative

The 'grand postwar arrangement' that Briand and Stresemann contemplated, and which had taken shape with the help of their assistants Berthelot, Seydoux and Schubert, hinged on a *quid pro quo* transaction that once again followed the principle 'economic concessions from Germany *versus* political concessions from France'. By mobilising parts of its railway bonds under the Dawes scheme Germany was to provide its western neighbour with the capital it urgently needed to restore public finances. In return, France would accelerate the

[19] Chamberlain to Crewe, 12 October 1926, FO 371/11331: C 10909/10060/18; Tyrrell memorandum, 26 July 1926, *DBFP*, IA, I, no. 103; Sargent memorandum, 9 October 1926, FO 371/11331: C 10930/10060/18.

[20] Treasury memorandum, 27 September 1926, FO 371/11331 10930.

[21] Kellogg address, 20 April 1926, *FRUS 1926*, I, p. 78; Hoover memorandum, 23 September 1925, Hoover Papers, Commerce, box 20.

[22] Stresemann notes, 17 and 20 September 1926, *ADAP*, B, I/II, nos. 88, 94. Hesnard minutes, 17 September 1926, MAE, Série Europe, Allemagne, Thoiry, vol. 398, Z 35–12; Briand statements to the Foreign Affairs Commission, 23 November 1926, Procès verbaux, C14763, no. 62, pp. 13–26. Cf. Jacobson and Walker (1975); Bariéty (1980).

evacuation of the Rhineland – to complete it by September 1927 – 'speed up the termination of military control and return the coal and steel region of the Saar. Further, Paris would promise to raise no objections against the German plan to 'buy back' the Eupen–Malmédy region from Belgium.[23]

The core components of this 'deal', then, were familiar to all key policy-makers and financiers. Essentially, as at the London conference, Germany was called on to reciprocate French advances with concessions that reached beyond the 'fulfilment' of Versailles and 'good behaviour'. In short, these concessions had to be financial – and were therefore inseparable from German reparations obligations. They were thus also inseparably bound up with the eventual final reparations agreement, in which both Britain and America had a considerable stake.[24] Because of this, and because Germany was still far from capable of pursuing an independent foreign financial policy, the scope for any Franco-German arrangements was very restricted from the start. This both Briand and Stresemann knew well. They also knew that their chances of success would largely be measured by the degree of London's and especially Washington's willingness to back their scheme – and the Anglo-American bankers' willingness to underwrite it financially.[25]

Given the extraordinary degree of German dependence on Anglo-American financial power and political consent under the Dawes regime, a bargain of Thoiry's complexity could not be realised any other way. More profoundly, then, its success hinged on an underlying compatibility of interests between not only two but four powers. In other words, it could not be realised without a constellation, and an Anglo-American engagement, comparable to what had made possible the London accords of 1924. Put differently, Thoiry threw into relief that further European stabilisation depended on how far three essential components of European and transatlantic politics could be reconciled: French security *caveats*, Anglo-American aspirations to promote Germany's inter-national integration and, last but not least, core financial interests on both sides of the Atlantic. Even more strikingly, the eventual fate of the Franco-German scheme underscored the extent to which essential levers of postwar international politics, and finance, remained in the hands of British and American policymakers – and financiers.

The failure of Thoiry thus also revealed distinct limits of Anglo-American stabilisation strategies after Locarno. Washington and Whitehall not only intended to determine or, in Britain's case, at least influence the terms and

---

[23] D'Abernon to Chamberlain, 29 September 1926, FO 371/11330; Chamberlain memorandum, 2 October 1926, FO 371/11331: C 10700/10060/18.

[24] Stresemann memorandum, 4 February 1926, *ADAP*, B, I/I, no. 80.

[25] *Ibid.*; Briand to Poincaré, 20 August 1926, MAE, Série Europe, Allemagne, Thoiry, vol. 398, Z 35–12.

timing of what all sides eventually sought: a revised reparations settlement. They were also determined to control and, if necessary, block any Franco-German attempts at *rapprochement* adversely affecting what they deemed pre-eminent national interests, both financial and political. From the outset, the success of the Thoiry design thus hinged on the question whether Briand and Stresemann could win sufficient Anglo-American support for their endeavour. Neither of them had any illusions about how critical this support was for implementing what could never come to pass as merely a bilateral agreement.

The Thoiry plan was not conceived on the spur of the moment, amidst the euphoria following Germany's return to the *Société des Nations* in September 1926. In fact, it had been immediately after Locarno that Briand had approached Berlin with the proposal that France would consent to an early Rhineland evacuation if Germany agreed to make substantial advance payments on reparations. Subsequently, he had come to view the Rhineland as France's essential pawn for a comprehensive post-Locarno agreement with Germany. And Stresemann had soon voiced interest in pursuing Briand's design.[26] What had motivated the French foreign minister to consider such far-reaching bilateral deals? Apart from pressing financial concerns, his actions sprang from a growing realisation that the French insistence on preserving the Versailles system was becoming ever less effective. While the *entente* with, and guarantees of, Britain remained essential, Briand had thus sought to widen the foundations of French security *through direct agreements with Germany*. And he was aware that such agreements had to be forged as long as France's bargaining-power as a victor of the Great War, ever more waning the closer the Versailles deadline for the Rhenish occupation approached, was still comparatively strong.[27]

It is therefore imperative to consider not only one but two dimensions of postwar politics to place subsequent Franco-German exchanges over the summer of 1926 and, finally, the Thoiry conversation in their proper context. On one level, these developments were a function of what has already been described: the stalling progress of Locarno diplomacy, especially over the Rhineland. Yet even more important was France's again worsening financial crisis – the ever more acute need to stabilise the franc and balance the budget. All of this made it more urgent than ever to attract foreign capital; or at least that was the common conclusion of Briand, Caillaux and the director of the

[26] Hoesch to AA, 1 December 1925; Stresemann to Hoesch, 8 December 1925, *ADAP*, B, I/I, pp. 10–11, 46–7. Cf. Wurm (1979), pp. 399ff.
[27] See Briand's and Berthelot's numerous memoranda on these issues, November 1925 – February 1926, MAE, Série Europe, Allemagne, 398/1–3; Briand statements to the Foreign Affairs Commission, 23 November 1926, C14763, no. 62, p. 13.

Banque de France, Moreau, which in August even Poincaré himself espoused.[28]
But Washington's loan embargo persisted. And though Briand strove hard for
it, the prospects of gaining a parliamentary endorsement of the Mellon–
Bérenger agreement were growing ever dimmer. The *Chambre* also still
had to approve the debt settlement with Britain. As Fleuriau warned from
London, Anglo-American financiers would not help rescue the franc until both
agreements had been ratified.[29]

Undoubtedly, without this impasse there would have been far less urgency
for the French government to hatch ambitious bilateral schemes with Germany. In early June, Briand even told Stresemann that the French 'financial
crisis' was so severe that the desired 'general agreement' had no prospects.[30]
Developments reached a climax when the Briand–Caillaux government,
formed on 23 June, had to resign, and Herriot's subsequent ministry fell on
21 July. Applauded for his efforts by Strong, Caillaux had once again tried to
consolidate the budget and institute special funds for debt payments.[31] But he
came up against impossible odds. As Ambassador Herrick had reported to
Kellogg on 8 June, 'the people of France are in a somewhat dangerous mood'.
An article in the newspaper *Rappel* had been 'complaining' that 'they must
sweat blood and gold to pay for the cakes of the Americans and English while
at the same time they are told to . . . ration their own bread'. Against this
background opposition to the debt agreement was 'assuming formidable
proportions'.[32]

It was at this point that, on 23 July, Poincaré returned to the helm of French
politics, forming an *Union Nationale* cabinet in which he acted both as premier
and his own finance minister. By mid-August, he had achieved a temporary
consolidation of the situation, and he had by and large balanced the budget.[33]
But if Poincaré wanted to implement a more fundamental consolidation programme, he still needed foreign capital. In a conversation with Parker Gilbert
in late August, the French premier and Moreau thus took up the idea of
liquidating a *tranche* of the German railway bonds under the Dawes scheme.[34]

For Briand, who stayed on as foreign minister, and senior *Quai d'Orsay*
officials such as Seydoux, a major incentive for seeking a deal with Germany

[28] Briand to Poincaré, 20 August 1926, MAE, Série Europe, Allemagne, Thoiry, vol. 398, Z 35–12.
[29] Fleuriau to Poincaré, 25 July 1925, Correspondance de Raymond Poincaré, Bibliothèque
Nationale, Paris. Cf. Pitts (1987), p. 136.
[30] Chamberlain to Tyrrell, 9 June 1926, FO 371/11898: W 5345/5199/98.
[31] Strong report to Harrison, 21 July 1926, Strong report to Jay, 9 July 1926, FRBNY Papers, C
261.1.
[32] Herrick to Kellogg, 8 June 1926, *FRUS 1926*, II, p. 96.
[33] See 12 July 1926, *JOC* F7/12954/25. Cf. Keeton (1987), pp. 170ff.
[34] Strong to Winston, 30 August 1926, Strong Papers; Phillips to Kellogg, 17 September 1926,
RG 39, box 62; Warren memorandum, 26 August 1926, Strong Papers. Cf. Moreau (1954),
pp. 78–82.

was not only the hope of redirecting international capital from German into French coffers, it was also the prospect of fortifying Franco-German *rapprochement*. Before the *Chambre*'s Foreign Affairs Commission, Briand argued in November that 'arrangements in the economic or financial sphere' could deepen political 'collaboration' between both countries. And this was 'the most solid guarantee for peace' once Germany had 'fulfilled the essential conditions' of Versailles.[35] By co-operating with Berlin, Paris also finally sought to escape what not only Seydoux perceived as 'the Anglo-American financial yoke' of the postwar era.[36] Briand nonetheless believed that France had to avoid alienating either the US creditor or the British guarantor – and creditor. Yet, careful though the *Quai d'Orsay*'s preparations were, the French foreign minister went to Thoiry without a clear mandate from Poincaré, who rejected the scope of his envisaged bargain.[37]

Parallel, while France's financial calamities were culminating and the Rhineland negotiations seemed at a dead end, Stresemann had from his side begun to take the initiative. In early August, he impressed upon Briand that the time had come to seek a 'strategic breakthrough' in Franco-German postwar relations. The German foreign minister had sought to seize upon Briand's overtures ever since December 1925, when he had authorised Ambassador Hoesch to explore them further. For what Briand outlined appeared to open the possibility of realising one of his principal goals – to 'liberate' the Rhineland not merely through concert diplomacy but also by employing Germany's most effective 'remaining weapon', its financial 'power'. In August, Stresemann underscored that, by offering France generous financial support, he essentially aimed to clinch the evacuation of the Rhineland. All other concerns were secondary.[38]

Stresemann also hoped to gain French acquiescence to German plans to 'buy back' Eupen–Malmédy from Belgium. Berlin had pursued negotiations with the Vandervelde government in Brussels from the spring of 1926.[39] On 30 July, however, Briand and Poincaré had told Vandervelde that France would not accept a scheme setting a dangerous precedent for a revision of the territorial *status quo* of 1919. Poincaré vowed that he would oppose any 'deal' that the Germans could then invoke to alter the status of the Saar, Upper Silesia and the 'Polish Corridor' as well. Briand reiterated this concern to Chamberlain on 20 August. Deliberately exaggerating, he complained that Berlin 'wanted in

[35] Briand statements to the Foreign Affairs Commission, 23 November 1926, C14763, no. 62, p. 13.
[36] Pitts (1987) p. 121; Seydoux memorandum, 15 June 1926, no. 56–26, MAE, Série Europe, Allemagne, vol. 389.
[37] Poincaré memorandum to Briand, 22 September 1926, MAE, Série Europe, Allemagne, Thoiry, vol. 398, Z 35–12.
[38] Stresemann to Hesnard, 5 August 1926, *ADAP*, B, I/II, pp. 15ff; Stresemann to Hoesch, 8 December 1925, *ADAP*, B, I/I, pp. 46–7.
[39] Cf. Enssle (1980).

every sphere to move too quickly', desiring everything at once – Eupen and Malmédy, 'a revision of the Danzig Corridor' and the 'Anschluss' of Austria.[40] As we have seen, the French foreign minister's views had markedly changed by September.

Despite French – and eventually also British – opposition, however, secret talks between Berlin and Brussels continued. Yet, like the Thoiry plans, they would come to naught. While the Eupen–Malmédy question was of no import to Washington, the prospect of a German arrangement with Belgium turned out to be an important reason for Britain's unease with the Thoiry scheme as a whole. When first confronted with the issue, Chamberlain had expressed profound concerns. He feared that the envisaged transaction would not only require renegotiating the Locarno treaty but also precipitate German calls for territorial revisions in the east. On 12 August, he noted: What 'chance . . . of political stabilisation' in Europe would there be 'if we begin *now* re-arranging frontiers'.[41]

Like Poincaré, the British foreign secretary felt that Eupen–Malmédy could set an unwelcome precedent; and it could raise highly inopportune questions, especially that of the 'Polish Corridor'. By contrast, the governor of the Bank of England, Norman, who in mid-August went to the Netherlands to confer with his counterparts Strong and Schacht, favoured supporting the German–Belgian scheme. As Norman informed Chamberlain, he deemed the transaction conducive to 'the general rehabilitation of Europe'. It seemed timely because Belgium urgently needed a sum like the $60 million that the German government had promised to stabilise the Belgian franc. The Foreign Office official Lampson originally encouraged Norman, telling him that Britain 'cared [not] much one way or the other who owned Eupen and Malmédy'. In view of Chamberlain's subsequent veto, however, Britain backed off from backing this particular attempt of Stresemann to pursue economic revisionism in the west.[42]

In the larger European picture, though, Eupen–Malmédy remained a side issue. The cardinal question in the autumn of 1926 was: had Briand and Stresemann indeed opened up a realistic perspective for a strategic break-through in Franco-German relations? Stresemann and Schubert – and no less Briand, Berthelot and Seydoux – strove hard to get London, Washington and leading Anglo-American financiers on board. Ultimately, everything depended on the Americans as they not only controlled the Dawes regime but also the necessary capital.

---

[40] Grahame to Chamberlain, 3 August 1926, FO 800.259; Chamberlain to Crewe, 20 August 1926, FO 425.398.

[41] Chamberlain minute, 12 August 1926, *DBFP*, IA, I, no. 142; Grahame to Chamberlain, 3 August 1926, FO 800.259.

[42] Lampson memorandum, 12 August 1926, *DBFP*, IA, I, no. 142.

Stresemann was painfully aware of Germany's actually severe capital short-age in the autumn of 1926. Since mid-1925, the Luther government had faced a *de facto* 'depression' of the German economy. Operating without formal SPD or DNVP support, Luther's minority cabinet, and particularly the new finance minister, Karl Reinhold, had struggled to overcome Germany's own financial crisis. In a speech to the *Reichstag* on 20 January 1926, Luther had called its mastery 'the most pressing task of the present time'.[43] Reinhold had first tried to minimise governmental spending and cut taxes that were hurtful to German business. Yet as such measures proved largely ineffective he eventu-ally resorted to deficit spending, particularly on 'work-creating' programmes to combat rising unemployment. This actually required Berlin to increase foreign borrowing, thus accentuating German dependence on US loans and the volatile global financial markets.[44]

At the same time, as the reparations agent Parker Gilbert never failed to remind Stresemann, he – and the Coolidge administration – had one priority: the unimpeded operation of the Dawes plan.[45] The United States, not the European powers, would set the time and terms of its eventual revision. In view of this, the transatlantic interdependence that Stresemann had deliberately fostered since 1923 now, three years later, imposed one vital limit on his policy: One of its key elements, financial leverage to effect political changes, was essentially under US control – and remained so for the foreseeable future.[46] Accordingly, Weimar Germany could not pursue an independent *Westpolitik*, particularly vis-à-vis France, or *Ostpolitik*, especially vis-à-vis Poland. Both remained fundamentally constrained. Yet the German foreign minister took these constraints into account. He consistently adjusted German aims to those which, in his judgement, Washington and Wall Street pursued.

Fundamentally, then, Stresemann did not alter his course when he contem-plated bilateral schemes with Briand. His policy of peaceful revision still rested on the premise that further US financial engagement in Germany was vital. It remained indispensable not only for Germany's economic recuperation *and* inner consolidation as a republic but also for its further international re-ascension. Following the precedent of 1924, Stresemann also maintained that this would be most effective in ensuring that the 'world creditor' would bene-volently back its German debtor when the reparations regime was finally up for revision.[47] As ever, though, a critical challenge for the German foreign minister remained to win sufficient domestic backing for the 'modern' great-power

[43] Stresemann memorandum, 4 February 1926, *ADAP*, B, I/I, no. 80; *SB*, vol. 338, p. 5146.
[44] Cf. McNeil (1986), pp. 112–33.
[45] Gilbert to Strong, 5 November 1925, Strong Papers, 1012.1; Schubert memorandum, 22 February 1926, *ADAP*, B, I/II, pp. 285–6.
[46] Stresemann speech, 19 December 1925, Stresemann Papers, vol. 274.
[47] Stresemann memorandum, 12 July 1926, *ADAP*, B, I/I, no. 276.

policy he envisaged – a policy that, under different auspices, the Federal Republic of Germany would successfully pursue after 1945. It ultimately required rising levels of prosperity, a firmer parliamentary base and the support of key interest-groups like the Association of the German Heavy Industry – and the *Reichswehr*. And all of this could only be assured through further notable successes of his policy, the sooner the better.[48]

In the short term, however, German dependence on the United States could limit Berlin's options considerably. At no point was this more conspicuous than in late 1926. The German foreign minister had already noted a year earlier that a crucial prerequisite for the success of any Franco-German scheme would be the commercialisation of a substantial *tranche* of the German railway bonds created under the Dawes scheme. And this could only be effected, with the consent of Washington and London, on the US capital market – the only market large enough to absorb the German bonds. From January 1926, the German government had sounded out the Republican administration as well as Anglo-American bankers on this issue. On 11 January, Ambassador Maltzan had met Mellon, Parker Gilbert, Strong and Norman in Washington to gauge their views. And all of them had left no doubt that they viewed the as yet vague Franco-German plans with suspicion.[49]

Eight months later, the main task for German and French policymakers had not changed. They still had to convince the Anglo-American powers that Thoiry was a 'grand bargain' worth supporting after all. This even outweighed their second major task: to convince their own domestic audiences of the same. In Stresemann's view, the key lay in dispelling British and American anxieties that a 'premature' liquidation of the railway bonds might undercut the Dawes plan as a whole. He tried to win over the US administration by placing Thoiry in the wider context of Europe's 'final' pacification, which also had to be in America's interest. And he characterised the Franco-German project as a natural consequence of the Dawes and Locarno agreements, which had met with so much US 'understanding and support'. Further, Stresemann tried hard to counter the impression that Berlin was pursuing a more fundamental policy shift – towards France and away from the 'Anglo-Saxon powers'. As he presented it, Thoiry by no means intended to go against American preferences and precipitate a 'premature' general settlement of reparations. German diplomacy made the same case in Britain.[50]

---

[48] Stresemann speech, 28 June 1926, Stresemann (1932), II, pp. 449–51.
[49] Stresemann to Hoesch, 8 December 1925, *ADAP*, B, I/I, pp. 46–7; Maltzan report about talks between Norman, Strong, Parker Gilbert and US Treasury Secretary Mellon, 11 January 1926, *ADAP*, B, I/I, p. 101.
[50] Stresemann speech, 2 October 1926, Stresemann (1932), III, pp. 33–6; Schubert memorandum, 9 October 1926, Stresemann instructions to German embassies in London and Washington, 15 October 1926, *ADAP*, B, I/II, nos. 139, 148.

In effect, Briand used very similar arguments to sway the administration in Washington. And he thought that he had early on won Chamberlain's general support when broadly outlining the envisaged *do ut des* scheme to him during a meeting in early June. Briand, too, described the plan as in no way directed against British reparations interests – and as a natural complement to the Locarno accords.[51] Overall, though, neither of the Thoiry interlocutors had any doubt that they faced an up-hill struggle in the arena of transatlantic politics and finance. Besides, both acknowledged that, even if Poincaré was originally prepared to explore it, their 'deal' would encounter considerable opposition in many French and even some German quarters. On the French right it was likely to spark outright resistance on account of its security implications for the Rhineland.[52] And, on the level of domestic politics, this resistance would matter most – more than parallel German fears about compromising chances for a major reduction of reparations in a later general settlement.[53]

The Anglo-American veto against Thoiry

As soon became clear after the proposal's publication, prevalent French definitions of security indeed still ran counter to a 'bartering' agreement with Germany on the scale of Thoiry. In the eyes of Poincaré and, notably, the French General Staff, the loss of the Rhenish occupation zones combined with a further rapid shift of power towards Germany raised unsettling prospects.[54] These concerns alone made a major Franco-German bargain very hard to legitimate less than one year after Locarno. But they were not the crucial impediment.

The main obstacles arose from precisely those 'intertwined political and financial interests' with Britain and America that had yielded such favourable results for Franco-German *rapprochement* since the end of the Ruhr crisis. As noted, weighing in against Thoiry from the beginning were hardly compatible financial interests, as defined by leading bankers such as Strong and Norman, yet also, and uncompromisingly, by the British and American Treasuries. Decisive, though, proved the refusal of key political decisionmakers in Whitehall and Washington to explore the Thoiry design's inherent potential. This stemmed from their unwillingness to subsume its immediate 'costs' in terms of loan, debt and reparations interests to the wider political and ultimately also financial

---

[51] Chamberlain memorandum, 2 October 1926, FO 371/11331; Chamberlain to Tyrrell, 9 June 1926, FO 371/11898: W 5345/5199/98.

[52] Schubert memorandum, 3 September 1926, *ADAP*, B, I/II, p. 157.

[53] Particularly Schacht articulated such concerns. See D'Abernon to Chamberlain, 1 October 1926, FO 371/11331.

[54] Cf. Maxelon (1972), p. 222.

benefits that it could generate. For a realisation of the Thoiry scheme could not only contribute to what Parker Gilbert considered imperative for Europe's economic consolidation: the stabilisation of French finances. It also, and above all, had the potential of reinvigorating the Franco-German peace process, which was and remained crucial for advancing Europe's political consolidation, also beyond Germany's eastern borders.[55]

Soon, however, within a month after the Thoiry meeting, it became obvious on which side the scales came down, at least for the Coolidge administration and a majority of Anglo-American financiers. All unequivocally rejected the scheme. Considering Washington's veto unchangeable, and unwilling to confront Churchill's entrenched opposition at home, Chamberlain soon followed suit. On 15 October, he concluded that British diplomacy should stress vis-à-vis Briand 'the serious, if not insuperable difficulties' in 'the successful accomplishment' of the Franco-German design.[56] Indeed, any chances of rescuing it had all but evaporated by that time. Capturing what aroused Anglo-American ill-will against the plans, Parker Gilbert summarised that they ultimately implied that France would obtain its money and Germany its land while Britain and the United States would have to foot the bill.[57]

In short, crucial for burying Thoiry was that no one among the British and American decisionmakers who determined the progress of peaceful change in Europe saw an urgent need, or a convincing rationale, to put his weight behind it. They indeed saw the complex arrangement as conflicting with two overriding American – and British – interests: first, to ensure that France did not elude its war-debt obligations; second, to ensure the Dawes regime's unhampered operation for the time being *and* to set the terms of its eventual *overall* revision when conditions seemed auspicious. As D'Abernon reported on 1 October, Parker Gilbert and US bankers then present in Berlin to discuss the Franco-German proposals deemed a revision of the Dawes plan only sensible once it had exhausted its usefulness and Germany faced full payments – at the earliest 'in two years'.[58] This was indeed when the Young plan negotiations would commence.

Most immediately detrimental to Franco-German designs was that key American policymakers and financiers considered them irreconcilable with the core premises of US war-debt policy. As Strong and Parker Gilbert had re-affirmed towards the governments in both Paris and Berlin throughout 1926, Washington continued to insist on a strict separation between reparations

---

[55] See Schubert memorandum, 9 October 1926, *ADAP*, B, I/II, no. 139.
[56] Chamberlain aide memoire, 15 October 1926, FO 371/11331: C 10060/18.
[57] Schubert memorandum, 22 February 1926, *ADAP*, B, I/I, pp. 285–6; Dieckhoff report from Washington, 27 September 1926, *ADAP*, B, I/II, pp. 238–9.
[58] D'Abernon to FO, 1 October 1926, FO 371/11331.

and war-debt questions. And, crucially, the US government made a ratification of the Mellon–Bérenger agreement the basic precondition for contemplating any support for the Thoiry scheme.[59] But this ratification was simply not yet on the cards. Essentially, the Coolidge administration not only sought to keep financial and wider security issues apart. It also insisted on setting the rules in all key areas of debts, loans and reparations, each either to be handled through bilateral negotiations or among the Europeans themselves – and without affecting US claims.[60] The administration did so largely in agreement with leading financiers in New York and the City of London.

Neither British nor American opposition was directed against Stresemann's underlying aim of regaining German sovereignty in the Rhineland by way of a 'businesslike' agreement with France. Nor was it mainly directed against Briand's political rationale of building further bridges across the Rhine. Yet especially Hoover remained suspicious that the hidden agenda pursued by both parties might be to renew efforts to form a 'closed' continental bloc. This time, France and Germany operated on co-operative premises. But what they envisaged was potentially no less harmful to US foreign commerce than Poincaré's coercive designs of 1923.[61] Although this remained a secondary concern in 1926, Republican decisionmakers thus placed Thoiry in the wider context of Franco-German initiatives that collided with America's 'open-door' policy.

The British government was less concerned about such wider implications. Instead, the Treasury concluded, and Niemeyer impressed on the Foreign Office, that the Thoiry scheme itself was not only 'financially unsound' but also 'injurious to Great Britain'.[62] At the core, it threatened to 'injure' cardinal interests of British debt and reparations policy. On the one hand, the Treasury feared that France might seek to circumvent the Churchill–Caillaux debt agreement. On the other, Churchill, Niemeyer and Norman anticipated that Thoiry's impact on the Dawes regime would be unsettling. In view of Britain's limited financial leverage, their main reaction was thus essentially defensive, if for different reasons than Washington's.

The central British aim remained to postpone any further reparation negotiations until conditions seemed conducive to a new overall settlement linking German obligations and allied war-debts. For only this linkage might allow Britain to reduce, and perhaps shed, its obligations to America, possibly in league with France. Mindful of this, and because he became convinced that the

---

[59] Schubert memorandum, 9 October 1926, *ADAP*, B, I/II, no. 139; D'Abernon to Chamberlain, 27 September 1926, *DBFP*, IA, I, no. 225, p. 403.

[60] Hoover memoranda, 23 September 1925 and ff, Hoover Papers, Commerce, box 20.

[61] Dieckhoff to AA, 27 September 1926, *ADAP*, B, I/II, pp. 238–9; Hoover to Kellogg, 28 November 1925, *FRUS 1925*, II, pp. 207–8.

[62] See Chamberlain's comments on a record of a conversation between Sargent and Niemeyer, 9 October 1926, FO 371/11331: C 10930/10060/18.

Thoiry project was ultimately 'impractical', Chamberlain opted against any serious engagement in its support. Fundamentally, he never altered his judgement that Franco-German accommodation could not be advanced through financial deals; it could only be sustained by building on Locarno and persevering with concert diplomacy.[63]

Yet, though eventually pouring cold water on it, not all Anglo-American decisionmakers had closed ranks against the Franco-German initiative from the start. For one thing, Parker Gilbert, whose backing was certainly critical for any attempt to implement the design, originally proposed his own recipe for transforming it into a workable plan. As D'Abernon reported on 12 October, the agent-general was 'firmly of the opinion that the time was not yet in sight even to start discussing about a general [reparations] settlement', as this would raise issues 'not yet ripe', namely 'the fixation of the amount of the German debt and the settlement of inter-Allied debts'. Yet he also thought that a 'partial settlement on the Thoiry lines', if implemented 'without prejudice to a general settlement later' could be 'useful, *if it led to the stabilisation of the French franc'*. Parker Gilbert suggested that the British and American Treasuries should jointly seize on the Franco-German proposals to stabilise the French currency, which in turn could underpin Europe's recuperation and permit Paris to discharge its debt obligations. To raise the requisite capital, the Anglo-American powers 'would put up the money against [a] ratification of the debt agreements'. Thus converted, Parker Gilbert concluded, the Thoiry conversations could 'provide a real opening'.[64]

In Washington, Treasury Under-Secretary Garrard Winston, whom the agent general had briefed about the scheme, was by no means oblivious to its obvious political significance. Winston concluded that it could be an important step on the path of Franco-German reconciliation, not to be dismissed lightly in the court of public opinion. He consequently enquired from the Morgan partner Morrow how far Wall Street deemed the time opportune for liquidating the German railway bonds on the American market.[65] But it soon transpired that the odds against such a transaction were stacked high. On behalf of the bank Dillon, Read & Co., the former US envoy Logan actually offered to underwrite the requisite bond sales. Yet not only Morgan & Co., whose opposition to any loans that were politically beneficial to Germany persisted, but also all other leading New York firms sent negative signals.[66]

In reaction to the bankers' verdict, what hardened was an underlying Anglo-American consensus that a commercialisation of the railway bonds was as misguided as the entire Franco-German scheme. Treasury Secretary Mellon

---

[63] Chamberlain to Crewe, 12 October 1926, FO 371/11331: C 10909/10060/18.
[64] D'Abernon to Chamberlain, 12 October 1926, FO 371/11331: C 10878/10060/18.
[65] Winston to Morrow, 27 September 1926, NA RG 39, box 85.
[66] *Journal of Commerce*, 17 October 1924. Cf. Kent (1989), p. 272.

and his British counterpart Churchill soon underscored their veto; and so did Strong and Norman.[67] Their main motive for vetoing the Thoiry project, however, was not financial but political. Neither side wished to precipitate a general revision of the Dawes scheme. And both also accentuated what remained the first, and steepest, hurdle in the autumn of 1926: as Parker Gilbert and Strong had already emphasised when meeting Moreau in Paris in July, there could only be a deal *after* Poincaré had pushed the Mellon–Bérenger agreement through the French parliament.[68]

In August, Coolidge and Kellogg had ruled out any further concessions to expedite the ratification process. Both rejected any new promises of lifting loan restrictions in return. And they had also rejected Mellon's proposal to complement the agreement with 'safeguard clauses' similar to those of the Dawes plan, which protected the debtor in adverse financial conditions.[69] Of course, Hoover also maintained his axiom that the US taxpayer should not be made liable to pay for the war through the backdoor, namely through concessions to Paris. After the Thoiry proposal had been publicised, the Coolidge administration was thus unwilling to isolate it from the wider interests of US war-debt policy. Treasury and State Department officials, including Castle, agreed that Washington must not soften its earlier stance to support a Franco-German bid that was ill-conceived in the first place.[70] Consequently, the US administration refused to get involved in any negotiations with Briand and Stresemann over Thoiry. It would not authorise the indirect supply of American capital to France via Germany.[71]

Clearly less inclined than Mellon to contemplate a 'generous' policy vis-à-vis France, Kellogg supported the US Treasury's firm line.[72] In the autumn of 1926, the State Department thus kept a distinctly low profile. No attempt was made to buttress the Franco-German initiative on political grounds. Kellogg's main concern after the plan's publication was to deflect responsibility for its expected failure from Washington. He hoped that the administration could

---

[67] Maltzan report about talks between Norman, Strong, Gilbert and Mellon, 11 January 1926, *ADAP*, B, I/I, p. 101; Schubert memorandum, 9 October 1926, *ADAP*, B, I/II, no. 139.

[68] Moreau (1954), pp. 113–14; Strong memorandum, 26 July 1926, FRBNY Papers, C 261.1; Strong to Mellon, 30 July 1926, Strong Papers, 1000.7. Cf. Leffler (1979), pp. 147–9.

[69] See Coolidge to Winston, 11 August 1926, RG 39, box 62; Castle Diary, 2 November 1926, vol. 10, p. 266a; Kellogg to Herrick, 16 July 1926, *FRUS 1926*, II, pp. 99–100.

[70] Hoover to Kellogg, 28 July 1926, RG 59 800.51 W89/199; A. Young to Kellogg, 11 October 1926, RG 59 462.00 R296/66/1/2; Castle Diary, 2 November 1926, vol. 10, p. 266a.

[71] While British criticism on grounds of 'free trade' remained subdued, the US government, though retaining high tariffs itself, also continued to oppose Franco-German bids to 'intertwine' economic interests through cartels, notably the steel cartel of May 1926. See US Commerce Department, *Annual Report*, 1926, pp. 34–7; Hoover memoranda, 23 September – 1 October 1925, Hoover Papers, Commerce, box 20; Treasury memorandum, 27 September 1926, FO 371/11331: C 10930/10060/18. Cf. Wurm (1993), pp.14ff; Pohl (1979), pp. 170–3.

[72] Kellogg to Herrick, 16 July 1926, *FRUS 1926*, II, pp. 99–100.

wait until opposition to Thoiry in Europe rendered any further discussion futile. As will be seen, Chamberlain pursued a very similar tactic. But Kellogg at least miscalculated. As he told Castle in early November, he could not believe press comments asserting that the scheme had failed because Washington 'had refused to allow the [railway] bonds to be sold'. Castle corrected him: 'this was the general impression'.[73]

Britain's eventual opposition to a 'cut + dried scheme'

Against the background of the mounting opposition to Thoiry in Washington and financial circles, the influence of the Baldwin government, and the Foreign Office in particular, was very limited. Britain could not have rescued the Franco-German scheme even if it had desired to do so. Yet warranting closer examination is the question why exactly British policymakers refrained from pursuing more than merely a face-saving strategy in support of Thoiry. Why did they make no harder efforts to explore, and foster, an initiative that at first glance appeared to tally well with the underlying aims of Chamberlain's Locarno policy – even if its implementation could be costly?

As mentioned, Briand and Stresemann did not spring the Thoiry bargain on the British foreign secretary as a *fait accompli*. When Briand informed Chamberlain in June that he and Stresemann would soon 'endeavour to make . . . a general agreement', he confided that he would even 'be prepared to consider' the 'occupied zones'. At that point, Chamberlain had 'warmly' welcomed this and the prospect of a 'general agreement' settling, notably, the Rhineland question. He had even observed that the Franco-German was 'one of those cases where a broad general agreement would be easier to secure and more likely to commend itself to public opinion in both countries' than any step-by-step negotiations over separate issues. And the foreign secretary had reiterated to Briand his verdict that, from the British standpoint, the number of troops in the occupied zones was absolutely 'indefensible'. It 'put' France and Britain 'wholly in the wrong'. Accordingly, Chamberlain suggested that if troop withdrawals had to be postponed they should definitely become part and parcel of the envisaged Franco-German agreement.[74]

Just before meeting Briand, Chamberlain had cabled Ambassador Crewe in Paris on 2 June that he welcomed 'any form of rapprochement between France and Germany' that would 'assist the development' of his 'policy of pacification'. British diplomacy had to avoid any impression of desiring to 'keep Franco-German antagonisms alive for some selfish purposes of our own' – neither on grounds of security concerns nor for the sake of British reparations

[73] Castle Diary, 2 November 1926, vol. 10, p. 266a.
[74] Chamberlain to Tyrrell, 9 June 1926, FO 371/11898: W 5345/5199/98.

policy. In the Foreign Office, Under-Secretary Tyrrell fully backed this orientation. He argued consistently that, not least to revitalise trade, British policy in western Europe should continue to centre on further efforts 'to reconcile Germany and France'. If the financial crises that beset both of Britain's Locarno partners spurred Briand and Stresemann into redoubling their reconciliation efforts, this could only further British objectives.[75] Such views struck a chord not only with Stresemann and Briand but also, naturally, with American ideas about the economic mainsprings of Europe's pacification.

Significantly, however, neither in June 1926 nor later did Chamberlain propose to act as a mediator in realising a Thoiry-like scheme. Desirable as he and Tyrrell considered its thrust in terms of overall policy, the Foreign Office would not make its implementation a core priority of the Locarno concert. When Briand first told him about the actual Thoiry conversation, on 2 October, Chamberlain again reacted overall favourably. But he also 'uttered a word of caution', remarking that he had earlier impressed on Stresemann not to 'base his arrangements with France on any preference for France or Belgium which would injure British interests'. He also told the French foreign minister that the British Treasury 'had considerable doubts' as to the 'practicability' of what he and Stresemann had suggested. Nonetheless, though markedly more cautious than in June, Chamberlain proposed that 'experts from all interested powers', including Britain and Italy, should convene to assess the scheme's prospects. He emphasised that its implementation would definitely require wider international co-operation and, eventually, make an involvement of the United States unavoidable.[76]

Yet, as the foreign secretary acknowledged in the British government's internal discussions, translating Thoiry into a workable scheme would be impossible unless the Treasury backed it and drew up constructive proposals, chiefly for marketing the German railway bonds. On 11 October, Chamberlain 'urged on' Niemeyer that Britain 'must not press [its] own interests too far; that we must not have the appearance of destroying for selfish reasons so promising a development in Franco-German relations; + that we must show a desire to help + not to hinder the rapprochement'.[77] But he did not sway the Treasury, which – conveniently – curtailed the Foreign Office's room to manoeuvre almost completely.

The British Treasury indeed raised serious financial concerns that would ultimately weigh most heavily in the balance against Thoiry. Niemeyer advocated that Britain should openly state its financial objections – essentially, that

---

[75] Chamberlain to Crewe, 2 June 1926, Tyrrell memorandum, 26 July 1926, *DBFP*, IA, II, nos. 40, 103.

[76] Chamberlain memorandum, 2 October 1926, FO 371/11331: C 10700/10060/18.

[77] Chamberlain minute, 11 October 1926, FO 371/11331: C 10722/10060/18.

the German railway bonds could not be liquidated on the US market against the will of Washington and the US bankers. He also argued that Chamberlain should warn French and German policymakers not to pursue illusions and subsequent myth-making, with Britain and America cast as the scapegoats once their designs should fail. In Niemeyer's expert opinion, 'the stabilisation of the franc, assuming that the American debt settlement were to be ratified, could be carried out without any need for raising such a large sum of money' as contemplated at Thoiry.[78] Clearly, the Treasury's primary interest lay in preventing a revision of the Dawes scheme that was disadvantageous to Britain, i.e. that lessened the chances of shirking its debt burden. Unsurprisingly, this objection proved decisive for the Baldwin government's stance. As Chamberlain noted on 15 October, the cabinet had by then 'come to the definite conclusion' that any modification of the Dawes plan '[could] not be envisaged unless and until it can be combined with a general revision of other international obligations' – chiefly, British war-debts. This remained Britain's maxim, although D'Abernon had reported that Parker Gilbert considered such a scenario as 'unlikely to materialize, at any rate as a state operation'.[79]

In early October, the Foreign Office official Orme Sargent had raised wider political concerns. In his view, British diplomacy faced the broader question 'whether for political reasons' it would 'not be prepared to sacrifice certain immediate . . . financial interests for the sake of the political advantage to be obtained from a Franco-German settlement', including 'the evacuation of the Rhineland'. To pursue this rationale would have required a convincing majority in cabinet. But, as the austerity-minded chancellor Churchill invariably stressed, Britain had nothing to give away in a phase of retrenchment, certainly not to promote a half-baked Franco-German plan.[80] And Chamberlain was not prepared to fight for what he soon deemed a hopeless cause, be it to convince his cabinet colleagues, the Treasury or the British public at large.[81]

The British government thus distanced itself from Thoiry on the international stage. On 14 October, Chamberlain declined Briand's request to mediate between France and the United States. While financial concerns were central, there was also an important political rationale for the course that Chamberlain eventually adopted. Following a period of hesitancy, he returned to the core premises of his self-accorded role in European politics. To the fore came his deep-seated reservations against 'unrealistic' Franco-German

[78] Sargent record of a conversation with Niemeyer, 9 October 1926, FO 371/11331: C 10930/10060/18.
[79] Chamberlain aide memoire, 15 October 1926, FO 371/11331: C 10792 /10060/18; D'Abernon to FO, 1 October 1926, FO 371/11331.
[80] Sargent record, 9 October 1926; Treasury memorandum, 27 September 1926, FO 371/11331: C 10930/10060/18.
[81] Chamberlain aide memoire, 15 October 1926, FO 371/11331: C 10792/10060/18.

initiatives that largely bypassed the British 'broker'. Ultimately, he could not favour bilateral approaches that discarded the rules of concert diplomacy as he defined them.[82]

As Chamberlain reminded Crewe on 12 October, Britain had to look ahead: 'Problems connected with Franco-German relations cannot be solved in a few weeks.' Nor could they be settled through proposals that raised unfounded expectations. For these only made his task of pragmatically balancing French and German interests all the harder. In private, Chamberlain noted that 'Briand & Stresemann at Thoiry dreamed dreams & saw visions that will not be easily realised, letting their imagination run away with them.' He did see their initiative as an affirmation of his course, concluding 'what an outcome since Locarno & what a justification of my policy!' In essence, though, he was also resolved to avoid being ever again 'faced by a cut + dried scheme on which both Germans and French have agreed, but which we cannot accept'.[83]

The lessons of Thoiry's failure

By late October, the Thoiry scheme's prospects were waning all around, not only due to the international difficulties but also because of mounting domestic opposition to it in France and even in Germany. Chamberlain was not alone in concluding that the initiative had lost its initial momentum. Accordingly, his main concern shifted: it now became to prevent Britain's opposition from having negative repercussions for the Locarno concert. Chamberlain took care to set himself apart from the blunter attitude of the British Treasury.[84] With no means to overcome unrelenting Anglo-American resistance, Briand and Stresemann had to concede that a project along the lines of Thoiry could not be realised in the foreseeable future.[85]

The longer concrete prospects for implementing the scheme remained elusive, the more susceptible it also became to criticism on the French and German home fronts. In Germany, Stresemann encountered increasing reservations not only in cabinet and the *Reichstag*'s Foreign Affairs Committee.[86] He also had to grapple with the scepticism of influential financiers, notably *Reichsbank* president Schacht. Throughout the autumn of 1926, Schacht

[82] Chamberlain to Fleuriau, 14 October 1926, FO 371/11331: C 10969/10060/18; Chamberlain minute, 21 December 1926, FO 371/12125/144.

[83] Chamberlain to Crewe, 12 October 1926, FO 371/11331: C 10909/10060/18; Austen to Hilda Chamberlain, 8 October 1926, Austen Chamberlain Papers, AC 5/1/395.

[84] Chamberlain minute, 26 October 1926, FO 371/11331: C 10824 /10060/18; Schubert memorandum, 27 November 1926, *ADAP*, B, I/II, no. 214.

[85] Stresemann instructions to German embassies, 26 October 1926, *ADAP*, B, I/II, pp. 373ff.

[86] Stresemann report to the Foreign Affairs Committee, 7 October 1926, Stresemann (1932), III, pp. 37–41; cabinet minutes, 13 October 1926, *AR Marx III und IV*, no. 89.

remained ambivalent. Yet his main argument was that a partial mobilisation of the Dawes *tranches* might be prejudicial to German interests when it came to the anticipated general reparations settlement. Then, he reckoned, Anglo-American support would be vital, so vital that it must not be jeopardised in advance. In France, it was chiefly growing *Bloc National* opposition to the 'betrayal' of vital security interests that forced Briand to distance himself from the plan. While the French cabinet had on 21 September given the go-ahead for pursuing the Thoiry deliberations further, ever more voices came out against a far-reaching agreement. These eventually included Briand's own chief aides at the *Quai d'Orsay*, Berthelot and Seydoux. Decisive, however, was Poincaré's intervention.[87]

In early October, Berthelot and Seydoux summed up their main *caveats*. Although both concluded that Stresemann's approach was supported by a majority of Germans desirous of seeing the Rhineland 'liberated', they advised against a swift evacuation. In their view, precipitated changes in the Rhenish *status quo* could encourage further German demands for revisions, both vis-à-vis France and Germany's eastern neighbours.[88] Berthelot maintained that in return for any bargain on the Rhineland, Germany should not only pay a financial price but also give what it had rejected at Locarno: *status quo* guarantees for eastern Europe. He also argued that French security depended on establishing a new control regime to ensure the Rhineland's continued demilitarisation following a French withdrawal. As Berthelot knew, Berlin would not be prepared to make such concessions, at least in the short term. Parallel, Seydoux raised financial objections. He supported Britain's position that the Dawes plan should be kept intact attendant to a general financial settlement, which might permit a revision of reparations *and* war-debts.[89]

Crucially, Poincaré shared all of these concerns. And he would draw his own consequences, overcome France's financial *malaise* 'from within' and thus nip all further discussions about reviving Thoiry in the bud. Following Briand's return from his tête-à-tête with Stresemann, Poincaré at first did not reject outright pursuing a 'grand bargain' with Germany. But he insisted that France's withdrawal from the Rhineland had to be *gradual*; and Germany had to take the

---

[87] Berthelot to de Margerie, 21 September 1926; Poincaré memorandum, 22 September 1926, MAE, Série Europe, Allemagne, vol. 398, no. 771, Z 35–12. Cf. Pitts (1987), pp. 155–64; Wurm (1979), pp. 465–9.

[88] *Quai d'Orsay* memorandum, 8 October 1925; Seydoux memorandum to Berthelot, 15 October 1926, MAE, Série Europe, Allemagne, vol. 399. The Franco-German scheme also generated anxieties in Poland. On 28 November, Britain's ambassador in Warsaw, Max Muller, reported a 'general apprehension that Franco-German negotiations entailing revisions of certain clauses of [the] Versailles Treaty may react unfavourably on Poland's tenure of her present frontiers'. But the ambassador also noted that the new foreign minister Zaleski held 'opposite views'; Max Muller to FO, 28 September 1926, FO 371/11331.

[89] Seydoux memorandum, 15 October 1926, MAE, Série Europe, Allemagne, vol. 399.

first step and ensure a *complete* mobilisation of the Dawes obligations. But Poincaré also pointed to Thoiry's essential security dimension when insisting that a complete evacuation of the occupied zones could only be considered once France's planned eastern fortifications – which then became the Maginot line – were complete.[90] The objections that Poincaré and Berthelot raised reflected a salient reality twelve months after Locarno: the limits that the European security question still placed on any comprehensive settlement that profoundly altered the postwar constellation. The underlying French concern remained that, irrespective of its abiding military weakness, a Thoiry-style bargain would have strengthened Germany's – inherently superior – position far more than that of France.

Any subsequent attempts to implement a modified Thoiry scheme were indeed rendered baseless by the fact that Poincaré managed to stabilise the franc, and consolidate French finances, without requiring external aid, either from Germany or the Anglo-American powers. He thereby initiated a significant development for France and postwar transatlantic relations. Showing first results in December 1926, France's internally driven consolidation continued through 1928 and, crucially, it greatly reduced French dependence on foreign capital. This meant that not only Germany but also Britain and America lost important leverage, not least concerning the ratification of the war-debt settlements.[91] Yet, as will be shown, the Thoiry idea was not completely dead.

It has been claimed that Chamberlain was essentially correct: the very fact that France was willing to consider an ambitious arrangement with Germany in 1926 was a success of Locarno politics and boosted it further.[92] In effect, however, Thoiry revealed both the positive impact *and the limits* of Locarno politics. Even more so, it underscored the possibilities that the nascent system of London and Locarno created. But it also threw into relief the constraints that this system imposed, especially if Germany and France tried to initiate changes which the Anglo-American powers considered disadvantageous. Thoiry did not fail because its domestic opponents on both sides of the Rhine were so powerful. Their hostility only peaked once the negative British and American reactions were known, and their veto unequivocal – in other words: when there was already no longer any real chance of striking a Thoiry-like bargain. For German foreign policy, thus Stresemann's summary on 26 October, further Franco-German initiatives that provoked a collision with British yet above all American interests would be out of the question.[93]

[90] Moreau account of a conversation with Poincaré, 23 September 1926. Moreau (1954), pp. 109–12; Crewe to Chamberlain, 30 September 1926, FO 371/11331.
[91] Cf. Keiger (1997), pp. 322–8.
[92] See Krüger (1985a), pp. 344–5.
[93] Stresemann instructions to the German embassies, 26 October 1926, *ADAP*, B, I/II, pp. 373ff.

The lessons that the makers of Weimar foreign policy had to draw were clear: German financial power was not (yet) sufficient for the pursuit of a self-reliant foreign economic policy. Stresemann's broader political aims – reconciliation and revision – could not be realised if he lost sight of what London, Washington and Wall Street desired. The only realistic alternative the German foreign minister saw was to adapt his strategies even more closely to what he perceived as core Anglo-American aims. After the interlude of Thoiry, he thus returned to *and accentuated* the 'general lines' of his policy of peaceful revision: the primary orientation towards the United States and towards the Locarno concert.[94] Most urgently, Stresemann signalled to the Coolidge administration that Berlin's highest priority was to continue its close co-operation with America, particularly on loans and reparations. If necessary, this would take precedence over German collaboration with any European power.[95] And the efforts of the *Auswärtige Amt* were appreciated in Washington. As Coolidge emphasised to Ambassador Maltzan in early December, while unable to support the ambitious Thoiry scheme Washington continued to desire close ties with Berlin. Yet collaboration had to proceed on a smaller scale. In Coolidge's view, Germany's accession to the League had increased the 'joint influence' that both nations could exercise on 'the development of international relations' if they focused on pertinent issues, particularly disarmament.[96]

Briand reached very similar conclusions. In late November, he acknowledged that the intimately related questions of security and occupation had been an 'essential' part of all of his conversations with Stresemann. In his estimation, to 'come to terms with' him could be achieved either 'quickly or slowly' – and Thoiry had been an attempt to choose the former path. Never envisaged as 'an easy or a short-term operation', it was bound to 'encounter obstacles'.[97] And the chief obstacle that the French foreign minister made out mirrored both Parker Gilbert's and Chamberlain's verdict: '[I]t was not possible for France and Germany to decide *à deux* financial questions, tending on reparations and the Dawes plan.' They could only be decided with the consent of '[o]ther parties, notably Great Britain, and . . . the United States', that could be 'deeply affected by any Franco-German arrangement'. Briand was thus 'determined that all matters of this sort could only be dealt with on a wider field'.[98] The key lesson that he, like Stresemann, had to absorb was that on this 'wider field' endeavours *à la* Thoiry were only feasible when a basis of common

---

[94] *Ibid.*
[95] Castle memorandum of a conversation with Maltzan, 1 November 1926, NA RG 59 751.62/73.
[96] Maltzan to AA, 6 December 1926, *ADAP*, B, I/II, pp. 495–6.
[97] Briand statements to the Foreign Affairs Commission, 23 November 1926, C14763, no. 62, pp. 18–22.
[98] Crewe to Chamberlain, 10 November 1926, FO 371/11331: C 4822/10060/18.

aims and understandings could be forged with those who directed British and American policies. Both for Paris and Berlin, then, engaging the Anglo-American powers – on terms that suited the latter's agendas – remained a *conditio sine qua non*. This would shape Euro-Atlantic politics until and beyond the Young plan negotiations.

All in all, the failure of Thoiry unquestionably marked a *caesura* in post-World War I international relations. After 1923, it was a second important turning-point in postwar politics, exemplifying that there was no automatic compatibility between Franco-German reconciliation and Anglo-American stabilisation precepts. Indeed, this compatibility could reach distinct limits as soon as the impetus of the former ran counter to paramount interests, and assumptions, of British and American decisionmakers. This had a significant impact on Locarno politics and transatlantic co-operation, essentially constraining both in a phase when greater dynamism was urgently required – and when such dynamism could have made the fledgling peace order of the mid-1920s more robust for harsher years to come. Ultimately, only Anglo-American forward engagement could have provided a real opening for invigorating the Franco-German peace process in its formative stage. As it turned out, such an opportunity would only come again – under more adverse conditions – in 1929, shortly before the repercussions of 'Black Friday' changed everything.

In one crucial respect, then, Thoiry was not a *caesura* at all. Its failure reaffirmed the basic ground-rules of Euro-Atlantic politics in the latter 1920s; and it re-affirmed the fundamental distribution of power and possibilities within the system of London and Locarno. By virtue of its financial strength and control of the Dawes regime, the United States remained this system's pivotal power. And Britain remained the pivotal arbiter within the Locarno triangle. If it chose to remain passive, the already narrow window of opportunity for Franco-German accommodation was closing even further. At the same time, Britain remained the lesser and America the essential senior partner of German policy. Both powers had a decisive say regarding the pace and extent of further revisions in postwar Europe. While opposing any French manoeuvres seemingly designed to cement the *status quo*, they were also wary of too far-reaching attempts at Franco-German *entente*. Both powers continued to favour a gradual, incremental approach to Germany's integration into a western system which mainly protected their interests.[99]

More fundamental still, the failure of Thoiry also confirmed the paradigmatic character of the 1924 London settlement for postwar politics. In the final analysis, a Thoiry-style grand bargain was only conceivable on the basis of congruent interests in sustaining a wider framework of financial *and* political

---

[99] Cf. Link (1970), pp. 624–5.

stability in Europe. This framework was being constructed, yet was still not sufficiently solid by late 1926. To solidify it remained a prime responsibility of Britain in the political and America in the financial spheres. And these processes could only advance if leading decisionmakers in London and Washington made fostering them a genuine foreign-policy priority. Yet after 1925 they only did so in a limited manner.

Did the obstruction of Thoiry bring out a basic paradox of British and even more strikingly of US stabilisation policy in the 1920s? Had a contradiction emerged between Anglo-American financial interests and both powers' aim to promote reconciliation between Europe's former archenemies? It seems more accurate to say that, from 1926, not a fundamental contradiction but a marked tension in British and American policies emerged – a tension that in the international constellation after the Great War was very hard to avoid. On the one hand, all principal policymakers and influential financiers in Britain and the United States desired further progress in Europe's stabilisation. They genuinely sought to overcome old prewar and postwar patterns of conflict through pragmatic co-operation. They did so not least because, as far as they succeeded, their efforts continually improved the conditions for capital investment in, and trade with, Germany, France and eventually also Poland and Czechoslovakia. But never far beneath the surface was an entrenched suspicion, notably in Washington. It was the suspicion that all efforts at Franco-German *détente* only disguised the formation of a debtors' coalition; and that these efforts were designed to create a new, exclusive economic bloc in continental Europe. Most Republican decisionmakers shared the perception that, implicitly or explicitly, all of this was directed against the United States and threatened to block the expansion of the US 'open-door' system in Europe.[100]

As noted, such misgivings were less of a factor in British policy. In Whitehall, other objectives – notably safeguarding the Locarno concert and British reparation interests – were of greater import. The core problem lay with US policy. And it stemmed not, at least mainly, from myopia. It was rather, plainly, the outgrowth of a once more aloof, financially orientated approach to European stabilisation – an approach that sought to promote stability by extending a liberal-capitalist model *and* informal US pre-eminence, *not* political responsibilities. Besides, a central Republican axiom remained that it should not be the American people, and voters, who in the end funded Europe's reconstruction without recompense – after the European powers had wrought the havoc of the Great War in the first place. The Republican administrations of the 'New Era' would not abandon this stance until the repercussions of the Great Depression left Hoover no other choice.[101]

[100] Commerce Department, *Annual Report*, 1926, pp. 34–7.
[101] Kellogg to Hughes, 12 August 1924, NA RG 59 462.00 R296/491. Also see the epilogue.

As the role-definition of its primary yet politically constrained power did not change in the later 1920s, the international system of the era of London and Locarno remained distinctly asymmetric. Basically self-reliant in terms of security and – if it chose to – economically, the United States did not 'need' anything vital from Europe. By contrast, Europe – and above all Germany and France – 'needed' many vital commodities from America: more long-term capital, a more unrestricted access to the US market, yet chiefly more commitment to peaceful change *and* European security. On balance, while structural difficulties abounded and European approaches to mastering them still left much to be desired, the Locarno powers' means were and remained limited. It was chiefly America's 'retrogressive' approach to international stabilisation that made any further – groundbreaking and legitimacy-enhancing – advances on the road to a more durable postwar system difficult.

The return to the European concert – a 'rougher road' to travel, 1926–7

The main conclusion that Chamberlain had drawn from the difficulties into which Stresemann and Briand had run was unequivocal. The future of European politics lay not in bilateral 'grand designs' *à la* Thoiry. It lay in pragmatic, sober compromises forged within the Locarno concert. As the hopes of Thoiry began to fade, he noted that 'the world moves tho' it has to travel a rough road'.[102] Indeed, the road on which he, Briand and Stresemann would have to travel became distinctly rougher from late 1926. But the British foreign secretary's confidence in the power and concomitant legitimacy of what (his) professional diplomacy could accomplish remained undiminished. He thus proposed to return to the core principles of Locarno to settle what he still regarded as the essentially political questions of Europe's further pacification in a spirit of 'reciprocity'.[103]

Chamberlain argued that the Locarnite powers should focus on making incremental progress on those issues that the Europeans could resolve amongst themselves, without US interference – notably the Rhineland question. In the aftermath of Thoiry, however, first a smaller, if hardly less contentious, matter had to be addressed: the end of inter-allied military control. From late October, British diplomacy demanded that Berlin redouble its efforts to meet, at last, all French disarmament requirements. And it simultaneously pressed Paris to be conciliatory, stressing that from the British standpoint Germany had '*de facto* disarmed'.[104]

---

[102] Chamberlain aide memoire, 15 October 1926, FO 371/11331: C 11024/10060/18; Austen to Hilda Chamberlain, 8 October 1926, Austen Chamberlain Papers, AC 5/1/395.
[103] Chamberlain to Crewe, 12 October 1926, FO 371/11331: C 10909/10060/18.
[104] Chamberlain to Tyrrell, 6 December 1926, *DBFP*, IA, II, no. 326; Chamberlain minute, 21 December 1926, FO 371/12125/144. Cf. Fox (1969), pp. 156–61.

Stresemann and Schubert essentially followed Chamberlain's exhortations. They, too, saw no alternative to 'intensified co-operation with England' in the European concert, not only to eliminate military control but also to reach their main goal: a 'political solution' of the Rhineland problem. Yet the *Auswärtige Amt* braced itself for a 'policy of small steps'.[105] Tough negotiations ensued, which again revealed two familiar characteristics: strong French reluctance to abolish an important control instrument of the Versailles system, yet also Paris' overriding interest in salvaging co-operation with Britain – and Germany.[106] They produced a settlement that was then finalised on the margins of the League Assembly's December session. The IMCC was to be withdrawn at the end of January 1927, to be replaced by a new control mechanism under the auspices of the League.[107] Essentially, though still resurfacing at times, notably at the Hague conference in 1929, the controversies over military control thus disappeared from the European agenda. Yet despite this step forward, Locarno politics entered rougher waters around the turn of 1926/7.

---

[105] Stresemann instructions, 26 October 1926, Stresemann memorandum, 24 November, *ADAP*, B, I/II, no. 209, pp. 373–4.
[106] Crewe to Chamberlain, 18 November 1926, *DBFP*, IA, II, no. 279.
[107] See British and German records of the Geneva meetings, 5–12 December 1926, *DBFP*, IA, II, nos. 323–33 and ff; *ADAP*, B, I/II, nos. 237, 258, 260.

22   Towards peaceful change in eastern Europe?
The crux of transforming Polish–German relations

German attempts at achieving a peaceful revision of the postwar *status quo* were of course not limited to Franco-German relations. They also extended to eastern Europe, above all to relations with Poland. The problem of how to pave the way for a settlement of Polish–German disputes had been comparatively sidelined at Locarno to achieve a conclusion of the western security pact. But it is also worth noting again that it was at Locarno, too, that the problem of how to settle the inevitable disputes over the contested border of 1919 and the status of minorities on both sides of that border had been seriously broached for the first time since the victors had created it at Versailles. In a wider perspective, only the advances of London and Locarno created a modicum of what preconditions had to be established to embark on the up-hill trajectory of approaching a postwar accommodation between Warsaw and Berlin. And only these advances had set the stage for ultimately even envisaging an 'eastern Locarno' which extended the European concert to a wider security system that also regulated relations between Weimar Germany, the states situated uneasily between it and the Soviet Union – and eventually also the Soviet Union itself.

What impact did the politics of London and Locarno have on Polish–German relations in the latter 1920s? How far could these relations indeed be pacified, and how far could and did the Anglo-American powers make any contributions to this process? All of these were open questions in the mid-1920s. And it also remained to be seen, of course, what effect any progress here, or lack thereof, would have on the Locarno concert, Germany's relations with the United States and its western orientation as such. In more general terms, after Locarno policymakers on all sides still faced the challenge of effecting no less than a sea-change in the structurally strained relations between a revisionist Germany and an unconsolidated Polish nation-state, which could then also have a stabilising impact on wider eastern Europe. Essentially, such a sea-change was imperative to forestall an eventual return to aggressive German revisionism and power-political competition between revisionist and *status quo* powers for zones of influence and domination in that most volatile part of postwar Europe.

409

The ubiquity of more or less openly hostile claims for revision in Germany has been noted. But, due to the preponderant security concerns arising from these claims, Warsaw had also pursued an antagonistic course vis-à-vis its western neighbour ever since Versailles.[1] After 1925, the 'pro-Locarno' course pursued by the foreign ministers Skrzyński and August Zaleski at first prevailed. And following his *coup d'état* in May 1926 Piłsudski stressed the continuity of Polish foreign policy. Yet the Marshal soon put his weight behind a course that did not further Poland's gravitation towards the Locarno system, nor the prospects for settling the postwar conflict with its western neighbour. Rather, Piłsudski's core aims became to revitalise the alliance with France and to observe strict neutrality between Germany and Soviet Russia, all to strengthen Polish security.[2]

Since negotiations over a trade agreement had foundered in the summer of 1925, a 'commercial war' between Poland and its most important trading partner, Germany, had broken out. It exacerbated Poland's already acute financial crisis. Amid newly rising inflation, the Polish economy suffered an acute shortage of capital, which following the Dawes agreement had not only bypassed France.[3] This scenario had spawned different strategies within the *Auswärtige Amt*, all centring on using Poland's economic weakness, to press political concessions from Warsaw. Concretely, some policymakers envisaged making German credits and participation in international loans to Poland dependent on Polish compliance with Germany's territorial demands. One faction, and notably a senior official of the eastern department, Herbert von Dirksen, advocated an aggressive course, namely that Berlin should turn the financial screws on its neighbour, doing everything possible to bring it to its knees, at least financially. Sooner rather than later, this was to force the Polish government to satisfy German claims. This approach was also supported by Schacht. The *Reichsbank* president favoured making Polish territorial concessions an integral part of any international loan scheme.[4]

Realising how sensitive this subject was both for Franco-German relations and Locarno politics, Stresemann and Schubert, who eventually took charge of the matter, pursued a more gradual and collaborative approach. While seeking to achieve the same outcome, namely a modification of Germany's post-Versailles eastern borders, they hoped to prepare the ground for territorial revision in co-operation with the western powers and, ultimately, through more or less consensual agreements with Poland. As both the German foreign

---

[1] Cf. Schattkowsky (1994a); Cienciala and Kormanicki (1984).
[2] Cf. Wandycz (1961), pp. 32ff, 50ff.
[3] Max Muller to FO, 25 January 1926, *DBFP*, IA, I, p. 411. Cf. Orde (1990), pp. 302–5; Rieckhoff (1971), pp. 161–72.
[4] Dirksen memorandum, 29 December 1925; Dirksen memorandum, 17 April 1926, *ADAP*, B, II/I, no. 148, pp. 71–2.

minister and his chief assistant reckoned, such agreements could only be sought in the medium, not in the short term.[5] After Locarno, Stresemann indeed saw fresh prospects for loosening the ties between France and its eastern alliance-partner through Germany's *rapprochement* with Paris. And he saw new opportunities for gaining the support, or at least benevolent neutrality not only of France but also of Britain and America should Germany eventually seek an 'overall rectification' of its eastern borders in its favour.

Not only in the west but also with a view to the highly precarious issue of – peaceful – territorial changes in the east, Stresemann sought to rely on the preferred tools of his foreign policy: economic power and the 'congruence of world-economic interests'. As he outlined behind closed doors on 14 December 1925, he did not intend to solve the 'eastern questions' through 'war-like conflicts'. Rather, while keeping Poland economically frail, Germany had to create a 'basis of political reconciliation' and 'common economic interests' with the 'world powers which have a decisive say', namely the Anglo-American powers and France. Should 'European peace' and 'economic consolidation' ever be jeopardised by 'developments in the east', Berlin had to impress upon them that this could mainly be attributed to the 'impossible borders' of 1919. Then, and only then, could Germany realise its revisionist aims.[6]

As he confided to Chamberlain on 28 January 1926, Briand thought that the Polish–German differences burdening Europe's postwar order could not be left unattended. He emphasised that 'obviously there was much that was intolerable in the present situation', and he basically deemed the east European *status quo* untenable in the long run. Singling out the intertwined problems of minorities, the 'Polish Corridor' and Danzig, Briand observed that 'one could not look at the map of East Prussia without feeling that sooner or later some accommodation must be discovered'. The French foreign minister had avowedly 'begged' his Polish counterpart, Count Skrzyński, not to 'close his mind to any possibility of an arrangement'.[7] And in late 1927, he even – privately – discussed details of such an arrangement with Stresemann.[8] Officially, however, Briand of course had to tread very carefully, both on the diplomatic stage and in the court of French opinion. He was caught between those – Poincarists and the General Staff – who still thought that French security depended on preventing its eastern alliance-system from unravelling, and those – like Berthelot and Seydoux – who at any rate did not want to open the door to

[5] Schubert to Rauscher (Warsaw), 6 January 1926, Stresemann instructions, 19 April 1925, *ADAP*, B, II/I, nos. 31, 150. Cf. Krüger (1985a), pp. 307–8.
[6] Stresemann speech, 14 December 1925, *ADAP*, B, I/I, pp. 743–5.
[7] Chamberlain memorandum, 1 February 1926, circulated to the cabinet, *DBFP*, IA, I, no. 233.
[8] Stresemann memorandum, 11 December 1927, *ADAP*, B, VII, no. 200.

assertive German revisionism. His room to manoeuvre thus remained very narrow indeed.[9]

In principle, Chamberlain agreed with Briand's assessment. In practice, though, and particularly in the short term, he likewise remained highly wary of any German attempts to put pressure on Poland.[10] While having to cultivate French 'understanding', it was thus crucial for Stresemann to win over those powers without whose backing any scheme of his economically underpinned *Ostpolitik* would remain stillborn: Britain and the United States. In the first half of 1926, the German Foreign Office made repeated efforts to convince political and financial leaders in London, Washington and New York that it was also in their interest to promote east European 'consolidation' the German way.[11]

In Britain, it was Montagu Norman who was most favourably disposed towards what the counsellor at the German embassy, Dufour Feronce, outlined to him about Germany's wider intentions.[12] The governor of the Bank of England generally sought to keep a certain distance from overt involvement in politically so highly delicate affairs. But he was convinced that by itself Poland did not have the means to master its financial crisis. In February 1926, Norman thus proposed, and he later concretised with Strong and Parker Gilbert, an international stabilisation package for the Polish state and economy. It was to be jointly funded by the Bank of England and the Federal Reserve Bank of New York; yet the German *Reichsbank* could also participate. Crucially, Norman envisaged that political questions, notably border revisions, could be explicitly included with this package. As he told the Foreign Office in August, he fundamentally saw no problem in allowing Germany practically to 'buy back' lost territories such as the 'Corridor' – much in the same way that they could also re-acquire Eupen–Malmédy from Belgium.[13]

FRBNY Governor Strong had a pronounced interest in both extending US capital export in eastern Europe's emerging markets, where British competition was to be surpassed, and supporting a stabilisation of Poland's currency and finances. In the summer of 1925, the FRBNY had provided the Polish National Bank with an emergency loan. The private banking-house Dillon Read & Co. had also lent money to the Polish government. Unlike his British

[9] Briand statements to the Foreign Affairs Commission, 19 December 1925, C14763, no. 46, pp. 15–21; *Quai d'Orsay* memorandum, 8 October 1925, Seydoux memorandum, 15 October 1926, MAE, Série Europe, Allemagne, vol. 399.

[10] Chamberlain memorandum, 1 February 1926; Chamberlain to Max Muller, 8 February 1926, *DBFP*, IA, I, nos. 233, 252.

[11] *ADAP*, B, II/I, nos. 21, 97, 116.

[12] *ADAP*, B, II/I, nos. 10, 21.

[13] Norman to Strong, 2 February 1926, Strong Papers, 1116.6/2; Norman to Gilbert, 3 June 1926, quoted after Orde (1990), p. 304; Lampson memoranda, 11 and 12 August 1926, *DBFP*, IA, II, nos. 142, 143.

counterpart, however, and in clear opposition to German plans, Strong deemed it neither wise nor prospective to link such financial transactions with sensitive political matters like territorial revision. Instead, he essentially favoured organising Poland's financial recovery much like that of Germany: under US supervision, perhaps aided by the Bank of England, yet ultimately controlled by an informal, 'unpolitical' US representative in Warsaw, who would advise the newly established Pilsudski regime.[14]

In May 1926, Strong sought to convince both Norman and Schacht to extend a joint central bank loan to Poland.[15] And he warned both of his colleagues that any further German manoeuvres to thwart his Polish consolidation agenda for political reasons would have very negative repercussions for Germany in US financial circles. In March 1927, the FRBNY governor was then instrumental in realising a successful $60 million stabilisation scheme and a first central bank credit of $20 million to Warsaw, officially arranged by the governor of the *Banque de France*, Moreau.[16] Following the pattern of the Dawes plan, yet commanding weaker control powers than Parker Gilbert, the American Charles Dewey was appointed as adviser to the Pilsudski government.[17]

Strong kept the State Department abreast with these developments, and it came to view them in a positive light. But they basically evolved below the threshold of what Kellogg considered major priorities.[18] The Commerce Department welcomed the success of central bank co-operation.[19] In the wider political context, however, the Republican administration saw even less need than in 1923/4 to abandon its non-intervention maxim and reliance on informal 'financial diplomacy'. Of course, Washington never considered becoming officially involved in efforts to stabilise Polish finances. Nor however – and more importantly – did it contemplate pursuing an assertive policy vis-à-vis Poland, and France, to precipitate changes in eastern Europe's territorial *status quo*.

Although personally not averse to Stresemann's arguments, Hoover and Kellogg at that stage clearly rejected an active promotion of potentially unsettling frontier revisions in eastern Europe.[20] Kellogg thus retreated to a position not unlike Chamberlain's. He let it be known that Washington would welcome any peaceful agreements that Germany and its eastern neighbours, Poland as

[14] Strong to Harrison, 15 May 1926; Strong to Harrison, 3 August 1926; Strong to Norman, 15 February 1927, Strong Papers, 1000.7, 1116.7/1.

[15] Strong to Harrison, 15 May 1926, Strong Papers, 1000.7.

[16] Cf. Orde (1990), pp. 306–7.

[17] Cf. Costigliola (1979), pp. 85–105; Pease (1986).

[18] Kellogg (1928a); Maltzan to Stresemann, 17 October 1925, Stresemann Papers, RM 27, no. 422.

[19] Commerce Department, *Annual Report*, 1925, pp. 35ff; *ibid.*, 1926, pp. 50–1.

[20] Castle notes of a conversation with Hoover, Castle Diary, 14 May 1926, vol. 8, p. 114.

well as Czechoslovakia, might reach amongst themselves.[21] Fundamentally, US policymakers also hoped that issues of territorial revision would lose their virulence over time once Germany had become more firmly anchored to a prosperous western system.

In London, the Foreign Office was not surprised that Berlin attempted to exert pressure on a Polish neighbour in political and financial disarray. Yet the central concern was not Poland's fate; it was to block any assertive or even confrontational moves on the part of Germany that would alarm Paris and ultimately jeopardise the west European concert. Chamberlain thus cold-shouldered all of Berlin's diplomatic soundings. From February 1926, he condemned what he perceived as German designs of waging a trade war against Poland to precipitate territorial concessions. The foreign secretary thus also poured cold water on Norman's unwelcome overtures on the issue of the 'Polish Corridor'. He distanced the Foreign Office from any involvement in attempts to link financial and political concerns in order to effect changes on Germany's eastern border. On 8 February, he told Poland's ambassador Konstanty Skirmunt that it would be 'unwise' for him to 'intervene' in 'matters . . . of a purely financial and business character' like Warsaw's negotiations with the Bank of England.[22]

Considerable though British and American understanding for German revisionist desires was, there was never enough common ground between their approaches to peaceful change and Berlin's wider aims to implement Stresemann's concepts. At least, the German foreign minister could not hope to succeed with his 'political–cum–economic' case for eastern Europe's territorial consolidation in the short term. Given that the Locarno powers and the United States had not yet found ways of actively tackling the cardinal security problems they raised, territorial revisions could not be realised, or even facilitated, by economic means – neither by incentives nor by pressure on Poland.

In exchanges with French, German and Polish diplomats, Chamberlain always returned to his position that Locarno politics could serve as an exemplary model for regional security agreements, which could and should be emulated to pacify relations between Germany and the states of eastern Europe. The emphasis of British diplomacy continued to lie on promoting the extension of basic ground–rules for conflict resolution, as encapsulated in Locarno's arbitration treaties.[23] The British foreign secretary also maintained that by interacting in the League German and Polish policymakers could learn to

---

[21] Kellogg speech, 14 December 1925, Kellogg Papers; Castle Diary, 17 and 29 January 1927, vol. 10, pp. 20, 34–5.

[22] Chamberlain to Max Muller, 8 February 1926; Orde to D'Abernon, 9 February 1926, *DBFP*, IA, I, nos. 252, 254.

[23] D'Abernon to Chamberlain, 29 July 1926; Chamberlain memorandum, 1 February 1926, *DBFP*, IA, I, no. 233; Tyrrell memorandum, 26 July 1926, *DBFP*, IA, I, nos. 233, 103, pp. 196–7.

adopt reasonable standards of arbitration and compromise, not least to deal with minority disputes. Yet, as he told D'Abernon in February 1926, though the League's minority treaties could be useful, it was ultimately the responsibility of the governments and minorities concerned to 'settle' the most 'contentious' issues through direct negotiations. Conveniently, Chamberlain thus set little store by outside interference. Neither in 1925 nor thereafter, when Briand made numerous proposals for an 'eastern Locarno', did he contemplate extending Britain's role, brokerage and, especially, guarantees eastward.[24] In his judgement, there were still no tenable borders warranting Locarno-style guarantees. Even if the *status quo* could have been altered peacefully, however, Chamberlain could not have convinced the Baldwin cabinet that Britain should underwrite the new state of affairs. Even less, of course, would Kellogg have been in a position to alter the Coolidge administration's rejection of security commitments in Europe, which had already foreclosed even informal US guarantees in support of the west European Locarno pact and would have been categorical in the case of eastern Europe. It need not be emphasised, though, that the American secretary of state never contemplated such commitments in the first place.

For his part, Chamberlain was not without concern about German tendencies of assertive revisionism. Overall, however, he remained confident that Stresemann would be able to contain them. He remained convinced that the German foreign minister himself did not contemplate a policy of stepped-up revision in the east. Ultimately, Chamberlain concluded, Stresemann would not want to risk undermining the concert of the Locarno powers, and British support, thus risking to frustrate German ambitions for peaceful change in western *and* eastern Europe. This assessment of Weimar Germany's *Ostpolitik* was actually largely borne out. In the 'Stresemann era', the German interest in maintaining the European concert and Anglo-American support indeed far outweighed revisionist ambitions vis-à-vis Poland. The maxim of Stresemann's and Schubert's pursuits remained that any pacific modifications of the eastern *status quo* could only be made in negotiations with Warsaw and in co-operation with the Locarno partners and the United States.

In practice, the politics of London and Locarno kept the sensitive issue of territorial revision largely off the European agenda. At best, this could de-escalate this issue while opening up prospects of settling it later, once Germany had been integrated more firmly in the emerging western system of the post-World War I era. And the British expectation that buttressing German *Westpolitik* under Stresemann created the best possible preconditions for any pacific solutions in this sphere was essentially confirmed.

---

[24] Chamberlain to D'Abernon, 4 February 1926, *DBFP*, IA, I, no. 245; Austen to Ida Chamberlain, 18 April 1926, Austen Chamberlain Papers, AC 5/1/379.

At the same time, however, the degree of insecurity still prevailing on Germany's eastern borders made such solutions inconceivable without external arbiters and guarantees. And the lack of Anglo-American engagement in promoting peaceful change in eastern Europe made any progress in this direction all but impossible. This meant that, while the eastern question did not complicate European politics the way it had done in the early 1920s, the decade's latter half saw no concrete, prospective steps to settle it either. How volatile the situation remained was thrown into relief when from early 1927 the looming danger of a war between Poland and Lithuania prompted fears, especially in Paris, that the entire post-Versailles *status quo* in eastern Europe might unravel, opening the door not only for eventually uncontrollable German revisionism but also for a revisionist collusion between Germany and the Soviet Union. As will be shown, prior to the Great Depression the Locarno system functioned remarkably well to pre-empt any such scenarios. Fundamentally, though, the structural problems that beset eastern Europe were left simmering, to be seized upon by less conciliatory German leaders in the 1930s.[25]

---

[25] For the Polish–Lithuanian conflict and the further evolution of Locarno-style security politics with a view to eastern Europe, see chapter 23. For a re-appraisal of the deterioration of stability in central and eastern Europe, see the epilogue.

The European security system of the latter 1920s

In April 1928, the British *Observer* proclaimed that the past year had witnessed movements 'Towards a New World-Order', which hinged on the 'Return of America' to European and world politics. This verdict was based on the negotiations over what became known as the Kellogg–Briand pact, the 'pact to renounce war as an instrument of national policy', which was then formally concluded in August 1928. The *Observer* posited that Locarno had marked one 'stage' in the evolution of postwar policy after the idealism of 1919 had failed. Yet it also called the Locarno pact 'the indispensable prelude to the renewal of American interest in Old-World affairs'.[1]

Later accounts have mostly pictured a distinctly different, bleaker 'reality'. According to some hitherto prevalent interpretations, less than two years after the security pact, the European concert was beginning to show serious cracks. Allegedly, the Locarno system could not bear the pressure of renewed Franco-German tensions over the velocity and extent of further postwar changes – and it was beyond Britain's means to overcome this tension.[2] Even harsher verdicts have been cast concerning the consolidation of anything resembling a trans-atlantic international order. What amounted to a re-assertion of earlier US isolationism purportedly precluded any advances towards such an order.[3] Realists have particularly regarded the Kellogg–Briand pact as a rather mean-ingless agreement that nourished further illusions about international pacifica-tion in the 1920s and had no significant impact on the European situation. At worst, it was regarded as further proof of where the misguided path to international stability begun at Locarno had led – further proof that the western powers discarded the essential task of containing Germany.[4]

To fathom what really marked the evolution of the Locarno system and transatlantic security relations in the later 1920s, two different sets of questions

---

[1] *Observer*, 15 April 1928, NA RG 59 711.4112 Anti-War.

[2] See Jacobson (1972b), pp. 101ff; Knipping (1987), pp. 32ff; Girault and Frank (1988), pp. 152–3; Pitts (1987), pp. 178ff.

[3] See Kennedy (1988), pp. 423ff; Leffler (1979), pp. 158ff; Costigliola (1984), pp. 184ff.

[4] See Marks (2002), pp. 262–3; Ferrell (1952); McKercher (1984), pp. 107ff; Keeton (1987), pp. 239ff; Buchheit (1998).

have to be answered. What has to be explored first are the prospects of consolidating the treaty system of 1925 as the central pillar of European security. How far could it create the 'certainty' required to settle the still intractable disarmament problem? How far could the European concert provide the wherewithal to come to terms with Europe's remaining postwar challenges? To what extent did the concert allow key policymakers to address these challenges so quickly and convincingly that the concert system itself acquired a greater degree of legitimacy? Then, a second set of questions is to be examined: how far was it indispensable and *possible* – to widen the European nucleus into a transatlantic security system after all? To what extent could Washington be engaged to play a more active role in bolstering peaceful change, and disarmament, in Europe? And what was the Kellogg–Briand pact's underlying significance in this context? Did it really extend the Locarno system in any substantive manner?

As will be shown, the European concert came under strain between early 1927 and the autumn of 1928. But it could be consolidated as the main framework and anchor of European security. Noteworthy about European politics in this phase was *not* that no further great leaps on the road to durable stability could be made. In view of the problematic constellations weighing down on policymakers on every level – security constraints, political constraints in transatlantic relations, domestic constraints which again tightened in Germany and France – this was beyond reasonable expectation. What can be called remarkable was rather that, although Chamberlain and Briand increasingly emphasised their *entente*, none of the principal European powers contemplated departing from the principles and ground-rules that each had come to identify with the Locarno concert.[5] Nor did any of these powers depart from the basic transatlantic bargain forged at the London conference. While Washington had retreated to premises of maximal 'non-involvement', those shaping policies in London, Paris and Berlin continued to regard the approaches inaugurated in 1924 and 1925 as most conducive not only to realising their short-term aims but also to safeguarding their more permanent interests.

In concrete terms, too, the Locarno politics of appeasement were bearing fruit. For all the difficulties that Chamberlain, Briand and Stresemann still faced, and though they were never quite even-handedly applied, Locarno's principles of 'reciprocity' proved effective. And, fundamentally, not only British but also French and German policymakers came to see Locarno-style diplomacy as the only way to resolve their differences and foster wider European stability, with no realistic alternative in sight. Indeed, all came to view the concert system as worth preserving for its own sake. But by their very nature

---

[5] Austen to Hilda Chamberlain, 17 December 1928, Austen Chamberlain Papers, AC 5/1/463.

Locarno politics simply could only produce *step-by-step* progress towards a 'resolution' of Europe's underlying security question. For not only had Briand and Stresemann to reckon with deteriorating domestic conditions for their pursuits after the failure of Thoiry, more importantly, no European protagonist could change the fundamental paradigm of the era of London and Locarno: the more international relations 'normalised' the more French fears of German preponderance resurfaced – if more in the public domain than on the part of Poincaré and the *Quai d'Orsay*. In a still competitive European international system that was just emerging from under the shadow of a legacy of more than a century of imperialist rivalry and a cataclysmic war, no rapid transformation was possible. Qualitative changes necessarily had to be incremental.

Yet the prevailing piecemeal progress in European politics also affected the very foundations of the Locarno concert. It made it much harder to effect the very changes that were crucial for increasing the system's legitimacy, particularly in Weimar Germany – above all, a mutually acceptable Rhineland agreement. What became clear in 1927, and what the fate of the Thoiry project had foreshadowed, was that neither Chamberlain's 'honest' brokerage nor, more broadly, European diplomacy could promote decisive steps in this direction. In different ways, this led to renewed attempts of both French and German policymakers to draw America into the European political process and, more specifically, European security politics. Briand and Berthelot thus essentially sought to fortify the *status quo*, Stresemann and Schubert to generate new possibilities for peaceful change. Yet the underlying aim of both sides was to improve their positions for what came to be viewed, eventually also in Britain, as the only way to 'liquidate' the war's consequences: a further comprehensive settlement including both a revision of the reparation regime and a Rhineland compromise. While requiring British support, such a settlement was inconceivable without the assent of the United States.

What was the significance of the Kellogg–Briand pact for all of these processes? In its final form of August 1928, the pact indeed constituted a significant complement to the Locarno system. But it did not mark a turning-point on the path towards a more solid Euro-Atlantic security order. Eventually signed by most European powers as well as Japan, but not Soviet Russia, the war-renunciation pact manifested an overarching postwar trend towards enhanced procedures and standards for the pacific settlement of disputes. In Kellogg's judgement, it constituted a 'valuable, practical and psychological reinforcement of existing efforts to maintain world peace'.[6]

Essentially, the US secretary of state indeed managed to transform Briand's original proposal for a *status quo*-orientated Franco-American pact, made in April 1927, into a universal war-renunciation treaty that promoted peaceful

---

[6] Kellogg to Lippmann, 21 July 1928, Kellogg Papers, roll 31.

change. Washington's approach corresponded with the fundamental aims of British Locarno policy. And it was even more conducive to German attempts to develop its revisionist policy into an internationally sanctioned procedure, which ultimately was to permit 'stabilising' revisions in eastern Europe. In itself, lacking sanction clauses for its enforcement, the pact had indeed little prospect to prove effective in restraining aggressors and thus pacifying international relations. Yet nor did the treaty of 1928 undermine a regional security mechanism like the Locarno pact. For it prescribed that signatories would be released from their commitment not to resort to war as soon as one state violated its pledge.

But the main transatlantic problem that re-emerged between 1927 and 1929 lay outside the immediate scope of the Kellogg–Briand pact. In short, neither the Coolidge administration nor the Hoover administration following it saw its – distinctly general – commitments under the pact as a precursor for wider engagement in fostering European security. Kellogg blocked all attempts to link the treaty with mechanisms that could engage Washington to this end. And British policy basically reinforced this, because Chamberlain still regarded the Locarno concert as Europe's crucial, and sufficient, security system. Thus, the latter 1920s did not see decisive steps towards a consolidation of the 'New World Order' that could not be created in 1919 but had taken shape since 1924.[7]

At best, the Kellogg–Briand pact had the potential of furthering a more long-term US reorientation – a gradually increasing awareness of the need for broader commitments to underpin 'efforts to maintain world peace', particularly in Europe. In the shorter term, it could not serve to address the Old World's deeper security problems. And it notably failed to provide what the Coolidge administration had hoped for: a new impetus for disarmament. It was precisely because of the necessarily gradual progress on core security issues that the Preparatory Commission's negotiations at Geneva continued to prove so unchangeably frustrating. There were still no sufficient foundations for a compromise between France's interest in retaining a reassuring superiority and Germany's call for 'armaments parity', be it through French disarmament or an internationally sanctioned German re-armament.[8]

In this critical domain, the limits of the British and even more so the American approach now became distinctly apparent. Following the breakdown of the 1927 Geneva naval conference, both powers became chiefly concerned with containing their profoundest bilateral crisis since 1919 through a new naval compromise underpinning the Washington system. Yet this could not be clinched until 1930. In the wider picture, which remained basically unchanged

---

[7] *Observer*, 15 April 1928, NA RG 59 711.4112 Anti-War.
[8] Cardogan memorandum, 2 February 1928, *DBFP*, IA, IV, no. 267.

after 1926, more tangible progress in consolidating a transatlantic security architecture, and wider British and American commitments, still had to precede the establishment of any effective disarmament regime. But this could not be achieved between 1927 and 1929. In view of the domestic constraints placed on Anglo-American decisionmakers in the realm of international security yet also the basic orientation of their policies, particularly the Republican policy of strategic 'non-entanglement', it was impossible to achieve.[9]

The dynamism of Locarno politics noticeably lessened in the spring of 1927. It seems symptomatic that Chamberlain warned against a 'demise of the spirit of Locarno', which he blamed on Germany's voracity for further concessions and unwillingness to placate French concerns.[10] Briand and Stresemann also deplored a stagnation of the 'politics of reconciliation'. For Stresemann, the main reason for this was not Briand's recalcitrance but the fact that a growing array of French political forces seemed to turn against the entire Locarno approach.[11] Confronting nationalist opposition in parliament and the press, Briand felt compelled to assert in the *Chambre*'s Foreign Affairs Commission on 19 January that 'no one' in the French government proposed to 'draw into question again . . . the policy of Locarno' – 'rapprochement' between France and Germany was a *'fait acquis'* not to be surrendered.[12]

Against this backdrop, the French foreign minister grew increasingly irritated at German demands for a hastened Rhineland evacuation, particularly as, in his eyes, they went together with German defiance on sensitive issues like *Reichswehr* connections with 'patriotic societies', which were grist to the mills of his domestic critics. Yet, as ever, he also seized on such concerns to strengthen his more *status quo*-orientated position in the concert and especially vis-à-vis Chamberlain. While Stresemann still invoked domestic pressures to accelerate changes, Briand was determined to make the formula *'festina lente'* ('make haste slowly'), which Berthelot had recently proposed, the maxim of European diplomacy.[13]

As is clearly discernible in retrospect, what accounted for the 'stagnation' of Locarno politics was *not* that it was eroding. Rather, it was a quite familiar constellation now turning for the worse. On one level, always existing domestic impediments in France and Germany grew more challenging. On another, international level of Locarno diplomacy, there was no immediate scope for decisive advances, and certainly no scope for a revival of Thoiry. The means of

---

[9] Kellogg to McCormick, 21 July 1928, Kellogg Papers, roll 31.
[10] Chamberlain to Lindsay, 12 January 1927, no. 62, FO 408.47.
[11] Stresemann to Sthamer, 18 January 1926, *ADAP*, B, IV, no. 36.
[12] Briand statements to the Foreign Affairs Commission, 19 January 1927, C14764, no. 57, 2–3; MAE, Série Europe, Allemagne, 400/76–8.
[13] Hoesch to Stresemann, 13 January 1927, no. 45, PA, 2406 H: D 504806; Phipps to Chamberlain, 15 December 1926, FO 371/12125. Cf. Pitts (1987), pp. 194–5.

policymakers in Berlin and Paris to set the agenda were limited – with the exception that, with Chamberlain's aid, Briand could stall further changes in the *status quo*. At the same time, and crucially, neither British nor American decisionmakers saw compelling reasons to propel the Locarno process further. Each side was counting on a gradual success of their stabilisation strategies of limited commitment.

Closing ranks with France – Britain's defensive approach to peaceful change in the latter 1920s

At the beginning of 1927, British diplomacy perceived no fundamental crisis of the European concert. But the Foreign Office registered unmistakable tensions stemming from a now prevalent atmosphere of mutual discontent between Paris and Berlin.[14] The more Chamberlain sensed this, however, the more he was inclined, not to question his approach but to re-accentuate his core maxims – 'co-operation' and 'reciprocal concessions'. In his view, there was no alternative to the (west) European concert.[15] Yet as Locarno politics turned into a piecemeal process, the foreign secretary's underlying penchant for strengthening the *entente* with France also became even more pronounced. He thus accepted that the pace of all further developments would be slow. Essentially, Chamberlain deemed it unwise to force this pace through British initiatives.

The rationale behind Britain's overall conservative approach sprang not so much from German attempts to step up changes in the Versailles system in the aftermath of Locarno. British caution was accentuated by a plethora of other European and global preoccupations, some central, some more peripheral. They included a burgeoning dispute with the Soviet Union, the protection of British interests in the Chinese civil war – and looming Anglo-American tensions over naval arms control. In Chamberlain's view, there was 'too much trouble in this world' at the dawn of 1927.[16] At that point, the Foreign Office did not yet foresee major disagreements with Washington over readjusting the global naval regime. Yet, as Chamberlain and Ambassador Howard noted, what proved increasingly divisive was the setting of quotas for the construction of new cruisers, which both Washington and London deemed vital to protect their respective global interests. Indeed, discord on this issue, which became virulent in the summer of 1927, particularly at the Geneva conference, had important implications not only for Anglo-American relations but also for

---

[14] Crewe to Chamberlain, 5 February 1927; Lindsay to Chamberlain, 16 February 1927, *DBFP*, IA, III, pp. 13–15, 36–9.

[15] Chamberlain to Lindsay, 5 February 1927, *DBFP*, IA, III, pp. 11–12; Chamberlain to Lindsay, 12 January 1927, FO 408.47.

[16] Austen to Hilda Chamberlain, 30 January 1927, Austen Chamberlain Papers, AC 5/1/407.

European security. Notably, it further stifled the work of the League's Preparatory Commission. In August, the Commission's proceedings were again adjourned without concrete results.

Ever since Locarno, Chamberlain had no longer considered disarmament a core Foreign Office concern; and the formulation of British disarmament policy had soon fallen to a specially created cabinet committee in which Cecil was the dominating influence. Cecil continued to favour a comprehensive approach linking naval and land disarmament in the framework of the Preparatory Commission. And from mid-1926 he had sought to strike a bargain with the French delegation at Geneva, according to which Britain was to advance proposals on naval questions and France was to 'take the lead on land & perhaps air questions'. But this came to naught not only because the Americans still objected to such linkage. It also foundered because, at least in the spring of 1927, Britain and France could not agree on standards for measuring each country's arms requirements.[17]

In view of these complications, Chamberlain favoured disentangling naval from land disarmament and concentrating on the search for new agreements between the principal naval powers – provided that the American government took the lead and called for a conference to this end. Mindful of French concerns, the British foreign secretary adhered to his position that, in Europe, any progress required first further improvements in overall security. As such improvements were not immediately attainable, he recommended a separate naval agreement with the Americans and, as far as possible, Japan, France and Italy to adjust the Washington system in a way that safeguarded the Empire's security. Above all, the British government sought to establish clear ratios in the newly central field of cruiser construction. Unlike more hard-line imperialist members of the cabinet like Birkenhead, for whom imperial defence superseded budgetary considerations, Chamberlain still fundamentally believed that, for reasons of economy, it was in Britain's interest to pursue disarmament.[18]

More immediately, though, Chamberlain's attention was absorbed by not merely one but multiple crises arising in the spring of 1927. In the Far East, he had 'the full weight of China' on him as London still struggled to bolster Chiang Kai-shek's nationalist forces without getting drawn into an uncontrollable civil war. Closer to home, relations with Moscow were sharply deteriorating over what Churchill and Chamberlain condemned as subversive Soviet

[17] Cecil minute, 18 August 1926, FO 371/11886: W 7802/78/98; Cecil to Chamberlain, 27 March 1927, *DBFP*, IA, III, no. 85. On British disarmament policy February–September 1927, see *DBFP*, IA, III, nos. 332–506.

[18] Minutes of 205 CID meeting, 17 November 1925, CAB 2/4; Chamberlain minute, 14 February 1927, *DBFP*, IA, III, no. 344; Cardogan memorandum, 2 February 1928, *DBFP*, IA, IV, no. 267.

interference in British domestic politics, particularly during the general strike of 1926. In late May 1927, this culminated in the Baldwin government's decision to break off diplomatic relations with the Soviet regime. Chamberlain had long sought to prevent an open 'breach'. As he noted on 27 February, he 'dread [ed] it 'not for the sake of Russia but for its reaction on Europe & especially on Germany & the Baltic States'.[19] Yet, as will be shown, the basic robustness of the Locarno system prevented Anglo-Russian altercations from having serious international repercussions.

These preoccupations did not outright sideline the Franco-German problem; it remained the weightiest question for British diplomacy. But Chamberlain clearly devoted less energy to shaping the Locarno process than before, not least because he thought he could afford to loosen the reins to a certain extent. Ever more doggedly, the foreign secretary pursued a policy of incremental and restrained peaceful change, concentrating on minor rather than core issues. Essentially, the harder compromises appeared – especially on the cardinal Rhineland question – the more Chamberlain insisted that his Locarno approach, and his rules of 'reciprocity', had to be strictly followed, especially by Berlin. This marked the thrust and dynamics of British policy – or lack thereof – between 1927 and 1929, leaving little room for widening the scope of the European concert – be it towards the east, be it towards the inclusion of salient financial questions, or be it towards broader co-operation with the United States.

By mid-January 1927, Chamberlain felt the need to dampen German hopes for further major revisions in the Rhenish *status quo* and to re-assert his definition Locarno-style *quid pro quo*. He responded to what he saw as an unwholesome combination of increasing German claims and – albeit minor – attempts to evade Versailles' disarmament clauses. These concerned for example the import of arms-industrial machinery and the halting of destruction of German fortresses along the border with Poland. As the British foreign secretary wrote to Ambassador Lindsay on 12 January, he considered the French public's 'growing irritation' in this respect justified, observing that if 'the average Frenchman asks himself what practical benefits have hitherto accrued to France since the Locarno treaties were initialled . . . he must be hard put to find the answer'.[20]

Chamberlain thus impressed on Stresemann that 'mutuality', as he understood it, remained 'the only possible basis of reconciliation, i.e. of the Locarno spirit'. Yet 'during the last fifteen months' Berlin had only tried to 'exact

---

[19] Austen to Hilda Chamberlain, 30 January and 27 February 1927, Austen Chamberlain Papers, AC 5/1/407, 411. Cf. Gorodetsky (1977), pp. 198ff.

[20] Chamberlain to Lindsay, 12 January 1927, FO 408.47; Chamberlain to Roberts (Warsaw), 12 January, *DBFP*, IA, II, no. 393.

concessions' without giving anything in return. To reverse this trend, the foreign secretary sought to 'encourage' Berlin to engage in confidence-building measures vis-à-vis Paris – and a policy of small steps. German policymakers were to honour their Locarno commitments and behave responsibly on 'smaller' issues, notably disarmament and relations with Poland, to prepare the ground for future agreements on the bigger issues of Locarno politics. Chamberlain remained 'gravely disturbed lest a more intractable spirit' should govern future French policy 'unless M. Briand can show the French public . . . practical benefits accruing to France from his policy.' In the Foreign Office's perception, Briand's volatile situation persisted. As Crewe reported from Paris on 5 February, French policy remained 'undoubtedly apprehensive as to German intentions' after the fall of the centre-ground Marx government in Berlin.[21] Against this background, Chamberlain basically concluded that an evacuation compromise was receding into the distance.

Fundamentally, Britain's Rhineland policy did not change. The Foreign Office re-asserted in April 1927 that, 'politically', the British view was and remained that, 'as a result of Locarno and Germany's entry into the League, the whole *raison d'être* of the occupation has fallen to the ground'. Its continuation tended to 'hinder instead of help the Locarno policy'. Chamberlain therefore told Stresemann that it remained the 'considered policy' of the British government to 'do all in their power to facilitate' a complete evacuation. In practice, though, he saw no scope for achieving concrete results in the short term. Instead, he concentrated on what in his eyes was a more urgent, and feasible, step ahead: a gradual diminution of the occupying forces as a sign of Anglo-French goodwill, yet only effected as a reward for good German behaviour.[22]

At the Locarno powers' December meeting in Geneva, Chamberlain had aired a proposal, co-ordinated with Briand, to accelerate troop withdrawals by establishing a permanent civilian control- commission. But Stresemann had outright rejected this because it contradicted Germany's cardinal aim of seeing a 'free, sovereign Rhineland'.[23] Subsequently, Chamberlain had practically endorsed Briand's line that an early evacuation could only be envisaged if Germany offered satisfactory 'equivalents' in terms of security and disarmament, to be determined by Paris and London.[24] Yet in the year following the

---

[21] Chamberlain to Lindsay, 12 January 1927, FO 408.47; Crewe to Chamberlain, 5 February 1927, *DBFP*, IA, III, no. 7.

[22] Foreign Office memorandum, 26 April 1927, *DBFP*, IA, III, p. 789; Chamberlain to Lindsay, 11 April 1927, *DBFP*, IA, III, no. 143.

[23] Stresemann to AA, 8 December 1926, *ADAP*, B, I/II, no. 244.

[24] Memorandum of a conversation between Chamberlain and Stresemann, Geneva, 5 December 1926, *ADAP*, B, I/II, no. 235.

failure of Thoiry the British Foreign Office also re-asserted its maxim that security issues like evacuation should be separated from reparations and wider financial questions. And the British Treasury still intended to link reparations not with Franco-German reconciliation but with a reduction of British war-debts.[25]

Lack of British forward engagement in Europe was thus not only attributable to Chamberlain's absorption by other crises. It also sprang from ever more ingrained British assumptions about what Locarno had already achieved and what consequently should be Britain's chief concerns. An important Foreign Office memorandum, updated in April 1927, concluded that the principal 'question of the future' in Europe was 'what Germany [will] make of her new position' after Locarno. It was revealing, however, that the same memorandum only listed Britain's Locarno and League commitments under point eighteen in an outline of priorities ranked in order of importance. In other words, the solidity of these commitments, and the sustainability of the Locarno system, was largely taken for granted. No less revealing was that the Foreign Office concluded that it was by then 'unnecessary to enlarge upon such ephemeral questions as military control, the Rhineland régime, the Saar, &c.' as 'the remaining restrictions' imposed by the Versailles treaty would be 'indubitably swept away' in the near future. 'Bigger questions' by contrast were those of 'Danzig, Upper Silesia, Austria and general disarmament'.[26]

While London was slithering into a crisis with Moscow, Germany's future relations with Soviet Russia also remained a notable concern. But the Foreign Office still accepted Stresemann's definition of a western-orientated Germany also having to protect its interests in the east, not that it was playing the western powers off against the Soviet Union. Significantly, though, none of these 'bigger concerns' led British policymakers to develop more engaging policies, let alone concrete initiatives for stabilising eastern Europe. Instead, Chamberlain continued to fend off Briand's various attempts to forge an 'eastern Locarno' that fortified the east European *status quo*, and France's alliances, against German and Soviet encroachments. And he persisted in his belief in the exemplarity of Locarno politics and its beneficial impact on what he envisaged as widening circles of stability in the east.[27]

---

[25] Treasury memorandum, 27 September 1926; Chamberlain memorandum, 2 October 1926, FO 371/11331 10930: C 10700/10060/18.

[26] Foreign Office memorandum, 26 April 1927, *DBFP*, IA, III, pp. 786–90.

[27] Chamberlain memorandum, 18 May 1927, *DBFP*, IA, III, no. 201; Chamberlain to D'Abernon, 4 February 1926, *DBFP*, IA, I, no. 245; Lindsay to Chamberlain, 16 February 1927, *DBFP*, IA, III, no. 17.

'The only practical approach' – the American 'school' of security policy in the latter 1920s

It is only a slight exaggeration to say that in the spring of 1927, prior to Briand's proposal for a war-renunciation pact, the Coolidge administration basically did not have any concrete security policy vis-à-vis Europe. The basic premise of the State Department, which the entire administration shared, was overwhelmingly that no such policy was required; that the stabilisation processes set in motion in 1924 could, and should, run their course with continued US involvement but minimal political interference on the part of the American government. The State Department drew up no plans for promoting Franco-German accommodation or for bolstering wider European stability by other means than through 'economic diplomacy', general calls for disarmament and an eventual revision of the Dawes scheme.

Not only Hoover but also Kellogg and Castle deemed some stagnation in Franco-German reconciliation efforts unavoidable, and all thought that they could safely be left to the care of the Locarno concert. They did not regard the shifting balance of influence and power between a recuperating Germany and its neighbours to the west and to the east as so significant as to be worrisome. And, at any rate, they did not consider this shift as a development on which Washington should or could have a major impact – apart from continuing its informal efforts to link Germany with the western capitalist system, both through the Dawes regime and through US loans and commerce.

In January 1927, Kellogg even felt the need to counter Congressional criticism of continued US involvement in the League's Preparatory Commission. The secretary of state did so by distinguishing an 'American', or rather Republican, approach to international security from that espoused by a European, essentially French, 'school of thought'. As he explained to the chairman of the House of Representatives' Foreign Affairs Committee, Porter, on 11 January, the European school espoused five 'fundamental principles'. The first was that 'security must be guaranteed' by 'military assistance against aggression', viewed as 'a necessary condition' for disarmament. The second was that arms limitation 'must be guaranteed by an international inspection'. The third stipulated that there was 'a complete interdependence of armaments'; thus no 'category' could be treated separately. Further, Europeans believed that it was 'not sufficient' to deal with 'actual peace-time armaments'; 'industrial, financial' and other factors also must be considered. And, finally, they demanded that any agreements 'in order to be effective must be universal'.[28]

---

[28] Kellogg to Porter, 11 January 1927, *FRUS 1927*, I, pp. 163–6.

In marked contrast to this, Kellogg outlined what in his judgement were quintessentially American principles of disarmament and security. Most fundamental was that 'there should be a direct approach' to arms limitation 'without awaiting complicated measures for providing security'. For the US government believed that disarmament promoted 'the cause of security', essentially by eliminating 'suspicion'. Second, effective agreements could only be premised on 'the good faith of the contracting parties' not an inspection 'machinery' creating 'new elements of suspicion'. Third, different categories of disarmament should be dealt with separately as a 'joint consideration of land, sea, and air armaments' would render any agreement 'needlessly complicated', if not impossible.[29] By the same token, Kellogg re-affirmed that 'the only practical approach' was to deal with 'visible armaments at peace strength' because considering industrial strength and other factors forestalled any concrete agreements. And, thus the final US precept, no arms-limitation system 'could be made either applicable or acceptable to all countries of the world'. Therefore, regional solutions had to be sought. And 'naval armament' could best be accomplished by the principal maritime powers – the underwriters of the Washington system. In Kellogg's eyes, the Preparatory Commission's troubles had confirmed 'the soundness' of American views.[30]

Both the secretary of state and his main adviser Castle reckoned that the differences between the European and the American approaches could at best be partially reconciled. They thus considered it pointless to 'call a general world conference' on disarmament. Yet, following his regional approach, Kellogg conceded that some 'features' of 'the European school' could be 'entirely applicable to the special needs of other countries'. *De facto*, US policymakers had come to view the Locarno accords as just such a feature, and they had some hopes that in the medium term the security pact could pave the way for disarmament. But its existence also made it easier for the administration to maintain, and justify, its 'traditional policy of noninterference in European affairs'.[31]

In fact, though, America's commanding informal influence on European and particularly German affairs even expanded in 1927 and 1928. Washington continued to pursue bilateral approaches vis-à-vis London, Paris and Berlin. Concerted Franco-German 'conciliation' remained a less critical issue, and east European problems were still deemed peripheral.[32] By and large, most decisionmakers, notably Hoover and Mellon, continued to trust in the

---

[29] *Ibid.*

[30] *Ibid.*; Kellogg to Herrick, 3 February 1927, NA RG 59 500.A15a 1/a; Kellogg (1928b), pp. i–xi.

[31] Kellogg to Porter, 11 January 1927, Kellogg to Wilson, 15 November 1927, *FRUS 1927*, I, pp. 163–6, 211; Castle Diary, 6 May 1927, vol. 11.

[32] Kellogg to Herrick, 3 February 1927, NA RG 59 500.A15a 1/a; Grew to Houghton, 21 February 1927, *FRUS 1927*, I, p. 16; Castle Diary, 6 May 1927, vol. 11. pp. 121–3.

groundbreaking pacifying effect of Europe's expanding financial consolidation, promoted through private agents. In Germany, Parker Gilbert was largely left to his own devices in overseeing the operation of the Dawes regime.[33] Particularly Hoover still regarded direct involvement in European security politics as unnecessary and harmful to US interests. And the commerce secretary still saw the disarmament problem through the prism of economic modernisation, as ever admonishing France to abandon outmoded reliance on military force. In February 1927, Coolidge authorised the dispatch of a US delegation to the World Economic Conference, which then took place in Geneva in May. He underlined Washington's interest in further promoting Europe's economic stabilisation and in 'contributing to the development of sound economic foundations of friendly intercourse and prosperity'. Yet he also emphasised that America would 'not be bound' by the conference's results or accept any general trade and tariff principles that conflicted with Congressional interests.[34]

In the State Department, more nuanced assessments of the European situation prevailed. But Kellogg and Castle also persisted with their policy of official non-involvement in European politics. In one respect, they were glad to see European policymakers resolve differences amongst themselves. Chiefly, though, they sought to keep a 'free hand' should relations between Germany and its neighbours again deteriorate, even if apart from Castle no one anticipated such a turn for the worse even in the medium term. Crucially, all of these tendencies countervailed what all European powers – apart from Britain – desired most: that Washington gravitated towards more engagement in the Old World.

Among US diplomats, perceptions of the evolving 'German problem' differed. In July 1927, Ambassador Schurman reported to Kellogg that the Norwegian king had severely criticised Stresemann, who had recently been awarded the Nobel Peace Prize together with Briand and Chamberlain. The king insisted that Stresemann based his policy not 'on a genuine love of peace but on the compulsion of circumstances'. Schurman disagreed, concluding that 'if German foreign policy has regard to self-interest' it was no 'less altruistic or honest than that of other nations'. The US ambassador agreed with the king that the Germans – like the Confederates in 1865 – were still in denial about their defeat in 1918. But he saw no disconcerting 'growth in militarism' among Germany's younger generations. Kellogg by and large concurred. The secretary of state held that the Norwegian king had 'probably set too high a standard for German public opinion' when it came to its acceptance of a still recent defeat. He reckoned that deeper changes in mentality required time and

---

[33] Mellon letter to Hibben, 15 March 1927, *FRUS 1927*, II, pp. 732–8.
[34] Hoover memorandum, 1927, Hoover Papers, box 365; Hoover statement, 6 October 1931, in Hoover (1952b), pp. 88–9; Coolidge message to Congress, 5 February, *FRUS 1927*, I, pp. 238–9.

peaceable conditions. And he had no reason to doubt that Stresemann pursued a by and large reliable policy that contributed to creating such conditions. Besides, Kellogg still thought that German leaders were far too interested in preserving their good and politically as well as financially beneficial relations with Germany's European neighbours and, notably, with the United States to be seriously tempted to revert to a more militaristic course.[35]

Yet Castle's more pessimistic stance had hardened as well, not only because of what he saw as the brittle domestic base of Stresemann's policy. Having monitored the collapse of Marx's government in December 1926, the new assistant secretary accepted Maltzan's assurances that 'Stresemann would continue to direct foreign policy' in Berlin. But his scepticism went more deeply. He shared the view that, for all their conciliatory pursuits, Stresemann was still an 'opportunist' and Schubert still 'really a servant of the old regime'. More generally, Castle believed that as long as European militarism persisted in many quarters, and both communism and fascism gathered followers, Europe's durable pacification remained doubtful – and so did the success of US-induced economic stabilisation. But precisely because of this, Castle consistently advised Kellogg to keep a distance from European quarrels and, notably, the machinations of French – or British – power politics.[36]

The Republican administration retained its objections to basic tenets of French disarmament policy. In March 1927, Kellogg rejected the draft for a Preparatory Commission statement that France had prepared with British support because it contained provisions for 'international supervision' and the 'punishment' of aggressors. At the same time, however, the State Department drafted a treaty of friendship and commerce with Paris 'similar' to that which Washington had concluded with Berlin in 1923. As Kellogg conveyed to Poincaré in June, the US proposal 'embodie[d] no attempt whatever' to 'attain by sharp bargaining undue advantages over a friendly State'.[37] In fact, though, the administration sought to use American preponderance to assert its open-door interests while still refusing to press Congress to lower US tariffs. As Castle laconically explained to Ambassador Claudel, Paris had to realise 'that under our law it was impossible' to 'negotiate any treaty containing reciprocal tariff favours'.[38] Parallel, Washington and Paris had opened commercial negotiations concerning a new French tariff decree, which the Poincaré government

---

[35] Schurman to Kellogg, 25 July 1927, Kellogg to Schurman, 19 August 1927, Kellogg Papers, roll 27.

[36] Castle Diary, 20 December 1926, vol. 10, p. 307; *ibid.*, 19 January 1927, vol. 11, p. 23a; *ibid.*, 29 January 1927, vol. 11, pp. 34–5.

[37] Kellogg to Herrick, 26 March 1927, 3 February 1927, NA RG 59 611.5131/514, 500.A15a 1/a; Kellogg to Gibson, 26 March 1927, *FRUS 1927*, I, p. 186; Kellogg to Whitehouse, 26 June 1927, *FRUS 1927*, II, p. 655.

[38] Castle memorandum, 19 September 1927, *FRUS 1927*, II, p. 677. Cf. Leffler (1979), pp. 178–9.

finally issued in August. Here, too, the main US aim was to lower French tariff levels. In both cases, French decisionmakers were incensed by what they – rightly – regarded as American double-standards. The talks over the envisaged commercial treaty faltered; and equally unresolved remained, of course, the question as to when, finally, the French parliament would ratify the Mellon–Bérenger agreement.

In 1927, the State Department began to register growing resentment not just in France but also in Germany against America's uncompromising pursuit of creditor interests and commercial expansion. Such resentment did not yet take a strong hold in the highest echelons of government and finance, at least not in Weimar Germany; nor did it as yet undercut the legitimacy of what Hoover envisaged as Europe's *Pax Americana*. But the policies of the Republican administration certainly did not help to make the 'Progressive' remedies to Europe's postwar problems that Washington still advocated more convincing or attractive to Europeans. For Kellogg at least, the underlying reasons for this were clear. As he noted in July 1927, he sensed 'a very general feeling of hostility toward us by many Nations of the World growing partly out of misunderstanding and partly out of envy of our prosperity'.[39]

The fiasco of the Geneva naval conference and the limits of Anglo-American security co-operation

Against such a more sombre background, preserving cordial, pragmatic relations with Britain remained a strategic priority for the Coolidge administration. But both powers' conflicting naval interests began to militate against this. Following Kellogg's advice, Coolidge finally, in early February 1927, called for a naval conference – not in Washington but in Geneva. And his chief proposal for the negotiations was to extend the Washington naval ratio of 5:5:3 between the three principal powers, Britain, the United States and Japan to the newly crucial cruiser class; the 'ratios of France and Italy' also were to be settled accordingly. America's representative at the Preparatory Commission, Gibson, headed the US delegation, accompanied by the 'very strong' Navy representative, Rear-Admiral Hilary Jones.[40] Britain was represented by a more high-profile delegation that was headed by Cecil and Navy Secretary William Bridgeman. As the responsibility for the conference fell to the special

---

[39] Kellogg to Herrick, 26 March and 13 April 1927, NA RG 59 611.5131/514, 517; Herrick to Kellogg, 1 and 9 April 1927, *FRUS 1927*, II, pp. 633–5; Kellogg to Ogden, 13 July 1927, Kellogg Papers, roll 27.

[40] Kellogg memorandum to the French government, 3 February 1927, NA RG 59 500.A15a 1/a; Kellogg to MacVeagh (Tokyo), 3 February 1927, *FRUS 1927*, I, pp. 5–6; US naval disarmament proposals, 10 February 1927, CAB 24/185, CP 59(27); Kellogg to Coolidge, 27 May 1927, Kellogg Papers, roll 27.

cabinet committee on disarmament, Chamberlain was not directly concerned. Unlike Kellogg, he thus had no major bearing on policymaking in a critical field of Anglo-American relations at that critical stage.

The failure of the Geneva conference which opened on 20 June and ended without agreement on 4 August 1927 manifested that Britain and the United States had manoeuvred their naval relations, and the global naval regime, into a veritable deadlock.[41] The conference was hampered from the start by the fact that France and Italy rejected Washington's rationale of separating naval from land armament issues and refused to attend the proceedings.[42] The Geneva negotiations thus became a tripartite affair. Both the British and the American delegations paid some attention to Japanese concerns. And Japan's high-level delegation, led by the distinguished Admiral Saito Makato and the diplomat Ishii Kikijuro, made considerable efforts to play a mediating role. But the key question was whether the world's two principal naval powers could find a strategic compromise. And it was their inability to reach an understanding that caused the breakdown of the proceedings.[43]

At the core of Anglo-American differences still lay the cruiser question – the principal sticking-points being, in Kellogg's words, 'first, the total tonnage of cruisers, and second, the size of cruisers and the gun calibre of their armament'. The State Department instructed Gibson to work towards a limitation of naval expansion but also parity with Britain in all classes, including cruisers. But the British delegation, following a proposal by the Earl of Birkenhead, demanded to divide cruisers into two classes. This was to allow Britain to retain the 'one-power' standard in the smaller class to defend the Empire's long lines of communication while conceding *de facto* parity with the American fleet in the larger class.

On 22 July, Kellogg warned Coolidge that he was no longer 'very hopeful of any practical result from the Conference'. The secretary of state considered an agreement along British lines 'injurious' to US interests. He failed to comprehend 'against whom Great Britain [felt] it necessary to have such sized armament' as there were 'no other navies in the world which could possibly endanger her commerce or her colonies'. Kellogg doubted that London would accept an agreement that the US administration 'could get ratified in the Senate'. This prediction was indeed borne out.[44]

The State Department's lack of comprehension regarding the other side's underlying motives was mirrored in London. And at Geneva Cecil and

---

[41] On the American perspective see *FRUS 1927*, I, pp. 5–158; on the British *DBFP*, IA, III, nos. 332–506. Cf. McKercher (1984), pp. 64ff.

[42] See Toynbee and Macartney (1924–30), 1927, I, pp. 1–21, 43–64.

[43] Kellogg to MacVeagh, 3 February 1927, Gibson to Kellogg, 2 August 1927, *FRUS 1927*, I, pp. 5–6, 146–8.

[44] Kellogg to Coolidge, 22 July 1927, Kellogg Papers, roll 27.

Bridgeman were likewise unable to see how they could forge a compromise that was acceptable to the cabinet's core imperialists. Churchill and the Earl of Birkenhead indeed preferred to have no agreement at all rather than concede complete parity with the United States or compromise what they deemed the Empire's vital need for a preponderance in smaller cruisers. Chamberlain supported this position. He was decidedly more Empire-minded than Cecil, who desperately sought to salvage an agreement and eventually resigned, on 9 August, when it became elusive. But in contrast to Churchill, the British foreign secretary remained anxious to prevent an open rupture in Anglo-American relations. And for the same reason, Kellogg, too, was anxious to avoid a 'break-up and final abandonment' of the Geneva talks.[45]

Chamberlain took charge of brokering a compromise against strong cabinet reservations. Eventually, the Baldwin cabinet endorsed a proposal for extending new ratios, favouring Britain, for smaller (6″) rather than larger (8″) armaments, which the Admiralty had demanded, in an agreement to be valid until 1936. When this still proved unacceptable to Washington, Chamberlain tried to advance an alternative compromise proposal formulated by the British and Japanese delegations at Geneva. But this, too, was outright rejected by the Coolidge administration.[46]

As has been shown, what really lay behind this dispute, and polarised British and American elite opinion, was on one level a fundamental strategic disagreement. Two core strategic aims, deriving from each side's experiences during the Great War, came into conflict: Britain's desire to preserve its ability to 'enforce maritime belligerent rights', essentially to protect the Empire's life-lines and globe-spanning sphere of influence in a future war; and America's priority to ensure the protection of 'neutral trading rights' in the same event.[47] This was undoubtedly critical. But in the larger picture, Anglo-American tension arose from an underlying transition and adjustment process already delineated. The long-time naval hegemon had to come to terms with a rising American power essentially claiming parity, particularly to safeguard its expanding interests in the western hemisphere and the Far East. The former increasingly lacked the resources even to maintain such parity but still featured a strong Conservative 'Royal Navy' segment that clamoured for a navy inferior to none. The latter was financially ever more superior. And it, too, featured a strong 'Big Navy Party' in the Senate, intent on US primacy 'inter pares' vis-à-vis

---

[45] Chamberlain speech, Commons, 27 July 1927, *Hansard*, 5th series, vol. 209, cols. 1246–7; Churchill memorandum, 29 June 1927, CAB 24/187; *DBFP*, IA, III, nos. 332ff; Kellogg to Coolidge, 29 July 1927, *FRUS 1927*, I, pp. 138–9.

[46] Gibson to Kellogg, 2 August 1927, Kellogg memorandum, 4 August 1927, Kellogg to Coolidge, 4 August 1927, *FRUS 1927*, I, pp. 146–8, 154–6; cabinet minutes, 3 and 4 August 1927, CAB 23/55, CC 47 and 48 (27).

[47] McKercher (1984), p. 69.

Britain. The underlying question was how far London and Washington could find mutually acceptable naval standards, and limits, that also satisfied Japanese interests; and how far they could thus ultimately sustain a functioning global maritime regime.

The collapse of the Geneva conference not only raised the spectre of a sharp deterioration in Anglo-American relations. Some commentators even warned that the long-term result could be a drift towards war between the two rival powers. But key decisionmakers on both sides deemed such scare-mongering greatly exaggerated. The consequences of the Geneva 'fiasco' both for Anglo-American relations and world politics were in fact serious but not disastrous. One effect was indeed that both Kellogg and Chamberlain were driven to redouble their efforts to pre-empt further estrangement, which in the short term propelled the conclusion of the Kellogg–Briand pact in 1928.

Not only the Foreign Office but also the State Department were deeply concerned about more far-reaching repercussions of Anglo-American discord for the global order. On 29 July 1927, Kellogg had underscored that a failure of the conference would be 'disastrous to all the world as an example that the two leading naval powers are unable to come to any agreement'. The 'moral effect' of such an outcome would be 'out of all proportion to the material interests involved'.[48] Chamberlain dismissed talk of a possible Anglo-American war as nonsense, underlining that no member of the Baldwin cabinet thought of it as 'anything but a crime'. In private, however, he remained highly critical of Republican policy, commenting in mid-December that he found it 'really a heartbreaking task to try to improve our relations'. Britain had been told that 'the payment of the [British war] debt had produced such a greatly improved feeling'. But in his assessment it remained as taxing as ever to 'twist' the American 'lion's tail' and forge a naval compromise. Nonetheless, Chamberlain was keen to minimise further damage.[49]

Despite such good intentions, however, what proved most consequential for the European situation was that the mutual search for Anglo-American *rapprochement* had distinct limits. Washington and London had a prevailing interest in resolving naval differences. And both sides sought other areas of agreement, notably in delimiting their spheres of strategic prerogatives. In the spring of 1928, this would lead both governments to agree to an informal recognition of each power's very own 'Monroe Doctrine'.[50] Crucially, though,

---

[48] Kellogg to Coolidge, 29 July 1927, *FRUS 1927*, I, p. 138; Kellogg to Phillips, 9 August 1927, Kellogg Papers, roll 27.

[49] Chamberlain to Howard, 10 August 1927, *DBFP*, IA, III, no. 503; Austen to Hilda Chamberlain, 17 December 1927, Austen Chamberlain Papers, AC 5/1/44; Chamberlain memorandum, 16 October 1926, *DBFP*, IA, IV, no. 215; cabinet minutes, 22 July 1922, CAB 23/55, CC 43(27); Castle Diary, 6 May 1927, vol. 11, p. 122.

[50] See chapter 24.

the Geneva crisis did not spur efforts either in London or in Washingon to go beyond this – to contemplate more substantial changes in their security policies. There was no intention on either side to deepen co-operation in this field to such an extent that it could also underpin future common engagement in Europe.

Mutual suspicion still ran deep. The naval dispute served to reinforce long-held mutual assumptions about the other side. In Washington, it accentuated suspicions of deep-seated British imperialism and high-handedness vis-à-vis natural US claims for an equal status not only in naval affairs but in world politics in general. And it did nothing to induce key policymakers like Castle to alter their judgement that 'behind all the words the British policy is exactly what it always has been, to maintain a balance of power'.[51] In London, it reinforced the perception that US decisionmakers were in the grip of a both swashbuckling and parochial Congress and, with the thrusting arrogance of the newly arrived, unable to strike 'reasonable' bargains. These not surprising but for each side absorbing developments in Anglo-American relations formed the essential backdrop to what took place on the stage of European diplomacy. They reinforced the separation of the two parallel processes that continued to shape postwar politics in the Euro-Atlantic sphere: US-dominated financial consolidation, or lack thereof, and the Locarno process.

Between piecemeal progress and stagnation – Locarno politics in 1927

Growing dissonances between Berlin, London and Paris in the first half of 1927 revealed the entire array of domestic and international impediments that made further decisive advances in Locarno politics both harder and ever more imperative. The utmost Chamberlain, Briand and Stresemann could accomplish was to contain their divergences over the Rhineland and disarmament, as no compromise on either issue was in sight in the immediate future.[52] If one lesson could be drawn after Thoiry, and was absorbed both in the *Wilhelmstraße* and the *Quai d'Orsay* – yet not in Whitehall – it was the lesson that resolving the critical Rhineland question would most likely require a further comprehensive financial-cum-political arrangement. And such an arrangement would essentially require Washington's approval to initiate a revision of the Dawes plan. Yet the leading policymakers in both Paris and Berlin came to conclude that this could hardly be envisaged prior to the next presidential

---

[51] Castle Diary, 6 May 1927, vol. 11, p. 121.

[52] Minutes of the French National Defence Council, 3 December 1926; memorandum of a conversation between Briand and Stresemann, Geneva, 5 December 1926, PA, General Files, 2466H: D516550–4. Cf. Pitts (1987), pp. 185–6.

elections in the United States, which were to be held in November 1928.[53] However strongly Chamberlain insisted on the primacy of European diplomacy, this was the fundamental constellation moulding not only transatlantic relations but also Locarno politics between the spring of 1927 and the autumn of 1928.

In the interim, though with different motivations, all Locarno powers thus came to pursue their own versions of a policy of small steps. All sought to pave the way for agreements on the salient issues by first engaging in co-operation on smaller and, so they hoped, more manageable problems. Chamberlain once again came to focus on 'the more urgent matter' of securing 'a reduction in the number of the occupying troops'. To alleviate German grievances, he now urged his recipes of confidence-building on Stresemann. In the British foreign secretary's calculation, any progress hinged on Berlin showing goodwill on issues that might seem minor yet were central to Paris. Rather than persist with its 'clamorous demand for further relief', Germany had to overcome its 'singular dilatoriness' and give 'precise guarantees' to reduce its stocks of 'war material' and dismantle its eastern fortifications. Besides, the German government had to take a clear stand against *Reichswehr* collaboration with 'Nationalist societies'.[54]

Under increasing domestic pressure to block any further major concessions to Germany, Briand was glad to espouse the British approach, which caused many frustrations in Berlin.[55] Fundamentally, though, what Chamberlain envisaged did correspond with the general strategy that Stresemann and Schubert had adopted by then. Particularly Schubert's recommendations were premised on the realisation that, under the circumstances, only consistent progress on 'minor' questions could widen the window of opportunity for a comprehensive Rhineland settlement. More broadly, Schubert and Stresemann deemed consistent Locarno-style co-operation – in Geneva as much as vis-à-vis eastern Europe – not only critical for Germany's wider revisionist agenda. They had come to view it as an important principle of German foreign policy as such.[56] In February, Chamberlain could thus praise Stresemann's 'statesmanship' in resolving the questions of war-materials and the eastern fortifications 'against

[53] Hoesch to Stresemann, 9 February 1927, PA, General Files, 3058H: D606516–20; Crewe to Chamberlain, 4 January 1927, FO 371/12125; Stresemann memorandum, 6 March 1927, PA, General Files, 3058H: D606531–5.

[54] Chamberlain to Lindsay, 12 January 1927, FO 408.47; Chamberlain to Lindsay, 15 March 1927, Austen Chamberlain Papers, AC 54/335.

[55] Memorandum of a conversation between Briand and Hoesch, 17 February 1927, MAE, Série Europe, Allemagne, vol. 400; Hoesch to Stresemann, 3 March 1927, PA, General Files, 3058 H: D 606531ff.

[56] Schubert memorandum, 8 December 1926; Stresemann memorandum, 9 December 1926, PA, General Files, 4587 H: E 183072–5, 183097–9.

domestic opposition', which advanced the policy of 'reciprocal concessions' that both he and the German foreign minister had 'at heart'.[57]

But even minor advances, such as partial French troop withdrawals, became more difficult in this phase because of more entrenched domestic fronts against Locarno politics on both sides of the Rhine.[58] Though he won a vote of confidence in the *Chambre* on 18 January, Briand had to be more assertive in countering allegations that he was an overly conciliatory 'sentimentalist' – that he had 'offered the towers of Notre Dame and even more' to Stresemann. *Mutatis mutandis*, his German counterpart confronted much the same criticism from German nationalist circles. As Briand observed, a film then very success-ful in Germany had portrayed Stresemann as having ordered workers to 'dismantle' the Brandenburg Gate, the symbol of 'the power of the old Germany', to send it to Paris.[59]

Briand's leeway was also noticeably curtailed, yet not critically diminished, by Poincaré, who had regained clout through his successful policy of '*le franc fort*'. By this time, the French premier no longer questioned the Locarno policy of *rapprochement* as such. But he argued that France should pursue it, as far as possible, from a position of strength, bargaining for financial concessions not only from Germany but also from the United States. Despite numerous internal disputes, however, the 'Cabinet of National Union' remained intact, and with it the basic foundations for Briand's policy. As Berthelot told Hoesch in mid-January, his chief could still build on this prevailing elite consensus in approaching further agreements with Germany. But he had no choice but to pursue a course of 'making haste slowly'.[60]

Confirmed beyond doubt in early 1927 was that the *Quai d'Orsay* no longer conceded any legal – or moral – grounds for evacuating the Rhineland on the basis of Locarno. And however urgently German politicians insisted that Berlin had met its obligations under the Versailles treaty, this could no longer be the basis for any agreement either.[61] To buy time, Briand sought to claim the 'power of definition' as to what conditions he would ultimately attach to French concessions. But for the time being the 'price' for the evacuation of the Rhineland remained unclear.

---

[57] Chamberlain to Lindsay, 5 February 1927, *DBFP*, IA, III, no. 6. For the strong domestic pressure on Stresemann to deliver results see Stresemann to Hoesch, 23 April 1927, PA, 1344/ 2466/516703; records of the *Reichstag* debates, 22–3 March 1927, Stresemann (1932), III, pp. 120ff.

[58] Schubert memorandum, 21 March 1927, *ADAP*, B, V, no. 27. Cf. Krüger (1985a), pp. 364–5.

[59] Briand statement to the Foreign Affairs Commission, 19 January 1927, C14764, no. 57/11.

[60] Poincaré to Briand, 2 June 1927, MAE, Etats-Unis, 243; Hoesch to Stresemann, 13 January 1927, no. 45, PA, General Files, 2466 H: D 504806; Phipps to Chamberlain, 15 December 1926, FO 371/12125. Cf. Keiger (1997), pp. 326–7.

[61] Memorandum of a conversation between Briand and Hoesch, 17 February 1927, MAE, Série Europe, Allemagne, vol. 400.

At the same time, France's search for wider bases of security vis-à-vis a reinvigorated neighbour continued, both with and in control of Germany. French leaders had to acknowledge that no further tangible commitments could be expected from either London or Washington. Nevertheless, while not reneging from Locarno co-operation with Germany Briand tried his utmost not only to cement the Anglo-French *entente* but also to pave the way for a *rapprochement* with Washington.[62] Paris also sought to reinforce the League security regime along the lines of the abortive Geneva Protocol of 1924. Unsurprisingly, that particular initiative received not even lukewarm British support. Backed by the Committee of Imperial Defence, Chamberlain essentially prevented a resuscitation of the Protocol in the latter 1920s. He still considered it too inflexible and involving too far-reaching commitments. Moreover, it could only diminish the Locarno concert's centrality. Instead, the British foreign secretary sought to intensify co-operation with Briand on key Locarno issues.[63] This the French foreign minister reciprocated.

Following the unsuccessful Thoiry initiative, Briand re-accentuated his *entente* policy, most demonstratively when accompanying President Doumerge on a state visit to Britain in mid-May 1927. Facing American pressure and German demands, Paris and London theoretically had a strong common interest in co-ordinating their disarmament policies in the Preparatory Disarmament Commission. But the French side remained dead-set against any change in the constellation of real armament superiority vis-à-vis Germany. Under the circumstances, any more than merely superficial compromise with Britain was elusive. What did become discernible, however, yet only after the Anglo-American fiasco at Geneva, were the contours of an understanding on the lowest common denominator. Those overseeing disarmament policies in the Baldwin cabinet and the Poincaré government began to envisage simply supporting the other side where it mattered most: Britain would support France on core issues of land disarmament and France would in turn back Britain's positions on naval arms control. Eventually, this would give rise to the infamous Franco-British disarmament compromise of August 1928.[64]

But crucial for European politics was something else. With Chamberlain's help, Briand by and large managed to reinforce his *de facto* dominance in determining the velocity and scope of 'progress' in the Locarno process. Both in parliament and vis-à-vis the French press he began to emphasise that no 'premature' evacuation of the Rhineland was conceivable without new, firmer

[62] Briand statement to the Foreign Affairs Commission, 19 January 1927, C14764, no. 57/11; Hoesch to Stresemann, 19 January 1927, PA, General Files, 2466 H: D 504822–8.

[63] *Quai d'Orsay* memorandum, 8 October 1926, MAE, Série Europe, Allemagne, vol. 399; Chamberlain minute, 24 May 1926, Cecil to Chamberlain, 22 May 1926, FO 371/11880: W 7802/78/98.

[64] Cabinet minutes, 25 July 1928, CAB 23/58, CC 41(28). See chapter 24.

German guarantees. As he told Hoesch, these not only pertained to reparations but also to security. The German industrialist Fritz Thyssen wrote Stresemann in February 1927 that, as a French coal-magnate had assured him, Paris would not agree to a complete evacuation before its eastern fortifications, the future Maginot Line, were completed.[65] In August, the British chargé Phipps augured that any 'quickening of the pace' in French policy seemed 'unlikely' because what still 'reign[ed] supreme' in Paris was anxiety vis-à-vis Germany, 'her numbers [and] efficiency'. Although it increasingly relegated them to the background, the French government also still had to consider the concerns of its most important eastern allies Poland and Czechoslovakia. While Prague continued its efforts to co-operate with all three Locarno powers, the Piłsudski regime exhorted Paris not to hasten further concessions to Germany, particularly a withdrawal from the Rhineland, which could set the wider postwar *status quo* in flux.[66]

But it would not suffice for the new German government to prove its 'good intentions' in the sphere of security. Ultimately, as Ambassador Crewe noted, the Poincaré government would not withdraw from the Rhineland 'until some new compensation of value to France [could] be discovered'. And as both Briand and Berthelot realised, it would be hard to find such compensation without 'the consent of America', which they did not expect to obtain before a new president had been elected in Washington in the autumn of 1928. Briand thus strove – successfully – to delay further troop reductions – essentially, to keep the Rhenish asset for an eventual bargaining-process with Germany.[67]

In many ways, Stresemann's domestic freedom of action became even more curtailed than Briand's. When in January 1927 the DNVP became part of Marx's second *Bürgerblock* coalition Stresemann calculated that drawing the German Nationals' leaders into government responsibilities would allow him to control and moderate their opposition to his foreign policy. But time and again the new constellation also made tenuous intra-governmental compromises almost unavoidable. In Ambassador Lindsay's assessment, it remained 'quite obscure' how far the DNVP would really accept the main condition for entering the government: an 'unambiguous adherence to Locarno'. This indeed remained a very contentious issue. Lindsay concluded nonetheless that, given Stresemann's authority, German policy was 'unlikely to undergo any serious modification'.[68]

[65] Hoesch to Stresemann, 19 January 1927, no. 67, PA, General Files, 2466 H: D 504822–3; Thyssen to Stresemann, 6 February 1927, Stresemann Papers, 7146 H: H 150700–1.
[66] Phipps to Chamberlain, 28 August 1927, *DBFP*, IA, III, no. 315. Cf. Wandycz (1988), pp. 63–72.
[67] Crewe to Chamberlain, 4 and 5 February 1927, *DBFP*, IA, III, pp. 15–16.
[68] Lindsay to Chamberlain, 29 December 1926, *DBFP*, IA, III, no. 376.

Yet the *Wilhelmstaße*'s 'policy of small steps' increasingly came under attack in Germany, not just in the right-wing press. The demands of its critics included not only that Stresemann at last present tangible compensations for his Locarno concessions, most of all in the Rhineland, but also that he should finally press for revisions of the Polish–German border; even the 'Anschluß' of Austria re-appeared on the horizon of public debate.[69] The German foreign minister thus confronted a very familiar yet ever harder challenge: how to make progress in implementing his policy of co-operation and peaceful change in the face of growing external *and* domestic constraints.

Behind closed doors, neither Stresemann nor Schubert doubted that it would be hard to fall back behind the precedent of Thoiry. They realised that achieving an early end of the occupation would require a German 'price' in terms of reparations. But they were also even more aware than their French counterparts that any arrangement they might contemplate could hardly be carried out successfully if it ran counter to US interests – particularly those articulated by Parker Gilbert. Yet this would require careful preparation and, ultimately, an *American* initiative to revise the Dawes regime, all of which conflicted with Berlin's cardinal interest in swift, conspicuous changes in the Rhenish *status quo*. As no public German appeal for complete evacuation on the grounds of Locarno bore fruit, nor any bid to strike a separate deal on the Saar question, Stresemann decided to focus on intermediate advances, which only seemed possible in the area of further French troop removals. In April 1927, he again used the threat to resign in order to put pressure on Chamberlain and Briand, telling both Locarno partners that the future of Locarno politics as such would be at stake unless headway was made on this issue.[70]

As from the spring of 1927 Stresemann's health became increasingly frail, the operative guidance of German policy hence often fell to his key adviser, Under-Secretary Schubert. And Schubert concluded that the German Foreign Office's maxim had to be to reinforce its Locarno policy of peaceful change – and resist all alternative temptations. Following his lead, Germany opted against all attempts to exploit possible differences between Britain and France or between France and its eastern allies to accelerate a corrosion of the postwar *status quo*. This was not to be Berlin's way of furthering its ambitions, notably in eastern Europe. Rather, the underlying rationale of Weimar German foreign policy became, ever more, to strengthen the European concert. Schubert therefore laid the emphasis on proving that Germany was willing to fulfil its

---

[69] Painlevé to Briand, 30 August 1927, MAE, Série Europe, Autriche, vol. 79; report by the *Bureau de Contrôle des Etrangères*, 31 January 1927, Série Europe, Allemagne, vol. 380.

[70] Stresemann memorandum, 1 November 1926, Stresemann Papers, 7334 H: H 162860–72; Stresemann to Marx, 14 January 1927, *AR Marx III und IV*, no. 167; Stresemann minutes, 28 April 1927, PA, General Files, 3058 H: D 606571–3.

new responsibilities as a Locarno power – even in instances where such responsibilities conflicted with more immediate revisionist interests.[71] As will be shown, this especially informed German attitudes vis-à-vis the escalating Polish–Lithuanian dispute over the status of Vilna.

Following the same rationale, Germany embarked on a new security initiative. Developed by Schubert, and launched in the summer of 1927, it sought to offer Britain and France a long-term bargain. Germany's conciliatory co-operation in strengthening the League's system of collective security was to be rewarded by a final Anglo-French recognition of its equal status as a European great power. In Schubert's calculation, this in turn was to pave the way for a solution to the Rhineland problem – ending an occupation no longer compatible with Germany's reinforced new status. And in the medium term it was to permit an approximation of equal armament levels agreed upon in the framework of a general disarmament conference. This strategy informed Germany's work in the League's security committee in 1927 and the spring of 1928. As a corollary, Schubert also developed a new German policy on arbitration and the pacific settlement of international disputes. Backed by Stresemann, he thus sought to devise new methods for advancing Berlin's agenda of peaceful change, sanctioned by international law under the League Covenant. Both Schubert and Stresemann reckoned, or at least hoped, that such methods could eventually also be used to effect a peaceable revision of Germany's eastern borders.[72]

Fundamentally, then, the two years following the failure of Thoiry saw a high-point in the evolution of Weimar Germany's western-orientated policy. Like Schubert, Stresemann had internalised that Germany's novel *realpolitik* first and foremost commanded developing the Locarno system and deepening 'intertwined interests' with the United States. The German foreign minister sought to convince his domestic audience that, in view of the catastrophe of 1914, preparing for renewed war was no longer a responsible option for German foreign policy – for Germany had nothing to gain from such a war and would only become its main battlefield. In his by then unequivocal judgement, the only realistic way to achieve postwar Germany's main aim – to re-emerge as a power 'with equal rights', unimpeded by Versailles' strictures – was to strengthen mechanisms like the new European concert.[73] In principle, the thrust of Stresemann's policy corresponded very much with what Chamberlain – and

[71] Stresemann instructions, 23 November 1926, quoted after Krüger (1985a), p. 390; Schubert memorandum, 26 January 1928, *ADAP*, B, VIII, no. 45.

[72] Schubert memorandum, 26 January 1928, *ADAP*, B, VIII, no. 45; Schubert memoranda, 21 and 24 March 1927, *ADAP*, B, V, pp. 27ff., 57ff.

[73] Stresemann speech, 28 January 1927, *ADAP*, B, IV, pp. 584–604; Stresemann *Reichstag* speech, 23 June 1927, in Zwoch (1972), pp. 251ff. Cf. Wright (2002), pp. 416–17.

Kellogg – sought to further. Yet how far would this suffice to settle the larger unresolved questions of postwar Europe?

From the peripheral to the core? The concert politics of small steps

Important developments in Locarno politics in 1927 and 1928 underlined that, while not achieving notable progress on core issues, the Locarno powers could pursue effective crisis-management on many smaller matters that would have caused grave complications in the early 1920s. The European concert proved its operability when all three powers had to cope with two crises that were only very partially of their own making, both originating from eastern Europe's unsettled *status quo*. That Chamberlain, Stresemann and Briand could achieve net-gains in confidence-building by settling highly sensitive issues of this nature threw into relief how entrenched Locarno politics had become by then, also in Berlin.

Albeit not related, both crises erupted in neuralgic areas of eastern Europe. One centred on the controversy between Poland and Lithuania over the future status of Vilna, which had been under Polish occupation since 1920. But it also raised wider problems. They stemmed from Moscow's opposition to further Polish encroachments on its sphere of influence and the German interest in preventing a Polish expansion encircling Eastern Prussia should the Piłsudski regime be victorious in a possible war. The conflict also heightened Berlin's concern to protect the German minority of Memel from Lithuanian encroachments, which had intensified after a 1926 coup in Vilna.[74]

As he found not only the Poles and Lithuanians but also the Germans 'irritable & irritating to one another', Chamberlain sought to calm tensions, concluding that his 'bed-side manner' as Europe's 'honest broker' was again required, this time in the east. Above all, he strove to prevent the conflict from unsettling Polish–German relations. The British foreign secretary tried to defuse tensions by mediating on the question of Germany's eastern fortifications. He assured the Piłsudski government that while he was open to the 'idea of some concession' to Berlin he would not accept a compromise that 'menaced the security of Poland'. Chamberlain also sought to promote what he deemed encouraging talks between Schubert and the Polish foreign minister Zaleski over the long-disputed Polish–German commercial treaty. He hoped that a breakthrough on the economic front could also foster a 'better feeling' in the

---

[74] Cf. Hiden (1987). In a similarly co-operative fashion, the Locarno powers also handled the Italo-Yugoslav crisis of 1927. See Chamberlain to Kennard (Belgrade), 29 March 1927, Chamberlain to Lindsay, 31 March 1927, *DBFP*, IA, III, nos. 90, 94.

political relations between Warsaw and Berlin.[75] But while the fortification issue could be settled, this breakthrough was not achieved until 1929.

Yet even in 1927 neither British nor French policymakers had cause for suspicion over Berlin's *Ostpolitik*. Stresemann and Schubert pursued a course of utmost restraint in the Polish–Lithuanian question.[76] In mid-February, Schubert confidentially told Ambassador Lindsay that it was 'no use' for Germany 'to pretend that they did not hope some day, by purely peaceable means, to bring about a change' of the 'Eastern frontiers'. But Berlin recognised that this was a 'remote contingency not to be realised for many years' and only to be approached in accordance with Germany's Locarno commitments. Schubert emphasised that, in the near future, Berlin was 'anxious' to maintain friendly relations with Warsaw. The *Wilhelmstraße* had no interest in a Polish state 'in financial chaos'. As Weimar Germany never completely abandoned the aim of 'rectifying' its postwar border with Poland, a certain tension in its *Ostpolitik* was and remained inescapable. But Berlin at no point sought to precipitate an escalation of the Polish–Lithuanian dispute or, more generally, a destabilisation of the eastern *status quo*.

By contrast, Briand of course retained a keen interest in doing everything to fortify that very *status quo* as far as possible. From early 1927, the French foreign minister faced not only German revisionist ambitions that in his perception could at best be contained but never quite be overcome. From his vantage-point, the spectre of a Polish–Lithuanian war also raised the danger that such a conflict might escalate into a confrontation between Poland and the Soviet Union, which ultimately threatened to drive Moscow to seek what France dreaded most: a power-political *entente* with Berlin.[77]

Briand thus had an obvious interest in exploring schemes to pre-empt any such scenario, which could affect not only France's eastern alliance system but alter the entire power constellation in eastern Europe. While also struggling to moderate Polish policy under Pilsudski, he returned to his previous approach and eventually came to propose different, more or less ambitious versions of an 'eastern Locarno'. Briand had long promised France's Polish ally that he would pursue such a guarantee pact once an end of the French Rhineland occupation was on the horizon. Yet when in late 1927 Zaleski confronted him with a revived proposal for an 'eastern Locarno' involving direct French and British guarantees for the sanctity of the Polish–German border, all the French foreign minister could do was to deflect it. For he rightly considered it a scheme that

---

[75] Austen to Ida Chamberlain, 22 January 1927, Austen Chamberlain Papers, AC 5/1/406; Chamberlain to Roberts (Warsaw), 12 January 1927, *DBFP*, IA, II, no. 393.

[76] *ADAP*, B, V, nos. 20, 25. Cf. Krüger (1985a), pp. 367–8.

[77] See the French documents on the Polish–Lithuanian conflict and eastern Europe in MAE, Pologne, 75/120-1, 150-81. Cf. Keeton (1987), pp. 265-83.

would never find Chamberlain's approval. Instead, Briand went on the offensive. At the League Council meeting at Geneva in December, he came to promulgate a far-reaching scheme for a Locarno-style eastern pact. As he outlined it to his Locarno partners, the pact he envisaged would not only involve the Locarno powers, Poland, the Baltic states and Soviet Russia – as well as Rumania. It would also comprise a highly precarious Polish–German bargain: the exchange of the 'Polish Corridor' for the German-held Memel region.

Yet although not only Chamberlain and Stresemann but also Marshal Piłsudski were at first favourably disposed towards Briand's idea, the Soviet regime was not, and the scheme never came to fruition. In the wider picture, the overall prevailing, and still daunting, constraints imposed by east European insecurity and regional rivalries after Versailles did not (yet) permit any other outcome. Moreover, not only German and Polish leaders but also the British government would have found it extremely difficult to underwrite such a 'grand bargain' in the east, had it actually been carried to its final stages.[78] Instead the Locarno powers came to focus on more immediate concerns at Geneva. Stresemann successfully joined forces with Chamberlain and Briand to dissuade Piłsudski from resorting to force against Lithuania.[79] Ultimately, Piłsudski was more interested in placing relations with Germany on a less contrary footing than in starting a war in the east.

The second crisis affecting European international politics had culminated in a break-off of diplomatic relations between Britain and Soviet Russia in May 1927, which even led to – exaggerated – fears of an open conflict or even war between the two powers. Chamberlain had long sought to calm the waters, conveying to the Soviet commissar for foreign affairs, Chicherin, that while Anglo-Soviet relations continued 'notoriously to be of unsatisfactory nature', Moscow was mistaken in concluding that Britain was 'plotting against the USSR'.[80]

But in the view of more conservative cabinet members, Soviet propaganda slandering the Empire had become unbearable. And so had been Moscow's 'interference with purely British concerns', notably the 1926 general strike. More concretely, they suspected the Soviet government of having launched

---

[78] See MAE, Pologne, 75/200–40; Stresemann memorandum of a conversation with Briand, 11 December 1927, *ADAP*, B, VII, no. 200; Chamberlain to Tyrrell, 12 December 1927, FO 800/361; Chamberlain record of a conversation with Stresemann, 12 December 1927, *DBFP*, IA, IV, no. 91. Cf. Wandycz (1988), pp. 73–105. Chicherin persisted with attempts to divide the Locarno powers when it came to eastern Europe. To relieve western pressure on Moscow, he instead sought to intensify bilateral arrangements with Germany and to pursue a bilateral non-aggression pact with France. Yet the latter was only concluded in 1932. Cf. Jacobson (1994), pp. 161–5.

[79] Lindsay to Chamberlain, 16 February 1927, *DBFP*, IA, III, no. 17; Austen to Ida Chamberlain, 12 December 1927, Austen Chamberlain Papers, AC 5/1/440.

[80] Tyrrell minute, 18 February 1927, *DBFP*, IA, III, no. 19. Cf. Gorodetsky (1977), pp. 198ff.

subversive activities from the site of the Russian trade delegation in London. Churchill and Birkenhead seized on this to press for what they had long desired: a diplomatic rupture with Moscow, which could also be used domestically to put Labour on the defensive. The Baldwin government officially broke off relations with Soviet Russia on 26 May.

This had important, and potentially disconcerting, implications for the Locarno concert. In February, Chamberlain had noted that the Soviet leadership, with Stalin 'now the biggest force', were 'beginning to realise that world revolution does not pay them'. But he still dreaded a an open 'breach', mainly because of its repercussions for Britain's relations with Germany and the Baltic states.[81]

Indeed, German diplomacy found itself in a difficult position. Schubert made clear to Lindsay that Anglo-Soviet tensions 'caused the gravest anxiety in Germany'.[82] Following the Berlin treaty of 1926, the *Auswärtige Amt* sought to maintain pragmatic relations with Soviet Russia, even though this had become increasingly unavailing since Stalin had begun to dominate the Soviet regime. Despite a German 300 million mark loan, economic relations remained sluggish. And Stresemann's efforts to check the secret co-operation between the *Reichswehr* and the Red Army had caused irritations in Moscow. Essential, however, was that the time when Berlin would have been tempted to seize on the Anglo-Soviet conflict to create new revisionist possibilities in eastern Europe was over. In short, German policymakers did not want to have to take sides. Generally, Stresemann and Schubert still sought to position Germany so that it could perform a bridge-function between the western powers and the Soviet Union. At the outset, they only refrained from mediating in the Anglo-Soviet quarrel for fear of being instrumentalised by either London or Moscow.[83]

But Chamberlain's principal interest, too, was to de-escalate the crisis. He thus reassured Stresemann and Briand at the League Council meeting in June that London would desist from further measures against Moscow, and he also underscored that what remained imperative for British diplomacy was to reach a close understanding between all three Locarno powers on how to deal with the Soviet regime. This was indeed achieved. Chamberlain and Briand even came to press Stresemann to exert a moderating influence on the Soviet delegation present at Geneva. And the German foreign minister, who had all along advised Chicherin to exercise restraint vis-à-vis Britain, completed this Locarno task successfully.[84] Stresemann's reliability not only reassured

---

[81] Chamberlain to the Soviet chargé d'affaires, 23 February 1927, Chamberlain to Lindsay, 1 March 1927, *DBFP*, IA, III, nos. 21, 32; Austen to Hilda Chamberlain, 27 February 1927, Austen Chamberlain Papers, AC 5/1/411.

[82] Lindsay to Chamberlain, 16 February 1927, *DBFP*, IA, III, no. 17.

[83] *ADAP*, B, V, nos. 20, 25.

[84] Minutes of a conversation between Chamberlain and Stresemann, 14 June 1927, *DBFP*, IA, III, no. 240; Stresemann statement, Geneva, 14 June 1927, *ADAP*, B, V, no. 209.

Germany's western partners, most importantly Briand. It also underscored how the European concert began to have a stabilising impact in the east, curtailing Soviet options to sow discord between the Locarno powers and even more crucially pointing beyond the uncertainties of a revisionist Germany that manoeuvred between east and west.

In contrast to such encouraging signs, the key negotiations over the 'consequences of Locarno' became ever more a tug-of-war, particularly between Paris and Berlin. They turned into a struggle for minimal mutual concessions in which British mediation-efforts had very limited effects. At their Geneva meeting in March 1927, Briand had impressed on his Locarno partners that inner-French opposition to his policy had become so intense that his hands were tied on the Rhineland – and even on minor troop reductions.[85] The discussions between Stresemann and Briand reminded Chamberlain of 'similar combats at Locarno'. Yet he also observed that this time 'business' was no longer done 'à deux' but 'à troix', which allowed him to prevent a situation where 'France & Germany left to themselves were unable to come together.' The foreign secretary regretted that British papers underestimated 'the decisive rôle which England played' in Locarno politics. For it alone had 'sufficient authority' and was 'sufficiently possessed of the confidence of both parties'.[86]

Eventually, Chamberlain's leaning on Briand was indeed again instrumental in forging a compromise. If less than in his judgement, Britain was still 'the key of the situation'. But by this time the 'honest broker' could only foster largely symbolical agreements. During President Doumerge's state visit to London in mid-May, Chamberlain not only re-affirmed his *entente* policy. He also managed to convince Briand that advances on troop reductions were indispensable if Britain and France wanted to win the battle 'for the soul of Germany' with Moscow. The British foreign secretary came to act on the assumption that the more intractable relations with the Soviet Union became, the more important it was that he and Briand 'should attach Germany solidly to the Western Powers'. Following the Anglo-French summit, Chamberlain had to counter German suspicions that 'the prominence given to the Entente between Great Britain and France portended a weakening of the Locarno policy'. Yet he reassured Stresemann that he and Briand would be 'the chief mourners at the funeral of that great instrument of peace' and no change in Britain's Locarno 'engagements' had occurred.[87]

---

[85] Stresemann memorandum, 6 March 1927, *ADAP*, B, IV, no. 219.
[86] Austen to Hilda Chamberlain, 14 March 1927, Austen Chamberlain Papers, AC 5/1/412; Chamberlain to Lindsay, 15 March 1927, *DBFP*, IA, III, no. 46.
[87] Austen to Hilda Chamberlain, 14 March 1927, Austen Chamberlain Papers, AC 5/1/412; Chamberlain memorandum, 18 May 1927, *DBFP*, IA, III, no. 201; Chamberlain to Lindsay, 27 May 1927, *DBFP*, IA, III, no. 218.

In fact, Chamberlain brought pressure to bear in Berlin's favour. He managed to overcome Briand's reservations on the issue of troop withdrawals, although the latter again invoked growing resistance against any concessions in Poincaré's cabinet and French military circles. Yet the final go-ahead was not given until August. Then, Paris and Brussels finally endorsed Chamberlain's proposal to remove a further 10,000 troops, 1,050 British, 900 Belgian and 8,050 French, which cut the occupying forces back to a total of 60,000. For the German public, this was an unimpressive result. But in view of the *tendences profondes* still marking post-Locarno Europe, it remained an arduous task to dynamise concert politics beyond taking such small steps. Most profoundly, thus Phipps' albeit overstated reminder from Paris, 'Fear, with a capital F' still dominated French attitudes. In the assessment of the British chargé, it could only be diminished by further 'tangible efforts by the party of reason in Germany'. More generally, though, not only such efforts but also time and a functioning international system, such as that founded but by no means finished at London and Locarno, were needed to diminish fear and suspicion – not just in France.[88]

From 1927, stagnation in Locarno politics on this profound level led policymakers in Germany and France to explore alternative, transatlantic avenues. Schubert's long-term aim was to widen the European into a transatlantic concert. He thus hoped to broaden Germany's room to manoeuvre not only regarding the salient reparations issue but also in the interlocked areas of security and territorial revision. As this orientation corresponded with his core strategy, Stresemann backed Schubert's bid to extend America's engagement as Germany's senior partner of peaceful change. The German foreign minister's policy still relied strongly on political-cum-economic bargaining, which – with the requisite support of Washington and Parker Gilbert – finally was to achieve his main aim: to 'liberate' the Rhineland.[89]

For their part, Briand and Berthelot were also eager to effect a *rapprochement* with the United States and to improve France's strained relations with the Coolidge administration. Yet the *Quai d'Orsay*'s strategy markedly differed from that of the *Wilhelmstraße*. In essence, it aimed to induce Washington, which in French eyes had hitherto backed Germany and pressed for changes in the Versailles system, to gravitate towards France. In short, Briand sought American support in his quest to buttress French, and European, security by solidifying the *status quo rebus sic stantibus*.[90]

---

[88] Chamberlain memorandum, 18 May 1927, *DBFP*, IA, III, no. 201, pp. 310–11; Stresemann memorandum, 6 March 1927, *ADAP*, B, IV, no. 220; Crewe to Chamberlain, 10 August 1927, Phipps to Chamberlain, 28 August 1927, *DBFP*, IA, III, nos. 312, 315, p. 543. Cf. Jacobson (1972b), pp. 132ff.

[89] Schubert memorandum, 21 March 1927, *ADAP*, B, V, no. 27; Stresemann (1932), III, pp. 255–65.

[90] MAE, Etats-Unis, 66/24–9. Cf. Keeton (1987), pp. 238–9.

24 No 'new world order'

The limits of the Kellogg–Briand pact

On 6 April 1927, marking the tenth anniversary of America's entry into the Great War, Briand made a statement to the Associated Press proposing a bilateral pact of perpetual peace between France and the United States. Positing that the two 'great democratic nations' were inspired by an 'identity of aims' in their peace policies, he declared that they should set an example to the world by signing a treaty committing both to 'the renunciation of war as an instrument of national policy'. More than two months passed before Kellogg signalled, on 11 June, that the Coolidge administration was willing to 'enter into diplomatic conversations' about Briand's proposal. Ten days later, Washington received a formal note with the French draft treaty.[1]

Thus, a complex process of transatlantic negotiations was set in motion, which went on for more than a year and evolved from 'soundings' between Paris and Washington to a series of 'multilateral' exchanges, which were largely steered by the US State Department. At its end, on 27 August 1928, the United States concluded, not a bilateral treaty with France but a multilateral pact signed not only by all Locarno powers and their European neighbours to the east (though the Soviet Union abstained) but also by Japan and a plethora of other states.

From the outset, Kellogg had suspected that Briand's plan amounted to 'a defensive treaty with France' that would allow Paris to buttress the postwar *status quo* and 'leave it open to her to take what action she liked in Europe' while ensuring Washington's 'neutrality'.[2] This he flatly rejected. Instead, and in line with British – and German – interests, the American secretary of state seized upon the French initiative to advance his own war-renunciation agenda. In short, Kellogg transformed Briand's design into a universal pact that was essentially non-committal, and indeed included no international sanctions against aggressors. Yet its overall thrust was to buttress peaceful change by

---

[1] Briand statement, 6 April 1927, Kellogg to Herrick, 11 June 1927, *FRUS 1927*, II, pp. 611–13, 614.

[2] Kellogg memorandum, January 1928; Marriner memorandum, 24 June 1927, Kellogg Papers, roll 27.

advancing arbitration and, more broadly, the pacific settlement of international disputes.

Even more strikingly, however, Kellogg thus demarcated the limits of US engagement in European security politics in the latter 1920s. At most, the making of the Kellogg–Briand pact can thus be regarded as a very early stage in a very long process of US strategic reorientation vis-à-vis Europe and the solidification of a transatlantic security order in the twentieth century. Both processes only culminated after 1945. More immediately, the pact negotiations cast a glaring light on the challenges that the Locarno system confronted in the latter 1920s. At their core lay the already familiar, yet persistent, difficulty of preserving the European concert while reconciling, as far as possible, France's more *status quo*-orientated policies and Germany's policies of peaceful change. As it was never seriously taken on by the US administration, this remained the critical task for the British 'honest broker'.

What motives lay behind Briand's pact proposal? Most narrowly construed, the French foreign minister appears to have calculated – erroneously – that by concluding a bilateral neutrality pact he could indeed draw the United States towards finally backing France's security policy and eastern alliance-system. At a minimum, the pact could serve to deflect unabated US criticism of French postwar militarism. In his April declaration, Briand had stressed that France was still striving to achieve a 'limitation of armaments' to ease the burden of decades of 'heavy military charges'.[3] The underlying aim of the *Quai d'Orsay*, then, was to reinforce the European state of affairs of the mid-1920s. Yet Briand's hopes reached further. His proposal was an attempt to seize the initiative, to move from the defensive to the offensive in the *grand jeu* of striving for a strategic *rapprochement* with Washington, ahead of Berlin. The French foreign minister sought to improve France's position not only in the arid field of security and disarmament but also in the tug-of-war over French debts and, crucially, future negotiations over a 'final' reparations settlement.

In Briand's perception, France had a cardinal interest in overcoming the post-Versailles deadlock in relations with the United States, if only to avoid repeating the mistakes of 1923 and 1924, when France had lost its commanding position in postwar Europe. The *Quai d'Orsay* reckoned that within the following two years not only the reparations – and debt – question would top the international agenda. With it, also the future of Franco-German security relations would be determined. French policymakers had no doubt that this would re-calibrate the European balance of political influence and financial power for the coming decade. And they also thought that central though it remained, the *entente* with Britain would not suffice to secure French interests

---

[3] Briand statement, 6 April 1927, *FRUS 1927*, II, p. 612.

in this process.[4] The strategic objectives that France pursued with the pact initiative were thus quite plausible. In retrospect, though, most remarkable about Briand's proposal was the extent to which it was based on basic misperceptions of the mainsprings and limits of Republican foreign policy.

Kellogg and the 'outlawry of war' – from *status quo* preservation to peaceful change

Briand's overture met with a distinctly chilly reception in Washington. Kellogg originally had distinct reservations towards the treaty draft that the French ambassador Paul Claudel submitted on 22 June 1927. These were shared by the State Department officials who would be instrumental in crafting the American counter-strategy, Castle and the chief of the Division of Western European Affairs, J.T. Marriner. Castle noted that Washington would 'be treading on dangerous ground' if it accepted Briand's terms. A bilateral anti-war pact would enable Paris to 'feel safe to do what it likes in Europe'. In the assistant secretary's view, such a pact was even, 'to a certain extent, a threat at nations excluded' from it. Marriner concurred. On 24 June, he warned Kellogg that Briand intended to found 'a kind of perpetual alliance between the United States and France, which would seriously serve to disturb the other great European Powers – England, Germany and Italy'.[5]

Kellogg took these concerns to heart, making them the core premise of US pact policy. There would be no 'negative alliance' with France that gave it free rein 'to take what action she liked in Europe'. The secretary of state also suspected that Briand's initiative might 'be used internally in France to postpone the ratification of the Debt Settlement and to create a feeling that payment was unnecessary'. Personally, he felt that until France showed a 'willingness to observe her present obligations', i.e. to ratify the war-debt settlement, Washington 'should not consider entering upon new ones'. Yet, for all these reservations, the State Department concluded that there was a prevailing US interest not in opening but rather in *shaping* further discussions with Paris.[6]

That Kellogg took this step had two principal reasons, one domestic, one pertaining to his general outlook on America's role in international affairs. Most immediately, he did so to satisfy the American war-outlawry movement,

---

[4] MAE, Etats-Unis, 66/1–7, 24–8; MAE, Série Europe, Grande Bretagne, 34/8ff. Cf. Keeton (1987), pp. 238–9.
[5] Castle Diary, 6 May 1927, vol. 11, pp. 123–4; Marriner memorandum, 24 June 1924, Kellogg Papers, roll 27.
[6] Kellogg memorandum, January 1928, Kellogg to Ogden, 13 June 1927, Kellogg Papers, roll 27; Kellogg to Herrick, 11 June 1927, *FRUS 1927*, II, p. 614.

which had powerful adherents in the Senate, above all Borah. More profoundly, he came to view a pact on American terms as a 'valuable, practical
and psychological reinforcement of existing efforts to maintain world peace'.
In his final assessment, it could be an 'added guarantee' impeding nations
from resorting to war 'without involving the United States affirmatively in
purely European problems' or 'exposing' it to any dangers 'latent in the
doctrine of military sanctions'. At the same time, the secretary of state aimed
to seize on Briand's initiative to counter what he by then clearly perceived as an
ever more pronounced European resentment against the new world power,
stemming from America's economic superiority yet also from the lack of
political US engagement in Europe. This became a less important but hardly
negligible motive for Kellogg's engagement on behalf of the war-renunciation
pact.[7] In July 1928, the secretary would note that 'a great deal of bitterness
against the United States' had arisen in Europe 'in the last few years' and
Washington's position 'would be made immeasurably worse' if Congress
rejected his pact.[8]

The importance of the domestic mainsprings of US policy should by no
means be understated. Making their weight felt were numerous associations
and academics campaigning for the outlawry of war who also had influence in
Washington and, in Marriner's view, represented a sizeable segment of voters'
opinion. Leading voices of this mostly, yet not exclusively, pacifist movement
were Professor J.T. Shotwell of the Carnegie Endowment for Peace, the
Columbia Professor J.P. Chamberlain and the head of the Chicago-based
'Outlawry of War Organisation', Salmon Oliver Levinson.[9] Responding to
public pressure, Kellogg assured the *New York Times*' editor-in-chief, Rollo
Ogden, on 13 June 1927 that he had 'no intention of slighting M. Briand's
proposal'. Castle had earlier predicted that the administration would have 'to
discuss the matter with France' as there was 'too much pacifist feeling in this
country to permit a refusal'. While there was 'a lot of French politics in the
scheme' Castle thus thought that the State Department also had to reckon with
'a certain amount of American politics'. For as he rightly stressed, the concept
'outlawry of war' was 'not a French idea at all', and lobbyists like Shotwell and
Levinson had to be handled carefully.[10]

---

[7] Kellogg to Lippmann, 21 July 1928, Kellogg to Ogden, 13 June 1927, Kellogg Papers, rolls
   31, 27.
[8] Kellogg to Whitelaw Reid, 24 July 1928, Kellogg Papers, roll 31. Kellogg advised Coolidge not
   to overstate 'the superiority of the United States' in a planned speech, wary of the 'effect it
   would have abroad'. See Kellogg to Coolidge, 3 August 1928, Kellogg Papers, roll 31.
[9] Cf. Ferrell (1952), pp. 24ff.
[10] Kellogg to Ogden, 13 June 1927, Kellogg Papers, roll 27; Castle Diary, 6 May 1927, vol. 11, pp.
   123–4.

Shotwell, who had discussed the proposal with Briand on 22 March, naturally urged the Republican administration to adopt the French plan, albeit with some modifications. Subsequently, he published a comment on the draft treaty entitled 'An American Locarno'. Exceeding French suggestions, he argued that the pact could be 'framed in terms' applicable not only to France and the United States but also to 'any other signatory of Locarno and other non-American powers' including Japan. In analogy to Locarno, the treaty was to create a nucleus of rules and obligations 'between the great civilized Powers'. Shotwell hoped that by proceeding from a regional to a global scope, 'the instruments of universal peace may finally be discovered'. He called his proposal a 'compromise between American history and the new experiments of Europe'. Thus, to internationalise Briand's design was from the start a central aim of the American anti-war movement. Eventually, the State Department would seize upon this. What ultimately appealed to Kellogg was that the war-renunciation pact could emulate Locarno in promoting peace and disarmament through 'measures of international insurance' while avoiding the Rhine pact's actual guarantee commitments.[11] On these grounds, the secretary of state deemed Shotwell's proposal worth considering.

An even more important motive for the State Department's decision to enter into negotiations with France, however, was that prominent senators, particularly Kellogg's mentor and close confidant William Borah, were among the leading advocates of war-renunciation.[12] Kellogg was in constant exchange with Borah, seeking to accommodate the senator's positions and to check possible Congressional opposition. This he expected chiefly from the 'Big Navy Party', which feared that US pacifists might use the treaty to prevent passage of the planned Naval Bill for an expanded cruiser programme. From his 'rather intimate knowledge of the sentiment in Congress', Kellogg was convinced that a sweeping treaty on Briand's terms, threatening the Congressional prerogative to declare war, would receive little support there. Yet he later obtained strong Senate backing for his multilateral treaty approach. Following a 'successful talk', the Foreign Relations Committee in December endorsed Kellogg's maxim that 'a treaty outlawing war . . . could not possibly be made with a single nation' but only 'with all the principal powers'.[13]

More profoundly, Kellogg's pact engagement was spurred by the fact that from early on he, Castle and Marriner saw an opening for taking Briand's 'offer' as the starting-point for a high-profile peace initiative. It was to be an

---

[11] J.T. Shotwell, 'An American Locarno', June 1927 [?], Butler statement, 31 May 1927, Kellogg Papers, roll 27.
[12] Kellogg to Coolidge, 27 June 1927, *FRUS 1927*, II, pp. 619–21.
[13] Correspondence between Kellogg and Borah, 26, 27 July 1928; Kellogg to Ogden, 13 June 1927, Kellogg Papers, rolls 31, 27; Castle Diary, 22 December 127, vol. 11, p. 313.

initiative that would suit all of the administration's principal interests, both domestic and international. And it would bear the stamp of a distinctly Republican endeavour: a universal – and non-committal – scheme for the outlawry of war. For the one commitment that US policy maintained vis-à-vis Europe – in very general terms – was the commitment to expanding an international order *that did not impede* peaceful change. In other words, Republican policymakers sought to further the evolution of principles and rules that fostered peaceable conflict-resolution and, if necessary, gradual changes in the international *status quo*. Crucially, though, the Coolidge administration was still not prepared to support international mechanisms for upholding and at the last resort enforcing such principles, particularly outside the western hemisphere. It was precisely on these grounds that the State Department resisted what it perceived as the *Quai d'Orsay*'s attempt to pull the United States to France's side in order to *cement* the European *status quo*.

On these premises, Kellogg sought to transform Briand's treaty proposal and place the negotiations over a new war-renunciation pact on a broader international footing.[14] On 27 June 1927, he told Coolidge that he would begin 'diplomatic conversations' not only with France but also the other main powers of the Washington system, Britain and Japan. As the secretary of state impressed on Briand, he would not commit himself publicly to a bilateral pact.[15]

The State Department's *spiritus rector*, Castle, also left his imprint on America's evolving pact strategy. He recommended concentrating on two aims. One was to extend any war-renunciation treaty to all major European powers, including Germany. The other was to link it with the conclusion of a series of arbitration treaties, as those the United States had concluded with France, Britain and Japan after the war were up for renewal in 1928. In mid-August 1927, Castle 'frankly' told the international press that he did not 'personally have much use' for a 'bilateral treaty'. If, however, 'France wanted to make similar treaties with Germany and Italy and England' Washington would be willing to 'do the same'.[16]

Following Castle's advice, Kellogg indeed sought to complement the envisaged pact with a series of improved arbitration treaties, which were premised on the Bryan Treaty of 1913 and the Root Treaty of 1908. The latter provided for the establishment of a Commission of Conciliation between two countries in case of dispute and obliged both parties not to resort to force during on-going

---

[14] Kellogg to Coolidge, 21 June 1927, *FRUS 1927*, II, p. 615. For Briand's draft treaty, received on 22 June, see Whitehouse to Kellogg, 22 June 1927, *FRUS 1927*, II, pp. 615–16.
[15] Kellogg to Coolidge, 27 June 1927; Kellogg to Whitehouse, 27 June 1927, *FRUS 1927*, II, pp. 619–20, 617–18.
[16] Castle Diary, 6 May, 19 August 1927, vol. 11, pp. 123, 180; Marriner memorandum, 24 June 1924, Kellogg Papers, roll 27.

investigations. Yet the State Department also had a keen interest in altering the system of arbitration treaties in accordance with Washington's growing desire after 1918 to demarcate exemptions. When informing France and Britain of US plans to extend the Root Treaty, Kellogg underlined that the Republican administration would insist on the new proviso that arbitration should not affect 'the vital interests, the independence or the honour of the two Contracting States'. Under these categories, he subsumed all questions touching upon core 'political' or 'domestic' matters and, notably, the Monroe Doctrine.[17]

Borah, who considered Shotwell's proposal impracticable, even argued that Washington should focus solely on renewing the Root treaties with France, Britain and Japan, thus avoiding the risk of finally falling into some power-political trap set by Briand. And Kellogg went so far as to promise him to oppose any treaty that submitted 'political' questions to 'compulsory arbitration' which, Borah assured him, the Senate would never accept. Fundamentally, Kellogg and Borah shared two basic, if contradictory, assumptions. On the one hand, they agreed that a war-renunciation treaty was of little practical value unless a 'machinery' existed 'to settle the questions which bring on war'. On the other hand, though, their main concern was that Washington should have no part in creating such an 'international machinery', be it through the League, or be it by gravitating towards a Euro-Atlantic concert, as 'pacifists' like Shotwell hoped. Indeed, this remained the basic problem marring US efforts to banish war in the decade after Versailles. Instead of contemplating extended commitments, Kellogg focused on limiting any obligations that the envisaged pact might confer on its signatories. And both in front of international and domestic audiences, he took pains to stress that the 'European conception' of 'treaties of alliance' was entirely different from the American, noting that the United States had not entered into an alliance since that with France, in 1793.[18]

Shotwell had earlier captured an underlying problem of the transatlantic negotiations over the war-renunciation pact when remarking that the 'fact that there is no real crisis in world affairs at the present moment' should not lead US decisionmakers to conclude that America had 'no immediate need' for a firmer 'framework of peace'. In Shotwell's judgement, the descent into war in 1914 had demonstrated 'the need for a definite agreed program for times of international crisis'. And he cited Stresemann's comment of March 1926 that

---

[17] Kellogg to Atherton (London), 28 December 1927, *FRUS 1927*, II, p. 628. Kellogg to E. Lape (American Peace Foundation), 21 July 1927; Kellogg to Ogden, 13 June 1927, Kellogg Papers, roll 27. Cf. McKercher (1984), pp. 104–5.
[18] Kellogg to Coolidge, 27 June 1927, *FRUS 1927*, II, pp. 619–21; Kellogg to Howard, 29 June 1927, Kellogg Papers.

the world war could have been prevented if the 'implements of international understanding' embodied in the Locarno agreements had already existed in 1914.[19] Fundamentally, though, there was indeed no urgency for the Coolidge administration to support more robust 'implements' of this kind in 1927. Nor, alas, did the administration include policymakers who had drawn Shotwell's lessons from the Great War.

On 29 June, Kellogg proposed not to give Briand a formal answer before it could be given on American terms. And Coolidge approved that, if at all, the French proposal should be 'discussed informally and through regular diplomatic channels'. Briand and Berthelot took pains to stress that they had no intention to 'sidetrack the informal diplomatic conversation' that Kellogg had demanded to prevent interference by 'too zealous' activists like Shotwell. But what followed were almost six months of diplomatic silence while the State Department was preparing its own draft for a 'multi-lateral' treaty that incorporated Kellogg's *caveats*.[20]

It was not until 28 December 1927 that the American secretary of state officially presented his counterproposal. He stated sardonically that France and the United States, 'instead of contenting themselves with a bilateral declaration of the nature suggested by M. Briand', should make 'a more signal contribution to world peace'. They were to join in 'an effort to obtain the adherence of all of the principal Powers of the world to a declaration renouncing war as an instrument of national policy'. This could then also lead other powers to follow suit, 'perfecting' what had become not a French but an American blueprint for the outlawry of war.[21]

From January 1928, Washington, not Paris, set the parameters of the pact negotiations. And what ensued was indeed not a bilateral but a multi-level process. It proceeded on two levels. On one, the United States discussed not only with France but also with Britain, Germany and other major powers, notably Japan, how far Kellogg's design was compatible with already existing treaties and obligations, above all French obligations in Europe and the precepts of Locarno and the League Covenant. On another level, the Anglo-American powers embarked on an attempt to reconcile war-renunciation with their self-accorded rights and commitments in the realms of hemispheric, viz. imperial security.

[19] Shotwell, 'An American Locarno', June 1927 [?], Kellogg Papers, roll 27.
[20] Kellogg to Coolidge, 27 June 1927, Coolidge to Kellogg, 29 June 1927, Whitehouse to Kellogg, 29 June 1927, *FRUS 1927*, II, pp. 619–22; 'Draft Treaty of Permanent Peace', 1927, Kellogg Papers, roll 27.
[21] Kellogg to Claudel, 28 December 1927; Kellogg to Atherton, 30 December 1927, *FRUS 1927*, II, pp. 627, 629; Kellogg to Root, 23 December 1927, Kellogg Papers, roll 30; Castle Diary, 21 December 1927, vol. 11, pp. 311–12.

Locarno and the emergence of a British 'Monroe Doctrine' – Britain and the war-renunciation pact

From Washington, Ambassador Howard had kept Chamberlain informed about US reactions to Briand's proposal throughout the summer and autumn of 1927.[22] But Britain only actively engaged in the pact process following Kellogg's official counterproposal. Essentially, Chamberlain had to toe a line between accommodating Washington and preserving the *entente* with Briand. Characteristically, the British foreign secretary sought to make a virtue of necessity by again assuming, or at least trying to assume, the role of a mediator. From January 1928, he ostensibly came to act on behalf of common Anglo-French interests in the transatlantic pact deliberations. In substance, however, he often saw more eye to eye with Kellogg's – and Stresemann's – agenda of peaceful change and limited commitments.

Nonetheless, closing ranks with Briand remained a principal concern for Chamberlain. In early January 1928, the foreign secretary assured his French counterpart that he was keen to hammer out a common platform with him. Britain agreed with France that, as a League member, it could not accept any treaty 'incompatible with our obligations'.[23] As he later told Houghton, Chamberlain still 'held the profound conviction that the friendship of France and Great Britain was an essential element in the peace of the world'. While 'sympathetic' to Kellogg's proposals, he had to consider the legitimate concerns of those states 'living in circumstances wholly different, with different obligations and different interests' from those of the United States. In other words, in negotiating over the pact Britain had to respect France's security concerns and particularly its alliance interests in eastern Europe. It could not 'sacrifice' an old friendship for the sake of supporting the United States on war-renunciation.[24]

The critical challenge for British diplomacy became to bridge the gap between America and France while also safeguarding Britain's interests both as a Locarno and as an imperial power. Chamberlain set out to achieve this by brokering a compromise that made Kellogg's draft treaty compatible not only with what became known as 'the British Monroe Doctrine' but also with the unhampered operation of the European concert. Not least, fostering such a compromise also was to offer him a way of 'building bridges' for Briand. During the critical stages of the pact negotiations, not only Chamberlain came to define Britain's role in this manner. In the spring of 1927, Cecil too had

---

[22] Howard to Chamberlain, 9 June 1927, *DBFP*, IA, III, no. 361.
[23] Chamberlain to Crewe, 6 January 1928, *DBFP*, IA, IV, no. 247.
[24] Chamberlain memorandum, 24 January 1928, *DBFP*, IA, IV, no. 262.

emphatically affirmed that '"England must always be an intermediary between the old and the new worlds."'[25]

In the eyes of Ambassador Howard, who became one of the pact's most outspoken British advocates, Kellogg's December note presented London with an opportunity. On 2 February 1928, he cabled Chamberlain that it was in Britain's 'particular interest' to support a 'general pact' – 'even without sanctions' and even if France chose not to pursue it any further. Britain should focus on 'the main question' whether it might not be beneficial to 'the peace of the world', and British interests, if America, 'now the most powerful [country] in the world', could be 'brought to subscribe to some general Treaty renouncing war'. And the British ambassador's verdict was clear. He argued that Britain should actively bolster a pact that could gradually foster a 'more positive and concrete' US security policy than Washington had 'up to the present been willing to commit itself to'. In Howard's view, this was critical for European and global stability, and it could also have positive implications for the future of the Washington naval system and security in the Far East. The ambassador also reported that, led by Borah, particularly the Middle West was 'beginning to clamour for some definite action on the outlawry of war' as it was 'tired of playing the rôle of "Der Geist der stets verneint" ("The spirit who always negates").'[26]

In charting a British war-renunciation policy, Chamberlain never went as far as Howard had recommended. But he showed a new willingness to consider possible benefits of co-operating with Washington. Substantially, he and most Foreign Office officials – like their American counterparts – saw little inherent merit in the pact. At best, they deemed it a more symbolical than tangible complement to the Locarno concert. Britain still had a strategic interest in promoting peaceful change in western and eastern Europe. But the Foreign Office still sought to achieve this, not through universal declarations without sanctions, but by operating through the concert.

Chamberlain nonetheless concluded that the envisaged treaty could do more than merely promote 'the formation of a "world opinion for peace"'. It could at least 'tend to draw the United States away from a policy of complete isolation'. Fundamentally, however, the British foreign secretary remained sceptical as to how far this could be achieved, and how far it could indeed be beneficial for Europe given the persistent domestic strictures of US foreign policy. He thus pursued more concrete, medium-term aims. In one – important – respect, British interests commanded improving Britain's position vis-à-vis America

---

[25] *Ibid.*; Houghton to Kellogg, 27 April 1928, NA RG 59 711.4112 Anti-War/15. Cf. McKercher (1984), pp. 504–27; Johnson (2004a).
[26] Howard here obviously cited Goethe's *Faust*. See Howard to Chamberlain, 2 February 1928, *DBFP*, IA, IV, no. 268.

in the run-up to the expected revision of the Dawes plan. This interest was less pronounced than in Paris or Berlin but still tangible. As Chamberlain noted on 24 January 1928, backing Kellogg's proposal could help 'a better understanding' in Washington 'of European problems, such as the reparations and debt questions' – though this could only be 'a faint hope' at present.[27]

More importantly, as noted, Chamberlain and Tyrrell saw the need to mend fences with Washington after the breakdown of the Geneva naval talks. As the foreign secretary put it in late January, a 'rebuff' to the Republican administration could 'drive [it] still further into the isolationist camp'; and it would strengthen the Big Navy party in Washington, thus making any future naval agreement even harder to clinch than before. Continuing naval tensions and the pact negotiations themselves would confirm Chamberlain's deep-seated impression that the United States remained a very problematic strategic partner. For in US domestic politics, as he observed in December, 'at any moment an international question may be made an instrument of party warfare regardless of the international consequences'.[28]

Two Monroe Doctrines – towards a strategic accommodation between London and Washington

But what spurred eventual Anglo-American agreement over the war-renunciation treaty were two overriding common interests keenly perceived by policy-makers both in the Foreign Office and the State Department. As we have seen, on both sides an underlying political will existed to re-establish a platform for pragmatic co-operation and to prevent a further escalation of naval tensions.[29] And it became increasingly clear in the spring of 1928 that both powers shared an interest in protecting their strategic prerogatives and global freedom of action. In short, therefore, Britain and the United States came to engage in a process of mutually defining their respective 'Monroe Doctrines' for the post-World War I era.

From the start, Chamberlain saw the 'dangers inherent in the very vagueness' of the 'phrase "renunciation of war as an instrument of national policy"'.[30] The Foreign Office identified two critical areas: how could the treaty be reconciled with Britain's legitimate self-defence and obligations under the Locarno treaties and the League; and how could it be reconciled with the special requirements of imperial defence. After Kellogg had submitted a draft proposal of the

---

[27] Chamberlain memorandum, 24 January 1928, *DBFP*, IA, IV, 1928, no. 262.
[28] *Ibid.*; Austen to Ida Chamberlain, 8 December 1928, Austen to Hilda Chamberlain, 17 December 1927, Austen Chamberlain Papers, AC 5/1/462, 441.
[29] Howard to Vansittart, 10 January 1928, *DBFP*, IA, IV, no. 250, pp. 488–9.
[30] Chamberlain memorandum, 24 January 1928, *DBFP*, IA, IV, no. 262.

envisaged pact on 27 February 1928, Chamberlain asked the Foreign Office's legal expert, Hurst, to study it in-depth. Hurst originally concluded that Britain and the Empire 'would stand to gain more than they would lose by accepting the proposal and agreeing to sign a multilateral treaty'. On the other hand, the United States would 'stand to lose all round'. Essentially, he concluded that the treaty would drastically curtail the Monroe Doctrine, which *inter alia* stipulated that Washington would not tolerate any European interventions in the western hemisphere. And it would also 'render the wonderful new [American] fleet useless' for enforcing this doctrine. For such as it was the pact would debar the United States from intervening in the case of disputes between Latin American and European countries, for example should London have to act in legitimate defence of British interests in Venezuela.[31]

One month later, however, Hurst gave a far more sceptical reading of the treaty's possible implications. He now argued that accepting Kellogg's formula of renouncing 'war as an instrument of national policy' could also bar Britain from defending key imperial interests, notably in Egypt, where also the safety of the Suez Canal and, thus, the access to India were at stake. Hurst underlined that Britain's 'position in Egypt [was] precisely similar' to that which America claimed in the western hemisphere.[32]

Chamberlain agreed with his legal adviser that a core question he had to resolve with Washington was what 'bearing' the proposed treaty would have on Britain's 'declaration' that had granted 'a qualified independence to Egypt'. The foreign secretary also thought that this case was 'exactly comparable' to cases involving the US Monroe Doctrine.[33] The immediate background to his deliberations was furnished by continual rows between Britain's and Egypt's leaders over the size of the Egyptian army and British troop-stationing rights. With relief, Chamberlain noted on 9 May that he had seen to a 'successful conclusion of the immediate Egyptian trouble', thus achieving, in Tyrrell's words, 'a miracle'.[34] But the underlying problem remained unresolved.

Britain's decisive note to Washington of 19 May thus included, as a key requirement for accession to the pact, the claim for a British equivalent of the Monroe Doctrine. The note emphasised that – in analogy to what the United States claimed for the western hemisphere – Britain had to safeguard its interests in 'certain regions of the world the welfare and integrity of which constitute a special and vital interest for [its] peace and safety'. There was no question that Kellogg would ever sign a treaty that impinged on the Monroe

[31] Hurst memorandum, 15 March 1928, *DBFP*, IA, V, no. 314.
[32] Hurst minute, 20 April 1928, *DBFP*, IA, V, no. 324.
[33] Chamberlain to Howard, 26 April 1928, *DBFP*, IA, V, no. 325, pp. 631–2.
[34] Austen to Hilda Chamberlain, 9 May 1928, Austen Chamberlain Papers, AC 5/1/453.

Doctrine or risked alienating Congress by curtailing its power to declare war.[35] Yet Houghton told Chamberlain on 25 May that the American secretary of state considered his reference to 'the British Monroe Doctrine' very 'unfortunate'. In the assessment of the State Department, it 'opened a veritable Pandora's box of difficulties'. If, following London's example, France, Italy and Japan now also found it 'expedient to develop a Monroe Doctrine of their own' this would create a 'serious situation'.[36] Chamberlain could merely express his hope that Britain's action would not set an unwelcome precedent, underlining that he had only meant 'to reassure Parliament over Egypt'. In fact, though, this particular Pandora's box of postwar international politics remained sealed in 1928. Neither France nor Germany, or for that matter Italy or Japan, began to claim strategic privileges of the kind the Anglo-American powers invoked for themselves.

Thus, following Kellogg's lead, London and Washington could concentrate on reaching an informal bilateral understanding. As a result, neither power's 'Monroe Doctrine' was specifically mentioned in the eventual war-renunciation treaty; but the tacit agreement between them was that each side's prerogatives were unaffected by the pact. On this basis, Chamberlain confirmed Britain's acceptance of the Kellogg–Briand pact on 18 July 1928.[37] This bilateral accommodation underscored the special status that Britain and the United States accorded themselves, and each other, in the post-World War I international system. It was indubitably contrary to the 'spirit' of what was to be a universal pact to renounce war.

Towards a transatlantic system of peaceful change? The Kellogg–Briand pact and the Locarno system

More significant for the evolution of transatlantic security relations, though, was the question of how far the treaty could not only be made compatible with but actually reinforce the existing Locarno system. While Chamberlain considered himself the essential mediator, it was Kellogg who really held the reins of the negotiating-process commencing in January 1928 to address that question. Not decisively, but noticeably, the American position was reinforced by Germany's unequivocal backing for Kellogg's design. More profoundly, what shaped the making of the Kellogg–Briand pact was one common interest

---

[35] Chamberlain memorandum to Kellogg, 19 May 1928, NA RG 59 711.4112 Anti-War 77; Hurst minute, 20 April 1928, *DBFP*, IA, V, no. 324. As ever a League advocate, Cecil severely criticised Britain's 'Monroe Doctrine'.
[36] Houghton to Kellogg, 25 May 1928, NA RG 59 711.4112 Anti-War.
[37] Chamberlain to Kellogg, 18 July 1928, NA RG 59 711.4112 Anti-War.

pursued by Washington, London and Berlin: the interest to make the pact an instrument for the promotion of peaceful change, not *status quo* preservation.

Crucially, however, the war-renunciation pact that gained contours in the spring and summer of 1928 would provide no mechanisms that could either serve to enforce its clauses or lead to more direct US engagement in settling the security questions at the heart of European concert diplomacy. Transatlantic deliberations soon centred on devising a treaty that indeed complemented this concert insofar as it promoted the pacific settlement of international disputes. But beyond this the Kellogg–Briand pact could not substantially contribute to fostering European security, at least not in the short term. In part, this was due to persistent, and unavoidable, tensions between German and French security strategies, which also shaped their pact policies. While German diplomacy sought to make the treaty a platform for peaceful change, Briand's preoccupation became to prevent it from increasing the fluidity of the European *status quo* and impinging on French alliance interests.

Chiefly, though, the limitations of the war-renunciation pact derived from persistent American reservations, which were further reinforced by British concerns. In Chamberlain's eyes, there was simply no prospect of obtaining Washington's support for any enforcement mechanisms; and there was no need for them as the Locarno concert provided precisely the kind of 'machinery' for settling disputes that Europe required.[38] The decisive American *caveat* remained indeed that the pact must not contain any 'universal' provisions that implied US commitments to European security.

Kellogg's counterproposal of December 1927 had played the ball back into France's court. As the US chargé Whitehouse reported from Paris, Briand was 'much disappointed' by the American reply 'as he had hoped it was possible to have a bilateral convention'.[39] And he was not yet prepared to accept the idea of a multilateral treaty.[40] But the French foreign minister had little alternative but to play the treaty game on Kellogg's terms if he wanted to salvage any aspect of his original initiative and avoid unwelcome domestic repercussions. He thus reacted swiftly, telling Whitehouse on 30 December that his 'attitude would be entirely sympathetic' if Kellogg wished to 'invite the leading states of the world' to sign a war-renunciation pact.[41]

On 1 January 1928, Castle asked Ambassador Claudel what effect an exclusive German–American treaty outlawing war would have in France. And Claudel had to concede that 'people would say that Germany was purchasing security from attack by the U.S. so that she could more readily attack her

[38] Chamberlain memorandum, 24 January 1928, *DBFP*, IA, IV, no. 262, pp. 510–14.
[39] Whitehouse to Kellogg, 31 December 1927, *FRUS 1927*, II, p. 630.
[40] Thus Claudel to Castle, Castle Diary, 1 January 1928, vol. 12, pp. 1–2.
[41] Whitehouse to Kellogg, 31 December 1927, *FRUS 1927*, II, p. 630.

neighbours.' 'Purchasing' security and support from the United States had indeed been a central motive for Briand's overture. But it was unmistakable that his initiative now began to backfire. In Castle's judgement, Briand had 'made his first suggestion for political reasons solely' and 'now got a bad case of cold feet'. They would be 'positively frozen' if Washington managed to 'make him do something' that 'on paper at least is a step toward [the] prevention of war'.[42]

But the *Quai d'Orsay* was not willing simply to follow suit. Briand's defensive tactics hinged on two elements, one procedural, the other substantial. Claudel was authorised to suggest that while France would gladly sign a 'renewed pact of friendship and arbitration' with the United States, both powers should work out a treaty between themselves and sign it first; only then should they 'invite' other states.[43] In terms of substance, Paris now faced the difficulty of averting negative repercussions of Kellogg's multilateral proposal on France's existing alliance commitments. To square this circle, Briand came to argue that the US draft threatened to weaken the League's collective security provisions because it proposed an unqualified outlawry of war instead of including specific provisions on 'the subject of aggressive war' and a definition of the aggressor. He therefore proposed that Kellogg's 'general draft' should be altered to exempt legitimate defensive wars, thus safeguarding French commitments to its eastern allies Poland and Czechoslovakia.[44] With Chamberlain's originally strong backing, Briand long defended these cardinal positions. But he could not afford to insist too adamantly on French terms if he wanted to rescue any prospects of drawing the United States closer to France.[45] The French foreign minister had to rescue what he could, also in relations with his Locarno partners, while trying to save face.

Kellogg immediately countered and checked Briand's new proposals. He told Claudel that signing a bilateral treaty first would be 'open to the objection' that it 'might for some reason be unacceptable to one of the other great Powers'. To prevent this, the views of all governments concerned should be 'accommodated through informal preliminary discussions'.[46] Yet the secretary of state also re-asserted his more fundamental objection. He declared that the Coolidge administration would refuse to conclude an exclusive pact that could be 'construed by other friendly Powers as in the nature of a defensive

---

[42] Castle Diary, 1 January 1928, vol. 12, pp. 2–3.
[43] Crewe to Chamberlain, 9 January 1928, *DBFP*, IA, IV, no. 249; Claudel to Kellogg, 5 January 1928, *FRUS 1928*, I, pp. 1–2.
[44] Crewe to Chamberlain, 5 and 9 January 1928, *DBFP*, IA, IV, nos. 246, 249; Claudel to Kellogg, 5 January 1928, *FRUS 1928*, I, pp. 1–2.
[45] Crewe to Chamberlain, 9 January 1928; Chamberlain memorandum, 24 January 1928; Howard to Chamberlain, 27 January 1928, *DBFP*, IA, IV, nos. 249, 262, 263.
[46] Kellogg to Claudel, 11 January 1928, *FRUS 1928*, I, pp. 3–5.

treaty with France' and would give France free rein in Europe by assuring it of American 'neutrality'.[47]

More broadly, Kellogg insisted that the envisaged treaty should not limit its scope to 'wars of aggression'. It indeed remained a core maxim of US pact policy that all signatories should 'unequivocally' renounce war 'as an instrument of national policy'. After the State Department had at first limited the circle of desirable signatories to the great naval powers, Kellogg for the first time mentioned Germany on 11 January 1928. Subsequently, including the German government became part and parcel of his strategy to pre-empt a bilateral pact and win the consent of all European powers to America's design. Castle seconded the secretary of state. Alluding to the envisaged arbitration treaty with France, he told the new German ambassador Friedrich von Prittwitz on 10 February that he 'should be very glad to have a similar treaty with Germany'.[48]

Profound parallel interests? Kellogg's pact proposal and Germany's policy of peaceful change

The demonstratively swift and affirmative reaction of German diplomacy underscored how keenly Stresemann felt that Kellogg's multilateral pact proposal presented Berlin with a real opportunity. This applied even more to Schubert who came to oversee German pact policy in the spring of 1928. In the eyes of both policymakers, aligning Germany with the American plans was in part desirable because they could serve to weaken France's eastern alliance system by limiting French options to come to the aid of its partners. Schubert quickly sought to seize upon Kellogg's proposal to achieve this. He held that Germany's main concern could not be to safeguard formal possibilities for waging offensive war; rather, it should be to 'devalue as far as possible the superior position of military power of states like France through legal commitments'.[49]

More importantly, however, the American overture seemed to open up a possibility to further a cardinal strategic interest of German policy. As particularly Schubert reckoned, it could be used to involve Washington, as far as possible, in attempts to establish enhanced international rules for the peaceable settlement of disputes – including agreements on eventual border revisions in eastern Europe. In this sense, the rationale behind what Schubert

---

[47] Howard to Chamberlain, 27 January 1928, *DBFP*, IA, IV, no. 263, p. 527.
[48] Kellogg to Claudel, 11 January 1928, *FRUS 1928*, I, pp. 4–5; Castle Diary, 10 February 1928, vol. 12, p. 36.
[49] Schubert directives, 12 January 1928; Schubert to Hoesch, 19 January 1928; Stresemann memorandum, 13 April 1928, *ADAP*, B, VIII, pp. 34ff, 64, 486–7; *AR Marx III und IV*, no. 463.

and Stresemann came to pursue was to promote exactly the opposite of what Briand's initial proposal had intended. In the German view, the war-renunciation treaty could become a critical complement to the Locarno pact, an instrument for widening the corridors of internationally acceptable alterations in the postwar *status quo*. At the same time, the German Foreign Office calculated that successful pact negotiations might also reinvigorate the dead-locked arms limitation talks at Geneva – and strengthen US support for German disarmament policy.[50]

Yet Berlin's espousal of the US war-renunciation agenda was of course also motivated by a further, and weightier, concern, relevant both in the short and in the long term. It sprang quite logically from the 'grand strategy' Stresemann had pursued since the turning-point of 1923. In short, the pact offered Germany an important opportunity to stand 'should to shoulder' with the power whose support would again be indispensable for achieving a satisfactory 'final settlement' of reparations. The reparations agent Parker Gilbert had just outlined the contours of such a settlement in December 1927, thereby placing it on the international agenda. And Stresemann seized on this constellation to win the support of the Marx cabinet for Kellogg's pact proposal. As he duly warned his colleagues, any suspicion that Germany was linking up with France in forming an anti-American front had to be avoided by all means. The Marx government authorised the foreign minister to proceed without delay. And Germany would in fact be the first power to declare its 'unconditional acceptance' of the Kellogg–Briand pact, a demonstration of goodwill that was well received in Washington.[51]

There were fundamental convergences between German and American conceptions of peaceful change. Both were directed against French plans to fortify a rigid system of collective security *de facto* allowing France to maintain its power-political preponderance in Europe as long as possible. And both sought to supersede such plans with strategies that aimed to create a far less rigid international order, an order permitting gradual adjustments to improve security yet also to accommodate other national interests.[52] This general German–American accord was underlined by the conclusion of a bilateral arbitration treaty on 5 May 1928.

Stresemann's support for Schubert's pact strategy indicated that he endorsed the under-secretary's longer-term objectives. Germany was to contribute to

[50] Stresemann circular to German embassies, 12 January 1928; *ADAP*, B, VIII, no. 18. Cf. Krüger (1985a), pp. 386ff.

[51] Cabinet minutes, 19 and 27 April 1928, *AR Marx III und IV*, nos. 463, 466; Kellogg to Coolidge, 13 July 1928, Kellogg Papers, roll 31.

[52] Schubert to Hoesch, 19 January 1928, Schubert directives, 12 January 1928, *ADAP*, B, VIII, pp. 34ff, 62–4.

making the war-renunciation pact the nucleus of a wider Euro-Atlantic security system – a Locarno system that also gradually integrated the United States. Ultimately, this approach indeed had the potential of transforming Weimar Germany's policy of revision into 'a comprehensive policy of conciliation with the other great powers and a generally accepted procedure of international law'.[53] Stresemann could not fulfil such high hopes prior to his death. But to the end he maintained a definition of peaceful change that was reconcilable with American, British and – if less so – French and Polish approaches. As the German foreign minister put it in September 1929, he worked towards 'preventing a rigidifying of all conditions by fostering a positive evolution by peaceful means' in postwar Europe.[54]

Yet it should not be overlooked that parallel interests between Germany and the United States would quickly have reached their limits if German policymakers had shown tendencies of pursuing a more aggressive revision agenda. Both Stresemann and Schubert realised that this especially applied to initiatives that, in Washington's perception, threatened to unsettle European stability rather than strengthen it, at least in the short term – chiefly stepped-up pursuits of territorial revisions vis-à-vis Poland. American reservations towards German attempts to put economic pressure on Warsaw in 1926 had been a clear sign. Indeed, there were still marked, and unavoidable, discrepancies between what Germany sought to advance and what not only France but also less influential powers like Poland sought to decelerate or even block. In fact, the Polish foreign minister Zaleski had presented his own proposal for a non-aggression pact during the League assembly's autumn session in September 1927. What he outlined was designed to reinforce the *status quo* in eastern Europe. Predictably, though, Zaleski's proposals were not welcomed by either Germany or Britain, and they received only lukewarm French support, because they again raised the irksome issue of guarantees for the Polish–German border.[55]

In May 1928, the Polish foreign minister conveyed to Chamberlain 'in a vein of light sarcasm' that the Pilsudski government in principle favoured the idea of a war-renunciation treaty along the lines that Kellogg had proposed. Yet Zaleski also contrasted the enthusiastic response the US initiative had received with the 'chilly reception given to the almost identical suggestion' he had made in Geneva. He underlined Warsaw's concerns over 'the settled policy of Germany', confirmed by Stresemann's embrace of the pact, 'to enlarge the scope of arbitration as eventually to embrace territorial questions definitely settled in the Treaty of Versailles'. He made clear that the Pilsudski

---

[53] Krüger (1974), p. 257; Stresemann statement, 27 April 1928, *AR Marx III und IV*, no. 466.
[54] Stresemann speech to the League assembly, 9 September 1929, Stresemann (1929), pp. 67–71.
[55] Stresemann memorandum, May 1928, *ADAP*, B, VIII, pp. 468ff.

government remained highly wary of German ambitions to refer to arbitration 'at some future date . . . such matters as the return to her of the Polish corridor'. Polish reservations to the pact could eventually be removed. But the deeper worries of Germany's eastern neighbours, including those of Czechoslovakia, had not (yet) disappeared.[56]

For international policymakers on all sides the key task remained to create a framework in which mutually acceptable changes not only became possible but also conducive to European stability. And one cardinal problem in meeting this task – if it could be met at all – remained unaltered as well: it was the problem of widening the commitments of all great powers, yet particularly Britain and America, to a still fledgling European security system. The Soviet Union, for that matter, never even took part in the negotiations over the Kellogg–Briand Pact, and did not sign it.

The final road to the pact to renounce war

The *grand jeu* of transatlantic diplomacy over the war-renunciation treaty not only showed how central Washington's behaviour remained for any advances in post-World War I security politics. It also shed a striking light on the tensions that the Locarno concert confronted in the latter 1920s. Above all, the concert's protagonists had to preserve its cohesion while balancing the high stakes involved in each power's relations with the American world creditor. And they had to cope with the structural pressures exerted by Germany's pursuit of accelerated peaceful change and French efforts to impede it.

On 6 February 1928, France and the United States agreed on a new treaty of friendship and arbitration, essentially following the State Department's line.[57] But the wider questions of war-renunciation remained in dispute – albeit with the balance shifting inexorably in favour of Kellogg's proposal. Kellogg was well aware that what lay behind Briand's objections to his treaty blueprint were the very alliance obligations in eastern Europe that the State Department considered detrimental in the first place. The American secretary of state essentially sought to overcome French opposition by making France's Locarno obligations the central reference-point. On 27 February, Kellogg told Claudel that, in his interpretation, the 'difference between the bilateral and multilateral form of treaty' seemed 'one of degree and not of substance'. He could not see how a multilateral pact should violate France's obligations as a League member and signatory of Locarno, which Claudel had raised as stumbling-blocks. If

---

[56] Erskine (Warsaw) to Chamberlain, 22 May 1928, *DBFP*, IA, V, no. 354. On Poland and the Kellogg–Briand pact see Larroche to Briand, 24 August 1928, no. 336, MAE Série Europe, Pologne, vol. 113. Cf. Wandycz (1988), pp. 121–4.
[57] Cf. McKercher (1984), p. 105.

they did violate them, however, this would equally apply to a bilateral 'unqualified anti-war treaty'.[58]

Britain certainly did not desire to reinforce French *status quo* politics. But, for the sake of the Anglo-French *entente*, and the Locarno pact, Chamberlain saw it as his duty to accommodate Briand's interests as far as possible. *De facto*, though, Britain clearly gravitated towards accepting the American treaty, once minor revisions had been made, and the Foreign Office's main concern became to re-establish common ground within the European concert. Because he took Briand's concerns seriously Chamberlain insisted till mid-May that the revised American draft treaty, sent to London in late February, had to be modified as it was still 'incompatible both with the terms of the covenant of the League' and Locarno.[59]

In charting a new course to reconcile British obligations under Locarno and vis-à-vis France with the envisaged pact, the British foreign secretary again relied on Hurst's recommendations. Hurst had at first been optimistic that the American treaty proposal would not prejudice Locarno or the Covenant as long as certain conditions were met. As with respect to the Monroe Doctrine, however, Hurst subsequently altered his assessment, suggesting important *caveats*. On 20 April, he recommended that Britain should reject Kellogg's revised draft, because in its present form it could weaken rather than complement the Locarno treaty. Hurst concluded that the US blueprint would collide with the central premise of Locarno-style collective security as, ultimately, a signatory that came to the aid of a pact partner attacked by a third party could be held in breach of the new treaty.[60]

In short, Hurst thus advised Chamberlain to insist, first, on including all Locarno powers into it and, second, on incorporating a provision that released the other signatories from their obligations should one of them break the pact. He concluded that, if these conditions were fulfilled, the pact could actually strengthen the Locarno edifice. Concretely, Britain could then legitimately aid France or Belgium if Germany attacked either of these powers.[61] This was to be Chamberlain's platform vis-à-vis Kellogg. The British foreign secretary eventually found the formula that whereas the 'purpose' of British war-prevention policy was the same as Washington's, Britain's position, interests and 'duties' as a Locarno power 'differed from those of the United States'.[62]

---

[58] Kellogg to Claudel, 27 February 1928, *FRUS 1928*, I, pp. 9–10.
[59] Chamberlain memorandum, 24 January 1928, *DBFP*, IA, IV, 1928, no. 262, p. 511; Chamberlain to Lindsay, 27 April 1928, Chamberlain to Howard, 26 April 1928, *DBFP*, IA, V, no. 326, 325; Houghton to Kellogg, 27 April 1928, NA RG 59 711.4112 Anti-War/15.
[60] Hurst memorandum, 15 March 1928, Hurst minute, 20 April 1928, *DBFP*, IA, V, nos. 314, 324.
[61] Hurst minute, 20 April 1928, *DBFP*, IA, V, no. 324.
[62] Chamberlain to Howard, 26 April 1928, *DBFP*, IA, V, no. 325, p. 631.

By this time, the *Quai d'Orsay* had accepted that it would be impossible to obtain a treaty that met France's main condition, only banning a 'war of aggression'. More broadly, the Poincaré government had to acknowledge that whatever compromise would ultimately be forged was unlikely to bolster France's position as a European *status quo* power. To limit further damages, Briand basically fell in line behind Britain's position. Yet both he and Chamberlain were also aware that Berlin took a different view, deeming Kellogg's draft reconcilable with all existing treaty obligations under Locarno and the League Covenant. Seeking to revive a Locarno concert badly frayed during the early stages of the pact negotiations, Chamberlain in late April proposed a meeting of jurists to resolve differences 'in accordance with Locarno procedure'. And he asked Stresemann to send Gaus to London to confer with Hurst.[63]

But while the German side responded favourably Kellogg rejected this overture. He viewed with 'disfavour' attempts to finalise the pact in a high-profile conference where the Europeans might close ranks against Washington. The secretary of state thus conveyed to Chamberlain that he desired to approach the treaty 'from a broad point of view, not a narrow legalistic one'. He thought it 'absurd' to determine the 'question whether the nations of the world should renounce war' by a jurists' commission. Subsequently, Chamberlain promised to 'call . . . off' the meeting. Yet in early July, Hurst and the French legal expert Fromageot nevertheless went on a secret mission to confer with Gaus in Berlin and co-ordinate the Locarno powers' positions. And all three agreed on a common platform.[64]

While Chamberlain and Stresemann remained cautious to avoid any semblance of a European understanding behind Washington's back, Locarno procedures had thus ultimately produced the desired modicum of unity. Yet the jurists only had to resolve details. On the central stage of transatlantic diplomacy London and Washington managed to settle their core differences over the treaty remarkably quickly in the spring of 1928. And Kellogg set the tone. This left Briand little leverage to redirect the negotiations. Between mid-March and late April, the US secretary of state embarked on a series of diplomatic and public initiatives to forge a treaty that not only Britain but also France and its east European allies could accept. German and Japanese assent could already be taken for granted at that stage. In substance, however, Kellogg

---

[63] Chamberlain memorandum, 24 January 1928, *DBFP*, IA, IV, 1928, no. 262; Claudel letter to Kellogg, 5 January 1928, *FRUS 1928*, I, pp. 1–2; Chamberlain to Lindsay, 27 April 1928, *DBFP*, IA, V, no. 326; Houghton to Kellogg, 3 May 1928, NA RG 59 711.4112 Anti-War 29.

[64] Kellogg to Houghton, 30 April 1928, *FRUS 1928*, I, pp. 41–2; Houghton to Kellogg, 3 May 1928, NA RG 59 711.4112 Anti-War 29; Hurst to Chamberlain, 9 July 1928, *DBFP*, IA, V, pp. 764–7. Cf. McKercher (1984), pp. 123–4.

never lost sight of his underlying aims to preserve the pact's universal scope and to minimise any concrete commitments that it could entail. His efforts culminated in a speech before the American Society of International Law in Washington on 28 April.[65]

On the key questions, Kellogg had already laid down his essentials in mid-March. In a speech before the Council on Foreign Relations, he had reiterated his objection to limiting the anti-war treaty to 'mere wars of aggression'. And he had approvingly cited Chamberlain's recent memorandum to the League's Preparatory Commission, which stated that any attempt to define the aggressor would be 'a trap for the innocent and a signpost for the guilty'. Kellogg insisted that introducing any 'exceptions and qualifications' in this respect, which could always be contested, would 'greatly weaken' the pact's effect. As he had earlier told Ambassador Claudel, its 'positive value as a guaranty of peace' would be 'virtually destroyed'.[66]

Instead, preceding Hurst, Kellogg proposed his own solution as to how the pact could complement the Locarno accords. On 19 March, he noted that it 'would be an easy way around' the Anglo-French objections 'for each party of the Locarno treaty to sign' the proposed pact. More specifically, the State Department recommended that its first signatories should also include Belgium, Poland and Czechoslovakia. If any of these powers subsequently violated the pact, Locarno's guarantees could again become operative and '[n]obody [would] claim that the proposed treaty prevents anybody from defending itself in any event'. Thus, both pacts could be reconciled without any undesirable reference to 'definitions of aggressor'.[67] This was essentially the case that Kellogg then publicly made in his speech to the American Society of International Law.

Reacting favourably to these pronouncements, Chamberlain wrote on 19 May that he now 'saw eye to eye' with Kellogg on the pact and that the British government would support it 'to the utmost of their power'. The British foreign secretary no longer saw any 'serious divergence' between the French and American drafts. Having 'carefully considered' French concerns, he welcomed Kellogg's assurance that Washington regarded the right of self-defence as 'inalienable' and respected Locarno's obligations. On this understanding, the final war-renunciation treaty indeed merely included a 'broad statement of principle, to proclaim without restriction or qualification that war shall not be used as an instrument of policy'.[68] This compromise paved the way for the

---

[65] Kellogg speech, 28 April 1928, Kellogg Papers; Kellogg to Houghton, 30 April 1928, *FRUS 1928*, I, pp. 41–2.

[66] Kellogg speech, 15 March 1928, Kellogg Papers, roll 31; Kellogg to Claudel, 11 January 1928, *FRUS 1928*, I, p. 5.

[67] Kellogg to Wickersham, 19 March 1928, Kellogg Papers, roll 31.

[68] Chamberlain to Kellogg, 19 May 1928, NA RG 59 711.4112 Anti-War 77.

high-profile ceremony in Paris where, on 28 August, the Kellogg–Briand pact was signed. Kellogg clearly relished the prestige that the pact brought him and the Republican administration. As he confided to Senator Borah, that all major powers attended the ceremony amounted to an 'impressive demonstration' of the American government's success.[69]

The Kellogg–Briand pact and the limits of transatlantic security politics – an appraisal

When all was basically decided, Kellogg characterised the negotiations with France as 'a good piece of bargaining' in which he had turned Briand's original proposal for a 'bilateral treaty' into a 'multilateral scheme'. And he stressed that the pact sprang from 'one of the fundamental policies of this administration which has been earnestly endorsed by both Mr. Coolidge and Mr. Hoover' – the policy 'to make any "reasonable move"' to 'prevent a recurrence of such a calamity as was inflicted upon the world in 1914'.[70] Kellogg conceded that neither the pact nor the conciliation and arbitration agreements that Washington had signed could afford 'a certain guarantee' against future international conflicts. But he maintained that they could buttress peace by arousing 'public conscience against the utter horror and frightfulness of war'. And ultimately statesmen could only 'abolish' war if they created conditions in which 'the peoples of the world' enjoyed prosperity and 'a peaceful mind'.[71]

That the pact was essentially concluded on US terms undoubtedly went against the grain of Briand's efforts to solidify the European situation. That it furthered cardinal interests of the evolutionary policy devised by Stresemann and Schubert was unmistakable. This was registered with dismay in Paris and satisfaction in Berlin. Yet the main concern in both capitals was the impact of the treaty on the real *grand jeu* of transatlantic relations in the latter 1920s: the revision of the Dawes settlement.[72] The emphasis of the British evaluation of the pact was somewhat different. Chamberlain could rightly claim that he had managed 'to guard the Covenant & Locarno'. And he had indeed effectively 'built a bridge for the French' by fostering a compromise between Washington and Paris. In the foreign secretary's final assessment, the resultant

[69] *Ibid.*; Houghton to Kellogg, 19 May 1928, NA RG 59 711.4112 Anti-War 77; Toynbee and Macartney (1924–30), 1928, pp. 1–47; Kellogg to Borah, 16 and 19 July 1928, Kellogg Papers, roll 31.

[70] Kellogg to Borah, 27 July 1928, Kellogg to Reid, 19 July 1928, Kellogg Papers, roll 31.

[71] Kellogg, 'The War Prevention Policy of the United States', 15 March 1928, Kellogg Papers, roll 31.

[72] Stresemann report to the cabinet, *AR Marx III und IV*, no. 463; 'The End of the Poincaré Ministry, June 1928 – 11 November 1928', Herriot Papers, vol. 3. Cf. Pitts (1987), p. 248.

pact could be an 'additional bulwark to what had been accomplished at Locarno'.[73]

Yet the Kellogg–Briand pact's limits with respect to European security were also clearly perceived, not only by British policymakers. Chamberlain reminded Kellogg that there was still one decisive difference between the new treaty and the Locarno accords: Locarno's 'machinery' went 'further than a renunciation of war', because it provided 'certain sanctions for a breach of their obligations'.[74] This constituted 'the burden of the guarantee' that Britain had undertaken in 1925. In Chamberlain's view, this 'machinery' and guarantee remained the cornerstones of Europe's postwar order, well effective without additional US involvement. And the Republican administration in Washington neither desired nor was in a domestic position to share the British 'burden'.

Indeed, the Kellogg–Briand pact did not (yet) complete the logic of Locarno in a sense corresponding with the aspirations of some of its American proponents – and Schubert.[75] Kellogg's engagement, pursued in consonance with Republican Progressive policy, did not signify that America was 'ready once more to take her place in the world's councils'.[76] Above all, it did not mean that the Coolidge administration was willing to play a more active role in European security. Towards domestic critics, particularly in Congress, Kellogg could underscore that the pact by no means implied that Washington now 'recognised' the Versailles treaty or the League. It remained crucial for the administration that the pact would not embroil it in the 'squabbles of Continental Europe'. As the secretary of state had told Robert McCormick of the *Chicago Tribune* on 21 July, the United States would neither sign up to 'any affirmative obligations of the Locarno Treaties' nor 'become involved in any obligation to apply sanctions' against a violator of the war-renunciation treaty.[77]

In sum, Kellogg's approach to the pact underscored the underlying continuity of Republican security policy. No one among the administration's principal policymakers had seen the pact negotiations as an opening for extending America's role in the stabilisation of the postwar Euro-Atlantic order – and US financial interests in Europe. The Coolidge administration had managed to reinforce its maxims of informal, ultimately non-committal yet publicly impressive measures to promote peace. In the Republican perception, Washington was globalising US standards of pacific settlement and conflict resolution; yet

---

[73] Austen to Ida Chamberlain, 9 July, 20 May 1928, Austen Chamberlain Papers, AC 5/1/ 459, 454.

[74] Chamberlain to Kellogg, 19 May 1928, NA RG 59 711.4112 Anti-War 77.

[75] Shotwell, 'An American Locarno', June 1927 [?], Kellogg Papers, roll 27.

[76] *Observer*, 15 April 1928, NA RG 59 711.4112 Anti-War 22.

[77] Kellogg to Reid, 19 July 1928, Kellogg to McCormick, 21 July 1928, Kellogg Papers, roll 31.

there were still no security interests at stake in Europe that warranted more far-reaching commitments to reinforce such standards. Unless a fundamental crisis and change in the transatlantic constellation occurred, this set distinct limits on widening the European nucleus into a transatlantic security system. Indeed, the Kellogg–Briand pact would mark the greatest extent of US engagement on behalf of war-prevention – not only in the 1920s but, essentially, before Hitler's challenge to the international order in the 1930s and the postwar planning of the 1940s.

The unresolved disarmament problem and the abiding challenge of European insecurity

In the short term, more fundamental security divergences prevailed, not only between the 'old' and the 'new world' but also within Europe. They had become particularly apparent when one month prior to the high-spirited signing of the war-renunciation pact, France and Britain agreed on a disarmament compromise that highly irritated both Washington and Berlin. Aggravating the consequences of the abortive Geneva conference, it sparked a real crisis in Anglo-American relations in the second half of 1928. And, as the new British ambassador Horace Rumbold reported from Berlin, it greatly 'disturbed' the German government. Stresemann not only saw the Anglo-French disarmament compromise as proof of resurgent *entente* thinking. He also feared that Britain had made far-reaching concessions to France 'in regard to land armaments'.[78]

Any prospects that a universal disarmament convention might emerge from the work of the Preparatory Commission had dimmed even further in the spring of 1928. In view of this dilemma, and of what London perceived as Washington's immense pressure to accept US terms in the cruiser dispute, a basic Anglo-French understanding had emerged. On 25 July, the Baldwin cabinet endorsed an earlier compromise between British and French naval representatives. To Kellogg's consternation, Chamberlain announced this in the Commons on 30 July – before communicating it to Washington, thus presenting him with a *fait accompli* and, as Marriner observed, 'something of a bomb-shell'. *Nota bene*, the German Locarno partner had also been presented with a *fait accompli*. Concretely, France accepted the British position that new naval restrictions should only apply to larger cruisers above a certain size (10,000 tons), whereas they would not apply to the smaller class of cruisers that the British government deemed vital for imperial defence. In return,

---

[78] Rumbold to Chamberlain, 4 August 1928; Cardogan memorandum, 2 February 1928, *DBFP*, IA, IV, nos. 429, 267. Cf. McKercher (1984), pp. 150–70.

Britain backed the French core demand of neither imposing any limits on the number of a country's, i.e. France's, trained military reservists nor including them in the overall calculation of force levels, and, more broadly, the Baldwin government endorsed the French land disarmament agenda.[79]

That Chamberlain backed this compromise, and thus risked further estrangement from Washington after Geneva, also stemmed from his fear that France and the United States might reach a naval agreement isolating Britain. Essentially, though, his decision sprang from the basic rationale of his Locarno policy.[80] As the British foreign secretary had emphasised after meeting Joseph Paul-Boncour at Geneva on 9 June, the preoccupations that they and Schubert had were 'the same': 'Unless we make some progress in the question of disarmament we shall be faced inevitably by Germany's repudiation of the disarmament provisions' of 1919. And this would have unpredictable consequences for 'the immediate and future peace of the world'. Germany had accepted the original provisions of the Versailles treaty only 'under duress' and it only 'respected them in the hope that they were but the first step to a general limitation of armaments'. As Chamberlain saw it, a complete breakdown of the Geneva talks would provoke a situation in which Berlin would no longer feel under any 'moral obligation' to observe Versailles' disarmament regime. It would practically become 'a dead letter'.[81]

The British chancellor of the exchequer, Churchill, had earlier proposed a power-political remedy for this dilemma. He spoke out against disarming France, arguing that the main continental power should remain 'so strong as to deprive Germany of any prospect of success and therefore of any wish to break the peace'. But Chamberlain opposed such a course for fear that it would sooner or later only spur German rearmament efforts. Also mindful of the importance that British public opinion attached to disarmament, the foreign secretary thus insisted on 'the international dangers' that would arise from a 'complete breakdown' of the Preparatory Commission's talks.[82] This position was shared by his key advisers at the Foreign Office, notably Orme Sargent.

Sargent warned Chamberlain that if the disarmament negotiations collapsed 'the Germans [would] seize this opportunity of fishing in troubled waters'. He held that Germany was not actually seeking a 'cancellation' of 'military clauses' of the Versailles treaty to 're-introduce military service' and restore its massive prewar armament industries. For such a 'retrogressive policy' would 'arouse

---

[79] Cabinet minutes, 25 July 1928, CAB 23/58, CC 41 (28); Chamberlain to Chilton, Dormer, Grahame, 30 July 1928; Cushendun to Chilton, 10 August 1928, *DBFP*, IA, IV, nos. 428, 440. Cf. Carlton (1968/9), pp. 141–62.
[80] This has been rightly stressed in Grayson (1997), p. 160.
[81] Chamberlain memorandum, 9 June 1928, *DBFP*, IA, IV, no. 377; Cardogan memorandum, 2 February 1928, *DBFP*, IA, IV, no. 267.
[82] Chamberlain to Cushendun, 9 June 1928, FO 800/262.

the fiercest opposition among those political parties & classes who dread the return of Prussian militarism'. More likely, Berlin would 'adopt a purely opportunist policy', putting public pressure on the ex-allied powers to meet their alleged obligations to disarm 'down to the level of Germany'. This could engender a 'gradual process' allowing the Germans to 'step by step resume their liberty without having to make any formal demand'.[83]

Chamberlain had never considered the League's universal approach to disarmament promising. But he concluded that France and Britain were 'prisoners of past decisions'. And, following Sargent's advice, he maintained that the British government had every interest in preventing the Geneva talks from ending without any result. Characteristically, however, the foreign secretary reckoned 'on grounds of high policy' that this could only be achieved by first forging a common disarmament platform with Paris.[84] Yet the Anglo-French compromise proved counterproductive and short-sighted. It not only split the Locarno concert – if only temporarily – but also thwarted any more far-reaching Anglo-American co-operation on disarmament, at or beyond Geneva.

When after a break of nearly two years the final round of the Preparatory Commission's talks opened in April 1929, it soon became clear that any German hopes of approaching 'armament parity' by way of inducing the other powers, and chiefly France, to disarm were receding into the distance. By this time, French policy sought a general arms-limitation convention that instead of prescribing arms reduction essentially fixed the armament levels of 1929 – *rebus sic stantibus* – for an interim period of several years. Paris also still insisted on linking land and naval disarmament, resisting American pressure to forge a naval settlement outside the Geneva negotiations.

After Washington's opposition to any naval compromise had basically rendered the Anglo-French bargain of 1928 useless, British policymakers found their influence on Paris on the critical land-armament issues severely constrained. But they basically kept supporting the French line. Like Washington, London first and foremost sought a separate agreement that finally laid to rest the Anglo-American quarrels over the future of the Washington system. To improve the chances for this, the American delegation at Geneva in late April 1929 effectively broke off the always tenuous alliance of expedience with Germany. Abandoning its former resistance, it sided with France on the most controversial issue of the envisaged final disarmament convention: Gibson endorsed the premise that the British delegation had already accepted, namely that trained reserves (notably those of France) would not feature as a category

[83] Sargent memorandum, 7 February 1928, *DBFP*, IA, IV, no. 269.

[84] Chamberlain memorandum, 9 June 1928, *DBFP*, IA, IV, no. 377; Chamberlain to Cushendun, 9 June 1928, NAL., FO 800/262.

in the assessment of international armament levels, i.e. basically be excluded from any disarmament convention.

As a consequence, Germany now faced a common front at Geneva. With increasing calls to pursue a more assertive policy, even in the *Auswärtige Amt*, Stresemann and Schubert confronted a situation that offered few alternatives. Should their efforts to obtain French disarmament fail, both favoured a modest German re-armament to achieve greater military 'equality', which they deemed consistent with Germany's new Locarno status. Their maxim remained to seek an international compromise that did not undermine the European concert. And Germany remained represented at the Geneva talks. But nothing even approaching a 'general convention' on disarmament could be envisaged.[85]

The basic problem underlying the frustration of disarmament efforts in the 1920s remained unchanged. In essence, it was and remained a problem that could only be 'solved' in the longer term, on the basis of what the Foreign Office's disarmament expert Cardogan in February 1928 called a greater 'sense of security'. In Cardogan's assessment, the victors had pledged in 1919 and thereafter that they would follow German disarmament with voluntary force-reductions 'to "the lowest point consistent with national safety"'. And, unlike France, Britain had actually reduced its army to levels far lower than those of 1914. But neither power had pledged to support a 'reduction to the German level' or a 'general convention for all-round proportional reduction of armaments'.[86] Cardogan pointed to what was and remained the *crux*: German disarmament, even 'carried to the point to which we believed it has been carried', did not yet 'produce sufficient sense of security' that enabled other European nations, and particularly France, to disarm.[87] But nor could the Locarno system – yet – provide the requisite foundations and environment for greater security. While Washington no longer placed any hope in the Geneva talks, these fundamentals continued to contravene all US pressure on France to use its 'horrendous' armament expenses for more productive purposes.[88]

It was Chamberlain's policy of *rapprochement* with the American government *after* the Anglo-French compromise of 1928 that came to prepare the ground for the landmark Anglo-American agreement on naval ratios. It was finally reached at the London naval conference, held from January till April 1930. Yet the breakthrough on the path to London only came after direct negotiations between the new British premier MacDonald and the new US president Hoover in the autumn of 1929. At the following naval summit, both powers

---

[85] Foreign Office memorandum, 16 August 1928, *ADAP*, B, IX, no. 236. Cf. Krüger (1985a), pp. 435–6.

[86] Cardogan memorandum, 2 February 1928, *DBFP*, IA, IV, no. 267.

[87] *Ibid.*

[88] Kellogg to Borah, 27 July 1928, Kellogg Papers, roll 31.

agreed to accommodate their cardinal cruiser interests while fundamentally upholding the 5:5:3 ratio with Japan, which remained the cornerstone of the Washington system. The United States was allowed to build a higher percentage of heavier cruisers; in return, Britain could build a proportionately higher share of lighter cruisers, still deemed integral to imperial defence. Washington and London also finally settled their long-standing dispute over belligerent rights. Characteristically, at the end of the first decade after the Great War, Britain and the United States thus finally managed to establish ground-rules for a bilateral settlement in an area that both powers considered strategically vital: naval arms control. But they could not underpin a wider framework for security and disarmament – at least not a framework beyond the confines of Locarno and the war-renunciation treaty of 1928.[89]

In the shorter term, however, the successful negotiations over the Kellogg–Briand pact had more tangible consequences, if in a different area. They set the stage for a more consequential development than the fruitless disarmament discussions: the making of the 'final' grand bargain of Euro-Atlantic international politics before the Great Depression. It hinged on the revision of the Dawes regime and, unachievable without it, the termination of the Rhineland occupation.

---

[89] See *DBFP*, IA, VI, nos. 359–434; MacDonald memoranda, 25 June and 4 October 1929, MacDonald to Dawes, 9 September 1929, *DBFP*, II, I, pp. 10–11, 106–7, 69–71; Hoover (1952a), pp. 345–6; *FRUS 1929*, III, pp. 1–37. Cf. McKercher (1984), pp. 171–99, and (1999), pp. 32–62; Carlton (1970), pp. 72ff.

25   The initiation of the Young process
The final bid to fortify the system of London
and Locarno

The pre-history of the Young plan and the settlement ending the Rhineland occupation, which were both finalised at the first Hague conference in August 1929, has often been portrayed as a history of decline, not only in European politics but also in transatlantic stabilisation efforts. Unavoidably, later interpretations have been coloured by what occurred so shortly thereafter: the outbreak of the Great Depression and the demise of the post-World War I international order.[1]

With regard to European diplomacy, an ever sharper deterioration of Locarno politics has been delineated, with all sides becoming ever more uncompromising under mounting domestic pressures. And attention has been drawn to Stresemann's feeling so disappointed in 1929 that at one point, though rescinding it later, he spoke of the western powers' 'deception' of Germany and the failure of his own Locarno policy. Is it indeed justified to conclude that the co-operation between the Locarno powers was abandoned long before the World Economic Crisis escalated? Was Locarno diplomacy already degenerating into an ever fiercer Franco-German competition for political and financial preponderance that Britain could no longer mediate?[2] By contrast, American policies in this critical period have been described as 'old approaches' in changing times – attempts to repeat the informal strategies adopted in forging the London settlement of 1924, especially in the promotion of the Young plan.[3]

A more critical interpretation has placed US and European efforts in 1928 and 1929 in a different, already familiar continuity, that of the 'misguided' approaches of the mid-1920s. In this assessment, they finally undermined any prospects of enforcing the Versailles system, basically setting the stage for the

---

[1] Nonetheless, the Dawes and Young settlements have never been systematically compared. For US policy see Leffler (1979), pp. 158ff; Costigliola (1984), pp. 196ff; for the reparations problem see Kent (1989), pp. 287ff; for the French and German perspectives see Knipping (1987), pp. 32–93; Heyde (1998), pp. 35–75.
[2] See Jacobson (1972b), pp. 239ff; Knipping (1987), pp. 220–1.
[3] See Leffler (1979), pp. 194–219; Link (1970), pp. 411ff.

destruction of international order in the 1930s. In other words, was Europe's deceptive interlude of peace now coming to its inevitable close – *before* the Great Depression?[4] There has also been a scathing critique of the Young process from two different angles – reparations diplomacy and international finance. It has been concluded that the Young plan was 'foredoomed to failure' because the policies of the interested powers, yet chiefly the domestic constraints that decisionmakers faced, only permitted short-lived compromises.[5] And it has been asserted that the financial flaws of the new reparation – and debt – regime were so grave that it had to collapse.[6] Were these the spheres where the critical fault-lines of postwar stabilisation now surfaced?

Indeed, the domestic road-blocks on the path to further international accommodation were becoming ever more daunting, especially in Germany. There, the increasingly radical opposition to the entire orientation of Stresemann's *Westpolitik* culminated in the referendum against the Young plan instigated by the press magnate Alfred Hugenberg and Hitler (even though it failed) in December 1929.[7] Yet the crux was not how far financial experts could finally propose a 'rational', financially coherent reparations scheme. Any 'final' reparations settlement remained irreducibly bound up with decisive political considerations on all sides. It not only involved core inter-state debt concerns on the part of the ex-allied powers but also core revision interests on the part of Germany, both regarding reparations and the Rhineland. As will be shown, politics even gained a new pre-eminence between early 1928 and the summer of 1929 as compared with the crisis situation of 1923.

The reparations conundrum could not just be 'liquidated' for good. Even in retrospect it remains highly doubtful whether financial experts could ever have found an 'objective formula' to determine Germany's 'real' capacity to pay that could have been accepted as 'fair' not only by the creditors but also by the debtor. At best, they could provide more or less equitable recommendations. Crucially, however, it was the task of policymakers to build on such recommendations and forge – as far as possible – a balanced *political* settlement. This was not only particularly challenging because decisionmakers on both sides of the Atlantic, yet especially in Berlin and Paris, faced generally more adverse domestic constellations than in the mid-1920s. All principal powers would be particularly hard-pressed to make substantial concessions in a period when in all four critical countries elections were due or expected between the spring of

[4] See Marks (2002), pp. 295–8; Bell (1986), pp. 31–47.
[5] Kent (1989), p. 287.
[6] These questions certainly featured prominently in the contemporary debate. See Hoover address, 15 October 1928, Hoover Papers, Commerce, 1928; Strong to Gilbert, 7 November 1925, Norman to Strong, 2 February 1926, Strong Papers, 1012.1, 1116.6/2; Leffingwell to Lamont, 20 July 1927, Lamont Papers, 103–12. Cf. Eichengreen (1992), pp. 241–6.
[7] Cf. Heyde (1998), pp. 65–75.

1928 and the spring of 1929. What was therefore all the more required was, once again, the political will to reconcile disparate national interests and domestic expectations. Called for most of all was a further compromise that strengthened the Locarno concert, which in turn required more than anything else finally to settle the Rhineland dispute. No less required was a new arrangement placing not only the reparations regime but also transatlantic co-operation on more solid – and legitimate – foundations than the Dawes regime. In short, it had to be a further political *quid quo pro* agreement in the vein of London and Locarno – an agreement underpinned by effective, commonly accepted ground-rules and mechanisms, which essentially consolidated the settlements of the mid-1920s.

The Young plan and the first Hague settlement indeed built on the premises of, and were intended to 'complete', what had been commenced at the London conference and then been complemented by the Locarno accords. They indeed produced a 'new deal' on reparations – though few thought at the time that it could stand the test of time as the 'final settlement'. And, essential for European politics yet only achievable through the transatlantic Young process, they brought a 'resolution' of what had been at the core of the Locarno era's Rhineland dispute: an early termination of the French, and Belgian, occupation. These were important achievements.

Undoubtedly, the actions of decisionmakers both in Europe and in the United States were influenced by more short-term tactical considerations, domestic pressures, electoral calculations and, in particular, financial even more than security concerns. This was a sign of a certain 'normalisation' of international politics after the initial postwar period of fragmentation and crisis. But it also made more long-term solutions more difficult to achieve, because the key decisionmakers, and especially those in Washington, were no longer spurred into more substantial engagement by the requirements of acute crisis-management.

To a remarkable extent, however, all leading policymakers, and financiers, of the postwar era's 'strategic quadrangle' – comprising the Anglo-American powers, France and Germany – sought to build on the precedents of the mid-1920s in forging the new settlement. More precisely, they sought to build on what each interpreted, in different ways, as the key lessons of these settlements – and as the consequences to be drawn from how the Dawes regime and Locarno politics had worked thereafter. While the Europeans sought to recur on the rules of London *and* Locarno, both the Coolidge and the Hoover administrations sought to premise their approach on what they now clearly construed as earlier successes of US 'economic diplomacy'. As will be shown, though, not only parochial interests but also some of the core lessons that policymakers had absorbed, particularly in Whitehall and Washington, actually *countervailed* further progress in 1929. In short, the making of the

Hague settlement did not mark a departure from Locarno politics. But it did mark a regression from the politics of London.

All three principal European powers pursued approaches that were overall designed to preserve the concert system and co-operative relations with the United States. Despite the difficulties still strewn on the path towards lasting European stability, this seems significant in itself; it manifested how far the Locarno powers had travelled since 1923. Germany and particularly France were less prepared to accept Anglo-American prescriptions than after the crisis of 1923. But both powers ultimately desired to negotiate a further 'grand bargain' that considered all sides' financial interests and political concerns. Crucially, French security concerns did *not* block the central bargain: the exchange of financial reassurance (in terms of reparations) against land (the 'liberated' Rhineland). Rather, Briand *and* Poincaré pursued a course commensurate with further Franco-German accommodation.[8] And to achieve its main political objective, evacuation, Berlin was indeed prepared to accept what the reparations agent Parker Gilbert called 'an expensive arrangement' on reparations.[9]

But in contrast to 1924, there was this time no decisive 'honest' broker crafting a further grand Euro-Atlantic settlement after the Great War. The potential of British diplomacy to take on such a role was diminished from the start because the Baldwin government lacked not only the required political-cum-financial clout but also, for a long time, a comprehensive strategy. Only once the path to the Hague conference had already been determined by others, especially Parker Gilbert, did British policy transcend its heretofore separate agendas: the Treasury's insistence on blocking a revision of the Dawes plan under the primacy of debt-reduction; and the Foreign Office's dogged pursuit of European diplomacy under the primacy of *entente* preservation. Consequently, Britain only came to foster the new bargain at a very late stage. And in the end the MacDonald government was indeed instrumental in mediating the final Rhineland agreement. Overall, however, Britain could not play a decisive part as policymakers in London, like those in Paris and Berlin, could only operate within the bounds and limits that were largely set by Washington.

Yet at this juncture the Coolidge government and, even more categorically, the Hoover administration succeeding it in 1929 refused to re-assume the essential mediating-role that the United States had fulfilled in 1924, that of an 'aloof' but decisive arbiter. Neither Hoover nor Kellogg, who was clearly less influential at this stage, saw a case for reviving the strategy of the Hughes

---

[8] Minutes of a conversation between Poincaré and Gilbert, January 1928, Poincaré Files, Archives Économiques et Financières, Paris, B 32/210; Moreau (1954), pp. 453ff. Cf. Artaud (1978), pp. 875–6.
[9] Schubert memorandum, 1 October 1928, *ADAP*, B, X, no. 53.

plan. All key decisionmakers viewed a political engagement of this nature as incompatible with cardinal American war-debt interests, and domestic constraints. But above all they deemed it incommensurate with core rationales of what by then clearly dominated US policy: Hooverian Progressivism.[10] This was the crux, not only for US policy but for postwar world politics as a whole.

Hoover believed that a revision of the Dawes regime could be achieved on the basis of a new 'apolitical' expert plan – without embroiling Washington politically and without any 'sacrifice' on its part, either in terms of political commitments or debt-relief. Consequently, US policy was premised on the central lesson that the commerce secretary and future president had drawn from the London settlement and its consequences in the mid-1920s: that it would be misguided to depart from the Republican 'depoliticisation' paradigm in crafting the new reparations settlement. If the Europeans desired to seize upon such a settlement to forge a Rhineland agreement, that was their business; it was only a distinctly secondary concern for the Republican administration. In sum, Washington abstained from pursuing a policy consonant with America's financial pre-eminence and the political clout accruing from it.

This was the crucial departure from the politics of the London conference. It did not preclude a new reparations agreement or undermine its longevity from the start. But it was one of the cardinal reasons why European policymakers found it exceedingly difficult to achieve not only a comprehensive settlement but also something more fundamental before the Great Depression overshadowed everything else. They could only make very limited progress in seizing on the Young process to make the system of London and Locarno more resilient, to strengthen not only its political but also its financial pillars and to imbue it with greater legitimacy. The nascent Euro-Atlantic order of the 1920s did by no means erode or show *serious* cracks before the World Economic Crisis. But international policymakers did not succeed in developing it qualitatively further; those in Washington saw no need to do so, those in Europe did not have the means to compensate for US neglect.

Towards the 'final liquidation' of the war's consequences?

Yet this was by no means a foregone conclusion when, in the autumn of 1927, first steps were taken to achieve no less than a 'final liquidation' of the war's consequences. In the formative twelve months that followed, the contours of a comprehensive Euro-Atlantic arrangement emerged. It was to comprise two basic elements: the 'final' reparations agreement which remained inextricably bound up with the issue of inter-allied war-debts; and a solution of the central

---

[10] Hoover (1952a), p. 182; Kellogg to Armour, 26 December 1928, NA RG 59 462.00 R296/2560.

problem of Locarno politics, which had hitherto eluded the European powers: the Rhineland question. The impetus for this settlement came from two directions, first from American financiers, above all Parker Gilbert, then, spurred by their proposals, from the French and German protagonists of Locarno. Each side entered the process from very distinct premises, and with equally distinct priorities and expectations.

Over the summer and autumn of 1927, consultations that Parker Gilbert held with key US financiers – notably Strong, Young and the Morgan partners Lamont and Morrow – and with Treasury Secretary Mellon produced the blueprint for an indeed ambitious endeavour. The scheme they drew up was to permit the settlement of all obligations accruing from the war – to settle, once and for all, not only reparations but also inter-allied debts. By and large following the example of the Dawes inquiry, this entire complex of problems was to be extracted from the realm of political controversy and once again defused through financially 'objective' repayment schemes, crafted by experts. Crucially, the reparations agent not only agreed with his interlocutors that the time had come to fix Germany's total obligations. He also envisaged withdrawing all foreign control – and transfer protection – mechanisms of the Dawes regime to boost what all US financiers and politicians deemed critical: *German* efforts to reform the country's 'irresponsible' financial policies. Thus, the new reparations regime was to guard against the transfer crisis that Gilbert saw looming and at the same time enhance Germany's 'capacity to pay', not least by giving the German economy new certainty through its 'finality'.

Crucially, Gilbert and Lamont also proposed, and Mellon at least contemplated, a departure in US postwar debt policy. To give all European debtors incentives, they suggested that the settlement's guiding principle should be overall debt reduction – a scaling-down of reparations and, if necessary, concomitant reductions in French and British war-debts. No less a departure was that the financial experts also envisaged the creation of a new international mechanism not only to oversee reparations transfers but also, potentially, to under-gird the still unconsolidated Euro-Atlantic financial system. First outlines for a Bank for International Settlements were circulated.[11] That the revision of the Dawes regime could also foster political change, especially in the Rhineland, was regarded as a desirable side-effect; it was not a central aim of American planning, which this time, in marked contrast to 1922/3, was essentially 'private'. No second New Haven plan was drafted on Kellogg's final watch.

---

[11] Lamont to Morrow, 6 May 1927, Lamont Papers, box 113; Strong to Gilbert, 13 September 1927, Strong to Jay, 10 November 1927, Strong Papers, 1012.2, 1012.3. Cf. McNeil (1986), pp. 192–3; Leffler (1979), pp. 183–4.

Following the initial American deliberations, the summer and autumn of 1928 saw the crystallisation of a second – European – set of expectations and strategies for the envisaged 'final' reparations settlement. On one level, all Locarno powers eventually concluded that such an agreement – largely following US precepts – was the only realistic way of tackling their pressing financial problems, exacerbated by the speculative boom on Wall Street, which was 'draining' American capital away from Europe. In Germany, there was an ever more acute shortage of foreign funds, which went hand in hand with economic uncertainty under the 'provisional' Dawes regime. In France, there was also a resurfacing demand for capital; yet the main French concern was finally to acquire a firm (reparations) basis for repaying war-debts. And in Britain, Churchill eventually drew the same conclusion as Poincaré on this matter.[12]

Yet the Locarno triumvirate also had to recognise the limits of its power in the fundamental realm of European concert diplomacy. Chamberlain finally came to adopt the premise that Stresemann and Briand had accepted long before him, namely that a comprehensive reparations settlement, which had to involve the United States, was the *conditio sine qua non* for settling the crucial Rhineland dispute. By 1928, no European leader any longer expected this process to yield a major breakthrough. But all hoped that terminating the evacuation and reparations disputes could provide largely stagnant Locarno politics with a much-needed boost, and an equally needed surge in its domestic legitimacy. This was especially vital for Stresemann to persevere with his policy in the face of not only unremitting nationalist opposition but also growing disenchantment in more moderate circles of Weimar politics. But it was also necessary to strengthen Briand's position in the Third Republic's ever-fluctuating environment. And, last but not least, Chamberlain required proof that his approach was yielding results. For he had to assuage mounting domestic criticism of his 'passivity' and pro-French orientation, especially from the Labour opposition, yet also among Conservatives.[13]

It casts a revealing light on the making of the Young settlement that, in contrast to 1923, the key impulse for a revision of the Dawes plan did not come from the Republican administration in Washington. It did not derive from a consistent US strategy pursued in co-operation with eminent financiers, and British leaders. Instead, it was the semi-official reparations agent in Berlin who gained a remarkable influence in the constellation of the late 1920s. From December 1927, Parker Gilbert proceeded not only to initiate a conclusive reparations settlement but also to guard US interests in the process. He became

---

[12] Churchill memorandum, 19 October 1928, FO 371/12878/231–2.
[13] Selby minute, 22 August 1928, Chamberlain to Tyrrell, 18 December 1928, *DBFP*, IA, V, nos. 135, 292.

the essential instigator of what became the 1920s' second formative experts' inquiry, that of the Young committee in 1929; and he also became a critical and tireless 'mediator' between French, British and German positions in setting the – essentially American – 'terms of reference'. Aware that, as Castle put it, almost all European affairs intimately 'relate[d] to' the Dawes plan, the State Department eventually sought to control Parker Gilbert's efforts. But Kellogg never saw the need to follow in Hughes' footsteps against the administration's clear determination, epitomised by Hoover, to steer clear of involvement.[14]

Having long been an international agent whose main task was to monitor the working of the Dawes regime and to admonish Berlin to exercise fiscal responsibility, Gilbert began to extend his brief. In his annual report of 10 December 1927, he concluded that the time had come to replace the Dawes system – to settle Germany's reparations obligations *in toto* and once and for all. Gilbert repeated his recommendations to the Reparation Commission in February 1928. Essentially, he argued that the Dawes regime should be replaced because both its creditors and Germany's economy required reassurance that only a long-term arrangement could provide – yet also because the old regime had actually encouraged German irresponsibility.

The reparations agent argued that more 'productive of reparations for the creditor Powers' than the Dawes plan's 'system of protection' would be one giving Germany 'a definite task to perform on her own responsibility, without foreign supervision and without transfer protection'. For only this would induce all levels of German government, the federal, the state and the municipal, finally to implement urgently needed structural reforms – and produce sufficient reparations, allowing America's debtors to repay their obligations. Besides, of course, the reparations agent reckoned that such reforms would also allow Berlin to keep servicing private US loans.[15] Gilbert proposed that once again a committee of politically 'independent' experts should settle the details of the settlement. By and large, these were the remedies that FBRNY Governor Strong had recommended throughout 1927.[16]

What Gilbert's initiative triggered were, at least from Washington's vantage-point, two clearly distinct yet in fact of course intricately linked developments. In contrast to 1923/4, there was only a very late, and limited, mutual reinforcement between the ensuing expert process, which eventually led to the Young report and became distinctly 'politicised', and a reinvigorated process of political negotiations, which essentially took place between the Locarno

---

[14] Castle Diary, 29 January 1927, vol. 10, pp. 34–5.
[15] Gilbert report, 10 December 1927, Gilbert memorandum, 24 February 1928, in Gilbert (1925–30), V, quoted after McNeil (1986), p. 192.
[16] Strong to Gilbert, 13 September 1927, Strong to Jay, 10 November 1927, Strong Papers, 1012.2, 1012.3.

powers. Yet only this latter process could pave the way for a sustainable settlement. In the realm of transatlantic relations, by contrast, drawn-out preliminary talks evolved. Here, Washington's aloof pursuit of a tightly controlled debt-policy agenda long conflicted with the underlying rationales of French and especially British policies. For the latter powers of course sought maximal debt reductions. Yet the US stance also limited German options to lighten the reparations burden to an absolute minimum. This constellation led to shifting informal alliances between the world creditor United States and the members of the Locarno concert. Unavoidably challenging this concert was thus the fact that it was divided into two: reparations creditors and war-debtors, on the one hand, and the reparations and loan debtor Germany on the other.

Parallel to this first process, and markedly affected by the divisions it caused, evolved a very tense inner-European negotiating-process in which the Locarno powers sought to hammer out the terms for terminating the Rhineland occupation. For Chamberlain, Briand and Stresemann, maintaining their concerted approach and reinforcing the Locarno system were still core aims in themselves. And eventually all three powers sought to seize on the expert recommendations to achieve, at last, a mutually acceptable Rhineland agreement. At the same time, though, decisionmakers on each side, and particularly Churchill and Poincaré, also sought to establish the best possible bargaining-position for the expected 'final' deal on reparations – and debts. This became a recipe for tough, often acrimonious yet at no point corrosive negotiations within the European concert.

The deadlock of Locarno politics

Prior to Parker Gilbert's decisive December report, the Locarno powers had all but reached a complete deadlock on the thorny Rhineland question. At their regular tripartite meeting at Geneva in September 1927, Briand and Chamberlain had impressed on Stresemann that, though the Nationalists beleaguered him at home, resolving the evacuation problem on the terms he suggested represented an 'absolute impossibility'. There was no prospect in solely recurring to the guarantees of 1925 and Germany's subsequent responsible behaviour.[17]

Behind closed doors, Chamberlain continued with his two-pronged approach of gently prodding Briand while also reinforcing the Anglo-French 'axis' in order to hasten evacuation. He maintained that their mutual co-operation could

---

[17] Chamberlain memorandum, 14 September 1927, Chamberlain to Tyrrell, 16 September 1927, *DBFP*, IA, IV, nos. 8, 11.

only be strengthened if both powers made sure to 'anticipate' rather than 'exceed' Versailles' dates for ending the occupation. The British foreign secretary urged the French government to complete its 'defence of the new frontier', the later Maginot line, 'as rapidly as possible' to reassure the French public and General Staff. Any further delays would make it ever harder for him to defend his cautious policy in the British parliament. But his exhortations had no significant effect. Instead of achieving even incremental progress, Chamberlain had to content himself with at least maintaining the *status quo*. In October 1927, he insisted vis-à-vis Briand that 60,000 troops had to remain 'an absolute maximum'.[18]

Facing what Stresemann increasingly perceived as a common Anglo-French front on this critical issue, German policy underwent a process of reckoning in the twelve months following Gilbert's report. At the outset of 1928, Stresemann and Schubert, who increasingly became its *spiritus rector*, desperately sought for new ways to hasten the end of the occupation. More than any other consideration – including the interest in reducing reparations – this remained their cardinal aim. It shaped the *Wilhelmstraße*'s pursuits because with its realisation stood and fell the legitimacy of its entire Locarno approach.

Stresemann had welcomed Parker Gilbert's call for a revision of the Dawes plan, which clearly corresponded with his US-orientated 'policy of interdependence'.[19] But in early 1928, the German foreign minister still strove to avoid tying the crucial Rhineland issue to those of reparations and war-debts. However seriously he took the need to assure American backing for a definite reparations settlement, Stresemann reckoned that no progress would be possible before the US presidential elections in November. Yet a swift arrangement with France and Britain over the Rhineland was critical. And the German foreign minister still sought to guard against Poincaré's attempts to use the occupation as a pawn in the eventual reparations negotiations.[20] Thus, backed by Marx's *Bürgerblock* cabinet, Stresemann and Schubert began their diplomatic 'Rhineland offensive' of 1928. They reverted to a tactic that Berlin had in fact used on numerous occasions since early 1926, yet never so assertively, and that, from June 1928, also the new Social Democratic chancellor Hermann Müller would pursue. In short, Stresemann put public pressure on Briand, and Chamberlain, by arguing, as he did in the *Reichstag* on 30 January, that

[18] Chamberlain memoranda, 14 September and 13 October 1927, Chamberlain to Crewe, 13 October 1927, *DBFP*, IA, IV, nos. 8, 20, 21.
[19] Schubert memorandum, 28 February 1928, Stresemann circular to German embassies, 30 January 1928, *ADAP*, B, VIII, pp. 264–5, 224–31.
[20] Stresemann circular to German embassies, 30 January 1928, *ADAP*, B, VIII, pp. 264–5, 222–31; Schubert memorandum, 28 February 1928, *ADAP*, B, VIII, pp. 264–5.

overcoming the Rhineland impasse was the litmus test not only for Franco–German relations but also the future of Locarno politics as such.[21]

Such German appeals, however, were as ineffective as further attempts to invoke the 'spirit' and 'due consequences' of Locarno to change the Rhenish *status quo*; and the same held true for renewed German attempts to make 'legal' claims under the Locarno treaty. The Poincaré government still flatly refused to espouse this logic and interpretation of Locarno; and Chamberlain essentially continued to back the French interpretation. Taking up Stresemann's publicly delivered challenge, Briand laid out the French case before the *Sénat* on 2nd February. He claimed that France did not rule out an early evacuation. But he also underlined that, while he could trust Stresemann, French policy had to reckon with changes for the worse in Germany; and he could not defy deeply held concerns of French 'public opinion'. The real thrust of Briand's remarks, however, was that Germany could not evade paying a price. He duly suggested that Berlin should propose a new, concrete political-cum-financial arrangement.[22]

After Thoiry, Paris had in fact never retreated from the premise that evacuation was inconceivable without 'some tangible *quid pro quo*' in the sphere of reparations.[23] In varying forms, Briand reiterated this *conditio sine qua non* to Stresemann as well as, later, to Chancellor Hermann Müller until the expert commission convened in February 1929 – and thereafter. He was unable yet also unwilling to renounce it. French policy thus linked any concessions on the occupation unequivocally with German financial compensations, which became distinctly more important for Briand and Poincaré than extended security guarantees. And, following the French foreign minister's rebuke of Stresemann's public demands, Berlin agreed to explore France's overtures, which first centred on reviving a Thoiry-like scheme.[24]

At their Geneva meeting in March, Stresemann again impressed on Briand that everything depended on rapid progress. No substantive 'deal' could proceed without Washington's approval; but it would be too late for it after the US elections as then the occupation would soon have to end under the Versailles treaty anyway. Briand responded that he could not make any commitments before the French elections, which were scheduled for May and in the event strengthened the position of Poincaré, who still vetoed any separate Franco-German scheme.[25] Stresemann also doubted that the Americans would

[21] Stresemann *Reichstag* speech, 30 January 1928, *SB*, vol. 394, cols. 12494–6.

[22] Briand speech, 2 February 1928, *JOS*, 1928, pp. 64–72. Cf. Jacobson (1972b), pp. 148–9.

[23] Crewe to Chamberlain, 4 February 1927, *DBFP*, IA, III, no. 7.

[24] Hoesch report, 1 February 1928, *ADAP*, B, VIII, no. 60; Briand speech, 2 February 1928, *JOS*, 1928, pp. 64–72.

[25] Stresemann memorandum of a conversation with Briand, Geneva, 5. March 1928, *ADAP*, B, VIII, no 143.

abandon their opposition to the crucial mobilisation of German reparation bonds, which had already thwarted the Thoiry scheme, particularly because Gilbert sought a different, general settlement.[26] Resuscitating Thoiry was indeed a hopeless cause in the spring of 1928. Hence, it became a tacit assumption of Locarno politics that no progress would be possible until, with American support, a comprehensive *do ut des* settlement involving reparations and evacuation appeared on the horizon.

While Briand and Stresemann were vying for a new bargain, Chamberlain was not only preoccupied by the 'brewing troubles' in China and vis-à-vis Soviet Russia. He also strove to improve relations with Washington through the war-renunciation pact. Thus, core Locarno issues were not the most pressing concern for the British Foreign Office at the time. Yet Chamberlain of course refused to back Stresemann's 'un-Locarnite' public campaign for evacuation. Though still sympathetic to the rationale that resolving the Rhineland problem was critical for Locarno politics, he remained adamant in the face of Berlin's overt pressure. Chamberlain's chief concern remained to preserve the *entente* within the European concert. He thus resisted demands, notably by opposition leader MacDonald, to exert 'conspicuous' pressure on France by threatening a separate withdrawal of British occupation troops.[27]

Systemic continuities and changes – the recast constellation of the latter 1920s

It seems instructive to compare not only the policies and outcomes but also the systemic constellation of 1928/9 with those of 1923/4. This can illuminate how far international policymakers sought to recreate, or develop further, what had proved successful five years earlier. And, no less, it can show what constraints and structural factors had changed in the meantime. Not least, it can also shed light on what lay behind the more restrained policies of Britain and the United States in the late 1920s; and it can illuminate under what altered conditions French and German policymakers had to operate. One difference was fundamental, if perhaps all too obvious. Whereas Locarno's edifice was creaking, and the reparations agent warned that the Dawes regime could founder unless it was revised, there was no crisis in 1928 on the scale of the Ruhr conflict that could spur more fundamental systemic reforms. In other words, there was no crisis – yet – perceived as so deep and serious that it could lead policymakers to heed the requirements of long-term stability,

---

[26] Schubert memorandum, 28 February 1928, *ADAP*, B, VIII, pp. 264–5.
[27] Chamberlain to Lampson, 12 February 1928, Chamberlain to Howard, 15 May 1928, Austen Chamberlain Papers, AC 55/303, 270; Foreign Office memorandum, 5 April 1928, FO 371: W 3961/2193/50.

both political and financial, rather than focus on satisfying more immediate interests.

In fact, rather than on the brink of disintegration or economic and political turmoil, Weimar Germany had (re)emerged as a comparatively strong power in the international system, though it remained a state highly dependent on foreign capital, with a still unstable parliamentary system, and a financial system that at least in American eyes was in urgent need of reform. And it also of course still remained a state that was subject to foreign control through the occupation and the Dawes regime. As we have seen, the resurgence of German power had nonetheless even become a notable security concern again, especially to its western and eastern neighbours. Yet while Warsaw repeatedly underscored to the Poincaré government its anxieties at the prospect of a 'liberated' Rhineland, such concerns could not prevent Paris from seeking a 'new deal' with Berlin.[28]

At the same time, though, the domestic climate in which Stresemann sought to sustain his course was becoming ever harsher. As Chancellor Müller's more assertive style exemplified, impatience with what many regarded as the painfully piecemeal progress of Locarno politics grew even among Social Democrats, who still remained the most loyal supporters of Stresemann's policy. Far more pronounced, of course – and rising – was criticism from nationalist circles. These demanded an immediate 'liberation' of the Rhineland; and, under the press magnate Hugenberg and Hitler, they would eventually clamour not only for rejecting the Young plan but for abandoning Stresemann's quest for *rapprochement* with the west as such.

France also still laboured under considerable structural problems, particularly the Third Republic's unstable parliamentary system. But while the sword of Damocles of the unresolved debt problem with America still hung over Paris, Poincaré's financial consolidation successes put France in a much stronger international position than in 1924.[29] This position was fortified through the Locarno concert and what was still a close *entente* with Britain. France was thus under much less pressure to agree to Anglo-American terms than after Poincaré's miscarried Ruhr invasion in 1923.

It should not to be overlooked that east European and especially Polish concerns were as secondary in the transatlantic processes of 1928 and 1929 as they had been during the Dawes process. Once the outline of a possible Rhineland settlement between the western powers became apparent, the Polish foreign minister Zaleski persistently demanded compensatory assurances or even guarantees for Poland. But his demands were practically brushed aside,

---

[28] Minutes of a conversation between Poincaré and Gilbert, January 1928, Poincaré Files, Archives Économiques et Financières, B 32/210.
[29] Cf. Mouré (2003), pp. 101–44.

both in the summer of 1928 and during the League's autumn session. Briand and Poincaré were no more prepared than the British government to let Warsaw's anxieties interfere with their overriding aim of reaching an agreement with Germany; nor was, *mutatis mutandis*, the German government. While an eastern Locarno was still out of the question for Berlin, both Paris and London still refused to extend further commitments to the Pilsudski government.[30]

In the wider picture, however, it has to be stressed that the Locarno powers' resolve to concentrate on an agreement amongst themselves, and with the United States, was the most promising practical course in the constellation of 1928. The lack of western engagement in fostering political and financial stabilisation in eastern Europe remained deplorable. But, if successful, a new Euro-Atlantic bargain in the west could ultimately also serve Polish interests – the more so the more it strengthened those German politicians and forces who backed Stresemann's bid to anchor the Weimar Republic to a western system. In short, a reparations and Rhineland settlement had to precede any further advances in the east.[31]

Fundamentally, what of course distinguished the constellation of 1928 from that of 1923 was the very progress in European politics that had been achieved in the intervening years. Four years earlier there had not been any functioning political *modus operandi*, particularly between Britain, France and Germany. This was now in place. On the European side, then, a certain 'primacy' of international politics had been re-established. States were less 'susceptible' to expert recommendations unless they suited their political interests. As will be shown, they essentially relied more on intergovernmental negotiations to hammer out the new settlements they sought. Thus, the two years preceding the Wall Street crash did by no means witness an abandonment of the rules and practices of the European concert.[32] By contrast, the management of political relations between the Europeans and an elusive American arbiter remained far more problematic.

Yet, as Thoiry's frustration had shown, there was also one systemic requirement that had not changed since 1924. If it was to be realised, and realised in a fashion germane to Europe's long-term consolidation, the envisaged new bargain had to be approached as a transatlantic bargain. Indeed, as Gilbert and US financiers saw clearly, the desired wider settlement could not be realised by financial experts alone – or, for that matter, by the Europeans themselves. It was hardly conceivable without a modicum of intergovernmental

---

[30] Lindsay to Chamberlain, 20 June 1928, Chamberlain to Erskine (Warsaw), 29 June 1928, *DBFP*, IA, V, nos. 62, 73; Larroche to Briand, 24 August 1928, MAE, Série Europe, Pologne, vol. 113.

[31] Cf. Wandycz, Krüger and Soutou (1981); Wandycz (1988), pp. 106ff.

[32] Cf. against this Knipping (1987), pp. 32ff.

co-operation across the Atlantic. Failing that, no real advances either on reparations and war-debts or in the interlocked sphere of Rhineland diplomacy, which lay at the heart of European security, could be achieved. For, however reluctant Washington was to use it *directly*, it still had the power to set the parameters for, or prevent, the complex 'deals' on which progress on all fronts depended. Given the extent to which both France and Germany were still tied up with US financial power, no bilateral arrangements between Paris and Berlin could succeed. This remained a basic constant. In other words, a new agreement had to involve not only the Locarno powers but also the United States. A basic degree of collaboration between all four powers was indispensable if a new expert plan was to be converted into a further *sustainable* settlement, one fortifying the system of London and Locarno.

Taking any major steps in this direction called, in particular, for a resuscitation of Anglo-American co-operation. But the conditions for such co-operation had changed; and so had – not radically, but in the nuances that mattered – the attitudes of British and especially of key American policymakers towards it. When first moves were made towards a revision of the Dawes plan in September 1927, decisionmakers on both sides of the Atlantic were eager to mend fences after the fiasco of the Geneva naval conference. Chamberlain and Kellogg were personally concerned to prevent a serious rift; and Castle agreed with Baldwin during the prime minister's visit to Washington in November that this had to be a strategic priority for both powers.[33]

But all these good intentions were overshadowed by the fact that between those who shaped policies on the critical issues of debts and reparations – in Whitehall, Churchill, in Washington, Hoover – a major clash of interests had erupted. This drove the most obvious wedge between London and Washington when both governments had to decide how far they could build on the Dawes settlement and again develop a joint approach. In short, two agendas came into conflict with each other. On the one hand, Churchill originally sought no revision of the Dawes plan at all until at least the requirements of the Balfour note could be satisfied. This essentially meant that he preferred to await a constellation in which British war-debts could be reduced so that Britain could then scale down its reparation demands accordingly. Yet the Treasury also still calculated that an eventual 'transfer crisis' or breakdown of the Dawes system might allow Britain to shed all of its obligations. This of course ran diametrically counter to the red line of US policy that Hoover drew most uncompromisingly: America would not countenance any concessions on its debt-claims. Indeed, Washington would use all its power to pre-empt any attempt to establish a direct or indirect linkage between these claims and reparations.[34]

[33] *DBFP*, IA, VI, nos. 359–434; Castle Diary, 16 November 1928, vol. 13, pp. 337–9.
[34] Kellogg to Armour, 26 December 1928, NA RG 59 462.00 R296/2560.

But perhaps even more important for limiting Anglo-American and wider transatlantic co-operation in 1928 and 1929 were fundamentally different assumptions then prevailing in London and Washington – assumptions about what kind of settlement was required not only to settle the reparations conundrum but also to reinforce German and European stability. These concerned a wide array of decisions, notably on the key questions: how much Germany could and should pay and who ultimately would control, and safeguard, the 'final' reparations regime. Informing these decisions were often incompatible notions about the need for political engagement – and political rules – to keep Europe on a path of consolidation. These differences also extended to the question of how to strengthen the back of those French and German leaders who pursued moderate policies – and who were sailing ever more closely to the wind. Indeed, a closer look at what determined British and American approaches to the Young settlement casts a striking light on more fundamental problems of international politics ten years after the Great War.

Accentuated aloofness – Hoover's case for non-engagement in the Young process

The Republican administration's policy on debts, reparations and wider European stabilisation emerging in 1928, and implemented in 1929, was intentionally only an attempt to pursue 'old approaches', namely those of the mid-1920s, to deal with the new situation.[35] In effect, what Washington pursued was a retrograde approach. It not only failed to build on the premises of 1924 but actually fell back behind them. And this was mainly due to the 'rising star' in Republican politics. In his last year as commerce secretary, then as president-elect and finally, from March 1929, as the new president, Hoover ever more became the key decisionmaker in Washington. Crucially, the consequence that he – and Coolidge – had drawn from the success of 1924 was that it had been one of US economic diplomacy – the promotion of a financially 'rational' settlement, insulating the administration from all political ramifications. In fact, though, it had precisely been Hughes' cautious but effective steering of US policy – his interplay with Britain and Anglo-American financiers – that had converted the Dawes plan into a more legitimate political settlement.

In 1928, Hoover's option for a more detached approach, which reflected prevalent views in the administration, led Washington to abstain from such a role in the Young process. As ever, Hoover advocated an economically orientated strategy of aloofness. And he did so partly out of consideration for what

---

[35] See Leffler (1979), pp. 194–219.

he rightly perceived as strong Congressional opposition to any more pronounced political engagement, which not least could have jeopardised US debt-interests.[36] Yet this was not the decisive motive for America's official non-involvement. What the administration pursued, or chose not to pursue, still hinged on fundamental Progressive premises. Nowhere was this 'vision' more accentuated than in Hoover's own mind. In his view, Europe had basically turned the corner from crisis to rising prosperity and stability – with decisive American help. And it was now time for the European governments to assume wider responsibilities in recasting their political economies, settling reparations, paying their war-debts and, in the German case, servicing reparations and loans. As Hoover saw it, this could be achieved *on American terms* yet without embroiling Washington in European disputes, and without raising the danger of a united European front calling for American debt-relief.[37]

While sharing Hoover's basic outlook, other protagonists of the Coolidge administration, notably Mellon and Kellogg, were more prepared to bolster European efforts. As noted, particularly the Treasury secretary considered offering the Locarno powers rewards in the form of future debt-relief or a more concerted loan policy.[38] But neither he nor Kellogg could shape American policy at a time marked by Hoover's final ascent, which culminated in his election victory over Al Smith in November 1928. Hoover assumed his presidency under the banner of 'Four More Years of Prosperity'.

On 19 December 1927, Mellon had commented favourably on Parker Gilbert's recommendation for a final reparations settlement in his recent report. Yet from the beginning he and the administration took great care to deflect all attempts to link the war-debt question with the revision of the Dawes plan. This also became a core determinant of greater US detachment in 1929. Mellon still sympathised with Gilbert's original plan for a comprehensive and lenient reparations agreement. Officially, however, he came to support Washington's uncompromising course.[39] And so did Kellogg and Castle. In view of the reigning consensus, neither saw any sense in proposing an alternative policy. While privately observing that, had he been a younger man, he would have gone on the 'stump' to promote debt cancellation, Kellogg publicly backed Hoover's line.[40] In March 1927, the president of Princeton University, J.G. Hibbon, and 115 further faculty members had called for a

[36] Campbell to Cushendun, 21 September 1928, *DBFP*, IA, V, no. 165.
[37] 'Memorandum on War Debt Settlements', 1927, Hoover Papers, Commerce Department, box 365.
[38] Gilbert to Strong, 14 November 1927, Strong Papers, 1012.2.
[39] Mellon statement, *New York Times*, 20 December 1928; Strong to Gilbert, 13 September 1927, Strong Papers, 1012.2.
[40] Castle to Maddox, 10 February 1928, Castle Papers, box 3; Rowe-Dutton to Waley, 28 January 1929, *DBFP*, IA, V, no. 72. Cf. Leffler (1979), p. 181.

re-assessment of US debt policy. They had demanded a departure from imposing 'tremendous burden of taxation' on 'friendly countries' such as Britain and France at the very time when America was 'amassing a national fortune'.[41] In a public letter, Mellon had replied that a fair settlement of ex-allied debts was indeed a prerequisite to the 'restoration of economic prosperity in the world'. But he had also asserted that the administration had already paved the way for this through lenient debt settlements with Britain and France, which these powers should and indeed could honour.[42]

Instead of encouraging fresh Anglo-French attempts to raise the debt issue in conjunction with reparations, the Treasury secretary came to pursue a more familiar priority. He kept up pressure on Poincaré finally to put his weight behind ratifying the Mellon–Bérenger accords. The main 'incentive' that Mellon offered was that the envisaged reparations agreement would provide a clear basis for France's future payments. The Coolidge administration had actually lifted its *de facto* loan embargo against France in early 1928 without prior French fulfilment of the key condition. But in the prevailing financial situation, with Wall Street speculation absorbing most available funds, this had not stimulated new flows of US capital.[43] Mellon and Hoover reckoned nonetheless that, once the debt agreement was operative, France could become as much a field for excess American funds and wider US expansion as Germany had been since 1924.

On 9 December 1928, Mellon underscored to Ambassador Prittwitz that America desired to commence the envisaged expert deliberations in order to 'expedite the ratification of the Mellon–Bérenger Agreement'.[44] For the same reason, the US government and Gilbert had earlier resisted Franco-German attempts to embark on another Thoiry-style deal. The reparations agent also impressed on Schubert that overheated US bond markets were indeed not ready to absorb reparation bonds. Crucially, however, despite Mellon's encouragement, the Coolidge administration remained very reluctant throughout 1928 to place official weight behind Gilbert's proposal for a general reparations settlement. Coolidge assured the reparations agent that Washington would not hinder his efforts. Yet nor would it officially aid him in this task.[45]

Hoover emerged as the driving force behind this policy. As from early on it was widely anticipated not only in Washington but also in Europe that he would succeed Coolidge, consideration for the course he steered became a potent factor in the Young process. Hoover had always been more adamant than Mellon that the US Debt Commission not only had exercised 'fairness'

---

[41] Harrison to US Diplomatic Officers, 23 March 1927, *FRUS 1927*, II, pp. 731–2.
[42] Mellon letter to Hibben, 15 March 1927, *FRUS 1927*, II, pp. 732–8.
[43] Cf. Leffler (1979), pp. 176–7.
[44] Prittwitz to AA, 9 December 1928, *ADAP*, B, X, pp. 474–5.
[45] Kellogg to Armour, 31 October 1928, NA RG 59 462.00 R 296/2425.

towards debtor-nations but also a 'duty' to the American taxpayer. And any downscaling of debts had to be purchased by raising taxes at home, which was out of the question. At the same time, the commerce secretary was convinced that America's principal debtors received more than sufficient reparations from Germany to service their obligations. This connection always figured prominently in the administration's internal calculations. Officially, though, the key members of the administration of course insisted on denying it. And they withstood all Anglo-French attempts to make it a central premise of the Young settlement.[46]

Fundamentally, all leading Republican policymakers adhered to one central postwar assumption. As Mellon put it, if a debtor was asked 'to pay substantially less than it [was] able to without undue burden on its people' this would be 'an injustice to our own taxpayers'. And if such reductions were to be linked to corresponding reductions in reparations, 'the net effect' would be 'to transfer the reparation payments from the shoulders of the German taxpayer to those of the American taxpayers'. The administration was resolved to prevent any such contingency from arising in the first place.[47]

Hoover cherished 'a personal resentment' against the French government because of their failure to ratify the debt 'arrangement'.[48] And he consistently called any 'further cancellation' both 'inequitable and impolitic' – the former because he considered European nations well capable of paying without undue sacrifices for their populations; the latter because it would have sent the wrong signal to Paris and London.[49] This also became a central plank of Hoover's election platform in 1928. Indeed, any move towards debt-relief remained anathema not only to the administration but also to a majority of both parties in Congress – Republicans and Democrats. Borah and other leading Republican senators unanimously condemned any moves towards cancellation.[50]

In 1929, the debt policy of the Hoover administration would overthrow Stresemann's rationale. More precisely, it would override the interests of the German government and international bankers in scaling down reparations, and thus benefit America's loan debtor. Yet Hoover's policy would also override Anglo-French interests in reducing their obligations. Washington's stance left Gilbert little choice but to forge a 'final' settlement that, rather than revise reparations, followed a different rationale. It was the rationale that

---

[46] Hoover to Coffman, 27 April 1926, Hoover memorandum, 23 September 1925, Hoover Papers, Commerce; Howard to Chamberlain, 30 December 1927, *DBFP*, IA, IV, no. 104.

[47] Mellon letter to Hibben, 15 March 1927, *FRUS 1927*, II, pp. 736–8.

[48] Campbell to Cushendun, 21 September 1928, *DBFP*, IA, V, no. 165; Hoover statement, 8 October 1931, Hoover (1952a), pp. 334–5.

[49] 'Memorandum on War Debt Settlements', 1927, Hoover Papers, Commerce Department, box 365.

[50] Lindsay to Sargent, 10 February 1928, *DBFP*, IA, IV, no. 140; Howard to Cushendun, 23 November 1928, *DBFP*, IA, V, no. 234.

Germany would have to pay a considerable price for gaining certainty – sufficient reparations to satisfy the claims of all creditors: France, Britain and the United States.[51]

In May 1928, Gilbert told the British ambassador Lindsay that the general 'American opinion' on reparations and debts would 'harden still further' if the European governments were 'seeking to delay a settlement with Germany for extraneous or purely selfish purposes'. The 'mere existence' of US 'investments' would 'not suffice to keep alive any beneficent interest in European affairs'. And their 'loss' in the event of a crisis 'would only affect a couple of hundred thousand bondholders'. The 'broad mass' of Americans – and therefore also the government – would still mainly be interested 'in the regular collection' of war-debts. American bankers were indeed keen to avoid accusations of caring more about their profits than about the interests of US taxpayers. They hence altogether avoided raising the issue of debt-cancellations.[52]

The underlying premises of US non-engagement

But the Republican administration not only adopted a course of detachment because of its debt preoccupations. On a deeper level, official US role-behaviour was informed by already familiar precepts of Hooverian 'economic diplomacy'. Hoover's approach to the 'final' reparations agreement was premised on two core premises. One pertained to his assumption that all European states had, or could gain, the capacity to pay their war obligations without burdening the American budget. The other, even more consequential, concerned the very nature of the international settlement that he envisaged, not only to solve the reparations problem but also to consolidate European stability – without Washington's official involvement.

Not just Hoover espoused, and constantly reiterated, the first premise. Mellon, Kellogg and Parker Gilbert also shared it. All believed that the key to remedying the reparations problem lay not in the hands of the American government. It lay, instead, in inducing France yet above all Germany to implement the 'correct' US-style reforms. If Berlin could summon the political will to stop using its funds, and US credits, for 'wasteful' purposes – such as welfare spending and public-infrastructure projects – it could pay sizeable reparations. And if Britain and particularly France could finally adopt equally stringent public-finance policies, reduce military spending – and rely on steady German reparations – they, too, could easily honour their debt obligations.[53]

[51] Gilbert to Strong, 10 July 1928, Strong Papers, 1012.2.
[52] Lindsay to Chamberlain, 30 May 1928, DBFP, IA, V, no. 43. Cf. Costigliola (1984), pp. 206–7.
[53] 'Memorandum on War Debt Settlements', 1927, Hoover Papers, Commerce Department, box 365; Hoover, 8 October 1931, Hoover (1952a), pp. 334–5. Gilbert note, 20 October, annex 1, Report, 10 December 1927, in Gilbert (1925–30), V. Cf. McNeil (1986), pp. 194–5.

In his revision proposals, the reparations agent Parker Gilbert clearly emphasised the need for a final, reliable schedule for reparations that transferred responsibility to German authorities. Subsequently, too, his emphasis was *not* on reducing reparations annuities as such; those he proposed nearly equalled the full Dawes rates. From a distance, not only Hoover but also Mellon had even less patience with the intricacies of German federalism and the complex interrelations between Berlin, German state governments and the country's municipalities. They tended to see the Müller coalition's inability to reduce 'politically motivated' public spending as indicative of misguided policies, not as reflecting the constraints facing any government in Berlin that was intent on preserving the Weimar Republic's precarious stability.[54]

Crucially, the American focus was no longer on buttressing Weimar's moderate political elites, which backed Stresemann's course against ever more vocal nationalist counter-forces. Rather, despite Schurman's increasingly concerned reports, US policymakers had concluded that Germany's political system was solid enough to implement incisive reforms. Vital in any case remained that Berlin did not suddenly 'announce that it either could or would not pay further reparations'. In Kellogg's view, this would have dealt the most 'disastrous' blow to 'the peace of Europe' – and US debt interests.[55]

At the same time, though, even if some expected transfer problems unless the Dawes plan was revised, no leading US decisionmaker anticipated a major crisis in Germany, either under the old or a new reparations regime. Once the German government pursued Progressive financial policies – thus the prevalent view, shared by Gilbert and Strong – Germany's potential for overcoming its on-going economic *malaise* was considerable. Progress did *not* depend on America altering its protectionist tariff policies, as Stresemann demanded.[56] And the same held, *mutatis mutandis*, for France. In 1927 and 1928, Gilbert's assessments led to repeated German remonstrations that both the reparations agent and the US government were overestimating Germany's capacity to pay. Yet American, and French, observers suspected that as in 1924 Berlin deliberately understated this capacity for political reasons.[57]

Even more profoundly, though, US policy at the end of the 1920s was guided by a second core tenet. It derived from Hoover's Progressive outlook

[54] Gilbert to Strong, 10 July 1928, Strong Papers, 1012.2; Gilbert note, 20 October, annex 1, *Report*, 10 December 1927, in Gilbert (1925–30), V.
[55] Schurman to Kellogg, 26 April 1927, Kellogg to Schurman, 11 April 1927, Schurman Papers, box 6; Castle memorandum, 29 September 1927, NA RG 59 862.51/2508; Gilbert report, 10 June 1927, in Gilbert (1925–30), IV, pp. 122ff. Cf. Berg (1990), 297–9.
[56] Gilbert memorandum, 24 February 1928, *ADAP*, B, VIII, pp. 241–4; Strong memorandum, 22 October 1927, NA RG 59 862.51/2519.
[57] Gilbert note, 20 October, annex 1, *Report*, 10 December 1927, in Gilbert (1925–30), V; Ritter directives, 27 December 1927, *ADAP*, B, VII, pp. 576–8.

and, more specifically, his interpretation of the Dawes process and the road that Europe had travelled since 1924. Hoover maintained that the Dawes commission 'succeeded beyond our hopes' in setting Europe 'on the way to peace and progress'. For it had addressed the reparations problem while keeping the interference of European power politics strictly at bay.[58] In principle, the commerce secretary thus advocated that the new settlement should again be based on the rational economic analysis of 'independent' experts. And it was once again to be divorced from the manoeuvres of European governments. Till the end of 1928, however, the Coolidge administration refused to endorse involving US experts in a new committee. Essentially, it feared that they would be too exposed to political pressures. And when Washington finally did consent, Coolidge impressed on the chosen delegates, Owen Young and J.P. Morgan, to eschew the Europeans' political battles. They were to emulate the work of their predecessors, concentrating solely on the task of 'finalising' the Dawes plan – and protecting US debt interests.[59]

To this extent, then, the Republican administrations of the latter 1920s followed the precedent of the Dawes proceedings. Crucially, though, Hoover subsequently departed from this precedent. When it came to turning the Young report into a Young settlement, he declined the European request to involve the US government in even the most informal, indirect manner. At the first Hague conference, the United States would only be represented by one 'unofficial observer', who largely confined his activities to informing Washington about the proceedings.[60] Under the outgoing Coolidge administration and, even more pronounced, under Hoover in 1929, Republican policy thus abandoned Hughes' approach. The United States no longer acted as a self-interested but overall constructive 'neutral' arbiter in transatlantic affairs. The central lesson of Hughes' critical engagement in 1924 had been cast aside.

When assuming office, Hoover found the United States 'still under the spell of reaction from the war', still 'so isolationist that [its] proper responsibilities were neglected'.[61] Crucially, however, he did not see these responsibilities in areas where US political leadership was critical. In particular he did not see them in forging an international framework in which not only reparation and war-debt problems but also their wider political implications could be addressed, a framework that permitted an effective management of international disputes, and crises. In the eyes of the new president, US influence had been instrumental in overcoming Europe's initial postwar crisis; and it was

[58] Hoover (1952a), p. 182.

[59] Young to Gilbert, 19 November 1928, R-30, Young Papers; Coolidge to Hoover, 9 April 1929, NA RG 59, 462.00 R296/2775/1/2.

[60] Howard to Cushendun, 23 November 1928, *DBFP*, IA, V, no. 234.

[61] Thus Hoover's retrospective verdict. See Hoover (1952b), p. 330.

now up to the European governments to settle the reparations problem, essentially by implementing the experts' recommendations. Once again, they were to accept American 'terms of reference'; yet they must not expect any concomitant US commitments in return.

In the same vein, the new Hoover administration was little concerned with the reparation settlement's possible repercussions for Franco-German relations, Locarno politics and wider European security. Nor, unlike Gilbert and bankers such as Strong and Lamont, did it seek to use this settlement to spur desirable political changes, notably a Rhineland agreement. Albeit more attentive to political ramifications, the State Department largely concurred that it was not Washington's role to aid the Locarno powers in settling issues whose resolution was regarded as a matter of course. Interestingly, then, Kellogg, who had been a prominent figure at the London conference of 1924, four years later distinctly refrained from emulating his predecessor Hughes. He did so because he, like Castle, shared Hoover's view about European responsibilities. And he also held that Washington was well advised not to get enmeshed in European bargaining over reparations and the Rhineland.[62] Ultimately, then, the view in Washington was that if the Locarno powers desired to use the reparations settlement to make further political agreements, this had to be strictly separated from implementing the envisaged new expert recommendations.[63] As the British ambassador Howard reported in November 1928, the 'appearance at least of complete American official isolation must be maintained'. In addition, Mellon and Kellogg made clear that whereas Washington welcomed the expert inquiry, 'war debts were to be entirely excluded and not to be brought up as a subject for discussion'.[64]

More important than these maxims were their political consequences. In essence, they reinforced the administration's aloofness from the Young process. Compared with the Dawes process, there was indeed a significantly reduced level of co-operation and co-ordination between Washington, the experts and bankers like Morgan and Strong. This applied even more to any efforts at forging a common political agenda with the European governments. Crucially, Republican policymakers concluded that the US government must not commit itself in any way to underpinning a political framework for the new settlement, even if the Europeans – or the experts – might deem such a framework indispensable. From the outset, there was thus a deep antipathy

---

[62] Castle Diary, 29 September 1928, vol. 13; Kellogg to Armour, 31 October 1928, Kellogg memorandum, 31 October 1928, NA RG 59 462.00 R 296/2425.

[63] Campbell to Cushendun, 21 September 1928, *DBFP*, IA, V, no. 165.

[64] Howard here endorsed Ambassador Prittwitz's view. See Howard to Cushendun, 23 November 1928, *DBFP*, IA, V, no. 234; Kellogg to Armour, 26 December 1928, NA RG 59 462.00 R296/2560.

towards attempts to involve the government, or federal reserve officials, in attempts to create instruments such as an international bank, which had first been proposed by Gilbert and Young. Washington desired no part in any international mechanism that would hence not only oversee reparations transfers but could also serve to contain a possible transfer crisis, which ultimately threatened to place the main political and financial burdens on the United States. This would remain a constraining constant of Republican policy throughout 1928 and 1929.[65]

Nor did Hoover of course change his opposition to firmer controls, and bail-out provisions, for private US loans to Europe. In short, Washington was not to be held liable as the world's lender of last resort. It was primarily for this reason that the commerce secretary from early on favoured replacing the Dawes regime with a mechanism no longer overseen by a US agent. Distinctly less a concern of his was that maintaining the Dawes system's controls would unduly interfere with German domestic politics, further sparking nationalist resentment.[66]

Essentially, then, Hoover's disparagement of old-style European politics had been confirmed by the latter 1920s. And so had his conviction that the real remedy not only for the reparations and debt problems but also Europe's wider stabilisation lay, not in the realm of international politics but in pressing all Europeans to pursue determined Progressive reform efforts. A basic overhaul of Europe's governmental, financial and economic structures could then serve to buttress political pacification. This remained the clarion call of Hooverian Progressivism.[67]

US foreign commercial policy – one set of rules for America, another for the world

At the same time, Hoover still believed that Washington could pursue its debt and stabilisation objectives without having to be conciliatory in another vital area: US foreign economic policy. Indeed, the commerce secretary pursued an equally hard-nosed approach to trade and tariffs. His was a less than benign way of defining how to act as the new pre-eminent power in the world economic system. Essentially, following Hoover's view Washington could determine trade and tariff rules as befitted its interests, and refuse to accept any general rules while still serving the cause of world prosperity and peace.[68]

---

[65] See chapter 26.
[66] Castle Diary, 29 September 1928, vol. 13.
[67] Hoover (1952b), p. 330. Cf. Hawley (1974), pp. 101–19.
[68] Hoover address, 15 October 1928, Hoover Papers; 'Memorandum on War Debt Settlements', 1927, Hoover Papers, Commerce Department, box 365.

Hoover's position was comparatively mild when seen against the background of strong pressures from the Republican majority in Congress to expand the US tariff regime, which ultimately produced the protectionist Smoot–Hawley Tariff Act in 1930.[69] Substantially, though, Congress merely championed a more excessive version of Hooverian commercial policy. The commerce secretary continued to argue that pursuing the 'open-door' abroad and selective protectionism at home did not amount to an inconsistent policy. And during the 1928 presidential campaign, he spoke out against the Democrats' criticism that high American tariffs prevented the United States from importing goods from debtor countries 'necessary to repay interest and capital upon [their] loans'.[70] While the Democratic 'platform' was to reduce tariffs, the Republican presidential candidate claimed that Republican tariff policy since 1922 had proved very effective, not only for the United States but also for its debtors and overall world trade.

What Hoover proposed to overcome the debt (and reparations) impasse was to invigorate 'a polyangular course of trade'. America's debtors were to increase their exports to raw-material-producing countries, which in turn were to export more products to the creditor countries, above all the United States. Thus, America would be able to maintain its dominance in trade relations with Europe, ensure debt-collection and further expand a 'profitable market' for US surplus capital, above all in Germany. In Hoover's reading, 'polyangular trade' could foster a system not marked by 'dictation' or 'domination' but by 'organised co-operation', in which 'every nation [could] gain by the prosperity of another'. Yet this vision hardly corresponded with the reality of transatlantic trade relations in the latter 1920s. To mention but one case in point: in 1927, Germany had incurred the highest trade deficit since the war, particularly vis-à-vis the United States. In fact, Hoover's policy created an ever more asymmetrical playing-field of international trade.[71]

French governments continually protested against US tariff and commercial policy. Chastising America's commercial tyranny of course also served Poincaré's domestic agenda, and from 1928 he and Briand sought to revive the idea of a Franco-German 'continental bloc' to resist that tyranny. Yet the German government remained careful to distance itself from any moves in this direction, since what Stresemann called the value of 'intertwined interests' with the United States was too high to be jeopardised. Like the British government, Berlin thus also held back with any public criticism of US tariffs.[72]

[69] Kellogg to Hawley, 26 February 1929, Stimson to Smoot, 26 June 1929, NA RG 59 611.003/ 1472, 1673a.
[70] Hoover address, 15 October 1928, Hoover Papers.
[71] *Ibid.*; Stimson to Hoover, 8 June 1929, *FRUS 1929*, II, pp. 998–9.
[72] Kellogg to Hawley, 26 February 1929, NA RG 59 611.003/1472; Stresemann press statement, 14 November 1928, *ADAP*, B, X, pp. 597–9.

The search for a comprehensive strategy – Britain and the quest for final postwar settlement

The limits of official US policy had the most decisive bearing on the shape of the Young settlement. But what was the British outlook in 1928? And what this time could be the role of the power that had performed a key mediating-function in forging the London reparations agreement in 1924? Between January and November 1928, a notable change in Britain's Rhineland and reparations policies occurred. First came a reorientation of the Foreign Office's concert diplomacy – essentially spurred by the recognition that evacuation could only be achieved through a further 'comprehensive' bargain, not by virtue of Locarno politics alone. Then followed a change in the Treasury's attitude. After a long period of prevarication, Churchill came to acknowledge that Britain had to depart from its long-standing reparations maxims. Ever since the London conference, the Treasury had maintained that no revision of the Dawes plan should be envisaged until there were prospects for combining it with a substantial reduction of British debts. In the autumn of 1928, Churchill finally altered his course, now also backing a new, 'final' reparations settlement roughly along the lines that the reparations agent Parker Gilbert had proposed. In other words, the Conservative chancellor of the exchequer espoused the premise that Britain's financial interests were best served by ensuring regular – and high – German payments, which covered (at a minimum) British obligations to America.[73]

Both British reorientations did not so much derive from active forward planning or underlying changes in policymaking assumptions. They were driven more by the momentum that Gilbert's initiative had generated. And, in Chamberlain's case, they were a response to obvious Franco-German aspirations to explore new ways of forging a 'grand' postwar settlement. Over the summer of 1928, an extension of the *entente* within the Locarno concert emerged, not only on disarmament but also on the Rhineland question. Here, Chamberlain essentially came to espouse Briand's core demand: sizeable financial compensation on Germany's part as the essential precondition for evacuation. What emerged thereafter can indeed be described as a second Anglo-French *entente*. Essentially, though, it was a temporary alliance of expedience between two reparations creditors and debtors of the United States.[74] That alliance was forged between the unlikely collaborators Churchill and Poincaré in October and November 1928; but it only held until disagreements over the distribution

---

[73] Churchill memorandum, 19 October 1928, FO 371/12878/231–2.
[74] This has been rightly emphasised in Jacobson (1972b), pp. 217–18.

of reparations superseded ex-allied unity at the first Hague conference in August 1929.

However many good reasons for this two-pronged *entente* orientation may have existed in the short term, it should not be seen as a sign of strength of British policy. In the sphere of reparations policy, it was hardly surprising and accorded with the Treasury's natural preoccupations. In the more important sphere of Locarno politics, however, Britain's course reflected Chamberlain's retreat from a leading role in shaping the European system and balanced agreements between the Locarno partners. Yet it was also informed by frustrations within the Foreign Office, which had not achieved any major results since 1925, particularly on the core evacuation issue, and was increasingly criticised in the Commons for its passivity.[75]

Chamberlain never abandoned either his self-perception or the role of the 'honest broker' between Paris and Berlin. But it was simply beyond his, and Britain's, means to forge the complex settlements on which the progress of Locarno politics by then depended. Yet the British foreign secretary also long refrained from developing strategies for such settlements and from co-ordinating them with the Treasury, which would have been the prerequisite for a coherent British strategy. His defensive insistence on closing ranks with Briand constrained British policy further. Ultimately, forced by the prevailing international constellation, Chamberlain came to pursue an approach quite closely resembling MacDonald's in 1924. From the autumn of 1928, he would seek to foster an experts' inquiry on US terms – with the aim of seizing on it to broker, at last, a Rhineland agreement. But he would be out of office before this came to fruition. With a certain historical irony, it again fell to a MacDonald government, his second, to forge the final compromise in August 1929.

Beyond Locarno politics – Chamberlain and the need for a Franco-German *quid pro quo* agreement

In principle, Chamberlain never abandoned his maxim that Britain's task was to strengthen the proponents of Locarno policy in Germany. Yet he reckoned that this could never be achieved by giving in to insistent German demands but only on the basis of 'sweet reasonableness', with Germany fulfilling Anglo-French conditions before reaping rewards. There were encouraging signs. As the foreign secretary told Crewe on 30 May 1928, it was 'clear' that 'the steady improvement in Germany's foreign relations, which has flowed from Locarno, has cut the ground from under the Nationalists'. Britain's Locarno policy had made it 'possible for the republic to live'; and the

---

[75] Chamberlain to Howard, 15 May 1928, Austen Chamberlain Papers, AC 55/270.

subsequent victory of the Social Democrat Hermann Müller was 'the reward' of British 'moderation'. This 'striking proof' of the German people's 'desire for peace' should encourage the Locarno powers 'to go further on the same lines'.[76]

Chamberlain thus impressed on Briand that both powers should respond to the developments in Berlin by showing 'that to a peaceful Germany we accord willingly and promptly what a Germany pledged to a policy of revenge would never have wrung from us.' And the most 'obvious' measure to end the 'abnormal relations between the German and the ex-Allied Governments' in accordance with Locarno was finally to open negotiations 'for the early evacuation of the occupied Rhineland'. More generally, Chamberlain and Lord Cushendun, who represented Britain at the crucial Geneva talks of September 1928, were keen to maintain the position of a mediator between French, German – and British – interests.[77]

In practice, however, the British foreign secretary was not willing to alter his definition of Locarnite 'reciprocity' and his maxim that further strengthening the close bonds with Briand still held the key, also to resolving the evacuation problem. In the Commons, Chamberlain thus maintained that Britain would be most ill-advised to put any overt pressure on France in this matter. Beyond the public's gaze, his priority remained hammering out a common platform with Briand before entering into any substantive negotiations with Stresemann. He thus consistently refuted Berlin's fresh appeals to Locarno to hasten evacuation.[78] Deflecting Foreign Office frustration with the piecemeal progress of its 'appeasement' policy, Chamberlain grew increasingly irritated at what he deemed the Müller government's departure from the principles of Locarno: 'sound policy & reasoned common sense'. Convinced that Britain had 'helped the Germans out of the waste' of the postwar crisis, he now asked German leaders 'for common sense, not gratitude'. In July 1928, he thus reminded Stresemann of 'a favourite Bismarckian maxim' – 'Do ut des'. The German government had to acknowledge that this was the only way of obtaining concessions from France, and Britain, on the occupation.[79]

Ultimately, this not only meant that Chamberlain kept deferring to Briand's concerns instead of moulding the Locarno agenda. It also had one concrete

---

[76] Chamberlain memorandum, 28 July 1928, Chamberlain to Crewe, 30 May 1928, *DBFP*, IA, V, nos. 112, 42.

[77] Chamberlain to Crewe, 30 May 1928; Cushendun to Rumbold, 30 October 1928, *DBFP*, IA, V, nos. 42, 199.

[78] Chamberlain statements, Commons, 8 February and 18 July 1928, *Hansard*, 5th series, vol. 213, cols. 115ff, vol. 220, cols. 386–9; Chamberlain to Howard, 15 May 1928, Austen Chamberlain Papers, AC 55/270; Chamberlain to Nicolson, 4 July 1928, *DBFP*, IA, V, no. 79.

[79] Chamberlain memorandum, 28 July 1928, Nicolson to Chamberlain, 4 July 1928, *DBFP*, IA, V, nos. 80, 112.

consequence: by April 1928, official British policy had accepted the need for a wider *do ut des* approach to the Rhineland problem. In general, as yet vaguely defined terms, a solution had to hinge on satisfying France's demand for military yet also financial compensations from Germany – essentially 'assurances' for the payment of reparations – in return for the withdrawal of all occupation troops. As Chamberlain told Schubert at Geneva on 8 June, no French government could 'carry through the anticipated evacuation without being able to show the French people some *quid pro quo*'. The latter essentially had to be financial.[80] Thus, less than three years after the security pact's conclusion, Chamberlain had to concede that the impasse at the heart of Locarno politics was not amenable to a Locarno-style resolution.

It shed some light on the overall still good state of relations between the Locarno powers in the spring of 1928 that, despite Briand's protestations, the Foreign Office could safely downgrade security as a major factor in the envisaged settlement. Correctly gleaning the main preoccupations of the *Quai d'Orsay*, and Poincaré, Britain instead focused on financial questions. Chamberlain called the occupation 'useless' because it was bound to end under the Versailles treaty 'long before any danger from Germany could materialise'. He therefore encouraged attempts to find a 'scheme' making early evacuation 'acceptable to French public opinion', eventually backing, apart from financial compensations, the creation of a new control and conciliation commission in the Rhineland for the time following the evacuation. The Foreign Office considered the practical value of this commission very low, anticipating that not even in the medium term would a new threat emerge from Germany once it had re-acquired its key strategic base.[81]

Yet how did Chamberlain envisage realising a wider European *quid pro quo* settlement? He never changed his basic assessment that any plans to revive the Thoiry scheme, about which Phipps and Lindsay reported from Paris and Berlin, were both impractical and injurious to British reparations interests. The British foreign secretary thus warned Stresemann that the Locarno powers 'could not afford a second Thoiry with its immense expectations and absolutely negative result'.[82] Instead, the Foreign Office concluded that it was very 'unlikely' that 'the problem of a premature evacuation of the Rhineland' could be solved 'otherwise than as part of a general financial settlement', which had to include not only reparations but also war-debts. And in this core field, Gilbert's proposal opened up new prospects and should be seized upon. What made the entire issue not only 'important' but also 'difficult' from the British

---

[80] Chamberlain statement in the Commons, 8 February 1928, *Hansard*, 5th series, vol. 213, cols. 115ff; Chamberlain memorandum, 9 June 1928, *DBFP*, IA, V, no. 55.

[81] Chamberlain to Grahame, 12 April 1928, *DBFP*, IA, IV, no. 194.

[82] *Ibid.*; Chamberlain memorandum of a conversation with Schubert, 9 June 1928, *DBFP*, IA, V, no. 55.

perspective was 'the fact that no settlement on the lines indicated will be possible without the active co-operation of the United States Government'.[83]

Grudgingly, Chamberlain thus accepted that the most important Locarno issue unresolved since 1925 could only be approached the American way. The British foreign secretary by no means underestimated the wider complications that such an approach raised. As he emphasised in April 1928, the crux was that 'any readjustment of reparations . . . inevitably raised the question of our respective indebtedness to the United States'. At the same time, however, all indications were that America would refuse to 'link a reduction of her claims on Europe' with any reparations scheme. Chamberlain rightly foresaw that this would immensely complicate any political negotiations with Washington.[84] Nevertheless, for reasons of overall policy, and in the interest of concluding a new naval settlement, he saw the need to bolster co-operation with the Coolidge administration.

Yet, mindful of the Treasury's *caveats*, the Foreign Office long kept aloof from concrete efforts to forge a comprehensive reparations settlement. Indeed, Chamberlain never managed to play a leading part in this process, neither vis-à-vis Washington nor vis-à-vis his Locarno partners. Only in December 1928, when all major decisions had been made, especially by the Americans, did he finally put his weight behind the expert inquiry. In part, Chamberlain was reluctant because he thought that any attempt to influence American policy would be futile, particularly before the US presidential elections.[85] Fundamentally, though, the Foreign Office never developed a convincing *quid pro quo* strategy because the foreign secretary clung to his preference for Locarno politics. In December, Chamberlain and Howard would even be instrumental in ensuring an American participation in the inquiry. But he still regarded the expert approach as a necessary evil, believing that the European powers had to make the final decisions.[86]

Against the transatlantic tide – the British Treasury and the 'final' reparations settlement

Within the Baldwin government, the main requirement now emerging was to balance the Foreign Office's wider political aims with the Treasury's more

[83] Foreign Office memorandum, 5 April 1928, FO 371: W 3961/2193/50; Gilbert report, 10 December 1927, in Gilbert (1925–30), V, p. 171.

[84] Chamberlain to Grahame, 12 April 1928, *DBFP*, IA, IV, no. 194; Chamberlain memorandum, 25 April 1928, *DBFP*, IA, V, no. 9; Balfour note, 1 August 1928, Cmd 1737.

[85] Foreign Office memorandum, 5 April 1928, FO 371: W 3961/2193/50; Lindsay to Chamberlain, 30 May 1928, *DBFP*, IA, V, no. 9.

[86] Chamberlain to Tyrrell and Grahame, 26 November 1928, *DBFP*, IA, V, no. 236; Austen to Hilda Chamberlain, 17 December 1928, Austen Chamberlain Papers, AC 5/1/463.

narrowly circumscribed financial objectives. In short, it proved very hard to forge a common strategy reconciling a Rhineland solution with the essentials of British debt and reparations policy. This turned Britain's policy of 'appeasement' into one of frustration in 1928. The Foreign Office and the Treasury co-ordinated basic responses, particularly through Tyrrell, then still under-secretary, and the reparations expert Frederick Leith-Ross.[87] But the separation of interests and responsibilities, already notable after Thoiry, had not lessened. If anything, it had become more accentuated, with the Foreign Office overseeing 'high politics' and Churchill and First Comptroller Sir R. Hopkins assiduously guarding the Treasury's debt and reparations prerogatives. The latter and, from June 1929 Churchill's successor Snowden, naturally had Britain's financial interests, not wider Locarno concerns, closest to their hearts.

In November 1927, enforcing the Treasury line, Tyrrell had instructed Ambassador Lindsay in Berlin to 'dry nurse' Gilbert and contain his efforts to initiate a general reparations settlement. Yet the under-secretary and Hopkins also agreed that Britain had to have 'some scheme or policy ready in our pockets' should the reparations agent or Poincaré raise this issue. Once Gilbert had launched his initiative, the Treasury saw 'trouble . . . brewing in regard to German reparations'. Its highest echelons regarded his proposals as 'diametrically opposed' to what Britain desired, because they deemed a revision of the Dawes plan premature. Till October 1928, the Treasury's 'strategy' thus became 'to prevent the [reparations] problem from becoming active as long as possible'. Originally, the earliest time it envisaged for a final settlement was March 1929, when a new US president would have taken office. In Gilbert's words, the Treasury pursued a policy of 'non-interference' in the hope of provoking a general reduction of all intergovernmental obligations.[88] This meant that Treasury policy was based on a distinctly unrealistic premise. Even at the time, some Treasury officials considered the scenario of an all-round cancellation of debts far-fetched – unless a major financial and transfer crisis erupted. Officially, the Baldwin government thus maintained that, in its assessment, the Dawes plan still functioned satisfactorily.[89]

British financial experts studied the reparations agent's reports on the Dawes plan and German structural problems very carefully. And, confidentially, they largely accepted Gilbert's assessment that, under the Dawes scheme, Germany was 'over-borrowing and over-spending'. But they did not agree that this made a revision of the system imperative to prevent 'early

---

[87] Sargent to Phipps, 5 January 1928, *DBFP*, IA, IV, no. 107.
[88] Tyrrell to Lindsay, 17 November 1927, Tyrrell to Hopkins, 5 December 1927, Sargent to Phipps, 5 January 1928, *DBFP*, IA, IV, nos. 44, 84 (enclosure), 107.
[89] Foreign Office memorandum, 5 April 1928, FO 371: W 3961/2193/50.

economic and financial disaster'. Rowe-Dutton, the Berlin embassy's financial adviser, took a more cautious view, making the case for an early general settlement. He warned that the first year of full Dawes annuities, 1929–30, could be 'a year of economic depression in Germany'. And this could be 'exploited' by German politicians to clamour for drastic reductions of 'the intolerable weight' of reparations. Yet these were secondary concerns for the Treasury. They did not – yet – warrant a British engagement on behalf of a final settlement. As Hopkins told Tyrrell on 11 April 1928, there was 'good ground for hope' that Germany would be able to pay annuities till 1930–1, the second year of full 'standard annuities'. For not only could an overall increase in German exports be expected. Above all, there was 'every reason to suppose that foreign loans will continue to be needed by and obtained by Germany'.[90]

What precisely lay behind the Treasury's policy? Ever since Thoiry, Churchill had insisted that Britain should only seek a comprehensive reparations settlement when the time was ripe, not any partial arrangement, even if it served Franco-German accommodation. And the chancellor's underlying rationale for the desired settlement was tantamount to a re-affirmation of the long-standing premise of British policy: the Balfour note.[91] As Kellogg had noted in 1927, the Treasury thus insisted that Britain 'was to receive enough . . . reparations and foreign obligations . . . to pay the United States'.[92] Britain was indeed prepared to scale down its reparation-claims, yet only in proportion to scaled-down US debt-claims.[93] After the publication of Gilbert's December report, the Treasury maintained this uncompromising stance. As Ambassador Lindsay told Gilbert on 12 June 1928, London was 'as firmly convinced as ever' that the entire 'present régime of vast inter-governmental payments was radically wrong' and thus 'anxious' to bring it 'to an end'. This was a tall order. And until it could be met, Churchill of course insisted on a ratification of the Anglo-French debt settlement.[94]

With regard to Germany, the Treasury operated on assumptions distinctly different from those that Gilbert and the Coolidge administration espoused. Overall, Treasury officials estimated Germany's future capacity to pay as rather limited. Some British economists concluded that foreign loans were

---

[90] Perowne memorandum, 22 November 1927, *DBFP*, IA, IV, no. 53; Lindsay to Chamberlain, 26 May 1928, *DBFP*, IA, V, no. 40; Tyrell to Hopkins, 26 March 1928, Hopkins to Tyrrell, 11 April 1928, *DBFP*, IA, V, nos. 6, 7.

[91] Hopkins memorandum, in Tyrrell to Lindsay, 17 November 1927, *DBFP*, IA, IV, no. 44; Chamberlain memorandum, 25 April 1928, *DBFP*, IA, V, no. 9.

[92] Kellogg memorandum, 27 November 1927, NA RG 59 462.00 R296/2487.

[93] Lindsay to Sargent, 13 April 1928, *DBFP*, IA, IV, no. 199.

[94] Sargent to Lindsay, 10 April 1928, *DBFP*, IA, IV, no. 193; Lindsay to Chamberlain, 30 May and 15 June 1928, Chamberlain to Crewe, 12 July 1928, *DBFP*, IA, V, nos. 43, 48, 88. Cf. Kent (1989), pp. 281–2.

used to 'finance reparation cash transfers to the Allied Powers' and to stimulate an artificial boom, but not to strengthen German export industries and thus 'facilitate' reparation-payments.[95] Essentially, though, British observers were more sceptical than American experts because they deemed the basic ability of Weimar Germany's embattled governments to reform public finance as prescribed by the Americans highly questionable.

While there were always suspicions that German politicians would instrumentalise financial difficulties, this was largely taken for granted. Even less was there noticeable anxiety that German leaders could try to provoke an outright crisis in the reparations regime – at least as long as moderate governments stayed in power.[96] What proved decisive was a different consideration. The British government shared the American view that German budgetary policies had exposed 'an increasing tendency towards extravagance and improvidence'. The Marx government not only made 'objectionable' expenditures like increasing the *Reichswehr* budget but also postponed a 'final settlement' of 'the financial relations between the Reich, the States and the communes'. And Müller's coalition continued that trend. Ultimately, this could jeopardise the working of the Dawes plan, and Leith-Ross came to anticipate a crisis. Yet the Foreign Office also noted that it was 'the weak position of the German Cabinet' as such that made it 'unable to insist on stringent measures' vis-à-vis the *Reichstag* and German public opinion to 'put the German financial house in order'.[97] This was essential.

Therefore, the reduction of reparations – and British debts – held the key. As long as achieving it seemed impossible, the Treasury refused to revise the Dawes regime. Yet Washington's firm line afforded no prospects at all in that direction. For the better part of 1928, British reparations policy was thus at odds not only with Gilbert's designs but also with US war-debt policy. This not only created tensions with the Coolidge administration but also severely limited the foundations of any meaningful Anglo-American co-operation. No joint efforts that even came close to those of 1924 could be contemplated. Churchill only altered his course in mid-October 1928 once – prodded by Gilbert – he concluded that Britain's reparation-claims could most effectively be protected by a new policy. His new approach was premised on finally accepting a revision of the Dawes plan, yet only after forging agreements with Poincaré that ensured maximal German payments – payments *at least* satisfying the core demands of the Balfour note.[98]

[95] Perowne memorandum, 22 November 1927, *DBFP*, IA, IV, no. 53.

[96] Rowe-Dutton record of a conversation with Schacht, 12 October 1928, *DBFP*, IA, V, no. 180.

[97] Perowne memorandum, 22 November 1927, *DBFP*, IA, IV, no. 53; Rumbold to Cushendun, 14 September 1928, *DBFP*, IA, V, no. 153.

[98] Sargent to Lindsay, 10 April 1928, *DBFP*, IA, IV, no. 193; Churchill memoranda, 20 September and 19 October 1928, FO 371/12878/71–3, 231–2.

It should be noted that in all of these manoeuvres the role of the governor of the Bank of England, Montagu Norman, was far less central than in 1924. The Baldwin cabinet's emphasis in 1928 clearly lay on forging an intergovernmental settlement. And it was assumed that private – US – loans would continue to flow to Germany. Rather than focus on the settlement of reparations, Norman pursued what was and remained his main concern: to consolidate British finances on the basis of the gold standard – and to seek ever new ways to reverse the drain of capital and gold reserves from Britain to America, which the Wall Street boom had precipitated. In 1929, he would explore how far British involvement in the envisaged Bank for International Settlements could serve this underlying interest. Norman thus intensified collaboration with US Federal Reserve officials, seeking to convince them – largely in vain – to raise interest-rates to redirect capital flows to Britain.[99]

Chamberlain's policy under strain – frustrations and domestic pressures

With the Foreign Office and the Treasury pursuing separate agendas, British policy remained incongruous during most of the critical year 1928. At crucial junctures, notably the critical September summit at Geneva, it was represented by Lord Cushendun rather than an illness-plagued Chamberlain. Overall, Britain's Locarno diplomacy was losing force. In the aftermath of the Anglo-French disarmament compromise, this provoked growing dissatisfaction with Chamberlain's entire course both in the Commons and the British press. Particularly the Labour leaders MacDonald and Arthur Henderson, yet also Lloyd George, chastised what they regarded as the foreign secretary's Janus-faced approach of invoking Locarno while practically reverting to old-style *entente* politics with France. The main criticism remained that Britain should press France harder to evacuate the Rhineland, essentially by threatening unilateral troop withdrawals. MacDonald also demanded that Britain should do more to support Weimar Germany's government.[100]

Such domestic criticism but also the often Sisyphean pursuits of British diplomacy in a complex transatlantic constellation provoked some soul-searching in the Foreign Office's higher echelons. Notably J.V. Perowne and Sargent, both influential advisers of Chamberlain, vented their frustrations. They not only blamed Germany for ingratitude but now also emphasised their suspicion that Stresemann was pursuing a wider agenda potentially inimical to Britain's longer-term interests. They saw it as an agenda in which 'freeing' the Rhineland

---

[99] Cf. Eichengreen (1992), pp. 216–19.

[100] Chamberlain to Tyrrell, 18 December 1928, Selby minute, 22 August 1928, *DBFP*, IA, V, nos. 292, 135.

was only a stepping-stone for revisions of the 'Polish Corridor' and 'armaments parity'. As noted, the observations of Perowne and Sargent revealed no shocking secret. From 1927, it had been a core Foreign Office premise that Europe's 'big questions' lay in the east. Yet in late 1928, both officials nonetheless began to question the entire rationale of Britain's concert policy. And both advocated what, in fact, Chamberlain pursued anyway: an emphasis on controlling Germany, on the basis of a strengthened *entente* with France.[101]

Against the backdrop of growing parliamentary and public pressure, the British foreign secretary dug in his heels. He made a point of publicly standing even more closely shoulder-to-shoulder with Briand than before. On the other hand, he accentuated his criticism of German calls for ever further concessions. In late August, an exasperated Chamberlain reminded Stresemann and Schubert that the Müller government's categorical evacuation demands undermined Locarno-style reciprocity and 'bore some resemblance to [the policy] pursued by Germany before the war', as captured in Eyre Crowe's key memorandum of 1907. There, Crowe had indicated 'how every concession made to Germany only whetted her appetite for more'.[102] But, critical though he was of German behaviour, Chamberlain never went as far as his advisers. He never seriously doubted either Stresemann's underlying motives or the wisdom of *his* Locarno approach. Yet the actions of Europe's 'honest broker' were no longer decisive for shaping postwar politics at the end of the 1920s.

Paving the way for the Young plan – the new transatlantic 'terms of reference'

However aloof Washington remained, the policies of the Republican administration had not only a salient effect on Gilbert's attempt to pave the way for a final reparations settlement – far more critical than the interests of Wall Street. The administration's course, and particularly the limits that Hoover set, were probably also the decisive forces shaping the subsequent Young plan itself – its scope, its limits and the extent to which the European powers could forge a viable political agreement on its basis. Not only Germany but also Britain and France eventually had to fall in line behind the non-negotiable interests of the US government.[103]

In the spring of 1928, it was pressure from Mellon and Hoover that led Gilbert to change his course. Instead of advocating a settlement based on

[101] Austen to Hilda Chamberlain, 17 December 1928, Austen Chamberlain Papers, AC 5/1/463.
[102] Chamberlain memorandum, 28 July 1928, Selby minute, 22 August 1928, *DBFP*, IA, V, nos. 112, 135.
[103] Minutes of a conversation between Müller and Briand, Geneva, 5 September 1928, minutes of six-power meeting, Geneva, 16 September 1928, *AR Müller I und II*, nos. 20, 28.

overall debt reduction, the reparations agent hence sought a 'final' arrangement conforming to Washington's debt interests vis-à-vis London and Paris, essentially by proposing that Germany would have to pay basically undiminished reparations. On this basis, he sought to obtain first French, then British backing for his approach. In the end, his manoeuvres spurred successful Anglo-French attempts at accommodating their policies, finalised in the Churchill–Poincaré agreement of mid-October 1928. What emerged was the understanding that neither power would retreat from the principle that each had to receive enough reparations to pay its obligations to the United States – and, in France's case, also 'surplus' indemnities for war damages.[104] This finally paved the way for the deliberations of the Young committee, which commenced in early 1929.

What also proved critical for preparing the ground for this inquiry, however, was Germany's new strategy on reparations and evacuation, developed by Schubert over the summer of 1928. Schubert proposed a tactically ingenuous way of simultaneously approaching a settlement of both issues without officially linking them, and effectively sought to use a reparations agreement as a 'bait' to accelerate the French troop withdrawals.[105] More broadly, Gilbert's initiatives triggered successive Franco-German attempts to settle 'outstanding great questions' no longer through a modified Thoiry scheme but by fortifying their negotiating-positions for a 'grand bargain'. In effect, such a bargain could not be separated from the envisaged 'final' reparations settlement. European efforts culminated in the crucial Geneva six-power meeting in September, where the decision to call for an expert inquiry analogous to the Dawes commission was made. In this process Britain only played a marginal role.

Parallel, though, France and Germany had also continued to explore different bilateral arrangements. Encouraged by Ambassador Hoesch, Stresemann persisted with efforts to achieve a *swift* 'unconditional evacuation' through direct agreements with Briand. And, over the summer, both Briand and Poincaré also made a last bid to pursue a 'continental' orientation, essentially a further attempt to draw Germany into a continental bloc arrangement to create a counterweight to America's financial predominance. At the same time, Paris also sought to lure Berlin into a debtors' coalition with the – vague – offer of potentially reducing future reparation-claims if Germany backed French debt-reduction demands vis-à-vis Washington.[106] Yet, though still critical of US trade policy, Stresemann carefully resisted all French overtures that threatened to push the German government into an anti-American coalition.

---

[104] Churchill memorandum, 19 October 1928, FO 371/12878/231–2.

[105] Cf. Krüger (1985a), pp. 438ff.

[106] Cabinet minutes, 1 September 1928, MAE, Herriot Papers, 20/MS, 28–9.

The core aim of his long-term policy remained to foster peaceful change with Germany's essential senior partner, the United States.

The general tendency towards Franco-German *rapprochement* in the realms of trade and economic questions had earlier been underscored by both powers' co-operation at the 1927 World Economic Conference.[107] And above all it had been strengthened through the Franco-German trade treaty of 17 August 1927, granting both sides most-favoured-nation treatment. Within the bounds set by Stresemann's priority not to alienate Washington, economic relations were indeed the most active element of bilateral relations. But ultimately both sides had to acknowledge, as in 1924, that they could not settle the critical issues dividing them without the Anglo-American powers, and most of all the elusive US administration.

The priority of 'liberating' the Rhineland – the German quest for a 'final' postwar settlement

It has been concluded that the main rationale of Stresemann's US-orientated course – that the American creditor's interest in the well-being of its German debtor would lead to a downscaled reparations settlement – did not produce the desired result.[108] Or did Stresemann's Locarno policy even enter a more fundamental crisis – and was he, crucially, beginning to depart from its premises?[109] In terms of reparations, Germany indeed had to pay a high or at least not lower 'price' under the Young settlement. In contrast to the developments of 1923 and 1924, the making of the Young plan even witnessed a certain reversal of dynamics. This time, Stresemann's rationale primarily benefited France and Britain: the interest of the US government in the liquidity of its debtors, and thus sufficient German reparations, overrode the interest of American bankers, and politicians, in Germany's short-term liquidity. The Republican administration also aimed to preserve Germany's capacity to service private US loans – yet only after Berlin had discharged its reparation-obligations, if necessary through further private credits.

But the overriding political aim uniting Stresemann and Chancellor Müller was a different one: to accelerate the evacuation of the Rhineland. And this they indeed achieved, if only after a further complex settlement involving substantial concessions on reparations. Yet, as we have seen, the willingness to pay a high financial toll for political advances had been a guiding principle of German foreign policy ever since 1923. And this remained so in 1929. In the end, Stresemann was justified in seeing the first Hague settlement as

---

[107] See *The World Economic Conference, Geneva, May 1927: Final Report* (Geneva, 1927).
[108] Cf. Kent (1989), pp. 283ff; McNeil (1986), pp. 194–5.
[109] Cf. Knipping (1987), pp. 25ff.

a – hard-won – vindication both of his Locarno policy and, if less so, his cultivation of 'parallel interests' with the United States. Throughout, his remained a policy building on international co-operation, not the provocation of crisis, to shed German obligations and foreign controls.

As noted, the situation in Germany changed through the elections in June 1928. Stresemann fought hard to establish a grand-coalition government, then formed under Müller and including the Social Democrats, the *Zentrum*, the German Democratic Party (DDP) and the foreign minister's own German People's Party (DVP). He saw such a broad coalition as the only way to ensure the continuation of his policy, and Müller indeed put his weight behind it. Yet, introducing his own new emphasis, the chancellor launched what in Paris and London was quickly viewed as an aggressive campaign for an immediate end of the Rhineland occupation. From his inaugural speech in the *Reichstag* on 3 July, Müller based his call for an 'unconditional' evacuation on the conviction that a Social Democrat would find it easier to achieve Germany's cardinal aim than the previous conservative *Bürgerblock* coalition.[110] As Chamberlain's reaction had shown, Müller's 'offensive' was not helping Stresemann's diplomacy. But it was a clear sign of how impatient even the Locarno-orientated left in Germany had become for tangible results.[111]

For all of Müller's assertiveness, though, Stresemann and Schubert had by this time clearly acknowledged that realising Germany's evacuation demand was ultimately inseparable from a final reparations arrangement. Against growing domestic opposition, Stresemann thus returned to the 'general line' of his foreign policy. He began to 'redirect' the reparations problem, and all political questions connected with it, 'into the current of a more economic and financial treatment'. And he sought to align German interests closely with those of Washington.[112] This clearly sidelined all further efforts by the German ambassador in Paris, Hoesch, to promote a separate settlement with the French government. And it led the German foreign minister himself to cold-shoulder all further bilateral overtures by Briand and Poincaré.[113]

Having welcomed Gilbert's call for a revision of the Dawes plan all along, Stresemann hence sought to apply the lessons that he had drawn from the Dawes process. He hoped that by unequivocally endorsing the American approach, Germany could once more enlist Washington's powerful support in achieving the 'conclusive liquidation of the war's consequences in the

---

[110] Müller inaugural speech, *Reichstag*, 3 July 1928, *SB*, vol. 423, pp. 38–40. Cf. Feucht (1998).
[111] Chamberlain to Nicolson, 4 July 1928, *DBFP*, IA, V, no. 79; Chamberlain statement in the Commons, 18 July 1928, *Hansard*, 5th series, vol. 220, cols. 386–9.
[112] Memorandum of a conversation between Gilbert and Stresemann, 12 November 1928, *ADAP*, B, X, no. 147.
[113] Cabinet minutes, 22 August 1928, *AR Müller I und II*, no. 18. Cf. Keeton (1987), p. 248.

financial sphere'. This, in turn, was to enable him achieve the same on the main political battleground of the Rhineland.[114] In effect, Gilbert's initiation of the Dawes revision-process had confirmed Stresemann's long-term calculation.[115] Under the Dawes regime, he had actively sought to further an expansion of interdependent interests with the world creditor, and America's financial stake in Germany had indeed increased exponentially. Stresemann was aware that inter-allied war-debts would be a significant factor in the new reparations deal. But like Schubert, the new finance minister Rudolf Hilferding and Schacht, he clearly hoped that, in analogy to 1924, the powerful convergence of governmental and private interests in the United States in ensuring the well-being of their debtor would ultimately redound to Germany's advantage.

Reichsbank president Schacht, who would leave his mark on the Young plan negotiations, originally argued, much like the British Treasury, that Germany should seek to delay a new settlement until a transfer crisis might allow it to shed most of its obligations. Yet he subsequently came to heed Gilbert's warning that such a scenario could have severe consequences, undercutting Germany's international credit and all of its prospects of obtaining fresh US loans. Ultimately, Schacht also shared Stresemann's expectation that the interests of US bankers, and the administration in Washington, in Germany's continued liquidity would weigh in Berlin's favour. On these grounds, the *Reichsbank* president eventually became one of the most ardent German proponents of a 'final' reparations agreement on Gilbert's terms.

Far more than Stresemann, Schacht was also motivated by the desire to 'smack', and rid Germany of, the Dawes regime. As he wrote to the foreign minister in September 1928, most important for him was to see the 'last vestiges of restraints, controls, and unresolved questions' under the Dawes regime 'swept away' and to restore Germany's 'absolute diplomatic freedom'. This sentiment was espoused by an ever broader segment of German opinion, not only nationalists. As will be seen, it also became a central theme of the concerted campaign against the Young plan staged by Hugenberg and Hitler in 1929.[116]

Stresemann shared the aim of restoring Germany as an 'independent' great power; and he also desired to reduce the extent of US interference in German affairs. But he was still favouring a more gradual, co-operative approach, intent on preserving, if on more equal terms, the 'interconnection of interests' that had so effectively linked Germany with the United States since 1924.[117] More

---

[114] Stresemann circular to German embassies, 30 January 1928, *ADAP*, B, VIII, p. 109.
[115] Cf. Link (1970), pp. 411ff.
[116] Schacht to Stresemann, 20 September 1928, *ADAP*, B, X, no. 42.
[117] Memorandum of a conversation between Gilbert and Stresemann, 12 November 1928, *ADAP*, B, X, no. 147.

generally, 'freeing' the Rhineland and revising the Dawes plan remained part and parcel of Stresemann's long-term policy of co-operative revision. Yet neither was intended as a stepping-stone for a more assertive approach. The German foreign minister did not intend, as some British observers suspected, to use the widened room to manoeuvre that Germany hoped to achieve to push for 'armaments parity' or to step up pressure to revise the 'Polish Corridor'.

Instead, while the structural problems of Polish–German relations did not disappear, German policy vis-à-vis Warsaw remained consonant with Locarno principles. Like London, Berlin sought to prevent any complicating Polish interference in the process of settling the evacuation and reparations questions, which it essentially regarded as 'western' concerns. But both in continuing attempts to defuse the Polish–Lithuanian crisis and, above all, in its efforts negotiate a Polish–German commercial treaty, Stresemann and Schubert maintained a course that sought to 'normalise' relations with the Pilsudski government as far as possible. The commercial treaty would be the last hard-won success of their policy. Yet it was only signed in March 1930 and, due to mounting domestic impediments on both sides, never ratified.[118]

Stresemann understood Gilbert's worries about the extent of Germany's foreign borrowing and public finance. But he also saw the profound challenge of reducing public spending and of inducing German states and municipalities to balance their budgets. More importantly, the German foreign minister continued to see the need for changes in the global economic system. Since 1924, he had consistently argued that Germany should be put in a position to pay its reparations, not through foreign loans, but through export surpluses. But the structural problems of the postwar international economy persisted as much as the asymmetry in transatlantic trade. Internally, Stresemann joined other German critics of US tariff policies. But any changes in this sphere could only benefit Germany in the longer run. More immediately, Berlin had to clinch a 'final' reparations settlement that reinvigorated the flow of US capital to Germany. A vital concern of Stresemann's policy remained to prevent a crisis of the Dawes transfer-system, which would have sparked a massive credit crisis with potentially disastrous consequences for the political stability of Weimar Germany. And that stability was increasingly precarious. Both in cabinet and in public, the foreign minister thus repeatedly warned against an impending German 'bankruptcy' and the 'political dangers' of a crisis of the Dawes regime.[119]

---

[118] Cabinet minutes, 9 July and 22 August 1928, minutes of a conversation between Müller and Zaleski, Geneva, 12 September 1928, *AR Müller I und II*, nos. 7, 18, 22.

[119] Stresemann press statement, 14 November 1928, Stresemann (1932), III, p. 385; cabinet minutes, 1 May 1929, *AR Müller I und II*, no. 191, p. 623; Schacht to Stresemann, 20 September 1928, *ADAP*, B, X, no. 42.

On balance, however, the political aim to free the Rhineland outweighed all financial considerations. Against this backdrop, and due to the foreign minister's ever frailer health, it was Schubert who, with his backing, developed the decisive strategy of implicitly rather than explicitly linking the Rhineland evacuation with the revision of the Dawes regime. In July, it crystallised in the under-secretary's recommendation that Berlin should make a *démarche* to Paris and London on the evacuation question, yet without proposing any *quid pro quo* settlement as demanded by France. Thus, Germany would not be the power officially raising the complicated reparations issue. If however, the Poincaré government chose to raise the issue of German financial compensations – as Schubert expected – Berlin could then point to the possibility of revising the Dawes plan. This way, Germany could use the evacuation problem as a 'lever' vis-à-vis France to accelerate a final reparations settlement.[120]

Thus Schubert's reasoning. Indeed, what he outlined seemed to be the only way for Germany to influence the process leading to the coveted Rhineland agreement. At the same time, the German government thus avoided formally acknowledging the nexus that, not only in Chancellor Müller's view, the German public would neither understand nor accept. Even Müller himself resisted paying a price for what in his eyes should be a natural consequence of Locarno. But the *Auswärtige Amt* eventually won the government's backing for its strategy.[121] As Schubert envisaged it, the new approach was meant to strengthen the Locarno system. But it was also indicative of Berlin's by then mounting disappointment with Britain and what was seen as Chamberlain's kow-towing to Briand. Though Stresemann still needed Britain's influence on France to hasten the end of the Rhineland occupation he had lost a great deal of faith in the British broker.[122]

Yet, as Schubert conceded, neither British policy nor his own approach held the key to further progress. While revitalising relations within the Locarno concert was important, the positions of France and the United States were crucial. And Gilbert at least soon came to back Schubert's course. It was in his interest that Germany should instigate what he, as a 'semi-official agent', could not set in motion: a broader political process between the European powers, ending in a final reparations settlement.[123] In the autumn of 1928, however, everything depended on how far the German design would be compatible with the aims of French policy.

---

[120] Schubert to Stresemann, 24 July 1928, Stresemann to Schubert, 26 July 1928, Schubert memorandum, 27 July 1928, *ADAP*, B, IX, nos. 173, 183, 184; documents on the 'Revision des Dawes-Plans', 1928, PA, Büro des Staatssekretärs.

[121] Cabinet minutes, 22 August 1928, *AR Müller I und II*, no. 18. Cf. Heyde (1998), pp. 39–40.

[122] Schubert memorandum, *ADAP*, B, IX, no. 193; Nicolson to Chamberlain, 20 July 1928, *DBFP*, IA, V, no. 99.

[123] Close co-ordination between Schubert and Gilbert was essential. See Schubert memorandum, 27 July 1928, *ADAP*, B, IX, no. 184.

Financial certainty over security concerns – France's approach to the 'final' postwar settlement

Throughout 1928, the *Quai d'Orsay*'s policy was shaped by one overriding aim. It never lost sight of establishing what, officially at least, Berlin so strongly resisted: a clear 'junction' between the withdrawal of French troops and German compensations in terms of reparations. In consideration for the Müller government's domestic situation, Briand eventually agreed that there would not have to be 'a direct and clear connection' between these issues. In fact, though, this 'connection' and insistence on a *do ut des* arrangement remained the maxims of French policy until The Hague conference.[124]

As early as February 1928, Berthelot had proposed a 'grand settlement' to be forged between the Locarno powers and the United States and settling with a 'single stroke' all contentious issues – the Rhineland, reparations and war-debts. Needless to say, although Berthelot desired to build on Gilbert's original scheme, any such far-reaching plans had to founder on the rock of Washington's opposition. Yet although the same constraints applied to reviving the Thoiry design, Briand long refused to relinquish this option. Even at the Geneva talks in September, he still returned to it, essentially to force Berlin to accept the underlying French 'junction'.[125]

Critical for French policy in this phase was that Poincaré, who considered the Thoiry approach a dead end, gravitated towards an espousal of Gilbert's general scheme. Influenced by the reparations agent's campaign on its behalf, he came to see it as the best means of achieving his core objective: to forge a secure long-term basis for – high – German reparation payments, which ultimately covered, at a minimum, France's debts to America. To realise this aim, Poincaré was indeed prepared to accept an early termination of the occupation. He was willing to relinquish what he had long regarded as an essential security guarantee, yet also as a 'pawn' that France had to use as the Versailles deadline was approaching.[126]

Up to this point, the rationale of French reparations and debt policy that Seydoux had stipulated in 1926 still had not changed. France was to block any revision of the Dawes plan until one of two scenarios could be envisaged: either a way was found to cut French obligations both to Britain and America; or there were good grounds to expect that a 'final' settlement would fix reparations that covered not only these debts but also French war-damages. By the

[124] Minutes of six-power talks, Geneva, 5 and 11 September 1928, *AR Müller I und II*, nos. 20, 21; Briand speech, 2 February 1928, *JOS*, 1928, pp. 64–72; Suarez (1938–41), V, p. 238.

[125] Hoesch report, 1 February 1928, *ADAP*, B, VIII, no. 60; minutes of a conversation between Müller and Briand, Geneva, 5 September 1928, *AR Müller I und II*, no. 20.

[126] Minutes of a conversation between Poincaré and Gilbert, January 1928, MF, B32/210.

summer of 1928, the *Banque de France* supported the latter course. To its governor, Moreau, clear assurances of German reparations seemed preferable to the highly uncertain prospect of US debt-relief.[127]

To Gilbert's consternation, however, Poincaré at first sought – once again – to link reparations and war-debts, demanding at a campaign rally in Carcassonne on 1 April that any comprehensive settlement should combine a revision of both. And the French premier also persisted with his policy of procrastination on the Mellon–Bérenger agreement, further putting off its ratification. All of this was of course anathema to the administration in Washington. Yet Poincaré was not a leader who backed down easily and, as noted, France's bid to counter US pressure went even further. Throughout the summer, both the French premier and his foreign minister persisted with attempts to invigorate something akin to a Franco-German economic alliance. It was to complement the Locarno system but chiefly intended to resist American power (and to draw Germany away from deepening commercial ties with Moscow). Even after the Müller government had signalled its disinclination, the French plan to forge a debtors' *entente* and trade alliance – amidst an escalating Franco-American 'tariff war' – did not disappear.[128]

When Stresemann was in Paris for signing the Kellogg–Briand pact, Poincaré reiterated his proposal that France and Germany close ranks, yet without offering him any concrete compensation for backing France's debt-reduction agenda. Briand made further overtures in September 1928. But all were to no avail. The German government followed the American reparations agent, who sternly warned Schubert and Schacht against any bilateral manoeuvres with France.[129] When this became clear, and France and the United States had agreed on basic terms for an expert inquiry, Poincaré demonstratively changed his course. He now came to support Gilbert's scheme. In a speech at Chambéry on 30 September, the French premier declared that he was now prepared to back a general reparations settlement. Yet he also registered France's demand for a still to be specified 'indemnité nette' covering French reconstruction costs.[130] On these premises, Poincaré then came to an understanding with Churchill in October.

Thus, prominent as they remained, security concerns were not the key factor in France's approach to the 'final liquidation of the war'. The need for strategic

---

[127] Seydoux dossier, 15 July 1926, MF, F30, 1282; Moreau (1954), pp. 475–6. Cf. Kent (1989), pp. 276–7.

[128] Döhle (Paris) to AA, 11 June 1928, *ADAP*, B, XII, no. 22.

[129] Stresemann memorandum, 27 August 1928, *ADAP*, B, X, pp. 640–1; minutes of a conversation between Müller and Briand, Geneva, 5 September 1928, *AR Müller I und II*, no. 20; Schubert note, 6 September 1928, *ADAP*, B, X, no. 19, ft. 4.

[130] Record of conversation between Poincaré and Gilbert, 20 September 1928, minutes of a conversation between Gilbert and Schubert, 1 October 1928, *ADAP*, B, X, pp. 161–3.

reassurance, and for a close understanding with Britain, remained undiminished. Briand stressed that the French people were 'deeply attached to the idea of the Entente with England', which remained the backbone of his Locarno policy.[131] But political-cum-financial considerations had clearly become paramount. This seems remarkable. It signalled the relative 'normalisation' of Franco-German relations, the emergence of a more businesslike pattern in the era of London and Locarno. This pattern was by no means beginning to dissolve by 1928.

Anxieties over security, or what French 'public opinion' could stomach in this respect, prevented neither Briand nor Poincaré from opening negotiations. They were indeed prepared to relinquish the Rhineland 'pawn' in return for adequate financial compensations even if this had to be approached the American way, through a new expert inquiry. In early 1928, Paul-Boncour, then *rapporteur* for the *Chambre*'s Foreign Affairs Commission, had been most vocal among those urging Briand to re-assess the security consequences of a *quid pro quo* arrangement with Berlin. In his – long-held – view, Locarno had a critical 'gap': beyond its specific guarantees, there were no (military) controls to prevent Germany from remilitarising the Rhineland once French troops had left. As noted, these concerns were echoed by France's eastern allies, particularly the Polish foreign minister Zaleski. But Briand and Poincaré were no more prepared than the Baldwin government to let such anxieties derail their strategic bargaining with Germany.[132]

Briand was therefore at first very reluctant to take up Paul-Boncour's public demand to establish a permanent inspection-body in the Rhineland. And he likewise dismissed Polish pleas for compensatory guarantees. By September, though, and mainly for domestic reasons, the call for a new civilian 'Commission de Conciliation et Constatation' in the Rhineland featured prominently among the conditions that Briand presented to Müller at Geneva. Nonetheless, the *Quai d'Orsay* clearly emphasised the need for German assurances that ended France's 'financial insecurity' after the wider security question had been 'taken care of' at Locarno and the problem of German disarmament was no longer 'an obstacle'. In other words, Briand desired Berlin to assure that it would pay steady, and sufficient, reparations once France no longer commanded 'the pawn . . . of the occupation'.[133]

It seems even more noteworthy, but was in fact consistent with his underlying aims since 1923, that Poincaré pursued the same priorities.[134] A good five

[131] Cushendun memorandum, 7 September 1928, *DBFP*, IA, V, no. 146.
[132] Larroche to Briand, 24 August 1928, no. 336, MAE, Série Europe, Pologne, vol. 113; Erskine (Warsaw) to Chamberlain, 22 May 1928, *DBFP*, IA, V, no. 354. Cf. Wandycz (1988), pp. 106ff.
[133] Minutes of six-power talks, Geneva, 11 and 13 September 1928, minutes of a conversation between Müller and Briand, Geneva, 5 September 1928, *AR Müller I und II*, nos. 21, 23, 20.
[134] Cf. Keiger (1997), p. 337.

years after he had ordered French troops to occupy the Ruhr, the French premier sought to strike a deal with Germany – and the Anglo-American powers – viewing this as the best insurance for France's future security *and* financial certainty. After the French General Staff had commenced official planning for what later concretised in the Maginot line, Poincaré felt that Paris could afford to pursue such a 'grand bargain'. And he felt that he could sell it to a majority in France. As it seemed the best insurance for consolidating the financial stability of the *franc-fort* period, Moreau also supported this course whole-heartedly.[135]

Thus, considerations of financial certainty trumped security concerns. Of course, both Briand and Poincaré also sought to make the most of the Rhenish 'pawn' as long as it was still of value, i.e. before the occupation was set to end under the terms of Versailles. But it seems not too far-fetched to see this re-orientation of French policy as the result of deeper changes. French leaders had come to seek compromise settlements with Germany, Britain and the United States, all to safeguard national security and prosperity. They espoused this in preference to prolonging the occupation and sustaining a more assertive control of the eastern neighbour.

Setting the new 'terms of reference' – the Geneva compromise and its consequences

Yet before the new 'grand bargain' could be completed, the European powers still had to create the basic political preconditions for its success. And, concretely, they had to agree on the basic 'terms of reference' for what was to be the first step in the desired direction: the expert inquiry. To set these terms was the main significance of the six-power meeting at Geneva in September 1928. Although Stresemann and Chamberlain were absent for reasons of ill health, the Locarno powers – represented by Briand, Chamberlain's stand-in Lord Cushendun and Müller – managed to forge a framework for the Dawes plan's 'organic development'. In turn, this opened the only possible window for a Rhineland settlement. Essentially, it was achieved by adopting Schubert's strategy and implicitly linking the 'liquidiation' of both questions.[136]

In the talks' opening stages, Briand re-asserted France's essential conditions. He impressed on Cushendun that it would be 'useless' for Berlin to demand 'immediate evacuation . . . without offering some substantial *quid pro quo*'. The

---

[135] Moreau (1954), pp. 320ff, 475–6; Stresemann memorandum, 27 August 1928, *ADAP*, B, IX, no. 263. On French financial policy see Mouré (2003), pp. 145–79.

[136] Schubert to Stresemann, 24 July 1928, *ADAP*, B, IX, no. 173; *Quai d'Orsay* memorandum, 21 August 1928, PA, General Files, 3243 D 724934–49; minutes of six-power talks, Geneva, 11, 13, 16 September 1928, *AR Müller I und II*, nos. 21, 23, 28; *DBFP*, IA, V, nos. 149–61.

French foreign minister conceded that the whole problem was 'complicated by the question of the inter-allied debts'. But he also announced that France was still interested in re-examining how far Thoiry could be the blueprint for a new arrangement. Essentially, he thus sought to ensure that Müller would officially accept that the evacuation problem had to be 'linked' to 'that of a final financial settlement'. If Berlin were prepared to make fresh proposals, the French government would be ready to start simultaneous discussions over evacuation and reparations.[137]

Briand stressed that France was 'anxious to reach a solution' enabling it 'to evacuate the Rhineland' and that, because of Müller's domestic situation, this 'should not be made to appear in the light of too much of a bargain'. In substance, however, he insisted on what also remained Poincaré's key conditions: Germany had to 'assure' France that it could meet 'all the charges which had fallen upon her shoulders as a result of the war'. And, to assuage French public opinion, no longer a Commission of Investigation but a lower-key 'Commission of Constatation and Conciliation' had to be established to monitor the demilitarised Rhineland following France's withdrawal. Briand won Cushendun's support for the new arrangement.[138]

Responding to the French overtures, Müller essentially espoused Schubert's tactical design. Early on, he had told Cushendun that any revival of the Thoiry scheme seemed only a recipe for delaying evacuation because the basic problems it raised had not changed. The United States would not 'co-operate' in realising the scheme as long as France had not ratified the debt agreement. And, crucially, 'public opinion in Germany would not understand the linking of the two questions of evacuation and reparations'.[139] On 11 September, the German chancellor presented Briand and Cushendun with the essentials of Berlin's alternative approach. He stressed that his government could not propose any concrete financial arrangements in return for evacuation prior to a revision of the Dawes plan. For Washington and US financial circles had clearly signalled that no American support would be forthcoming 'until the reparations had been settled' and 'the definite sum' of German liabilities fixed. Making evacuation dependent on this would also 'involve [the] grave risk that evacuation would be postponed indefinitely', which would have serious domestic repercussions for the policy that he and Stresemann pursued. And the prevalent German expectation remained that evacuation should be unconditional, the 'logical conclusion' of 'the Locarno policy'. Nevertheless,

---

[137] Cushendun memorandum, 7 September 1928; minutes of six-power talks, Geneva, 11 September 1928, *DBFP*, IA, V, nos. 146, 151.

[138] Briand statement, 13 September 1928; Cushendun memorandum, 7 September 1928, *DBFP*, IA, V, no. 146.

[139] Cushendun memorandum, 8 September 1928, *DBFP*, IA, V, no. 149.

Müller finally signalled that he was prepared to discuss the terms of a general settlement of evacuation *and* reparations on the premise of implicit linkage.[140]

In a conversation with Briand on 5 September 1928, the German chancellor had sought to assuage French security concerns, and devalue arguments based thereupon. Following Stresemann's logic, he argued that Germany's on-going 'credit emergency' and dependence on American capital furnished France with the 'best guarantee' for its 'fulfilment' of the reparations obligations once France had withdrawn from the Rhineland. For Germany's international credit would be 'most severely affected' if Berlin were to cease or even reduce payments.[141] In Müller's view, this was a more effective insurance for France, also in terms of security, than any new verification commission, which would only spark resentment in German nationalist circles. As will be shown, the German government later essentially succeeded in making this case at The Hague.

Underlining the ineffectiveness of British diplomacy at this critical stage, Cushendun could play Chamberlain's broker-role even less convincingly than, had he been present, the foreign secretary himself. As the Foreign Office and the Treasury had still not agreed on a common approach by that time, Cushendun had only very limited authority at Geneva to foster political compromises. All he could do was to impress on Müller and Briand that he would not venture beyond Chamberlain's core principles. On the one hand, London would not 'separate' itself from Paris, as this 'could only result in defeating the purpose' all Locarno partners 'jointly had in view'. On the other hand, the British government was resolved to 'assist in finding a bridge' across the 'abyss' separating France and Germany. But, as Cushendun confessed in his reports to London, he was not 'unduly optimistic' that he could 'do [anything] to help' in this process.[142]

Cushendun confirmed Britain's opposition to any further explorations of Thoiry-style alternatives, demanding that the Locarno powers 'must start afresh'. And he made the – futile – suggestion to Briand that, also to placate domestic criticism in Britain, both powers should consider making a 'gesture'. They should announce an unconditional evacuation of the second occupation zone because – 'nearly mature for evacuation' under Versailles – it 'was really of very little bargaining value'. Overall, however, Cushendun closely followed Chamberlain's – and thus Briand's – new line, pressing Müller to follow suit.

---

[140] Minutes of six-power talks, Geneva, 11 September 1928, *DBFP*, IA, V, no. 151.

[141] Minutes of a conversation between Müller and Briand, Geneva, 5 September 1928, *AR Müller I und II*, no. 20.

[142] Cushendun memorandum, 8 September 1928, minutes of six-power talks, Geneva, 11 September 1928, Cushendun to Lindsay, 19 September 1928, *DBFP*, IA, V, nos. 149, 151 (enclosures), 162.

While reiterating that his government had long 'desired' to end the occupation as soon as possible, he also underlined that London 'did connect the two questions of reparations and evacuation' – 'one question involved the other'. Britain thus unequivocally backed France's demand for a *quid pro quo* agreeement.[143]

Thus, the real question at Geneva remained how to establish an informal linkage between evacuation and a general reparations settlement in a manner consistent with the interests of all three Locarno powers – and the United States. And a compromise on this issue was finally found on 16 September. As it turned out, though, it was originally more acceptable to Berlin and Paris than the British Treasury. The parties agreed that, on the one hand, 'official negotiations' over 'the early evacuation of the Rhineland' were to be opened and, on the other, 'a complete and definite settlement of the reparation problem' was needed. For this latter purpose, a 'committee of financial experts' was to be nominated by the interested governments. Also launched were negotiations on the constitution of a – *panacea* – Commission of Verification and Conciliation.[144]

On Britain's behalf, Cushendun had thus endorsed the premise that it was impossible to separate evacuation from a general settlement of reparations. Thereby, he had provoked a heated dispute with the Treasury.[145] For Churchill still maintained that the time was not ripe for a revision of the Dawes plan. As Britain's new ambassador in Berlin, Rumbold, put it, the Treasury policy remained 'to "stone wall" in the matter of reparations'. And this became the last remaining roadblock on the path to a new expert inquiry.[146]

On 15 September, Churchill had told Cushendun that a reparations settlement should only be approached after the American elections and 'then something like a united European position would develop in regard both to war debts and reparations', with the Rhineland evacuation 'acting as a stimulus'. After the Geneva meeting, Churchill sought to fortify Britain's defensive positions, insisting that the Balfour note remained 'the foundation of our policy'.[147] On 20 September, Churchill underscored that opening reparations negotiations was not only 'futile' but also 'dangerous', especially for British finances, because Washington still ruled out any debt-concessions. Both he and

---

[143] Cushendun memoranda, 8 September and 12 September 1928, minutes of six-power talks, Geneva, 11 September 1928, *DBFP*, IA, V, nos. 149, 151, 152 (enclosures).

[144] Minutes of six-power talks, Geneva, 16 September 1928, *DBFP*, IA, V, no. 161 (enclosure).

[145] *Ibid.*; Cushendun statement during six-power talks, Geneva, 11 September 1928, Cushendun record of a conversation with Briand, 12 September 1928; Rumbold to Cushendun, 14 September 1928; Cazalet to Birkenhead, 16 September 1928, *DBFP*, IA, V, nos. 151, 152, 153, 159; *AR Müller I und II*, no. 21.

[146] Rumbold to Lindsay, 20 September 1928, *DBFP*, IA, V, no. 164.

[147] Cazalet to Birkenhead, 16 September 1928, *DBFP*, IA, V, no. 153.

Leith-Ross feared that unless Britain made its European partners 'realise that we also have interests to defend', it would 'speedily' be manoeuvred into 'a position where France and Germany would confer upon each other mutual benefits at our expense'. At the same time, accepting the Franco-German compromise of Geneva would enable Washington to 'see its general debt [policy] permanently accepted by Europe', which had to be prevented by all means. At the very least, Britain had an interest in placing the 'onus' of 'arresting European appeasement and recovery' on the uncompromising US creditor. Churchill thus insisted on delaying the 'expert conversations' so that 'nothing [could] be settled for some time'.[148]

For Gilbert, overcoming the British Treasury's sustained opposition became the most pressing concern after Geneva. Yet he did manage to convince Baldwin and Churchill to change tack. When meeting the British chancellor in London in mid-October, the reparations agent assured him that Germany would be able to meet the Treasury's core requirement, as defined by Leith-Ross – to muster annuities of 2 billion marks. But this did not yet suffice to make Churchill alter his stance, which he announced to the cabinet on 17 October.[149] Ultimately, the chancellor only backed the expert inquiry once he could reach a favourable understanding with Poincaré. Meeting both the French premier and Gilbert in Paris, Churchill took charge and obtained Poincaré's consent not only to hasten the ratification of the Franco-British debt settlement but also to form an Anglo-French reparations alliance. Churchill wanted to 'make sure' that, prior to any expert inquiry a 'means of agreement exist[ed]' between the Great Powers concerned'. It had to ensure 'that France will not ask too much nor Germany offer too little' and Britain's 'legitimate claims' would be met.[150]

In short, France accepted that the Balfour declaration stipulated British essentials for the envisaged 'final settlement'; and Britain agreed that the 'reparations sum' accorded to France had to cover both 'the debt to America' and the 'reconstruction of destroyed territory'. Most importantly, though, accepting the American line, Churchill and Poincaré agreed that, instead of seeking debt-reduction, both powers should each receive maximal reparations sufficient to cover at least their obligations to the United States. They proposed a distribution-scheme settling annuities of 2 billion marks, which exceeded Germany's reduced payments under the Dawes plan and thus

---

[148] Churchill memorandum, 20 September 1928, Leith-Ross memorandum, 20 September 1928, FO 371/12878/1–73, 75–9. Rumbold to Lindsay, 20 September 1928, *DBFP*, IA, V, no. 164. Cf. Jacobson (1972b), pp. 203–4.

[149] Cabinet minutes, 17 October 1928, CAB 23/59/47; Fisher and Hopkins to Churchill, 16 October 1928, FO 371/12878/191–5; Dieckhoff (London) to AA, 18 October 1928, *AR Müller I und II*, no. 49.

[150] Tyrrell to Grahame, 19 October 1928, *DBFP*, IA, V, no. 182.

significantly higher than what Berlin hoped to obtain.[151] Gilbert could therefore report to Mellon that, with the Geneva compromise, the Anglo-French understanding prepared the ground for a general reparations settlement – without threatening US debt interests.[152] Irrespective of Washington's continued insistence on strictly divorcing reparations from debts, what thus emerged was indeed a powerful confluence of interests. This was one of the most powerful forces shaping the Young plan.

On one level, then, 1928 indeed saw at least a temporary *renversement des coalitions*. In 1924, the settlement had been driven by the 'parallel interests' that united Germany and its *de facto* patrons, the Anglo-American powers. It had been their common concern to prevent Germany's disintegration and link it with a western system, not least as a market for Anglo-American capital and capable reparations – and loan – debtor. In 1928, the strong bond of 'parallel interests' emerging between America, Britain and France was based on the common aim of finally settling the notorious war-debt problem. This was to be achieved largely by making Germany pay annuities that satisfied both Anglo-French demands and, following a finally ratified Mellon–Bérenger agreement, those of Washington. Crucially, such calculations outweighed Anglo-American worries that the envisaged settlement might financially overburden and politically destabilise Weimar Germany. For US policymakers – and most bankers – believed that Germany had the capacity to shoulder substantial burdens, and the British Treasury subdued its scepticism for reasons of political expedience.

In the wider picture, however, there was no fundamental re-alignment in the Euro-Atlantic 'strategic quadrangle'. If less forcefully than in the mid-1920s, Anglo-American influence and interests still served to promote the realisation of Weimar Germany's main aims, especially on the Rhineland. And, more broadly, they also still buttressed the Locarno process – even if they did so far less effectively than four years earlier. Nor should be overlooked that, as noted, the Müller government was indeed prepared to offer sizeable financial compensations for achieving what was politically crucial: the evacuation of the Rhineland. Ultimately, it was American power that propelled the making of the Young scheme, and it thus set the – brittle but indispensable – framework for the eventual political-cum-financial bargain at The Hague. And it was Britain's reinvigorated meditation, first pursued by Chamberlain, then by his successor Henderson and Prime Minister MacDonald, that again clinched the final settlement.

---

[151] *Ibid.*; Tyrrell to Cushendun, 19 October 1928, *DBFP*, IA, V, no. 183; Churchill memorandum, 19 October 1928, FO 371/12878/231–2.

[152] Poole to Kellogg, 28 September 1928, *FRUS 1928*, II, p. 871; Gilbert to Mellon, 23 October 1928, NA RG 59 462.00 R 296/2425.

Now that they had finally discovered common ground, Gilbert and Churchill sought to pressure Berlin to agree to a swift commencement of expert negotiations. And, as Churchill put it in early November, Berlin was to acknowledge the Anglo-French compromise 'confidentially' as the essential starting-point. From the German perspective, however, this compromise was seen as a 'finely-tuned manoeuvre' to abandon the Geneva compromise. Indeed, Stresemann came to criticise it as a step back to pre-Locarno politics – the formation of a creditors' front vis-à-vis Germany. On 17 November, he thus obtained Müller's backing for a formal German protest note against it.[153] Nonetheless, for Berlin a *de iure* independent expert commission still seemed to provide the best possible reassurance that, analogous to 1924, a more balanced agreement could be reached and America's powerful influence would work to Germany's advantage.[154]

The US embassy in Berlin confirmed that the Müller government was indeed prepared to follow Gilbert's 'leadership'. Washington's backing still seemed essential to prevent France and Britain from pushing through a separate understanding at Germany's expense. On 10 October, Schubert 'emphasised' to the US chargé in Berlin, Poole, Berlin's 'great desire for American co-operation' in the envisaged expert inquiry. Berlin was careful to avoid 'any action disturbing or unacceptable to the United States Government' and prepared to heed all 'American requirements', especially that of strictly separating reparations and war-debts. In a note of 30 October, Ambassador Prittwitz conveyed the German government's wish to proceed 'in the same manner as the first committee of experts instituted in 1923'.[155] Fundamentally, the *Auswärtige Amt* desired to re-enact as far as possible the success of the Dawes process.

Yet the outgoing Coolidge administration was long unwilling to accept any US role in the second major attempt to settle the reparations problem after Versailles. In response to a query by Gilbert, Kellogg confidentially outlined the basic guidelines of US policy on 31 October. The administration was 'in principle willing for American citizens to serve as independent experts on a committee similar to the Dawes Committee'. Crucially, however, Washington was not prepared to 'co-operate with other Governments concerned', neither in 'designating' the US experts nor any other way that could be construed as

---

[153] Dieckhoff to AA, 5 November 1928, *AR Müller I und II*, no. 68, note 4; Sthamer to AA, 15 November 1928, *ADAP*, B, X, no. 132; cabinet minutes, 17 November 1928, *AR Müller I und II*, II, no. 68.

[154] Record of a conversation between Stresemann and Gilbert, 13 November 1928, Stresemann (1932), III, pp. 376ff.

[155] Poole to Kellogg, 28 September and 11 October 1928, German memorandum, 30 October 1928, *FRUS 1928*, II, pp. 871–3.

giving the administration even indirect 'official responsibility' for the committee's recommendations.[156]

Privately, Kellogg was of course no less cognisant than Mellon of the fact that the administration's indirect interest in a long-term reparations settlement was considerable. But towards the Europeans he enforced the official line that the American interest in reparations was 'entirely too small' to 'justify' that Washington assumed commitments, 'either directly or indirectly'. By the end of 1928, the secretary of state had thus clearly espoused Hoover's maxims, and abandoned those of Hughes in 1924. His priority became to safeguard narrower US interests. Consequently, when Poincaré used public speeches – at Chambéry and Caen in mid-December – to re-establish the irksome linkage with France's debt situation, Kellogg lost no time to retaliate. He dictated to the international press that 'debts were to be entirely excluded' from the expert deliberations.[157] Yet however draconian Washington was on this point, it remained a highly contentious issue, providing the subtext to all subsequent proceedings.

Following the turn in Chamberlain's diplomacy, Britain finally propelled the negotiations that set the terms under which Washington in early January 1929 finally dropped its objections to the participation of Owen Young and J.P. Morgan. Authorised by Chamberlain, Howard – as 'dean of the Ambassadors' accredited in Washington – oversaw a process whereby the European governments nominated the experts after informally sounding the US administration's preferences; then the State Department officially confirmed their endorsement.[158] As noted, by this time, Chamberlain had come under acute pressure in the Commons for what not only MacDonald and Lloyd George saw as his collusion with Paris and old-style *entente* politics. As the British foreign secretary told Briand at Lugano in mid-December, not only 'the whole Liberal and Labour Parties' were 'openly advocating evacuation' and attacking him for not 'securing' it 'or at least withdrawing the British contingent'. A 'large section of the best conservative opinion' showed 'equal impatience'.[159]

It seems hardly surprising that the lacklustre progress of Locarno diplomacy against a backdrop of transatlantic complications should have spawned such

---

[156] Kellogg to Armour, 31 October 1928, NA RG 59 462.00 R 296/2425.

[157] Kellogg memorandum, 27 November 1928, Kellogg to Armour, 31 October 1928, Armour to Kellogg, 23 December 1928, Kellogg to Armour, 26 December 1928, NA RG 59 462.00 R 296/2494, 2425, 2560.

[158] Memorandum of conversation between Kellogg and Howard, 12 January 1929, Kellogg and Armour, 18 January 1929, NA RG 59 462.00 R 296/2613/1/2, 2623; Chamberlain to Tyrrell, 4 December 1928, *DBFP*, IA, V, no. 257; Howard to Chamberlain, 7 January 1929, *DBFP*, IA, VI, no. 24.

[159] Selby minute, 22 August 1928, Chamberlain to Tyrrell, 18 December 1928, *DBFP*, IA, V, nos. 135, 292.

criticism. Even more foreseeable, though, was that Chamberlain persevered with his 'policy of appeasement'. This culminated in his joint declaration with Briand at Lugano, where he again ruled out unilateral troop withdrawals. Chamberlain subsequently told the Commons that the only way to 'get' the French 'out' of the Rhineland was to aid Paris in obtaining a satisfactory reparations settlement – which would also satisfy Britain's interests. This was indeed the correct reading of the situation.[160]

After the Lugano meeting, Chamberlain noted on 17 December that 'if Stresemann, Briand and I were left alone to find a solution, I think we should manage to secure the evacuation of the Rhineland within a reasonable time'. But the three protagonists of Locarno diplomacy were not 'being left alone' – nor could they 'manage' evacuation politics on their own. Responding to Müller's renewed call for an immediate withdrawal of all occupation troops the British foreign secretary reiterated that 'the Germans were the most difficult people to help in this world' as they were 'always rolling back down the mountain the stone which [he had] laboriously rolled up it'.[161] In reality, though, Chamberlain could no longer be the pivotal broker rolling the key 'stones' up the mountain of European stabilisation. For Britain lacked the requisite power. Yet those who held the critical reins in Washington refused to take Britain's place.

Chamberlain concluded that to achieve his main aims – to preserve the *entente* and buttress the entire Locarno system – Britain essentially had to adopt a two-pronged approach. In fact, he thus reverted to what MacDonald had pursued in 1924. On the level of – transatlantic – reparations diplomacy, London now mediated between Washington, Paris and Berlin to implement the Geneva agreement. Then, once the experts had 'got to work', Chamberlain sought to use the new momentum and initiate 'diplomatic conversations' on a second, much preferred level – that of Locarno politics – to settle the evacuation question. On 26 November, the foreign secretary confirmed that an expert committee should be set up 'similar' to that of 1924, and with key US participants. As Poincaré told Tyrrell the following day, Paris was also 'strongly in favour' of 'following as close[ly] as possible [the] procedure of [the] Dawes Committee', though it insisted on duly respecting the Versailles treaty. Chamberlain therefore urged that the new inquiry should be constituted 'fairly soon' and that 'the Germans should enter it on a footing of equality'.[162] All of this was accomplished in early 1929.

[160] *Ibid.*
[161] Austen and Hilda Chamberlain, 17 December 1928, Austen Chamberlain Papers, AC 5/1/463.
[162] Chamberlain to Tyrrell, 18 December 1928, Chamberlain to Tyrrell, 26 November 1928, Tyrrell to Chamberlain, 27 November 1928, Chamberlain circular, 30 November 1928, *DBFP*, IA, V, nos. 292, 237, 242, 245.

In the realm of Locarno diplomacy, Chamberlain was resolved to hasten the end of the Rhineland occupation by persuading Berlin to accept Briand's demand for a 'Commission of Verification and Conciliation'. In his view, this was crucial for assuaging the French public's concerns. In practice, the commission was to monitor the demilitarised Rhineland as unobtrusively as possible once the ex-allied troops had withdrawn. Yet the British foreign secretary also increased pressure on Paris to 'show a really conciliatory disposition' in hastening the evacuation. Confidentially, he impressed on Briand that French prevarication weakened his domestic standing and ability to lend a helping hand.[163]

But Chamberlain's 'noble work of appeasement' was to remain unfinished, at least on his watch. He would be out of office before the final post-Locarno settlement could be approached. At what turned out to be the final meeting of the original Locarnites at the League Council's spring session in March 1929, Chamberlain reached agreement with Briand and Stresemann that the Geneva compromise of September 1928 still constituted the only basis for future progress. The terms of France's withdrawal from the Rhineland could only be negotiated after the Young committee, by then in session in Paris, had produced its report. Chamberlain thereby endorsed the process that would lead to the first Hague conference.[164] But he had to resign, with the Baldwin cabinet, on 4 June 1929, two months before that conference opened.

---

[163] Chamberlain to Tyrrell, 18 December 1928, Selby minute, 22 August 1928, Chamberlain to Rumbold, 19 December 1928, *DBFP*, IA, V, nos. 292, 135, 299.
[164] Chamberlain to Henderson, 19 April 1929, Rumbold to Chamberlain, 13 and 25 May 1929, Chamberlain to Rumbold, 19 December 1928, *DBFP*, IA, VI, nos. 122, 143, 155.

In his first annual message to Congress on 3 December 1929, President Hoover remarked that it had been a committee of distinguished experts 'under American leadership' that proposed a plan 'looking to a revision' of the ex-allied powers' reparations claims against Germany. In his words, his administration had 'denied itself any participation in the war settlement of general reparations' as US claims were 'comparatively small', arising mainly from 'the costs of the army of occupation'.[1] Thus, in effect, the calibration of US interest in adopting even an informal role in the process of forging a further, final reparations settlement was distinctly different from what had informed Hughes' policy in 1924. This was underscored by the Hoover administration's original refusal, still maintained in mid-January 1929, to endorse Owen Young as chairman of the expert committee.[2]

Subsequently, Kellogg informed Ambassador Howard 'in strict confidence' that while Washington still saw the political responsibility for settling reparations as lying with the European powers, it desired that they should have 'any advice or assistance' possible from American experts. Yet he also emphasised that the new US administration desired to leave matters largely 'in the hands of Mr. Young', after it had finally approved his chairmanship. As Castle noted, if the European governments 'got in a jam where they could not organise', Young would be asked to 'communicate confidentially with the President'. But there would be no decisive engagement. Once they had commenced, the Hoover administration took care to dissociate itself from the Paris proceedings. And it relied on such confidential communication not only to aid the experts in 'rendering assistance' but also, and chiefly, to limit what the committee discussed.[3] This meant above all keeping the debt question and wider political considerations – like the Rhineland or territorial revisions in eastern Europe – off its agenda.

[1] Hoover, 'First Annual Message to Congress', 3 December 1929, in Hoover (1934), pp. 143–4.
[2] Castle memorandum, 12 January 1929, NA RG 59 462.00 R296/2613; Kellogg to Armour, 7 December 1928, *FRUS 1928*, II, p. 876.
[3] Castle memorandum, 12 January 1929, NA RG 59 462.00 R296/2613.

In Paris, Young and Morgan were joined by the British experts Sir Josiah Stamp, who – with Young – became the main architect of the expert plan, and Lord Revelstoke, who died during the proceedings. France was chiefly represented by the financial expert Emile Francqui and central bank governor Moreau; Germany by his counterpart Schacht, the steel-magnate Albert Vögler and the eminent Hamburg banker Carl Melchior. Stresemann had sought to build a 'community of responsibility' beyond party lines in assembling the German delegation, largely to defend the expert approach against the fierce assaults of the nationalist Hugenberg press.

The complex process of the committee's deliberations need not be reassessed in detail here but only insofar as it shaped the further course of transatlantic relations.[4] In short, it revolved around two major issues. First, the experts focused on a re-assessment of Germany's capacity to pay and, subsequently, the size of German annuities and a conclusive timetable for their payment. This was inseparable from heated debates over the new distribution scheme, chiefly concerning the percentages to be accorded to Britain and France. The second key item on the agenda was 'the question of an international settlement and credit bank', whose central task would be to handle 'all the German obligations'.[5]

In Young's assessment, the German delegates had started off the deliberations by presenting the 'economic situation in Germany' in a light supporting their main 'contentions'. They had based their arguments on the claim that, given its continuing dependence on foreign loans, 'Germany could not safely assume obligation to pay annually over the frontier [of] one billion marks on reparations', particularly if the new scheme abolished 'transfer protection'. Towards the US experts, Schacht also stressed that Berlin had to consider the 'out-payment service of her private loans', which added a further 1 billion marks in annual obligations. As to the number of annuities, the German experts argued that the Versailles treaty 'in express terms looked to [the] discharge of all war obligations in one generation'. Citing this unusual yet expedient precedent, Schacht underlined that Germany could not be 'yielding' on this position 'merely because the Allied Governments have extended their [debt] payments over two generations or more'. Yet in the face of stern Anglo-French opposition, premised on the Churchill–Poincaré accord and the demand for basic annuities of 2 billion marks, Germany would have to yield on all fronts. Ultimately, the Müller government accepted a payment schedule spanning fifty-six years, or two generations.[6]

---

[4] For the Young committee proceedings see Vogt (1970); *FRUS 1929*, II, pp. 1025ff; *DBFP*, IA, VI, nos. 109–72. Cf. Knipping (1987), pp. 48ff.

[5] Young memorandum, 3 March 1929, NA RG 59 462.00 R 296/2768. Cf. Schuker (1983), pp. 122–30.

[6] Young memorandum, 3 March 1929, NA RG 59 462.00 R 296/2768; Schacht (1931), pp. 58ff.

In the second week of the proceedings, a subcommittee 'on unconditional payments' under Lord Revelstoke was established to recommend a new 'machinery' for the transfer of unconditional reparations and 'to handle their mobilisation' should this become necessary 'sometime in the future'.[7] The French delegate Francqui proposed establishing an international bank that, in Young's assessment, would be 'a mere shell to hold the German obligations'. The chairman of the committee noted that France desired to 'have all the German obligations out in one basket' to prevent the debtor from reneging on payments by partially writing them off as 'political debts'. Schacht duly launched a counterproposal. He envisaged 'an international credit bank' into which Germany would pay a 'substantial amount of capital', yet not all annual obligations, while shares would be 'issued against that capital' and distributed to Germany's creditors. Under Schacht's scheme, Germany would even become a 'stockholder' in the bank. And the bank would be empowered to grant loans in order to stimulate trade. In particular, this was to increase German exports and eventually allow Germany to fund reparations through surpluses rather than foreign loans.[8]

Seeking to encourage the Hoover administration to support the proposed international bank, Young left no doubt about what was at stake, not only with respect to Europe's financial architecture. He told Kellogg that if the German and French ideas could 'be combined', the emerging bank could not only become the new central 'trustee' organisation for reparations. It could also 'act as credit bank and promote international trade'. In turn, this would permit the interested governments to 'rid' the world of all 'war agencies'. It would allow them to 'abolish' the Reparations Commission, 'withdraw from Germany all the receivership machinery of the Dawes Plan, obtain military evacuation and leave Germany a free and responsible power to deal, through the bank, with her own indebtedness'. Subsequently, Young suggested that the governor of the Federal Reserve Bank should become the director of the new institution to give it the requisite clout and vital US support.[9]

Indubitably, no successful effort to consolidate the postwar financial system could be undertaken without the backing of the 'world creditor'. And, concretely, there was no hope of establishing an effective international bank if it did not receive some support from the Hoover administration and, sanctioned by it, the Federal Reserve Bank of New York. Superficially at least, the bank

---

[7] A further subcommittee, chaired by Stamp, had been established to study the transfer of 'conditional payments' which, in contrast to unconditional payments, were to be 'subject to a moratorium which Germany may declare', not to exceed two years. See Young memorandum, 3 March 1929, NA RG 59 462.00 R 296/2768.

[8] Schacht (1931), pp. 58ff; Ritter memorandum, undated, Ruppel to Ritter, 18 April 1929, *ADAP*, B, XI, nos. 179, 213.

[9] Young memorandum, 3 March 1929, NA RG 59 462.00 R 296/2768.

schemes contemplated in Paris seemed to conform with Hoover's Progressive approach of 'depoliticising' not only reparations but also international finance – to lay the management of both in the hands of experts. Yet, unsurprisingly, the Hoover administration cold-shouldered Young's attempts to promote US engagement. For the time being, it vetoed the participation of any 'official of the Federal Reserve System' in the envisaged international bank. As Mellon told Young in early April, he essentially feared that the contemplated institution would be at the hub of a new financial edifice in which the American government would end up 'collecting reparations from Germany in satisfaction of the allied debt'. It threatened to become an instrument created by American experts yet eluding both the administration's and the Federal Reserve Bank's control while effectively subverting US debt policy. Not only for Mellon and Hoover but also for Kellogg's successor Stimson, this seemed a most undesirable prospect.

The new secretary of state conveyed to Young on 8 April that he and Mellon had been 'much disturbed' at his attempts to promote his vision of a settlement publicly, through articles in the *New York Times*, and without prior consultations with the administration.[10] Sojourning in Paris, Kellogg was asked by Stimson to consult with Young and Morgan to convey the State Department's misgivings. And so he did, unequivocally. Via Kellogg, Treasury Secretary Mellon admonished that through the experts' recommendations the position 'consistently taken' by Republican administrations after the war – that US debt claims were 'entirely independent' from reparations – was 'being most effectively nullified'.[11]

The expert proceedings came to the brink of breakdown in late April because persistent Anglo-French disagreements over the distribution of annuities escalated, and were compounded by Schacht's introduction of far-ranging political considerations.[12] The German delegate Melchior told the American financiers that the conference was 'as good as wrecked' because, while Germany was 'ready to assume [a] heavy burden' the 'Allied figures' so 'vastly' exceeded its capacity to pay that no agreement seemed within reach. Yet the real 'break' was caused by Schacht. Without consulting the Müller government, and clearly abusing his relative freedom of action, the *Reichsbank* president argued that Germany could only accept the proposed high annuities if the ex-allied powers granted political compensations in return. Schacht envisaged highly controversial concessions: apart from a lowering of European

[10] Mellon statement, 8 April 1929, NA RG 59 462.00 R 296/2773b.
[11] Stimson to Armour, 9 April 1929, Kellogg memorandum, 11 April 1929, Mellon statement, 8 April 1929, NA RG 59 462.00 R 296/2773c, 2775, 2773b. Cf. Costigliola (1984), pp. 210–17.
[12] Treasury memorandum, April 1929; Churchill memorandum, 8 May 1929, *DBFP*, IA, VI, no. 136; Hoesch to AA, 14 April 1929, *ADAP*, B, XI, no. 173.

tariff barriers to encourage German exports, a revision of the 'Polish Corridor' and a redistribution of colonial mandates in Germany's favour. Thomas Lamont, in Paris as an observer close to the American delegation, cabled to Morgan & Co. on 19 April that Schacht seemed to 'go quite off the rails', desiring to be 'the original author of political changes on the map of Europe'.[13]

In London, Chamberlain told Fleuriau that the consequences of a failure at Paris would be 'so serious that the representatives would find themselves obliged to reach an agreement'. But Schacht's demands had been immediately cited in *The Times*, and especially Germany's alleged colonial aspirations caused a major stir in Britain. When faced with a different scheme of this nature in early April, presented by the *Wilhelmstraße's* former permanent secretary, Richard von Kühlmann, without Stresemann's authority, Chamberlain had left the latter in no doubt: Britain 'could not contemplate returning to Germany . . . her former colonial possessions'. Nor would the British government 'ever transfer a mandate to Germany'.[14]

Yet the crisis of the Paris talks could be defused. Highly anxious to prevent their collapse, the German government recalled Schacht to Berlin and finally prevailed on him to moderate his position. Britain accepted 'sacrifices' in the distribution question. And in Lamont's verdict Young did 'a heroic piece of work holding the conference together'.[15] On 3 May, Stresemann instructed the German representatives that accepting Young's compromise proposals was 'unavoidable'. Even relatively high annuities had to be countenanced because Germany could not afford a failure, while key provisions of Young's scheme, such as the proposed international bank, the transfer moratorium and the 'liberation from controls' actually were in Germany's vital interest. As not only Stresemann realised, and the flight of US capital from Germany during the subsequent crisis showed, a 'final' break-up of the expert negotiations would have had a very 'unsettling effect upon the markets' because most international financiers had 'counted upon a settlement as certain'.[16]

Young had warned Washington that due to its inflexible debt policy the European powers might blame the administration should the expert negotiations fail. And in return Castle indeed underscored that the State Department was anxious to avoid a further deterioration of the 'international atmosphere' after Schacht had raised divisive political demands in what should remain a

[13] Chamberlain to Henderson, 19 April 1929; Rumbold to Chamberlain, 20 April 1929, *DBFP*, IA, VI, nos. 122, 125; Leffingwell to J.P. Morgan & Co., 19 April 1929; Lamont to J.P. Morgan & Co., 19 April 1929, Lamont Papers, TWL 178–21.

[14] Lindsay to Rumbold, 2 April 1929, *DBFP*, IA, VI, no. 109. Stresemann disclaimed any official support for Kühlmann's actions.

[15] Schacht to Müller, 27 April 1929, cabinet minutes, 29 April 1929, *AR Müller I und II*, nos. 184, 185; Lamont to J.P. Morgan & Co., 19 April 1929, Lamont Papers, TWL 178–21.

[16] Stresemann to German representatives, Paris, 3 May 1929, *ADAP*, B, XI, no. 214.

purely financial inquiry. Yet all the Hoover administration did to defuse the crisis was to rely on the US experts using their influence on the ground.[17] From afar, Stimson sought to steer the experts, and the proceedings, back to the financial plain. He 'officially' told Young on 2 May that 'Allied needs' rather than Germany's 'capacity to pay' was playing 'a preponderant part' in Paris, which had introduced an undesirable 'political element' that had been 'absent' during the Dawes deliberations. To counter this, Young should do his best to 'attack the problem from a purely economic point of view' – to 'reconcile' what Germany considered its capacity with what the experts 'believe[d] the Germans [were] able to pay'. All 'political questions' should then 'properly' be considered by the interested European governments *after* they had received the expert report. And in these considerations, as the secretary of state made clear, Washington would have no part.[18]

The path to the first Hague conference

On 7 June, the work of the expert committee concluded with a result, soon referred to as the Young report, that has been severely criticised, both at the time and, even more so, with hindsight. Notably, it has been branded as an inherently brittle compromise, dominated by the creditors' short-term interests, which clearly outweighed their will to attempt an economically prudent reform of the Dawes regime and the wider Euro-Atlantic financial order. In this interpretation, German attempts to trade financial 'sacrifices' for political revisions, as launched by Schacht, aggravated difficulties; but ultimately Berlin had no choice but to accept the creditors' demands. As is well known, when it was published there was widespread disenchantment with the Young plan in Germany where particularly nationalist circles soon decried its 'enslavement' of Germany for two generations. This would soon stir the unprecedented campaign of Hugenberg and Hitler against it.[19]

Per saldo, however, and taking into account the international and national pressures under which it was forged, the Young scheme can be seen as a less than disastrous compromise. It indeed contained key elements, such as the Bank for International Settlements (BIS), which had *the potential* of becoming cornerstones of a more sustainable world financial order.[20] What made the plan overall acceptable, not least for the German government, was the fact that,

---

[17] Armour to Stimson, 10 May 1929, *FRUS 1929*, II, pp. 1067–8; Prittwitz to AA, 20 April 1929, *ADAP*, B, XI, no. 185.

[18] Stimson to Armour, 2 May 1929, Armour to Stimson, 10 May 1929, *FRUS 1929*, II, pp. 1066–8.

[19] Rumbold to Henderson, 9 June 1929, *DBFP*, IA, VI, no. 174. Cf. Kershaw (1998), pp. 309–10.

[20] Cf. Link (1970), pp. 469ff; Eichengreen (1992), pp. 262–4.

while fixing a reparations total, it also provided for a distinct reduction in payments for the immediate future (the years between 1929 and 1932). And it was the fact that it proposed to end all foreign financial controls of the Dawes regime, thus re-establishing Germany's 'financial sovereignty'.

For Stresemann, the US-led expert negotiations had certainly not brought the desired breakthrough. But sober calculation led him to put his entire political weight behind the new scheme.[21] One important reason for this remained the German foreign minister's deep concern to pre-empt a collapse of the Dawes regime. In his eyes, such a collapse would have precipitated the flight of US short-term capital and conjured up the threat of German 'bankruptcy', with uncontrollable political consequences. But Stresemann's crucial motive for supporting it remained that only the Young scheme could open the door to the Rhineland evacuation. Against this backdrop, the Müller government became determined to do everything in its power to implement the Young plan.[22]

More generally, it is important to note when appraising the Young plan's implications that it was indeed a highly politicised outcome. It reflected negotiations suffused with political interests on all sides. But the real problem did not lie with the Young scheme itself. For it was impossible under the circumstances of the late 1920s, and less conceivable than in 1924, to forge a financially 'rational' settlement of the still politically charged reparations issue. Particularly the constraints of domestic politics, as perceived by the main actors, played a major part in determining the scheme's fate.[23] Yet the cardinal challenge was once again, as in 1924, to convert the plan into a financially *and* politically viable agreement – as well as to re-consolidate the political framework indispensable to this end, which in some form had to include the United States. This challenge had to be met, and would only be partially met, at the first Hague conference – without the involvement or support of the Hoover administration. To sustain such a framework thereafter, once the World Economic Crisis struck, would be beyond the means of policymakers on both sides of the Atlantic.

The Hoover administration and the Young plan – the refusal to jump on the European train

In the United States, Young promoted the expert plan as a means to overhaul the international economic order and boost the fortunes of capitalism against

---

[21] Stresemann letter to *Reichstag* president Löbe, 29 September 1929, *ADAP*, B, XIII, no. 26.
[22] Stresemann press statement, 14 November 1928, Stresemann (1932), II, p. 385; cabinet minutes, 1 May 1929, *AR Müller I und II*, no. 191.
[23] Cf. Kent (1989), pp. 287–303.

the threat of Bolshevism. He particularly campaigned once again on behalf of the proposed Bank for International Settlements, which in his eyes had to play a central part in the scheme. On 6 June, Young called it the mechanism of 'that mutual co-operation which the world's expanding economic era must have'.[24]

US bankers were largely satisfied with the outcome of Paris. J.P. Morgan & Co. thanked Young for 'sacrificing himself to the world's need'. Above all, they hoped that the report would act against further unsettling the world's financial markets by ending the continued uncertainty over reparations. As Ambassador Prittwitz reported, there was 'satisfaction' among financiers that once again US experts had shown Europe the path to stability. By 'further liquidating' the war's financial consequences, the Young plan could not only bolster European recovery but also shore up 'political stability' in the Old World.[25]

Wall Street also came to be 'strongly in favour' of having a Federal Reserve official as a permanent member on the directorate of the proposed international bank. For, as J.P. Morgan publicly declared, the bank could constitute a 'great instrument for the preservation of world peace'. The new FRBNY governor, George L. Harrison, was relatively sympathetic to such positions. He maintained Strong's keen interest not only in making the Young scheme a success but also in widening central-bank co-operation to solidify the global financial order – under US control. But a majority on the Federal Reserve board was wary of losing control if they collaborated too closely with Norman and other European central bankers.[26]

The Hoover administration remained even more adamant, at least in the summer of 1929. It was at this very juncture that Hoover asserted, in his own peculiar way, that '[the] colossal power of the United States overshadows scores of freedom-loving nations and thus made concomitant American leadership in world affairs indispensable'.[27] But in the president's outlook this did not extend to assuming political responsibilities in underpinning the Young regime and the international bank. On the administration's behalf, Stimson reiterated Mellon's earlier veto, stressing not least that Congress remained dead-set against official US support for the international bank. Neither he nor Hoover ever became 'particularly enamoured' with the BIS as an integral part of the Young scheme. On 29 August, Stimson told Howard that despite Young's 'glowing account' of the bank, Hoover was at heart 'an old engineer'

---

[24] Wilson to Stimson, 4 June 1929, NA RG 59 462.00 R296/3000; Howard to Henderson, 14 June 1929, *DBFP*, IA, VI, no. 181.

[25] Morgan to Lamont, 4 June 1929, Lamont Papers, TWL 178–28; Prittwitz to AA, 9 June 1929, *ADAP*, B, XII, no. 17.

[26] Howard to Henderson, 14 June 1929, *DBFP*, IA, VI, no. 181; Lamont (1930), pp. 336–63. Cf. Leffler (1979), p. 204.

[27] Hoover (1929).

and he himself a circumspect lawyer – and before they got onto 'a wagon of that sort' they liked to 'know where [they were] going to get off'. Yet the bank 'might have very far reaching results', burdening America with bail-out obligations 'impossible to for[e]see'. Particularly the manoeuvres of Moreau and Schacht in Paris had aroused such US suspicions.[28]

Even more important, though, was that Hoover and Stimson saw eye to eye in regarding the expert scheme as the best guarantee available for ensuring that Washington received steady and assured debt-payments from Britain and France. Yet, as Howard noted, the Young plan had not only raised the hopes of an 'enlightened minority' in the United States that was intent on seeing America 'play her part in world co-operation'. It had also accentuated 'the fears of the majority who [sought] safety in isolation' and distance from what they essentially regarded as a 'settlement of intra-European differences'. Isolationists like Senator Howell of Nebraska were alarmed at any expert reference to the beneficial effect of future debt-reductions for the new scheme. In the end, however, though not contemplating an active US role in buttressing them Hoover was 'unwilling to obstruct the efforts of Europe to put her house in order' and thus ensure that the 'vast' US investments in Germany were safe. He came to declare his official support for the Young plan. More profoundly, it did 'flatter the national pride to feel that a United States citizen [had] once again solved Europe's problems for her'. That was precisely how the administration would present the Young scheme to Congress. On 4 June, the president thus officially congratulated Young and Morgan on 'the outcome of their exertions'.[29]

Stimson unequivocally backed Hoover's line. Taking office on 28 March 1929, the new secretary of state had immediately confronted the Young committee deliberations in Paris.[30] But European affairs had until then been rather remote on the horizon of his concerns. Stimson had just served for one year as the US governor of the Philippines, returning from Manila only in the spring of 1929, and was at first still preoccupied with Philippine affairs. And he seemed to take over the helm of the State Department in an era marked by prosperity and the absence of serious problems in transatlantic relations, apart from the then still unresolved naval difficulties with Britain. A far more pressing preoccupation for him was to become the situation in China,

[28] Howard to Henderson, 29 August 1929, *DBFP*, IA, VI, no. 347. Cf. Schuker (1983), pp. 336ff.
[29] Lamont memorandum, 25 June 1929, NA RG 59 462.00 R296/3036/1/2; Howard to Henderson, 14 June 1929, *DBFP*, IA, VI, no. 181; Foreign Office memorandum, 17 June 1929, FO 800/280.
[30] Stimson to Armour, 9 April 1929, NA RG 59 462.00 R 296/2773c; Stimson, 'Memorandum of Events since Being Secretary of State', 28 August 1930, Stimson diary, vol. 10, Stimson Papers; Hoover (1952a).

particularly once the Manchurian railway crisis escalated, first between the Chinese and the Soviets, then through Japan's involvement.[31]

Relying on Castle, who remained assistant secretary for western Europe, Stimson saw no reason during his first year in office to develop a distinct policy line on war-debts, reparations and the extent of US involvement in forging a European settlement. In private, the new secretary of state had not shared the reigning Republican consensus on war-debts during the 1920s. He had expressed the opinion that it might be best for all sides if America simply cancelled allied debts to expedite Europe's postwar reconstruction. But Stimson felt that he was 'fighting a minority battle'. And once in office, he quickly adapted, strictly enforcing the administration's maxims vis-à-vis the experts and European governments. He did so mainly because he believed that no politician could abandon the premise that Britain and France had to repay their full obligations without undermining his position vis-à-vis Congress and the American public.

Stimson acknowledged that Young had had 'a desperately hard job' in Paris yet had also done 'a very good job' in discharging his responsibilities. But he had also conveyed to him, in 'conciliatory' but clear language, that the State Department would not countenance further expert efforts that 'would connect the collection of reparations from Germany with the payment of Allied debts to the United States'. In his view, it was natural that Britain and France should seek to link war-debts and reparations because 'they were very poor and they depended on getting money from Germany to help them pay their debts to us'. Yet nor could the United States afford to run the risk of 'drift[ing] into the position of debt-collector against Germany', as this would excessively burden the American government and prevent a further 'reconciliation' with Germany.[32]

Stimson characterised himself first and foremost as an 'old lawyer' who shunned ambitious foreign entanglements with unforeseeable consequences; and his actions in 1929 bore out this characterisation. Officially, he underscored his reliance on the Kellogg–Briand pact, and public opinion, to resolve international disputes. But soon he also sought to distinguish his own approach to international affairs, essentially one of restraint and non-interference, from other, more ambitious approaches, notably that of Woodrow Wilson. The Republican secretary of state highlighted the 'dangers' that had sprung from Wilson's foreign policy, characterising it as 'a blend of high idealism with [an] absolute inability to foresee the reaction which his views and efforts would

---

[31] Stimson, 'Memorandum of Events since Being Secretary of State', 28 August 1930, Stimson diary, vol. 10, Stimson Papers; Stimson and Bundy (1948), pp. 19–26, 69ff. Cf. Ferrell (1963), pp. 159ff, 207.

[32] Stimson diary, 23 November 1932, Stimson Papers, Stimson to Armour, 9 April 1929, NA RG 59 462.00 R 296/2773c; Stimson, 'Memorandum of Events since Being Secretary of State', 28 August 1930, Stimson diary, vol. 10, Stimson Papers.

produce on other people'. As Stimson saw it, neither the United States nor other countries had much to gain from a policy that, like Wilson's, sought to 'delve into their internal policies and . . . to reform them according to his own views and his own forecast of world movements'.[33] Moreover, Stimson was as mindful as his predecessor Kellogg of the undercurrents of isolationism and economic nationalism prevailing in Congress, and the constraints they imposed on US policy vis-à-vis Europe.[34]

Thus, it was to a large extent President Hoover himself who continued to shape, and limit, Washington's role in the Young process. In August, Stimson would conscientiously pursue, and justify, the administration's policy of detachment from the Hague conference. Further eschewing any formal entanglement, the Hoover administration again exerted all its informal influence to implement the Young scheme. Parallel, it used the same levers to ensure the ratification of another key settlement. The French *Chambre* finally ratified the Mellon–Bérenger agreement on 21 July, albeit only by the narrowest margin of eight votes.[35] On 28 July, Hoover could thus inform the American press that he was 'very much gratified to learn' that France was 'disposing' of 'one more of the great financial problems left over by the World War'. The settlement foresaw a 'complete discharge' of French obligations, exceeding $4,000,000,000 over a sixty-two-year period, starting with an initial eleven-year period of reduced annuities. Addressing 'world opinion', the US president underscored that the settlement, based on US lenience, 'mutual sacrifice and consideration', would 'promote a better understanding' between the 'two great nations', and it would thus also give a boost to Europe's further recovery after the war.[36] While the new Franco-American 'understanding' remained limited, the Mellon–Bérenger agreement did give Washington and Paris a substantial common stake in the ratification of the Young plan. The British assessment of the expert recommendations was distinctly more ambivalent.

The second Labour government and the bid for a second London settlement

On 30 May, just days before the expert report was published, the Labour opposition had won its most decisive election victory yet. But MacDonald nevertheless had to form his second minority government, again counting on the support of Lloyd George and the Liberals. By a certain historical

[33] Stimson, 15 September 1930, Stimson Papers.
[34] Howard to Henderson, 29 August 1929, *DBFP*, IA, VI, no. 347; Stimson to Smoot, 26 June 1929, NA RG 59 611.003/1673a; Stimson to Hoover, 8 June 1929, NA RG 59 462.00 R296/2941/1/2; Stimson (1932).
[35] Cf. Moreau (1954), pp. 566–74; Artaud (1978), pp. 870ff.
[36] Hoover press statement, 28 July 1929, in Hoover (1934), pp. 81–2.

coincidence, then, it was once more a government under his leadership that had to see through a major postwar settlement, and protect 'British interests', in a bid to amend the results of the 1924 London conference. MacDonald was determined to re-assume the reins of British foreign policy. He especially sought to shape policy on two strategic issues: mending relations with Washington by finally forging a naval compromise; and co-operating with America to regain what, in his eyes, Baldwin's government had renounced – a leading role in Europe's pacification.[37]

In the assessment of the Labour government, Chamberlain's overly passive and pro-French course had to give way to a forceful bid to buttress Weimar Germany's social democratically led government. To achieve this, Britain above all had put pressure on France to accept the long-overdue evacuation of the Rhineland as one further and decisive step on the path of European reconciliation. Unlike 1924, MacDonald did not also become his own foreign secretary. He – reluctantly – agreed to give this post to Arthur Henderson, mainly because he could not afford to sideline him for part-political reasons. Yet the most pronounced conflicts over Labour's European policy in 1929 did not erupt between MacDonald and Henderson. Rather, they found both of them opposing the man who would leave his mark on The Hague settlement by his nationalist defence of British interests – Labour's returning 'iron chancellor', Philip Snowden.

His leadership of the Labour opposition between 1925 and 1928 had reinforced MacDonald's central assumptions about foreign affairs. He saw enlightened great-power co-operation, if possible directed by a progressive British government, as the key to achieving the main aims of Labour's internationalist policy. He regarded a re-establishment of close Anglo-American ties as the cornerstone for consolidating European and global peace. Likewise, he still considered an active pursuit of Germany's stabilisation as a westernorientated power in a manner also satisfying France as Britain's critical task. In sustaining this orientation, the prime minister was indeed noticeably influenced by Sir Maurice Hankey, who was then still secretary to the cabinet and the Committee of Imperial Defence. Publicly, MacDonald still couched his pursuits in terms of Labour internationalism, as laid down in the Labour executive committee's resolutions on 'International Peace and Co-operation' of 1928.[38] And from the opposition-benches he had criticised Chamberlain's lack of 'moral leadership' in international politics. Yet by 1929 the Labour premier had essentially accepted the Locarno concert as an important anchor of European stability.[39]

---

[37] MacDonald diary, 4 June 1929, MacDonald Papers, 30/69/8/1. Cf. Carlton (1970), pp. 15ff; Boyce (1987), pp. 197–8.
[38] *Report of the 28th Annual Conference of the Labour Party* (1928), pp. 212ff.
[39] Chamberlain to Tyrrell, 18 December 1928, *DBFP*, IA, V, no. 292.

Like MacDonald and all leading Labour internationalists, Henderson had long been a strong advocate of the need for groundbreaking revisions of the Versailles treaty and the rehabilitation of Germany. While generally little concerned with international economics, and a proponent of free trade, Henderson had early on called for a 'solution of the vexed problem of reparations', also through major British concessions. On similar grounds, he had backed the London settlement of 1924, particularly because it buttressed Weimar Germany's return to the comity of nations.[40] By contrast, the new foreign secretary had only given his support to the Locarno treaty 'with strong reservations'. A more faithful proponent of Labour internationalism than MacDonald, he maintained that the security pact could not be seen as a 'definite step calculated to lead to the abolition of war as a method of settling national disputes'. The 'restricted security' it provided was insufficient to allow for 'decisive steps towards disarmament'. Instead, Henderson – like Cecil – was a fervent proponent of the Geneva Protocol. And he championed the wider aim to transform the League into an effective organisation overseeing 'international peace and co-operation' and enforcing a tight regime of collective security, binding arbitration and disarmament. As he stressed at the annual Labour conference in 1929, the British government must not waver in its commitment to 'strengthening the League of Nations and all its machinery'.[41]

For all their different emphases, though, it should not be overlooked that both on the Young settlement and the Rhineland question Henderson and MacDonald pursued largely a common agenda; an agenda that came to conflict with Snowden's. Their priority was a politically viable reparations settlement 'solving' the Rhineland problem; his was the dogged pursuit of what he saw as Britain's rightful financial claims, culminating in his brutal insistence on British reparation 'percentages' at The Hague. In this sense, indeed, two Labour foreign policies emerged in the first year of MacDonald's second government.

More importantly, though, both MacDonald and Henderson were committed to securing the 'immediate and unconditional' evacuation of all occupation troops from the Rhineland. And they, like Snowden, were equally committed to a 'complete and definite settlement of the German reparations problem'.[42] But the methods that they proposed notably differed from Chamberlain's Locarno diplomacy. De facto, MacDonald built on the basic premises that underpinned the politics of London and Locarno. He accepted the basic

[40] Henderson speech, 23 February 1924, Times, 25 February 1924.
[41] Henderson speech, Report of the 29th Annual Conference of the Labour Party (1929), pp. 215–16. Cf. Wrigley (1990), pp. 151–66.
[42] Report of the 29th Annual Conference of the Labour Party (1929), p. 208. Cf. Carlton (1970), p. 29.

ground-rules of the integrative politics of *quid pro quo* between Britain, France and Germany. And he accepted that whatever compromise settlements the Europeans made had to be forged on terms that the government in Washington could endorse. Henderson shared these premises.

What chiefly set Labour foreign policy apart from Chamberlain's, however, was that neither of its protagonists believed that European stabilisation could be advanced by relying first and foremost on a British *entente* with France. Instead of emphasising the need for bilateral reassurance, both MacDonald and his foreign secretary were convinced that Paris had to be markedly pushed to make progress, not only on the Rhineland issue but also regarding disarmament. If necessary, Britain had to side demonstratively with Germany. Concretely, MacDonald and Henderson still reckoned that the main lever in Britain's arsenal was the threat of unilaterally withdrawing British troops from the Rhineland. Particularly the new foreign secretary favoured keeping this arrow in Britain's quiver, and he would pull it out at the decisive stage of the Hague negotiations. In short, then, the Labour view was that the pendulum within the European concert had to swing from Paris to Berlin to enable more balanced solutions to Europe's outstanding problems. And this indeed began to happen; it became most obvious at the first Hague conference itself.[43]

But the new British government also acknowledged that no success on the critical evacuation question was possible in the international constellation of June 1929 without first clinching a solution to the reparations question that was acceptable not only for the European powers but also for the United States. Particularly MacDonald had absorbed the central lesson of his success at the London conference; in analogy to 1924, his government had to begin by securing the adoption of a largely US-style expert scheme, with due consideration for the interests of Washington and the Anglo-American bankers. A pre-eminent concern of MacDonald remained to prepare the ground for a naval agreement with the Hoover administration, and thus place the strategically vital relations with America on a firmer footing. In his judgement, this far outweighed any possible gains Britain could make by fighting for higher reparations-annuities – and risking a collapse of the Young scheme.[44]

In the Foreign Office's assessment, a failure of the Young plan would not only produce a 'breakdown' of German credit with 'unforeseen consequences'. It would also have serious political consequences, furnishing 'definite proof' in Germany and France that 'the Locarno policy of appeasement had failed' and strengthening isolationist sentiment in the United States. As Sargent underlined, while the Americans had desired to revise the Dawes scheme mainly to

---

[43] Henderson to Lindsay, 30 August 1929, FO 408/54, no 65; Henderson memorandum, 3 October 1929, CAB 24/206, CP 263(29).

[44] MacDonald memoranda, 25 June and 4 October 1929, *DBFP*, II, I, pp. 10–11, 106–7.

re-establish 'financial "normalcy"' and stabilise German finances 'once and for all', the Locarno powers had always approached the revision under a broader 'political aspect'. They viewed the reparations issue as part of a wider task: the 'complete re-entry of Germany into the European comity of nations'.[45]

By the summer of 1929, the Foreign Office concluded that French public opinion, long haunted by the dread of German vengefulness, had finally 'been brought to realise' that Locarno provided 'a sufficient substitute' for the military guarantee of the Rhineland occupation. On these grounds, Britain could promote a settlement, no longer by threatening separate troop-withdrawals but by fostering a '*quid pro quo*' agreement that afforded France 'some sort of financial compensation' for foregoing its treaty rights. For cardinal political reasons, the Foreign Office therefore warned against rejecting the Young scheme.[46]

As so much depended on finalising the reparations settlement, Snowden's position carried substantial weight, even more so than in 1924. But the chancellor of the exchequer came to espouse a different, distinctly more negative view. In short, he did not regard the Young plan as even approximating 'an absolutely final and definitive settlement of the whole problem' of reparations – and debts. Snowden held that Churchill's consent to negotiations had been more injurious to British interests than the Treasury's previous policy of procrastination. Particularly irritating to him was that, while France had increased its net receipts under the new scheme, Britain's share of overall annuities was to be reduced to 20 per cent (down from 22 per cent under the Dawes scheme). Snowden also criticised that German payment through deliveries in kind, which had previously harmed British trade, was set to continue. Finally, echoing US sentiments, the chancellor maintained that, as it was 'not relevant', the Rhineland question should not be introduced into the consideration of the Young report's 'purely financial aspects'.[47]

The Treasury's critique of the Young plan was not unanimous though. Stamp saw the Young plan in a more positive light. In his assessment, Britain had not only achieved satisfactory annuities and largely averted the threat to British exports through excessive German payments-in-kind. He also considered the establishment of a Bank for International Settlements as a step in the right direction, crucial to overcome the then prevalent play of 'uncoordinated and uncontrolled forces which settle our fate through the fortuitous value of a single metal' – gold. Essentially, Stamp hoped that the bank might serve to co-ordinate monetary policies between the major European gold-standard states. Snowden agreed that Britain should 'accept in principle the constitution of the International Bank', yet only provided that the 'necessary safeguards'

[45] Foreign Office memorandum, 17 June 1929, FO 800/280.   [46] *Ibid.*
[47] Snowden memorandum, 15 July 1929, *DBFP*, IA, VI, no. 234.

could be established and Britain carried no disproportionate share of the 'transfer risk' in the event of a crisis. Ultimately, though, the Treasury left this matter in the hands of Norman, because it desired the 'unpolitical' Bank of England to oversee not only the set-up of the complex BIS arrangements but also monetary stability in Europe. Norman's attitude towards the international bank remained guarded. The one real advantage he saw was that it might lead to greater co-operation with US Federal Reserve bankers and 'enlighten' them about the need to cut the intricate node of reparations and debts.[48]

On the cardinal political-cum-financial issue, however, Snowden remained adamant, overruling Stamp. As he noted on 15 July 1929, Britain could have considered 'making a final sacrifice now' if the settlement could really be expected to be 'absolutely final and definitive'. But he reckoned that it was 'not likely to last more than a few years'. And, consequently, his overriding aim at the subsequent Hague conference would be to redress even the minor 'sacrifice' that British delegates had accepted under the Young scheme. Snowden was determined that, at the very least, Britain's reparations share under the Dawes scheme, based on the Spa percentages, had to be re-established. In his view, Britain had 'unstintingly' supported its 'Continental Allies' during the war yet never got 'anything substantial' in return for its 'enormous sacrifices'. Now the time had come to stop being 'the milch-cow for every European need'.[49] The British government had to avoid being blamed for a breakdown of the Young scheme. But in actual fact, thus Snowden's rationale, a reversion to the Dawes scheme would be far from disastrous – and more beneficial to Britain than accepting the Young scheme such as it was.

The making of the first Hague settlement

The conflicts of the first Hague conference, held between 6 and 31 August 1929, did not sound the Locarno system's death-knell. Nor was the five-power summit, attended by the Locarno *trias*, Belgium and Italy, predestined to mark the closing of the era of London and Locarno.[50] But the Hague settlement, and the way in which it was reached, did mark a third major *caesura* in post-World War I international politics – after those of 1924 and 1925. Its historical significance was that, as it turned out, it constituted the last 'grand bargain' concluded – this time between the western *European* powers and Germany – in accordance with the ground-rules and understandings established since the

---

[48] Stamp memorandum, 4 July 1929, quoted after Boyce (1987), p. 193.
[49] Snowden memorandum, 15 July 1929, *DBFP*, IA, VI, no. 234.
[50] For the first Hague conference see *DBFP*, IA, VI, nos. 296–349; *ADAP*, B, XII, nos. 155–230; documents on the first Hague conference, 1929, PA, Büro des Staatssekretärs. Cf. Jacobson (1972b), pp. 309–49.

Ruhr crisis, and on preconditions largely set by the United States. Essentially, it was the last significant settlement premised on the politics of London and Locarno before Hitler came to power.

In fact, then, while the degree of tactical manoeuvring and acrimonious dispute in the summer of 1929 was indeed staggering, the international system founded in the mid-1920s had not withered away. That the American government this time refused to assume even a semi-official arbitrating-role, and that the British government was a less consistent and 'disinterested' broker than in 1924, made it exceedingly difficult to reach more than a basic agreement. Yet this was in fact achieved. The outcome of The Hague centred on another Franco-German compromise whereby 'land' – the erstwhile French security base of the Rhineland – was exchanged for 'money' – final German reparation commitments under the Young regime. At the outset of the proceedings, Henderson declared that 'history would judge the consequences of the present Conference by its political rather than by its financial results'.[51] Although not all later observers have agreed, this verdict was indeed confirmed.[52] The British foreign secretary noted correctly that while the financial discussions had 'loomed largest in the public eye', the 'political side' had been no less vital. The 'final evacuation of the Rhineland' was indeed the single most important result of the first Hague conference, potentially of greater consequence for Europe's further 'appeasement' than any gains or losses that Britain or other creditor powers made in their reparation shares.[53]

In the summer of 1929, there was no further breakthrough, let alone a qualitative leap comparable to that of the London conference. But it should be emphasised again that the international and domestic conditions in Europe had changed significantly. Germany was no longer an isolated 'underdog' whose interests on the international stage had to be represented by two *de facto* senior partners, Britain and America. France had ample means, not least replenished financial strength, to resist a settlement that its government deemed disadvantageous. In many ways, The Hague negotiations thus reflected, and continued, the 'normalisation' of postwar European politics and transatlantic relations that had already marked the process leading up to them. One symptom of this normalisation was that during the conference the influence of international financiers was significantly less weighty than in 1924.

Behind the scenes of the intra-European negotiations, leading bankers such as Lamont impressed their interest in a success of the Young plan on the governments concerned.[54] And they were also asked by the Hoover administration to

---

[51] Henderson to Lindsay, 8 August 1929, *DBFP*, IA, VI, no. 296.

[52] Cf. Kent (1989), pp. 307–13; Knipping (1987), pp. 58–67.

[53] Henderson to Lindsay, 30 August 1929, *DBFP*, IA, VI, no. 349.

[54] Lamont to J.P. Morgan & Co., 19 April 1929, Lamont Papers, TWL 178–21.

make a compelling financial case for the swift implementation of a new reparations agreement. Yet shaping the talks of The Hague, far more than those of London, was a hard-fisted *intergovernmental* bargaining process. It was an attempt to reconcile the disparate interests and publicly raised expectations of France, Britain and Germany with those laid down by the US government, which were less conspicuous but always present in the background.

In fact, the tight limits that Washington had set, chiefly on debts, accounted at least as much for The Hague's acrimony as the fact that the Young proposals had left German and British interests unsatisfied. Snowden for one certainly had no qualms about safeguarding national interests in tough bargaining with a 'normal' German negotiating-partner, even if the result significantly burdened Weimar's predominantly Social Democrat government. And, as noted, the Hoover administration was even less concerned that the envisaged 'final reparations settlement' would place unbearable, perhaps existential, burdens on Germany. Besides, for President Hoover himself postwar 'normalisation' also meant greater US distance from the European debtors' attempts to settle their political differences.

With the Republican administration guarding its distance, Britain played a more dominant role at The Hague than at London in 1924. But its role was also very ambivalent. This ambivalence was thrown into relief by Snowden's uncompromising pursuit of British percentages with scant regard for its wider political implications and Henderson's effective mediation between Stresemann and Briand. Mainly on account of Snowden's 'Britain first' rationale, the Labour government's search of a 'rational' financial agreement indeed degenerated into the 'feckless pursuit' of 'short-term interests'.[55]

It should not be overlooked, though, that this regression occurred against the background of a deteriorating financial situation and rising British unemployment. The impact of the Wall Street boom, which not only cut the flow of US loans to Europe but also actively withdrew gold and capital from Britain, was becoming palpable. And that constellation made it ever harder for both the Treasury and the Bank of England to maintain financial stability on gold-standard premises. Though it did not yet escalate in the summer of 1929, this brewing crisis further curtailed the MacDonald government's already tight room to manoeuvre, making a more balanced approach difficult.[56] Nonetheless, Snowden played a distinctly obstructive part in the making of the Young settlement. By contrast, and with MacDonald's backing, Henderson made an important contribution to the last major political agreement of the 1920s, that of settling the Rhineland evacuation. It was thrashed out in the final days of August.

---

[55] Cf. Kent (1989), pp. 305–6.   [56] Cf. Eichengreen (2004), pp. 314–43.

Yet necessary concentration on Henderson's diplomacy, or Snowden's lack thereof, should not obscure the fact that what led to the Hague agreements was the second major transatlantic *'quid-pro-quo* process' in the decade after the Great War. Only such a process produced the agreement that had been elusive since Locarno and the like of which would not be seen again before 1933. It was based on Germany paying a financial price in the form of a 'final reparations settlement' that certainly fell short of fulfilling revisionist expectations of financiers like Schacht, let alone more radical German nationalists. And it was premised on strategic French concessions in the form of (occupied) territory, and with little of the security assurances – apart from a largely token *Commission de Constatation* – on which Briand and Poincaré had originally insisted. In the wider picture, however, it was an agreement that only became possible, once again, because of an American initiative, even though this time – in contrast to 1924 – it was not the initiative of a US secretary of state but largely that of the semi-official reparations agent Parker Gilbert. But the Hoover administration's eventual – self-interested – decision to back the new scheme and join forces with financiers in pressuring the Europeans to adopt it was again a very critical factor.

At the conference itself, the United States was only represented by Edmund Wilson, the long-serving US minister in Switzerland. At the behest of Hoover and Stimson, Wilson indeed acted as no more than an 'unofficial observer' with specifically limited authority. Stimson notified the president that Kellogg had attended the London conference of 1924 'to put in force the provisions of the Dawes plan' and that this could furnish a 'precedent'.[57] Significantly, however, neither he nor Hoover regarded it as a precedent in Hughes' vein. The Hoover administration saw no need to repeat either the forceful political intervention or the intensive co-operation with US financiers that had characterised Washington's pursuits in the mid-1920s. American policymakers thus exerted their influence only in the most informal fashion. They basically relied on the European governments' self-interest in *not* acting against US wishes. And they relied on key US financiers, apart from Lamont, especially J.P. Morgan himself, to lean on London and Berlin to ensure that the Young scheme would be adopted.[58] Theirs echoed US efforts *after* rather than *at* the London conference. Only on this level, then, the pattern of 1924 re-emerged.

Planning for the conference, the Labour government had agreed to propose that financial and political discussions should be pursued 'concurrently' at The Hague and that two commissions should be established for this purpose. Henderson became the chairman of the Political Commission, while Snowden

---

[57] Howard to Henderson, 19 July 1929, *DBFP*, IA, VI, no. 243; Armour to Stimson, 31 May 1929, NA RG 59 462.00 R296/2910.
[58] Lamont (1930), pp. 336–63.

dominated the other, the Financial Commission. Subsequently, deliberations at The Hague indeed fell into two parts, centring on two main issues: the distribution of annuities among Germany's reparations creditors; and the terms for ending the Rhineland occupation. The time and energy spent on the first, which dominated the proceedings, stood in inverse proportion to its historical significance. Yet it soon emerged that it had to be settled – and that, concretely, France and Belgium had to satisfy Snowden's reparations demands – before the second, more important Rhineland compromise could be forged. As Henderson observed, this was then achieved 'without much difficulty'.[59]

In the judgement of Henderson, the British delegation's overriding task at The Hague was to secure the withdrawal of all allied troops from the Rhineland at the earliest possible date. MacDonald had put pressure on the French government by announcing that he desired to have British troops home 'by Christmas'. Yet the Labour premier, who sought to steer Britain's delegation from London, and Henderson, who strove to do the same at the conference itself, had to master a twofold challenge to realise this objective. On one level, while also seeking some concessions on annuities to satisfy parliament and public opinion at home they had to restrain Snowden from undermining a financial agreement through his assertive demands. On another, they had to mediate a Rhineland agreement between France and Germany that – as ever – could not only be accepted by Stresemann and Briand but also find the approval of their respective domestic audiences. Concretely, Henderson reckoned that British diplomacy had to use its 'influence and ingenuity' in preparing a compromise that covered the French demand for a 'Comité de Conciliation et de Constatation' yet also was 'sufficiently anodyne' to satisfy the Germans.[60]

In mid-July, France had established rigid conditions for the compromise that the British government desired. And Briand, who had succeeded Poincaré as interim premier, lost no time in asserting France's bargaining-position. He stressed that an early evacuation of all occupation zones hinged on settling the reparations question 'in a final manner' and 'accepting the Young Plan as a whole', i.e. without major revisions in Britain's or Germany's favour. He also insisted that there not only had to be a 'Comité de Conciliation et de Constatation' but that this committee also had to be sufficiently robust to satisfy French public opinion and the French General Staff.[61] Briand's demands left the French delegation a wide array of possible interpretations.

[59] Henderson to Tyrrell, 5 July 1929; Sargent memorandum, 9 July 1929, DBFP, IA, VI, nos. 221, 224.

[60] Henderson to Lindsay, 9 and 30 August 1929, DBFP, IA, VI, nos. 300, 349; Schubert memorandum, 9 August 1929, ADAP, B, XII, no. 157.

[61] Tyrrell to Henderson, 18 July 1929; Briand to Tyrrell, 9 July 1929, DBFP, IA, VI, nos. 241, 225 (enclosure).

While the French premier assured Stresemann that he no longer desired to impose anything 'in the nature of military control', these basic criteria had to be met. In the French interpretation, the *comité* was a natural extension of the Locarno pact, filling a gap that the treaty had left for the time following the occupation. Finally, though, Briand introduced further important *caveats*. He maintained that Paris had always distinguished between the different occupation zones and, given the size of France's forces, it would be more difficult for him than for his British and Belgian colleagues to give a precise evacuation date for the final, third zone. On 9 August, Briand privately told Henderson that 'some regrettable delay' in the evacuation of that zone would be unavoidable because the *Chambre* first had to ratify The Hague settlement, which was inconceivable before mid-October.[62]

Presented with such hardly surprising French conditions and *caveats*, Stresemann nonetheless felt the need to counter Briand's overtures and stake out Germany's bargaining-essentials in what even sympathetic British observers deemed a wooden, almost ritualistic fashion. Yet what the German foreign minister asserted merely reflected the Müller government's overriding concern. It was the concern that a combination of French prevarication and British hard-line defence of financial interests would converge to prevent once again the realisation of the German delegation's chief aim at The Hague: to return home with a fixed termination date for the Rhineland occupation. Stresemann thus began by returning to 'the old German argument' that there was 'no real connexion between the political question of the evacuation and the financial questions arising out of the [reparation] settlement'. He insisted that, as Berlin had not only fulfilled Versailles' disarmament obligations and accepted fresh commitments through Locarno but also conscientiously paid 'the sums due under the Dawes Plan', the occupation was no longer 'legally justified'. Playing his part in the Franco-German ritual, Briand of course immediately refuted Stresemann's arguments.[63]

The German foreign minister also sought to impress on his interlocutors that, despite French offers to make it less military in character, the establishment of a verification and control commission would create major domestic troubles for the Müller coalition. Not least, Kaas and Wirth, the leaders of the *Zentrum* party, which was part of the coalition and represented the Rhineland's mainly Catholic population, had already vehemently protested against any such schemes. Even more, a new commission would be grist to the mills of the nationalist forces that, under Hugenberg and Hitler, were already militating

---

[62] Briand to Tyrrell, 9 July 1929, *DBFP*, IA, VI, nos. 241, 225 (enclosure); Tyrrell to Henderson, 18 July 1929, Henderson to Lindsay, 8 and 9 August 1929, *DBFP*, IA, VI, nos. 241, 296, 300.

[63] Schmidt memorandum, 8 August 1929, *ADAP*, B, XII, no. 155; Henderson to Lindsay, 8 August 1929, *DBFP*, IA, VI, no. 296.

against the Young plan. Like Finance Minister Hilferding, Stresemann also feared that Snowden's intransigence could further jeopardise a Rhineland compromise. But he maintained that at the London conference 'similar situations' had arisen and would have undermined the proceedings 'unless MacDonald had assumed a balancing position'. In fact, both the British prime minister and Henderson sought to achieve the same in 1929.[64]

Snowden's nationalism and the necessary evil of the 'distribution question'

In the far-ranging disputes over the distribution question, which took centre-stage during the negotiations' first three weeks, the British chancellor retained his 'unbending attitude', much deplored by Briand. He kept up his pressure for substantial rises in Britain's share of unconditional and conditional reparation annuities. But French attitudes in the Financial Commission were long no less 'unbending'. The leading French delegate, Finance Minister Henri Chéron, defined on 7 August what would remain his delegation's bottom-line till the eleventh hour: Paris 'accepted' the experts' emphasis that the Young plan 'must be regarded as an indivisible whole' that was not to be tampered with 'though it involved considerable sacrifices' for France. The French delegation underscored its resistance to revisions in Britain's favour by forming a common front with the Belgian premier Henri Jaspar. On 21 August, Briand still countered Snowden's pressure by insisting that it was 'politically impossible' for his government 'to accept any alteration in [the] Young table of distribution'.[65]

For their part, Hilferding and the German economics minister Curtius told Snowden that Germany was already showing its readiness for financial concessions by accepting the proposed Young scheme. Berlin could not accept any 'new German sacrifices', especially increases in unconditional annuities. But the German delegation undertook to ensure that the newly proposed deliveries in kind – mainly coal-deliveries – would be made in ways least injurious to British commercial interests. And Stresemann impressed on Snowden that the longer The Hague negotiations dragged on, 'the more difficult the situation in Germany would become as the movement against the Young Plan would grow ever stronger'.[66] Yet this was to no avail.

---

[64] Schmidt memorandum, 8 August 1929, *ADAP*, B, XII, no. 155. Germany also sought to discuss the Saar question and French sanctions under the Young regime. Both issues could only be settled in 1930. Cf. Krüger (1985a), pp. 496ff.

[65] Henderson to Lindsay, 7 August 1929, Snowden to MacDonald, 22 August 1929, *DBFP*, IA, VI, nos. 292, 328 (enclosure); Schmidt memorandum, 8 August 1929, *ADAP*, B, XII, no. 155.

[66] Schubert memorandum, 9 August 1929, Schmidt minutes, 17 August 1929, *ADAP*, B, XII, nos. 157, 180.

By mid-August, the proceedings had reached serious roadblocks. Both the Hoover administration and MacDonald viewed the developments at The Hague, and particularly Snowden's pursuits, with growing unease. And both sought to prevent not only a collapse of the negotiations but also a collapse of the entire Young scheme. Republican decisionmakers in Washington were very negatively impressed by Snowden's 'opposition' to the Young scheme which they essentially saw as a 'political manoeuvre'. As Ambassador Howard reported on 12 August, while the Hoover administration 'outwardly' maintained its 'usual aloofness to all matters affecting reparations', it actually followed the Hague talks very closely; and, like Wall Street, the administration signalled that the United States would be distinctly 'disappointed' if a 'complete breakdown' ensued.[67]

But the State Department's attempt to prevent such a contingency was restricted to pressing MacDonald, through Lamont and the new ambassador in London, General Dawes, to rein in his chancellor. Moreover, the department informed Ambassador Howard that should the conference fail US 'resentment' would be 'directed against Great Britain'. Howard observed that Snowden's intransigence had one beneficial effect: it drew American attention to the fact that Europe in 1929 was 'very different from Europe when M. Poincaré was in the Ruhr' – yet also to the unchanged debt and reparations quagmire. The *New York World* had underlined that because they had not addressed these problems Americans 'live[d] in a glass house and could throw no stones at Mr. Snowden'. But Howard also noted that the 'process of re-education' of US opinion had only just begun. Arguably, this process would only be substantially advanced after another world war.[68]

Urged by Dawes and Lamont, MacDonald on 10 August sent a plea for moderation to Snowden, warning him that Britain could not afford to block an agreement at The Hague and proposing to send Lamont across the Channel to find a solution. Yet the prime minister's telegram was mistakenly sent 'en clair', thus exposing the Labour government's internal divisions. Snowden, who of course rejected Lamont's offer, retorted that this had undermined his bid to convince the other delegations that he was 'not bluffing'. In fact, the revelation came as no surprise to either the German or the French delegates. Schubert and Berthelot concluded, correctly, that it was unlikely to alter the course of the proceedings. More importantly, the 'telegram affair' revealed the central nexus of interests that linked Washington, US high finance and a pragmatic Labour premier who was intent on reinvigorating Anglo-American collaboration. If less pronounced than in 1924, this nexus again became the

---

[67] Howard to Henderson, 12 August 1929, *DBFP*, IA, VI, no. 310.
[68] *Ibid.*; Howard to Henderson, 23 August 1929, *DBFP*, IA, VI, no. 333.

most powerful propellant for the eventual Hague agreement, the adoption of the Young plan and the Rhineland settlement.[69]

Despite Snowden's rebuke MacDonald persisted with his efforts and on 24 August obtained cabinet backing for his position that the British delegation should accept anything approximating 'a substantial offer' from the other powers, '70 or 80 per cent of [Britain's] claim'. His rationale remained that it was crucial to 'avoid the unknown but certainly troublesome repercussions, political and financial, that would follow a complete breakdown', especially in Germany. The blame for any such scenario must not be laid at London's doorstep.[70]

But the British chancellor of the exchequer remained even more persistent. He was not swayed by the cabinet resolution. And he also rejected Stresemann's proposal to work out an interim arrangement rather than risk complete failure and a return to the Dawes plan. When subsequently Chéron and Jaspar took furtive steps towards meeting British claims, Snowden dismissed their proposals as 'impertinent'. The situation was further complicated by Italy's resolve to refuse any concessions regarding its reparations shares.

In the end, though Snowden claimed to be 'sympathetic to German anxieties', he always returned to his 'granite' position that if Britain's demands were not accommodated the Dawes scheme should continue. And he confidentially told the German delegation that it should welcome this because in the event of a major transfer crisis Germany could still end up with far lower obligations than under the proposed Young scheme.[71] Snowden indeed negotiated in an imperiously nationalist manner. He devalued the other powers' claims as merely selfish rather than legitimate – yet he at the same time far exceeded his interlocutors in just such selfishness. At one point, the chancellor privately confessed that while he had always considered himself 'an internationalist' he became 'incredibly imperialist' when he saw the Union Jack hoisted in a foreign country. And for him, as Snowden told Stresemann on 17 August, not merely minor reparations sums were at stake. Rather, the Labour government had to prove, both domestically and in the international sphere, that it could assert its interests vis-à-vis the other powers; and he had to 'preserve' the 'prestige' that had been largely lost under Chamberlain.[72] In 1929, Snowden was to achieve the former but hardly the latter goal.

---

[69] Snowden to MacDonald, 10 August 1929, *DBFP*, IA, VI, no. 304; Snowden (1934), p. 799; Sthamer to AA, 8 August 1929, Schubert memorandum, 13 August 1929, *ADAP*, B, XII, nos. 156, 171.

[70] MacDonald to Snowden, 24 August 1929, *DBFP*, IA, VI, no. 337.

[71] Schmidt memorandum, 17 August 1929, *ADAP*, B, XII, no. 180; Snowden to MacDonald, 22 August 1929, *DBFP*, IA, VI, no. 328 (enclosure).

[72] Grigg (1948), p. 229; Schmidt memorandum, 17 August 1929, *ADAP*, B, XII, no. 180. Cf. Boyce (1987), pp. 208–9.

The hard-won agreement on the distribution of the 'final' shares of reparation-annuities was not hammered out until 27 August – and it was ultimately only reached through Franco-Belgian concessions and the other powers' combined pressure on Italy. Essentially, as Hankey cabled to MacDonald, the other creditors had agreed to 'secure to Great Britain an additional 40 million marks a year for 37 years' and to readjust 'the frame-work of the Young plan' so as to grant it 96 million marks per annum 'as unconditional annuity'.[73] Finally, Rome had been persuaded to accept that the Italian state railways would purchase an annual supply of 1 million tons of British coal to compensate for British losses through German deliveries in kind.

So much, then, for the glorious horse-trading that, ten years after Versailles, allowed the victors and the vanquished of the Great War to forge a settlement supposed to 'liquidate' that war's consequences once and for all. For all it was worth, the compromise on annuities did pave the way for the establishment of the Young regime – and it enabled a settlement of the central 'political' problem, the evacuation dispute, just two days later, on 29 August. This was achieved in what became the last instance of functioning, effective Locarno politics – or rather: London- and Locarno-style search for compromise – in the interwar period.

The 'resolution' of the Rhineland question? The final evacuation agreement of 1929

If Chamberlain had sought to steer the Locarno concert through a privileged *entente* with Briand, Henderson proved at The Hague that he could successfully recalibrate British policy towards a more equidistant mediating-position between Paris and Berlin. Notably on the Rhineland issue, the Labour government desired to step up peaceful change, thus favouring a re-orientation towards German positions. Yet, backed by MacDonald, Henderson was also very careful not to alienate Briand by too openly siding with Stresemann. Instead, he acted on the premise that in order to achieve what London sought, a swift and definite evacuation, he had to foster what had always been at the heart of Locarno politics: a mutually acceptable arrangement that could win domestic support in both France and Germany.

Parallel to the acrimonious altercations in the Financial Commission, Henderson embarked on this mediation-process, both in the Political Commission and through separate private meetings with Briand and Stresemann. Early on, he signalled to the German foreign minister that the Labour government sympathised with his insistence on finally setting a definite evacuation date, as this was not only crucial for winning the *Reichstag* vote on the Young plan but

---

[73] Hankey to MacDonald, 28 August 1929, *DBFP*, IA, VI, no. 344.

also for the Müller coalition's survival. Yet Henderson also told Briand that he sought to effect the Rhineland evacuation in a manner permitting him, too, to save face – and preventing a demise of his centre-left government. In effect, both politicians were equally anxious to avoid a scenario in which a right-wing government would take over in Paris and refuse to accept a dissatisfactory Rhineland agreement.[74]

On the one hand, the British foreign secretary thus took pains to reassure the French premier. He underlined that his government had 'purposely refrained' from carrying out the election pledge of immediately withdrawing British troops because it desired to retain 'cordial relations' with Paris. On the other, he told both Stresemann and Briand that MacDonald was earnestly committed to bringing home all British troop contingents by the end of the year, which remained an important lever vis-à-vis France. Henderson's core aim remained to convince the French delegation to accept a fixed deadline, and he at first proposed late December 1929. But the British foreign secretary sought to forge compromises with, not against, Briand. He thus refrained from outright dismissing Briand's domestically motivated demand for a new control commission, even though he was no more convinced of its usefulness than before the conference. Instead, Henderson attempted to build a bridge that spanned the Franco-German gulf on this issue – even if in British eyes the new commission's main quality had to be that it was unobtrusive and thus did not spark German resentment.

Fundamentally, Henderson was as convinced as MacDonald that the time for trying to contain Weimar Germany through Versailles-style control bodies had definitely passed. In their judgement, the only effective way of ensuring that Germany continued to respect the basic demilitarisation provisions of 1919 and, more generally, the emerging postwar order lay in strengthening moderate, centrist forces within Weimar's parliamentary system. They had to be strengthened against those who were clamouring against the Young plan and for a more aggressive German policy. And this in turn required eliminating all manifestations of treaty enforcement – in order to accelerate Germany's integration into a 'comity of nations' whose European core was the Locarno concert, though MacDonald and Henderson did not call it that.[75]

By the time that the Political Commission convened for what became a groundbreaking meeting on 22 August, Stresemann had reached agreement with Henderson on 'the main point of principle', the final evacuation date for

---

[74] Henderson to Lindsay, 9 August 1929, Henderson to Briand, 22 August 1929, Briand to Henderson, 22 August 1929, *DBFP*, IA, VI, nos. 300, 329; Schmidt minutes of talks between Stresemann and Briand, 8 August 1929, *ADAP*, B, XII, no. 55.

[75] Henderson to Lindsay, 9 and 25 August 1929, Sargent to Nicolson, 20 August 1929, *DBFP*, IA, VI, nos. 299, 325, 339.

French troops. Both consented that if the Müller government was to have any chance of presenting the envisaged settlement as a success, the deadline had to be no later than 1 April 1930. Briand had prevaricated for nearly three weeks on this critical issue, invoking the impasse in the Financial Commission's deliberations. He eventually agreed to consult French military experts on the earliest feasible date for completing troop withdrawals from the decisive third occupation zone. And on 21 August he informed Stresemann that 'under no circumstances' could he meet the deadline that Britain and Germany had proposed. Briand maintained that the size of 50,000 French troops still stationed in the Rhineland had to be considered; and he also argued that it would be very difficult to remove them in wintertime. Thus, the end of September 1930 seemed the earliest realistic date that the French delegation could suggest. One day later, however, the French premier informed Henderson that if the *Chambre* could be brought to endorse the conference agreements by late October the occupation could be terminated earlier, by 30 June 1930.[76]

At The Hague, then, there were clearly no longer any fundamental French reservations to ending the occupation on grounds of security. The only remaining sticking-points were the evacuation's *modus procedendi* and timing. To make French acceptance easier, and protect Britain's financial interests, Henderson had earlier proposed that, as a 'gesture of friendship', Germany should waive all of its restitution-claims against the occupying powers. And Stresemann had promised to deal with them 'in a large and conciliatory spirit'. Yet he also tried to use this conciliatory offer as a bait, assuring Henderson on 22 August that Germany was prepared to satisfy all restitution demands provided that France and Belgium agreed to an early evacuation date. Parallel, a special commission had provided a basic formula for a 'Comité de Conciliation et Constatation', to be established 'in conformity' with 'the arbitration agreements concluded at Locarno'.[77] In practice, however, the commission would never become operative – it fell victim to the turbulence of the early 1930s.

In the final stages of the negotiations, Henderson became more assertive in bringing Britain's weight to bear in Germany's favour. He now announced that irrespective of the discussions' outcome Britain would begin pulling out its occupation troops in September. Yet, in short, the crucial understanding between the Locarno powers remained elusive. France refused to commit to any 'fixed date' as long as the fate of the Young plan remained uncertain. In the

---

[76] *ADAP*, B, XII, nos. 202–27; Briand to Henderson, 22 August 1929, Henderson to Lindsay, 12 August 1929, *DBFP*, IA, VI, nos. 329, 313.

[77] Conference minutes, 21 August 1929, Henderson to Lindsay, 30 August 1929, *DBFP*, IA, VI, nos. 326, 349; Schmidt minutes of talks between Stresemann and Briand, 21 August 1929, *ADAP*, B, XII, no. 196.

end, it was not Henderson's finesse as mediator but the compromise in the distribution dispute that generated the critical final momentum. As the British foreign secretary himself noted, 'the moment [that] a settlement on the financial side was in sight, both M. Briand and Dr. Stresemann showed the most conciliatory spirit'. On 29 August, Briand's final offer, the deadline of 30 June 1930, became the cornerstone of the agreement that ended the Rhineland occupation five years ahead of the Versailles treaty's original deadline.[78]

Throughout The Hague negotiations, official US policy had maintained a nearly complete detachment from the Rhineland question. Symptomatically, before the conference Stimson had only referred to this 'political' issue to underline that Washington had never been 'interested' in the occupation 'for its own sake' but only 'acting on the request of its associates' when supporting it in the early 1920s. In his view, Washington had already made 'substantial concessions' in terminating its participation and agreeing to reduce its army-cost claims vis-à-vis Germany.[79]

The American secretary of state now essentially expected Britain to induce the French government, at last, to end what he and Hoover had long come to regard solely as proof of French militarism. In other words, Washington left it to the Europeans to settle The Hague's thorniest political problem. The main US concern had been that newly escalating disputes over evacuation could derail the adoption of the Young scheme. Yet this had soon seemed unlikely. In any case, Stimson was not prepared to get involved in Henderson's deliberations with Stresemann and Briand even through intermediaries such as the unofficial American observer Wilson. Nor was the State Department prepared to exert pressure on France in analogy to what Hughes had pursued five years earlier with regard to the Ruhr. US bankers, notably the Morgan partners, were this time equally reluctant to interfere in anything beyond their main concern of seeing the new expert plan adopted.[80]

The outcome of The Hague conference – a balance-sheet

The Labour government was on balance very satisfied with The Hague settlement, not least because it won praise for it both in the Commons and in the British press. Like MacDonald, Henderson accorded the outcome an epochal significance, noting that the conference had 'at long last taken the final step for bringing the world war to an end'.[81] It was revealing, though, that most British papers particularly hailed Snowden's 'triumph' in the distribution

---

[78] Henderson and Lindsay, 30 August 1929, FO 408/54, no. 65; Hankey memorandum, 31 August 1929, *DBFP*, IA, VI, no. 346; *ADAP*, B, XII, nos. 222–7. Cf. Knipping (1987), pp. 67–73.
[79] Stimson to Armour, 11 May 1929, *FRUS 1929*, II, p. 1069.
[80] Lamont (1930), pp. 336–63.
[81] *Report of the 29th Annual Conference of the Labour Party* (1929), p. 208.

question, and the chancellor received an enthusiastic reception on his return to London. He won praise for his re-assertion of Britain's 'international rights'. Yet not only Henderson but also the Conservatives' 'Francophile circles', and notably Chamberlain, concluded that Snowden had 'smashed a lot of political china' at The Hague.[82] Indeed, Labour's 'iron chancellor' had won concessions at a considerable price for Britain. He had not only damaged already strained relations with the erstwhile French *entente* partner but also Britain's standing in Germany and the United States, which Montagu Norman deplored. Nevertheless, both Briand and André Tardieu, the former French interior minister who succeeded him as premier in October, were relieved to have attained a compromise at The Hague and keen to see it implemented.[83]

After the Hague conference, the Labour government did not desire to revive Chamberlain's *entente cordiale*. But both MacDonald and Henderson were intent on mending fences with Paris, albeit without making any fresh commitments to France. To prevent 'années d'amertume' in Anglo-French relations, which the French ambassador Fleuriau anticipated, MacDonald had conciliatory talks with Briand soon after the conference. For the British prime minister, the success of The Hague was to provide new foundations for regaining a leading role in pacifying Europe, in concert with France *and* Germany. He soon publicly asserted that Britain had a vital interest in remaining a pivotal European power – rather than follow the orientation that the press magnate Lord Beaverbrook recommended after The Hague: to seek distance from European affairs and focus instead on imperial consolidation. The British government thus put its diplomatic weight behind a swift ratification of The Hague accords, not least to facilitate what remained a strategic priority for MacDonald: the conclusion of a naval agreement with the Hoover administration that prevented a further parting-of-ways with the United States not only in that strategically vital domain. As noted, it was on this front that the Labour premier would achieve the final major success of his foreign policy at the London naval conference of 1930.[84]

In the United States, both official and press reactions to the Hague agreements were muted. On 29 August, Stimson told Howard that he felt 'much relieved at the prospective final settlement'. The tenor of 'principal organs of the American press', notably the *New York World*, was that 'any settlement of European differences [was] better than none'. The Hoover administration generally welcomed that there were now concrete prospects for implementing

[82] Dieckhoff to AA, 2 September 1929, *ADAP*, B, XII, no. 230. Cf. Boyce (1987), pp. 210–11.

[83] *Chambre* minutes, Sessions Extraordinaires, 1929, pp. 50–9; Tardieu statement, 8 November 1929, *ADAP*, B, XIII, no. 124. Cf. Heyde (1998), pp. 54–8.

[84] Henderson to Tyrrell, 4 October 1929, *DBFP*, IA, VII, no. 21; Dieckhoff to AA, 2 September 1929, *ADAP*, B, XII, no. 230; MacDonald to Dawes, 9 September 1929, MacDonald memorandum, 4 October 1929, *DBFP*, II, I, pp. 69–71, 106–7.

the Young scheme. And it pressed both the Tardieu government and the Müller coalition to expedite their parliamentary ratification. Yet Hoover and Stimson did so without great verve. Their weightiest concern remained to shield the US government from any unwanted political consequences, 'impossible to for[e]see', that the settlement could produce.[85]

For fear that the Europeans might find ways of re-introducing the loathed connection between debts and reparations, the administration declined any role in underpinning the Hague settlement. It was mainly for this reason that Hoover and Stimson also remained wary of even informally endorsing the Bank for International Settlements. Ultimately, they did not want to fall prey to the European powers' political manoeuvrings, suspecting that Britain, yet above all France and Germany, were aiming to instrumentalise the BIS to prepare the ground for debt-relief.

The Hoover administration's negative attitude towards the international bank – or any more 'far-reaching' international financial institutions – also stemmed from more general reservations. In the view then prevailing in Washington, the bank was bound to become 'much more than a clearing house' for reparations transfers. It could also challenge US financial independence as the BIS board would include members 'from various countries'. In other words, no country, not even the United States, would be able to retain control over its financial policy. And not only US bankers suspected that particularly Paris and Berlin would seek to limit the bank's independence from political interference. In turn, this would inevitably lead Congress to raise 'considerable reservations' not only to the bank but the entire Young scheme. Ultimately, however, and this was decisive, the president himself entertained and 'inspired' such reservations.[86]

Hoover's fundamental misgivings would not change; yet nor would they stand in the way of at least encouraging the co-operation of international bankers in the framework of the BIS. The president was resolved to proceed the informal, Republican way. After The Hague, his administration continued to impress on the European governments that unless they ceased their attempts to use the envisaged international bank to their political ends, Washington would not even tolerate unofficial links of FBRNY officials with the new institution. And it would also make it impossible for the bank to liquidate any reparations bonds on the US market, which was crucial for regulating the Young scheme's transfer-system. But Hoover did eventually authorise US bankers to attend the critical Baden-Baden meeting in November 1929. There, the American representatives played a leading part in instituting the Bank for International Settlements. With Hoover's approval, the erstwhile chairman of

---

[85] Howard to Henderson, 29 August 1929, *DBFP*, IA, VII, no. 347.   [86] *Ibid.*

the FBRNY-board, Gates W. McGarrah, became its first president. In view of America's previous reticence, this was all the more a sign of the dominance of US financial power in the post-World War I international system.[87]

The attitude of leading British decisionmakers towards the new bank remained very sceptical throughout. Norman desired wider co-operation with the other principal central bankers. He particularly sought to draw the US Federal Reserve into stabilising the gold-standard system. In his view, they had to be alerted to the mounting imbalances within the financial order that the outpouring of gold and capital from Germany and Britain to America had caused, and US protectionism was aggravating. But neither the governor of the Bank of England nor the British Treasury considered the – politicised – Bank for International Settlements the appropriate instrument to foster such co-operation.[88]

Yet the bank's main weakness was and remained something else: it was the lack of firmer commitments on the part of the interested governments to making it more than a 'clearing house' for reparations. In other words, the bank suffered from the very deficiency that suspicions in Washington and London against the institution had engendered in the first place. With a view to the entire Young regime, US policy certainly did not follow the maxim that Walter Lippmann had publicly set for the European powers prior to the Hague agreement. Lippmann had observed that the advantages to be gained by any one nation 'through standing out for its own particular interests' were 'insignificant as compared with the gains which would accrue to that nation and to the whole world from a general liquidation of the remaining post-war problems'.[89]

With hindsight, and even without it, the aftermath of the first Hague conference seems an appropriate juncture to draw up a balance-sheet of what progress in Euro-Atlantic stabilisation after the Great War had been made in the 1920s – and of what remained the core challenges to its sustenance. The Hague agreement obviously did not become, in Henderson's words, the 'final step' that brought 'the world war to an end'.[90] Under the circumstances of 1929, no settlement could accomplish this. But, had it not been for the Wall Street collapse less than two months later, the outcome of August 1929 may later well have been viewed, deservedly, as a further hard-won but tenable compromise, setting the stage for further advances on the road to more durable stability in postwar Europe.

---

[87] Cf. Leffler (1979), pp. 215–16.
[88] Notes of a conversation between Snowden, Francqui and Gutt, 14 November 1929, *DBFP*, IA, VII, no. 73. Cf. Boyce (1987), pp. 212–13.
[89] Howard to Henderson, 9 August 1929, FO 840/6/11/10.
[90] *Report of the 29th Annual Conference of the Labour Party* (1929), p. 208.

The Locarno concert had emerged from The Hague scathed and battered but not defunct. Anglo-French relations had been strained by the distribution dispute. And the German government faced a hard struggle to present the outcome domestically as a convincing success of its co-operation with the western powers. But the leading decision makers of all three powers had proved that even under the constraints that Washington's draconian debt policy imposed they could still succeed in settling, as far as possible, the immensely complicated reparations dispute. And they had shown as well that, if with great difficulty, they could draw a line under the most virulent political dispute of the latter 1920s: the Rhineland dispute – or, more precisely, its most virulent aspect: the occupation. That this had been achieved through Locarno-style negotiations created some prospects for sustaining – or rather reviving – the European concert.

In the wider perspective, the post-Hague constellation saw Weimar Germany still linked up with the nascent Euro-Atlantic order of the mid-1920s. It still had a government pledged to upholding the commitments to peaceful change that Germany had assumed under Stresemann's direction – though the Müller coalition was increasingly assailed by nationalist forces lambasting a policy that only yielded piecemeal revisionist results. By and large disarmed in accordance with the provisions of Versailles, Germany was also still respecting the premises of the Geneva disarmament conference. It was not (yet) pushing for marked changes in the military *status quo* – changes towards 'armament parity'. Yet the deadlock in efforts to agree on mutually acceptable standards that regulated either French disarmament, measured German rearmament or a combination of both *without* unhinging European stability remained one of the greatest international liabilities four years after Locarno. In this highly sensitive area, future French and German attitudes would be crucial. But no less critical would be how far British and American leaders could at last foster long-sought disarmament agreements in continental Europe, also through wider security commitments. From the perspective of 1929, such commitments seemed a remote prospect.

An even remoter prospect remained a pacific consolidation of the east European *status quo*. It was still an open question, even in the medium term, how this could be achieved – be it through peaceful 'adjustments' of the Polish–German frontier through international agreement; be it by an eventual German acceptance of the frontiers of 1919, and compensatory minority agreements with Warsaw, based on the recognition that there was no peaceful way of regaining the 'Polish Corridor'. This remained not only an issue neglected by British and American decisionmakers. It also remained at least as great a liability to European stability as the unresolved disarmament problem. Yet nor was there an inescapable road leading to future escalation.

Under Stresemann, German policy towards Poland – and towards Soviet Russia – was still proceeding in clear consonance with the commitments undertaken under Locarno and the Kellogg–Briand pact. The aforementioned conclusion of a Polish–German commercial treaty in the autumn of 1929, practically the last act of Stresemann's foreign policy, underscored this.[91] It also highlighted that, although much was left unachieved in this field, the best assurance for Polish – and Czechoslovak – security was still that the system of Locarno and the Young regime remained intact, and that Weimar Germany remained an integral part of both of these systems. The underlying challenge had not changed. Only if moderate German policymakers were in a position to pursue their western orientation, and to contain more assertively revisionist forces by presenting further concrete 'consequences' of their policies, would they also be able to persist with a moderate *Ostpolitik*.

Finally, in 1929 there was still a government in Berlin that was prepared to accept the new reparations regime – and to fight for its implementation against mounting domestic opposition. More broadly, the Müller cabinet was resolved to keep Germany tied to the web of interdependent interests that had under-girded the country's economic and political rehabilitation after the nadir of 1923, although this meant shouldering substantial reparation-burdens.

Both US policymakers and financiers reckoned that the Young scheme was workable. And they reckoned as well that the new 'certainty' it provided could revitalise the German economy and also alleviate Berlin's chronic budgetary shortfalls – if that 'certainty' finally gave rise to internal reforms. All of this was to prop up Weimar Germany's political stability.[92] Indeed, if the Young settlement delivered what its makers desired, the new regime and the Locarno concert had the potential of providing the Euro-Atlantic international system with two necessary, if still not sufficient, 'backbones'. Yet if this could not be accomplished, all sides would be hard put to implement the Hague agreements. And they would find it exceedingly hard to weather any major storm – unless particularly the Hoover administration recast its approach to Europe's con-tinued consolidation. And this seemed very unlikely in the summer and autumn of 1929.

If, as more cautious British experts like Stamp had long warned, a graver deterioration of economic conditions in Germany were to occur, and prompt a full-blown transfer crisis, the means available under the Young scheme to master it – for example through the new international bank – were distinctly limited. Even more consequential, though, could be the political ramifications of such a crisis, particularly in Germany. There, as both British and American diplomats reported, the agitation not only of the extremist Hitler–Hugenberg campaign but also more moderate nationalists against the Young plan

---

[91] *AR Müller I und II*, no. 480; *ADAP*, B, XIII, no. 7. Cf. Krüger (1985a), pp. 501–4.
[92] Lamont (1930), pp. 336–63.

foreshadowed ominous developments.[93] The key challenge remained to win further legitimacy not only for the Young plan but also for a continuation of the arduous accommodation process between Germany and the west.

At stake was not only whether the Müller coalition could ensure the Young plan's ratification. It was, more generally, how far centre-ground governments would be able to continue Stresemann's policy of accepting substantial international obligations in return for what many critics saw as very limited revisionist benefits. This would have a decisive bearing on how far not only Stresemann but also his successors would be in a position – and willing – to sustain the Weimar Republic's western orientation.

Otherwise, a scenario could emerge in which a German power that had shed the controls of the occupation and the Dawes regime could be tempted to adopt a more assertive course. In turn, greater German assertiveness could provoke a backlash in France. *Mutatis mutandis*, then, the question would become how far French leaders could continue the course to which Briand and Poincaré had committed themselves by 1929: to consolidate French security and prosperity by co-operating with Berlin. Had the scope for such policies reached its limits at The Hague? In short, any of these developments could place severe constraints on the further operation of the European concert, because – as ever – it hinged on all of its members' sustained commitment.

In the final analysis, one fundamental question posed itself anew in the summer of 1929. It was the question what further concessions or commitments Anglo-American policymakers would find necessary, and domestically possible, in order to advance further a still fragile Franco-German peace process: how far London could promote further – legitimating – peaceful change through the European concert; and how far Washington could take more concrete measures to stabilise the Young regime. Should their policies prove insufficient, the gravest danger on the horizon was that Europe's postwar system might unravel, through economic and subsequent political crisis or vice versa, from its most vulnerable end: Weimar Germany. Not surprisingly, at the time this danger was seen far more clearly by the MacDonald government than the Hoover administration.

At The Hague, the promotion of the Rhineland settlement and consolidation of the European concert that MacDonald and Henderson pursued had proved rather effective – despite Snowden's exploits. And the Labour government's commitment to taking the 'appeasement' of Europe further by brokering agreements between France and Germany, particularly on arms limitations, was genuine. Britain indeed retained its indispensable mediating-role in European politics – and potentially also in transatlantic relations. Yet, if measured

---

[93] Poole to Stimson, 17 September 1929, Schurman to Stimson, 11 November 1929, NA RG 59 462.00 R296/3352, 3461; Rumbold to Henderson, 3 November 1929, *DBFP*, IA, VII, no. 46.

against the realities of the Young process, the means that British policy had to maintain a decisive influence were actually rather limited.

After the Hague conference, the Labour government did not contemplate any more far-reaching strategic commitments – in western or eastern Europe – to advance its agenda of peaceful change and disarmament.[94] MacDonald simply did not see himself in a position to legitimate such commitments domestically. Yet he also remained in principle opposed to espousing what the Foreign Office eventually proposed: fresh military guarantees through a fortified Geneva Protocol, essentially to reassure France. British leverage to foster the Young scheme's implementation, and operation, was even more limited. It could only be exerted within a framework largely determined by Washington.

In retrospect, the Euro-Atlantic settlement process of 1928 and 1929, which still evolved in a phase of comparative stability, represents one of the most notable missed opportunities in international politics after the Great War. It was not so much an opportunity missed by the protagonists of British foreign policy, or Locarno politics, for their room to manoeuvre was indeed severely constrained. It was chiefly an opportunity discarded by decisionmakers in Washington. In short, there was indeed scope for taking greater strides towards a more solid Euro-Atlantic order of international politics and finance – and towards anchoring Weimar Germany to this system. There was significant scope for more progress in thus containing what remained the most fundamental threat of the postwar era: that of a resurgent aggressive revisionism in Germany, bent on destroying not only the order of Versailles but also the advances made since the Ruhr crisis.

Of most immediate consequence was that the Hoover administration persisted with its refusal to make any political commitments underpinning the Young regime. Thus, the Bank for International Settlements remained hamstrung. More generally, no effective mechanism existed for controlling the American loan flow to Europe and for regulating wider financial stabilisation. Nor, crucially, were there any effective instruments to deal with a crisis of the US-dominated reparation and debt regime. As noted, there were not only self-serving but also some legitimate reasons behind Hoover's option for an essentially unilateral policy of aloofness in the process of settling Europe's postwar questions at the end of the 1920s. But this should not distract from one basic conclusion. The Hoover administration's disengagement from the making of the Young settlement was critical in curtailing progress towards a more robust system of international politics, a system more capable of coping with crises.

---

[94] MacDonald to Dawes, 8 August 1929, *DBFP*, II, I, no. 12; Henderson memorandum, 19 February 1931, Simon notes of a conversation with Briand, 25 March 1931, *DBFP*, II, III, nos. 205, 207.

In many ways, Washington commanded the decisive financial means and concomitant political leverage to shape a more 'equitable' reparations and debt agreement, as outlined by the reparations agent Parker Gilbert and broadly supported by Mellon in 1927. But taking the lead in this direction this would have involved sacrifices and commitments that Hoover was not prepared to shoulder. Making them would have required hard – and perhaps futile – battles with a still predominantly isolationist Congress; and it would have required making a strong case for an alternative, more internationally engaged US policy to an electorate that key Republican decisionmakers deemed as isolationist as its elected representatives. Fundamentally, though, Hoover rejected commitments of this kind as a matter of principle. His axiom remained that the United States should not ultimately fund Europe's reconstruction without recompense – after the European powers had caused the havoc of the war, and drawn America into it, in the first place.[95] Formally, a change in this stance never occurred. In practice, however, relinquishing America's debt-claims became unavoidable under the impact of what soon engulfed Hoover's administration: the Great Depression.

The more general problem that the developments between 1925 and 1929 threw into relief was that in the asymmetric Euro-Atlantic system of the post-World War I era the United States was ultimately unwilling to fulfil the role that its financial hegemony accorded it in a manner consolidating this system. Republican elites of the 1920s were still far from having reached the conclusions of those who drafted the Marshall plan and envisaged the North Atlantic Alliance after another world war, namely that it was in America's own best interest to make wider political and financial commitments to rebuilding postwar Europe. More precisely, in the absence of immediate foreign threats they had not yet begun, or deemed it necessary, to develop comprehensive strategies that committed the American government not only to underwriting European security but also to providing rather generous financial assistance, all in order to buttress what Washington ultimately desired: Europe's political and economic revitalisation, the American way.

In 1929, it seemed that the United States could afford to pursue a policy of 'having the best of all worlds'. On the one hand, the Hoover administration continued to assert 'open-door' principles abroad; on the other, and driven by the US Congress, it enforced an ever more restrictive protectionist tariff policy at home. What highlighted the underlying disparities affecting transatlantic relations was that at the very time that the European powers were approaching the adoption of the Young scheme, the American Congress began serious debates over a new, even more protectionist tariff bill to replace the 1922

---

[95] Hoover (1952b), pp. 89–90; Kellogg to Hughes, 12 August 1924, NA RG 59 462.00 R296/491.

Fordney–McCumber tariff. The Smoot–Hawley Act was then passed in May 1930. What raised commercial tensions between Europe and the United States in 1929 was not only the Congress's commercial nationalism. It was also the fact that the Hoover administration made little effort resist the proposed sharp tariff-raises on industrial and agricultural goods. Fundamentally, the president persisted with his aggressive, and one-sided, foreign economic policy, seeking to couple the 'open door' with rising US tariffs for the benefit of all mankind.[96]

The obvious double-standard implicit in this policy was gravely noted in Europe. Particularly in France, it sparked renewed calls for a united European front against US trade policy. For overriding political reasons, the Müller government still rejected retaliatory measures, let alone a common front with Paris. The pre-eminent interest in effecting a naval *rapprochement* with Washington also led the Labour government to shun overt criticism. Behind closed doors, however, political elites in both Germany and Britain were incensed by US tariff policy.[97]

Not oblivious to such reactions, Hoover became concerned about possible European retaliations. In practice, however, the president did little more than register his displeasure at more far-reaching Congressional proposals. He refused to veto the Smoot–Hawley Act. This provided an additional impetus to Briand's call for a 'United States of Europe' at the League Assembly of September 1929. His – vague – blueprint for a European federal union was indeed intended to countervail US predominance. And the French proposal led Stresemann to lay out his own, more economically orientated and prag-matic, vision of a future European federation. But the German foreign minister still studiously distanced himself from Briand's plans insofar as they still had an underlying anti-American thrust. He had no intention of dissolving the difficult but vital partnership with the United States.[98]

Towards the limits of Europe's stabilisation – the ratification of the Young settlement, 1929–30

For Stresemann and Schubert, the single most important political result of The Hague was indubitably the termination of the Rhineland occupation.[99]

---

[96] Stimson to Hoover, 8 June 1929, *FRUS 1929*, II, pp. 998–9; Stimson to Smoot, 26 June 1929, NA RG 59 611.003/1673a. Cf. Leffler (1979), pp. 195ff.

[97] Memorandum of a conversation between Stresemann and Briand, 11 June 1929, *ADAP*, B, XII, pp. 44–8.

[98] Castle to Smoot, 4 September 1929, NA, RG 59 611.003/1854; Briand speech to the League assembly, 5 September 1929, *Société des Nations* (1929), pp. 52–3; Stresemann speech, 9 September 1929, *ibid.*, pp. 70–1.

[99] Stresemann to Löbe, 19 September 1929, *ADAP*, B, XIII, no. 26.

Shortly before his death, the German foreign minister summarised that Germany was now once again 'master in its own house'. And he regarded this outcome as a – hard-won – vindication of a policy that had not only cultivated co-operation with Britain and France but also 'parallel interests' with the United States, however frustrating both had become at times.[100] Especially retaining close ties with America on the premises of the new reparations regime seemed critical to Stresemann if Germany was to steer clear of 'bankruptcy'. Though hardly enthusiastic about The Hague's results, a majority within Müller's cabinet shared the foreign minister's views. Thus an all the more vital task became to see through the ratification of the Young plan, and the Hague accords, amidst a rising storm of domestic opposition.

British and American diplomats monitored German reactions closely. The British ambassador Rumbold reported that the 'political atmosphere' in Germany was 'not healthy'. But he also observed that, though they only admitted it 'grudgingly', most Germans were 'relieved by the results attained at the Hague', especially the liberation of the Rhineland. In the ambassador's view, the settlement had strengthened Stresemann's position. *Reichspräsident* Hindenburg had made a point of congratulating the German delegation on their return.[101]

American observers were more anxious about the growing momentum of the nationalist 'anti-Young plan' movement. Schurman reported that the movement's wrath was directed against what a certain Adolf Hitler, who was gaining stature as its chief instigator, called 'the new Paris *Diktat*'. Hitler desired to organise a 'general peoples' resistance' to thwart what he termed a plot to enslave Germans for generations to come. Indeed, as US counsellor Poole rightly stressed, galvanising opposition and providing the Hugenberg press with 'strong matter for popular agitation' was not the inconceivable 'size' but the 'duration' of German obligations.[102] In the autumn, Hugenberg and Hitler launched a widespread referendum campaign to adopt the 'Draft Law against the Enslavement of the German People'. But, disconcerting though it was, the Hitler–Hugenberg campaign never managed to acquire a coherent platform or following; and it notably failed to attract less extreme nationalists. The referendum ended with a resounding defeat on 22 December 1929.[103]

More ominous for Müller's government was that *Reichsbank* president Schacht turned against the Young settlement, becoming its most prominent

---

[100] Stresemann interview with T. Wolff, 11 September 1929, Stresemann (1932), III, p. 566.

[101] Rumbold to Henderson, 11 September 1929, *DBFP*, IA, VII, no. 7.

[102] Schurman to Stimson, 30 August 1929, Poole to Stimson, 4 September 1929, NA RG 59 462.00 R296/3311, 3258.

[103] Rumbold to Henderson, 11 September, 10 and 11 October 1929, *DBFP*, IA, VII, nos. 7, 22, 23; Schurman to Stimson, 11 November 1929, NA RG 59 462.00 R296/3461. Cf. Schulze (1982), pp. 310–12.

'moderate' critic. He particularly admonished that the Hague agreement imposed on Germany heavier burdens than the original Young scheme had envisaged. By early December, Schacht not only criticised Germany's creditors but also pushed the Müller government to introduce draconian financial reforms to salvage Germany's international credit.[104]

By that time, the growing extent of Germany's financial, and political, impasse had become palpable. A further economic downturn following the US stock-market crash of October had led to decreasing tax revenues and spiralling costs through unemployment. But the government was unwilling to follow Schacht's call for slashing unemployment benefits, which would have hit its core working- and lower-middle-class electorate hardest. Inner-coalition disputes over this issue also eventually caused the Müller coalition's break-up in late March 1930, a watershed in the history of Weimar Germany.

On 12 March, Müller had still succeeded in finally winning the *Reichstag*'s ratification of the Young plan; yet this had already exerted immense centrifugal pressures on his coalition. At that juncture, not only the future of Stresemann's foreign policy but the Weimar Republic's very survival hung in the balance. The underlying question had become whether the deepening crisis could still be mastered by a parliamentary government as such. Schacht essentially argued that Germany required a kind of 'economic dictatorship'. And, as will be seen, the new chancellor Heinrich Brüning indeed saw the need for a more authoritarian government, no longer backed by the *Reichstag* but relying on President Hindenburg's emergency powers. Crucially, though, Brüning would turn his back on Weimar Germany's foreign policy of the latter 1920s.[105]

In this sense, Stresemann's death on 3 October 1929, uncannily only days before Wall Street's Black Friday, had a larger significance. The importance of any one personality in the evolution of larger historical processes should certainly never be overrated. And it should also be noted that Stresemann's successor, Curtius, strove hard to develop his own policy of 'peaceful revision'.[106] But it seems justified to conclude that with Stresemann Weimar Germany had not only lost its 'greatest statesman'.[107] It had also lost the central integrative figure, instrumental for pursuing, and legitimating, Weimar's policy of peaceful accommodation after the Great War.

Stresemann's passing foreshadowed more than the demise of his foreign policy. This was confirmed by Carl von Schubert's replacement as undersecretary at the *Auswärtige Amt* by Bernhard von Bülow in 1930. What

---

[104] Nicolson to Henderson, 6 December 1929, *DBFP*, IA, VII, no. 112; Schurman to Stimson, 7 December 1929, NA RG 59 462.00 R296/3472, 3474.
[105] See the epilogue.
[106] Rumbold to Henderson, 14 November 1929, *DBFP*, IA, VII, no. 72 . Cf. Rödder (1996).
[107] Rumbold to Henderson, 10 October 1929, *DBFP*, IA, VII, no. 22. Cf. Wright (2002), pp. 492–525.

followed threw into relief one of the vital requirements for sustaining the system of London and Locarno that ultimately could not be met: the requirement to strengthen the basis on which other proponents of Germany's western orientation could follow in Stresemann's footsteps – and to contain those forces seeking to undermine this course. Till the end, Stresemann had striven to hold the Müller coalition together, not only to ratify The Hague accords but also to continue his policy. He died deeply exhausted.

In France, the assaults of Hitler and Hugenberg against the Young plan rekindled concerns that Germany might yet seek to elude its reparation obligations once France had evacuated the Rhineland. At the same time, underlying fears resurfaced that a more nationalist government would come to power in Berlin – and France then face a more assertive neighbour without the former strategic buffer-zone. This also played a part in Briand's centre-left government being replaced by a more conservative one under Tardieu in October 1929. Essentially, however, Tardieu continued his predecessor's policy, if in a more assertive style. He still deemed it the most pragmatic way to safeguard French security and reparations interests – with Germany.[108]

At the second Hague conference, convening in January 1930 to settle the remaining issues to be resolved before the Young plan could come into force, France and Germany were largely left to their own devices. The new French premier again raised the controversial sanction question. Returning to the Versailles treaty, Tardieu sought to re-assert France's right to enforce sanctions in case Germany defaulted on its payments or otherwise failed to implement the Young regime. But he was ultimately not prepared to revive Poincaré's policy of 1923 and extend the occupation after all. With the backing of London and Washington, the new German foreign minister Curtius thus succeeded in eliminating what had been a core German concern since Versailles. The second Hague agreement certified that the era of French sanctions vis-à-vis Germany was over. France had to be content with rather superficial political and financial guarantees. The Permanent Court of International Justice was to be the last instance of appeal should a creditor deem Germany in breach of its obligations.[109]

In terms of the financial reassurance that the Tardieu government sought, the second Hague conference ended with a Franco-German compromise. Tardieu had demanded that Berlin participate in efforts to commercialise the first *tranche* of reparation-bonds without delay, not least by postponing any foreign borrowing for purposes of domestic crisis management. But Müller had insisted that his government urgently required fresh capital. In line with Britain, the Hoover administration's 'contribution' to what became the second

[108] Tardieu statement, 8 November 1929, *ADAP*, B, XIII, no. 124; Tardieu (1931), pp. 131ff.
[109] Cf. Kent (1989), pp. 314–15; Knipping (1987), pp. 96–104.

Hague compromise largely consisted in underlining its opposition to floating any large numbers of reparation bonds on the international market.[110]

Thus, a Franco-German solution had to be found. In the end, the German government pledged to refrain from taking out any long-term loans until the spring of 1931; and in return the French government granted Berlin the right to use a third of the first reparation-*tranche* to satisfy the acute credit-needs of the German railway and postal systems. By this point, then, the 'liquidation' of the war's consequences had turned into a wrangling over financial minutiae. But it was such wrangling, largely without any major Anglo-American involvement, that led to the follow-up agreement which finally paved the way for the Young plan's ratification in France and Germany, secured in the spring of 1930.

---

[110] Cf. Leffler (1979), pp. 217–19.

Epilogue
The disintegration of the unfinished transatlantic peace order, 1930–1932 – an inevitable demise?

Why did the nascent transatlantic peace order of the post-World War I era disintegrate so rapidly under the shock-waves of the World Economic Crisis? Why were its mainstays basically eroded within less than four years after the landmark settlement of the first Hague conference, to be finally swept away by Hitler after 1933? Did the Great Depression reveal that the system founded at London and Locarno was built on flawed premises? Did it reveal that the 'illusory' cease-fire that these settlements had allegedly instituted was merely one stage in the twentieth century's 'thirty years' war'? If so, then the stabilisation efforts of the 1920s had indeed prepared the ground for Hitler's ascent to power. Or was the unprecedented world crisis of the early 1930s the crucial *caesura*? Was the crisis simply too overwhelming to be mastered by policymakers on either side of the Atlantic? Did it not only wreck what had been forward-looking attempts at a 'European restoration'?[1] Did it also undermine America's bid for a Progressive reconstruction of the Old World?[2]

The key question is, indeed, a different one. What should be analysed is what made the international system of the 1920s, as altered through the Hague settlements and the Young regime, so *susceptible* to collapse when the World Economic Crisis escalated. In essence, the disintegration of the 'unfinished transatlantic peace order' between 1930 and 1932 was by no means an inescapable outcome. It was not mainly due to 'inherent contradictions' of Anglo-American attempts to recast the order of 1919 and constrain German power at the same time. There is no direct causal relationship between the advances of the mid-1920s and the Great Depression. In other words, the World Economic Crisis was *not* essentially a crisis of the system of London and Locarno, revealing that all achievements since 1924 pointed in the wrong direction.

---

[1] For a useful overview see Bell (1986), pp. 16ff, 35ff. For the wider context see Kindleberger (1973), pp. 95–231; James (2001), pp. 27–100, 187–99; Clavin (2000).
[2] Hoover statement, 6 October 1931, in Hoover (1952b), pp. 88–9. Cf. Leffler (1979), pp. 194ff; Costigliola (1984), pp. 216ff.

What foreshadowed the real escalation of calamities in 1931, the US stock-market crash of October 1929, was essentially an exogenous development. Except for Washington's failure to check Wall Street's hyper-speculation it was a calamity whose origins lay beyond the reach of what international policymakers could have influenced decisively.[3]

Undoubtedly, the mainsprings of the soon global crisis that first engulfed Europe and then spread to the United States between 1931 and 1933 were financial and economic. And the structural shortcomings of the gold-standard-based monetary system as well as Euro-Atlantic debt, loan and trade relations produced indeed disastrous consequences.[4] Yet that the central European financial breakdown of 1931 could spiral into a fundamental crisis of the Euro-Atlantic world also had different, political reasons. This deterioration was not just attributable to the upheaval caused by the Great War. Its roots lay not merely, as Hoover would claim, in the European states' failure to overcome this unprecedented upheaval by mending their old ways through Progressive reforms.[5]

What aggravated the crisis, and in many ways accounted for its escalation, was the inability of the predominant American power – and the major European powers – to establish a more solid financial and political architecture to manage the war's aftershocks. It was their limited progress towards fortifying the Young scheme and untangling the burdensome issues of reparations, debts and international loans prior to an acute crisis. This was encapsulated in the failure to turn the Bank for International Settlements into a more effective institution that provided emergency and long-term credits. It was compounded by the refusal of all Republican postwar administrations in Washington to create governmental bail-out mechanisms for international loans. Yet it should also be noted again that, for different reasons, even the bigger European powers – the victors as well as the vanquished of the war – were hardly capable of making further decisive advances towards a more durable postwar international system. For the principal policymakers on all sides faced more or less towering constraints, both international and domestic; and the domestic checks placed on the actions of American decisionmakers were considerable, too.

More generally, what made the system of London and Locarno founder in the end was chiefly that it remained unconsolidated, and indeed 'unfinished', in critical respects. Not least because they had failed to develop concerted stabilisation strategies further after 1925, neither British nor American policymakers found ways to cope with the greatest challenge to postwar stability in the critical sphere of international *politics*. Mainly because of the US government's strategically and domestically motivated refusal to underpin them, there

---

[3] Cf. Kennedy (1999), pp. 43ff; Link (1970), pp. 630ff.
[4] Cf. Eichengreen (1992), 246–86; Kindleberger (1973), pp. 95ff, 291–308.
[5] Hoover (1952b), pp. 89–90.

were as yet no effective rules, and still no effective transatlantic mechanisms, that could be relied on if a severe crisis of the Young regime erupted. In a nutshell, then, the international system of the 1920s was so susceptible to collapse because it was not yet sufficiently robust. In turn this was due to the fact that the powers which, if any, had the means to fortify it – above all, the United States, to a lesser extent Britain, France and Germany – were either no longer sufficiently committed to, or capable of, underpinning this system. And after 1929, even the Anglo-American powers no longer had the power or the wherewithal to enforce the rules of the system of London and Locarno, or to enhance them, in order to cope with the unprecedented crisis.

On balance, and crudely put, an international crisis can have two effects. It can spur policymakers into taking more decisive measures to come to terms with it – to adapt and advance existing rules, understandings and mechanisms to this end. Or it can lead them, ultimately, to revert to self-preservation approaches – approaches geared to the protection of seemingly more immediate national interests. And that reversal has one crucial consequence: it undermines any functioning international system. By and large, international politics in the world crisis of the early 1930s exemplified the latter variant. Some wider lessons were only drawn later, in the making of the transatlantic international order after World War II.

Though this was already becoming an ever steeper up-hill struggle by 1930, there were indeed prospects to sustain both the Young regime and the co-operation of the Locarno powers on the basis of the Hague settlements – if there had not been a shock of the magnitude of 1931. Without this shock they may well have gone down in history as a further arduous but necessary step on the road of Europe's long-term stabilisation in the twentieth century. As it was, however, the efforts of international policymakers and financiers at and around the Hague conferences had not sufficed to forge another landmark agreement. Crucially, the Young process provided neither Briand and Tardieu nor the Müller government with results further legitimating their adherence to the politics of London and Locarno.

Essentially, British and American stabilisation policies did not begin to founder because they sought to achieve mutually incompatible objectives: to strengthen Weimar Germany *and* to constrain German power, to accommodate it *and* to build European peace, to integrate it internationally *and* to foster French – and Polish – security. Rather, they came to fail because those who shaped these policies did not, or could not, do enough in a period of 'relative stability' to buttress the newly republican Germany and to back those in Berlin who were struggling to pursue peaceful change and a *rapprochement* with the west. In retrospect, it can be concluded that this became the Achilles' heel of the unfinished peace order after the Great War. Anglo-American policymakers had not succeeded in giving Weimar Germany's leaders of the Stresemann period sufficient incentives or a sufficient domestic mandate to keep Germany on a path of difficult yet continually closer integration with the predominantly western international order that had emerged since the Ruhr crisis of 1923.

It is hard to see how subsequently, when the real crisis struck, any outside power could have had a decisive influence in preventing, or reversing, the Weimar Republic's demise from within. Anglo-American decisionmakers had ever less incentives to offer, or other means, to prevent Stresemann's successors from renouncing the commitments that Weimar German governments had accepted between 1924 and 1929. The new German leaders came to withdraw from the Young regime and from the security system based on the Locarno and Kellogg–Briand pacts.

The beginning of this process, which greatly heightened European insecurity, predated the climax of the crisis in 1931. The departure from Stresemann's course was initiated under Brüning in the spring of 1930. It would be precipitated, with drastic consequences, by Franz von Papen and Kurt von Schleicher. Brüning's austerity measures and his bid to recast Germany through an assertive foreign policy were without a doubt still qualitatively different from what Hitler would later pursue. But it was Hitler who could build on the postwar order's initial demolition between 1930 and 1932 and bring it to an irreversible conclusion.[6] The governments in London and Washington tried to reverse this development. But with international and internal crises spinning out of control, they no longer had the means to keep Germany linked with the 'western system'. In this sense, the World Economic Crisis *turned into* a fundamental crisis of the system of London and Locarno – and made it disintegrate.

The more fundamental challenge that American and British decisionmakers confronted in this critical phase was to manage a taxing transition – the transition from integrative to containing policies vis-à-vis Germany. This became the core dilemma of the early 1930s. In the 1920s, the pursuit of balance-of-power containment would have precluded the advances of London and Locarno. And it would have precluded stabilising a republican Germany committed to a nascent Euro-Atlantic 'community', undercutting the domestic support of Stresemann or any other German leader who sought accommodation with the victors of the Great War. But in the early 1930s, the tables began to turn. Now the underlying problem became how to react once one power – Germany under Brüning – began to renounce the existing international ground-rules. How could these rules be enforced without undermining any prospects of a still republican Germany remaining within the western system (or returning to it)? In the final analysis, neither British nor American leaders found ways to come to terms with this dilemma before 30 January 1933.

[6] See Bracher (1978).

A vicious spiral of crises and insufficient responses

The developments of 1931 and 1932 can be described as a vicious spiral of crises spinning out of control, followed by successive international, then more and more nationally orientated attempts to contain them, which all proved increasingly inadequate. This certainly also applied to the responses given by Britain and, above all, to the vain efforts at 'crisis management' pursued by the Hoover administration.[7] The unprecedented deterioration process reached a nadir when mastering it came to elude the grasp of international decision-makers. Its stages are all too familiar. The Young regime ended, and reparations were abolished, less than two years after the Young plan's official launch. Its fate was 'settled' at the Lausanne conference in July 1932. What followed was the *de facto* abolition of all transatlantic intergovernmental debts.[8] In the realm of security politics, the crisis peaked with the collapse of the final round of the Geneva disarmament conference, provoked when, also in July 1932, Germany left the negotiations under Papen's 'cabinet of national concentration'. By December, the western powers declared that they accepted German 'equality of rights' regarding armaments – a final concession on which ultimately only Hitler could capitalise.[9]

That a shock of the kind of 'Black Friday' was to occur was not unlikely in view of the rampant and politically uncontrolled expansion of US *laissez-faire* capitalism. Not contingent at all, though, given the lack of mechanisms to cope with an upheaval of this kind, was the scope of its political consequences. Once the fundamental crisis struck, the United States was unwilling to extend its commitments. Britain no longer had the leverage to promote stabilising changes. France lacked Anglo-American reassurance to persevere with the accommodation of Germany. And most immediately damaging was that the increasingly semi-authoritarian German governments of the early 1930s abandoned Stresemann's policies.

What further limited the chances of preserving the transatlantic order was that, if to varying degrees, the ability of all governments to pursue international solutions was ever more severely constrained. It was constrained by the crisis' debilitating effect on internal politics and national economies. This was epitomised by the existential problems of the Weimar Republic and the concomitant rise of the National Socialists; but it also held true for the western powers.

In Hoover's assessment, what 'tore the [postwar] system asunder' were 'the malign forces arising from economic consequences of the war'. In his eyes,

---

[7] For the term 'vicious spiral' see Meier (2002), p. 423.
[8] *DBFP*, II, III, nos. 137–92. Cf. Kent (1989), p. 372.
[9] *DBFP*, II, II, nos. 235–70. Cf. Krüger (1985a), 546–51.

these forces were bound up with the treaty system of Versailles, 'the postwar military alliances with their double prewar armament', the Europeans' 'frantic public works programs to meet unemployment', 'unbalanced budgets' and partly politically provoked 'inflations'.[10] While to a certain extent it seems justified to seek the Great Depression's root-causes in the dislocations wrought by the Great War, this is not the entire picture. European developments indeed triggered the spiralling crisis of 1931. But what also tore the system asunder was the limited extent to which policymakers, especially in Washington, had found thorough remedies for the war's consequences since 1919. The repercussions of the stock-market crash exposed and aggravated the fault-lines of the Euro-Atlantic financial architecture and the 'interlocked problems' of European political stability, all converging on Weimar Germany.[11]

The consequences of Black Friday were by no means immediately felt. The decisive turn for the worse, towards an all-out 'Great Depression', occurred only in 1931. What reached a preliminary climax with the Hoover moratorium of 20 June 1931 was an accelerating chain-reaction of crises.[12] It threw into relief the weaknesses of the postwar order and the gathering momentum of those forces bent on undermining it. Feeding on the economic downturn and rising unemployment, yet also growing resentment against reparations and a propagandistically maligned *status quo*, the National Socialists had scored their first significant victory at the September elections of 1930. While still a minority in opposition, their success not only precipitated a rapid withdrawal of US investments from Germany. It also led Chancellor Brüning, in office since March 1930, to mount a counter-offensive. To contain domestic discontent, he proposed a customs union with Austria, dealing a disastrous blow to relations with Britain and France.

For a greatly disconcerted French government, this conjured up fears of the long-dreaded *Anschluß*. In turn, Austrian anxiety that Paris might use its still strong financial power to 'dry out' local banks in order to thwart Brüning's scheme led to a panic. It culminated in the closing of the country's largest bank, the Vienna *Kreditanstalt*, and soon sent shock-waves throughout central Europe. Many German banks closed as well, and the *Reichsbank* was threatened with the same fate. The outbreak of this truly historic financial crisis shook the Young system to the core. It debilitated the entire mechanism of debt- and reparation-payments; it struck the American world creditor; and – while France at first remained relatively unscathed – it precipitated Britain's hitherto gravest political-cum-financial crisis in modern times, the

---

[10] Hoover (1952b), pp. 61, 89.
[11] Foreign Office memorandum, 2 December 1931, CAB, 24/225, C.P. 301 (31).
[12] Kennedy (1999), p. 71.

Slump. All of this deeply unsettled the already tense political relations between the western powers and Germany.[13]

Indeed, it was *not* Brüning's underlying aim to wreck the Young plan in order to rid Germany of the reparations burden. The primary goal of the ruthless deflationary policy that he came to pursue – with severe consequences – was domestic: to put the German house back into order, to restructure the German state along more conservative, semi-authoritarian lines and thus to restore the country's financial strength. On the domestic front, Brüning of course achieved the opposite of what he intended. He not only aggravated Germany's financial crisis but thereby also strengthened the National Socialists. Most disconcertingly, by February 1932 German unemployment had reached its highest postwar level of over 6 million.[14]

Most consequential for the system of London and Locarno, however, was that Brüning not merely had a 'propensity for diplomatic adventurism', which first culminated in the customs-union project. Rather, under Brüning a fundamental change in the methods and maxims of German foreign policy took place. Berlin departed from Stresemann's policy of seeking peaceful change through international co-operation and *quid pro quo* agreements. In other words, the new government abandoned Germany's acceptance of the international rules and understandings of the latter 1920s.[15] Brüning and Curtius rejected any serious attempt at concerted crisis management with France, and sought no more than tactical, short-term collaboration with the Anglo-American powers. Essentially, they opted for an uncompromising pursuit of maximal aims – notably: a complete cancellation of reparations and, most unsettling, armament 'parity' and a revision of the 'Polish Corridor'. Both the chancellor and Stresemann's successor at the *Auswärtige Amt* did so not least, and increasingly, to contain the rising NSDAP, Hitler's Nationalist Socialist German Workers' Party.

Though insisting on the 'primacy of external policy', Brüning thus essentially instrumentalised his assertive foreign policy to effect a retrenchment of the German economy and polity. He sought to end Germany's embroilment in the Young system and dependence on foreign, chiefly American, loans, essentially by way of a shock therapy. His course undoubtedly exacerbated the adverse effects of the flight of US short-term capital following the Wall Street crash. In short, it was a course largely inverse to Stresemann's. Brüning could only pursue it because he no longer led a parliamentary government but a *Präsidialkabinett* that ultimately relied on President Hindenburg's emergency

---

[13] Cf. Becker and Hildebrand (1980); James (1986); Nicholls (1991).

[14] Brüning's policy has remained very controversial. See Kent (1989), p. 332; Kolb (1988), pp. 212–18; Evans (2003), pp. 248–83.

[15] Cf. Krüger (1985a), pp. 512–29; Knipping (1987), pp. 94ff, and Rödder (1996).

decrees. Yet this subordination of foreign to domestic policy was only one side of the coin. The chancellor's conduct also reflected ever more widespread frustration with what many influential voices in Germany now branded as the lacklustre revisionist 'progress' achievable through Locarno politics and the Young regime, a frustration that had been growing despite the 'liberation' of the Rhineland.

Notably Foreign Minister Curtius yet even more so the new permanent under-secretary at the *Auswärtige Amt*, von Bülow, espoused a distinctly more assertive and unilateral style to restore Germany to its rightful great-power status. Bülow thought that the time had come to abandon the arduous search for international compromises. He advocated pushing through German demands, especially on disarmament, without seeking preliminary understandings with the Locarno partners. As a consequence, while both Curtius and Brüning sought Anglo-American backing to accelerate revisions, the relationship with France turned from strained co-operation to open rivalry.[16] These were incisive qualitative changes. German policymakers mounted no less than a 'massive attack' not only on Versailles but also on the system of London and Locarno. Of course, this attack was even more ruthlessly pursued, from June 1932, under von Papen's 'cabinet of national concentration'.

In the early stages of these developments, French leaders had sought to obtain German and British support for a qualitative leap in a different direction. Essentially, they intended to tie the more restless eastern neighbour more firmly into a European *status quo* system. In May 1930, Briand flanked the official termination of the Rhineland occupation, which the new premier Tardieu had sanctioned, by specifying his earlier plans for a European Federal Union. He still sought to reassure the French electorate, this time by way of replacing the old territorial *glacis* with an extended framework of co-operation and control. It was to solidify the *status quo* through the establishment of institutionalised consultations between the Locarno powers, which were to cover both political and economic issues.[17]

Yet not only Brüning but also the MacDonald government poured cold water on this far-reaching scheme. Ever more, French governments found themselves caught between the rock of Germany's increasingly uncompromising revisionist policy – with French anxieties being fuelled futher by the rise of the 'Hitler element' – and the hard place of Anglo-American refusals to provide firmer security assurances, both strategic and financial. By the end of 1931, the Foreign Office concluded that France was 'unwilling either to disarm

---

[16] Bülow memorandum, 25 October 1929; AA to Sthamer, 31 December 1929, *ADAP*, B, XIII, nos. 76, 224; Curtius to Prittwitz, 9 March 1930, PA, 8591/H 216251–2; *AR Brüning I und II*, no. 158. Cf. the more affirmative analysis of Curtius' policy in Rödder (1996).

[17] Briand speech to the League assembly, 5 September 1929, *Société des Nations* (1929), pp. 52–3.

or to finance Europe, as she alone can, unless she is satisfied on the question of security'.[18] Failing such satisfaction, which by that time extended Anglo-American commitments could provide, the Tardieu government remained strictly opposed to even moderate German rearmament. And Paris indeed not only sought security from overt aggression but also guarantees against further revisions of the Versailles treaty and what in French eyes was its Locarno complement. Apart from disarmament, the most precarious issue on which France resisted any change was the 'Polish Corridor'.

Following the revelation of Brüning's customs-union plans, the national-conservative governments under Tardieu and later under Pierre Laval altered the course of French policy. From the spring of 1931, Paris, too, adopted a more assertive approach, though it did not perform as marked a turn in this direction as Berlin had done earlier. Essentially, both Tardieu and Laval came to pursue a distinctly more hard-fisted *quid pro quo* policy. In a reversal of earlier patterns of Franco-German relations after the war, they chiefly sought to press Germany into continued collaboration, and the fulfilment of its reparation obligations, by using what France, at that point comparatively least affected by the depression, still commanded: financial power.[19]

More precisely, French policymakers struggled to safeguard security through new bargains on two fronts, the German and the Anglo-American. Their attempts to rein in the Brüning government were premised on the assertion that any French concessions on reparations and, subsequently, any loans to Germany would only be forthcoming if Berlin showed moderation. Concretely, Tardieu demanded that Brüning depart from his pursuit of an outright cancellation of reparations. And the French premier also demanded that Germany rescind what he regarded as its dangerous bid to alter the continental European balance through the *Anschluß* of Austria, its ambitious arms-parity policies and the push for frontier revisions in the east.

On the eve of the crisis of 1931, a domestically ever more besieged Briand had suggested to Curtius that Germany should seek long-term loans from France to combat its acute financial problems. Yet by then French nationalists were already clamouring for a more drastic reversal of France's German policy. They advocated replacing the occupation's controls with new financial checks. In short, the threat of withdrawing French short-term loans was to function as a lever to contain German ambitions and enforce continued reparation payments.[20] As noted, after the éclat of Brüning's *Zollunion* manoeuvres France indeed put financial screws on Germany, aggressively opposing

---

[18] Foreign Office memorandum, 2 December 1931, CAB, 24/225, CP 301 (31); Tardieu speech, *Chambre*, 30 November 1930, in Tardieu (1931), pp. 185–8.

[19] Cf. Mouré (2003), pp. 181–99.

[20] Hoesch to AA, 9 July 1930, *ADAP*, B, XV, no. 129. Cf. Kent (1989), pp. 333–4.

German attempts to establish a financial domination over eastern central Europe. In March 1932, this would give rise to the Tardieu plan. Tardieu countered Berlin's schemes with the call for a preferential customs and economic union of all countries of the Danube region, yet excluding Germany (and Bulgaria).[21]

Parallel, French governments urgently sought more extensive strategic backing from Britain and the United States. Both Tardieu and Laval maintained that they could only afford a more conciliatory policy towards Germany, both on reparations and disarmament, if London and Washington were prepared to do more to buttress France's position. Essentially, both argued that the anxieties of the French electorate had to be calmed through fresh security guarantees. And they sought to persuade the Hoover administration finally to relent US debt-claims.[22]

As long as the Mellon–Bérenger agreement was still in force, the bond of Franco-American interest in preserving the Young plan – and in making Germany pay – remained unbroken; but no longer than that. Much thus depended on how far British and American policymakers found ways, and still had the domestic room to manoeuvre, to forge new bargains with France and contain the acute crisis of 1931. Beyond this, however, the MacDonald government and the Hoover administration faced a far more daunting task, no less a task than to salvage the international system hinging on Locarno and the Young scheme. The most pressing challenge was to prevent the system from fraying where it was most vulnerable. The Anglo-American powers had to prevent a further deterioration of the German situation while at the same time checking and canalising Brüning's demands. This was rapidly becoming too tall an order.

Too little, too late – changes and continuities in Hoover's policy in the face of the crisis

Once the shock-waves of the European crisis flooded back to America in late spring of 1931, Hoover concentrated on domestic initiatives to revive the US economy, believing that he could effect a recovery by balancing the budget through tax rises. The president was convinced that the United States could 'make a large measure of recovery independent of the rest of the world' and largely shield itself from the repercussions of a complete European collapse. In Hoover's judgement, it was the breakdown of the European loan and banking structures in 1931, not pre-existing shortcomings in America's financial

---

[21] Cf. Bariéty (1980), pp. 361–88.

[22] On Laval's visit to Washington in October 1931 see Stimson memorandum, 23 October 1931, in Stimson and Bundy (1948), p. 109; *DBFP*, II, II, nos. 275–80.

institutions of the 'new era', that had turned the recession into a veritable world depression.[23]

But within the ever tighter domestic and international constraints that the Republican president confronted, and to counter the unravelling of the international monetary and financial order in the spring of 1931, Hoover eventually began to alter his foreign policy of aloofness. He actually departed from his previous reliance on private agents and informal approaches to European stabilisation. Notably, Hoover moved towards proposing a debt moratorium. He also prodded FRBNY Governor Harrison to seek new ways of salvaging not only German finance but also the gold-standard system of the postwar era. And, after London's departure from the gold standard in 1931, he even contemplated revising the debt settlements with Britain and France to rescue the Young regime and prevent a complete collapse of international finance. In the sphere of international politics, Hoover and Stimson also came to pursue a wider yet ultimately half-hearted and unsustainable agenda of peaceful change. Their main aim, and futile hope, was to halt Germany's drift towards authoritarian government and away from the international structures and agreements of the 1920s.

In retrospect, Hoover averred that 'the leaders of the democratic regime in Germany' of the early 1930s had still been 'earnestly striving to maintain peace'. But the underlying problem that he saw even after a decade of peace was 'the continual spectacle of European power politics and imperialism'.[24] In October 1931, the president told leading senators and congressmen that the 'multitude of small democracies' created in 1919 were under the spell of 'excessive nationalism'. Beneath all lay 'the social turmoil of communism and fascism gnawing at the vitals of young democracies', most ominously in Germany. Yet the crux was that '[h]ates and fears' still dominated relations between the nations of Europe. Hoover thus still saw excessive European militarism, especially that of France and its eastern allies, as a cardinal evil. While Germany was 'still limited in arms except in the hearts of the military caste', most European countries had 'wasted the substance which should have gone into productive work upon these huge armies and massive fortifications'.[25]

To transform the political situation in Europe, Hoover and Stimson first sought to put financial pressure on France. Then they advanced *the possibility* of 'some *quid pro quo*', offering financial rewards through deb cancellation to prod Paris finally to accept substantial disarmament agreements.[26] And

---

[23] Hoover, message to Congress, 8 December 1931, *FRUS 1931*, I, p. xiii. Cf. Huthmacher and Susman (1973).

[24] Hoover (1952a), pp. 330–1. See also Stimson (1934).

[25] Hoover statement, 6 October 1931, in Hoover (1952b), pp. 88–9.

[26] Stimson diary, 23 November 1932, Stimson Papers.

they tried to use the same levers to promote a more conciliatory French policy towards Germany. The American president and his distinctly more sceptical secretary of state hoped not only to moderate the positions of the Tardieu and Laval governments on reparations but also to induce them to accept what they regarded as necessary changes in the Versailles treaty, particularly a revision of the Polish–German border. These aspirations culminated in talks with Laval in Washington in the autumn of 1931.[27]

In a similar vein, Hoover still relied on Germany's dependence on US goodwill and renewed credits. And, more generally, he counted on the Brüning government's self-interest in avoiding a total collapse of the Young regime, and the German economy. He reckoned that this would eventually moderate Brüning's policies. Satisfying German revisionist claims, notably regarding the 'Polish Corridor', which Hoover had always deemed untenable, was to buttress this process. Essentially, these changes were to alleviate German discontent and draw away popular support both from the National Socialists and the communists. The key, however, at least in Hoover's perception, lay in promoting Germany's financial and economic recovery.

Yet all of these schemes and efforts clearly fell under the rubric: 'too little, too late'. Above all, they were marred by Washington's unwillingness to embark on the most important reorientation required if there was to be any hope of re-stabilising Europe: to overcome the post-Versailles aversion to official strategic commitments in Europe. More precisely, the Hoover administration ultimately declined to assume responsibilities in two crucial areas. It did not move to prop up the international financial architecture, where it alone had – albeit waning – power to make a difference. And it declined to make any guarantees finally underpinning an international security system that reassured France and thus possibly permitted the desired peaceful revisions of the postwar order.

More consequential than America's strategic reticence, though, was that the Hoover administration never fundamentally altered its aloof position vis-à-vis the Young regime. It never embarked on the up-hill struggle of convincing Congress that the United States should accept commitments to this end. If any international way of mastering the fundamental crisis of the early 1930s was to be discovered, then the US government had to take the lead in finding it. But the crisis did not lead the administration to re-assess its essential policies. It never came to envisage supporting the creation of more robust political mechanisms and banking structures to rescue the beleaguered Euro-Atlantic order of the postwar era.

[27] Stimson diary, 8 June 1931, Stimson Papers; Stimson memorandum, 23 October 1931, in Stimson and Bundy (1948), p. 109; Lindsay (Washington) to the Marquess of Reading, 26 October 1931, *DBFP*, II, II, no. 280.

While still commerce secretary, Hoover had repeatedly called for governmental measures to control markets and contain speculation. But he had not been able to prevail against the preference of President Coolidge and the Federal Reserve to maintain a policy of *laissez-faire* and trust in the market's capacities for self-regulation.[28] Yet although Hoover later called America's banking and credit system 'the weakest link in our whole economic system', he would not take any serious steps to reform it or to establish governmental controls after the Wall Street crash.[29] Much less, then, was his administration (or the Federal Reserve) prepared to step into the breach in Europe and prop up the collapsing international credit structures – be it through debt-relief or through government-backed loans.

In keeping with Republican approaches of the latter 1920s, Hoover and his main advisers, Castle and the assistant secretary of the Treasury, Ogden Mills, first sought to transfer responsibility for mastering the crisis to private American bankers. Via FRBNY Governor Harrison, they were urged either to maintain their existing loans or even to widen their credit commitments in Europe. When the bankers predictably refused to take on such risks, Washington demanded that the Brüning government take charge instead. Castle publicly impressed on the European powers that Berlin, not Washington, had failed to restrict unproductive loans – and the Hoover administration would not be cornered into cleaning up a mess that Germany had inflicted on itself.[30] Yet coming to terms with this mess was of course beyond the grasp of the Brüning government.

The more severely the spiralling international crisis hit the US economy, the more doggedly the US administration persisted with its rationale that America should not have to bail out the Europeans, which had caused the *malaise* in the first place. Formally, Hoover never abandoned this position. *De facto*, however, relinquishing America's debt-claims became unavoidable amidst the widening depression, and it was anticipated through the Hoover moratorium. The moratorium, not debt cancellation, marked the greatest extent of Washington's willingness to make concessions vis-à-vis Europe. In this climate, Montagu Norman's proposal of early 1931 that the Bank for International Settlements should establish an agency that, anticipating the World Bank, could provide emergency lending to Germany through French and US surplus capital had to be futile. Predictably, the governments in Washington and Paris as well as French and American bankers came to oppose the creation of such an institution. Subsequently, yet only once the entire gold–dollar system teetered on the brink of collapse, Harrison and the Federal Reserve Board did come to contemplate the need for more far-reaching US commitments to the

---

[28] Cf. Galbraith (1992), p. 44.   [29] Quoted after Schlesinger (1956), p. 474.
[30] *FRUS 1931*, I, pp. 251ff. Cf. Leffler (1979), pp. 247–8.

international financial order. And they also came to consider fundamental revisions in America's debt policy. But their plans were not sanctioned by the administration and were rapidly overtaken by events.[31]

In the sphere of transatlantic security politics, the Hoover administration's domestic leeway was significantly more restrained. But Hoover and Stimson also remained strongly committed to a policy of steering clear of obligations in Europe, which they still deemed impossible to vindicate vis-à-vis Congress.[32] They not only rejected a return to Wilsonian approaches but also a reversal of the Republican shunning of security-pact entanglements in Europe. Such a reversal seemed all the more undesirable as an even greater Congressional majority admonished a strictly isolationist course in times of mounting domestic calamities. Hoover's actions were still informed by his assessment that after Wilson's 'idealism' had been 'mostly rejected' at Versailles, the League had not become 'an instrument for amending and revising' the postwar *status quo*.[33] Nor could the Locarno pact any longer be such an instrument, even if Washington had chosen to gravitate towards it.

The most striking and (in)famous instance of US 'restraint' in upholding international order in the depression era of course occurred not in relations with Europe but following the occupation of Manchuria through the Japanese Kwantung Army in September 1931 and the establishment of the puppet regime of Manchukuo in February 1932. In line with reigning Congressional *caveats*, Hoover not only declined to participate in international sanctions against Japan, notably an economic boycott through the League. He also refused to adopt any forceful American counter-measures in protest against Japan's violation of the Washington system's nine-power treaty, which guaranteed the territorial integrity of China.

While the League had to resign itself to a resolution condemning Japan's aggression, Washington's response was ultimately restricted to the so-called Stimson Doctrine. Stimson averred that the United States would not recognise either the Manchukuo regime or any further forced alterations in the east Asian *status quo*. Yet the secretary of state also implicitly acknowledged that the United States was not prepared to take any military or economic measures to enforce this doctrine. This remained the Hoover administration's policy even though Stimson himself had earlier advocated harsher sanctions against Japan; he had not been able to prevail over Hoover's *caveats*. Its reaction to the Manchurian crisis underscored to what extent America's international aloofness

---

[31] Cf. Kent (1989), p. 340; Eichengreen (1992), pp. 264ff.
[32] Stimson diary, 12 July 1931, Stimson Papers; Howard to Henderson, 29 August 1929, *DBFP*, IA, VI, no. 347.
[33] Hoover (1952a), pp. 330–1; Hoover statement, 6 October 1931, Hoover (1952a), pp. 88–9.

undercut any prospects of stabilising the postwar order, and reconstructing a functioning security system, on the shifting sands of the depression years.[34]

Vis-à-vis Europe, and especially vis-à-vis France, Stimson and an even warier Hoover also remained strictly opposed to new security commitments, not least, yet not only, because they considered any attempts to win a Congressional approval for them futile. Fundamentally, neither the president nor the secretary of state were any more inclined now than in 1929 to make clear distinctions between Locarno politics and the earlier European alliance manoeuvres that they had replaced. While seeking to promote disarmament, the US government was not to be involved in any European entanglements of this kind.[35]

It is essential to recall that Hoover did *not* see the Young regime, the Locarno concert and the Kellogg–Briand pact as steps towards more robust, permanent instruments of a post-Wilsonian world order in which Washington played a leading part. Rather, he regarded all of them as features of a Euro-Atlantic order that permitted the American government to retain an essential degree of international detachment, and to concentrate on expanding an economically underpinned *Pax Americana*. The crisis of the early 1930s did not alter this fundamental assessment. Yet it also has to be concluded that, by this time, the domestic constraints that weighed on Hoover's administration – the financial burdens that the crisis imposed and the ensuing Congressional and public pressure to restore 'America first' – had become overwhelming. They had become too overwhelming to leave room for any decisive steps in a different, more internationalist direction.

In sum, it was precisely because they faced a crisis of unprecedented proportions that Hoover and Stimson ultimately deemed it imperative to maintain the essentially non-committal US foreign policy of the latter 1920s. For what in their eyes the United States could least afford was to jeopardise its domestic recovery by over-extending its international responsibilities.[36] The limits of what a still weak executive in Washington could accomplish were further underscored by Hoover's inability to shape foreign economic policy. Although he intended to do so – without shedding his belief in the wisdom of measured protectionism – the president could not prevail on Congress to moderate the Smoot–Hawley tariff. This failure was a clear sign to the European powers that, instead of reversing the trends of the 1920s in view

---

[34] Stimson diary, 23 September 1931, 9 October 1931, Stimson Papers; US note to Japan and China, 7 January 1932, in Stimson and Bundy (1948), p. 80; Stimson (1936), pp. 39ff. Cf. Ferrell (1957); Kennedy (1999), pp. 93–4.

[35] Hoover disarmament proposals, 22 June 1932, *DBFP*, II, III, pp. 606–8; Stimson diary, nos. 27, 152, 168–72, Stimson Papers; Stimson and Bundy (1948), pp. 27–33; Dawes memorandum, 3 March 1931, *DBFP*, II, III, no. 206.

[36] Hoover to Stimson, Stimson diary, 29 September 1929, Stimson Papers.

of the worsening depression, America was adopting even more protectionist policies.[37]

Arguably, by 1932, and probably already by 1931, no US administration could any longer have succeeded in taking on decisive strategic commitments to stabilise the European and global situation – if leading decisionmakers in Washington had finally seen the need for making such commitments. Highly difficult to vindicate in the 1920s, they would have been impossible to legitimate in the domestic climate which by then prevailed in the United States.[38] Franklin D. Roosevelt's election victory in 1932, his concentration on nationally focused recovery policies and his unprecedented quest for resuscitating and reforming the United States 'from within', through what became the New Deal, confirmed this unequivocally.[39] Eventually, Hoover and Stimson sought to prevail on Britain to extend further guarantees to France in order to conciliate Germany.[40] But this, too, was to no avail.

The unbridgeable gap between aims and means: British policy in the face of the crisis

Of the four principal powers of the post-World War I Euro-Atlantic system, Britain pursued probably the most internationalist policies in response to the World Economic Crisis. The principal European broker of the 1920s came to develop approaches that in principle were most conducive to the postwar system's preservation. It did so both under Labour and, from August 1931, under the MacDonald-led National government, which included a dominant Conservative element and was later continued under Baldwin and Neville Chamberlain. Yet if the United States did not have the requisite political leadership, or government structures, Britain no longer had the power to prevent a collapse of Europe's postwar order. The erstwhile hegemon of the global economic and political order was even less capable of performing this task once it descended into the gravest financial and political calamity befalling Britain since the war, the Slump, in the summer of 1931.[41]

In December 1931, a Foreign Office memorandum characterised what it called the 'present world "confidence crisis"' as 'a series of interlocking problems, ranging from the purely financial and monetary problem at the one end to the purely territorial problem created by the Peace Settlements at the other end'. In the assessment of the Foreign Office, the 'links' in that

---

[37] Hoover (1952a), pp. 291–9.
[38] Hoover statement, 6 October 1931, in Hoover (1952b), pp. 88–9.
[39] Cf. Dallek (1995), pp. 23–34.
[40] Stimson diary, 17 October 1931, Stimson Papers.
[41] Cf. McKercher (1999), pp. 63–125; Clavin (1996).

'chain' were the following: the *'monetary crisis* [led] inevitably back to the *economic chaos* in Europe', which was bound up with 'the political questions of *reparations and war debts'*. These again were 'linked by the United States with the question of *disarmament'* and the latter, at least in the perception of the French government, hinged on 'the problem of *security'*. Yet that problem in turn raised the question of *'the territorial status quo* in Europe', notably 'the Eastern frontier question'. This meant that, ultimately, Britain faced 'the conflict between *the maintenance or revision of the Peace Settlements'*.[42] To disentangle this chain of 'interlocking problems', British policymakers came to pursue two major agendas. They sought to foster a stabilisation of the Locarno system through stepped-up peaceful change; and they sought to promote 'world recovery' through a reinvigoration of free trade and a reform of the gold-standard system of the 1920s.

The fundamental goal of British diplomacy was to ensure, as far as possible, that not only France and Germany but also the United States committed themselves to seeking international instead of national solutions to the spiralling financial and political crisis. But the cardinal aim was to shore up European security through further political and eventually also territorial changes of the postwar order. The MacDonald government hoped to accomplish these changes through international agreements that served to reverse Weimar Germany's slide into assertive nationalism and to stymie a further rise of 'the Hitler element'. Ultimately, it sought to prevent Germany's withdrawal from the Locarno system and, thus, the collapse of the system itself.

Yet British policy, which observed disconcerting changes in Berlin's international conduct from the summer of 1930, did not simply adopt a one-sidedly pro-German orientation. Particularly the Foreign Office aimed to revive co-operation with France on which in the view of the new permanent under-secretary, Robert Vansittart, both European peace and the desired gradual and peaceful revision of the *status quo* depended. Henderson, who still held the reins of the Foreign Office, consistently sought to overcome the Anglo-French tensions over reparations that had culminated at the Hague conferences and provoked an all-but collapse of the previous *entente*. And he also sought to bridge the marked differences separating French and British approaches to disarmament and security. Essentially, Henderson intended to build on the Hague approach of 1929. He aimed to stabilise the European situation by addressing German grievances one step at a time – through compromise settlements, not by ceding to the Brüning government's maximal demands.

MacDonald was sometimes at odds with Henderson's course because he had become increasingly frustrated with what he deemed France's 'militaristic'

---

[42] Ashton-Gwatkin memorandum, 2 December 1931, CAB, 24/225, CP 301 (31).

mentality and unwillingness to compromise with a Germany on the verge of collapse. But the Labour premier at first maintained his rationale that it was only in co-operation with France that Britain could hope to achieve stabilising revisions in Germany's favour. As Vansittart noted in February 1931, British diplomacy had to proceed 'gradually', to 'work *towards* – not immediately *for*' the further revision of the Versailles treaty. The Foreign Office favoured rewarding German moderation and Berlin's abiding by the rules of Locarno over a policy of making advance concessions. And it sought to make clear that the limits of British support were reached where the Brüning government sought to force revisions.[43]

From 1931, the Foreign Office saw wider security guarantees to France as the key to promoting peaceful change, and it recommended to extend them by signing up to a fortified Geneva Protocol. But the National government's cabinet eventually refused to follow this path. It was 'not prepared to enter into some form of guarantee over and above Locarno' which might lead British forces to have to fight a new war on the continent to uphold the *status quo* 'even in respect of the Eastern frontier of Germany'.[44] In March 1932, MacDonald defended his vision of League policy in the cabinet's disarmament committee, distinguishing it from the French approach. While France 'held the view that there could be no security without armaments', he saw the League as 'an instrument created for handling situations on a conciliation basis' and by way of creating 'a moral force strong enough to over-ride attempts to satisfaction by resort to arms'.[45]

The shortcomings of this approach in the rougher international climate of the early 1930s were most obviously exposed during the Manchurian crisis. This crisis also threw into relief the limits of Britain's political will, and means, to uphold the principles of the League Covenant and the Washington system. London's response to the Japanese military's aggression was even feebler than Washington's. The National Government concluded that Britain had neither the forces nor the financial resources to contain Japan's incursions in China. It even declined to accept Stimson's proposal for a strong joint condemnation of these incursions, supporting instead the motion to pass a – toothless – League resolution which called for a peaceful settlement of the Sino-Japanese conflict.[46]

---

[43] MacDonald diary, 12 February 1930, 14 July 1931, MacDonald Papers; Vansittart minute, 26 February 1931, *DBFP*, II, I, no. 352.
[44] Cabinet minutes, 15 December 1931, CAB 24/225, CP 322 (31).
[45] Minutes, cabinet disarmament committee, 21 March 1932, MacDonald Papers, 1/591. Cf. Marquand (1977), pp. 716–17.
[46] MacDonald diary, 30 January 1930, MacDonald Papers. Cf. Beasly (1987), pp. 175–97.

MacDonald had hoped that Tokyo would recognise his efforts at the London naval conference as an important step towards accommodating Japanese interests in east Asia. Yet he now faced a more fundamental dilemma. Neither Britain nor the League had the power to contain the Japanese aggression. Neither had the military power to enforce the very rules and principles of pacific settlement that the Labour premier had sought to foster ever since the Great War. The call of 'world opinion', made through the League resolution, could not be effective once the aggressor was turning its back on the League system itself. This was also the critical challenge that MacDonald's successors faced, and failed to meet, when Hitler began to dismantle both the League and Locarno system in Europe.

The second agenda that the British governments of the early 1930s pursued was simple, yet no less Sisyphean. In short, they sought to prevent not only Germany's financial collapse but also the disintegration of the entire world economic order of the postwar decade. For Britain's core financial and trading interests depended on the preservation of both – far more than those of France or the United States. London also tried to win American co-operation in efforts to recalibrate the gold-standard system and prevent even further tariff-barriers. Most of all, however, British policymakers pursued a revisionist reparations policy. And they sought to relieve Europe's financial crisis by finally achieving the abolition of all intergovernmental debts.

The British Treasury and banking circles, notably Norman, favoured pressing for rapid and fundamental changes in the Young regime to provide Germany with some breathing-space for recovery; yet, as ever, these had to be linked to revisions in the transatlantic debt settlements. Not least, the British rationale was to induce Washington to propose debt-cuts to promote French concessions to Germany, both on reparations and the postwar *status quo*. But up until the Hoover moratorium the Labour government remained reluctant to advocate this openly because MacDonald and Snowden feared the negative repercussions that such proposals would have for Britain's standing vis-à-vis Washington and Wall Street, which would only have aggravated already mounting financial problems facing the British government. At the same time, MacDonald sought to prevail on Tardieu to refrain from hard-line financial policies vis-à-vis Berlin. In private, he castigated French financial diplomacy as 'atrocious' at a time when Germany was 'on the edge' and its 'banks collapsing'. The British prime minister held that, instead of disrupting German finance and attaching harsh conditions to any reparations proposals, Paris should join forces with Britain in making controlled concessions – and even extending long-term loans – to the Brüning government.[47]

---

[47] MacDonald diary, 11 and 14 July, MacDonald Papers. Cf. McKercher (1999), pp. 87–94.

But Britain's diplomatic and financial bargaining-power for effecting any of these changes was severely circumscribed. And it became even more circumscribed when in the autumn of 1931 the deepening Slump and spiralling unemployment forced the National government to adopt two consequential measures. They not only contributed to the erosion of the Young scheme but also further weakened the entire postwar financial order. Under the new chancellor of the exchequer, Neville Chamberlain, Britain abandoned the gold standard. And it introduced a 10 per cent general tariff, which in 1932 was followed by the establishment of a protective system of imperial-preference tariffs through the Ottawa accords. Both compounded the negative impact of the American Smoot–Hawley tariff and German difficulties of ever obtaining export-surpluses to pay reparations.[48] London then openly called for a general cancellation of all intergovernmental debts. But the effect that any decision of the British government could have on the policies of the governments in Paris and Washington remained very limited. In 1931, only the United States could take decisive steps towards recasting the debt and reparations regimes – steps that opened up some prospects of containing the crisis.

The Hoover moratorium and the end of the Young regime

The Hoover administration was indeed finally forced to pursue what had been anathema to tight-fisted Republican debt policy ever since 1919: a comprehensive policy to prevent the interlocked reparations and debt regimes from being undermined by the spiralling crisis. Yet Hoover did not go so far as to contemplate breaking the *circulus vitiosus* of international indebtedness and relieve Austrian and German finance by reducing or even cancelling war-debts. Instead, he proposed on 20 June 1931 that all countries should observe a one-year moratorium on all 'intergovernmental debts, reparations and relief debts'. Less than a week later, the United States also granted an emergency loan of $100 million to the German central bank; yet that loan was already exhausted by early July.[49]

Given the extent of Congressional resentment against any concessions to the European powers – and against the indirect protection of Wall Street's loan interests – Hoover's was indeed a politically courageous act. And, although Senator Borah condemned the moratorium, Congress eventually sanctioned it. Yet the moratorium did not suffice to correct a decade of inflexible loan and debt policy or to prevent the failure of Hooverian economic diplomacy as a

---

[48] Cf. Eichengreen (2004), pp. 333–4; Kent (1989), pp. 323–4.
[49] Hoover (1952b), p. 70; Stimson diary, 15 and 18 June 1931, Stimson Papers; Lindsay to Henderson, 20 June 1931, *DBFP*, II, II, no. 62.

whole. Although the president subsequently prevailed on private US bankers to accept a 'standstill agreement' whereby they, too, pledged to refrain from collecting their dues in Europe, his measures could not halt the financial avalanche. German banks were only given a short respite and the United States could only temporarily be insulated from Europe's financial *malaise*.

Ultimately, Hoover's initiative was indeed more of a 'palliative' and stop-gap measure than the result of a sustainable new approach. The Republican administration was still unwilling to make fundamental adjustments; and it was not willing to co-ordinate its policy either with Britain or France, let alone Germany. Unsurprisingly, Hoover's main concern remained to forestall debt cancellation in the longer term. While the American president was worried about Germany's financial situation and newly cognisant of the financial interdependence linking America and its *de facto* principal debtor, his main anxiety was *not* that Germany's collapse was imminent. Rather, his main concern was to salvage US claims by pre-empting any German appeals for a moratorium, which could trigger the long-feared common European assault on the American world creditor.[50]

At the London financial conference of July 1931, the European powers accepted Hoover's moratorium programme, even though both Britain and Germany were left dissatisfied. But no fundamental adjustment could be envisaged. Washington refused to consider any revisions in the Mellon–Bérenger agreement as long as France still seemed capable of avoiding default. And Stimson, who attended the conference, naturally rebutted Snowden's call for more long-term readjustments, strongly rejecting a revision of the Young plan *and* the transatlantic debt settlements. The American secretary of state also refrained from openly supporting a revision of Europe's political *status quo* to allay German grievances.[51] Subsequently, British and German hopes for a major international conference to address all key issues that fuelled the European crisis – from the economic toll of armaments to reparations and debts – also came to naught because of America's unmistakable veto.

Meeting with Stimson, Henderson and the French premier Pierre Laval in Paris before the London conference, Brüning had underlined that a mere moratorium or 'standstill' agreement would not suffice; Germany needed short-term loans and more long-term credits of up to $500 million to weather out the crisis. MacDonald had urged France to contribute to a major long-term loan without pressing Berlin to make major concessions. Parallel, he sought to

[50] Schlesinger (1956), p. 233. Cf. Link (1970), pp. 500–2.

[51] *DBFP*, II, II, nos. 206–23; Stimson statement to the international press after his return from visits to London and Berlin, New York, 3 September 1931, Stimson diary, vol. II, Stimson Papers.

induce Brüning to abandon the unsettling customs-union scheme and to reduce military spending. But his efforts bore no fruit.[52]

Pursuing his own *do ut des* strategy, and indeed turning on the head the pattern that Briand and Stresemann had set in the 1920s, Laval had offered Brüning a loan of 2 billion marks. In return, the French premier demanded political concessions from Germany. The most pressing French concerns remained the abandonment of Berlin's ambitious armament-parity aims and its demands for frontier revisions in the east.[53] But Brüning refused to contemplate such bargains, confident that he could achieve far more radical revisions on the reparations front. His policy became to do everything in Germany's power to make the Hoover moratorium permanent. Before Brüning and Curtius had left for London, the German cabinet had passed a declaration, the so-called *Tributaufruf*. This *Tributaufruf* not only announced that the limits of what 'privation' the German people could endure had been reached. It also greatly alarmed the Hoover administration by stating that Germany's 'precarious economic and financial situation' made 'the removal of her intolerable reparation burden' imperative.[54]

This was to remain Brüning's cardinal aim. In January 1932, responding to mounting domestic pressures and seeking to aid Hindenburg's re-election against Hitler, the German chancellor swept aside a proposal for a revised reparations settlement which had been painstakingly forged between the United States, Britain and France. And he thereby managed to antagonise all three western powers. Brüning's bottom-line, and *idée fixe*, remained that nothing short of complete cancellation would go far enough to overcome Germany's crisis and prevent its slide into extremism.[55] By that time, the British government had jettisoned the gold standard and taken major steps towards erecting the imperial-preference system to combat the Slump.[56] MacDonald was thus more anxious than ever to achieve far-reaching debt cancellations – albeit through international agreements. Under British pressure, Herriot, who had once again become the French premier, ultimately consented to attend the Lausanne conference of July 1932. This conference effectively brought the end of the Young scheme, reparations and transatlantic debts little more than two years after the Young plan's official launch.

In the run-up to Lausanne, MacDonald had mounted a last-ditch attempt to forge a comprehensive agreement on reparations and debts under the

---

[52] Notes of international talks, Paris, 19 July 1931, record of a meeting between MacDonald, Henderson, Brüning and Curtius, Berlin, 28 July 1931, Tyrrell to Henderson, 10 July 1931, *DBFP*, II, II, nos. 219, 228, 179.

[53] Hoesch to AA, 21 July 1931, *ADAP*, B, XVIII, no. 67.

[54] *AR Brüning I und II*, nos. 1180–4. See also Kent (1989), pp. 341–2.

[55] *ADAP*, B XIX, no. 168.   [56] Cf. Eichengreen (2004), pp. 333–40.

debilitating conditions of the depression, essentially proposing an indefinite prolongation of the Hoover moratorium.[57] Yet, still fearful that it would finally have to relinquish its debt-claims, the Hoover administration had declined to attend the conference. But it could not contain its consequences. In the Lausanne accords, all European reparations creditors renounced their claims – and effectively decided to end their payments to the United States. The 'gentlemen's agreement' they concluded, which stated that the Lausanne accords' execution would hinge on first reaching an understanding with Washington, never came into force. Although the Hoover administration did not recognise this inner-European agreement, by the summer of 1932 all debts had *de facto* been abolished. In analogy to 1929, the administration's unwillingness, and inability, to propose meaningful debt-concessions in order to reform the reparations regime marred the effect of the Hoover moratorium. Ultimately, it did not even suffice to 'freeze' the *status quo* under the Young plan till the eventual end of the international depression. Little more than a year after Hoover's announcement, the fate of the Young regime, reparations and US debt-claims had been sealed.[58]

All of these political developments ensued against the background of a burgeoning financial crisis. And that its effects became so disastrous can be attributed to one cardinal deficiency of postwar structures that has already been noted and in turn derived mostly from Washington's *laissez-faire* precepts: the absence of a functioning, robust monetary system and international trade regime. The expanding gold-standard order of the 1920s had essentially never developed beyond a fair-weather system. For the reigning assumption on both sides of the Atlantic remained that gold was the indispensable anchor of Euro-Atlantic trade and finance, regulating both in a quasi-automatic fashion (and disproportionately benefiting the strongest power). On these grounds, leading European policymakers and financiers, yet above all their American counterparts, had not deemed it necessary to work towards creating a more solid framework 'beyond the gold standard'. Already before 1929, when no financial storm was on the horizon yet, the hallmark disequilibrium within the gold-dollar system had constantly grown, with the United States hoarding most gold and available capital. Most ominously, however, no provisions had been made to handle major shocks to the system. It therefore soon collapsed when the massive crisis engulfed central Europe and Britain in 1931.[59]

In a bid to avoid further deflation, depressed economies like Germany and Austria sought to prevent losing the last vestiges of their gold reserves. The

---

[57] See Stimson diary, 23 November 1932, Stimson Papers.
[58] Simon to Tyrrell, 11 July 1932, *DBFP*, II, III, no. 189; see also *ibid.*, nos. 137–92; Stimson diary 11 July 1932, Stimson Papers.
[59] See chapter 11. Cf. Eichengreen (1992), pp. 304ff.

Bank of England also soon faced the challenge of reversing the drain of gold and US capital from German and British markets, which threatened to turn Britain's recession into outright depression. The British Treasury and the Bank of England had long sought to stabilise the gold-standard system and to induce the US Federal Reserve to follow suit. When this was to no avail, the National government in September 1931 finally took the drastic step of withdrawing from gold altogether. Following a rush on the *Reichsbank*'s gold reserves, Germany came to pursue a similar yet idiosyncratic path, establishing various regimes of 'control and blocked currency regulations'.[60] Less affected by the financial turmoil, France retained the gold standard and came to lead the so-called 'Gold Bloc' also including Belgium. Yet it too had to abandon the standard in 1935, and the 'Gold Bloc' disintegrated.[61]

Combined with the creation of the imperial-preference bloc through the Ottawa agreements, what Keynes welcomed as the 'breaking of [Britain's] gold fetters' almost brought world trade and capital movements to a standstill.[62] The United States, on whose leadership the gold order had depended, could not prevent its demise. Hoover sought to effect a recovery within the system's constraints. But his successor Roosevelt saw no alternative but to jettison the gold standard in 1933. Like other states, the United States introduced capital export restrictions to attenuate the effects of the spiralling crisis. But US policymakers had already contributed the main share to precipitating these developments through their own protectionist policies.

A central premise of the Young regime had been that the export of private American capital would generate sufficient economic growth in Europe not only to 'solve' the reparations problem but also to underpin stabilisation in and beyond Weimar Germany and France. Yet precisely because of the advances of the 1920s the 'world creditor' saw no need to act in accordance with what a 'success' of this system would have required – namely, Germany's ability to pay reparations and US loans, and France's ability to repay war-debts. In fact, the latter 1920s had seen a widening rather than diminished negative trade-balance between the main European powers and America.[63] The Smoot–Hawley Act of 1930 thus did not cause this already existing asymmetry. But further US tariff raises aggravated the new trend toward protectionism, which then escalated amidst the worsening crisis. In 1930, Lamont had implored Hoover – in vain – to oppose the Smoot–Hawley tariff as it would spur 'nationalism all over the world'.[64] This was indeed the consequence.

In sum, between 1929 and 1933 the world financial system experienced a marked turn to 'everybody-for-himself' policies. The Euro-Atlantic economy

---

[60] Bell (1986), 144–5; Eichengreen (2004), pp. 330–54.   [61] Cf. Mouré (2003), pp. 181–99.
[62] Quoted after Chernow (1991), p. 331.   [63] Cf. Kindleberger (1973), pp. 71ff.
[64] Quoted after Burner (1979), p. 298.

fractured into protective monetary and trading blocs and protectionist states. What took place has been aptly called a process in which the leading decision-makers in all countries sought to sail their ships through the storm on their own, including those who steered the most capital ship.[65] By 1933, Roosevelt had no longer any mandate from Congress to discuss either debt or tariff reductions. Nor did his administration any longer make any serious effort to salvage the postwar monetary order.

Most infamously, Roosevelt declined to meet Britain's urgent plea to aid the stabilisation of the pound during the London economic conference of 1933. The new president informed the US delegation that his administration 'should avoid even a tentative commitment' to 'control fluctuations in the dollar', which would have been the key prerequisite for propping up the British currency. More broadly, pressed by Congress and resolved to concentrate all energies on initiating the 'New Deal', Roosevelt came to opt for self-reliant national approaches to all major issues – from financial stabilisation to disarmament. To preserve its resources, the United States turned inward. It turned its back on Europe and the international system – eventually to re-emerge revitalised and with a far stronger executive to take on a new global role, yet only after another world war.[66]

The demise of the European security order – the limits of Anglo-American crisis management

Of even graver consequence, though, was that a similar development of 'renationalisation' took place in the sphere of international security. The Great Depression did not precipitate, it *brought about*, the erosion of the European concert system. And the inability of western decisionmakers – and unwillingness of German leaders – to deal with the repercussions of the depression in a concerted manner also swept away all transatlantic attempts at crisis management in the realm of security. All furtive American and more substantive British initiatives that sought to alleviate German grievances and promote peaceful change came to naught. With them foundered all prospects of keeping a crisis-stricken Weimar Germany in some way integrated within the postwar international system. Ultimately, Anglo-American leaders could not give the Brüning government and its successors sufficient incentives, nor threaten them with effective sanctions, to stop them from abandoning Stresemann's policies. Because of this, Britain and the United States could no longer have a reassuring – and moderating – influence on French policymakers either.

---

[65] Kennedy (1999), p. 76.

[66] Roosevelt to Hull and US delegation, 4 July 1933, Roosevelt to MacDonald, 21 July 1933, *FRUS 1933*, I, pp. 683–4, 735.

What had been Locarno politics ever more descended into a Franco-German power struggle in which Britain no longer had the means and America refused to act as a strategic mediator.[67] This struggle crystallised in the dispute over armament 'parity' at the Geneva disarmament conference, which recommenced in February 1932. Fundamentally at stake was how far Berlin would succeed in brusquely recasting the strategic 'balance' of postwar Europe and how far Paris could block this. Also at stake was how far the Anglo-American powers could still find ways to promote negotiated settlements that prevented both a full-blown Franco-German antagonism and a complete dissolution of the Locarno security order. But while Brüning still sought tactical coalitions with London and Washington – behind France's back – the overall trend could not be reversed. It was a trend from *détente* to rivalry, especially in Franco-German relations. Though MacDonald and Henderson struggled to forge further strategic compromises, the rules of the European concert were indeed abandoned.

Hoover and Stimson were convinced that European stability could not be recovered by cementing an untenable *status quo*, one that was vehemently contested by Germany and only maintained by France's military preponderance. Particularly Stimson castigated what he saw as French aspirations to widen a continental European 'hegemony'. In September 1931, he remarked that Europe's 'underlying problems', also bedevilling all disarmament efforts, lay 'between France and Germany' and everything turned on '*the revision of the Versailles treaty*'.[68] Both for Washington and London, everything else seemed of secondary importance, including suspected attempts of the Stalin regime to fish in Europe's increasingly troubled waters, drive a wedge between the Locarno powers and draw Germany closer to the Soviet Union.

In the assessment of the Hoover administration, the key to consolidating the Old World thus lay in more assertive efforts to foster *controlled* peaceful change. Germany's remaining postwar grievances finally had to be abetted, particularly through disarmament and territorial revisions in the east. To make this possible, France finally had to be forced to permit serious progress at the next – and final – round of the Geneva disarmament conference. In American eyes, a descent into politically antagonising and economically ruinous arms-races in Europe could only be pre-empted if Paris finally accepted substantial military cuts.[69] In the autumn of 1931, Hoover and Stimson also ratcheted up their pressure on Laval to accommodate Berlin's desire to revise the 'Polish

[67] Cf. McKercher (1999), pp. 95–125.
[68] Stimson diary, 30 September 1931, Stimson Papers. See also *ibid.*, 30 July 1931, XVII, nos. 169–73, Stimson Papers.
[69] 1 Hoover (1952b), pp. 88–9; Stimson diary, January 1931, Stimson Papers. Cf. Craig (1980), pp. 106–17.

Corridor', which particularly the US president himself regarded as the crux, calling it the 'unstable spot of Europe and of the world'.[70]

The real crux, however, remained that both the Hoover administration and the British government were still unwilling – and domestically less in a position than ever since 1919 – to assume the security obligations indispensable to fostering, and stabilising, the changes they sought. When Laval visited Washington in October 1931 Hoover would not even consider a 'consultative pact' with France, as suggested by the French premier, in order to further disarmament and his political revision objectives in Europe. Prior to the Franco-American consultations, some higher State Department officials had developed plans to extend US capabilities in support of League anti-aggression efforts on the basis of the Kellogg–Briand pact. They thus hoped to encourage France to disarm and Britain to extend its security commitments. But Hoover rejected the State Department's approach, fearful that it would embroil Washington in enforcing League sanctions.[71]

Naturally, even less desirable for the Republican administration was to enter into what Hughes and Kellogg had successfully resisted throughout the 1920s, a bilateral pact with France that could foreshadow one-sided alliance commitments. And, as Stimson remarked, it was a 'political impossibility' in view of the US Senate's entrenched opposition to any such entanglements. Hoover subsequently confirmed that his cardinal aim was and remained precisely to rid Europe of war-prone 'military alliances'. Instead, from 1931 his administration reverted to the informal tactics of the era of London and Locarno, pursuing a familiar, yet by then no longer effectual combination of pressure and incentive. Both the president and his secretary of state impressed on all European powers that only once they had reached substantive disarmament agreements and revised the precarious 'Polish Corridor' would Washington be inclined to lower its debt-claims. And only then would it seek to canalise gold and capital flows back to Europe. For only then could the administration expect Congressional support for such controversial measures.[72]

Flanking these overtures, Stimson made increasing efforts to encourage Britain's National government to play a more committed part in European security. Yet all he could offer MacDonald were assurances that the United States would welcome it if Britain assumed wider responsibilities under the Geneva Protocol. The State Department indeed went out of its way to emphasise that possible British obligations would not interfere with US neutrality policy (as the Protocol's provisions governing blockades against aggressors

---

[70] Stimson diary, 23 October 1931, Stimson Papers. Cf. Leffler (1979), pp. 264–5.

[71] Hoover (1952a), pp. 330–1; Stimson diary, 4 and 6 March 1930, Stimson Papers.

[72] Stimson diary, 23 October 1931, Stimson Papers; Hoover statement, 6 October 1931, in Hoover (1952b), pp. 88–9; Stimson diary, 12 October 1931, Stimson Papers; *FRUS 1931*, I, pp. 549–50.

threatened to interfere with US trade).[73] Yet both Stimson's assurances and Hoover's half-hearted pursuit of Republican 'carrot-and-stick' strategies proved ineffectual. In retrospect, it seems indeed remarkable how little consideration both policymakers gave to the political implications of their disarmament and revision proposals, particularly as they were not accompanied by greater US reassurances. They clearly underestimated the extent of French anxieties vis-à-vis an eastern neighbour pursuing increasingly assertive policies, especially in the highly sensitive areas of disarmament and the east European frontiers. Tardieu and Laval constantly reiterated to Washington, and London, that advances in security had to precede any French moves even approaching armament 'parity' with Germany.[74]

For both MacDonald and Henderson, the promotion of a negotiated, and gradual, revision of the European *status quo*, particularly through disarmament, was central to achieving their underlying aim: to buttress Weimar Germany's republican order. This was not only meant to prevent further gains of the National Socialists but also, more broadly, to keep Germany anchored to the postwar international system. British policymakers were deeply concerned about the crisis-prone situation on Germany's eastern border and drafted vague designs to push for a negotiated settlement that would assemble such an 'army of forces as would overcome even Polish obduracy without bloodshed'.[75] Yet neither the Labour nor the subsequent National government were prepared, or in a position vis-à-vis Paris, to pursue what Washington admonished from afar: ambitious and necessarily unsettling initiatives to revise the 'Polish Corridor' that the Piłsudski government was hardly inclined to accept without major resistance.

Rather, MacDonald maintained that within an order still including Europe's main powers disarmament offered the best means for bolstering peace in the tense situation of 1931. Henderson continued his futile attempts to build bridges to successive French governments. But MacDonald increasingly shared American antipathies to France's assertive policies vis-à-vis Germany and its insistence on maintaining a massive armed preponderance. And so did, largely, the National governments of 1931/2. As early as February 1930, MacDonald had noted that the 'purely militarist' mentality of French leaders lay at the root of 'the peace problem of Europe'. The British prime minister thus sought all the more to prevail on Laval, then Tardieu, to initiate arms reductions.[76] But he also struggled to commit Brüning and Curtius to a moderate policy.

[73] Stimson diary, 17 October 1931, Stimson Papers.
[74] Stimson record of conversations between Hoover and Laval, 23 October 1931, Stimson Papers; Lindsay (Washington) to the Marquess of Reading, 26 October 1931, *DBFP*, II, II, no. 280.
[75] Foreign Office memorandum, 2 December 1931, CAB, 24/225, CP 301 (31).
[76] MacDonald diary, 12 February 1930, MacDonald Papers.

Meeting both at Chequers in June 1931, he insisted that Britain would only support Berlin if it curbed its claims and pursued them within the framework of a new disarmament conference.[77] This stance did not change thereafter.

Essentially, MacDonald hoped that by eliminating the disarmament clauses of Versailles he could convince Brüning to accept less than full 'equality', reconciling modest German rearmament with French concerns. Yet, as a Foreign Office memorandum noted in December 1931, Europe's 'political deadlock' could not be solved as long as Britain and America refused to 'meet France' on the matter of 'further commitments'. And 'the absence of American co-operation' made it still harder for Britain to make such commitments.

Henderson and Sargent thus began to explore alternative ways of reassuring France. Eventually, they indeed reverted to the instrument that had been sidelined during the Locarno period: the Geneva Protocol. The Foreign Office concluded that 'the risks entailed by accepting the principles of the protocol in full are less than those which [would] be upon [Britain], if we allow the present situation to drift'. In the Foreign Office's appraisal, the gains that seemed possible by using the Protocol as a lever – measured disarmament, a new reparations settlement and Britain's 'main object': '*European recovery and the restoration of confidence*' – outweighed its undesirable ramifications. These were, essentially, that Britain would have to extend its Locarno guarantee to eastern Europe and risk having to join France in a war against the (German) aggressor in the event that a conflict over the 'Polish Corridor' was to erupt.[78]

This was the response of Henderson and the British Foreign Office to France's continual demands for firmer guarantees. After Laval had returned from Washington empty-handed in October 1931, the efforts of his successor Tardieu indeed centred on obtaining British support for a more forceful Geneva Protocol. In Tardieu's view, however, the Protocol had to be an instrument whose purpose was to enforce the European *status quo*, also in the east. And he eventually complemented this by proposing to establish an international force to police the more muscular League regime that he envisaged. Thus, as ever, the underlying thrust of French policy was clearly to solidify the treaty system of Versailles and its complements of the mid-1920s by all available means. French policy conflicted ever more with British pursuits of peaceful change. And a French consent to a revision of the Polish–German frontier was essentially ruled out, with or without a reinforced League.[79]

Crucially, however, MacDonald was no more willing than when first supporting the Geneva Protocol in 1924 to extend Britain's military guarantees to France. And he enjoyed full backing from his Conservative coalition partners,

---

[77] Cf. Krüger (1985a), p. 544.
[78] Foreign Office memorandum, 2 December 1931, CAB, 24/225, CP 301 (31).
[79] Cf. Bariéty (1980), pp. 361ff.

notably Baldwin and Neville Chamberlain. Britain would not assume obligations beyond those assumed at Locarno; it would not enforce what was still deemed an unsustainable *status quo* in eastern Europe. On the same grounds, and because the Conservative majority refused to relinquish strategic decision-making powers to Geneva, the cabinet rejected not only the Protocol but also the proposed international policing-force.[80] In a time of acute financial crisis and soaring unemployment, the National government deemed it even less conceivable than in 1925 to vindicate the extension of costly commitments to Europe's still most highly armed power. More profoundly, though, MacDonald never changed his view that France's new Protocol policy was misguided. For, as he noted in March 1932, it threatened to change the emphasis of European politics from 'conciliation' and arbitration to military enforcement and *status quo* protection.[81] Yet in MacDonald's judgement this would only undermine what remained of the co-operative system of the 1920s.

By the time the final Geneva disarmament conference commenced in February 1932, the Hoover administration had reverted to a policy of strict non-entanglement both with the League and arms-limitation efforts in Europe. US efforts exhausted themselves in economic appeals for French disarmament which were no longer backed by financial pressure. Hoover was still not prepared to spur French arms-reductions with the 'carrot' of debt-relief.[82] And a frustrated MacDonald had meanwhile come to regard Tardieu's security and disarmament policies as 'an ever active influence for evil in Europe'. But in an ever deteriorating international situation, London's attitude only reinforced the French view that 'there could be no security without armaments'.[83]

Once the Geneva proceedings got under way – under the chairmanship of Henderson – the British government persisted with attempts at accommodating the vastly conflicting interests of Germany and France. Overall, however, Britain still leaned towards striking a 'balance' by way of reducing French armament-levels and allowing Germany to make moderate increases. The crucial aim of British policy was still to achieve such a balance through an international agreement, i.e. to prevent a complete breakdown of the Geneva efforts. For the main British fear remained that Germany would otherwise resort to uncontrolled rearmament, without regard to any international limitations.[84] But MacDonald and Henderson could neither contain Berlin's ambitions for armaments 'parity' nor overcome French resistance to German

---

[80] Cabinet minutes, 15 December 1931, CAB 24/225, CP 322 (31).
[81] MacDonald statement, 21 March 1932, MacDonald Papers, 1/591.
[82] Stimson diary, July 1931, Stimson Papers; *FRUS 1931*, I, pp. 501–4; Hoover statement, 6 October 1931, in Hoover (1952b), pp. 88–9.
[83] MacDonald diary, 7 April and 1 May 1932, MacDonald statement, 21 March 1932, MacDonald Papers.
[84] *DBFP*, II, II, nos. 235–52.

pressure in what increasingly turned into a Franco-German tug-of-war which eroded European security.

The Brüning government by this time insisted that substantial changes towards German equality in armaments were imperative, also to contain further gains of the National Socialists in Germany. Deeply dissatisfied with the *status quo*, neither Brüning nor the *Auswärtige Amt* were any longer pursuing policies on the premise of preserving the Locarno system. Rather, they sought to push through their demands in order to shore up the government's embattled domestic position – yet also to fulfil what they deemed rightful German claims. The revision of the 'Polish Corridor' remained a secondary issue. It was armament 'parity' that became, or rather was made into, the litmus test for Germany's craved-for 'equality' as a great power until and beyond Brüning's resignation in May 1932.[85]

Yet the more assertive and ruthless German conduct became the more French governments insisted that only more substantive security arrangements could make their stance on disarmament more conciliatory. By December 1932, MacDonald commented that French policies 'could drive Germany into war again'.[86] The *caesura* of the final round of League-based disarmament efforts had come earlier when, following the instructions of the new chancellor von Papen, the German delegation deserted the conference on 22 July. On 11 December 1932, the western powers finally passed a declaration stating that Germany was to be granted 'equality of rights' in the armament question. This completed the disintegrative process that had created the international constellation in which Hitler could seize his opportunity. And he would seize it – to wreck the post-World War I order and prepare the ground for a second world war.[87]

On 5 January 1933, Stimson observed to the German ambassador Prittwitz that unless the great powers succeeded in renewed disarmament efforts and in 'preventing wars some future war would probably destroy our entire civilisation'.[88] Unfortunately, this prediction was almost borne out. Fortunately, it did not entirely come true. But all hopes of salvaging the advances of the 1920s ended with the demise of the Weimar Republic, and the Nazi regime's ascent to power, less than a month after it had been made.

---

[85] Bülow minute, 14 January 1931, *ADAP*, B, XVI, no. 159; Weizsäcker memorandum, 2 March 1931, *ADAP*, B, XVII, no. 1.
[86] MacDonald diary, 3 December 1932, MacDonald Papers.
[87] *DBFP*, II, II, nos. 260–70. Cf. Krüger (1985a), pp. 546–51.
[88] Stimson memorandum, 5 January 1933, NA RG 59 793.94/5711.

Conclusion
The incipient transformation of international politics after World War I – learning processes and lessons

After the turning-point of the Ruhr crisis, not only British and American approaches to European stability were altered. Decisionmakers on both sides of the Atlantic began to recast international politics in Europe, and between Europe and America. They remade European order. More than the Ruhr crisis itself, it was the 'return' of the Anglo-American powers to the European continent in October 1923 and their intervention in the Franco-German conflict that marked the systemic *caesura* of post-World War I international history – at least in the western powers' relations with Germany.

The system of London and Locarno

In sum, what a comparative and systemic analysis of Euro-Atlantic politics after the Great War can bring to light are three distinct stages of what in effect was one overarching process of European stabilisation. It was a process that gained momentum from the autumn of 1923, and led to the two formative international settlements of the mid-1920s – the settlements of London and Locarno. It then continued through half a decade of limited, yet nonetheless remarkable postwar consolidation until it was brought to an end by the World Economic Crisis. The security pact of Locarno would have been impossible had it not been for the initial stabilisation of Europe brought about – to a large extent the American way, yet ultimately only through Britain's pivotal brokerage – through the agreements of London. Conversely, the Anglo-American peace initiated in 1924 would have remained ephemeral without Locarno. Essentially, then, British and American policymakers, and no less their French and German counterparts, had begun to reorientate policies and pursue new ways of international accommodation and peaceful change, ameliorating a *status quo* that had become untenable.

As has been described, after the London conference a certain dualism emerged. This was largely due to the American government's renewed espousal of unbridled economic diplomacy and the role of a distinctly informal, aloof arbiter in matters of international security. A process of political-cum-financial consolidation, essentially advanced on American terms, spurred and was complemented by a process of political stabilisation, essentially European advances towards solving the European security question. As the outcome of Locarno manifested, however, if all sides chose to foster both of these processes they could be *mutually reinforcing*. The overall outcome was a palpable gain in European stability and security within a remarkably short 'fulcrum period': the formation of a nascent transatlantic peace order.

From 1923, policymakers made not merely minor amendments to the old international order, that of 1919. They began to develop, and they brought to bear, new ground-rules altering it as such. Not only but chiefly because they were the first postwar agreements negotiated between the victors *and* the vanquished of the war, the London and Locarno settlements were indeed beginning to supersede the truncated Versailles system both in terms of quality and stability. Within two years nothing less than the contours of a new system of international politics had emerged. A change of paradigm had occurred. Those who shaped British and American international policies from the watershed of the Ruhr crisis – but also those who departed from strict treaty enforcement in France and uncompromising revisionism in Germany – began to achieve what the peacemakers at Versailles did and could not achieve in the immediate aftermath of the unprecedented cataclysm of 1914–18. They painstakingly forged complex, integrative compromises. They began to draw Weimar Germany into a western peace system while inducing France to co-operate in this process – and in fact taking into account French interests.

What all decisionmakers departed from was the really existing 'Versailles politics' that had marked the crisis period 1919–23 – on the American but also, after Lloyd George's fall, on the British side: withdrawal and non-engagement; on the French side, not least in consequence of this: coercive treaty 'execution' and, under Poincaré, even the bid to establish a continental hegemony *against* Germany. At the same time, the vanquished power of the war, whose initial rejection of the 'yoke of Versailles' undoubtedly remained the gravest threat to European peace, had been isolated, pushed ever further away from finding a place in the postwar order and, ultimately, on the verge of collapse in 1923.

Thereafter, Anglo-American decisionmakers were united by a common interest in preserving a – democratic – German state as bulwark of political and economic order in central Europe. At first, they also sought to preserve the Weimar Republic as a bulwark against the spread of Bolshevism; but, when the Bolshevik threat had abated, they mainly sought to preserve it as a counterweight to what they perceived as French ambitions to exceed the parameters of Versailles and gain not only a strategic foothold on Rhine and Ruhr but also control over a Franco-German economic bloc.

What the Ruhr crisis heightened was a sense among British and American policymakers that it was in their interest not only to buttress Weimar Germany economically and to establish a workable reparations regime. They also had an interest in strengthening the position of those German decision makers who endeavoured to 'play' by Anglo-American rules and struggled to legitimate this course domestically – notably Stresemann. Both sides acknowledged, albeit the British government at first more than the American administration, that this also required reintegrating Germany into the political decisionmaking processes of Euro-Atlantic reparations diplomacy and security relations. In many ways, legitimating the Dawes approach was tantamount to widening the legitimacy for Germany's postwar orientation to the west as such. The same of course also was true for the Locarno process.

The international stabilisation efforts of the mid-1920s can be called the first comprehensive, and to a remarkable degree successful, attempts to come to terms with the crux of the European situation. This was not 'merely' the unsettled German question but, inseparable from it, the Franco-German question – the unsettled relations between the arch-enemies of the prewar and postwar period. Once altered, Anglo-American pacification strategies clearly met the fundamental challenges of Europe's postwar instability far more effectively either than either the Versailles system or France's original postwar policy.

From the autumn of 1923, policymakers on both sides of the Atlantic – and on both sides of the Versailles divide – embarked on what under the conditions of the post-World War I era was a stony but arguably the only realistic path towards generating a modicum of international stability in Europe. It was a path of complex bargains. Undoubtedly, both Anglo-American powers had to compromise, and did compromise, least to foster advances on this path. They had to make few serious compromises either with regard to strategic commitments or in terms of financial sacrifices. And the United States invested even less in the critical postwar settlements than Britain.

If one takes into account each power's departure-point of 1919, the bulk of concessions on all fronts was for Germany and above all for France to make – not to mention the 'concessions' that Poland was pressed to make, and resisted. More than previously recognised, however, British and American policies were essential in fostering and catalysing the crucial international agreements and bargains after the Great War. Only their impact made the salient international accords of 1924 and 1925 possible. This, not least, may be seen as an indication of how Britain and the United States could, and did, operate, as pivotal powers in the post-World War I international system.

With a focus on the fulcrum period between the Ruhr crisis and the Hague settlement of 1929, it thus can be underlined that to a remarkable extent – and more than has been previously acknowledged – they began to promote broader reorientations towards the adoption, if not always explicit acceptance, of *shared* rules and – largely Anglo-American – practices of pacific settlement and transnational co-operation. These were not only espoused in Berlin, where in view of the defeat and the grappling of Weimarian policymakers for a new 'republican foreign policy' this was more foreseeable. They were also adopted – if grudgingly – in Paris.

The sea-change in international politics after the Ruhr crisis clearly manifests that under the systemic conditions of the 1920s it took the intervention of Britain and the United States even to begin overcoming the Franco-German antagonism. Since 1919, French and German leaders had not been able to find a bilateral *modus vivendi*. Not least of course, this had proved impossible because most of what divided these two powers was intricately connected with Europe's larger postwar problems – notably those of reparations, security and the unstable *status quo* in eastern Europe. These problems could not be resolved by the two powers alone. Even to approach their solution required a broader framework, and this could only be provided, however imperfectly, by the Anglo-American powers. Conversely, however, neither British nor American policies would have been successful if those who implemented them had merely encountered Franco-German exhaustion after the Ruhr conflict. In fact, not only German but also French decisionmakers accepted Anglo-American approaches to peaceful change because they partly saw no alternatives but also because they hoped that these approaches would allow them to pursue core national interests more effectively.

Anglo-American forward engagement had the most remarkable impact on the evolution of Weimar Germany's *Westpolitik* under Stresemann. In essence, they furthered Germany's pursuit of moderate policies of peaceful revision. It is worth emphasising once again that only America's pursuit of the Dawes settlement and Britain's promotion of the Locarno pact allowed Stresemann to lead Germany out of the Ruhr crisis and subsequently to pursue his co-operative course in the first place. By restraining France, they created the essential international conditions not only for his policy but also for the Weimar Republic's inner stabilisation and incipient inclusion in a western postwar system, which distinctly superseded all German temptations to gravitate towards a revisionist alliance with the Soviet Union.

Active Anglo-American policies, and pressures, also pointedly influenced the significant departures of French policymaking and decisionmaking from the autumn of 1923. France's postwar leaders, and notably Poincaré, moved with suspicion in the direction that Washington, London and New York set. And not only Poincaré but also Herriot and Briand engaged in extensive rearguard battles for a maximal preservation of French pre-eminence and the *status quo* of 1919 – from preserving the sanction powers of the Reparations Commission in 1924 to insisting on a more or less exclusive Anglo-French *entente* within the Locarno concert throughout the latter 1920s. Yet *de facto* French policy, too, gravitated towards Anglo-American principles and rules of pacific settlement and controlled peaceful change to a remarkable extent, finally even in the core sphere of security. It was on this basis that British and American stabilisation policies could give a decisive impetus to the 'relative stabilisation' of the Euro-Atlantic international system achieved by the mid-1920s, which in turn created the necessary, if as yet far from sufficient, preconditions for extending postwar stability from western to eastern Europe.

The nature of the post-World War I international system

What can a re-appraisal of the incipient transformation of Euro-Atlantic politics between 1923 and 1925 reveal about the nature of the post-World War I international system? Arguably, it was a hegemonic more than a multi-polar system. Yet it was also a system that to a certain extent was unsettled by the effects of what was essentially the first, and critical, stage in a long-term process of hegemonic transition. It was the transition from Britain's inter-national hegemony, which had culminated in the middle of the nineteenth century, to the global hegemony of the United States, which only reached its – likely – culmination-point after World War II, if not towards the end of the twentieth century.

Further, the international system after the Great War was marked by an un-precedented asymmetry between the United States and the European powers. In this sense, there was some justice to Hoover's verdict that while Europe needed America, no vital American interest was (yet) at stake, even in the economic sphere, that made far-reaching US commitments to European peace imperative.[1] Notably, while British leaders had more serious concerns in this area, no overriding threat to US national security seemed to emanate from Europe, even in the medium term – not from Germany and even less from the Soviet Union, which was essentially turning inward in the 1920s, and only beginning to develop an international policy of its own. Nevertheless, the United States pursued Europe's Progressive stabilisation.

Due to the American maxim of non-entanglement, Britain was and remained the politically pivotal power for peaceful change in postwar Europe, above all in the realm of security politics. Because of Britain's diminished financial capabil-ities after 1918, however, the United States clearly became the pivotal power not only for Weimar Germany's consolidation but also for the political-cum-financial stabilisation of France and wider post-Versailles Europe.

This cannot only be concluded from a retrospective assessment. As we have seen, it was to a greater or lesser extent a perception shared by contemporary decision-makers in London, Washington, Paris, Berlin and Warsaw. Thus, not only because of the power capabilities of the states they represented, the principal policymakers in Washington and Whitehall were the only actors

---

[1] Hoover memorandum, 23 January 1922, Hoover Papers, box 21.

who, if they could devise strategies to this end, also had the means to foster new ground-rules of European stabilisation after 1919. In other words, in the constellation of the 1920s, and once they co-operated, they were the only actors who could decisively change the hamstrung Versailles system, commit French and German policymakers to new principles of accommodation and thus shape the outcomes that not only Britain and the United States desired, the London and Locarno settlements and the international integration of Germany that these settlements fostered.

Learning processes – parallels and distinctions

As this analysis has sought to substantiate, what set Europe on a course of 'relative stabilisation' between 1923 and 1929 were deeper-level changes. Stabilisation was propelled by a pointed change in the concepts and rationales that underlay British and American approaches and also, prompted by the former, French and German postwar policies. And it took a crisis of the magnitude and possible repercussions of the Ruhr crisis to spur policymakers into decisive steps to implement these concepts. What had long merely been British and American 'grand designs' was finally brought to bear on the European situation.

What informed this departure most profoundly? Can Europe's incipient pacification indeed be characterised as the outcome of learning processes? Or is this a term with too normative, and positive, connotations for describing what decisionmakers underwent – and came to do differently by the mid-1920s? As I hope to have shown, what the protagonists of peaceful change painstakingly embarked upon can indeed be seen as idiosyncratic – and in many respects constrained – attempts to draw consequences. Hughes and MacDonald as well as Chamberlain and Kellogg drew consequences from the cataclysm of the Great War and the deficiencies of the Versailles system. But they also, and notably, drew lessons from the way in which the Franco-German postwar crisis had escalated in the Ruhr conflict. And so did, from their own specific vantage-points, Poincaré, Herriot, Briand and notably Stresemann and Schubert.

One of the main findings of this study can thus be summarised as follows: the orientations and ultimate ends of the individual and collective learning processes that not only Anglo-American policymakers but also their French and German counterparts underwent were in essence converging in the decade after World War I. And, at least until the end of 1925 and to a large extent until 1929, these processes, and the policies they generated, were overall commensurable. There were no steep learning curves. Far from progressing in a linear fashion, reorientations in post-World War I international politics were hardly informed by striking instances of a 'turning-around of the mind'. But they were nonetheless pointing in a new, forward-looking direction: overall balanced compromises supplanted coercion, reconciliation of interests as well as longer-term aims and requirements of legitimacy supplanted destabilising containment.

Rivalries were of course not overcome or extinguished; but they were partly addressed at their roots, partly submerged through new understandings and standards whose net-effect was integrative and stabilising. It is worth emphasising again that, after the failure of forging such understandings at Versailles, this development was unprecedented – not only in the twentieth century but also in the wider history of transatlantic relations. In European diplomacy, it seems justified to follow Chamberlain in arguing that, on a large scale, such advances were made for the first time since the heyday of the nineteenth century's Vienna system.

A systematic comparison of the origins and nature of British and American stabilisation strategies after World War I can serve to discern many parallel yet also very distinct reorientations. Both had a marked impact on how Anglo-American decisionmakers co-operated with each other, and on how far they sought to co-operate with the leaders of France, Germany and eastern Europe. What policymakers in Whitehall and Washington pursued from 1923 were for the most part not radically novel approaches to rebuilding international order. But their strategies departed significantly not only from what had informed each power's policies towards Europe before 1914 but also from the *caveats* or excessive ambitions that had originally limited the effectiveness of their engagement both at and after the Paris Peace Conference.

In view of the novel challenges of European instability after 1919 it seems hardly surprising that British and American leaders sought guidance from, *or they sought to develop futher or even transcend*, 'tried and tested' models of crisis-management taken from their own, specific foreign-policy traditions and realms of experience. A left-liberal proponent of 'new diplomacy' after 1918, MacDonald at first relied on sweeping internationalist maxims, rejecting what he saw as British balance-of-power traditions. Apart fom Wilson's, his undoubtedly was the most far-reaching departure by any Anglo-American leader after 1918. Yet, aided by Crowe and in a continuity of British foreign policy, he soon came to develop an evolutionary approach, pursuing British interests through negotiations with the other great powers, including Weimar Germany.

Chamberlain, by contrast, essentially endeavoured to build on Castlereagh's achievements of 1814/15. He sought to adapt to the twentieth century what he deemed Britain's tradition of shaping European peace orders *as a European power*. His was not the worldview of a politician too concerned with the transatlantic dimension or financial complexities of European reconstruction after 1919. Yet his promotion of the European concert decisively furthered Germany's inclusion into the Locarno system, which indeed anticipated the principles of post-1945 European integration.

By comparison, Hughes – like Hoover – devised policies that could hardly be based on a long tradition of American involvement in European and world affairs, or indeed the legacy of an American world-power role. Consequently his outlook was shaped by his pragmatic, yet also markedly legalistic, aim of internationalising his version of principles and practices taken from the Progressives' quest for domestic reform in the United States in the prewar era. On these premises, Hughes advocated a very limited governmental role and a maximum of 'depoliticisation', aiming to recast European power politics mainly through privately driven stabilisation initiatives. But he also oversaw a very important change in strategy: the carefully controlled yet essential reorientation of US postwar policy that paved the way for the implementation of the Hughes plan of 1922. The pre-eminent US secretary of state of the interwar period translated this plan into a pragmatic stabilisation policy that met the specific requirements of European conflict-resolution in 1924.

Hughes' successor Kellogg had far greater direct exposure to the European crisis. Yet he came to build both on the successful precedent of the Dawes settlement and on his predecessor's legacy in reinforcing what he regarded as the very effective rationales of aloof arbitration and non-entanglement. This placed severe limits on a more constructive American approach to European security in and after 1925.

Under both Hughes and Kellogg, Republican policy was informed by the assumption that America's financial power could be the most potent instrument of peaceful change. What evolved into a doctrine of US economic diplomacy was in fact spearheaded by Herbert Hoover. It was espoused not only by the Coolidge administration but also by leading US financiers like the Morgan partners and FRBNY Governor Strong. In essence, political and financial elites held that overcoming the Franco-German antagonism was compatible with, and could indeed be furthered by, America's interest in expanding its own sphere of financial influence and the open-door regime. Until the end of 1925, this rationale by and large proved valid. Yet, as has been shown, this constellation changed, and numerous transatlantic tensions over the priorities of consolidation and peaceful change arose, in the latter 1920s, once Europe's 'relative stabilisation' had been achieved.

In sum, Whitehall and Washington accentuated different stabilisation objectives and rationales. On balance, British policymakers sought to achieve European stability primarily by political means. They chiefly sought to promote intergovernmental co-operation in a reconstituted 'comity of nations', originally a concert of west European great powers that co-operated with the United States, pacified Germany's relations with its eastern neighbours and also served to draw Germany away from a potentially hazardous revisionist *entente* with the Soviet Union.

By contrast, American policymakers, who co-operated far more closely with financial leaders, mainly relied on allegedly 'apolitical' yet in fact economic *as well as* political consolidation strategies. They sought to pacify Franco-German relations and wider Europe by including Germany and France in a recast 'community of ideals, interests, and purposes'. And they essentially envisaged this community as a prosperity-enhancing and, apart from the US market, 'open' system of international politics and finance, controlled by the United States.

For all the distinctions between British and American approaches, however, what proved decisive between 1923 and 1925 was their combined impetus. It spurred a fundamental change of the principles and rules underlying Euro-Atlantic politics. Above all, the protagonists of Anglo-American peaceful change began to act on the common premise that European stability was neither to be regained by reconstructing an elusive postwar balance of power nor by erecting a far-reaching system of collective security through the League. Undoubtedly significant was that in Washington *and* Whitehall not only prewar *realpolitik* but also the Wilsonian approach to international politics had come to be regarded as highly undesirable. Both approaches were deemed not only unfeasible in the face of domestic opposition but also incompatible with the core national interests of two powers that sought to minimise formal – and especially military – commitments to postwar Europe. More profoundly, however, both sides concluded that Europe's cardinal postwar problems, above all the Franco-German question, were simply not amenable either to balance-of-power solutions or to solutions based on grand designs of universal collective security.

Irrespective of different ideological predilections, the maxim that a coercive containment that alienated Germany from the western powers did not further European peace was espoused not only by Hughes and MacDonald but also by Chamberlain, Kellogg and Hoover. On the other hand, with the exception of MacDonald indeed *no* leading Anglo-American decisionmaker believed that the solution to Europe's postwar ills lay in remaking the League into the main, universal instrument of international pacification. At the core, all protagonists rejected *static* supranational regimes of collective security not only as impinging on their strategic sovereignty but also, and essentially, as too rigid to further desirable peaceful change – *with* Germany.

Instead, if on different premises, Anglo-American policymakers came to adopt the common rationale that the best prospect for European stability – and French security – could be opened up by pursuing new ways of anchoring Weimar Germany to a western peace system. Thus, French leaders had to be induced, or if necessary pressed, to pursue this path as well. Further, albeit to varying degrees both British and American policymakers realised that Europe's core problems required transatlantic answers. Clearly, those who grappled with the reparations problem from the time of the Ruhr crisis, especially MacDonald and Hughes, realised this more acutely than those who strove to recast European security politics in 1925, notably Chamberlain. Further, those in London and Washington who sought to overcome Europe's postwar crisis had to learn to open up new avenues of concerted action with the political and economic leaders of France and Germany. And they had to chart new ways of collaborating with the transnationally operating elites of Anglo-American high finance.

Ultimately, what the British and American protagonists of peaceful change began to learn was how to fulfil their countries' critical roles in pacifying the Franco-German conflict and initiating a Franco-German peace process in the 1920s. This was not yet achieved in Polish–German relations. Yet, on balance, what they fostered was conducive to an international equilibrium in the widened Euro-Atlantic state-system, an equilibrium of rights, security and reciprocal responsibilities between the victors and the vanquished of the Great War. It was indeed more conducive to this than anything tried, in vain or to the detriment of international order, at Versailles.[2]

The 'paradox' of the unfinished peace after World War I – too little or too much progress?

It was perhaps complacency when Chamberlain reckoned that the deeper changes of mentality in Germany and France would require a long period of relative stability and a functioning European concert to pacify French and German conduct. As noted, the British foreign secretary at one point told King George V that he looked ahead to the 1960s or 1970s as the culmination-point of such processes.[3] While there is no explicit indication that US foreign-policymakers had similar perspectives in mind, the entire thrust of their economic pacification policies – and of refashioning Europe after the Progressive American model – was likewise one of gradual, long-term stabilisation. These outlooks were probably not unrealistic. Indeed, one factor not to be underestimated when gauging the prospects and limits of international stabilisation after the epochal Great War is simply that of *time*. Time was required for the complex and necessarily gradual process of peaceful accommodation between the western powers, Germany and possibly also Germany's eastern neighbours to bear fruit. And time was also required for the deeper changes in mentality indispensable to this end.

---

[2] Cf. Schroeder (1994), pp. vii–x.
[3] Chamberlain to George V, 9 February 1925, Austen Chamberlain Papers, AC 52/378.

In retrospect, however, it is of course clear that the time Weimar Germany and the new international system of the mid-1920s *de facto* had to achieve consolidation was highly constrained. Europe enjoyed only a short era of relative stability between 1925 and 1929. The larger question raised here thus relates to the limits of what any more or less stable and functioning international system can at best achieve, particularly in terms of consolidating not only international order but also the domestic politics and economies of its major actors. As the demise of the Weimar Republic after 1929 demonstrated most drastically, internal radicalisation in the wake of an international crisis may be the root cause for a regression into aggressive power politics and war.[4]

And yet it is worth underlining once again that all the limits of Anglo-American engagement *after* 1925, and the limits this placed on the further evolution of the system of London and Locarno, were not such, or of such a magnitude, that they inexorably led to its disintegration. The new European concert of the mid-1920s was not an inherently flawed construction or an inherently insufficient basis for European peace; nor was the American design for an economically founded transformation of European politics. To a large extent, they generated an astonishing measure of stability in the short period between 1924 and 1929.

But the fact that the system of London and Locarno remained in essential aspects nascent and incoherent made it vulnerable once a major crisis erupted. Crucial was that no generally accepted mechanisms existed yet that could have enabled policymakers to engage in concerted *transatlantic* crisis-management, both in the critical spheres of security politics and international finance. This was the main reason why British and American statesmen could not find the means to master the gravest challenge to international stability between 1919 and 1932, the World Economic Crisis.

As the developments following the Ruhr crisis manifested, both British and American stabilisation policies had indisputable limits and were marred by self-imposed restrictions and domestic constraints; but neither had serious inherent flaws. Both approaches were marked by inconsistencies, a certain tension between the professed aims of stabilising Europe and the political will to make robust commitments to this end, yet they were not marked by blatant contradictions. More importantly still, the Euro-Atlantic peace order that emerged in 1924 and 1925 was not doomed to founder. Rather, the core problem of European stabilisation after the Great War was that international policymakers, and above all those in Whitehall and Washington, did or simply could not make stronger commitments to sustaining, and extending, the processes of peaceful change that they had initiated at London and Locarno.

[4] See Bracher (1978).

Neither the Locarno concert nor the US-induced process of financial-cum-political stabilisation that followed the Dawes settlement were bound to remain ephemeral. And, rather than widen it, the settlements of London and Locarno in fact began to narrow the new twentieth-century divide between western and eastern Europe that had emerged after World War I. Locarno did create borders of different validity, which was unavoidable under the circumstances. But what the settlements of the mid-1920s achieved above all was something else: in the aftermath of a highly divisive, and imposed, Versailles peace settlement, and after more than five years of rising tensions in eastern central Europe, they prepared the only realistic ground for a peaceful change of Polish–German relations; and they also prepared the ground for what necessarily had to be a drawn-out, arduous process – a process of levelling, as far as possible, the disparate levels of stability, security and prosperity between western and eastern Europe, all the way to the Soviet Union.

Yet the evolution of international relations between the Locarno pact and the Great Depression was also marked by a paradox, or at least by what appears to be a paradox. On the one hand, for all its limitations the western powers' reinvigorated co-operation with Germany allowed for tangible – and in retrospect striking – progress in stabilising post-World War I Europe between 1926 and 1929. On the other hand, the nascent Euro-Atlantic peace order could ultimately not be fortified. And an important cause of its eventual dissolution was precisely that the London and Locarno settlements had so successfully generated *relative* stability in Europe. For this, in essence, encouraged Anglo-American disengagement from Europe, and above all from European international politics.

While their influence remained pivotal, particularly policymakers in London and Washington did not do enough to make the system of London and Locarno more storm-proof and effective. In the end, they failed to develop it into a more durable and legitimate international order, sufficiently solid to withstand major crises. It is also important to note, however, that the calamity that befell the world between 1929 and 1932 was one of unprecedented proportions. It would have been extremely hard, if not impossible, to master that crisis even in the framework of a far more entrenched, and legitimate, system of international politics and finance.

On the positive side of the post-World War I era's balance-sheet, it can be noted that the politics of London and Locarno did allow for genuine advances in the latter 1920s where it mattered most. They indeed furthered the foremost Anglo-American aim: Weimar Germany's increasing, if necessarily gradual, inclusion into a western-orientated peace system – both politically and economically. And they thus also improved further the security of France, Poland and Europe as a whole. Locarno politics and America's Progressive consolidation efforts converged to achieve this to an extent hardly imaginable at the nadir of the Ruhr crisis. Both gained steadiness, remaining the two decisive processes that shaped transatlantic relations and European developments up to the Great Depression.

A systemic analysis can underscore that Anglo-American ground-rules of political accommodation and liberal-capitalist reconstruction became the decisive rules of Euro-Atlantic politics in the decade after World War I. Despite all the setbacks they gained more legitimacy and more, not less, acceptance on the part of French and German policymakers after 1925, if more so in Berlin than in Paris. More precisely, as Hughes had anticipated in 1924, they gained ground first and foremost among political and financial elites.[5] With the exception of France, they were accepted most unreservedly in the circles of high finance on both sides of the Atlantic, circles that obviously had most to gain. Yet they were also adopted by those political decisionmakers who pursued peaceful, if competitive co-operation in postwar Europe. Among these, Briand and Stresemann stood out. Both positively and negatively, British and American strategies thus retained a marked impact on the on-going reorientation processes of French and German foreign policies in the latter 1920s. Despite increasing Anglo-American aloofness, both sides continued to see co-operation with London and Washington as the best, or at any rate the most realistic, way to solve cardinal political and economic problems.

Particularly in Germany, the approach that Stresemann and Schubert developed after 1923 to change the postwar *status quo* increasingly shaped the very ends of German policy. Under Stresemann, the objective of again becoming a great power of equal standing in Europe was ever more unequivocally pursued through strategies of peaceful settlement, bargaining within the Locarno concert and reliance on economic means. Demands for unsettling territorial revisions in the east did not disappear altogether, but they became more and more muted. They were not pushed forward at the price of destroying Germany's most vital relations – those with the western powers.

Although there were more pronounced divisions over the course of French financial and security policy among leading decisionmakers, notably between Briand and Poincaré, very similar developments came to mark France's post-Locarno policy. The governments of the postwar Third Republic came to pursue both financial crisis-management and security by seeking as much co-operation with, and backing of, the Anglo-American powers as possible. And they came to pursue the same ends by trying to co-operate with, and control, the *voisin d'outre-Rhin*. Both in Paris and Berlin, these orientations amounted to more than simply a lack of better alternatives. But, as the failure of the Thoiry initiative manifested, French and German policymakers were also

---

[5] Hughes to Kellogg, 20 September 1924, NA RG 59 462.00 R296/607.

driven to bilateral attempts at mastering their problems once not only America's but also Britain's political involvement in Europe began to slacken.

On the negative side of the post-Locarno balance-sheet, one finding is unavoidable: Between 1926 and 1929 neither the diplomacy of the European concert nor US pursuits of financial and political stability produced any further outcomes that were as groundbreaking as those of the mid-1920s – not in western Europe, and certainly not in eastern Europe. Neither bore fruit as quickly or convincingly as either Berlin or, on different grounds, Paris desired. Indeed, a core problem became that whatever was achieved in the wake of the London and Locarno settlements came to be viewed as falling short of the expectations that these successes had generated, particularly in Germany, yet also in France.

To his dismay, Stresemann could not reap, at least not immediately, what he considered the 'just' rewards of Germany's international engagement through the Locarno pact, especially a swift 'liberation' of the Rhineland. This had repercussions for the legitimacy of his conciliatory policy among German elites and also in wider German public opinion. Briand had not as yet found a new basis of French security that he deemed solid enough to accept further substantial changes in the postwar *status quo*, especially on the eastern bank of the Rhine. And more importantly, as Chamberlain predicted in 1925, it would require time, a solidified European concert and reliable German conduct to convince French elites that such changes could actually be in their own best interest.[6] Undoubtedly, far more of all of this was required to convince the postwar leaders of Poland, Czechoslovakia and the other east European states 'caught' between Germany and the Soviet Union of the same.

Yet European concert diplomacy was by no means ineffective or even malfunctioning. With US power continuing to act as the essential background force, Locarno politics became the *modus operandi* in Europe between 1926 and 1929. In the final analysis, however, only the politics of London *and* Locarno could yield tangible results on all core issues still dividing France and Germany – and Germany and Poland. But any advances simply took longer, and became more arduous, than all sides had originally expected. The Rhineland occupation was eventually terminated, and the Rhineland question thus, at least from the Anglo-American perspective, largely resolved. It has been shown why this could not be achieved in 1926 or even 1927 but only in 1929. But it was still accomplished more than five years before the original Versailles deadline.

Crucially, this key dispute could not be settled by virtue of European concert politics alone; it could only be settled through what was essentially an attempt to recreate the success of the Dawes negotiations. In other words, the basic constellation of Euro-Atlantic politics did not change in the latter

---

[6] Chamberlain to George V, 9 February 1925, Austen Chamberlain Papers, AC 52/378.

1920s: major advances could only be made through America's decisive intervention, however aloof the Republican administrations in Washington remained. Notably, it would have been impossible without the United States to forge the final, though arduous, international settlement of the era of London and Locarno, the Hague settlement of 1929.

In effect, then, what Chamberlain called the 'nucleus of certainty, security, and stability' of Locarno could actually be strengthened.[7] And it was also beginning to extend, if tentatively, to eastern central Europe. The Polish–German question remained a critical aspect of the Franco-German question – and one of the most precarious postwar problems that still had to be addressed. Crucially, Anglo-American policies began to foster Germany's departure from assertive revisionism also in eastern Europe. And this also began to have a positive effect on those who led Poland's postwar quest for security between Germany and Soviet Russia, chiefly Foreign Minister Skrziński. But in view of the burdensome legacies of the Great War and Versailles, and under the only slowly waning shadow of postwar European insecurity, particularly in the east, the tentative efforts of British and American policymakers could not prompt a sea-change, either in Warsaw or in Polish–German relations.

Seeking security and aiming to strengthen Poland's status as a first-rate European power, Marshal Piłsudski, who held the reins from mid-1926, pursued a relatively pragmatic course. But he did – and perhaps could – not depart from Poland's predominant reliance on power politics. While the German Foreign Office began to develop tentative, and still highly problematic, designs to effect a pacific revision of Germany's eastern frontier and address the mutual minority problems created in 1919, the Polish government understandably remained highly cautious. And until the Great Depression, and even thereafter, not only American but also British leaders basically refrained from any serious initiatives to broker a settlement between Warsaw and Berlin to widen Europe's 'circles of stability' in the east. Overall, the burdensome process towards an 'eastern Locarno', in whose later stages Polish–German differences might have been accommodated, could not be significantly advanced.

Undoubtedly, that progress in Franco-German accommodation was so hard to achieve between 1926 and 1929 can in part be attributed to salient domestic and structural factors affecting French and German policies. The constraints that both Briand and Stresemann faced hardly lessened after 1925, imposed as they were by the continuing opposition of important elite segments and pressure-groups in both countries as well as the continually tenuous parliamentary bases with which both policymakers had to operate. What hardly lessened either, but rather grew, was the abiding structural challenge of reconciling Germany's further revitalisation, and demands for further peaceful

---

[7] Minutes of the 192nd CID meeting, 16 December 1924, CAB 24/172, CP 125 (25).

revisions of the Versailles system, with the still deep-seated suspicions of its western and eastern neighbours. A prevalent fear in many quarters remained that for all of Stresemann's conciliatory pursuits one day other forces might seize power in Germany who could then capitalise on his achievements to cast away the 'yoke' of Versailles by force.

All of these factors weighed down heavily on any prospects of changing relations between Germany and Poland as well. Here, conditions were even more adverse. In view of the highly sensitive frontier issue at the heart of mutual animosities, not only between Berlin and Warsaw, and the depth of these animosities after Versailles, it was hardly surprising that peaceful change in eastern Europe stagnated in the latter 1920s. Yet what also accounted for this stagnation was the way in which Britain and United States defined and delimited their policies. Neither British nor US decisionmakers saw a cardinal national interest in pursuing an active mediation between Berlin and Warsaw.

Nor did they more broadly see a need for developing strategies to stabilise Europe's least consolidated geo-political terrain, that between Germany and the Soviet Union. Not least, the calculation both in London and Washington was that while the implementation of such strategies promised few short-term gains it could prove extremely burdensome. Consequently, Washington abstained completely from any political role in this sensitive area (prior to Hoover's haphazard attempts to pressure Poland into territorial concessions in the early 1930s). London, too, declined to extend its Locarno commitments eastwards. Both powers deemed it politically fruitless, and injurious to their definitions of national interests, to accept direct responsibility for eastern Europe's consolidation. Both counted instead on the pacifying effect of anchoring Weimar Germany to the western system. And they continued to hope that this would also – eventually – serve to stabilise the eastern *status quo* and to contain the threat of a resurgent Soviet–German revisionism for good. While the inherent gravity of the Polish–German conflict after Versailles can hardly be overstated, such Anglo-American attitudes contributed significantly to making the era of London and Locarno a period not of crisis but of stagnation on this critical frontier of postwar stabilisation. Concrete attempts at settling the most precarious issues dividing Germany and its eastern neighbours were postponed rather than stepped up.

There was thus a plethora of continental European factors that contributed to the incomplete consolidation of the Franco-German peace process and of the emergent postwar order. In the final analysis, though, this incomplete consolidation was also, and in many ways chiefly, due to a different development. It can be attributed to a further significant reorientation of British and American policies between 1925 and 1929. In effect, policymakers in Whitehall and Washington, though the latter more than the former, reverted to a course of relative passivity and disengagement from Europe. Thereafter, when the Great Depression reached its nadir, not only the United States but finally also Britain resorted to unilateral policies to safeguard their narrower national interests – and their national or imperial economic systems. It was of course no coincidence that domestic and economic pressures to forego multilateral, 'system-preserving' procedures for a resolution of the World Economic Crisis generally reached a new peak at this point. As a final result of these retrograde developments, the unfinished transatlantic peace order of the 1920s was to disintegrate.

What occurred after 1929 thus revealed all the more distinctly the constraints imposed on Europe's international stabilisation after the Great War not only by unfavourable domestic and economic conditions but also by distinct Anglo-American international policies of 'limited commitment'. Even more, however, it highlighted the constraints under which French, German and east European policymakers had to operate. Ultimately, neither Anglo-American nor continental European reorientations gained sufficient impetus to sustain peaceful change in the brief period of respite that the system of London and Locarno warranted prior to the storms of the 1930s.

An even greater crisis, another world war, and, ultimately, the Cold War's bipolar balance of mutually assured destruction between the American and Soviet superpowers would be required to advance to a new stage of co-operation between the United States, Britain, and – initially – the states of western Europe. Nevertheless, what emerged in the 1920s prefigured in many, yet by no means all, respects the rules and foundations of hegemonic pacification, collective security and concerted efforts at Europe's reconstruction that would foster the more permanent stability achieved after World War II. Rather than on a 'salutary' balance of power, this peace order depended and was later founded on a new international equilibrium under the *aegis* of a (largely) benign US hegemon.

The transatlantic international system of the post-1945 era would be built on the premises of a binding US commitment to European security through the North Atlantic Alliance, the more sustainable financial architecture of the Bretton Woods institutions and Washington's promotion of (west) European reconstruction, as well as integration, through the Marshall plan. This established the essential framework for finally resolving the Franco-German question of the twentieth century and anchoring Germany to a western system.[8] In the end, yet only after the order of Yalta dissolved forty years later, in 1989, the new Euro-Atlantic order could also open up comparable prospects to the states of eastern Europe. Then, a viable peace system could finally be extended from

---

[8] See Maier (1981); Hogan (1987); Milward (1984); Trachtenberg (1999).

a western nucleus to a wider European sphere, overcoming the continent's divisions after two world wars.

Undoubtedly, the sea-changes that gained momentum from the 1940s only took place in the way they did because they initially occurred in the context of a burgeoning Cold War confrontation between the world's two new superpowers. But those who shaped post-World War II policies in Washington – and London – also built on the lessons of the interwar period – the lessons drawn from thirty years of recurrent crises and, in particular, Europe's unfinished peace after World War I.[9] Though they – somewhat erroneously – came to see these as essentially negative lessons, the process of Europe's long-term pacification between 1919 and 1991 can thus in many ways be understood as an arduous learning process. Originally, it evolved under the auspices of a 'declining' yet still potent British world power. Ever more decisively, however, it was shaped, and limited, by the at first informal, then indisputable hegemony of the United States in what was to become, also in Europe, an American century.

---

[9] See Gaddis (1972) and (1997); Ikenberry (2001).

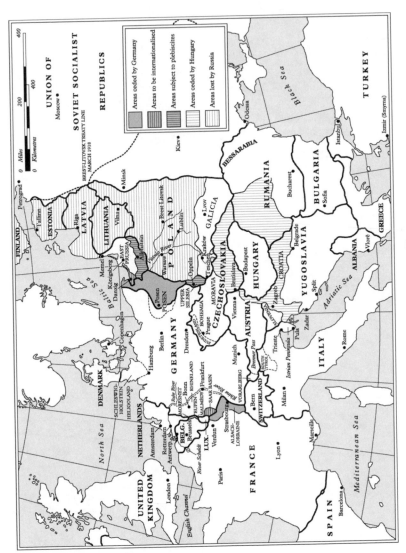

Post–World War I Europe after the peace settlement of Versailles

Bibliography

Primary sources

A   Great Britain

Government papers
NATIONAL ARCHIVE, LONDON
CAB 2: Committee of Imperial Defence Minutes.
CAB 23: Cabinet Conclusions.
CAB 24: Cabinet Memoranda.
CAB 27/275: Cabinet Committees – Foreign Policy – Security, 1924–32.
CAB 27/361–3: Cabinet Committees – Disarmament, 1927–32.
CAB 29/103–4: Proceedings of the London Reparations Conference, 2 vols.
FO 371: Foreign Office Political Files.
FO 800/220: Tyrrell Papers.
FO 800/243: Crowe Papers.
FO 800/256–63: Miscellaneous Correspondence of Austen Chamberlain, 1924–9.
FO 840/1: Papers of the Locarno Conference, 1925.
Treasury Papers, 1923–32.

Private papers
Stanley Baldwin Papers (Cambridge University Library).
Viscount Cecil Papers (British Library).
Austen Chamberlain Papers (University of Birmingham Library).
Winston Churchill Papers [Chartwell Papers] (Churchill College, Cambridge).
Marquis Curzon Papers (India Office Library and National Archive).
Viscount D'Abernon Papers (British Library).
Maurice Hankey Papers (Churchill College, Cambridge).
Ramsay MacDonald Papers (National Archive).
Robert Vansittart Papers (Churchill College, Cambridge).

Published sources
British Documents on Foreign Affairs. Reports and Papers from the Foreign Office Confidential Print, general ed. M. Dockrill 2/1, *The Paris Peace Conference of 1919* (Frederick, MD, 1989).

Documents on British Foreign Policy, 1919–1939, Series I, Volumes I–XXVII (HMSO, 1946–86).

Documents on British Foreign Policy, 1919–1939, Series IA, Volumes I–VII (HMSO, 1966–75).

Documents on British Foreign Policy, 1919–1939, Series II, Volumes I–III (HMSO, 1946ff).

Hansard, Parliamentary Debates: House of Commons, 5th series.

Cmd 1737: The Balfour note, 1 August 1922.

Cmd 1943: Papers relating to British Policy during the Ruhr Conflict (1923).

Cmd 2191: Cabinet Files relating to the London Reparations Conference (1924).

Cmd 2289: *League of Nations Fifth Assembly*, Report of the British Delegates relating to the Protocol for the Peaceful Settlement of International Disputes.

Cmd 2368: Papers relating to the Protocol for the Peaceful Settlement of International Disputes, 1925.

Cmd 2435: Papers respecting the Proposals for a Pact of Security, made by the German Government, 9 February 1925.

Cmd 2525: Final Protocol of the Locarno Conference, 1925.

Cmd 2692: *Agreement of the Settlement of the War Debt of France to Great Britain*, with additional materials, 1926.

B   United States

Government Papers

NATIONAL ARCHIVES, MARYLAND, MANUSCRIPT DIVISION

Department of Commerce: Record Group 39; Records of the Bureau of Foreign and Domestic Commerce: Record Group 151.

Department of State. General Files: Record Group 59.

Department of War. Records of the Military Intelligence Division: Record Group 165.

Federal Reserve Bank of New York Papers (Federal Reserve Bank Archives, New York).

Private Papers

William E. Borah Papers (Library of Congress, Washington, DC, Manuscript Division).

William Castle Diary, William Castle Papers (Houghton Library, Harvard University, Cambridge, Massachusetts).

Calvin Coolidge Papers (Library of Congress, Washington, DC, Manuscript Division).

William S. Culbertson Papers (Library of Congress, Washington, DC, Manuscript Division).

Charles G. Dawes Papers (Library of Congress, Washington, DC, Manuscript Division).

Joseph Grew Papers (Houghton Library, Harvard University, Cambridge, Massachusetts).

Warren G. Harding Papers (Library of Congress, Washington, DC, Manuscript Division).

Herbert Hoover Papers (Hoover Institution, Stanford, California; Hoover Presidential Library, West Branch, Iowa).

Alanson B. Houghton Papers (Corning Glass Archives, Corning, New York).

Edward. M. House Papers (Sterling Library, Yale University, New Haven, Connecticut).

Charles E. Hughes Papers (Library of Congress, Washington, DC, Manuscript Division).
Frank B. Kellogg Papers (Minnesota Historical Society, St Paul, Minnesota).
Thomas W. Lamont Papers (Baker Library, Harvard Business School, Cambridge, Massachusetts).
John P. Morgan Papers (Pierpont Morgan Library, New York).
Dwight D. Morrow Papers (Pierpont Morgan Library, New York).
Jacob G. Schurman Papers (Olin Library, Cornell University, Ithaca, New York).
Henry L. Stimson Papers (Sterling Library, Yale University, New Haven, Connecticut) [Microforms].
Benjamin Strong Papers (Federal Reserve Bank Archives, New York).
Owen D. Young Papers (Van Horne House, Van Hornesville, New York).

Published sources
Burnett, P.M. (ed.) (1940), *Reparation at the Paris Peace Conference*, 2 vols. (New York).
Congressional Record, 65th and 69th Congress, 1919, 1925.
Miller, D.H. (1928), *The Drafting of the Covenant*, 2 vols. (New York and London).
Papers relating to the Foreign Relations of the United States, 1919 (Washington, DC, 1932ff), *The Paris Peace Conference*.
Papers relating to the Foreign Relations of the United States, 1919–1933, US Department of State (Washington, DC, 1934ff).
Senate Committee on Finance: Hearings on the Sale of Foreign Bonds, etc. (Washington, DC, 1932).
Survey of American Foreign Relations, 1929 (New Haven, CT, 1929).

C   *Germany*

Government papers
POLITICAL ARCHIVE, FOREIGN OFFICE, BERLIN
Büro des Reichministers.
Büro des Staatssekretärs.
General Files of the German Foreign Office, 1919–32.
Handakten des Staatssekretärs Carl von Schubert.
Politische Abteilung II: Westeuropa.
Politische Abteilung III: Vereinigte Staaten.
Sonderreferat Wirtschaft.

Private papers
Friedrich Gaus Papers (Political Archive, Foreign Office, Berlin).
Gustav Stresemann Papers (Political Archive, Foreign Office, Berlin).

Published sources
Akten zur deutschen auswärtigen Politik 1918–1945. Aus dem Archiv des Auswärtigen Amts: Serie A: 1918–1925, vols. I–XIV (Göttingen, 1982ff).
Akten zur deutschen auswärtigen Politik 1918–1945. Aus dem Archiv des Auswärtigen Amts: Serie B: 1925–1933, vols. I–XIII (Göttingen, 1966ff).

Akten der Reichskanzlei. Weimarer Republik: Die Kabinette Brüning I und II, 2 vols., ed. T. Koops (Boppard, 1982).

Akten der Reichskanzlei. Weimarer Republik: Die Kabinette Luther I und II, 2 vols., ed. K.-H. Minuth (Boppard, 1977).

Akten der Reichskanzlei. Weimarer Republik: Die Kabinette Marx I und II, 2 vols., ed. G. Abramowski (Boppard, 1973).

Akten der Reichskanzlei. Weimarer Republik: Die Kabinette Marx III und IV, 2 vols., ed. G. Abramowski (Boppard, 1988).

Akten der Reichskanzlei. Weimarer Republik: Die Kabinette Müller I, ed. M. Vogt (Boppard, 1971).

Akten der Reichskanzlei. Weimarer Republik: Die Kabinette Müller II, ed. M. Vogt (Boppard, 1970).

Akten der Reichskanzlei. Weimarer Republik: Die Kabinette Stresemann I und II, 2 vols., ed. K.D. Erdmann and M. Vogt (Boppard, 1978).

Akten der Reichskanzlei. Weimarer Republik: Die Kabinette Wirth I und II, 2 vols., ed. I. Schulze-Bidlingmaier (Boppard, 1973).

Locarno-Konferenz, 1925. Eine Dokumentensammlung, Ministerium für Auswärtige Angelegenheiten der Deutschen Demokratischen Republik (Berlin, 1962).

Luckau, E. (ed.) (1941), *The German Delegation at the Paris Peace Conference* (New York).

Ursachen und Folgen. Vom deutschen Zusammenbruch 1918 und 1945 bis zur staatlichen Neuordnung Deutschlands in der Gegenwart. Eine Urkunden- und Dokumentensammlung zur Zeitgeschichte, IV–VIII: Die Weimarer Republik (Berlin, 1959ff).

Verhandlungen des Reichstags. Stenographische Berichte und Anlagen, vols. 344– (Berlin, 1921ff).

Verhandlungen der verfassunggebenden Deutschen Nationalversammlung. Stenographische Berichte und Anlagen, vols. 325–30 (Berlin, 1920).

D   France

Government papers

MINISTRY OF FOREIGN AFFAIRS, QUAI D'ORSAY, PARIS

Série B Amérique 1918–1940: Sous-série Etats-Unis 1918–29.
Série Y Internationale 1918–40.
Série Z Europe 1918–40: Sous-série Allemagne 1918–29.
Série Z Europe 1918–40: Sous-série Autriche 1918–29.
Série Z Europe 1918–40: Sous-série Europe 1918–29.
Série Z Europe 1918–40: Sous-série Grande-Bretagne 1918–29.
Série Z Europe 1918–40: Sous-série Pologne 1918–29.
Série Z Europe 1918–40: Sous-série Rive Gauche du Rhin.
Série Z Europe 1918–40: Sous-série Ruhr.
Série Relations Commerciales 1918–29: Dossier: Conférence de Londres.

ARCHIVES OF THE ASSEMBLÉE NATIONALE, PARIS

Procès-verbaux des séances de la Commission des Affaires Etrangères, 1923–9.
Procès-verbaux des séances de la Commission des Finances, 1923–9.

ARCHIVES NATIONALES, PARIS
Files, Ministère des Finances.

Private papers

Papiers d'Aristide Briand Papers (French Foreign Office, Paris).
Papiers d'Edouard Herriot Papers (French Foreign Office, Paris).
Correspondance de Raymond Poincaré (Bibliothèque Nationale, Paris).
Poincaré Files (Archives Economiques et Financières, Paris).

Published sources

Commission des Réparations, *Report of the First Committee of Experts* (Paris, 1924).
Geouffre de Lapradelle, A. (ed.) (1929–36), *La Paix de Versailles. La conférence de paix et la Société des Nations (la documentation internationale)*, 12 vols. (Paris).
Journal Officiel de la République Française. Débats Parlementaires (*Chambre des Députés*), 1923–9.
Journal Officiel de la République Française. Documents Parlementaires (*Sénat*), 1923–9.
Mantoux, P. (1992), *The Deliberations of the Council of Four (March 24 – June 28, 1919)*, trans. and ed. A.S. Link and M. Boemeke, 2 vols. (Princeton).
Paillat, C. (ed.) (1979–84), *Dossiers secrets de la France contemporaine*, 5 vols (Paris).

E   *League of Nations, Geneva*

League of Nations (1922), *Resolutions and Recommendations Adopted by the Assembly during its Third Session* (Geneva).
League of Nations (1929), *Official Journal*, Special Supplement no. 75 (Geneva).
Société des Nations (1924), *Société des Nations*, Supplément spécial no. 23 (Geneva).
Société des Nations (1929), *Journal Officiel: Actes de la dixième Session ordinaire de l'Assemblée*. Débats (Geneva).
The World Economic Conference, Geneva, May 1927. Final Report (Geneva, 1927).

Contemporary publications, diaries, letters, speeches and memoirs

Angell, N. (1913), *The Great Illusion. A Study of the Relations of Military Power to National Advantage* (London).
Baker, R.S., and Dodd, W.E. (eds.) (1925–7), *The Public Papers of Woodrow Wilson*, 6 vols. (New York).
Baldwin, Stanley (1937), *On England* (London).
Ball, S. (ed.) (1993), *Parliament and Politics in the Age of Baldwin and MacDonald: The Headlam Diaries, 1923–1935* (London).
Barnes, J., and Nicolson, D. (eds.) (1980), *The Leo Amery Diaries, I: 1896–1929* (London).
Bergmann, C. (1926), *Der Weg der Reparationen. Von Versailles über den Dawes-Plan zum Ziel* (Frankfurt am Main).
Boyden, R.W. (1924), 'The Dawes-Report', *FA* 2, pp. 583–97.

Brockdorff-Rantzau, U. v. (1920), *Dokumente* (Berlin).
Bulletin of the International Labour and Socialist Conference (Berne), 7 February 1919.
Burnett, P.M. (ed.) (1940), *Reparation at the Paris Peace Conference*, 2 vols. (New York).
Cecil, Viscount (1941), *A Great Experiment: An Autobiography* (London).
Chamberlain, A. (1928), *Peace in Our Time: Addresses on Europe and the Empire* (London).
   (1930), 'Great Britain as a European Power', *Journal of the Royal Institute of International Affairs* 9.
   (1931), 'The Permanent Bases of British Foreign Policy', *FA* 9, pp. 535–46.
   (1935), *Down the Years* (London).
   (1936), *Politics from the Inside: An Epistolary Chronicle, 1906–1914* (London).
Child, R.W. (1925), *A Diplomat Looks at Europe* (New York).
Churchill, W.S. (1929), *The World Crisis, IV: The Aftermath, 1918–1928* (London).
Clemenceau, G. (1930), *Grandeurs et misères d'une victoire* (Paris).
D'Abernon, E.V. (1929/30), *An Ambassador of Peace*, ed. M.A. Gerothwol, I: *The Years of Recovery, January 1924–October 1926* (London).
   (1930), *Foreign Policy* (London).
Danelski, D.J., and Tulchin, J.S. (eds.) (1973), *The Autobiographical Notes of Charles Evans Hughes* (Cambridge, MA).
Dawes, C.G. (1939), *A Journal of Reparations* (New York and London).
Dawes, R.C. (1926), *Wie der Dawes-Plan zustande kam* (Stuttgart).
Edwards, W.H. (1928), *This Pact Business* (London).
Einzig, P. (1931), *The World Economic Crisis, 1929–1931* (London).
Gilbert, M. (ed.) (1979), *Winston S. Churchill, V: Companion Part I: The Exchequer Years, 1922–1929* (London).
   (1981), *Winston S. Churchill, V: Companion Part II: The Wilderness Years, 1929–1935* (London).
Gilbert, S.P. (1925–6), 'The Meaning of the "Dawes Plan". An Address before the Council on Foreign Relations, New York, January 12, 1926', *FA* 4.
   (1925–30), *Deutschland unter dem Dawes-Plan. Die Berichte des Generalagenten für Reparationszahlungen*, 10 Halbjahresbände (Berlin).
Glasgow, G. (1925), *From Dawes to Locarno: Being a Critical Record of an Important Achievement in European Diplomacy, 1924–1925* (London).
Grey, Lord (1925), *Twenty-five Years* (London).
Grigg, P.J. (1948), *Prejudice and Judgement* (London).
Hart, A.B. (ed.) (1918), *Selected Addresses and Public Papers of Woodrow Wilson* (New York).
Headlam-Morley, J. (1972), *A Memoir of the Paris Peace Conference, 1919*, ed. A. Headlam-Morley *et al.* (London).
Headlam-Morley, J.W. (1930), *Studies in Diplmatic History* (London).
Henderson, H.D. (1955), *The Inter-War Years and Other Papers* (Oxford).
Herriot, E. (1924), 'The Program of Liberal France', *FA* 1.
   (1948), *Jadis*, 2 vols. (Paris).
Hoover, H. (1919), 'We Cannot Fiddle While Rome Burns', address, Palo Alto, 2 October 1919 (New York).
   (1922), *The European Situation and American Business: An Address* (Washington, DC).
   (1924), 'Government Ownership', an address by Herbert Hoover, delivered in Washington, DC, 29 September 1924 (Washington, DC).

(1926), 'The Future of our Foreign Trade', an address given in New York, 16 March 1926 (Washington, DC).

(1929), 'Address of President Hoover at the Ceremonies on the Eleventh Anniversary of Armistice Day under the Auspices of the American Legion', Washington, DC, 11 November 1929 (Washington, DC).

(1930), 'Address of President Hoover at the Twelfth Annual Convention of the American Legion', Boston, MA, 6 October 1930 (Washington, DC).

(1934), *The State Papers and other Public Writings*, ed. W. Starr Myers, I (New York).

(1952a), *Memoirs, II: The Cabinet and the Presidency, 1920–1933* (London).

(1952b), *Memoirs, III: The Great Depression, 1929–1941* (London).

(1961), *The Ordeal of Woodrow Wilson* (New York).

(1922), 'Deal Only with Upright States', *The Nation's Business* 10, pp. 10–11.

Hughes, C.E. (1923), 'Recent Questions and Negotiations', *FA* 2.

(1925), *The Pathway of Peace. Representative Addresses Delivered during his term as Secretary of State, 1921–1925* (New York).

Kellogg, F.B. (1926), 'Some Foreign Policies of the United States', *FA* 4.

(1928a), *Foreign Relations* (Washington, DC).

(1928b), 'The War Prevention Policy of the United States', *FA* 6.

Kessler, H. Graf (1996), *Tagebücher 1918–1937*, ed. W. Pfeiffer-Belli (Frankfurt am Main).

Keynes, J.M. (1919), *The Economic Consequences of the Peace* (London).

(1921), *A Revision of the Treaty* (London).

(1971), *The Collected Writings of John Maynard Keynes*, 29 vols. (London).

Kriegk, O. (1925), *Locarno, ein Erfolg? Eine kritische Studie der Verträge von Locarno und ihrer Vorgeschichte* (Berlin).

Labour Party Annual Conference Reports, 1922–9 (1923–30) (London).

Lamont, T.W. (1930), 'The Final Reparations Settlement', *FA* 8.

Laroche, J. (1957), *Au Quai d'Orsay avec Briand et Poincaré: 1913–1926* (Paris).

Link, A.S. (ed.) (1977), *The Papers of Woodrow Wilson*, 69 vols. (Princeton).

Lippmann, W. (1922), *Public Opinion* (New York).

(1923), 'The Outlawry of War', *Atlantic Monthly* (August).

(1925), *The Phantom Public* (New York).

(1943), *U.S. Foreign Policy: Shield of the Republic* (New York).

(1944), *U.S. War Aims* (New York).

Literary Digest (1919–32).

Lloyd George, D. (1932), *The Truth about Reparations and War Debts* (New York).

(1938), *The Truth about the Peace Treaties*, 2 vols. (London).

Luther, H. (1960), *Politiker ohne Partei* (Stuttgart).

MacDonald, R. (1914), 'From Green Benches', *Leicester Pioneer* 20 (March).

(1918), *National Defence. A Study in Militarism* (London).

(1919), 'Outlook', *Socialist Review* (July).

(1923a), *The Foreign Policy of the Labour Party* (London).

(1923b), 'Outlook', *Socialist Review* (February).

(1925), *Protocol or Pact* (London).

MacKenzie, N. (ed.) (1978), *The Letters of Sidney and Beatrice Webb, III: Pilgrimage, 1912–1947* (Cambridge).

Manchester Guardian (1923–9).

Miller, D.H. (1928), *The Drafting of the Covenant*, 2 vols. (New York and London).

Moreau, E. (1954), *Souvenirs d'un gouverneur de la Banque de France: Histoire de la stabilisation du franc, 1926–1928* (Paris).

New York Times (1923–9).

Nicolson, H. (1931), *Peacemaking in 1919* (London).

—— (1937), *Curzon: The Last Phase, 1919–1925. A Study in Post-War Diplomacy* (London).

Nicolson, N. (ed.) (1966), *Harold Nicolson: Diaries and Letters, 1930–39* (London).

Noel Baker, P.J. (1925), *The Geneva Protocol for the Pacific Settlement of International Disputes* (London).

Official Bulletin of the International Labour and Socialist Conference (Berne), 7 February 1919.

Petrie, C. (1939/40), *The Life and Letters of the Rt. Hon. Sir Austen Chamberlain*, 2 vols. (London).

Pogge von Strandmann, H. (ed.) (1985), *Walther Rathenau. Industrialist, Banker, and Politician. Notes and Diaries, 1907–1922* (Oxford).

Poincaré, R. (1928), *L'Œuvre financière et économique du Gouvernement. Discours prononcé à la Chambre des Députés par Monsieur Raymond Poincaré 2 et 3 février 1928* (Paris).

—— (1930), 'La Ruhr et ke Plan Dawes', *Revue de Paris* 1 (January).

—— (1933), *Au service de la France. Neuf années de souvenirs, X: Victoire et Armistice, 1918* (Paris).

—— (1977), *A la recherche de la paix, 1919*, ed. J. Bariéty and P. Miquel (Paris).

Rathenau, W. (1929), *Politische Briefe* (Dresden).

Rendel, G. (1957), *The Sword and the Olive: Recollections of Diplomacy and the Foreign Service, 1913–1954* (London).

Report of the Agent General for Reparations Payments. 10 June 1927 (1927), (Berlin).

Saint-Aulaire, Comte de (1953), *Confession d'un vieux diplomate* (Paris).

Schacht, H. (1931), *Das Ende der Reparationen* (Oldenburg).

—— (1953), *76 Jahre meines Lebens* (Bad Wörishofen).

Self, R.C. (ed.) (1995), *The Austen Chamberlain Diaries and Letters: The Correspondence of Sir Austen Chamberlain with his Sisters, Hilda and Ida, 1916–1937* (Cambridge).

Seymour. C. (ed.) (1926–8), *The Intimate Papers of Colonel House*, 4 vols. (Boston and New York).

Shaw, A. (ed.) (1924), *The Messages and Papers of Woodrow Wilson*, 2 vols. (Washington).

Smuts, J.C. (1918), *The League of Nations: A Practical Suggestion* (London).

Snowden, Viscount (1934), *An Autobiography, II: 1919–34* (London).

Stannard Baker, R. (ed.) (1927–39), *Woodrow Wilson: Life and Lettes*, 8 vols. (Garden City, NY).

Steed, W. (1925), 'Locarno and British Interests', *JBIIA* 4, pp. 286–99.

Stern-Rubarth, E. (1939), *Three Men Tried: Austen Chamberlain, Stresemann, Briand and their Fight for a New Europe* (London).

Stimson, H.L. (1932), *The Pact of Paris. Three Years of Development* (Washington, DC).

—— (1934), *Democracy and Nationalism in Europe* (Princeton).

—— (1936), *The Far Eastern Crisis* (New York).

Stimson, H.L., and Bundy, McG. (1948), *On Active Service in Peace and War* (London and New York).

Stresemann, G. (1919), *Von der Revolution bis zum Frieden von Versailles* (Berlin).

(1926), *Reden und Schriften. Politik-Geschichte-Literatur, 1897–1926*, 2 vols. (Dresden).

(1929), 'Speech at the General Assembly, League of Nations, 9 September 1929', *League of Nations Official Journal*, Special Supplement no. 75 (Geneva).

(1932), *Vermächtnis. Der Nachlaß in drei Bänden*, ed. H. Bernhard, 3 vols. (Berlin).

(1976), *Schriften*, ed. A. Hartung (Berlin).

Suarez, G. (1932), *Herriot, 1924–1932* (Paris).

Suarez, G. (ed.) (1928), *De Poincaré à Poincaré* (Paris).

(1938–41), *Briand. Sa vie, son œuvre avec son Journal et de nombreux documents inédits*, 5 vols. (Paris).

Tardieu, A. (1921a), *La paix* (Paris).

(1921b), *The Truth about the Treaty* (Indianapolis).

(1931), *L'épreuve du pouvoir* (Paris).

Times, 1924–9.

Toynbee, A.J., and Macartney, P. (eds.) (1924–30), *Survey of International Affairs, 1923–29* (Oxford).

Turner, C.R. (ed.) (1930), *Essays and Speeches on Various Subjects by Gustav Stresemann* (London).

Turner, H., Jr (1967), 'Eine Rede Stresemanns über seine Locarnopolitik', *VfZg* 15, pp. 412–36.

Union for Democratic Control Policy Statement (1919) (London).

Vansittart, Lord (1958), *The Mist Procession* (London).

Vogt, M. (ed.) (1970), *Die Entstehung des Young-Plans, dargestellt vom Reichsarchiv 1931–1933* (Boppard).

Weber, M. (1994), 'The Profession and Vocation of Politics', in M. Weber, *Political Writings*, ed. P. Lassman and R. Speirs (Cambridge), pp. 309–69.

Williamson, Ph. (ed.) (1988), *The Modernisation of Conservative Politics: The Diaries and Letters of William Bridgeman, 1904–1935* (London).

Williamson, Ph., and Baldwin, E. (eds.) (2004), *Baldwin Papers. A Conservative States-man, 1908–1947* (Cambridge).

Wilson, T. (ed.) (1970), *The Political Diaries of C.P. Scott 1911–1928* (London).

Young, O. D. (1925), 'Address by Owen D. Young at the Johns Hopkins University', 23 February 1925 (New York).

Zwoch, G. (ed.) (1972), *Gustav Stresemann, Reichstagsreden* (Bonn).

Secondary Sources

Adamthwaite, A. (1995), *Grandeur and Misery. France's Bid for Power in Europe, 1914–1940* (London).

Adler, S. (1957), *The Isolationist Impulse* (New York).

Agulhon, M. (1993), *The French Republic 1879–1991* (London).

Ahmann, R., Birke, A.M., and Howard, M. (eds.) (1993), *The Quest fot Stability. Problems of West European Security, 1918–1957* (London).

Aldcroft, D.H. (1970), *The Inter-War Economy. Britain 1919–1939* (London).

Amalvi, C. (1995–6), *Catalogue de la Troisième République*, 3 vols. (Paris).

Ambrosius, L. (1987), *Woodrow Wilson and the American Diplomatic Tradition. The Treaty Fight in Perspective* (Cambridge).

Artaud, D. (1978), *La question des dettes interalliées et la reconstruction de l'Europe, 1917–1929* (Lille and Paris).

(1979), 'Die Hintergründe der Ruhrbesetzung 1923. Das Problem der interallierten Schulden', *VfZg* 27, pp. 241–59.

Aster, S. (1991), *British Foreign Policy, 1918–1945: A Guide to Research and Research Materials*, 2nd edn (Wilmington, DE).

Baechler, C. (1996), *Gustave Stresemann (1878–1929). De l'impérialisme à la sécurité collective* (Strasbourg).

Bailey, T.A. (1947), *Woodrow Wilson and the Peacemakers* (New York).

Bariéty, J. (1975), 'Stresemann et la France', *Francia* 3, pp. 554–83.

(1977), *Les relations franco-allemandes après la première guerre mondiale, 10 Novembre 1918–10 Janvier 1925, de l'exécution à la négotiation* (Paris).

(1980), 'Finances et relations internationales à propos du "plan de de Thoriy" (septembre 1926)', *RI* 21 (Spring), pp. 423–31.

(1985), 'Die französische Politik in der Ruhrkrise', in Schwabe (1985c), pp. 11–27.

(2000), 'Aristide Briand et la sécurité de la France en Europe, 1919–1932', in Schuker (2000), pp. 117–34.

Barnett, C.J. (1972), *The Collapse of British Power* (London).

Bartlett, C.J. (1989), *British Foreign Policy in the Twentieth Century* (Basingstoke and London).

Bátonyi, G. (1999), *Britain and Central Europe 1918–1932* (Oxford).

Baumgart, C. (1996), *Stresemann und England* (Cologne, Weimar and Vienna).

Baumgart, W. (1999), *Europäisches Konzert und nationale Bewegung: internationale Beziehungen, 1830–1878* (Paderborn).

Baumont, M. (1966), *Arisitide Briand. Diplomat und Idealist* (Göttingen).

Beasly, W.G. (1987), *Japanese Imperialism, 1894–1945* (Oxford).

Becker, J., and Hildebrand K. (eds.) (1980), *Internationale Beziehungen in der Weltwirtschaftskrise 1929–1933* (Munich).

Becker, J., and Hillgruber, A. (eds.) (1983), *Die deutsche Frage im 19. und 20. Jahrhundert* (Munich).

Becker, J.-J. (1986), *The Great War and the French People* (London).

Becker, J.-J., and Berstein, S. (1990), *Victoire et frustrations 1914–1929* (Paris).

Bell, P.M.H. (1986), *The Origins of the Second World War in Europe* (London and New York).

Beloff, M. (1989), *Dream of Commonwealth, 1921–42* (London).

Benner, E. (2001), 'Is There a Core National Doctrine?', *NN* 7/2 (April), pp. 155–74.

Bennett, G.H. (1989), *British Foreign Policy during the Curzon Period, 1919–24* (London).

Berg, M. (1990), *Gustav Stresemann und die Vereinigten Staaten von Amerika. Weltwirtschaftliche Verflechtung und Revisionspolitik 1907–1929* (Baden-Baden).

Berg, P. (1963), *Deutschland und Amerika, 1918–1929: Über das deutsche Amerikabild der zwanziger Jahre* (Lübeck and Hamburg).

Berghahn, V.R. (1993), *Germany and the Approach of War in 1914*, 2nd edn (London).

Berghahn, V.R., and Kitchen, M. (eds.) (1981), *Germany in the Age of Total War* (London).

Bertram-Libal, G. (1972), *Aspekte der britischen Deutschlandpolitik 1919–1922* (Göppingen).

Bessel, R. (1993), *Germany after the First World War* (Oxford).

Birn, D.S. (1985), *The League of Nations Union, 1918–1945* (Oxford).

Blake, R., and Louis, R.W. (eds.) (1994), *Churchill. A Major New Assessment* (Oxford and New York).

Boadle, D.G. (1979), *Winston Churchill and the German Question in British Foreign Policy, 1918–1922* (The Hague).

Boemeke, M., Feldman, G.D., and Glaser, E. (eds.) (1998), *The Treaty of Versailles. A Reassessment After 75 Years* (Cambridge).

Bond, B. (1980), *British Military Policy between the Two World Wars* (Oxford).

Bonin, H. (1988), *Histoire économique de la France depuis 1880* (Paris).

Borchardt, K. (1980), 'Wirtschaftliche Ursachen des Scheiterns der Weimarer Republik', in Erdmann and Schulze (1980), pp. 211–49.

—— (1982), *Wachstum, Krisen, Handlungsspielräume der Wirtschaftspolitik* (Göttingen).

Bordo, M., and Goldin, W. (eds.) (1998), *The Defining Moment. The Great Depression and the American Economy in the Twentieth Century* (Chicago).

Borne, D., and Dubief, H. (1988), *La crise des années trente (1929–1938)* (Paris).

Boyce, R.W.D. (1987), *British Capitalism at the Crossroads, 1919–1932* (Cambridge).

Boyle, A. (1967), *Montagu Norman. A Biography* (London).

Bracher, K.D. (1978), *Die Auflösung der Weimarer Republik* (Düsseldorf).

Brandes, J. (1962), *Herbert Hoover and Economic Diplomacy* (Pittsburgh).

Braudel, F., and Labrousse, E. (1980), *Histoire économique et sociale de la France, t. 4, 2e vol., 1914–années 1950* (Paris).

Brinkley, D. (1995), *The End of Reform. New Deal Liberalism in Recession and War* (New York).

Buchheit, E. (1998), *Der Briand-Kellogg-Pakt von 1928 – Machtpolitik oder Friedensstreben?* (Münster).

Bunselmeyer, R.E. (1975), *The Cost of War, 1914–1919. British Economic War Aims and the Origins of Reparations* (Hamden, CT).

Burk, K. (1981), 'Economic Diplomacy between the Wars', *HJ* 24.

—— (1985), *Britain, America and the Sinews of War, 1914–1918* (London).

—— (1989), *Morgan Grenfell 1838–1988. The Biography of a Merchant Bank* (Oxford).

—— (1991), 'The House of Morgan in Financial Diplomacy, 1920–1930', in McKercher (1991a), pp. 125–57.

—— (1992), 'The Lineaments of Foreign Policy: The United States and a "New World Order" 1919–1939', *JAS* 26.

Burks, D.D. (1959), 'The United States and the Geneva Protocol of 1924: "A New Holy Alliance"?', *AHR* 64, pp. 891–905.

Burner, D. (1979), *Herbert Hoover. A Public Life* (New York).

Bussière, E. (1992), *La France, la Belgique et l'organisation économique de l'Europe* (Paris).

Calier, C., and Soutou, G.-H. (eds.) (2001), *1918–1925: Comment faire la paix?* (Paris).

Cain, P.J., and Hopkins, A.G. (2001), *British Imperialism 1688–2000*, 2nd edn (London).

Cairns, J.C. (1974), 'A Nation of Shopkeepers in Search of a Suitable France, 1919–1940', *AHR* 79, pp. 710–43.

Carlton, D. (1968), 'Great Britain and the League Council Crisis of 1926', *HJ* 11, pp. 354–64.

—— (1968/9), 'The Anglo-French Compromise on Arms Limitation, 1928', *Journal of British Studies* 8, pp. 141–62.

—— (1970), *MacDonald versus Henderson. The Foreign Policy of the Second Labour Government* (London).

Carr, E.H. (1939), *The Twenty Years' Crisis 1919–1939. An Introduction to the Study of International Relations* (London).

(1947), *International Relations between the Two World Wars, 1919–1939* (London).

Carsten, F.L. (1966), *The Reichswehr and Politics, 1918–33* (Oxford).

(1984), *Britain and the Weimar Republic* (London).

Case, J.Y., and Case, E.N. (1982), *Owen D. Young and American Enterprise* (Boston).

Cassels, A. (1980), 'Repairing the Entente Cordiale and the New Diplomacy', *HJ* 23, pp. 133–53.

Catterall, P., and Morris, C.J. (eds.) (1993), *Britain and the Threat to Stability in Europe, 1918–1945* (London and New York).

Ceadel, M. (1980), *Pacifism in Britain, 1914–1945. The Defining of a Faith* (Oxford).

Chandler, L.V. (1958), *Benjamin Strong, Central Banker* (Washington).

Chang, H.J. (2002), *Kicking Away the Ladder. Development Strategy in Historical Perspective* (London).

Chernow, R. (1991), *The House of Morgan. An American Banking Dynasty and the Rise of Modern Finance* (New York).

Cienciala, M., and Kormanicki, T. (1984), *From Versailles to Locarno, Keys to Polish Foreign Policy, 1919–1925* (Kansas City).

Clark, I. (1997), *Globalization and Fragmentation. International Relations in the Twentieth Century* (Oxford).

Clarke, P. (1994), 'Churchill's Economic Ideas, 1919–1930', in Blake and Louis (1994), pp. 77–94.

Clarke, S.V.O. (1967), *Central Bank Co-operation* (New York).

Claude, I.L. (1964), *Swords into Plowshares. The Problems and Progress of International Organizations*, 3rd edn (New York).

Clavin, P. (1996), *The Failure of Economic Diplomacy. Britain, Germany, France and the United States, 1931–36* (Basingstoke).

(2000), *The Great Depression in Europe, 1929–1939* (New York).

Clay, H. (1957), *Lord Norman* (London).

Clayton, A.J. (1986), *The British Empire as a Superpower, 1919–1939* (London).

Clemens, G. (ed.) (2001), *Nation und Europa* (Stuttgart).

Cohen, W.I. (1987), *Empire without Tears* (New York).

Cohrs, P.O. (2003), 'The First "Real" Peace Settlements after the First World War. Britain, the United States and the Accords of London and Locarno, 1923–1925', *CEH* 12/1, pp. 1–31.

(2004), 'The Quest for a New Concert of Europe. British Pursuits of German Rehabilitation and European Stability in the 1920s', in Johnson (2004b), pp. 33–58.

Conze, W. (1961), 'Deutschlands weltpolitische Sonderstellung in den zwanziger Jahren', *VfZg* 9, pp. 33–76.

Cook, C. (1975), *The Age of Alignment. Electoral Politics in Britain, 1922–1929* (London).

Costigliola, F.C. (1972), 'The Other Side of Isolationism. The Establishment of the First World Bank, 1929–1930', *JAH* 59 (December), pp. 602–20.

(1973), 'The Politics of Financial Stabilisation: American Reconstruction Policy in Europe, 1924–30', Ph.D. Diss., Cornell University, NY.

(1976), 'The United States and the Reconstruction of Germany in the 1920s', *BHR* 50, pp. 477–522.

(1977), 'Anglo-American Financial Rivalry in the 1920s', *JEH* 37, pp. 911–34.

(1979), 'American Foreign Policy in the "Nutcracker": The United States and Poland in the 1920s', *PHR* 48, pp. 85–105.

(1984), *Awkward Dominion. American Political, Economic, and Cultural Relations with Europe, 1919–1933* (Ithaca and London).

Cowling, M. (1971), *The Impact of Labour, 1920–1924. The Beginning of Modern British Politics* (Cambridge).

Craig, G.A. (1980), 'Die Regierung Hoover und die Abrüstungskonferenz', in Becker and Hildebrand (1980), pp. 106–17.

(1994), 'The British Foreign Office from Grey to Austen Chamberlain', in G.A. Craig and F. Gilbert (eds.) *The Diplomats 1919–1939* (Princeton), pp. 15–48.

Crowe, S.E. (1972), 'Sir Eyre Crowe and the Locarno Pact', *EHR* 87, pp. 49–74.

Crowe, S.E., and Corp, E. (1993), *Our Ablest Public Servant* (Braunton).

Dallek, R. (1995), *Franklin D. Roosevelt and American Foreign Policy, 1932–1945* (New York and Oxford).

Darwin, J. (1980), 'Imperialism in Decline? Tendencies in British Imperial Policy between the Wars', *HJ* 23, 3, pp. 657–79.

Dayer, R.A. (1991), 'Anglo-American Monetary Policy and Rivalry in Europe and the Far East, 1919–1931', in McKercher (1991a), pp. 158–86.

DeConde, A. (1978), *A History of American Foreign Policy, II: Global Power (1900 to the Present)*, 3rd edn (New York).

Dilks, D. (ed.) (1981), *Retreat from Power. Studies in Britain's Foreign Policy in the 20th Century, I: 1906–1939* (Basingstoke and London).

Dockrill, M., and Fischer, J. (eds.) (2001), *The Paris Peace Conference 1919: Peace without Victory?* (Basingstoke).

Dockrill, M., and Goold, J.D. (1981), *Peace without Promise. Britain and the Peace Conferences, 1919–1923* (London).

Dockrill, M.L., and McKercher, B.J.C. (1996), *Diplomacy and World Power. Studies in British Foreign Policy, 1890–1951* (Cambridge).

Dohrmann, B. (1980), *Die englische Europapolitik in der Weltwirtschaftskrise 1921–1923* (Munich and Vienna).

Doise, J., and Vaïsse, M. (1987), *Diplomatie et Outil militaire. Politique étrangère de la France, 1871–1969* (Paris).

Doß, K. (1984), *Das deutsche Auswärtige Amt im Übergang vom Kaiserreich zur Weimarer Republik. Die Schülersche Reform* (Düsseldorf).

Drummond, I. (1972), *British Economic Policy and the Empire, 1919–1939* (London).

Dülffer, J., Kröger, M., and Wippich, R.-H. (eds.) (1997), *Vermiedene Kriege: Deeskalation von Konflikten der Großmächte zwischen Krimkrieg und Erstem Weltkrieg (1865–1914)* (Munich).

Dunbabin, J.P. (1993), 'The League of Nations' Place in the International System', *History* 78/254, pp. 421–42.

Dupeux, L. (ed.) (1992), *La révolution conservatrice allemande sous la république de Weimar* (Paris).

Duroselle, J.-B. (1985), *La décadence 1932–1939. Politique étrangère de la France*, 3rd edn (Paris).

(1988), *Clemenceau* (Paris).

(1994), *La Grande Guerre des Français, 1914–1918. L'incompréhensible* (Paris).

Dutton, D. (1985), *Austen Chamberlain. Gentleman in Politics* (Bolton).

Ebersold, B. (1992), *Machtverfall und Machtbewußtsein. Britische Friedens- und Konflikt-lösungsstrategien 1918–1956* (Munich).

Edwards, M.L. (1963), *Stresemann and the Greater Germany 1914–1918* (New York).

Egerton, G.W. (1978), *Britain and the Creation of the League of Nations* (Chapel Hill, NC).

(1979), *Great Britain and the Creation of the League of Nations. Strategy, Politics and International Organization, 1914–1919* (London).

Eichengreen, B. (1992), *Golden Fetters. The Gold Standard and the Great Depression, 1919–1939* (Oxford).

(2004), 'The British Economy between the Wars', in Floud and Johnson (2004), pp. 314–43.

Ellis, L.E. (1967), *Frank B. Kellogg and American Foreign Relations, 1925–1929* (New Brunswick).

Enssle, M.J. (1980), *Stresemann's Territorial Revisionism. Germany, Belgium, and the Eupen-Malmédy Question 1919–1929* (Wiesbaden).

Erdmann, K.D. (1955), 'Das Problem der Ost- oder Westorientierung in der Außenpolitik Stresemanns', *GWU* 6, pp. 133–62.

(1966), *Adenauer in der Rheinlandpolitik nach dem Ersten Weltkrieg* (Stuttgart).

(1980), *Gustav Stresemann: The Revision of Versailles and the Weimar Parliamentary System* (London).

Erdmann, K.D., and Schulze, H. (eds.) (1980), *Weimar. Selbstpreisgabe einer Demokratie* (Düsseldorf).

Evans, R.J. (2003), *The Coming of the Third Reich* (London and New York).

Fausold, M.L., and Mazuzan, G.T. (eds.) (1974), *The Hoover Presidency. A Reappraisal* (New York).

Feis, H. (1950), *The Diplomacy of the Dollar, First Era 1919–32* (New York).

Feldman, G.D. (ed.) (1985), *Die Nachwirkungen der Inflation auf die deutsche Geschichte, 1924–1933* (Munich).

Feldman, G.D. (1993), *The Great Disorder. Politics, Economics, and Society in the German Inflation, 1914–1924* (Oxford).

Ferguson, N. (1992), 'Germany and the Origins of the First World War: New Perspectives', *HJ* 35.

(1997), 'The German Inter-War Economy: Political Choice vs. Economic Determinism', in Fulbrook (1997), pp. 258–78.

(1998a), 'The Balance of Payments Question: Versailles and After', in Boemeke, Feldman and Glaser (1998), pp. 401–40.

(1998b), *The Pity of War* (London).

(2003), 'Hegemony or Empire?', *FA* 82 (September/October).

Ferrell, R.H. (1952), *Peace in their Time. The Origins of the Kellogg–Briand Pact* (New York).

(1957), *American Diplomacy in the Great Depression. Hoover–Stimson Foreign Policy* (New Haven, CT).

(1963), *Frank B. Kellogg and Henry L. Stimson* (New York).

Ferris, J.R. (1989), *The Evolution of British Strategic Policy, 1919–1926* (London).

(1991), '"The Greatest Power on Earth": Great Britain in the 1920s', *IHR* 13, pp. 726–50.

Feucht, S. (1998), *Die Haltung Sozialdemokratischen Partei Deutschlands zur Außenpolitik während der Weimarer Republik (1918–1933)* (Frankfurt am Main).

Fink, C. (1979), 'Stresemann's Minority Policies, 1924–1929', *JCH* 14, pp. 403–22.

(1984), *The Genoa Conference. European Diplomacy, 1921–1922* (Chapel Hill and London).

Fink, C., Frohn, A., and Heideking, J. (eds.) (1991), *Genoa, Rapallo and European Reconstruction in 1922* (Cambridge and New York).

Fink, C., et al. (eds.) (1985), *German Nationalism and the European Response, 1890–1945* (London).

Fischer, C. (2003), *The Ruhr Crisis, 1923–1924* (Oxford).

Fischer, F. (1967), *Germany's War Aims in the First World War* (London).

Fleury, A. (1998), 'The League of Nations: Toward a New Appreciation of its History', in Boemeke, Feldman and Glaser (1998), pp. 507–22.

Floud, R., and Johnson, P. (eds.) (2004), *The Cambridge Economic History of Modern Britain*, II (Cambridge).

Fox, J.P. (1969), 'Britain and the Inter-Allied Military Commission of Control, 1925–26', *JCH* 4, pp. 143–64.

Franz, O. (ed.) (1981), *Am Wendepunkt der europäischen Geschichte* (Göttingen and Zurich).

Friedman, M., and Schwartz, A.J. (1963), *A Monetary History of the United States, 1867–1960* (Princeton).

Fry, M.G. (1998), 'British Revisionism', in Boemeke, Feldman and Glaser (1998), pp. 565–602.

Fulbrook, M. (ed.) (1997), *German History since 1800* (London).

Gaddis, J.L. (1972), *The United States and the Origins of the Cold War, 1941–1947* (New York).

(1997), *We Now Know. Rethinking Cold War History* (Oxford).

Galbraith, J.K. (1992), *The Great Crash 1929*, 2nd edn (London).

Gardner, L. (1984), *The Anglo-American Response to Revolution, 1913–1923* (Oxford).

Gasiorowski, Z.J. (1958a), 'Stresemann and Poland before Locarno', *JCEA* 18, 1, pp. 25–47.

(1958b), 'Stresemann and Poland after Locarno', *JCEA* 18, 3, pp. 292–317.

Gatzke, H. (1954), *Stresemann and the Rearmament of Germany* (Baltimore).

Gelfand, L.E. (1998), 'The American Mission to Negotiate Peace: An Historian Looks Back', in Boemeke, Feldman and Glaser (1998), pp. 189–203.

Gescher, D.B. (1956), *Die Vereinigten Staaten von Nordamerika und die Reparationen, 1920–1924* (Bonn).

Geyer, M. (1980), *Aufrüstung oder Sicherheit. Die Reichswehr in der Krise der Machtpolitik 1924–1936* (Wiesbaden).

Gilbert, M. (1966), *The Roots of Appeasement* (London).

(1976), *Winston S. Churchill, V: 1922–1939* (London).

Girault, R., and Frank, R. (1988), *Turbulente Europe et nouveaux mondes. Histoire des relations internationales contemporaines 1914–1941* (Paris).

Goldstein, E. (1991), *Winning the Peace. British Diplomatic Strategy, Peace Planning, and the Paris Peace Conference, 1916–1920* (Oxford).

(1996), 'The Evolution of British Diplomatic Strategy for the Locarno Pact, 1924–1925', in Dockrill and McKercher (1996), pp. 115–35.

(1998), 'Great Britain: The Home Front', in Boemeke, Feldman and Glaser (1998), pp. 275–312.

Gordon, M.R. (1969), *Conflict and Consensus in Labour's Foreign Policy 1914–1965* (Stanford).

Gorodetsky, G. (1977), *The Precarious Truce. Anglo-Soviet Relations, 1924–27* (Cambridge).

(1994a), 'The Formulation of Soviet Foreign Policy – Ideology and Realpolitik' in Gorodetsky (1994b), pp. 30–44.

Gorodetsky, G. (ed.) (1994b), *Soviet Foreign Policy 1917–1991: A Retrospective* (London).

Gottwald, R. (1965), *Die deutsch-amerikanischen Beziehungen in der Ära Stresemann* (Berlin).

Grathwol, R.P. (1980), *Stresemann and the DNVP. Reconciliation and Revenge in German Foreign Policy* (Kansas City).

Grayson, R. (1997), *Austen Chamberlain and the Commitment to Europe. British Foreign Policy, 1924–29* (London).

Grupp, P. (1988), *Deutsche Außenpolitik im Schatten von Versailles 1918–1920* (Paderborn).

Guinn, P. (1988), 'On Throwing Ballast in Foreign Policy: Poincaré, the Entente and the Ruhr Occupation', *EHQ* 18, pp. 427–37.

Hagspiel, H. (1987), *Verständigung zwischen Deutschland und Frankreich? Die deutsch-französische Außenpolitik der zwanziger Jahre im innenpolitischen Kräftefeld beider Länder* (Bonn).

Hall, C. (1987), *Britain, America and Arms Control 1921–1937* (London).

Hawley, E.W. (1974), 'Herbert Hoover and American Corporatism, 1929–1933', in Fausold and Mazuzan (1974), pp. 101–19.

(1979), *The Great War and the Search for a Modern Order* (New York).

Hawley, E.W. (ed.) (1981), *Herbert Hoover as Secretary of Commerce* (Iowa City).

Heinemann, U. (1983), *Die verdrängte Niederlage. Politische Öffentlichkeit und Kriegsschuldfrage in der Weimarer Republik* (Göttingen).

Heyde, P. (1998), *Das Ende der Reparationen. Deutschland, Frankreich und der Youngplan 1929–1932* (Paderborn).

Hiden, J. (1987), *The Baltic States and German Ostpolitik* (Cambridge).

Hildebrand, K. (1980), 'Das Deutsche Reich und die Sowjetunion im internationalen System 1918–1932: Legitimität oder Revolution?', in Stürmer (1980), pp. 38–61.

(1989), 'Europäisches Zentrum, überseeische Peripherie und neue Welt. Über den Wandel des Staatensystems zwischen dem Berliner Kongreß (1878) und dem Pariser Frieden (1919/1920)', *HZ* 249, pp. 53–94.

(1995), *Das vergangene Reich. Deutsche Außenpolitik von Bismarck bis Hitler* (Stuttgart).

Hillgruber, A. (1967), *Deutschlands Rolle in der Vorgeschichte der beiden Weltkriege. Die deutsche Frage in der Welt* (Göttingen).

(1969), *Kontinuität und Diskontinuität in der deutschen Außenpolitik von Bismarck bis Hitler* (Düsseldorf).

(1980), 'Unter dem Schatten von Versailles – die außenpolitische Belastung der Weimarer Republik: Realität und Perzeption bei den Deutschen', in Erdmann and Schulze (1980), pp. 51–67.

(1983), 'Revisionismus – Kontinuität und Wandel in der Außenpolitik der Weimarer Republik', *HZ* 237, pp. 597–621.

Hinsley, F. (ed.) (1977), *British Foreign Policy under Sir Edward Grey* (1977).

Hobsbawm, E.J. (1969), *Industry and Empire* (Harmondsworth).

(1987), *The Age of Empire, 1875–1914* (London).

(1992), *Nations and Nationalism since 1780: Programme, Myth, Reality*, 2nd edn (Cambridge).

(1994), *Age of Extremes. The Short Twentieth Century, 1914–1991* (London).

Hofstadter, R. (1955), *The Age of Reform. From Bryan to F.D.R.* (New York).

(1962), *The American Political Tradition and the Men Who Made It* (London).

Hogan, M.J. (1987), *The Marshall Plan. America, Britain and the Reconstruction of Western Europe, 1947–1952* (Cambridge).

(1990), 'Corporatism', *JAH* 6, pp. 153–60.

(1991), *Informal Entente. The Private Structure of Cooperation in Anglo-American Economic Diplomacy, 1918–1928*, 2nd edn (New York).

Holtferich, C.-L. (1984), 'Zu hohe Löhne in der Weimarer Republik?', *GG* 10, pp. 122–41.

Höltje, C. (1958), *Die Weimarer Republik und das Ostlocarno-Problem. Revision oder Garantie der deutschen Ostgrenze von 1919* (Würzburg).

Holz, K.A. (1977), *Die Diskussion um den Dawes- und Young-Plan in der deutschen Presse*, 2 vols. (Frankfurt am Main).

Howard, M. (1972), *The Continental Commitment. The Dilemma of British Defence Policy in the Era of the Two World Wars* (London).

(2001), *The Invention of Peace. Reflections on War and International Order* (London).

Huntington, S.P. (1989), 'American Ideals versus American Institutions', in Ikenberry (1989), pp. 223–58.

Huthmacher, J., and Susman, W. (eds.) (1973), *Herbert Hoover and the Crisis of American Capitalism* (Cambridge, MA).

Ikenberry, G.J. (ed.) (1989), *American Foreign Policy* (Boston and London).

(2001), *After Victory. Institutions, Strategic Restraint and the Rebuilding of World Order after Major Wars* (Princeton).

(2004), 'Illusions of Empire: Defining the New American Order', *FA* 83 (March/April).

Iriye, A. (1977), *From Nationalism to Internationalism. US Foreign Policy to 1914* (London).

(1993), *The Globalizing of America, 1913–1945* (Cambridge and New York).

(2002), *Global Community. The Role of International Organizations in the Making of the Contemporary World* (Berkeley, CA).

Jacobson, J. (1972a), 'The Conduct of Locarno Diplomacy', *RP* 34, pp. 67–81.

(1972b), *Locarno Diplomacy: Germany and the West, 1925–29* (Princeton).

(1983a), 'Is There a New History of the 1920s?', *AHR* 88, pp. 617–45.

(1983b), 'Strategies of French Foreign Policy after World War I', *JMH* 55, pp. 78–95.

(1994), *When the Soviet Union Entered World Politics* (Berkeley, CA).

(1998), 'The Soviet Union and Versailles', in Boemeke, Feldman and Glaser (1998), pp. 451–68.

(2004), 'Locarno, Britain and the Security of Europe', in Johnson (2004b), pp. 11–32.

Jacobson, J., Walker, J.T. (1975), 'The Impulse for a Franco-German Entente: The Origins of the Thoiry Conference, 1926', *JCH* 10, pp. 157–81.

Jaffe, L. (1985), *The Decision to Disarm Germany* (New York).

James, H. (1985), *The Reichsbank and Public Finance in Germany, 1924–1933. A Study of the Politics and Economics during the Great Depression* (Frankfurt am Main).

(1986), *The German Slump. Politics and Economics, 1924–1936* (Oxford and New York).

(2001), *The End of Globalisation. Lessons from the Great Depression* (Cambridge, MA).

(ed.) (2002), *The Interwar Depression in an International Context* (Munich).

Jeannesson, F. (1998), *Poincaré, la France et la Ruhr, 1922–1924* (Strasbourg).

Jenkins, F.A. (1960), *Defence by Committee. The British Committee of Imperial Defence, 1880–1959* (Oxford).

Jenkins, R. (1987), *Baldwin* (Basingstoke and London).

Jervis, R. (1976), *Perception and Misperception in International Politics* (Princeton, NJ).

Johnson, D. (1961), 'Austen Chamberlain and the Locarno Agreements', *University of Birmingham Historical Journal* 8, pp. 62–81.

Johnson, G. (2000), '"Das Kind" Revisited. Lord D'Abernon and German Security Policy', *CEH* 9, 2, pp. 209–24.

(2002), *The Berlin Embassy of Lord D'Abernon, 1920–1926* (Basingstoke and New York).

(2004a), 'Austen Chamberlain and the Negotiation of the Kellogg–Briand Pact, 1928', in Johnson (2004b), pp. 59–79.

Johnson, G. (ed.) (2004b), *Locarno Revisited. European Diplomacy 1920–1929* (London).

Joll, J. (1992), *The Origins of the First World War*, 2nd edn (Harlow).

Jones, K.P. (ed.) (1981), *U.S. Diplomats in Europe, 1919–1941* (Santa Barbara, CA).

Junker, D. (1975), *Der unteilbare Weltmarkt. Das ökonomische Interesse in der Außenpolitik der USA 1933–1941* (Stuttgart).

(1981), 'Die Außenpolitik der USA 1920–1940', in Franz (1981), pp. 200–17.

Kaiser, A. (1989), *Lord D'Abernon und die englische Deutschlandpolitik 1920–1926* (Frankfurt am Main).

Keegan, J. (2000), *The First World War* (London).

Keeton, E.D. (1985), 'Economics and Politics in Briand's German Policy, 1925–1931', in Fink *et al.* (1985).

(1987), *Briand's Locarno Policy. French Economics, Politics and Diplomacy, 1925–1929* (New York).

Keiger, J.P.W. (1983), *France and the Origins of the First World War* (London).

(1997), *Raymond Poincaré* (Cambridge).

(2004), 'Poincaré, Briand and Locarno: Continuity in French Diplomacy in the 1920s', in Johnson (2004b), pp. 95–108.

Kennan, G.F. (1951), *American Diplomacy 1900–1950* (Chicago).

Kennedy, D.M. (1980), *Over Here. The First World War and American Society* (Oxford and New York).

(1999), *Freedom from Fear. The American People in Depression and War* (Oxford and New York).

Kennedy, P.M. (1975), 'Idealists and Realists. British Views of Germany 1864–1939', *Transactions of the Royal Historical Society*, 5th series, 25, pp. 137–56.

(1981), *The Realities behind Diplomacy. Background Influences on British External Policy 1865–1980* (London).

(1983), 'The Tradition of Appeasement in British Foreign Policy, 1865–1939', in P.M. Kennedy, *Strategy and Diplomacy 1870–1945. Eight Studies* (London).

(1988), *The Rise and Fall of the Great Powers. Economic Challenge and Military Conflict from 1500 to 2000* (London).

Kennedy, P.M. (ed.) (1991), *Grand Strategies in War and Peace* (New Haven and London).

Kennedy, P.M., and Hitchcock, W.I. (eds.) (2000), *From War to Peace: Altered Strategic Landscapes in the Twentieth Century* (New Haven, CT).

Kent, B. (1989), *The Spoils of War. The Politics, Economics and Diplomacy of Reparations 1918–1932* (Oxford).

Kershaw, I. (1998), *Hitler, 1889–1936, Hubris* (London).

Kimmich, C.M. (1976), *Germany and the League of Nations* (Chicago).

Kindleberger, C.P. (1973), *The World in Depression, 1929–39* (Berkeley).

Kissinger, H.A. (1994), *Diplomacy* (New York).

Kitching, C.J. (1999), *Britain and the Problem of International Disarmament* (London).

   (2004), 'Locarno and the Irrelevance of Disarmament', in Johnson (2004b), pp. 161–77.

Klümpen, H. (1992), *Deutsche Außenpolitik zwischen Versailles und Rapallo. Revisionismus oder Neuorientierung?* (Münster and Hamburg).

Knapp, M., and Link, W. *et al.* (1978), *Die USA und Deutschland 1918–1975. Deutschamerikanische Beziehungen zwischen Rivalität und Partnerschaft* (Munich).

Knipping, F. (1987), *Deutschland, Frankreich und das Ende der Locarno-Ära, 1928–1931* (Munich).

Knock, T.J. (1992), *To End All Wars. Woodrow Wilson and the Quest for a New World Order* (Princeton).

   (1998), 'Wilsonian Concepts and International Realities at the End of the War', in Boemeke, Feldman and Glauser (1998), pp. 111–30.

Köhler, H. (ed.) (1984), *Deutschland und der Westen* (Berlin).

Kolb, E. (1988), *Die Weimarer Republik*, 3rd edn (Munich and Vienna).

Koszyk, K. (1972), *Deutsche Presse 1914–1945* (Berlin).

Krasner, S. (1976), 'State Power and the Structure of International Trade', *WP* 28, pp. 317–43.

Krasner, S. (ed.) (1983), *International Regimes* (Ithaca, NY).

Krieger, W. (1978), *Labour Party und Weimarer Republik. Ein Beitrag zur Außenpolitik der britischen Arbeiterbewegung zwischen Programmatik und Parteitaktik, 1918–1924* (Bonn).

Kruedener, J. v. (ed.) (1990), *Economic Crisis and Political Collapse. The Weimar Republic 1924–1933* (New York and Oxford).

Krüger, P. (1973), *Deutschland und die Reparationen 1918/19. Die Genesis des Reparationsproblems in Deutschland zwischen Waffebstillstand und Versailler Friedensschluß* (Stuttgart).

   (1974), 'Friedenssicherung und deutsche Revisionspolitik. Die deutsche Außenpolitik und die Verhandlungen über den Kellogg-Pakt', *VfZg* 22, pp. 227–57.

   (1980), 'Der deutsch-polnische Schiedsvertrag von 1925 im Rahmen der Locarno-Verträge', *HZ* 230, pp. 577–612.

   (1981), 'Das Reparationsproblem der Weimarer Republik in fragwürdiger Sicht. Kritische Überlegungen zur neuesten Forschung', *VfZg* 29, pp. 21–47.

   (1984), 'Die "Westpolitik" in der Weimarer Republik', in Köhler (1984), pp. 105–30.

   (1985a), *Die Außenpolitik der Republik von Weimar* (Darmstadt).

   (1985b), 'Struktur, Organisation und außenpolitische Wirkungsmöglichkeiten der leitenden Beamten des Auswärtige Dienstes 1921–1933', in Schwabe (1985a), pp. 101–69.

   (1993), 'German Disappointment and Anti-Western Resentment, 1918–1919', in Schröder (1993), pp. 323–36.

Krüger, P. (ed.) (1991), *Kontinuität und Wandel in der Staatenordnung der Neuzeit. Beiträge zur Geschichte des internationalen Systems* (Marburg).

Krüger, P., and Schroeder, P.W. (eds.) (2001), *The Transformation of European Politics, 1763–1848: Episode or Model in Modern History?* (New York).

Kupchan, C.A. (2003), *The End of the American Era. U.S. Foreign Policy and the Geopolitics of the Twenty-First Century* (New York).

LaFeber, W. (1989), *The American Age. United States Foreign Policy at Home and Abroad since 1750* (New York).

Lake, D. (1988), *Power, Protection, and International Trade: The International Sources of American Commercial Strategy, 1887–1939* (Ithaca, NY).

Langer, W.L. (1962), *European Alliances and Alignments 1871–1890*, 2nd edn (New York).
(1968), *The Diplomacy of Imperialism 1890–1902*, 2nd edn (New York).

Laubach, E. (1968), *Die Politik der Kabinette Wirth 1921/22* (Lübeck and Hamburg).

Lee, M.M. (1982), 'Gustav Stresemann und die deutsche Völkerbundspolitik 1925 bis 1930', in Michalka and Lee (1982), pp. 350–74.

Lee, M.M., and Michalka, W. (1982), *German Foreign Policy 1917–1933. Continuity or Break?* (Leamington Spa).

Leffler, M.P. (1977), 'American Policy-Making and European Stability 1921–1933', *PHR* 46, pp. 207–28.
(1979), *The Elusive Quest. America's Pursuit of European Stability and French Security* (Chapel Hill, NC).
(1981), 'Herbert Hoover, the "New Era" and American Foreign Policy', in Hawley (1981), pp. 148–79.
(1999), 'The Cold War: What Do "We Now Know"?', *AHR* 104, (April), pp. 501–24.

Lentin, A. (1985), *Guilt at Versailles. Lloyd George and the Pre-History of Appeasement* (London).

Levy, C., and Roseman, M. (eds.) (2002), *Three Post-War Eras in Comparison: Western Europe 1918–1945–1989* (Basingstoke and New York).

Lévy-Leboyer, A. (ed.) (1977), *La position internationale de la France. Aspects économiques et financières (XIXe–XXe siècles)* (Paris).

Link, A.S. (1979), *Woodrow Wilson. Revolution, War, and Peace* (Arlington Heights, IL).

Link, A.S., and Catton, W.B. (1973), *The Progressive Era and the First World War, 1900–1920*, 4th edn (New York).

Link, A.S., and McCormick, R.L. (1983), *Progressivism* (Arlington Heights, IL).

Link, W. (1969), 'Die Ruhrbesetzung und die wirtschaftspolitischen Interessen der USA', *VfZg* 17, pp. 373–82.
(1970), *Die amerikanische Stabilisierungspolitik in Deutschland, 1921–1932* (Düsseldorf).
(1974), 'Der amerikanische Einfluß auf die Weimarer Republik in der Dawesplanphase (Elemente eines "penetrierten Systems")', in Mommsen, Petzina and Weisbrod (1974), pp. 485–98.
(1978), 'Die Beziehungen zwischen der Weimarer Republik und den USA', in Knapp and Link *et al.* (1978), pp. 62–106.

Lippelt, H. (1971), '"Politische Sanierung" – Zur deutschen Politik gegenüber Polen 1925/26', *VfZg* 19, pp. 323–73.

Lloyd, T.O. (1993), *Empire, Welfare State, Europe. English History 1906–1992*, 4th edn (Oxford).

McDougall, W.A. (1978), *France's Rhineland Diplomacy, 1914–24: The Last Bid for a Balance of Power in Europe* (Princeton).

(1979), 'Political Economy versus National Sovereignty: French Structures for German Economic Integration after Versailles', *JMH* 51, pp. 4–23.

McDougall, W.A., Trachtenberg, M., and Maier, C.S. (1979), Special Issue on Versailles, *JMH* 51.

McKenna, M.C. (1961), *Borah* (Ann Arbor, MI).

McKercher, B.J.C. (1984), *The Second Baldwin Government and the United States, 1924–1929. Attitudes and Diplomacy* (Cambridge).

(1989), *Esme Howard. A Diplomatic Biography* (Cambridge).

(1991b), '"The Deep and Latent Mistrust": The British Official Mind and the United States, 1919–1929', in McKercher (1991a), pp. 209–38.

(1991c), 'Reaching for the Brass Ring: The Recent Historiography of Interwar American Relations', *DH* 15, 4.

(1999), *Transition of Power. Britain's Loss of Global Pre-eminence to the United States, 1930–1945* (Cambridge).

McKercher, B.J.C. (ed.) (1991a), *Anglo-American Relations in the 1920s. The Struggle for Supremacy* (Basingstoke and London).

Macmillan, M. (2001), *Peacemakers: The Paris Conference of 1919 and its Attempt to End War* (London).

McNeil, W.C. (1986), *American Money and the Weimar Republic: Economics and Politics in the Era of the Great Depression* (New York).

Maddox, R.J. (1970), *William E. Borah and American Foreign Policy* (Baton Rouge, LA).

Magee, F. (1995), '"Limited Liability"? Britain and the Treaty of Locarno', *Twentieth Century British History* 6, pp. 1–22.

Maier, C.S. (1979), 'The Truth about the Treaties', *JMH* 51, pp. 56–67.

(1981), 'The Two Postwar Eras and the Conditions for Stability in 20th-Century Western Europe', *AHR* 86, pp. 327–52.

(1987), *In Search of Stability. Explorations in Historical Political Economy* (Cambridge and New York).

(1988), *Recasting Bourgeois Europe. Stabilization in France, Germany and Italy in the Decade after World War I*, 2nd edn (Princeton).

(2002), 'An American Empire? The Problems of Frontiers and Peace in Twenty-First-Century World Politics', *Harvard Magazine* (November–December).

Maisel, E. (1996), *The Foreign Office and Foreign Policy, 1919–1926* (Brighton).

Mannock, J.W. (1962), 'Anglo-American Relations, 1921–38', Ph.D. Diss., Princeton University.

Marks, S. (1976), *The Illusion of Peace: International Relations in Europe, 1918–1933* (London).

(2002), *The Ebbing of European Ascendancy. An International History of the World, 1914–1945* (London).

Marquand, D. (1977), *Ramsay MacDonald* (London).

Maxelon, M.O. (1972), *Stresemann und Frankreich 1914–1929. Deutsche Politik der Ost-West-Balance* (Düsseldorf).

May, E.R. (1961), *Imperial Democracy. The Emergence of America as a Great Power* (New York).

(1973), *'Lessons' of the Past: The Use and Misuse of History in American Foreign Policy* (New York).

Mayer, A.J. (1967), *Politics and Diplomacy of Peacemaking. Containment and Counter-revolution at Versailles, 1918–1919* (New York).

Mayeur, J.-M. (1984), *La vie politique sous la Troisième République (1870–1940)* (Paris).

Mearsheimer, J. (2001), *The Tragedy of Great Power Politics* (New York).

Medlicott, W.N. (1968), *British Foreign Policy since Versailles, 1919–1963* (London).

Meier, C. (2002), *Caesar*, 5th edn (Munich).

Michalka, W. (1992), 'Die Außenpolitik von Weimar (I). Zwischen Revisionismus und Neuansatz 1918–1922', *NPL* 37, pp. 384–403.

Michalka, W. (ed.) (1994), *Der Erste Weltkrieg: Wirkung, Wahrnehmung, Analyse* (Munich).

Michalka, W., and Lee, M.M. (eds.) (1982), *Gustav Stresemann* (Darmstadt).

Middlemas, R.K., and Barnes, J. (1969), *Stanley Baldwin* (London, 1969).

Miller, K. (1967), *Socialism and Foreign Policy. Theory and Practice in Britain to 1931* (The Hague).

(1999), *Populist Nationalism: Republican Insurgency and American Foreign Policy Making, 1918–1925* (Westport, CT).

Milward, A.S. (1984), *The Reconstruction of Western Europe, 1945–1951* (London).

Miquel, P. (1961), *Poincaré* (Paris).

(1972), *La Paix de Versailles et l'opinion publique française* (Paris).

(1977), *La Paix de Versailles et l'opinion publique française* (Paris).

(1983), *La Grande Guerre* (Paris).

Moggridge, D.E. (1972), *British Monetary Policy, 1924–31: The Norman Conquest of $4.86* (Cambridge).

Möller, H. (1998), *Europa zwischen den Weltkriegen* (Munich).

Mollier, J.-Y., and George, J. (1994), *La plus longue des républiques 1870–1940* (Paris).

Mommsen, H. (1989), *Die verspielte Freiheit. Der Weg der Republik von Weimar in den Untergang, 1918–1933* (Berlin).

Mommsen, H., Petzina, D., and Weisbrod, B. (eds.) (1974), *Industrielles System und politische Entwicklung in der Weimarer Republik* (Düsseldorf).

Monroe, E. (1981), *Britain's Moment in the Middle East* (London).

Morgan, K.O. (1979), *Consensus and Disunity. The Lloyd George Coalition Government, 1918–1922* (Oxford).

Morgenthau, H.J. (1952), *In Defense of the National Interest. A Critical Examination of American Foreign Policy* (New York).

Mouré, K. (2003), *The Gold Standard Illusion. France, the Bank of France and the International Gold Standard, 1914–1939* (Oxford).

Néré, J. (1985), *Le problème de mur d'argent. Les crises du franc (1924–1926)* (Paris).

Newton, D. (1998), *British Policy and the Weimar Republic 1918–1919* (Oxford).

Newton, S. (1996), *Profits of Peace. The Political Economy of Anglo-German Appeasement* (Oxford).

Nicholls, A.J. (1991), *Weimar and the Rise of Hitler*, 3rd edn (London).

(1994), *Freedom with Responsibility. The Social Market Economy in Germany, 1918–1963* (Oxford).

Nicolson, H. (1952), *King George the Fifth. His Life and Reign* (London).

Niedhart, G. (1978), 'Appeasement. Die britische Antwort auf die Krise des Weltreichs und das internationale System der Zwischenkriegszeit', *HZ* 226, pp. 52–76.

(1980), 'Multipolares Gleichgewicht und weltwirtschaftliche Verflechtung. Deutschland in der britischen Appeasement-Politik 1919–1933', in Stürmer (1980), pp. 113–30.

(1999), *Die Außenpolitik der Weimarer Republik* (Munich).

Ninkovich, F. (1999), *The Wilsonian Century* (New Haven, CT).

Nipperdey, T. (1993), *Deutsche Geschichte 1866–1918*, II: *Machtstaat vor der Demokratie* (Munich).

Northedge, F.S. (1996), *The Troubled Giant. Britain among the Great Powers 1916–1939* (London).

Nye, J.S., Jr (1993), *Understanding International Conflicts. An Introduction to Theory and History* (New York).

Offner, A.A. (1975), *The Origins of the Second World War. American Foreign Policy and World Politics, 1917–1941* (New York).

Orde, A. (1978), *Great Britain and International Security, 1920–1926* (London).

(1990), *British Policy and European Reconstruction after the First World War* (Cambridge).

O'Riordan, E.Y. (2001), *Britain and the Ruhr Crisis* (London).

Otte, T.G. (1998), *Harold Nicolson and Diplomatic Theory. Between Old Diplomacy and New* (Leicester).

Oudin, B. (1987), *Arisitide Briand: la paix, une idée neuve en Europe* (Paris).

Parrini, C.P. (1969), *Heir to Empire. United States Economic Diplomacy, 1916–1923* (Pittsburgh).

Pease, N. (1986), *Poland, the United States and the Stabilisation of Europe, 1919–1933* (New York).

Perkins, D. (1956), *Charles Evans Hughes and American Democratic Statesmanship* (Boston).

Petricioli, M. (ed.) (1995), *A Missed Opportunity? 1922: The Reconstruction of Europe* (Bern and New York).

Pitts, V.J. (1987), *France and the German Problem. Politics and Economics in the Locarno Period, 1924–29* (New York).

Pogge von Strandmann, H. (1981), 'Rapallo – Strategy in Preventive Diplomacy. New Sources and New Interpretations', in Berghahn and Kitchen (1981), pp. 123–46.

Pohl, K.-H. (1979), *Weimars Wirtschaft und die Außenpolitik der Republik 1924–1926. Vom Dawes-Plan zum Internationalen Eisenpakt* (Düsseldorf).

Pollard, S. (1992), *The Development of the British Economy, 1914–1990*, 4th edn (London and New York).

Pusey, M.J. (1951), *Charles Evans Hughes*, 2 vols. (New York).

Rémond, R. (1997), *Notre siècle. 1918–1995* (Paris).

Reynolds, D. (1991), *Britannia Overruled. British Policy and World Power in the 20th Century* (London).

Rhodes, B.D. (1991), 'The Image of Britain in the United States, 1919–1929: A Contentious Relative and Rival', in McKercher (1991a), pp. 187–208.

(2004), *United States Foreign Policy in the Interwar Period, 1918–1941: The Golden Age of American Diplomatic and Military Complacency* (Westport, CT).

Richardson, D. (1989), *The Evolution of British Disarmament Policy in the 1920s* (London).

Rieckhoff, H.V. (1971), *German–Polish Relations 1918–1933* (Baltimore).

Riesenberg, K.E. (1982), 'Die SPD in der "Locarno Krise" Oktober/November 1925', *VfZg* 30, pp. 130–61.

Robinson, P.R., and Gallagher, J. (1953), 'The Imperialism of Free Trade', *Economic History Review*, 2nd series, 6, 1, pp. 1–15.

Rödder, A. (1993), 'Der Mythos von der frühen Westbindung. Konrad Adenauer und Stesemanns Außenpolitik', *VfZg* 41, pp. 543–73.

(1996), *Stresemanns Erbe. Julius Curtius und die deutsche Außenpolitik 1929–1931* (Paderborn).

Roskill, S. (1972), *Hankey, Man of Secrets* (London).

Rothwell, V.H. (1972), *British War Aims and Peace Diplomacy, 1914–1918* (Oxford).

Rowland, B. (ed.) (1975), *Balance of Power or Hegemony: The Interwar Monetary System* (London).

Rupieper, H.-J. (1979), *The Cuno Government and Reparations, 1922–23* (The Hague).

Salewski, M. (1966), *Entwaffnung und Militärkontrolle in Deutschland 1919–1927* (Munich).

(1980), 'Das Weimarer "Revisionssyndrom"', *Aus Politik und Zeitgeschichte* 2/80 (January), pp. 14–25.

Salzmann, S. (2003), *Great Britain, Germany, and the Soviet Union. Rapallo and after, 1922–1934* (London).

Saueressig, P. (1996), *Chancen und Grenzen informeller Diplomatie. Charles Evans Hughes und amerikanische Außenpolitik 1921–1925* (Munich).

Schattkowsky, R. (1994a), *Deutschland und Polen von 1918/19 bis 1925: deutsch-polnische Beziehungen zwischen Versailles und Locarno* (Frankfurt am Main and New York).

(1994b), 'Deutschland und Polen vor Locarno. Probleme ihrer Beziehungen 1923 bis 1925', in Schattkowsky (1994c), pp. 107–14.

Schattkowsky, R. (ed.) (1994c), *Locarno und Osteuropa* (Marburg).

Schlesinger, A.M., Jr (1956), *The Crisis of the Old Order* (Boston).

(1999), *The Cycles of American History* (New York).

Schmidt, G. (ed.) (1983), *Konstellationen internationaler Politik 1924–1932* (Bochum).

Schöllgen, G. (2000), *Das Zeitalter des Imperialismus*, 4th edn (Munich).

Schröder, H.-J. (ed.) (1993), *Confrontation and Cooperation. Germany and the United States in the Era of World War I, 1900–1924* (Oxford).

Schroeder, P.W. (1976), 'Munich and the British Tradition', *HJ* 19, 1, pp. 223–43.

(1987), 'The Nineteenth Century System: Balance of Power or Political Equilibrium?', *RIS* 15, pp. 135–53.

(1993), 'Economic Integration and the European International System in the Era of World War I', *AHR* 98, pp. 1130–37.

(1994), *The Transformation of European Politics 1763–1848* (Oxford).

(2004a), 'Alliances, 1815–1945: Weapons of Power and Tools of Management', in Schroeder (2004d), pp. 195–222.

(2004b), 'Embedded Counterfactuals and World War I as an Unavoidable War', in Schroeder (2004d), pp. 157–92.

(2004c), 'The Mirage of Empire versus the Promise of Hegemony', in Schroeder (2004d), pp. 297–306.

(2004d), *Systems, Stability, and Statecraft. Essays on the International History of Modern Europe*, ed. and with an introduction by D. Wetzel, R. Jervis and J.S. Levy (New York).

(2004e),'World War I as Galloping Gertie: A Reply to Joachim Remak', in Schroeder (2004d), pp. 137–56.

Schuker, S.A. (1972), 'Republican Policy and the Pax Americana, 1921–1932', in Williams (1972a), pp. 254–92.

(1976), *The End of French Predominance in Europe. The Financial Crisis of 1924 and the Adoption of the Dawes Plan* (Chapel Hill, NC).

(1983), 'American Foreign Policy and the Young Plan, 1929', in Schmidt (1983), pp. 122–30.

(1987), *American 'Reparations' to Germany* (Princeton).

(1998), 'The Rhineland Question: West European Security at the Paris Peace Conference of 1919', in Boemeke, Feldman and Glaser (1998), pp. 275–312.

Schuker, S.A. (ed.) (2000), *Deutschland und Frankreich. Vom Konflikt zur Aussöhnung* (Munich).

Schulze, H. (1982), *Weimar. Deutschland 1917–1933* (Berlin).

(1996), *States, Nations and Nationalism: From the Middle Ages to the Present* (Oxford).

Schulzinger, R. (1990), *American Diplomacy in the Twentieth Century* (Oxford).

Schwabe, K. (1971), *Deutsche Revolution und Wilson-Frieden. Die amerikanische und deutsche Friedensstrategie zwischen Ideologie und Machtpolitik 1918/1919* (Düsseldorf).

(1985b), 'Großbritannien und die Ruhrkrise', in Schwabe (1985c), pp. 53–87.

(1985d), *Woodrow Wilson, Revolutionary Germany, and Peacemaking, 1918–1919* (Chapel Hill, NC).

(1986), 'Die Vereinigten Staaten und die Weimarer Republik. Das Scheitern einer "besonderen Beziehung"', in Trommler (1986), pp. 367–78.

(1998), 'Germany's Peace Aims and the Domestic and International Constraints', in Boemeke, Feldman and Glaser (1998), pp. 37–68.

Schwabe, K. (ed.) (1985a), *Das Diplomatische Korps 1871–1945* (Boppard).

(ed.) (1985c), *Die Ruhrkrise 1923. Wendepunkt der internationalen Beziehungen nach dem Ersten Weltkrieg* (Paderborn).

Service, R. (2000), *Lenin. A Biography* (Cambridge, MA).

(2005), *Stalin. A Biography* (Cambridge, MA).

Sharp, A. (1984), *Lloyd George's Foreign Policy* (London).

(1991), *The Versailles Settlement: Peacemaking in Paris, 1919* (London).

Short, F. (2000), *Raymond Poincaré. Un homme d'Etat républicain* (Paris).

Siebert, F. (1973), *Aristide Briand, 1862–1932. Ein Staatsmann zwischen Frankreich und Europa* (Stuttgart).

Silverman, D.P. (1982), *Reconstructing Europe after the Great War* (Cambridge, MA).

Skidelsky, R. (1983), *John Maynard Keynes, I: Hopes Betrayed, 1883–1920* (London).

(1996), *John Maynard Keynes* (Oxford).

Smith, T. (1994), *America's Mission. The United States and the Worldwide Struggle for Democracy in the Twentieth Century* (Princeton, NJ).

Snidal, D. (1985), 'The Limits of Hegemonic Stability Theory', *IO* 39 pp. 579–614.

Snyder, G.H., and Diesing, P. (1977), *Conflict Among Nations* (Princeton).

Soutou, G.-H. (1989), *L'Or et le Sang. Les buts de guerre économique de la Première Guerre Mondiale* (Paris).

(1998), 'The French Peacemakers and their Home Front', in Boemeke, Feldman and Glaser (1998), pp. 167–88.

(2001), 'La France et la problématique de la sécurité collective à partir de Locarno: dialectique juridique et impasse géostratégique', in Clemens (2001).

Spenz, J. (1966), *Die diplomatische Vorgeschichte des Beitritts Deutschlands zum Völkerbund 1924–1926* (Göttingen).

Stamm, C. (1977), *Lloyd George zwischen Innen- und Außenpolitik. Die britische Deutschlandpolitik 1921/22* (Cologne).

Steiner, Z.S. (1993), 'The League of Nations and the Quest for Security', in Ahmann, Birke and Howard (1993), pp. 35–70.

Steiner, Z.S., and Neilson, K. (2003), *Britain and the Origins of the First World War*, 2nd edn (Basingstoke).

Stevenson, D. (1982), *French War Aims against Germany, 1914–1919* (Oxford).

  (1998), 'French War Aims and Peace Planning', in Boemeke, Feldman and Glaser (1998), pp. 87–109.

Stone, R. (1970), *The Irreconcilables. The Fight against the League of Nations* (Lexington, KT).

Strachhan, H. (2001), *The First World War, I: To Arms* (Oxford).

Stürmer, M. (1967), *Koalition und Opposition in der Weimarer Republik, 1924–1928* (Düsseldorf).

Stürmer, M. (ed.) (1980), *Die Weimarer Republik. Belagerte Civitas* (Königstein).

Taylor, A.J.P. (1954), *The Struggle for Mastery in Europe 1848–1918* (Oxford).

  (1957), *The Trouble Makers. Dissent over Foreign Policy* (London).

  (1964), *The Origins of the Second World War* (Harmondsworth).

  (1965), *English History, 1914–1945* (Oxford).

Temperley, H. (ed.) (1969), *The History of the Peace Conference of Paris*, 6 vols. (Oxford).

Thompson, A.S. (1997), 'Tariff Reform: An Imperial Strategy, 1903–1913', *HJ* 49, 4, pp. 1033–55.

Tillmann, S.P. (1961), *Anglo-American Relations at the Paris Peace Conference* (Princeton).

Tomes, J.H. (1989), 'Austen Chamberlain and the Kellogg Pact', *Millennium: Journal of International Studies* 18, 1, pp. 1–27.

Towle, P. (1993), 'British Security and Disarmament Policy in Europe in the 1920s', in Ahmann, Birke and Howard (1993), pp. 127–53.

Trachtenberg, M. (1979), 'Reparations at the Paris Peace Conference', *JMH* 51, pp. 24–55.

  (1980), *Reparation in World Politics. France and European Economic Diplomacy, 1916–1923* (New York).

  (1999), *A Constructed Peace. The Making of the European Settlement 1945–1963* (Princeton).

Trommler, F. (ed.) (1986), *Amerika und die Deutschen. Bestandsaufnahme einer 300-jährigen Geschichte* (Opladen).

Turner, A. (1999), *Britain and French War Debts in the 1920s* (London).

Turner, H.A., Jr (1963), *Stresemann and the Politics of the Weimar Republic* (Princeton).

Unger, G. (2005), *Aristide Briand: le ferme conciliateur* (Paris).

Urbanitsch, P. (1968), *Großbritannien und die Verträge von Locarno* (Vienna).

Walsdorff, M. (1971), *Westorientierung und Ostpolitik. Stresemanns Rußlandpolitik in der Locarno-Ära* (Bremen).

Walters, F.P. (1952), *A History of the League of Nations*, 2 vols. (London).

Waltz, K. (1979), *Theory of International Politics* (Reading, MA).

Walworth, A. (1986), *Wilson and his Peacemakers. American Diplomacy at the Paris Peace Conference* (New York).

Wandel, E. (1971), *Die Bedeutung der Vereinigten Staaten für das deutsche Reparationsproblem* (1971).

Wandycz, P.S. (1961), *France and her Eastern Allies, 1919–1925. French–Czechoslovak–Polish Relations from the Paris Peace Conference to Locarno* (Westport, CT).

(1980), *The United States and Poland* (Cambridge, MA).

(1988), *The Twilight of the French Eastern Alliance, 1926–36. French–Czechoslovak–Polish Relations from Locarno to the Remilitarization of the Rhineland* (Princeton).

(1998), 'The Polish Question', in Boemeke, Feldman and Glaser (1998), pp. 313–37.

Wandycz, P., Krüger, P., and Soutou, G. (1981), 'La Pologne entre Paris et Berlin de Locarno à Hitler (1925–1933)', *RHD* 95, pp. 236–348.

Watt, D.C. (1965), *Personalities and Policies. Studies in the Formulation of British Foreign Policy in the Twentieth Century* (London).

(1984), *Succeeding John Bull. America in Britain's Place, 1900–1975* (Cambridge).

Weidenfeld, W. (1972), *Die Englandpolitik Gustav Stresemanns* (Mainz).

Wengst, U. (1973), *Graf Brockdorff-Rantzau und die außenpolitischen Anfänge der Weimarer Republik* (Frankfurt am Main).

Westphal, A. (1942), *The House Committee on Foreign Affairs* (New York).

Widenor, W.C. (1980), *Henry Cabot Lodge and the Search for an American Foreign Policy* (Berkeley, CA).

Willert, A. (1952), *The Road to Safety* (London).

Williams, L.J. (1971), *Britain and the World Economy, 1919–1970* (London).

Williams, W.A. (1972b), *The Tragedy of American Diplomacy*, 2nd edn (New York).

Williams, W.A. (ed.) (1972a), *From Colony to Empire* (New York).

Williamson, Ph. (1992), *National Crisis and National Government. British Politics, the Economy and Empire 1926–1932* (Cambridge).

(1999), *Stanley Baldwin. Conservative Leadership and National Values* (Cambridge).

Winkler, H.A. (1985), *Der Schein der Normalität. Arbeiter und Arbeiterbewegung in der Weimarer Republik 1924 bis 1930* (Berlin and Bonn, 1985).

(1993), *Weimar 1918–1933. Die Geschichte der ersten deutschen Demokratie* (Munich).

(2000), *Der lange Weg nach Westen*, 2 vols. (Munich).

Winkler, H.R. (1956), 'The Emergence of a Labour Foreign Policy in Great Britain, 1918–1929', *JMH* 9, pp. 247–58.

Woods, N. (ed.) (1996), *Explaining International Relations since 1945* (Oxford).

Wormser, G. (1977), *Le septennat de Poincaré* (Paris).

Wright, J.R.C. (1995), 'Stresemann and Locarno', *CEH* 4, 2, pp. 109–31.

(2002), *Gustav Stresemann. Weimar's Greatest Statesman* (Oxford).

Wrigley, C. (1990), *Arthur Henderson* (Cardiff).

Wurm, C.A. (1979), *Die französische Sicherheitspolitik in der Phase der Umorientierung 1924–1926* (Frankfurt am Main, 1979).

(1980), 'Deutschlands Außenpolitik unter Stresemann, die USA und Westeuropa', *Geschichte und Gegenwart* 9, pp. 176–87.

(1993), *Business, Politics, and International Relations: Steel, Cotton, and International Cartels in British Politics, 1924–1939* (Cambridge).

Wurm, C.A. (ed.) (1989), *Internationale Kartelle und Außenpolitik. Beiträge zur Zwischenkriegszeit* (Frankfurt am Main and Wiesbaden).

Wyatt-Walter, A. (1996), 'The United States and Western Europe: The Theory of Hegemonic Stability', in Woods (1996), pp. 126–54.

Zeidler, M. (1993), *Reichswehr und Rote Armee 1920–1933. Wege Stationen einer ungewöhnlichen Zusammenarbeit* (Munich).

Zwehl, K.V. (1974), 'Die Deutschlandpolitik Englands von 1922 bis 1924 unter besonderer Berücksichtigung der Reparationen', Ph.D. Diss., Munich.

Index

Index

Index